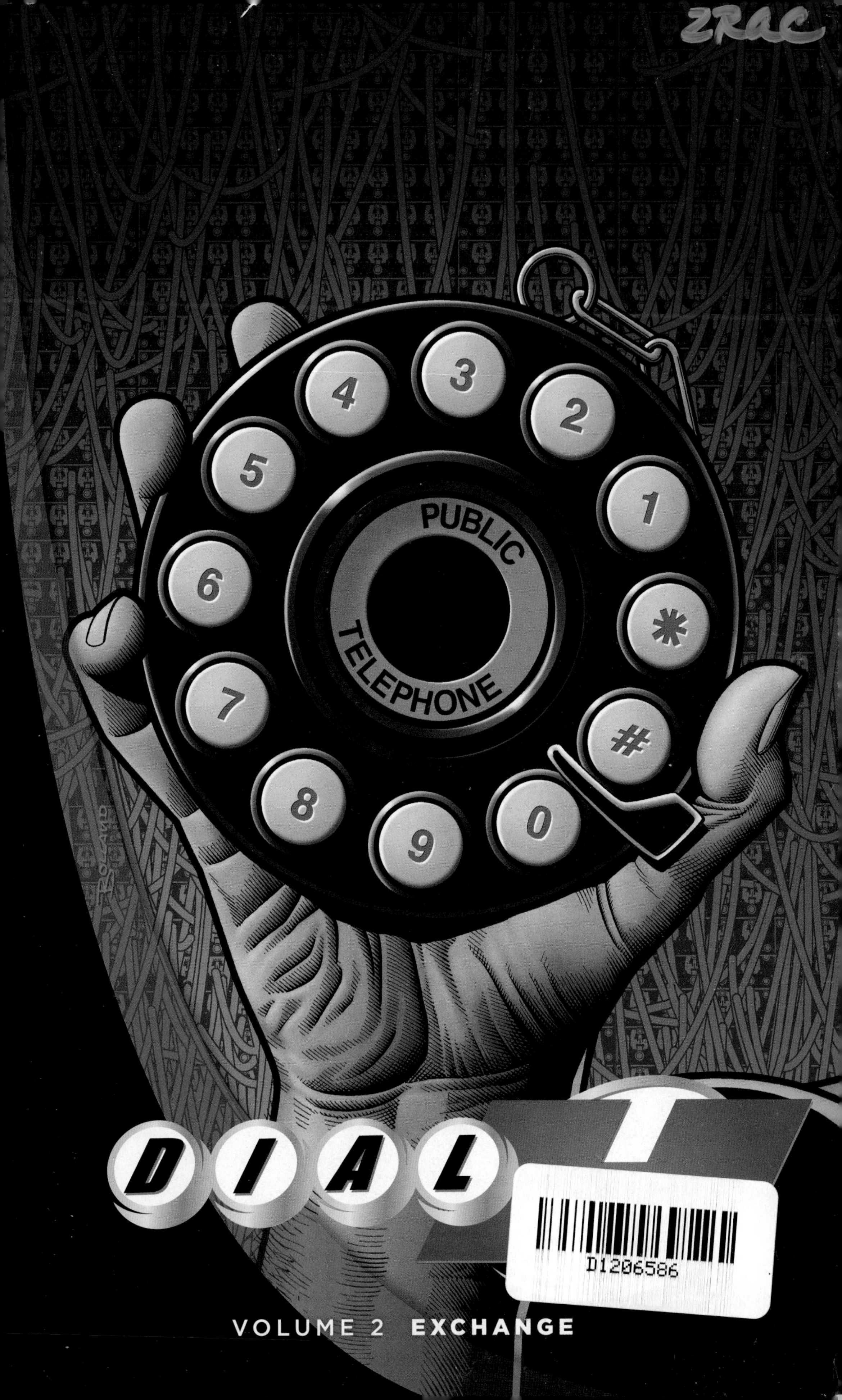
PUBLIC
TELEPHONE
1 2 3 4 5 6 7 8 9 0 * #

DIAL

VOLUME 2 EXCHANGE

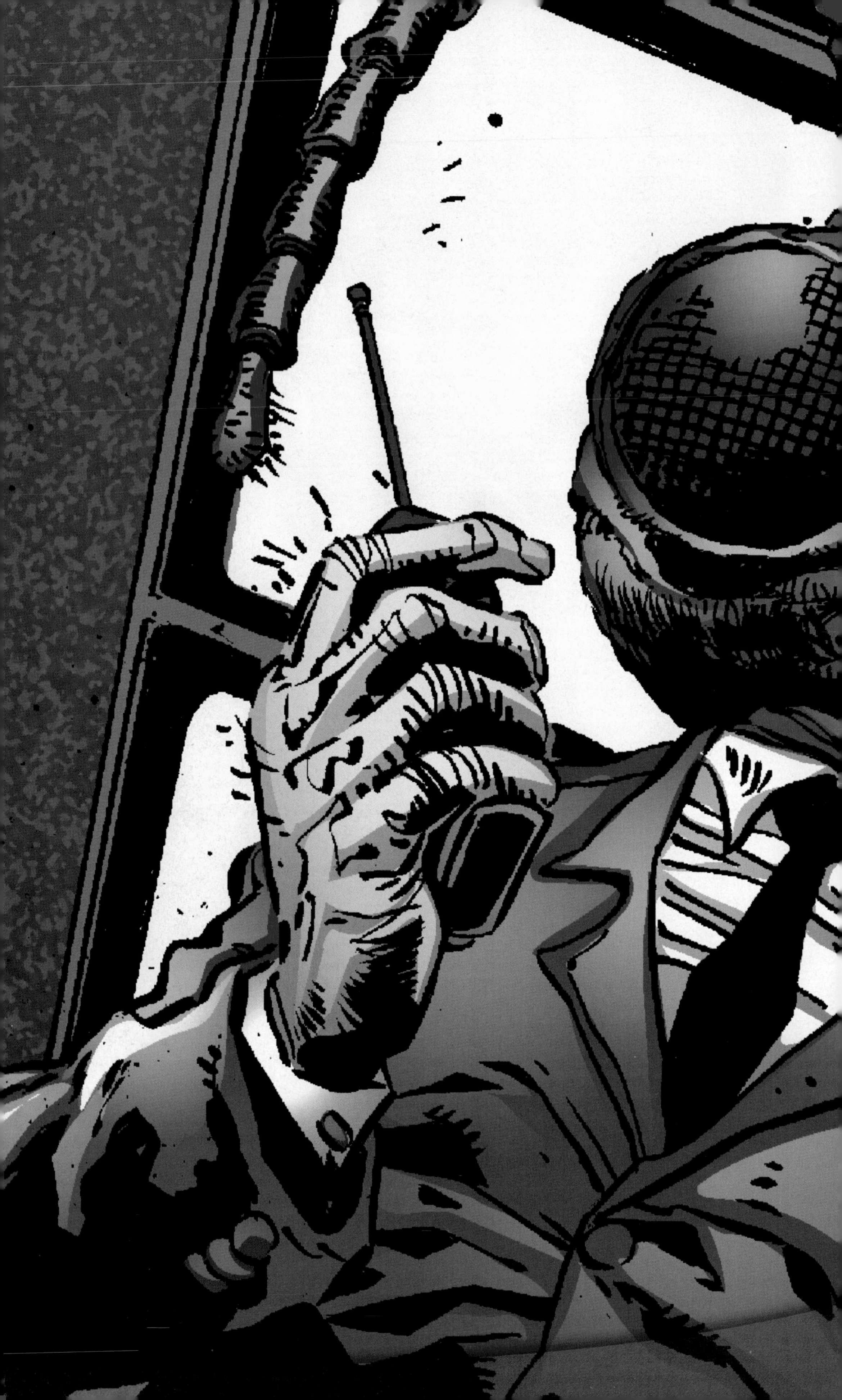

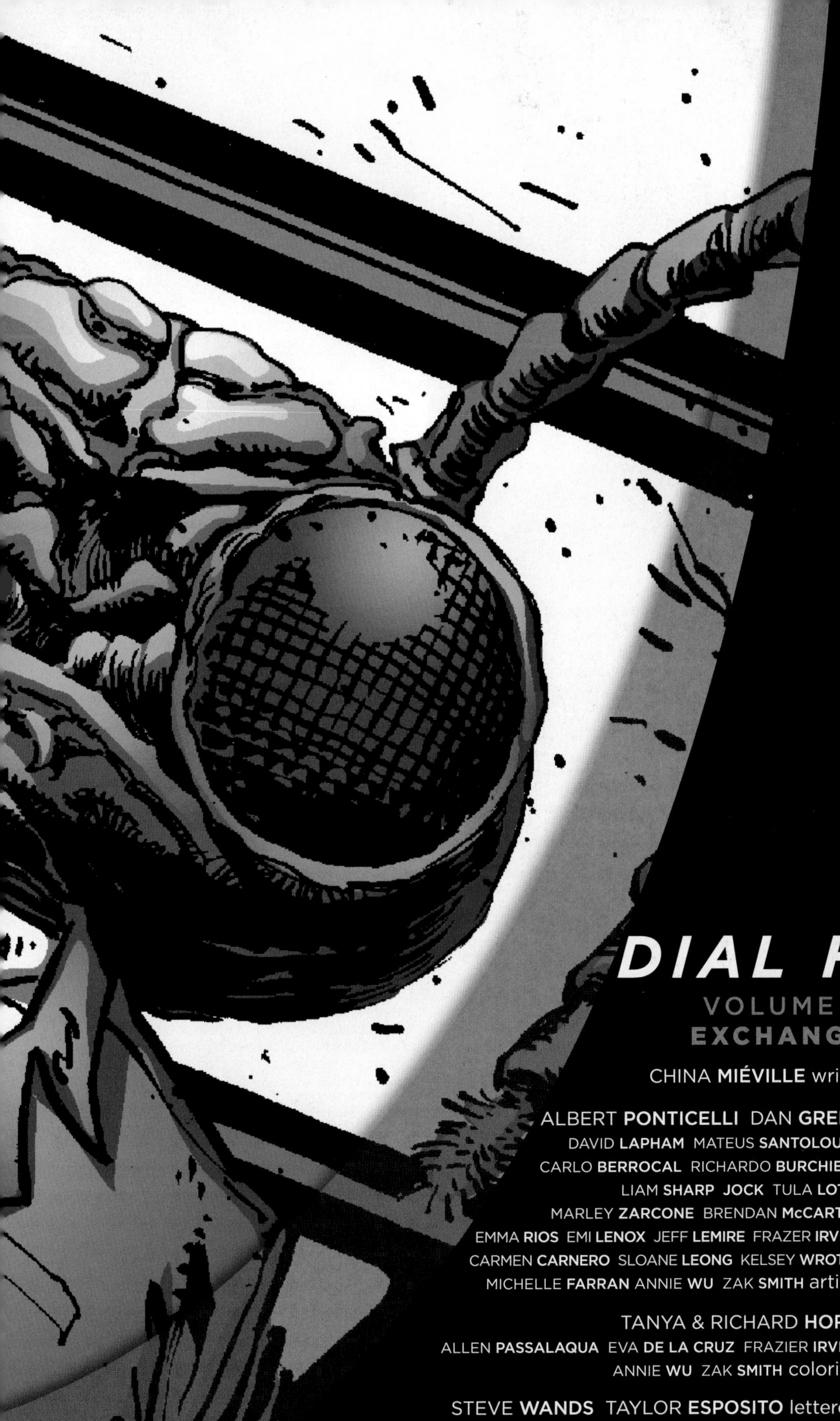

DIAL H

VOLUME 2
EXCHANGE

CHINA **MIÉVILLE** writer

ALBERT **PONTICELLI** DAN **GREEN**
DAVID **LAPHAM** MATEUS **SANTOLOUCO**
CARLO **BERROCAL** RICHARDO **BURCHIELLI**
LIAM **SHARP** **JOCK** TULA **LOTAY**
MARLEY **ZARCONE** BRENDAN **McCARTHY**
EMMA **RIOS** EMI **LENOX** JEFF **LEMIRE** FRAZER **IRVING**
CARMEN **CARNERO** SLOANE **LEONG** KELSEY **WROTEN**
MICHELLE **FARRAN** ANNIE **WU** ZAK **SMITH** artists

TANYA & RICHARD **HORIE**
ALLEN **PASSALAQUA** EVA **DE LA CRUZ** FRAZIER **IRVING**
ANNIE **WU** ZAK **SMITH** colorists

STEVE **WANDS** TAYLOR **ESPOSITO** letterers

BRIAN **BOLLAND** collection & original series cover artist

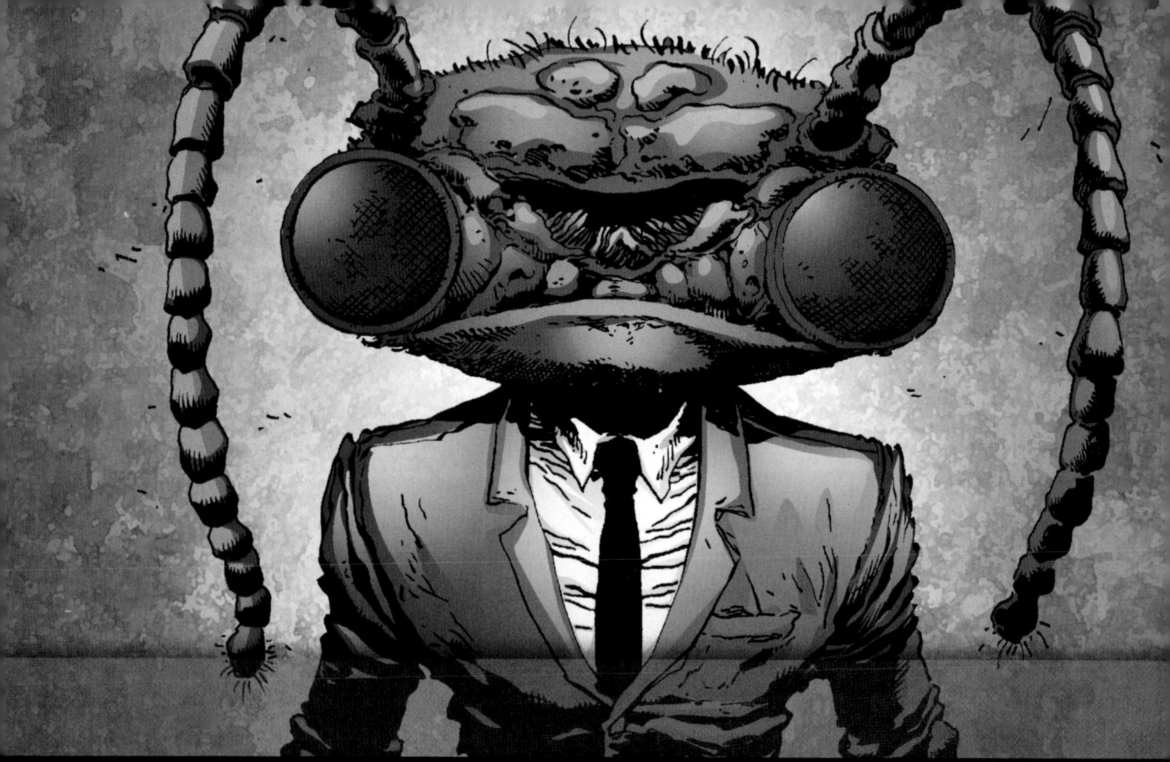

KAREN BERGER WILL DENNIS GREGORY LOCKARD Editors - Original Series
RACHEL PINNELAS Editor ROBBIN BROSTERMAN Design Director - Books
ROBBIE BIEDERMAN Publication Design

BOB HARRAS VP - Senior Editor-in-Chief, DC Comics

DIANE NELSON President DAN DIDIO and JIM LEE Co-Publishers
GEOFF JOHNS Chief Creative Officer
JOHN ROOD Executive VP - Sales, Marketing and Business Development
AMY GENKINS Senior VP - Business and Legal Affairs NAIRI GARDINER Senior VP - Finance
JEFF BOISON VP - Publishing Planning MARK CHIARELLO VP - Art Direction and Design
JOHN CUNNINGHAM VP - Marketing TERRI CUNNINGHAM VP - Editorial Administration
ALISON GILL Senior VP - Manufacturing and Operations HANK KANALZ Senior VP - Vertigo & Integrated Publishing
JAY KOGAN VP - Business and Legal Affairs, Publishing JACK MAHAN VP - Business Affairs, Talent
NICK NAPOLITANO VP - Manufacturing Administration SUE POHJA VP - Book Sales
COURTNEY SIMMONS Senior VP - Publicity BOB WAYNE Senior VP - Sales

DIAL H: VOLUME 2: EXCHANGE

DC Comics, 1700 Broadway, New York, NY 10019
A Warner Bros. Entertainment Company.
Printed by RR Donnelley, Salem, VA, USA. 1/03/14. First Printing.
ISBN: 978-1-4012-4383-8

Library of Congress Cataloging-in-Publication Data

Miéville, China, author.
Dial H. Vol. 2, Exchange / China Miéville ; [illustrated by] Alberto Ponticelli ; [illustrated by] Dan Green.
pages cm. -- (The New 52!)
Collects #7-15 of Dial H"-- Provided by publisher.
ISBN 978-1-4012-4383-8 (pbk.)
1. Graphic novels. I. Ponticelli, Alberto, illustrator. II. Green, Dan, illustrator. III. Title. IV. Title: Exchange.
PN6737.M53D54 2014
741.5'942--dc23
2013040734

SUSTAINABLE FORESTRY INITIATIVE
Certified Chain of Custody
At Least 20% Certified Forest Content
www.sfiprogram.org
SFI-01042
APPLIES TO TEXT STOCK ONLY

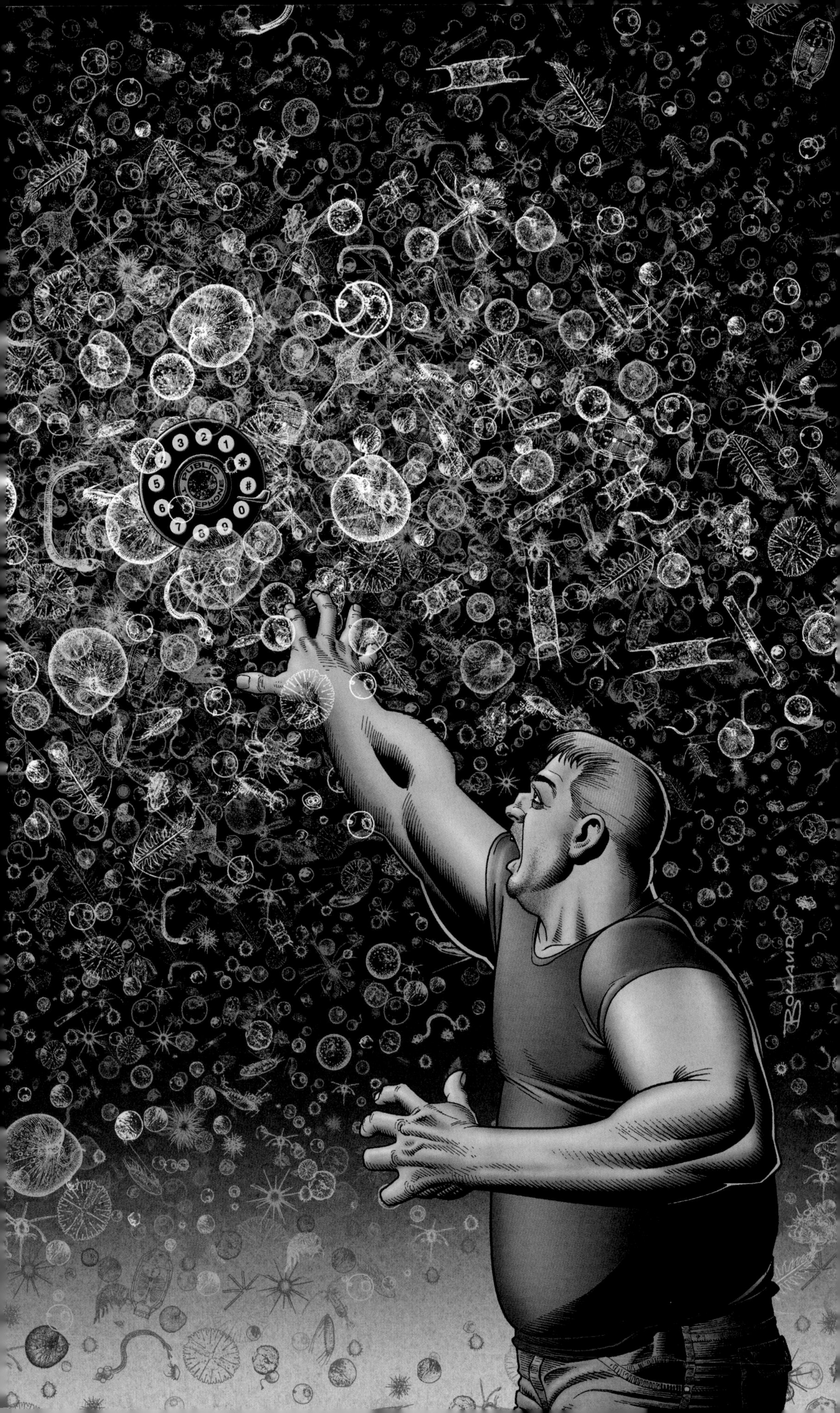
PUBLIC
BOLLAND

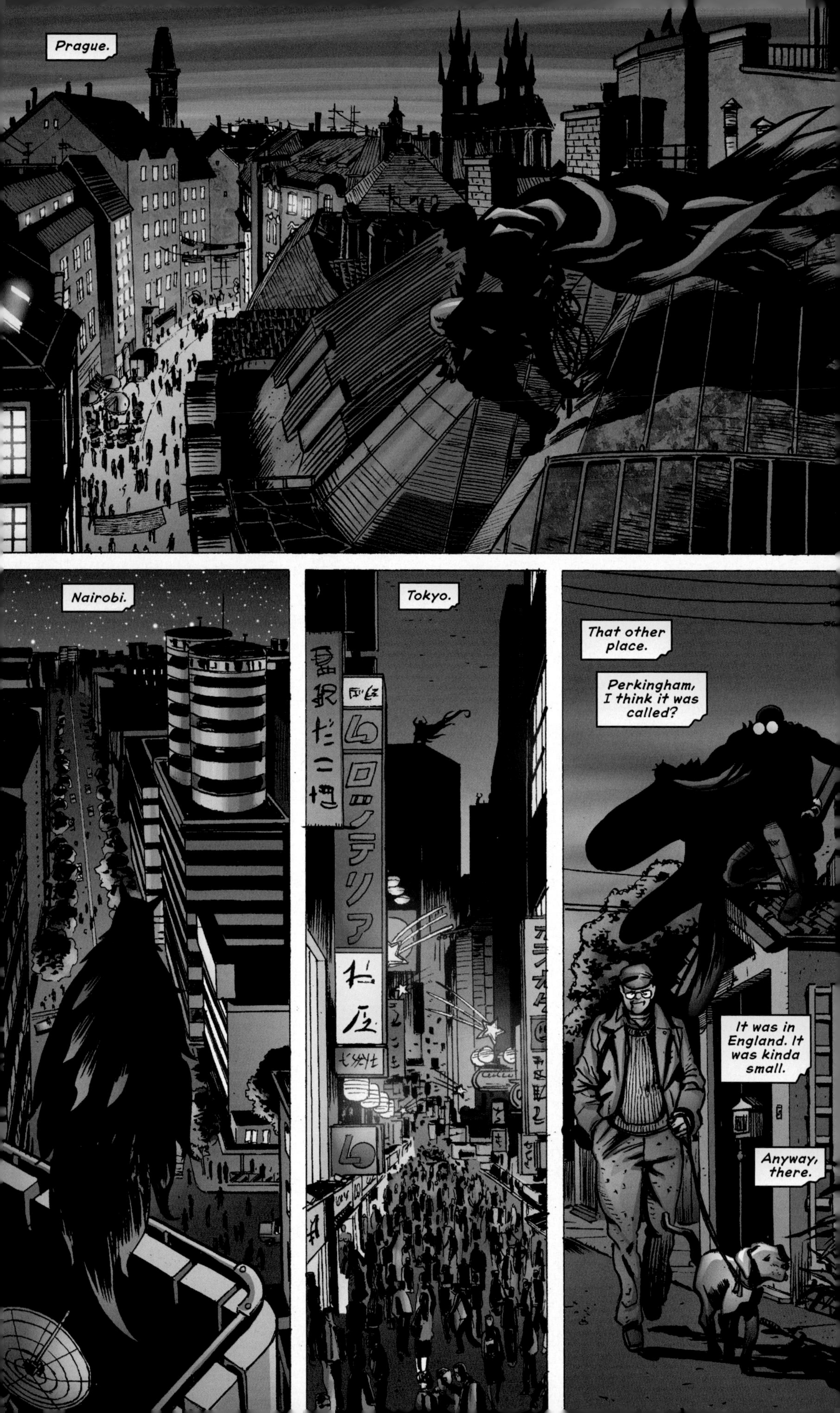
Prague.
Nairobi.
Tokyo.
That other place.
Perkingham, I think it was called?
It was in England. It was kinda small.
Anyway, there.

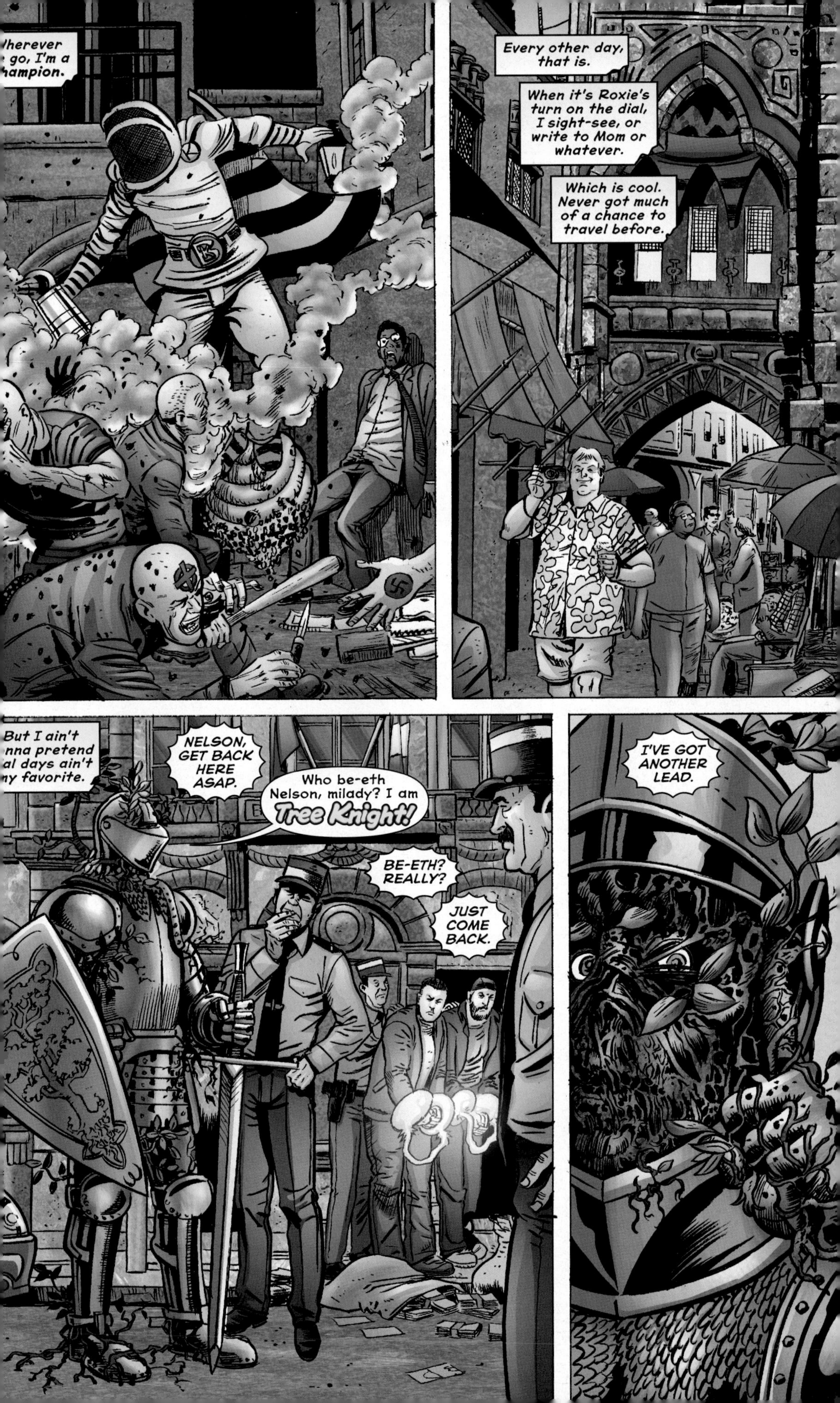
herever go, I'm a hampion.
Every other day, that is.
When it's Roxie's turn on the dial, I sight-see, or write to Mom or whatever.
Which is cool. Never got much of a chance to travel before.
But I ain't nna pretend al days ain't ny favorite.
NELSON, GET BACK HERE ASAP.
Who be-eth Nelson, milady? I am Tree Knight!
BE-ETH? REALLY?
JUST COME BACK.
I'VE GOT ANOTHER LEAD.

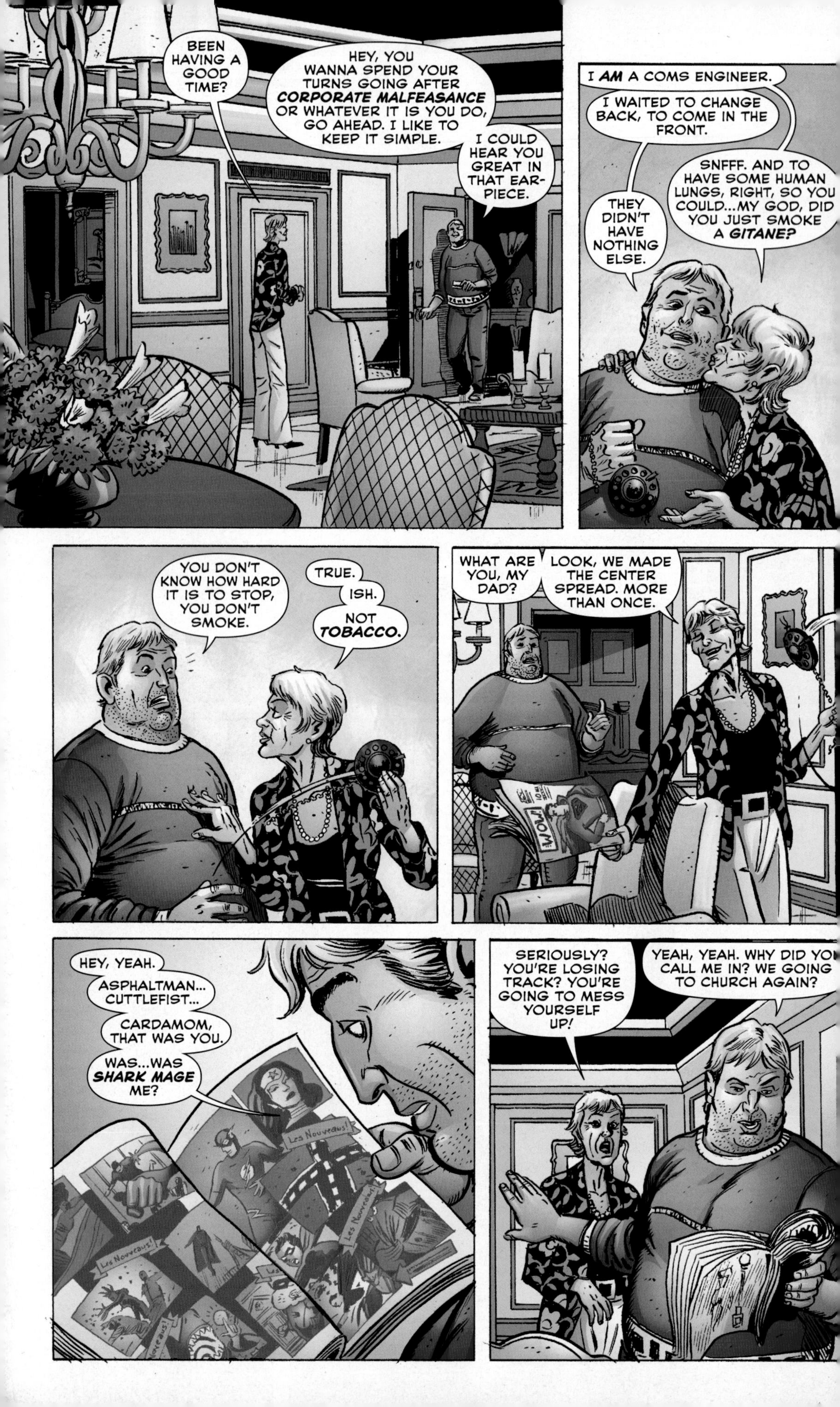
BEEN HAVING A GOOD TIME?
HEY, YOU WANNA SPEND YOUR TURNS GOING AFTER CORPORATE MALFEASANCE OR WHATEVER IT IS YOU DO, GO AHEAD. I LIKE TO KEEP IT SIMPLE.
I COULD HEAR YOU GREAT IN THAT EAR-PIECE.
I AM A COMS ENGINEER.
I WAITED TO CHANGE BACK, TO COME IN THE FRONT.
SNFFF. AND TO HAVE SOME HUMAN LUNGS, RIGHT, SO YOU COULD...MY GOD, DID YOU JUST SMOKE A GITANE?
THEY DIDN'T HAVE NOTHING ELSE.
YOU DON'T KNOW HOW HARD IT IS TO STOP, YOU DON'T SMOKE.
TRUE.
ISH.
NOT TOBACCO.
WHAT ARE YOU, MY DAD?
LOOK, WE MADE THE CENTER SPREAD. MORE THAN ONCE.
WOW!
HEY, YEAH.
ASPHALTMAN... CUTTLEFIST...
CARDAMOM, THAT WAS YOU.
WAS...WAS SHARK MAGE ME?
Les Nouveaus!
SERIOUSLY? YOU'RE LOSING TRACK? YOU'RE GOING TO MESS YOURSELF UP!
YEAH, YEAH. WHY DID YO CALL ME IN? WE GOING TO CHURCH AGAIN?

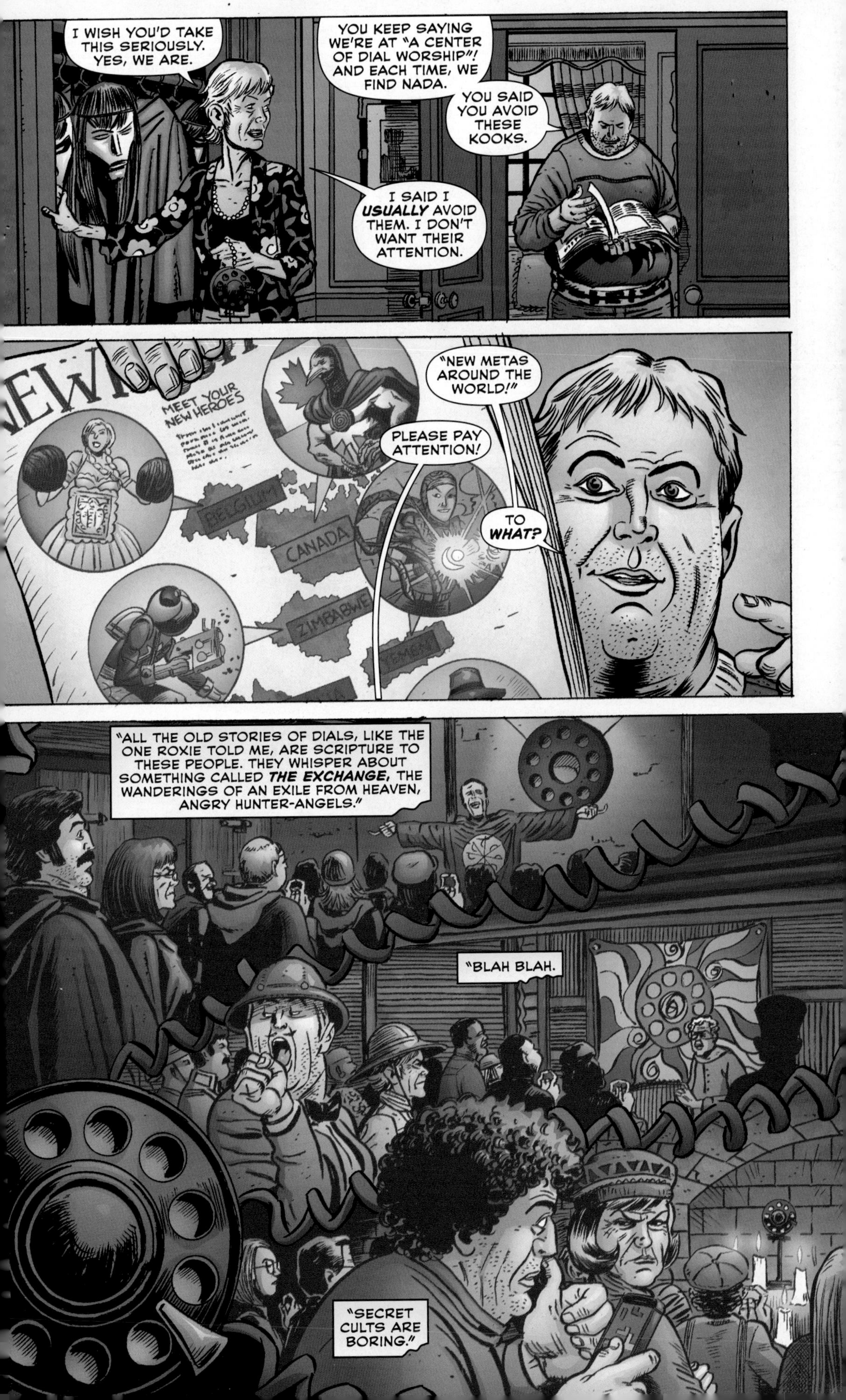
I WISH YOU'D TAKE THIS SERIOUSLY. YES, WE ARE.
YOU KEEP SAYING WE'RE AT "A CENTER OF DIAL WORSHIP"! AND EACH TIME, WE FIND NADA.
YOU SAID YOU AVOID THESE KOOKS.
I SAID I USUALLY AVOID THEM. I DON'T WANT THEIR ATTENTION.
MEET YOUR NEW HEROES
BELGIUM
CANADA
ZIMBABWE
YEMEN
"NEW METAS AROUND THE WORLD!"
PLEASE PAY ATTENTION!
TO WHAT?
"ALL THE OLD STORIES OF DIALS, LIKE THE ONE ROXIE TOLD ME, ARE SCRIPTURE TO THESE PEOPLE. THEY WHISPER ABOUT SOMETHING CALLED THE EXCHANGE, THE WANDERINGS OF AN EXILE FROM HEAVEN, ANGRY HUNTER-ANGELS."
"BLAH BLAH.
"SECRET CULTS ARE BORING."

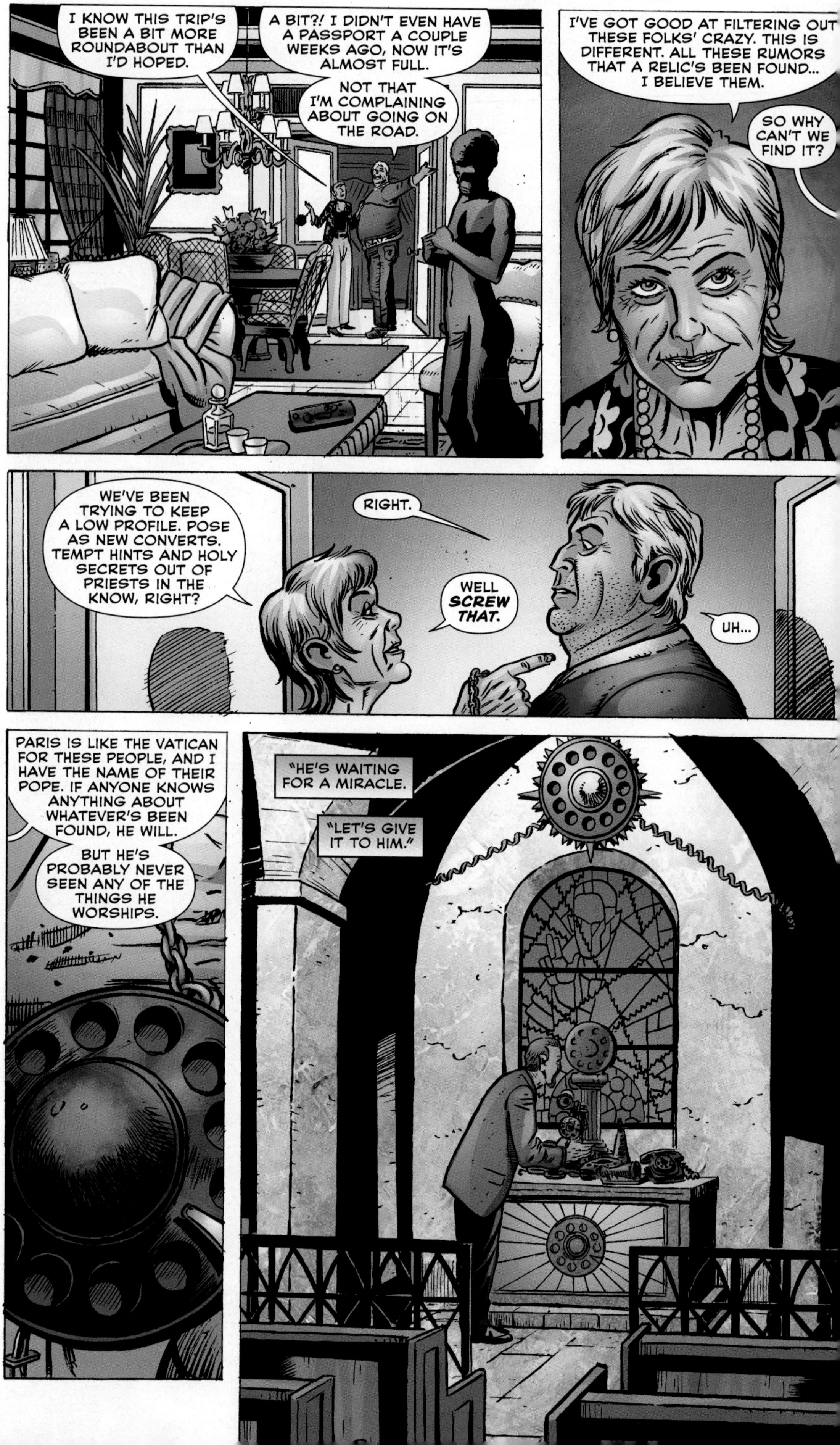
I KNOW THIS TRIP'S BEEN A BIT MORE ROUNDABOUT THAN I'D HOPED.
A BIT?! I DIDN'T EVEN HAVE A PASSPORT A COUPLE WEEKS AGO, NOW IT'S ALMOST FULL.
NOT THAT I'M COMPLAINING ABOUT GOING ON THE ROAD.
I'VE GOT GOOD AT FILTERING OUT THESE FOLKS' CRAZY. THIS IS DIFFERENT. ALL THESE RUMORS THAT A RELIC'S BEEN FOUND... I BELIEVE THEM.
SO WHY CAN'T WE FIND IT?
WE'VE BEEN TRYING TO KEEP A LOW PROFILE. POSE AS NEW CONVERTS. TEMPT HINTS AND HOLY SECRETS OUT OF PRIESTS IN THE KNOW, RIGHT?
RIGHT.
WELL SCREW THAT.
UH...
PARIS IS LIKE THE VATICAN FOR THESE PEOPLE, AND I HAVE THE NAME OF THEIR POPE. IF ANYONE KNOWS ANYTHING ABOUT WHATEVER'S BEEN FOUND, HE WILL.
BUT HE'S PROBABLY NEVER SEEN ANY OF THE THINGS HE WORSHIPS.
"HE'S WAITING FOR A MIRACLE.
"LET'S GIVE IT TO HIM."

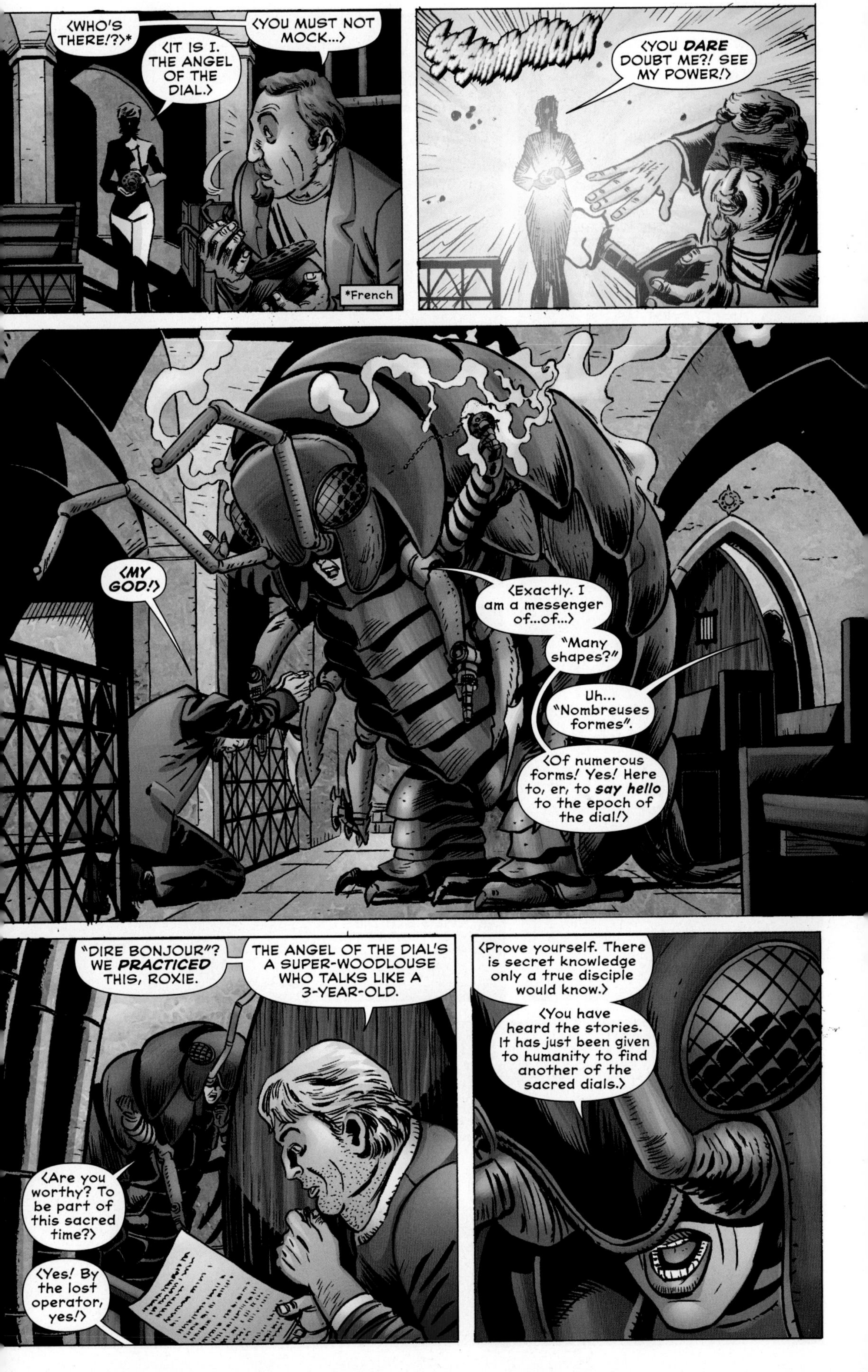
<WHO'S THERE!?>*
<YOU MUST NOT MOCK...>
<IT IS I. THE ANGEL OF THE DIAL.>
*French
<YOU DARE DOUBT ME?! SEE MY POWER!>
<MY GOD!>
<Exactly. I am a messenger of...of...>
"Many shapes?"
Uh... "Nombreuses formes".
<Of numerous forms! Yes! Here to, er, to say hello to the epoch of the dial!>
"DIRE BONJOUR"? WE PRACTICED THIS, ROXIE.
THE ANGEL OF THE DIAL'S A SUPER-WOODLOUSE WHO TALKS LIKE A 3-YEAR-OLD.
<Are you worthy? To be part of this sacred time?>
<Yes! By the lost operator, yes!>
<Prove yourself. There is secret knowledge only a true disciple would know.>
<You have heard the stories. It has just been given to humanity to find another of the sacred dials.>

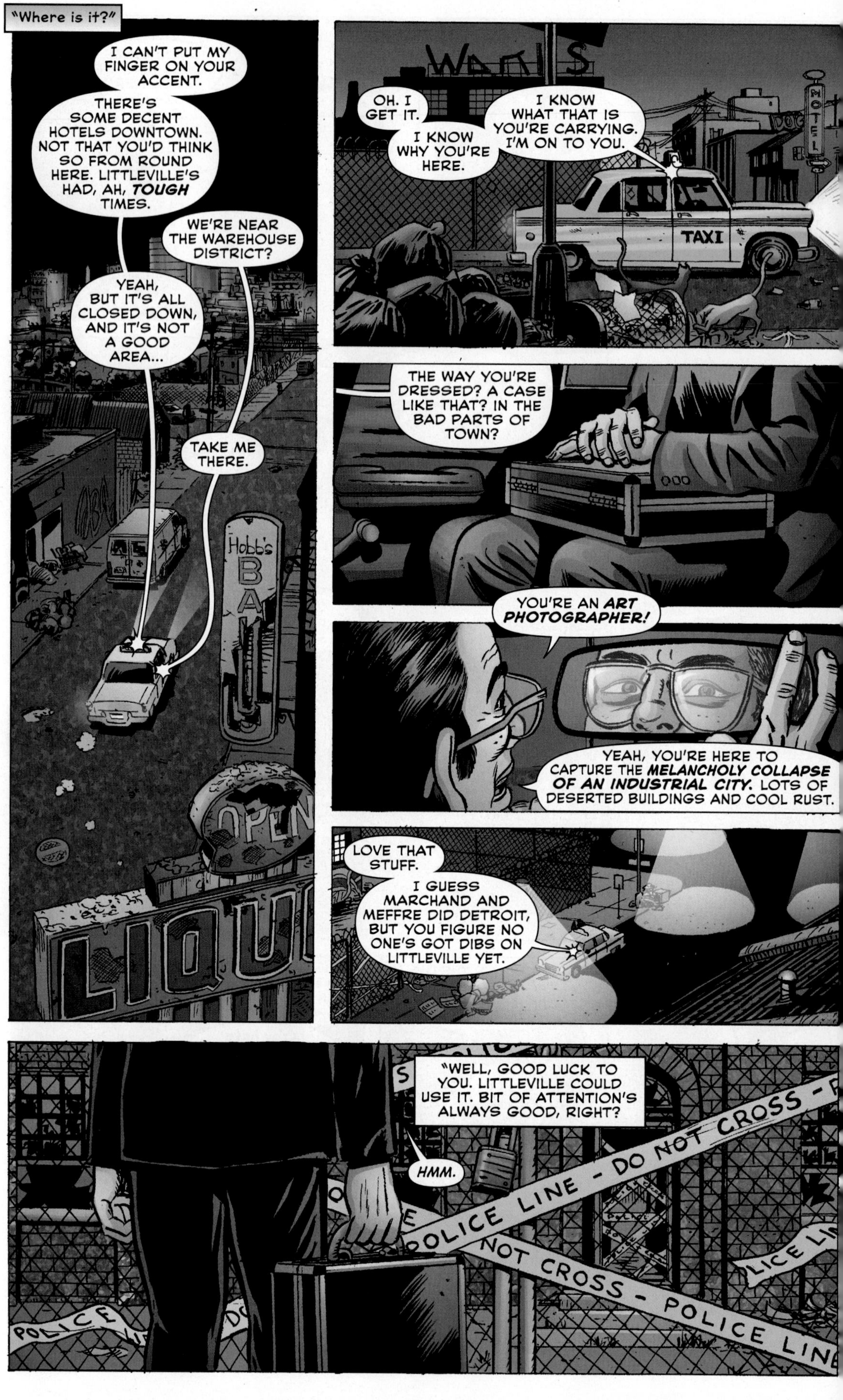

"Where is it?"
I CAN'T PUT MY FINGER ON YOUR ACCENT.
THERE'S SOME DECENT HOTELS DOWNTOWN. NOT THAT YOU'D THINK SO FROM ROUND HERE. LITTLEVILLE'S HAD, AH, TOUGH TIMES.
WE'RE NEAR THE WAREHOUSE DISTRICT?
YEAH, BUT IT'S ALL CLOSED DOWN, AND IT'S NOT A GOOD AREA...
TAKE ME THERE.
Hobb's
OPEN
LIQU
OH. I GET IT.
I KNOW WHY YOU'RE HERE.
I KNOW WHAT THAT IS YOU'RE CARRYING. I'M ON TO YOU.
TAXI
THE WAY YOU'RE DRESSED? A CASE LIKE THAT? IN THE BAD PARTS OF TOWN?
YOU'RE AN ART PHOTOGRAPHER!
YEAH, YOU'RE HERE TO CAPTURE THE MELANCHOLY COLLAPSE OF AN INDUSTRIAL CITY. LOTS OF DESERTED BUILDINGS AND COOL RUST.
LOVE THAT STUFF.
I GUESS MARCHAND AND MEFFRE DID DETROIT, BUT YOU FIGURE NO ONE'S GOT DIBS ON LITTLEVILLE YET.
"WELL, GOOD LUCK TO YOU. LITTLEVILLE COULD USE IT. BIT OF ATTENTION'S ALWAYS GOOD, RIGHT?
HMM.
POLICE LINE - DO NOT CROSS
NOT CROSS - POLICE LINE

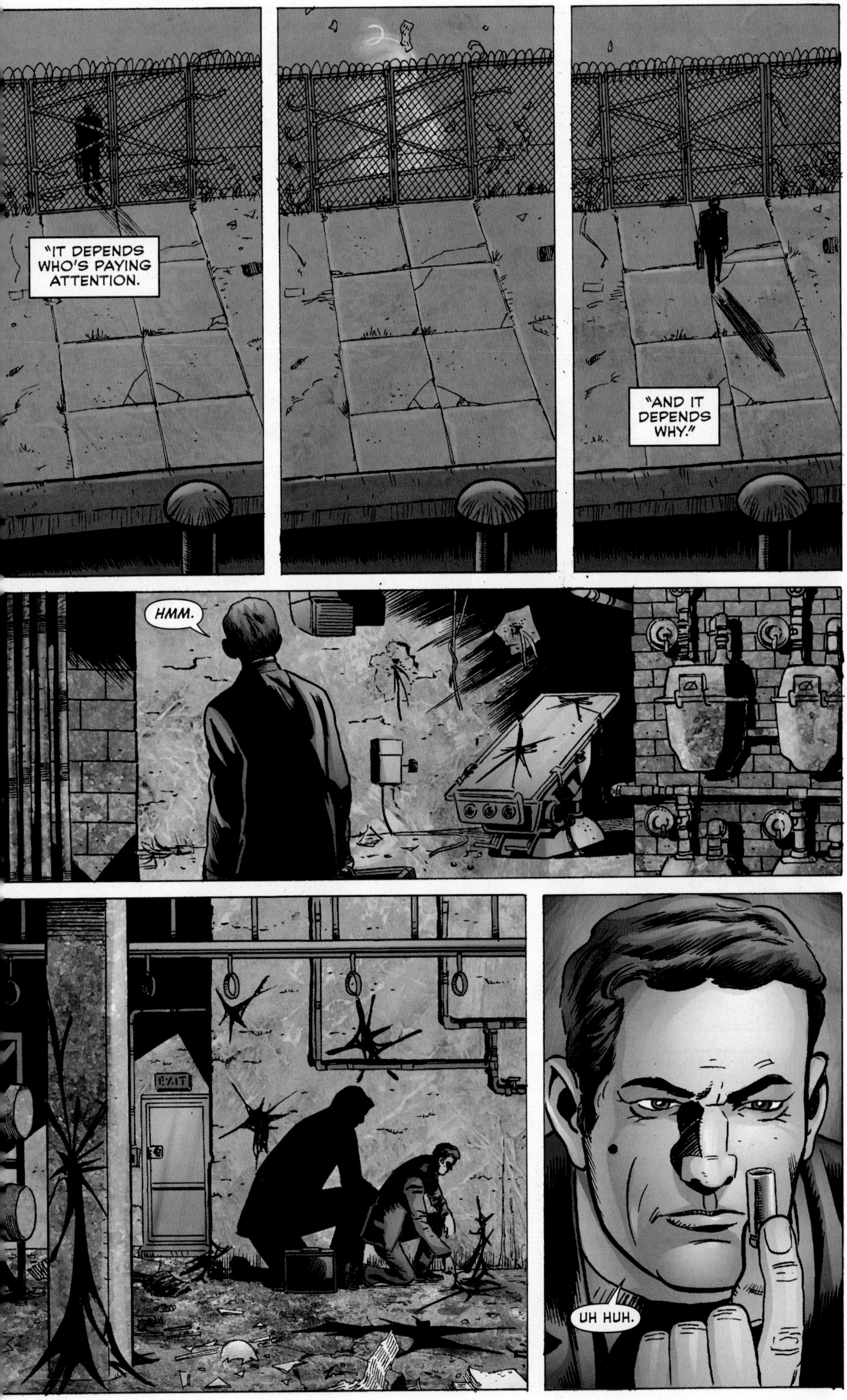
"IT DEPENDS WHO'S PAYING ATTENTION.
"AND IT DEPENDS WHY."
HMM.
UH HUH.

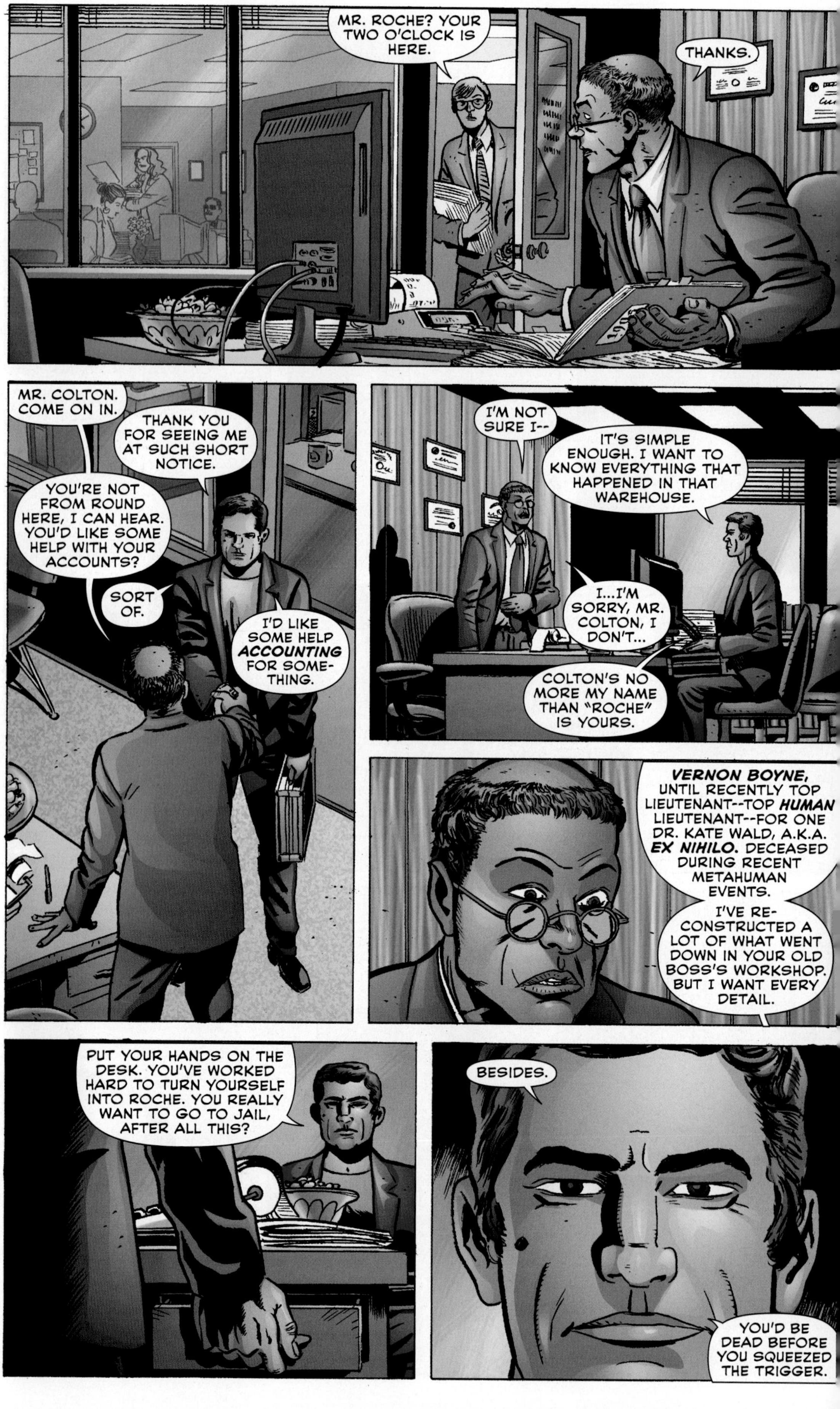
MR. ROCHE? YOUR TWO O'CLOCK IS HERE.
THANKS.
MR. COLTON. COME ON IN.
THANK YOU FOR SEEING ME AT SUCH SHORT NOTICE.
YOU'RE NOT FROM ROUND HERE, I CAN HEAR. YOU'D LIKE SOME HELP WITH YOUR ACCOUNTS?
SORT OF.
I'D LIKE SOME HELP ACCOUNTING FOR SOME-THING.
I'M NOT SURE I--
IT'S SIMPLE ENOUGH. I WANT TO KNOW EVERYTHING THAT HAPPENED IN THAT WAREHOUSE.
I...I'M SORRY, MR. COLTON, I DON'T...
COLTON'S NO MORE MY NAME THAN "ROCHE" IS YOURS.
VERNON BOYNE, UNTIL RECENTLY TOP LIEUTENANT--TOP HUMAN LIEUTENANT--FOR ONE DR. KATE WALD, A.K.A. EX NIHILO. DECEASED DURING RECENT METAHUMAN EVENTS.
I'VE RE-CONSTRUCTED A LOT OF WHAT WENT DOWN IN YOUR OLD BOSS'S WORKSHOP. BUT I WANT EVERY DETAIL.
PUT YOUR HANDS ON THE DESK. YOU'VE WORKED HARD TO TURN YOURSELF INTO ROCHE. YOU REALLY WANT TO GO TO JAIL, AFTER ALL THIS?
BESIDES.
YOU'D BE DEAD BEFORE YOU SQUEEZED THE TRIGGER.

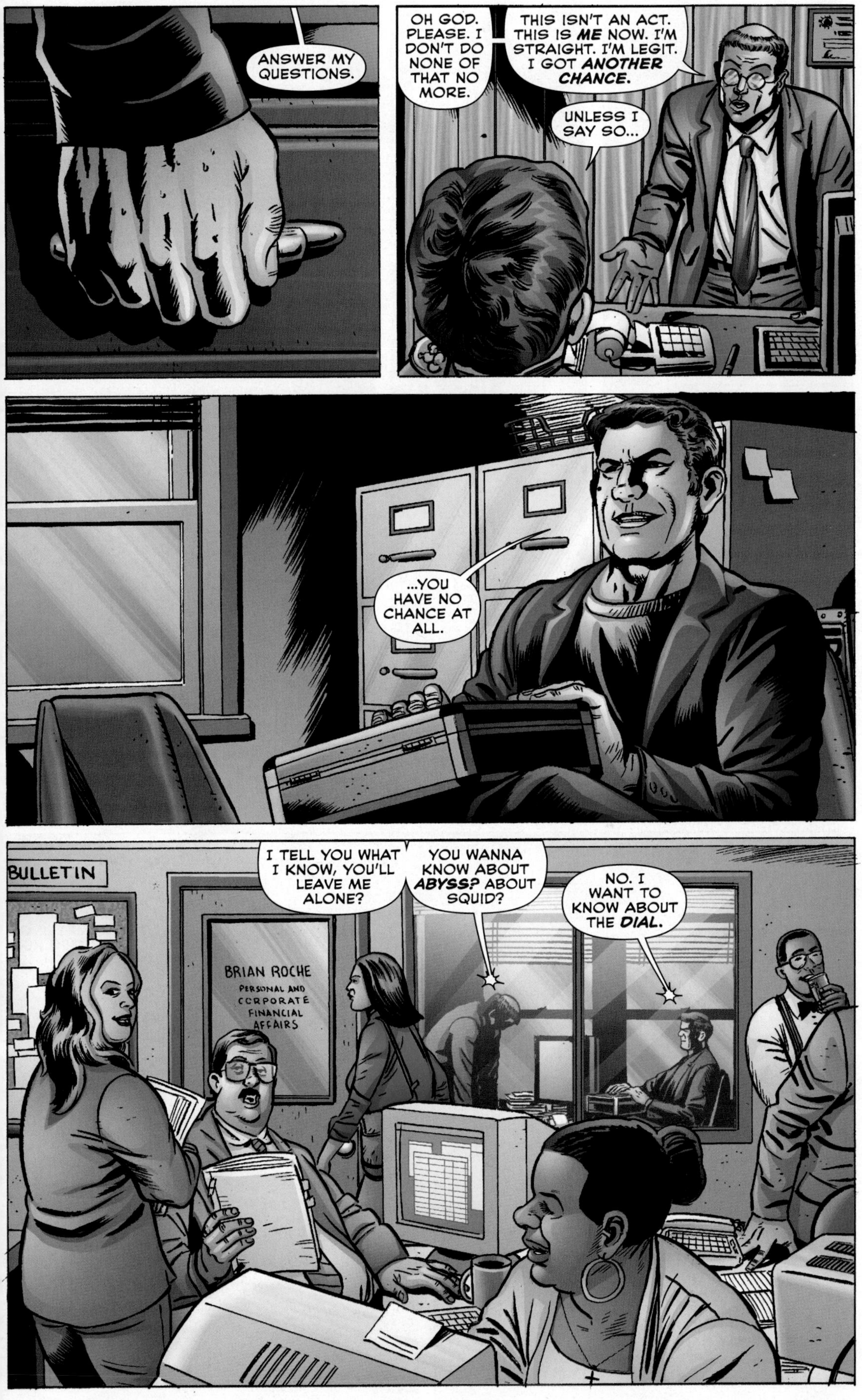

ANSWER MY QUESTIONS.
OH GOD. PLEASE. I DON'T DO NONE OF THAT NO MORE.
THIS ISN'T AN ACT. THIS IS *ME* NOW. I'M STRAIGHT. I'M LEGIT. I GOT ***ANOTHER CHANCE.***
UNLESS I SAY SO...
...YOU HAVE NO CHANCE AT ALL.
BULLETIN
BRIAN ROCHE
PERSONAL AND CORPORATE FINANCIAL AFFAIRS
I TELL YOU WHAT I KNOW, YOU'LL LEAVE ME ALONE?
YOU WANNA KNOW ABOUT ***ABYSS?*** ABOUT SQUID?
NO. I WANT TO KNOW ABOUT THE ***DIAL.***

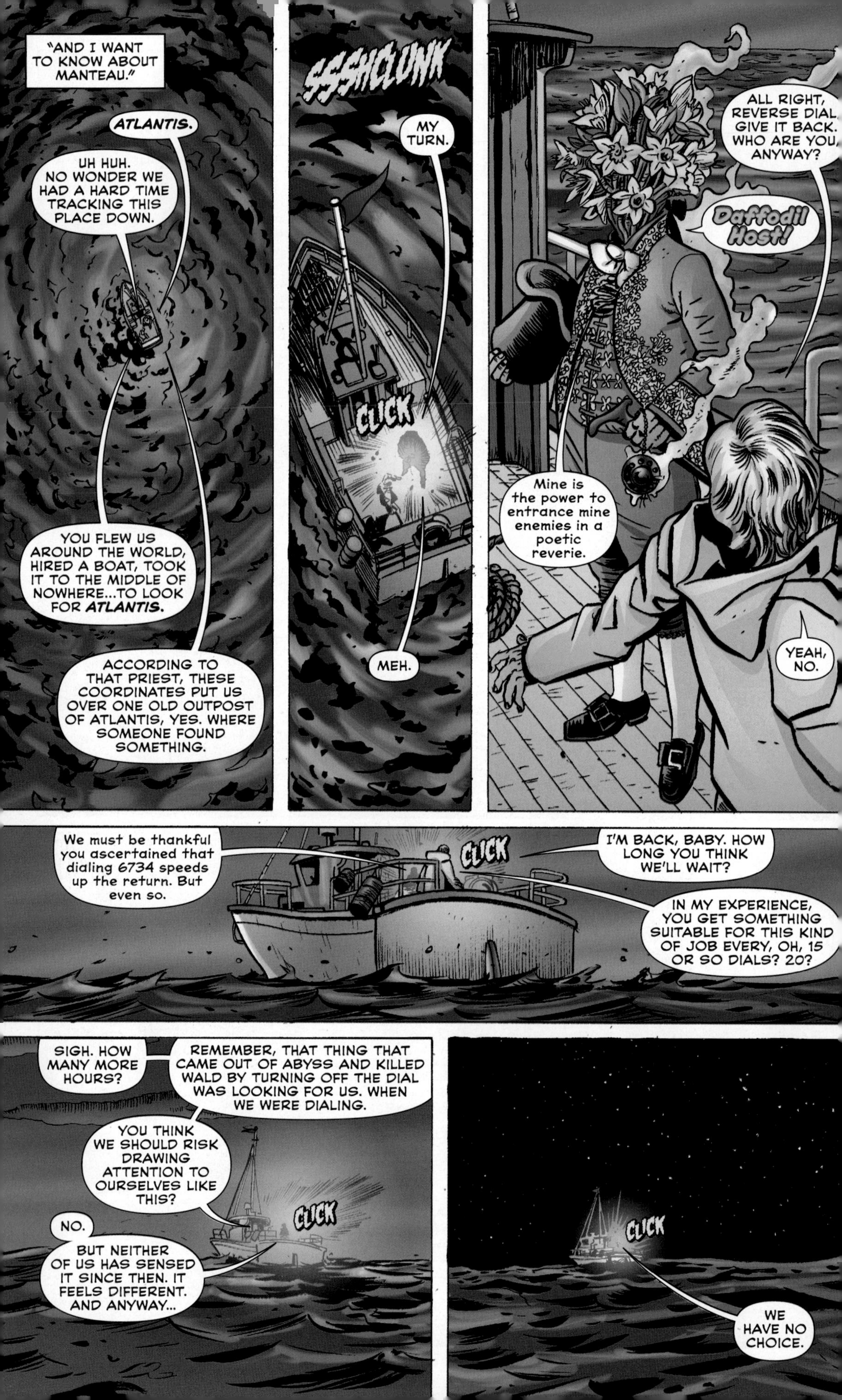
"AND I WANT TO KNOW ABOUT MANTEAU."
ATLANTIS.
UH HUH. NO WONDER WE HAD A HARD TIME TRACKING THIS PLACE DOWN.
YOU FLEW US AROUND THE WORLD, HIRED A BOAT, TOOK IT TO THE MIDDLE OF NOWHERE...TO LOOK FOR ATLANTIS.
ACCORDING TO THAT PRIEST, THESE COORDINATES PUT US OVER ONE OLD OUTPOST OF ATLANTIS, YES. WHERE SOMEONE FOUND SOMETHING.
SSSHCLUNK
MY TURN.
CLICK
MEH.
ALL RIGHT, REVERSE DIAL GIVE IT BACK. WHO ARE YOU, ANYWAY?
Daffodil Host!
Mine is the power to entrance mine enemies in a poetic reverie.
YEAH, NO.
We must be thankful you ascertained that dialing 6734 speeds up the return. But even so.
CLICK
I'M BACK, BABY. HOW LONG YOU THINK WE'LL WAIT?
IN MY EXPERIENCE, YOU GET SOMETHING SUITABLE FOR THIS KIND OF JOB EVERY, OH, 15 OR SO DIALS? 20?
SIGH. HOW MANY MORE HOURS?
REMEMBER, THAT THING THAT CAME OUT OF ABYSS AND KILLED WALD BY TURNING OFF THE DIAL WAS LOOKING FOR US. WHEN WE WERE DIALING.
YOU THINK WE SHOULD RISK DRAWING ATTENTION TO OURSELVES LIKE THIS?
CLICK
NO.
BUT NEITHER OF US HAS SENSED IT SINCE THEN. IT FEELS DIFFERENT. AND ANYWAY...
CLICK
WE HAVE NO CHOICE.

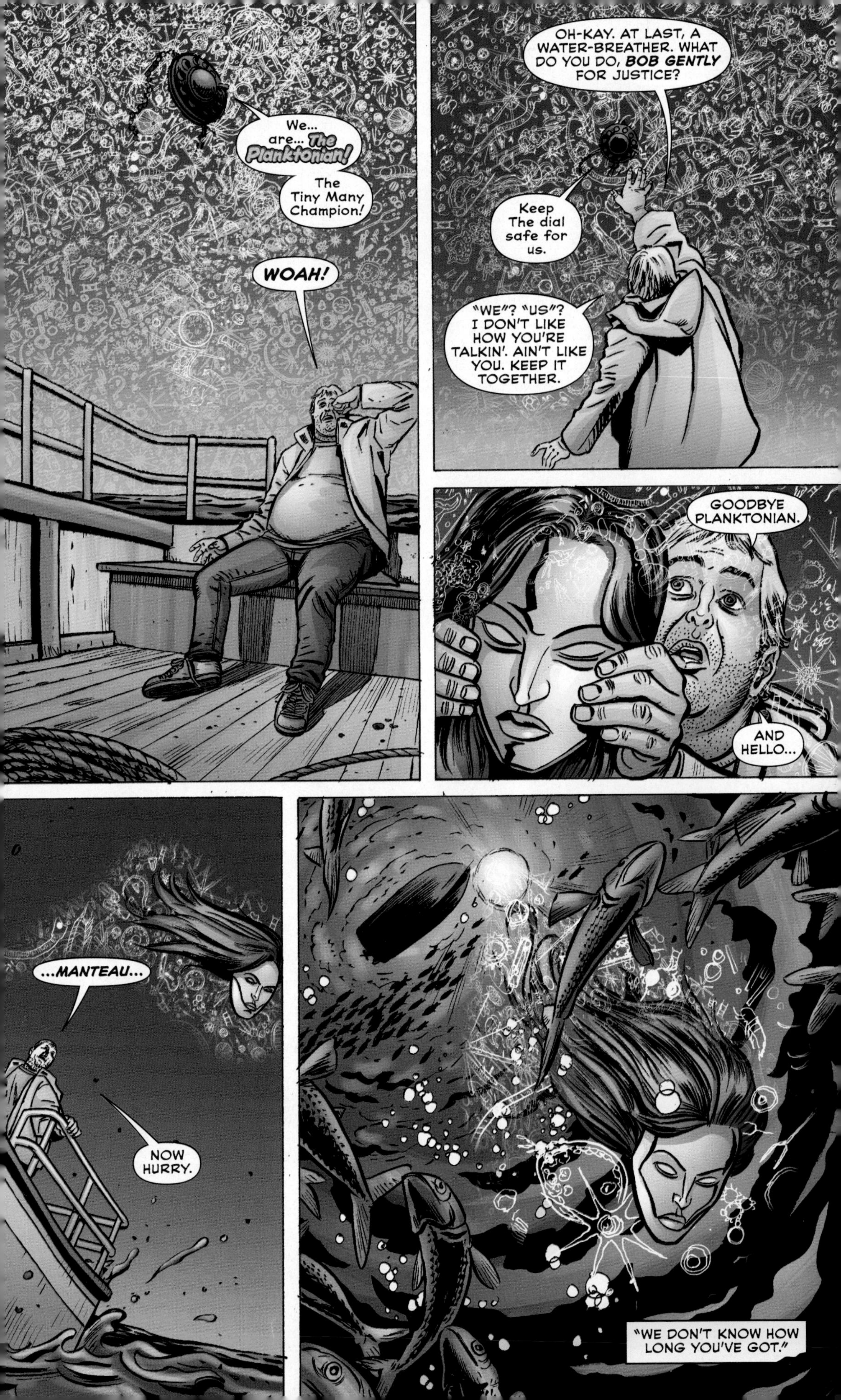
We... are... The Planktonian!
The Tiny Many Champion!
WOAH!
OH-KAY. AT LAST, A WATER-BREATHER. WHAT DO YOU DO, BOB GENTLY FOR JUSTICE?
Keep The dial safe for us.
"WE"? "US"? I DON'T LIKE HOW YOU'RE TALKIN'. AIN'T LIKE YOU. KEEP IT TOGETHER.
GOODBYE PLANKTONIAN.
AND HELLO...
...MANTEAU...
NOW HURRY.
"WE DON'T KNOW HOW LONG YOU'VE GOT."

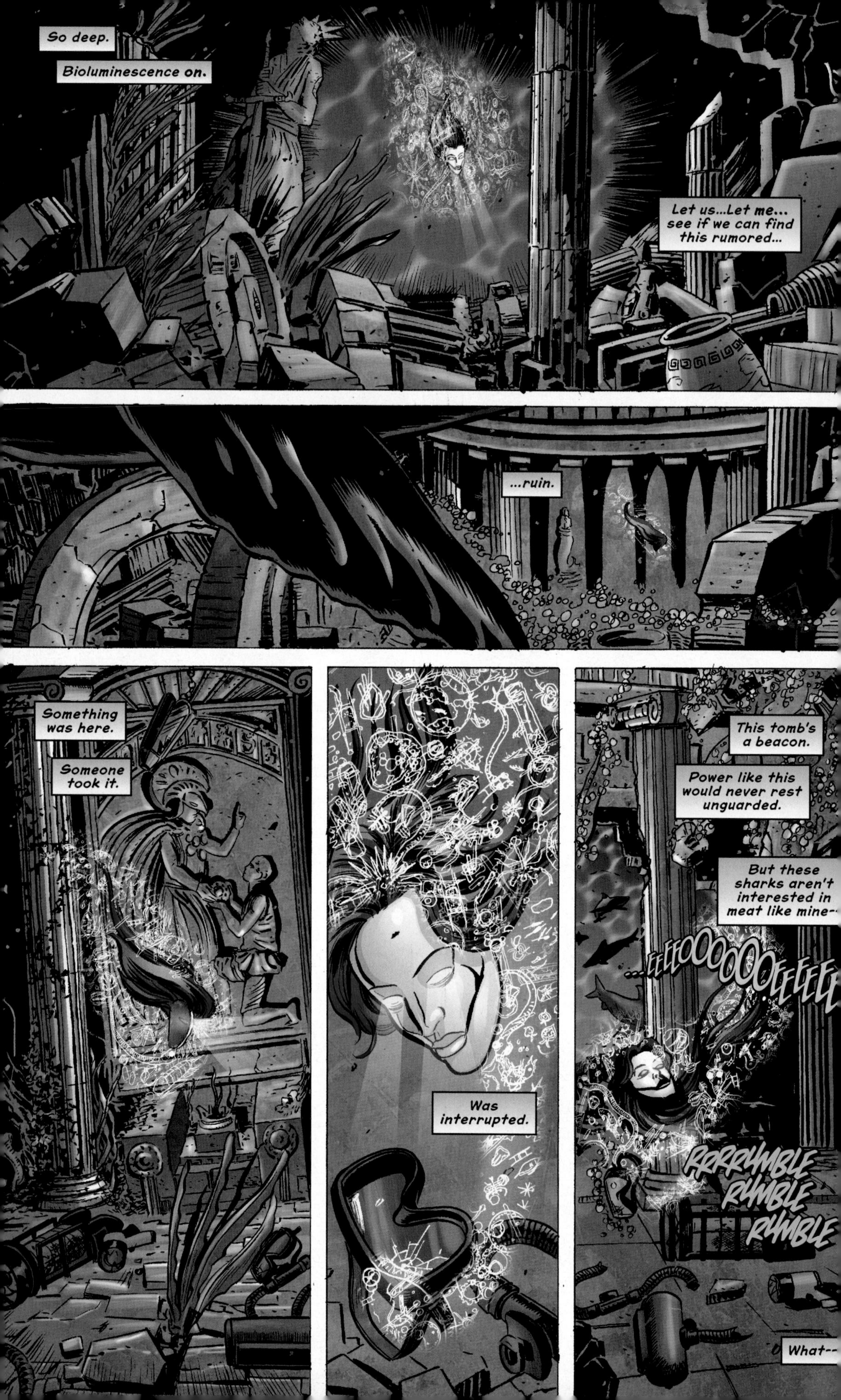
So deep.
Bioluminescence on.
Let us...Let me... see if we can find this rumored...
...ruin.
Something was here.
Someone took it.
Was interrupted.
This tomb's a beacon.
Power like this would never rest unguarded.
But these sharks aren't interested in meat like mine--
...EEEEOOOOOOOEEEEEE
RRRRUMBLE RUMBLE RUMBLE
What--

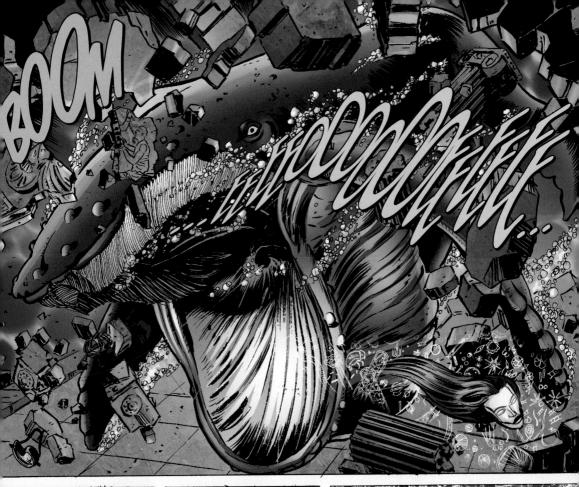

Old nemesis.

Great maw.

I...we... must focus.

Need all my...our... strength.

we

we

we

we

We are the rage of amphipods.

Krillstorm.

The vengeance of fry.

Our strategy is multitude.

No more masks.

We are

we

we

we

The Pelagic Paladin.

The Planktonian.

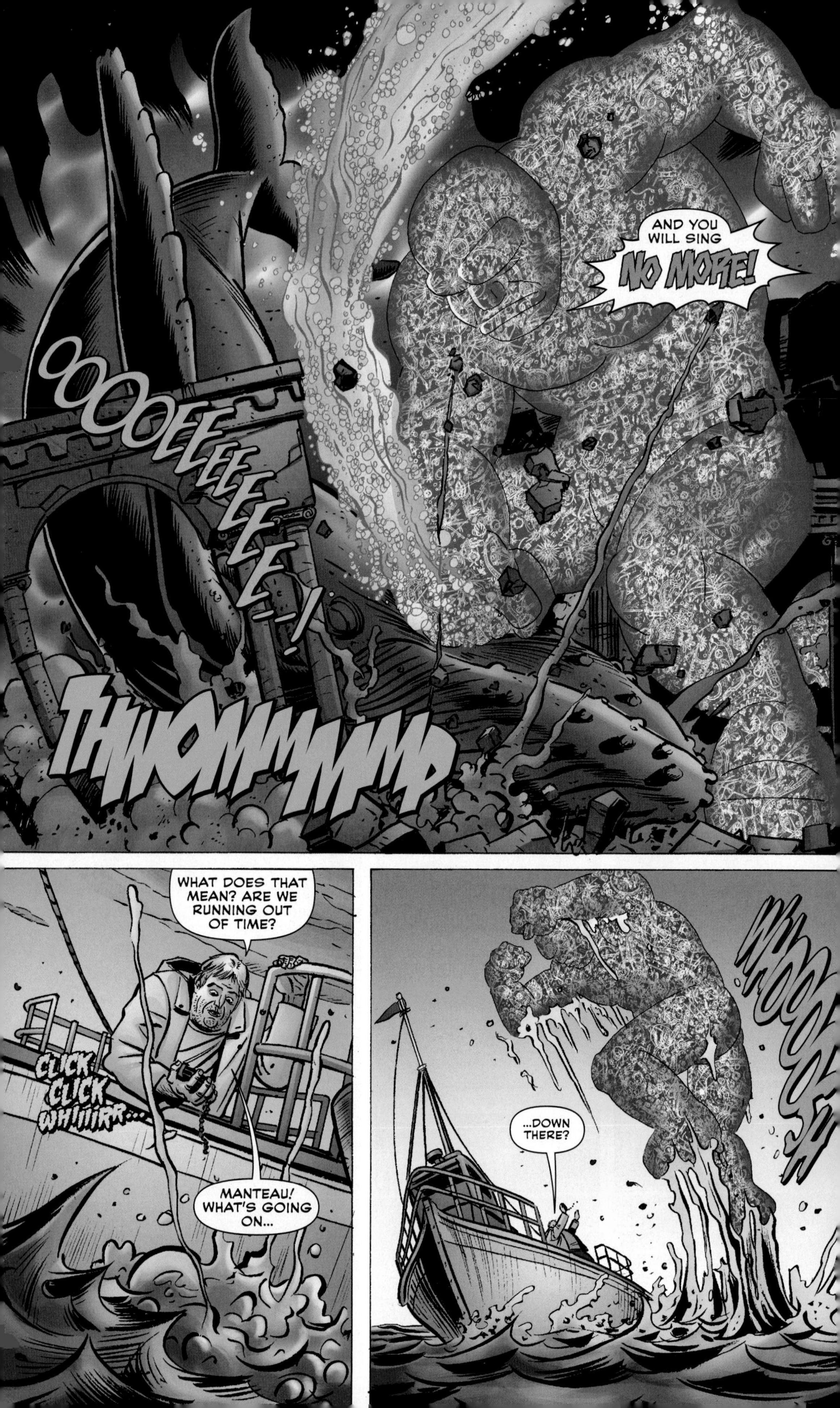
AND YOU WILL SING NO MORE!
OOOOEEEEEEEEE--!
THWOMMMMMP
WHAT DOES THAT MEAN? ARE WE RUNNING OUT OF TIME?
CLICK CLICK WHIIIRR...
MANTEAU! WHAT'S GOING ON...
WHOOOOSH
...DOWN THERE?

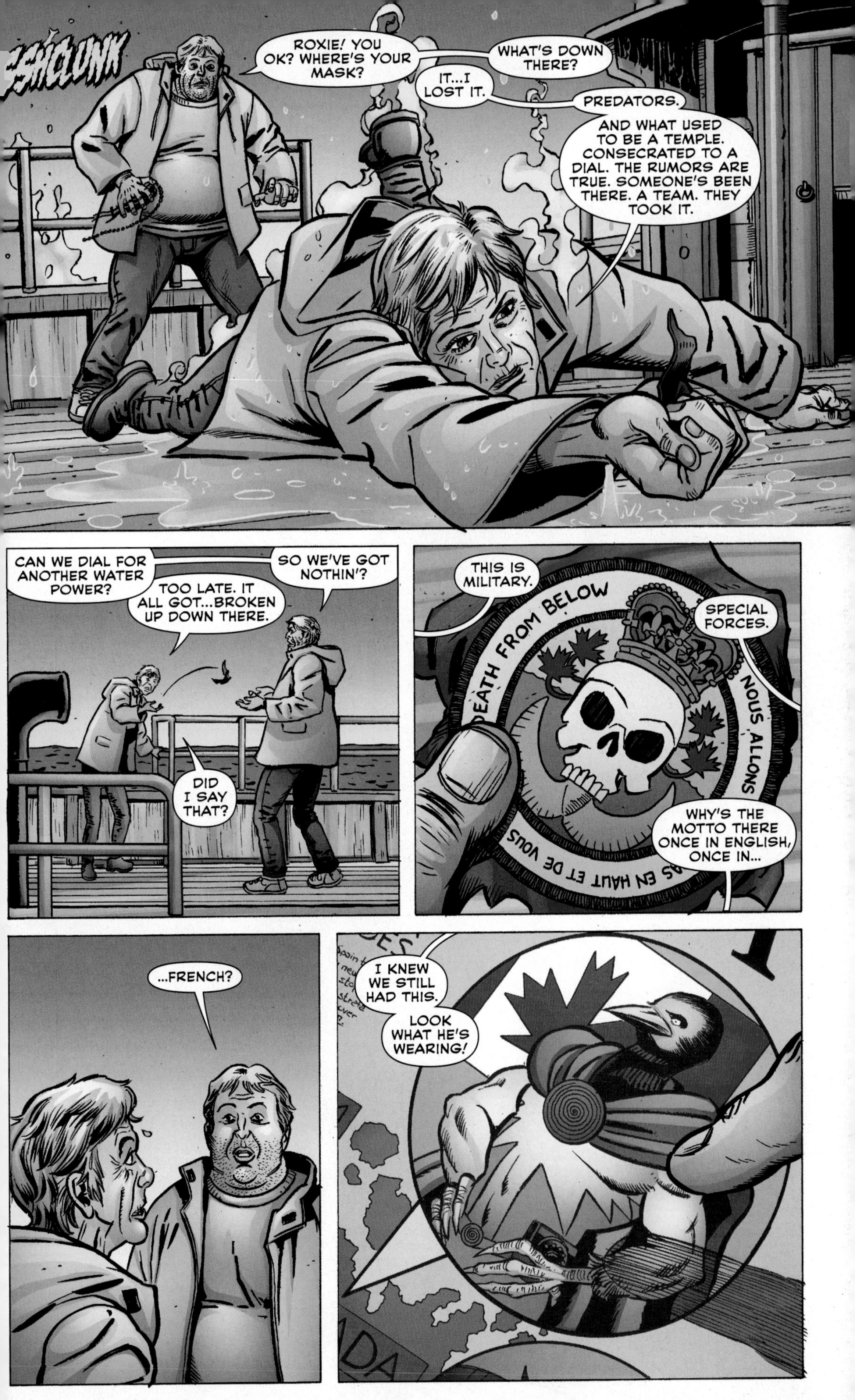
SHCLUNK
ROXIE! YOU OK? WHERE'S YOUR MASK?
WHAT'S DOWN THERE?
IT...I LOST IT.
PREDATORS.
AND WHAT USED TO BE A TEMPLE. CONSECRATED TO A DIAL. THE RUMORS ARE TRUE. SOMEONE'S BEEN THERE. A TEAM. THEY TOOK IT.
CAN WE DIAL FOR ANOTHER WATER POWER?
SO WE'VE GOT NOTHIN'?
TOO LATE. IT ALL GOT...BROKEN UP DOWN THERE.
DID I SAY THAT?
THIS IS MILITARY.
DEATH FROM BELOW
SPECIAL FORCES.
NOUS ALLONS
AS EN HAUT ET DE VOUS
WHY'S THE MOTTO THERE ONCE IN ENGLISH, ONCE IN...
...FRENCH?
I KNEW WE STILL HAD THIS.
LOOK WHAT HE'S WEARING!

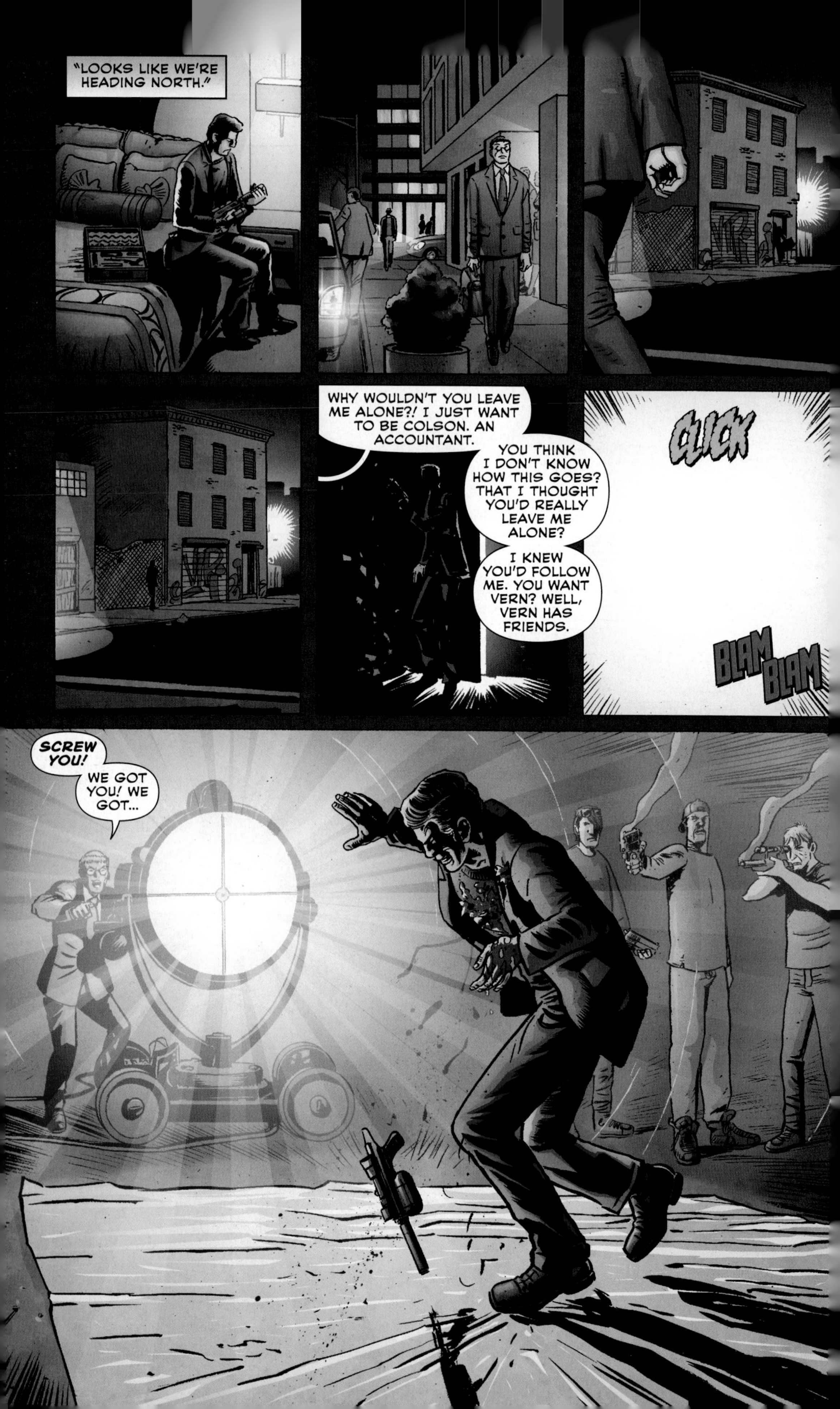
"LOOKS LIKE WE'RE HEADING NORTH."
WHY WOULDN'T YOU LEAVE ME ALONE?! I JUST WANT TO BE COLSON. AN ACCOUNTANT.
YOU THINK I DON'T KNOW HOW THIS GOES? THAT I THOUGHT YOU'D REALLY LEAVE ME ALONE?
I KNEW YOU'D FOLLOW ME. YOU WANT VERN? WELL, VERN HAS FRIENDS.
CLICK
BLAM BLAM
SCREW YOU!
WE GOT YOU! WE GOT...

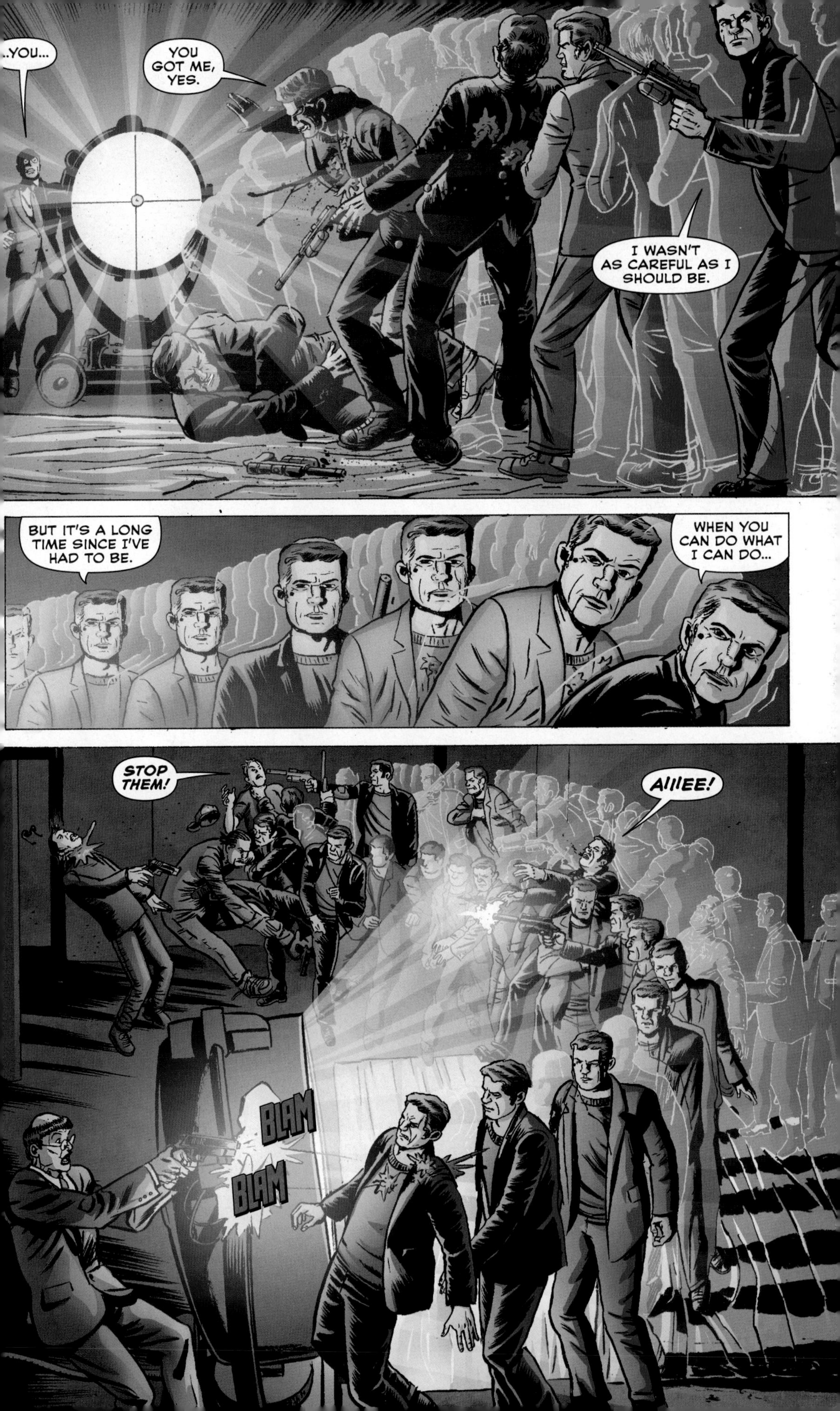
..YOU...
YOU GOT ME, YES.
I WASN'T AS CAREFUL AS I SHOULD BE.
BUT IT'S A LONG TIME SINCE I'VE HAD TO BE.
WHEN YOU CAN DO WHAT I CAN DO...
STOP THEM!
AIIIEE!
BLAM
BLAM

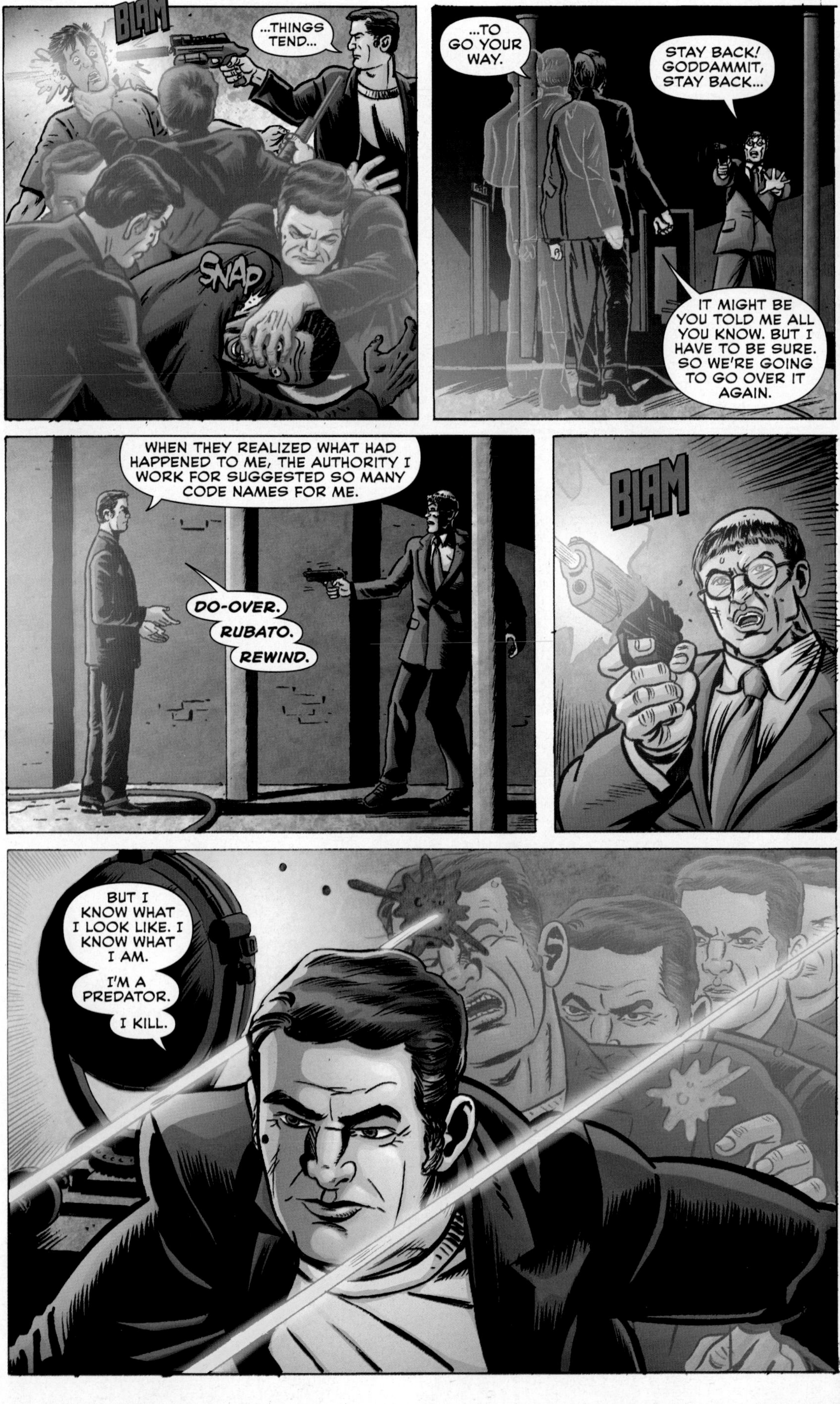

BLAM
...THINGS TEND...
SNAP
...TO GO YOUR WAY.
STAY BACK! GODDAMMIT, STAY BACK...
IT MIGHT BE YOU TOLD ME ALL YOU KNOW. BUT I HAVE TO BE SURE. SO WE'RE GOING TO GO OVER IT AGAIN.
WHEN THEY REALIZED WHAT HAD HAPPENED TO ME, THE AUTHORITY I WORK FOR SUGGESTED SO MANY CODE NAMES FOR ME.
DO-OVER.
RUBATO.
REWIND.
BLAM
BUT I KNOW WHAT I LOOK LIKE. I KNOW WHAT I AM.
I'M A PREDATOR.
I KILL.

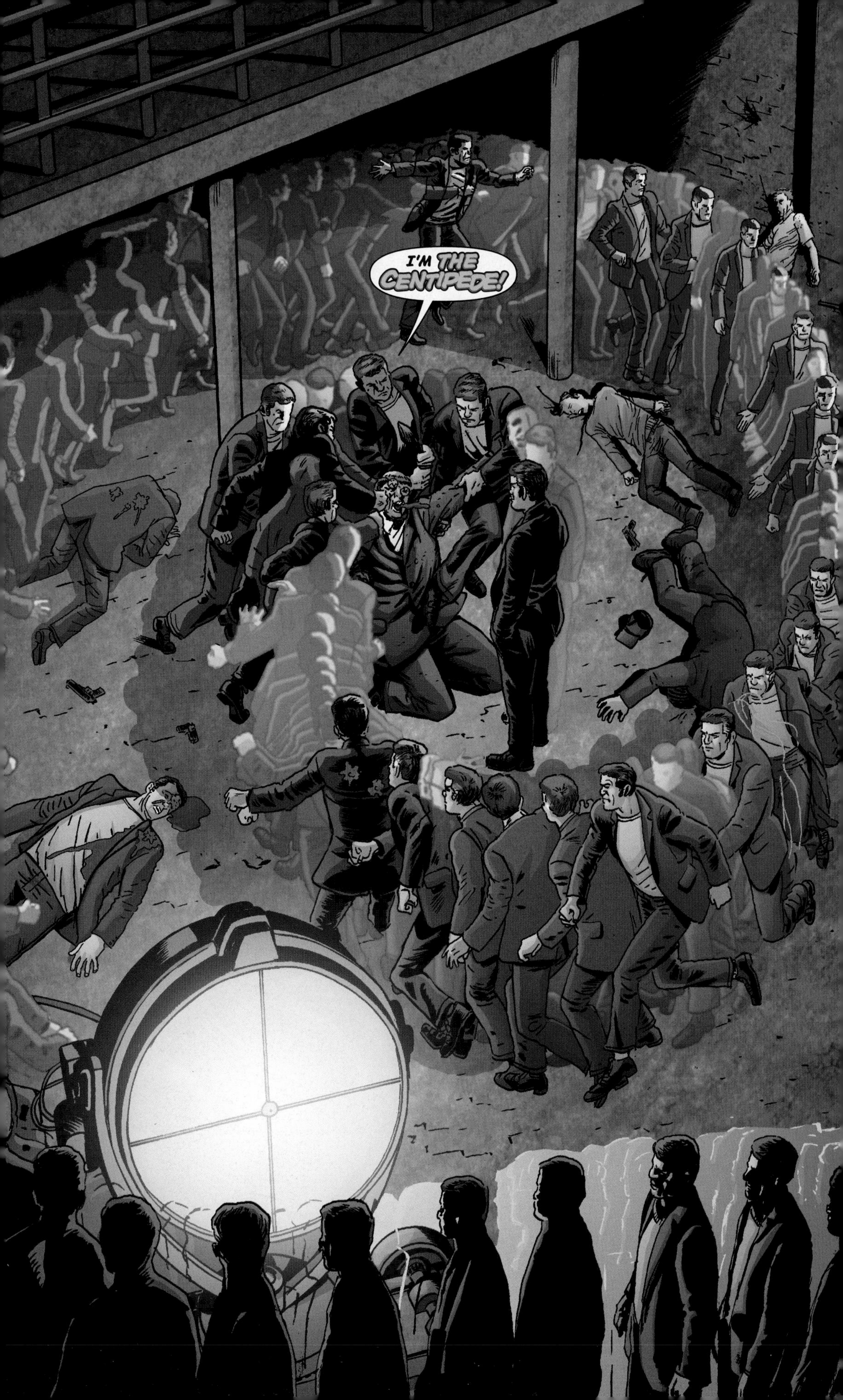
I'M THE CENTIPEDE!

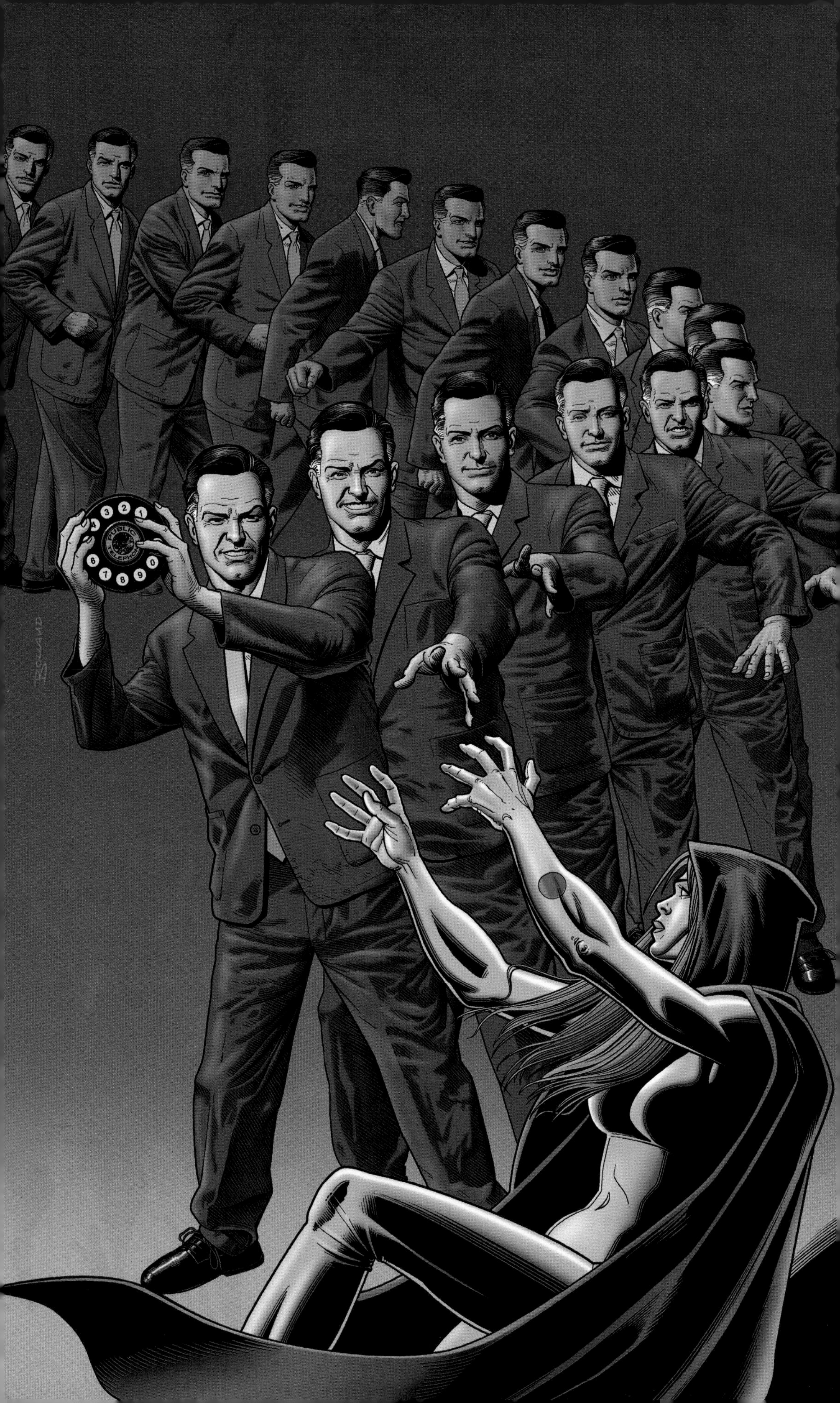

PUBLIC
TELEPHONE
BOLLAND

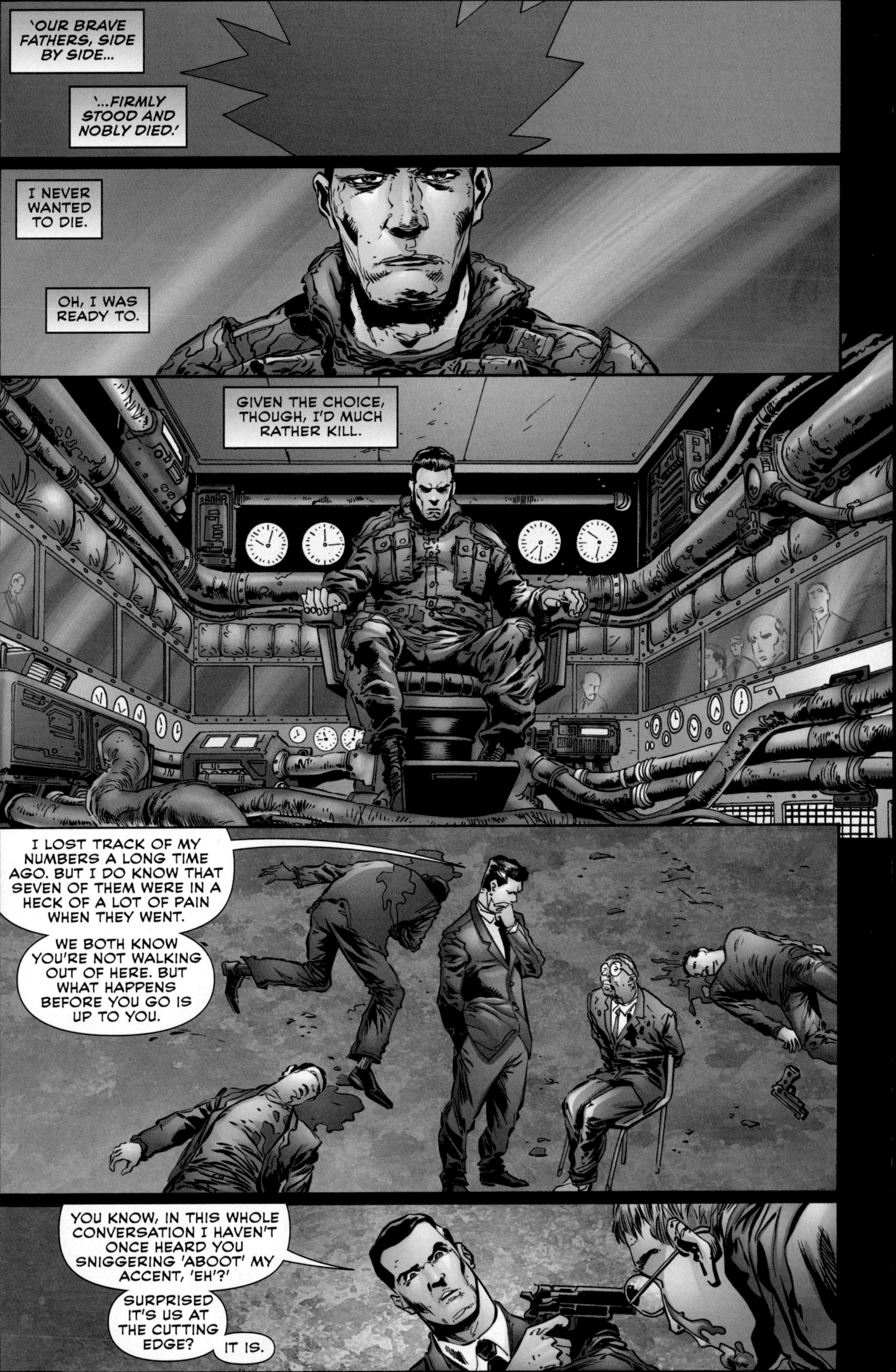
'OUR BRAVE FATHERS, SIDE BY SIDE...
'...FIRMLY STOOD AND NOBLY DIED.'
I NEVER WANTED TO DIE.
OH, I WAS READY TO.
GIVEN THE CHOICE, THOUGH, I'D MUCH RATHER KILL.
I LOST TRACK OF MY NUMBERS A LONG TIME AGO. BUT I DO KNOW THAT SEVEN OF THEM WERE IN A HECK OF A LOT OF PAIN WHEN THEY WENT.
WE BOTH KNOW YOU'RE NOT WALKING OUT OF HERE. BUT WHAT HAPPENS BEFORE YOU GO IS UP TO YOU.
YOU KNOW, IN THIS WHOLE CONVERSATION I HAVEN'T ONCE HEARD YOU SNIGGERING 'ABOOT' MY ACCENT, 'EH'?'
SURPRISED IT'S US AT THE CUTTING EDGE?
IT IS.

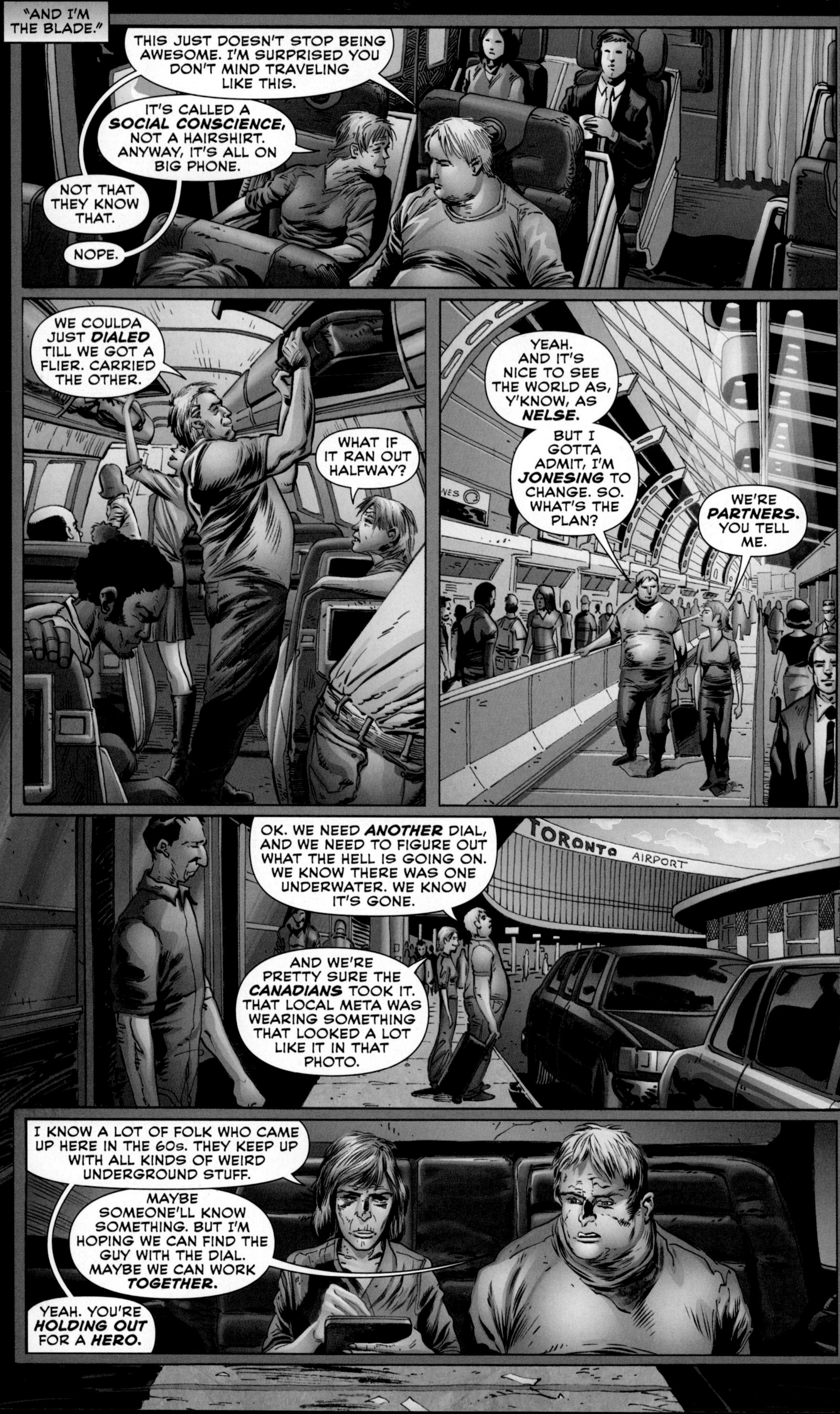
"AND I'M THE BLADE."
THIS JUST DOESN'T STOP BEING AWESOME. I'M SURPRISED YOU DON'T MIND TRAVELING LIKE THIS.
IT'S CALLED A SOCIAL CONSCIENCE, NOT A HAIRSHIRT. ANYWAY, IT'S ALL ON BIG PHONE.
NOT THAT THEY KNOW THAT.
NOPE.
WE COULDA JUST DIALED TILL WE GOT A FLIER. CARRIED THE OTHER.
WHAT IF IT RAN OUT HALFWAY?
YEAH. AND IT'S NICE TO SEE THE WORLD AS, Y'KNOW, AS NELSE.
BUT I GOTTA ADMIT, I'M JONESING TO CHANGE. SO. WHAT'S THE PLAN?
WE'RE PARTNERS. YOU TELL ME.
TORONTO AIRPORT
OK. WE NEED ANOTHER DIAL, AND WE NEED TO FIGURE OUT WHAT THE HELL IS GOING ON. WE KNOW THERE WAS ONE UNDERWATER. WE KNOW IT'S GONE.
AND WE'RE PRETTY SURE THE CANADIANS TOOK IT. THAT LOCAL META WAS WEARING SOMETHING THAT LOOKED A LOT LIKE IT IN THAT PHOTO.
I KNOW A LOT OF FOLK WHO CAME UP HERE IN THE 60s. THEY KEEP UP WITH ALL KINDS OF WEIRD UNDERGROUND STUFF.
MAYBE SOMEONE'LL KNOW SOMETHING. BUT I'M HOPING WE CAN FIND THE GUY WITH THE DIAL. MAYBE WE CAN WORK TOGETHER.
YEAH. YOU'RE HOLDING OUT FOR A HERO.

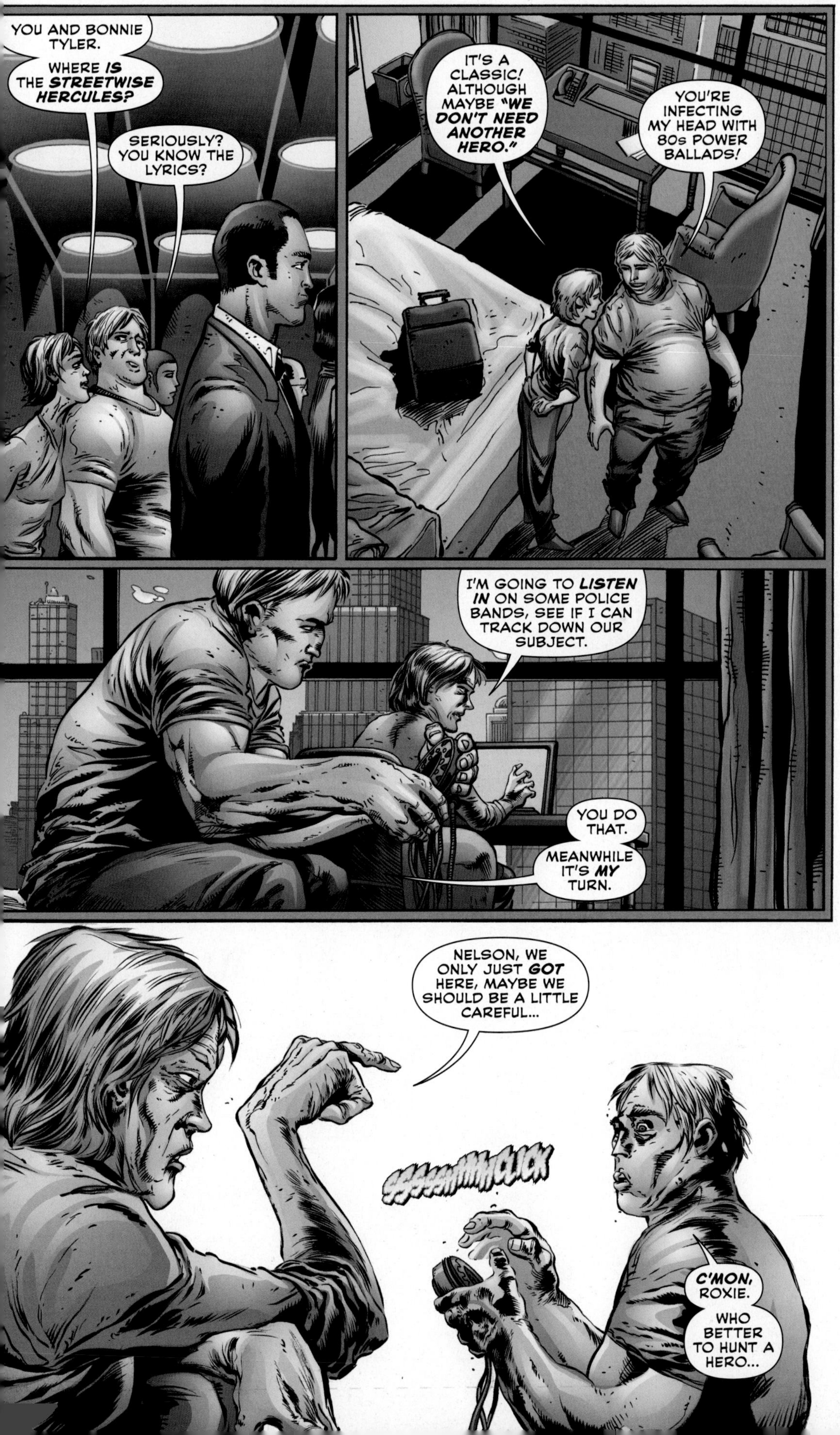
YOU AND BONNIE TYLER.
WHERE IS THE STREETWISE HERCULES?
SERIOUSLY? YOU KNOW THE LYRICS?
IT'S A CLASSIC! ALTHOUGH MAYBE "WE DON'T NEED ANOTHER HERO."
YOU'RE INFECTING MY HEAD WITH 80s POWER BALLADS!
I'M GOING TO LISTEN IN ON SOME POLICE BANDS, SEE IF I CAN TRACK DOWN OUR SUBJECT.
YOU DO THAT.
MEANWHILE IT'S MY TURN.
NELSON, WE ONLY JUST GOT HERE, MAYBE WE SHOULD BE A LITTLE CAREFUL...
SSSSSHHHHCLICK
C'MON, ROXIE.
WHO BETTER TO HUNT A HERO...

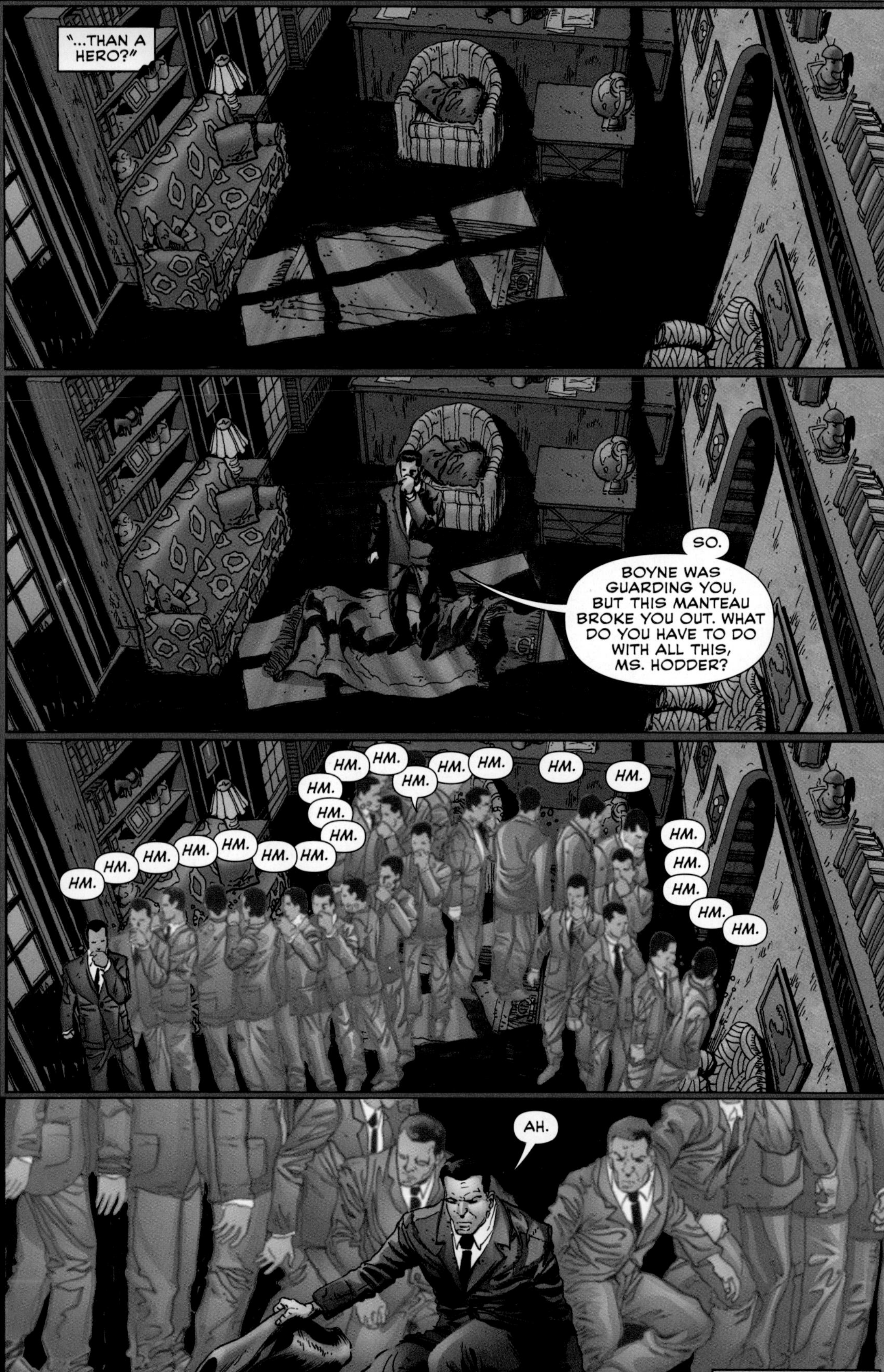
"...THAN A HERO?"
SO.
BOYNE WAS GUARDING YOU, BUT THIS MANTEAU BROKE YOU OUT. WHAT DO YOU HAVE TO DO WITH ALL THIS, MS. HODDER?
HM.
HM.
HM.
HM.
HM.
HM.
HM.
HM.
HM.
HM.
HM.
HM.
HM.
HM.
HM.
HM.
HM.
HM.
HM.
HM.
HM.
HM.
AH.
I REMEMBER THE DAY I CHANGED. WHEN I LEARNED WHAT I'D BECOME.

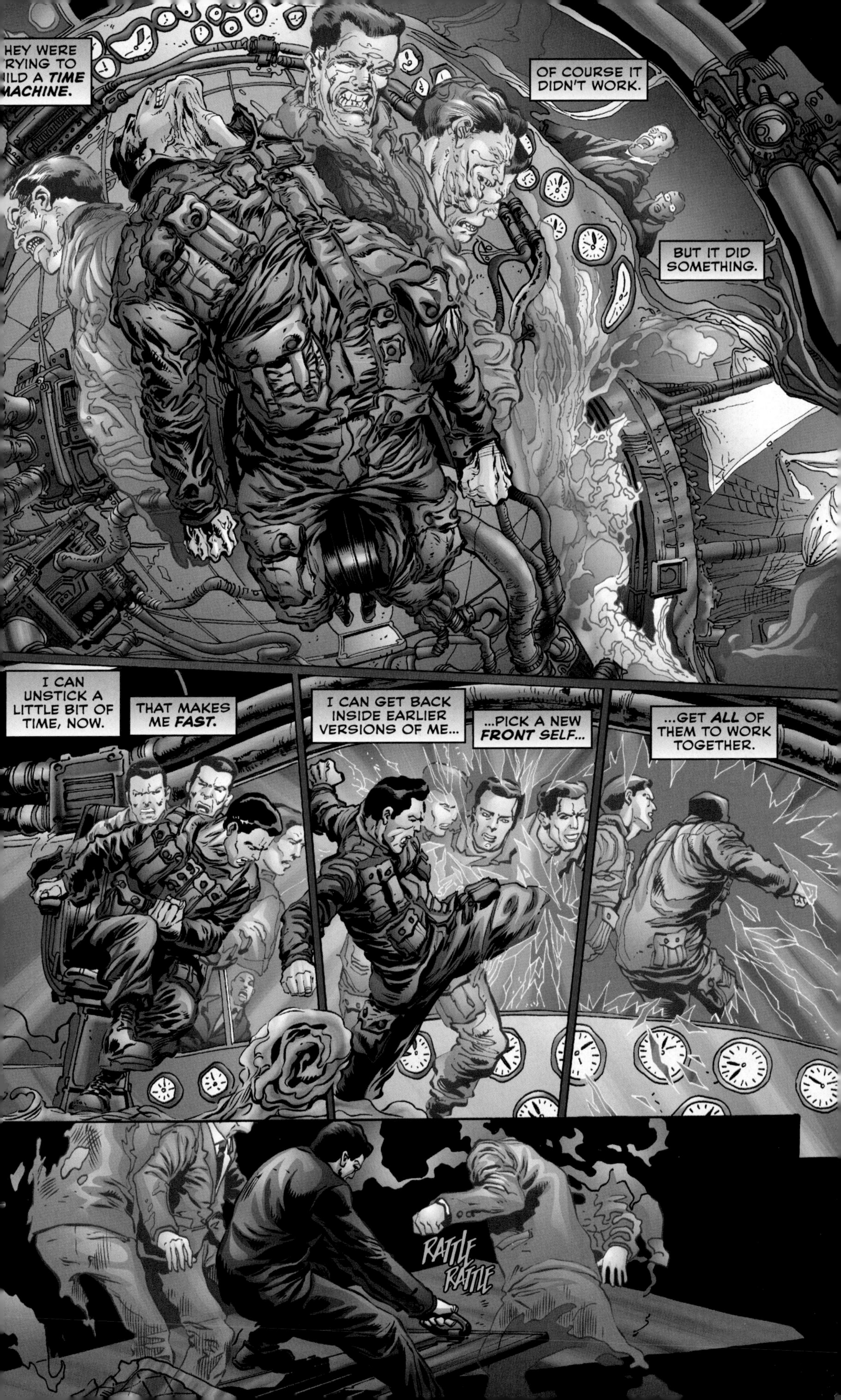

HEY WERE
RYING TO
ILD A TIME
MACHINE.
OF COURSE IT DIDN'T WORK.
BUT IT DID SOMETHING.
I CAN UNSTICK A LITTLE BIT OF TIME, NOW.
THAT MAKES ME FAST.
I CAN GET BACK INSIDE EARLIER VERSIONS OF ME...
...PICK A NEW FRONT SELF...
...GET ALL OF THEM TO WORK TOGETHER.
RATTLE RATTLE

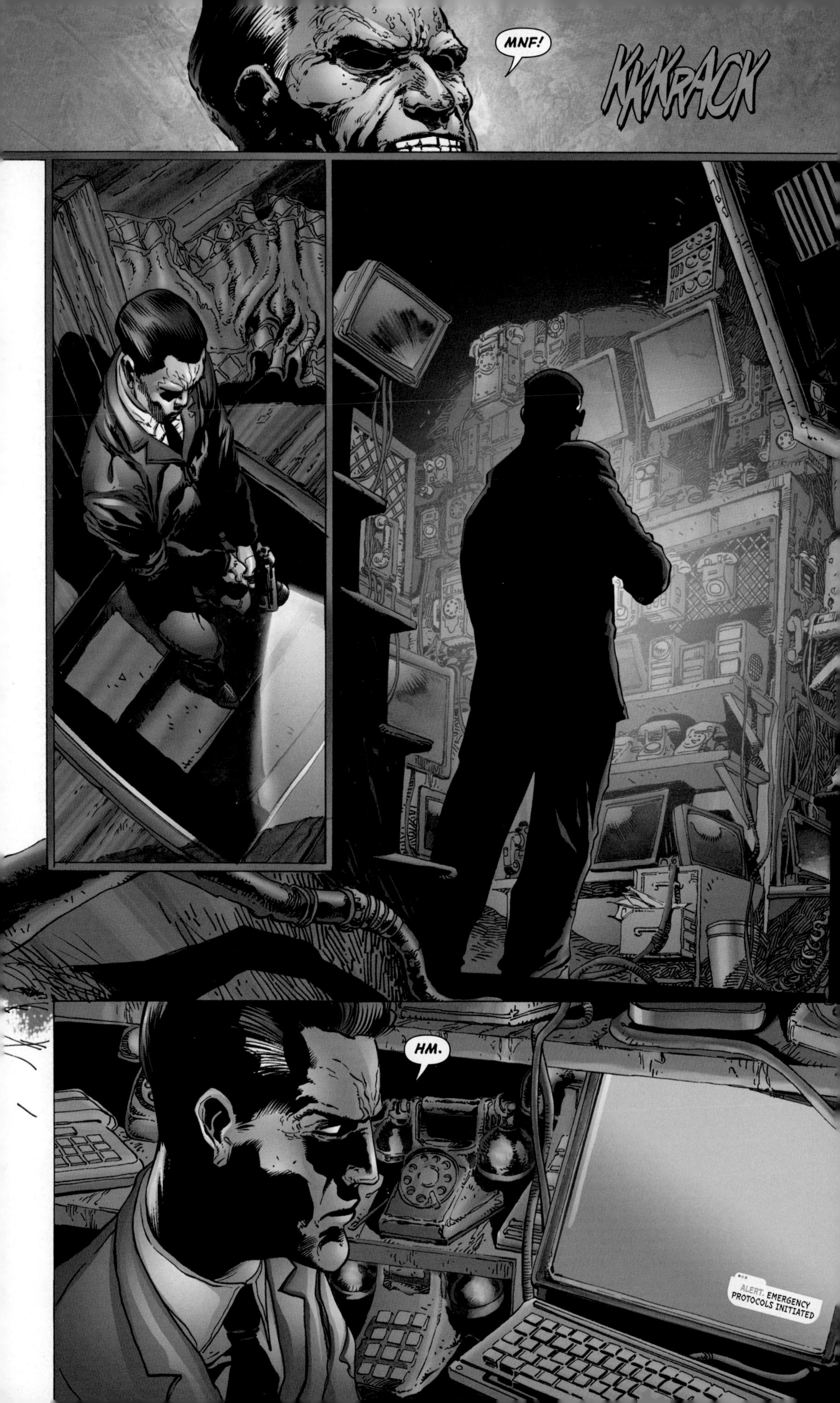
MNF!
KKKRACK
HM.
ALERT. EMERGENCY PROTOCOLS INITIATED

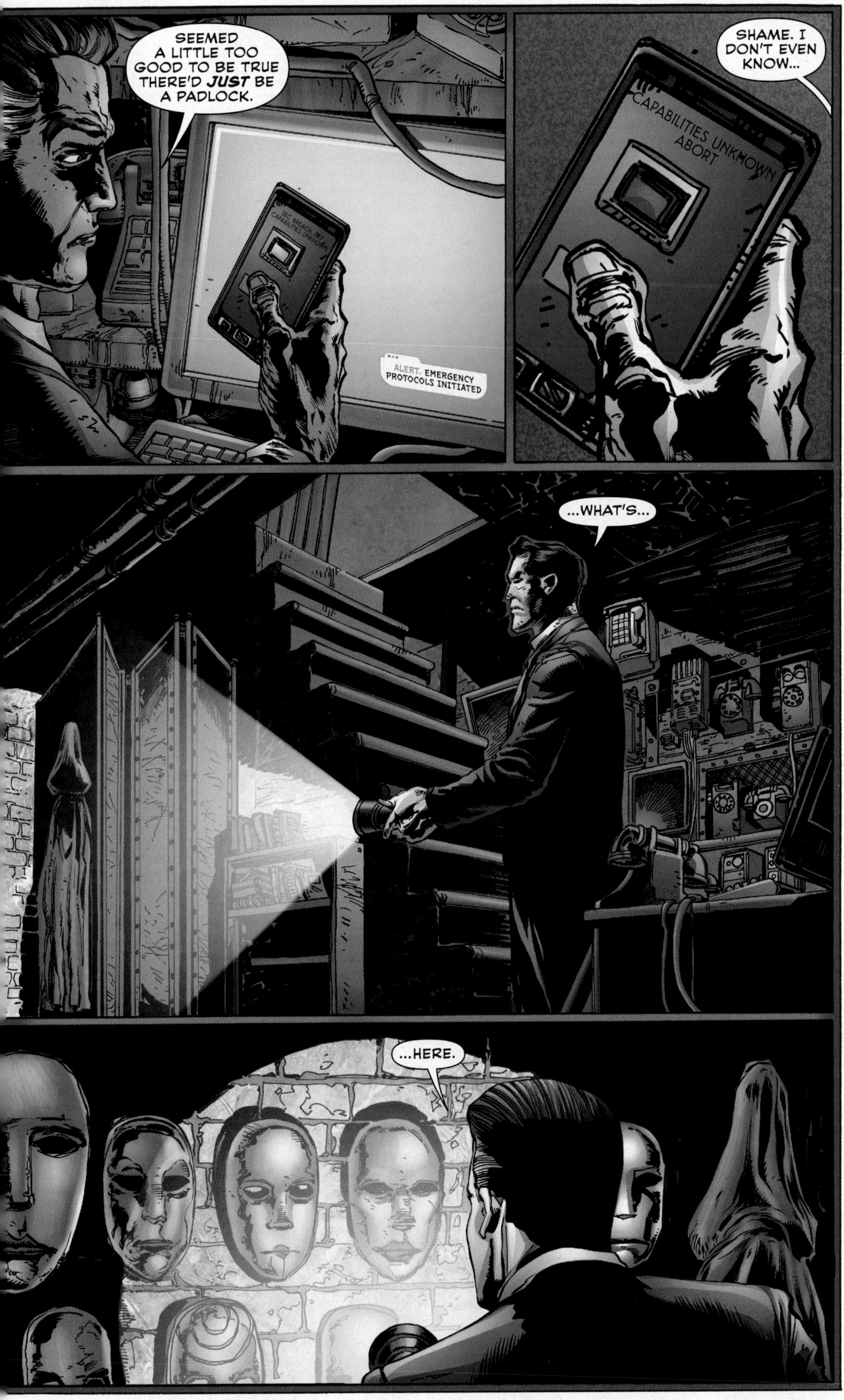
SEEMED A LITTLE TOO GOOD TO BE TRUE THERE'D JUST BE A PADLOCK.
SEC BREACH. DET CAPABILITIES UNKNOWN
ALERT. EMERGENCY PROTOCOLS INITIATED
SHAME. I DON'T EVEN KNOW...
CAPABILITIES UNKHOWN ABORT
...WHAT'S...
...HERE.

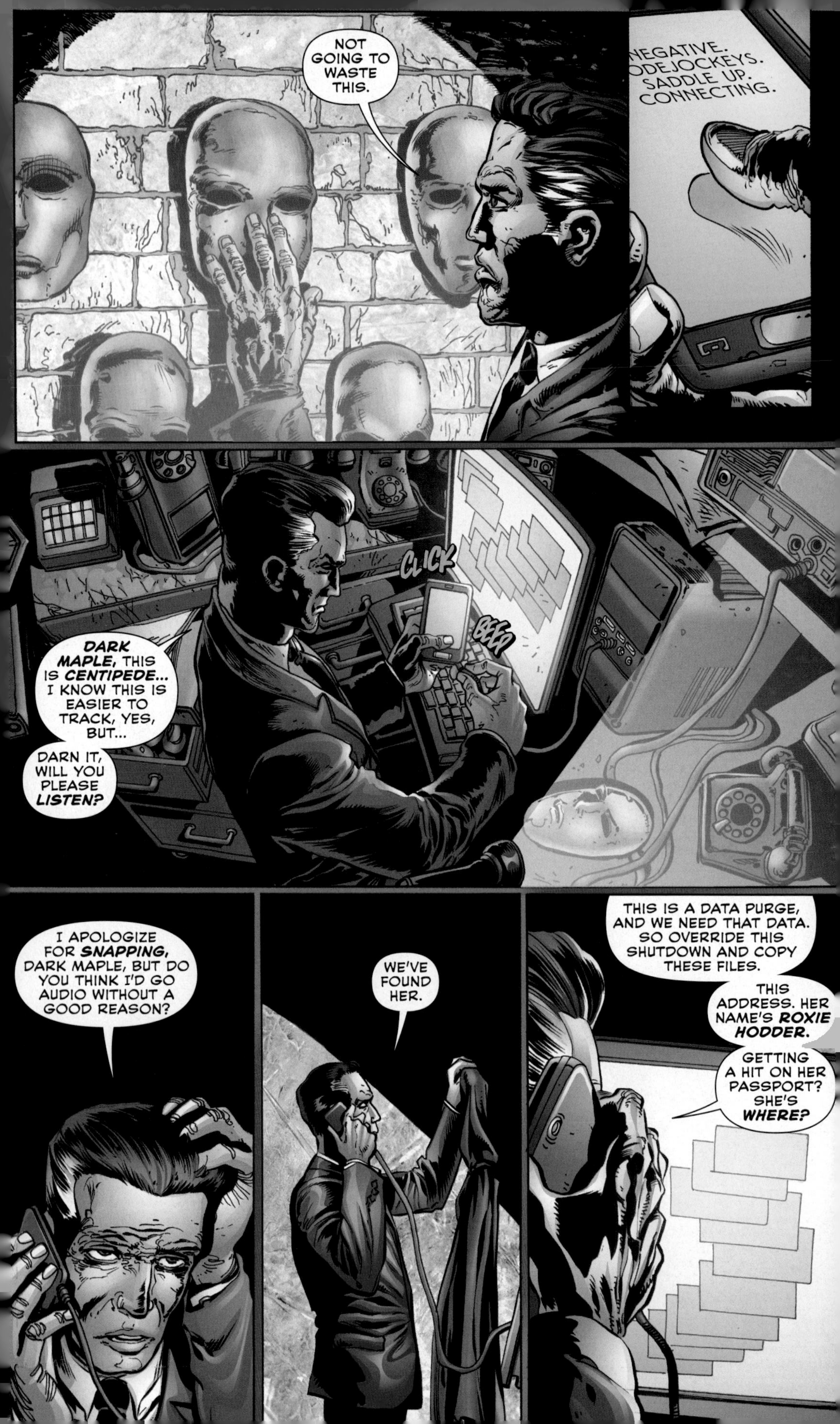
NOT GOING TO WASTE THIS.
NEGATIVE. ODEJOCKEYS. SADDLE UP. CONNECTING.
CLICK
BEEP
DARK MAPLE, THIS IS CENTIPEDE... I KNOW THIS IS EASIER TO TRACK, YES, BUT...
DARN IT, WILL YOU PLEASE LISTEN?
I APOLOGIZE FOR SNAPPING, DARK MAPLE, BUT DO YOU THINK I'D GO AUDIO WITHOUT A GOOD REASON?
WE'VE FOUND HER.
THIS IS A DATA PURGE, AND WE NEED THAT DATA. SO OVERRIDE THIS SHUTDOWN AND COPY THESE FILES.
THIS ADDRESS. HER NAME'S ROXIE HODDER.
GETTING A HIT ON HER PASSPORT? SHE'S WHERE?

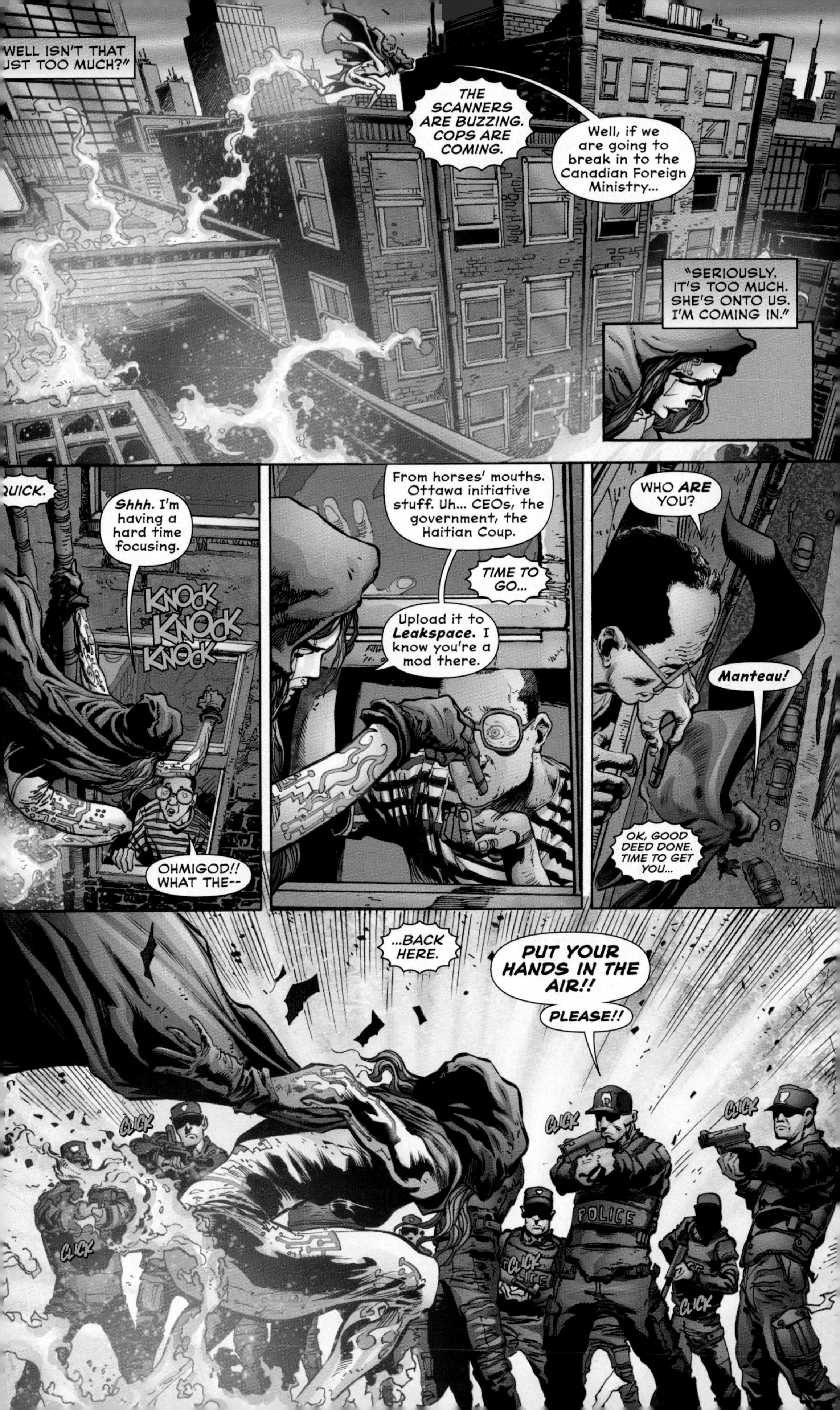

WELL ISN'T THAT
JUST TOO MUCH?"
THE SCANNERS ARE BUZZING. COPS ARE COMING.
Well, if we are going to break in to the Canadian Foreign Ministry...
"SERIOUSLY. IT'S TOO MUCH. SHE'S ONTO US. I'M COMING IN."
QUICK.
Shhh. I'm having a hard time focusing.
KNOCK KNOCK KNOCK
OHMIGOD!! WHAT THE--
From horses' mouths. Ottawa initiative stuff. Uh... CEOs, the government, the Haitian Coup.
TIME TO GO...
Upload it to Leakspace. I know you're a mod there.
WHO ARE YOU?
Manteau!
OK, GOOD DEED DONE. TIME TO GET YOU...
...BACK HERE.
PUT YOUR HANDS IN THE AIR!!
PLEASE!!
CLICK
CLICK
CLICK
CLICK
CLICK
CLICK
POLICE

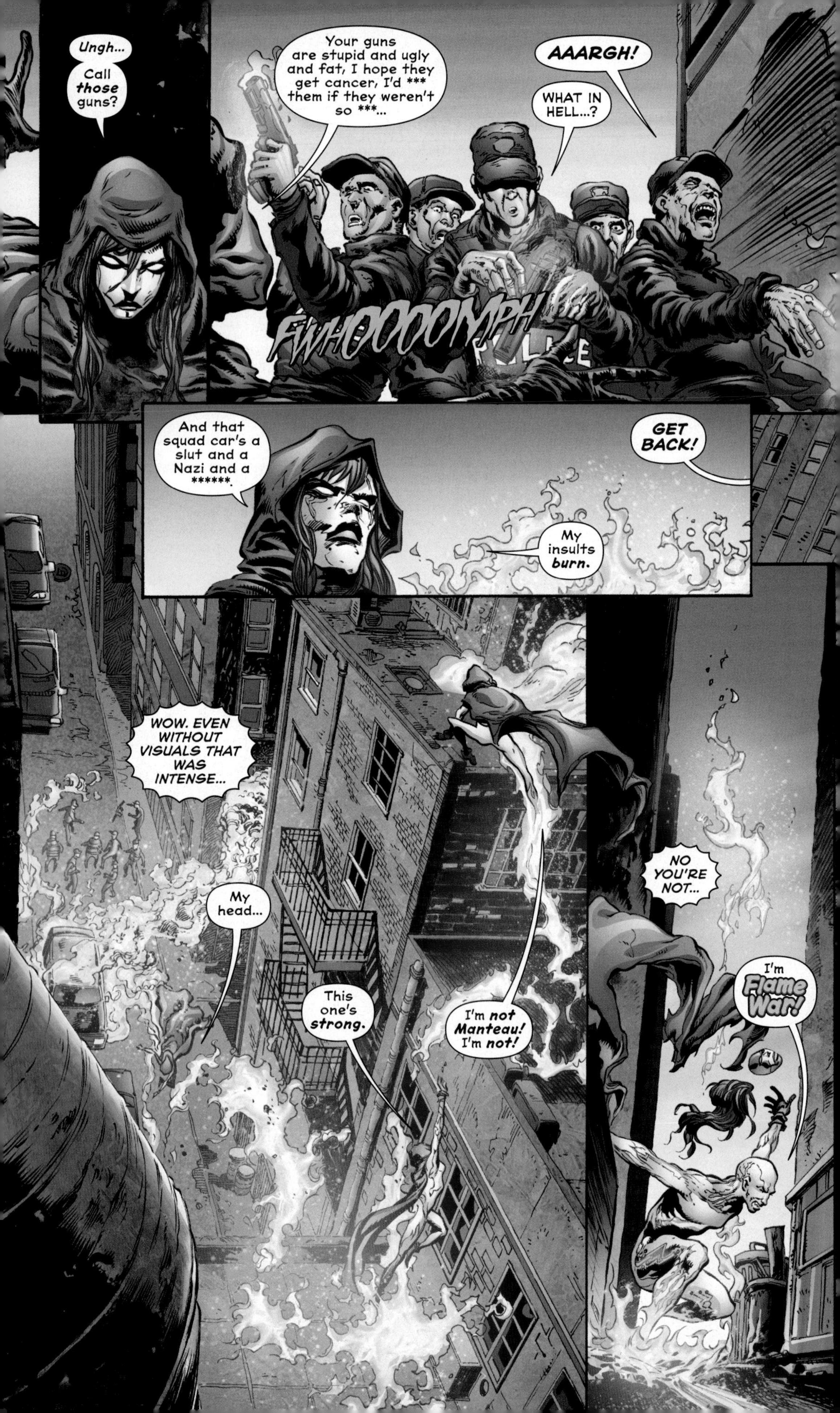
Ungh...
Call those guns?
Your guns are stupid and ugly and fat, I hope they get cancer, I'd *** them if they weren't so ***...
AAARGH!
WHAT IN HELL...?
FWHOOOOOMPH
And that squad car's a slut and a Nazi and a ******.
GET BACK!
My insults burn.
WOW. EVEN WITHOUT VISUALS THAT WAS INTENSE...
My head...
This one's strong.
I'm not Manteau! I'm not!
NO YOU'RE NOT...
I'm Flame War!

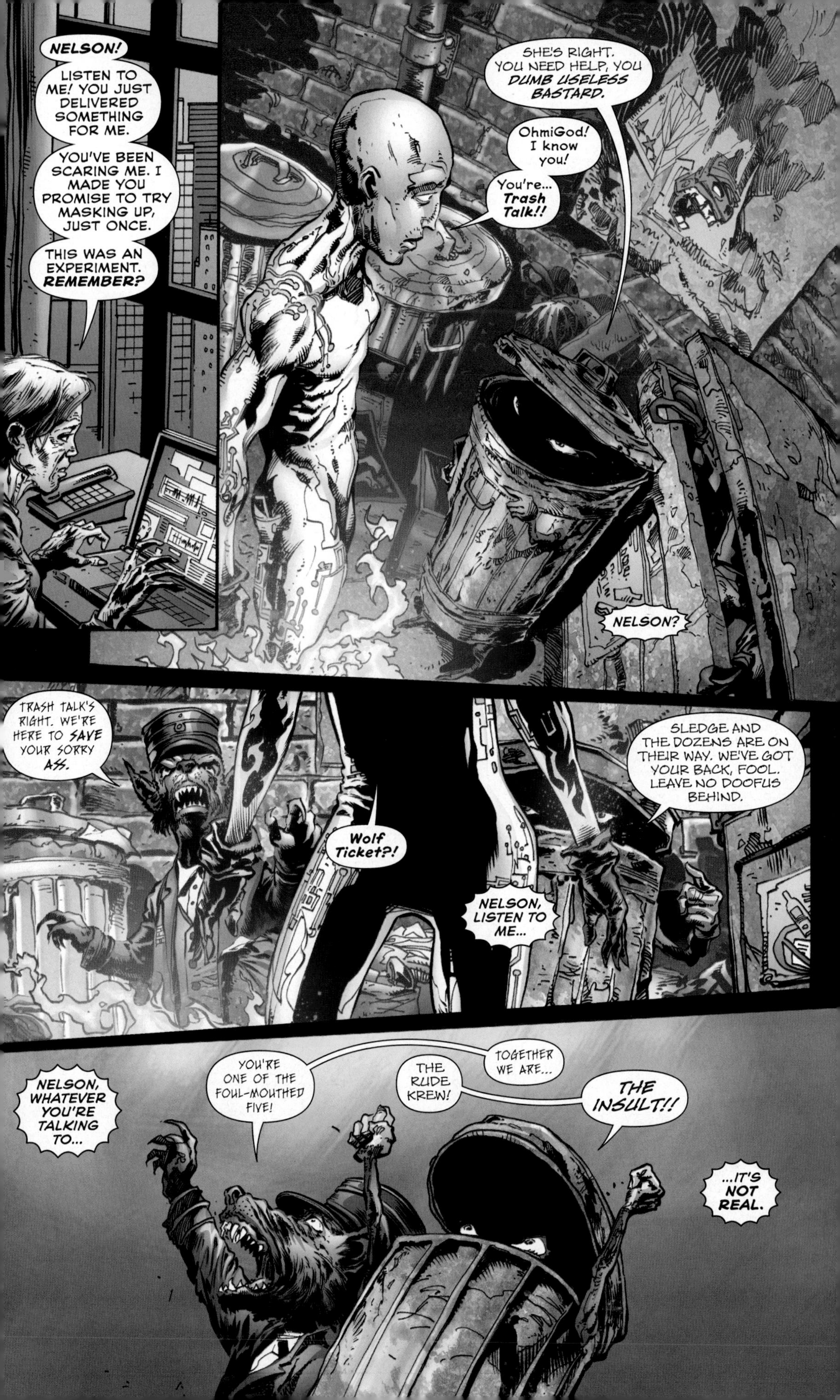
NELSON!
LISTEN TO ME! YOU JUST DELIVERED SOMETHING FOR ME.
YOU'VE BEEN SCARING ME. I MADE YOU PROMISE TO TRY MASKING UP, JUST ONCE.
THIS WAS AN EXPERIMENT. REMEMBER?
SHE'S RIGHT. YOU NEED HELP, YOU DUMB USELESS BASTARD.
OhmiGod! I know you!
You're... Trash Talk!!
NELSON?
TRASH TALK'S RIGHT. WE'RE HERE TO SAVE YOUR SORRY ASS.
Wolf Ticket?!
SLEDGE AND THE DOZENS ARE ON THEIR WAY. WE'VE GOT YOUR BACK, FOOL. LEAVE NO DOOFUS BEHIND.
NELSON, LISTEN TO ME...
NELSON, WHATEVER YOU'RE TALKING TO...
YOU'RE ONE OF THE FOUL-MOUTHED FIVE!
THE RUDE KREW!
TOGETHER WE ARE...
THE INSULT!!
...IT'S NOT REAL.

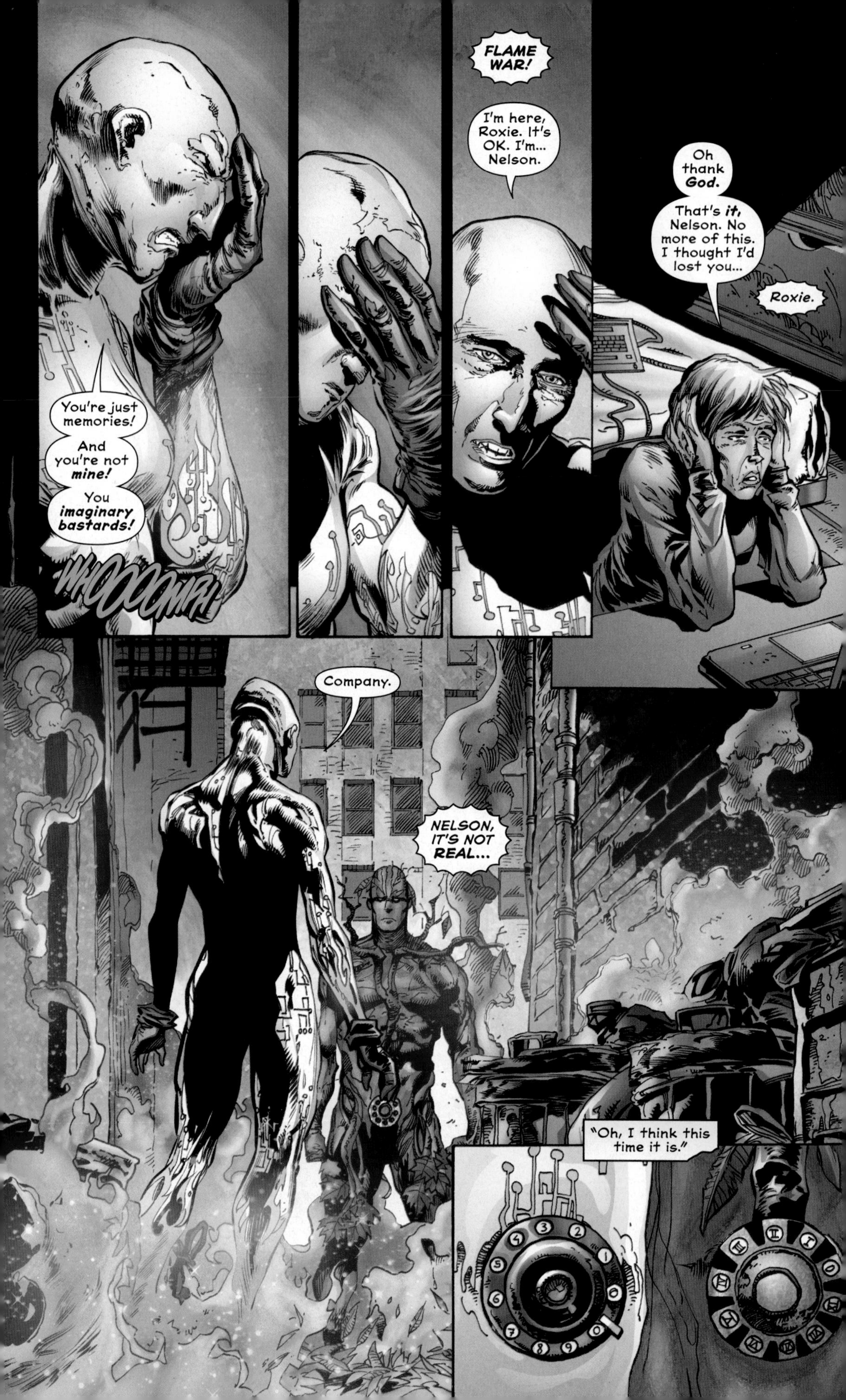
You're just memories!
And you're not mine!
You imaginary bastards!
WHOOOOOMPH
FLAME WAR!
I'm here, Roxie. It's OK. I'm... Nelson.
Oh thank God.
That's it, Nelson. No more of this. I thought I'd lost you...
Roxie.
Company.
NELSON, IT'S NOT REAL...
"Oh, I think this time it is."

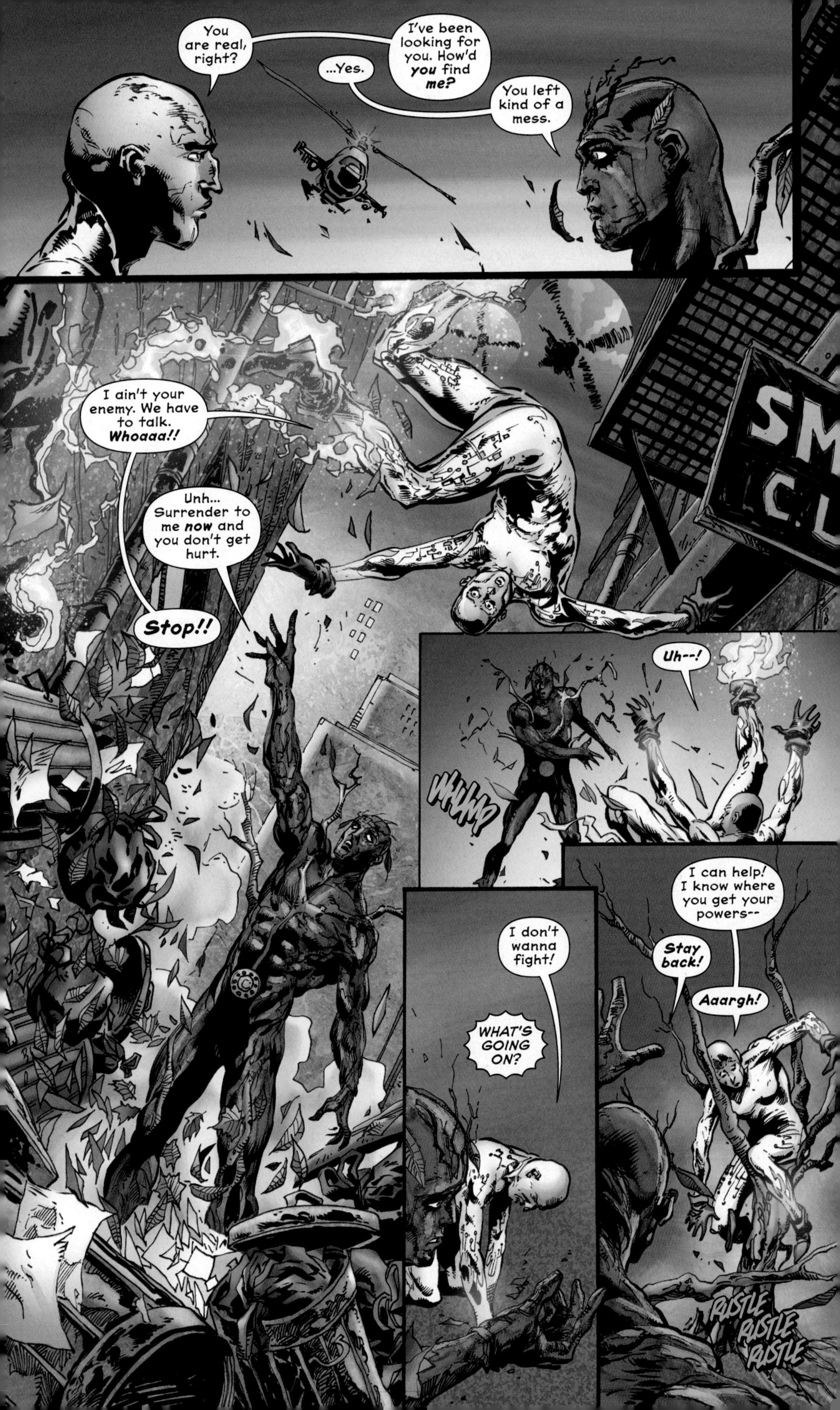

You are real, right?
I've been looking for you. How'd *you* find *me?*
...Yes.
You left kind of a mess.
SM
C.L
I ain't your enemy. We have to talk. ***Whoaaa!!***
Unh... Surrender to me *now* and you don't get hurt.
Stop!!
Uh--!
WHUMP
I can help! I know where you get your powers--
I don't wanna fight!
Stay back!
Aaargh!
WHAT'S GOING ON?
RUSTLE RUSTLE RUSTLE

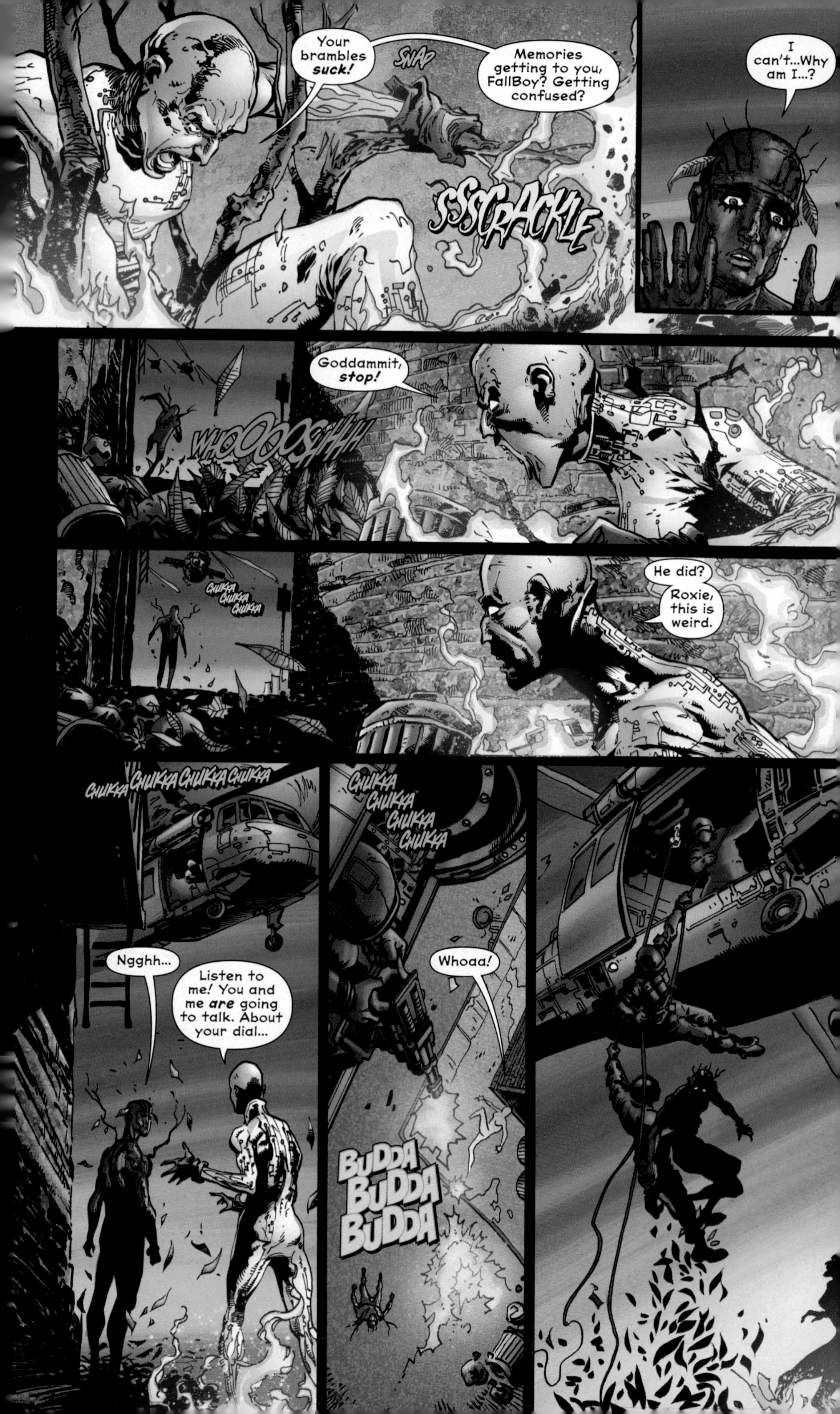
Your brambles suck!
SNAP
Memories getting to you, FallBoy? Getting confused?
SSSCRACKLE
I can't...Why am I...?
Goddammit, stop!
WHOOOOOSHHH
CHUKKA CHUKKA CHUKKA
He did?
Roxie, this is weird.
CHUKKA CHUKKA CHUKKA CHUKKA
Ngghh...
Listen to me! You and me are going to talk. About your dial...
CHUKKA CHUKKA CHUKKA CHUKKA
Whoaa!
BUDDA BUDDA BUDDA

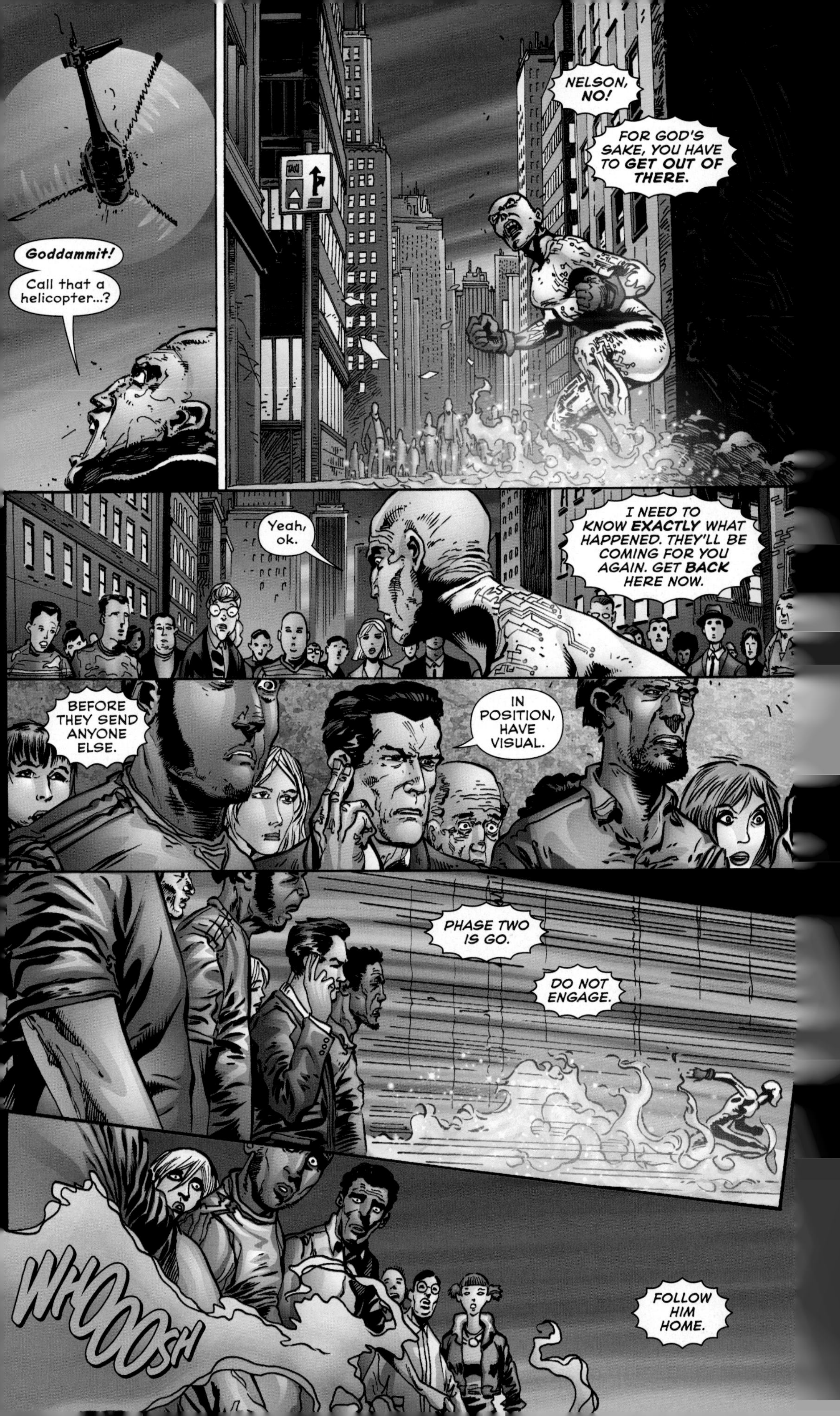
Goddammit!
Call that a helicopter...?
NELSON, NO!
FOR GOD'S SAKE, YOU HAVE TO GET OUT OF THERE.
Yeah, ok.
I NEED TO KNOW EXACTLY WHAT HAPPENED. THEY'LL BE COMING FOR YOU AGAIN. GET BACK HERE NOW.
BEFORE THEY SEND ANYONE ELSE.
IN POSITION, HAVE VISUAL.
PHASE TWO IS GO.
DO NOT ENGAGE.
WHOOOOSH
FOLLOW HIM HOME.

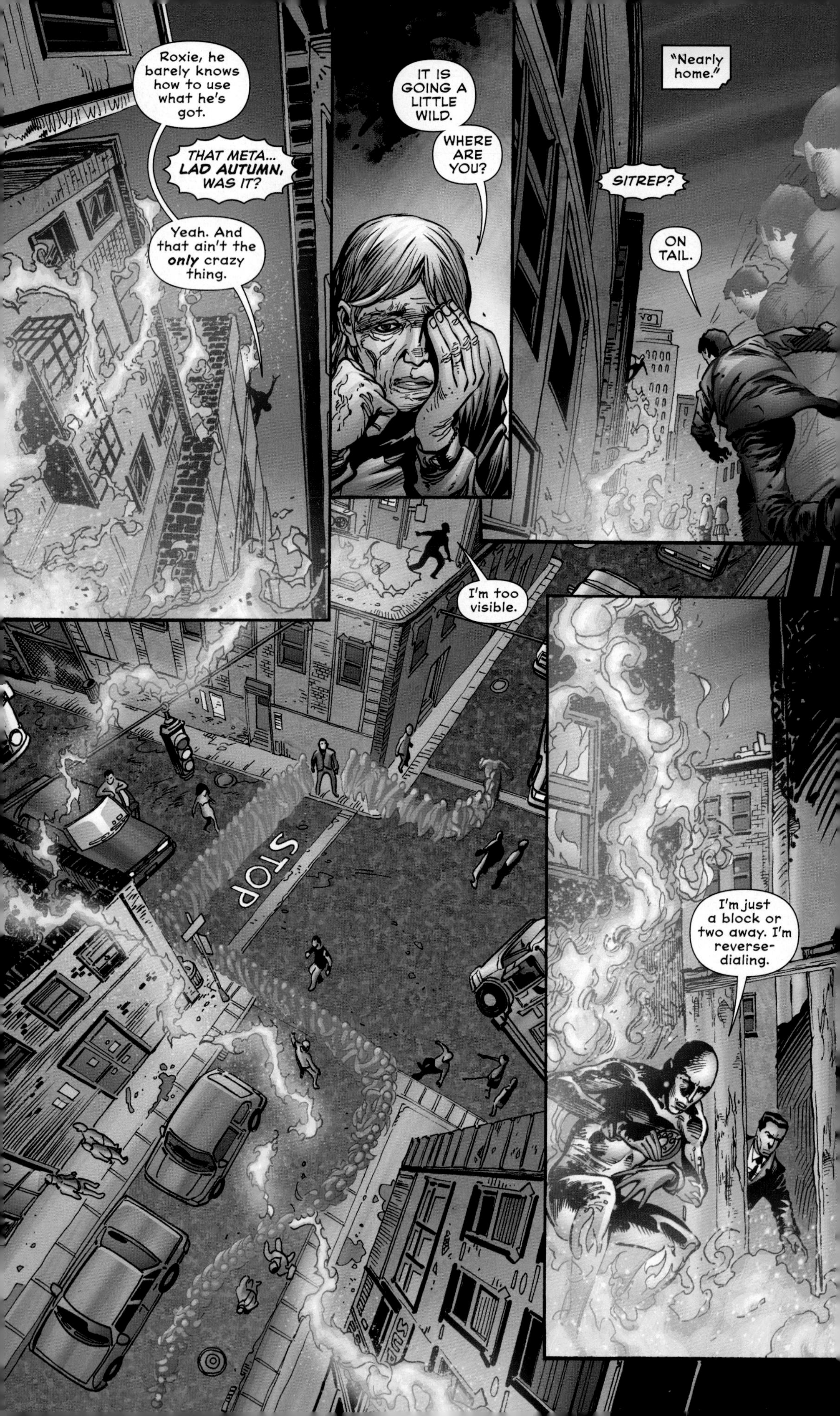
Roxie, he barely knows how to use what he's got.
THAT META... LAD AUTUMN, WAS IT?
Yeah. And that ain't the only crazy thing.
IT IS GOING A LITTLE WILD.
WHERE ARE YOU?
"Nearly home."
SITREP?
ON TAIL.
I'm too visible.
STOP
I'm just a block or two away. I'm reverse-dialing.

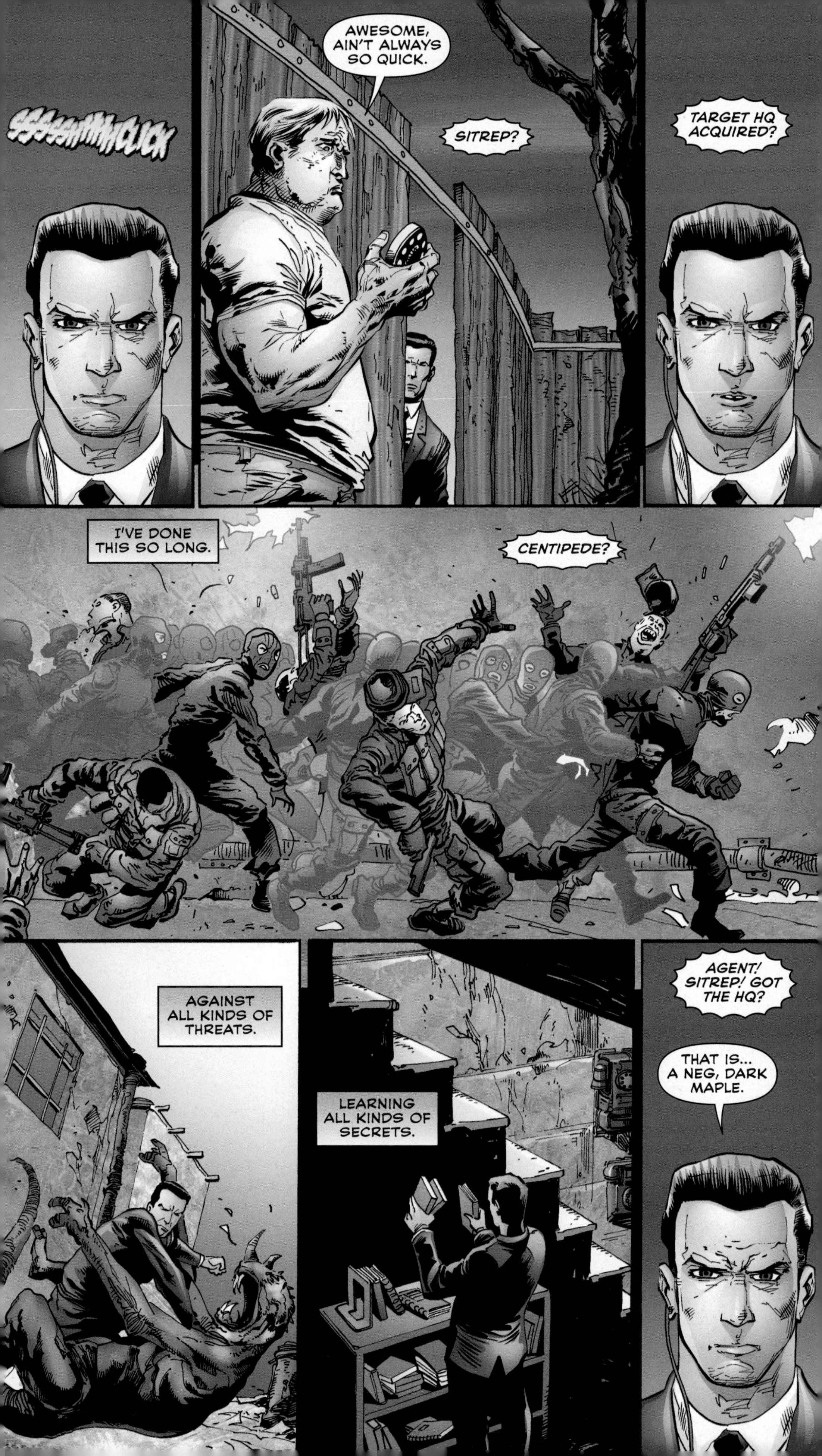
SSSSSHHHHCLICK
AWESOME, AIN'T ALWAYS SO QUICK.
SITREP?
TARGET HQ ACQUIRED?
I'VE DONE THIS SO LONG.
CENTIPEDE?
AGAINST ALL KINDS OF THREATS.
LEARNING ALL KINDS OF SECRETS.
AGENT! SITREP! GOT THE HQ?
THAT IS... A NEG, DARK MAPLE.

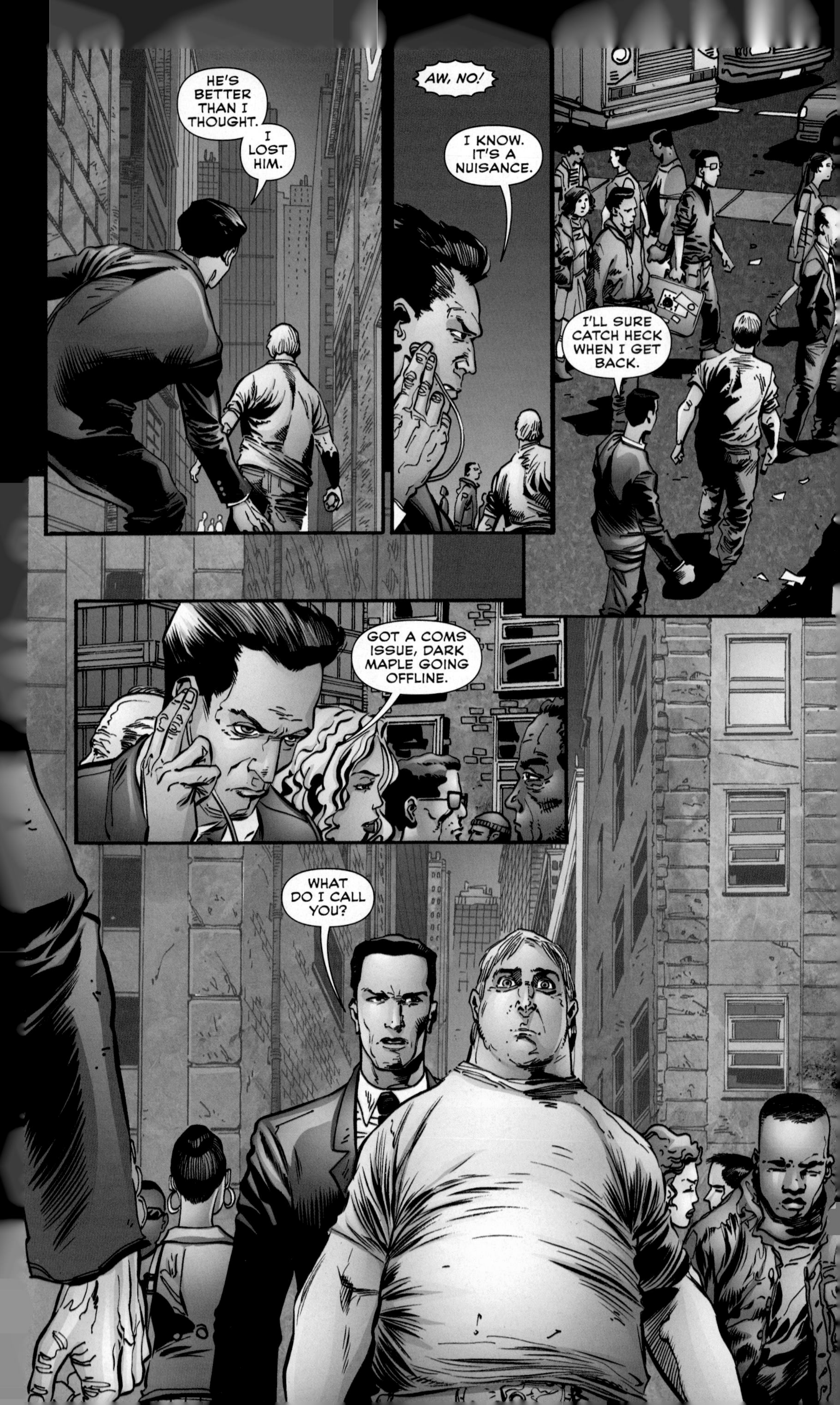
HE'S BETTER THAN I THOUGHT.
I LOST HIM.
AW, NO!
I KNOW. IT'S A NUISANCE.
I'LL SURE CATCH HECK WHEN I GET BACK.
GOT A COMS ISSUE, DARK MAPLE GOING OFFLINE.
WHAT DO I CALL YOU?

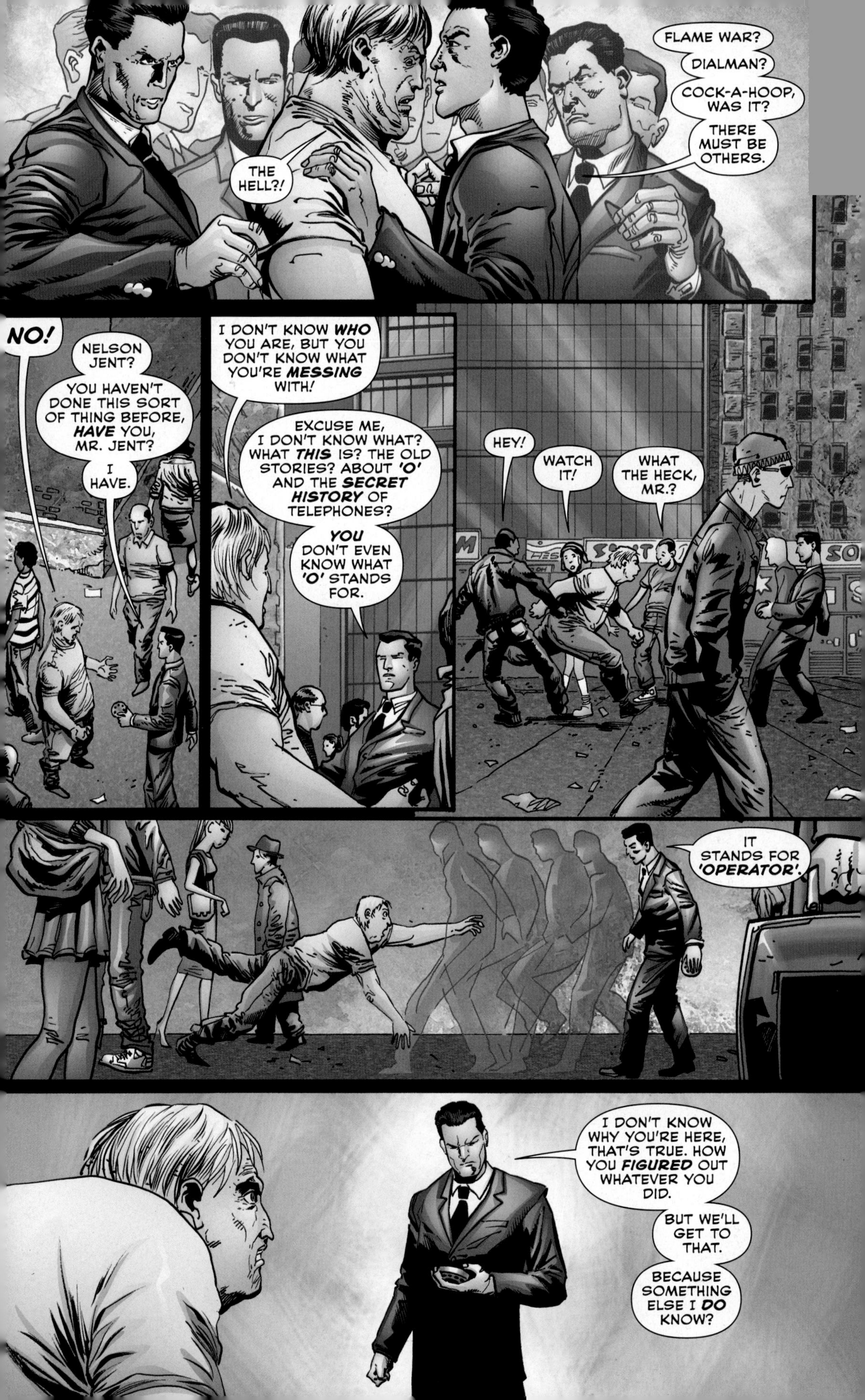
FLAME WAR?
DIALMAN?
COCK-A-HOOP, WAS IT?
THERE MUST BE OTHERS.
THE HELL?!
NO!
NELSON JENT?
YOU HAVEN'T DONE THIS SORT OF THING BEFORE, HAVE YOU, MR. JENT?
I HAVE.
I DON'T KNOW WHO YOU ARE, BUT YOU DON'T KNOW WHAT YOU'RE MESSING WITH!
EXCUSE ME, I DON'T KNOW WHAT? WHAT THIS IS? THE OLD STORIES? ABOUT 'O' AND THE SECRET HISTORY OF TELEPHONES?
YOU DON'T EVEN KNOW WHAT 'O' STANDS FOR.
HEY!
WATCH IT!
WHAT THE HECK, MR.?
IT STANDS FOR 'OPERATOR'.
I DON'T KNOW WHY YOU'RE HERE, THAT'S TRUE. HOW YOU FIGURED OUT WHATEVER YOU DID.
BUT WE'LL GET TO THAT.
BECAUSE SOMETHING ELSE I DO KNOW?

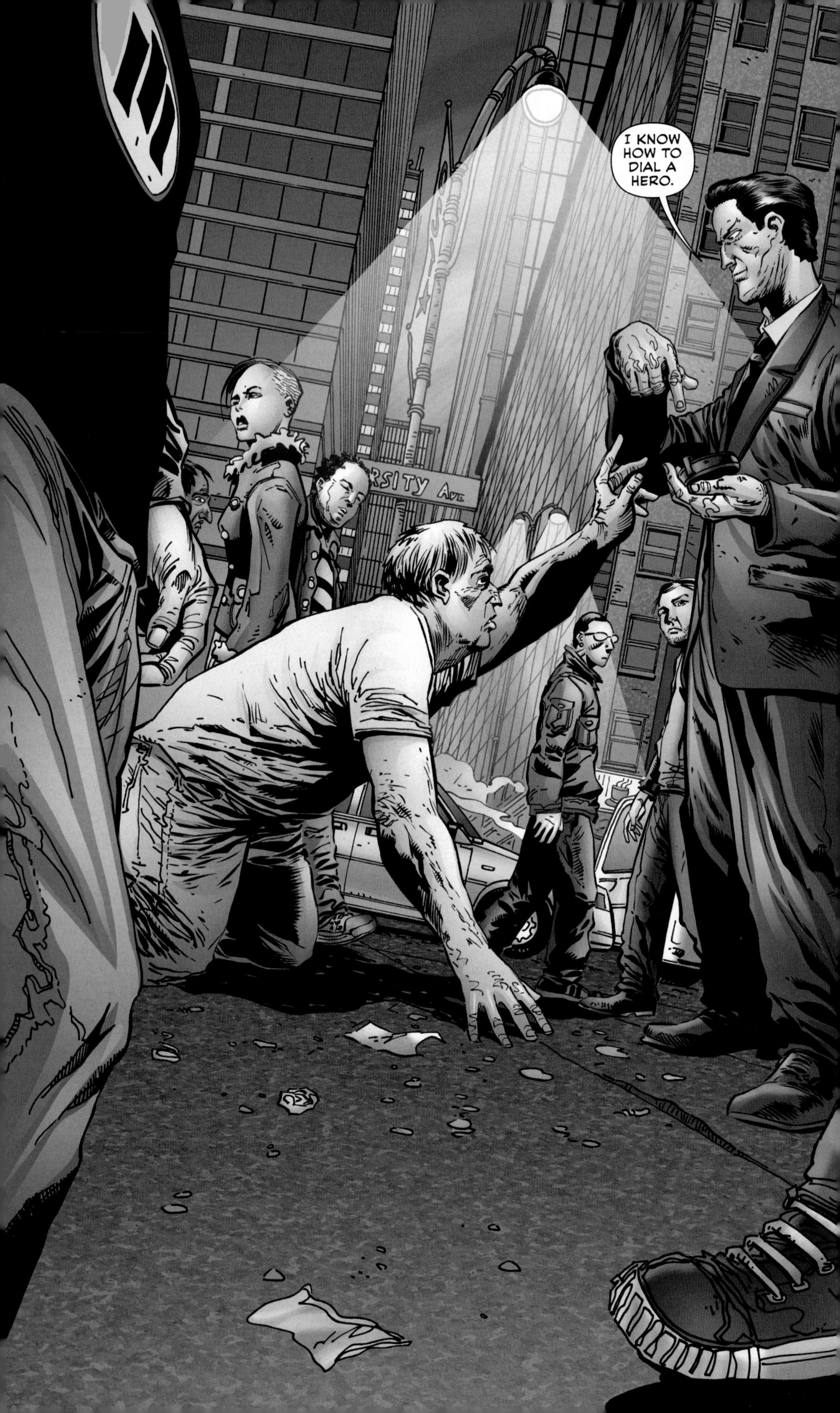
I KNOW HOW TO DIAL A HERO.

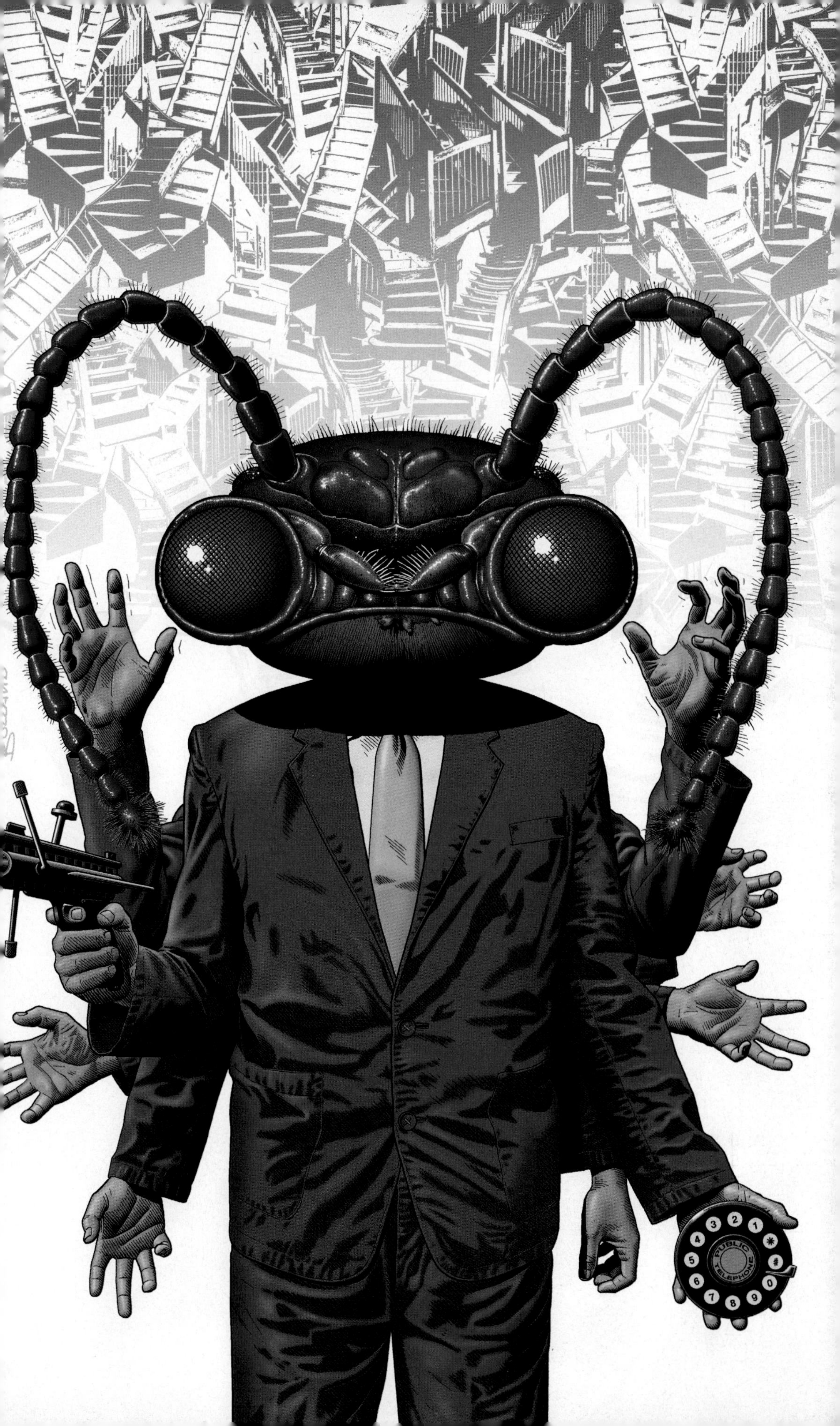
PUBLIC TELEPHONE

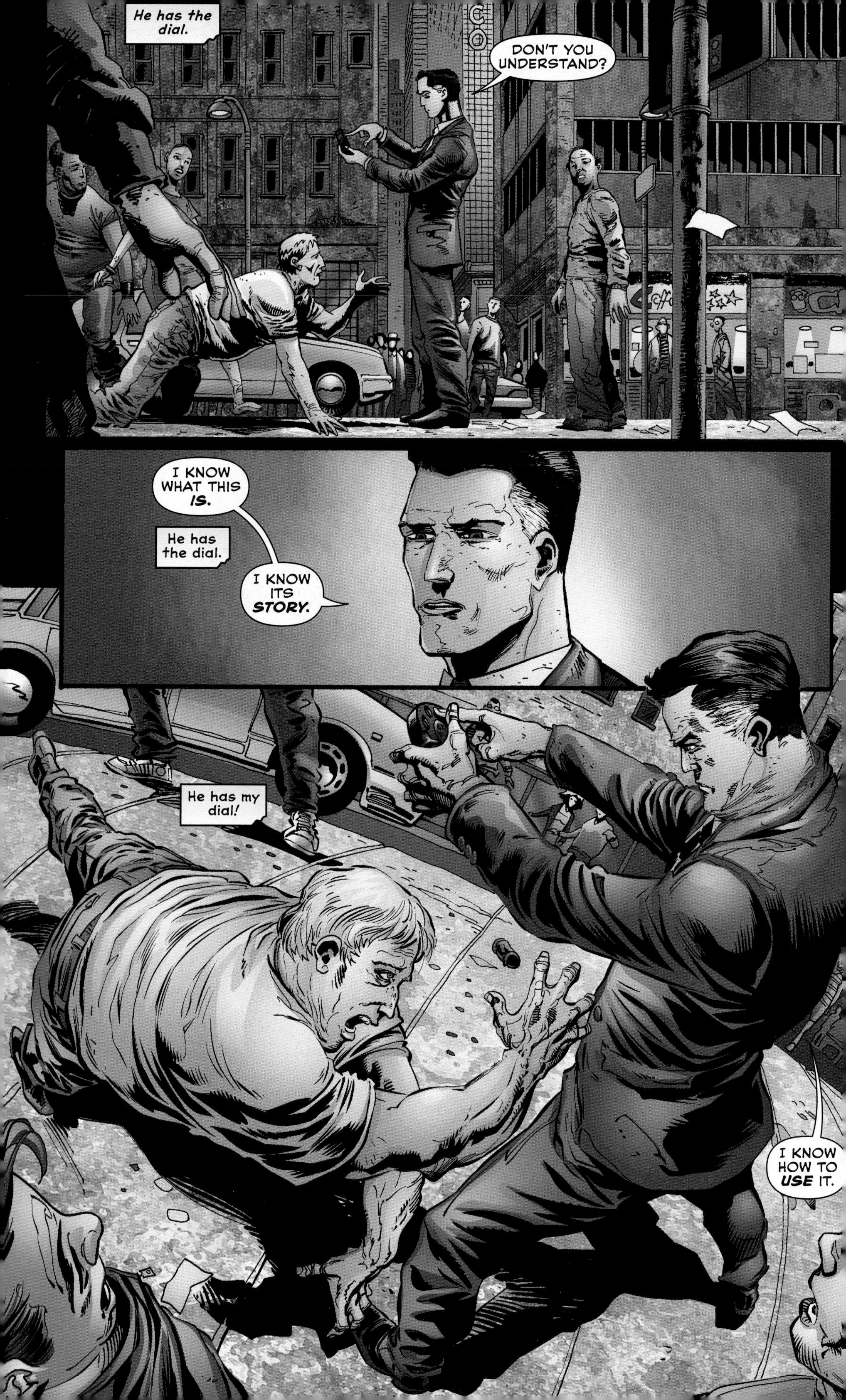
He has the dial.
DON'T YOU UNDERSTAND?
I KNOW WHAT THIS IS.
He has the dial.
I KNOW ITS STORY.
He has my dial!
I KNOW HOW TO USE IT.

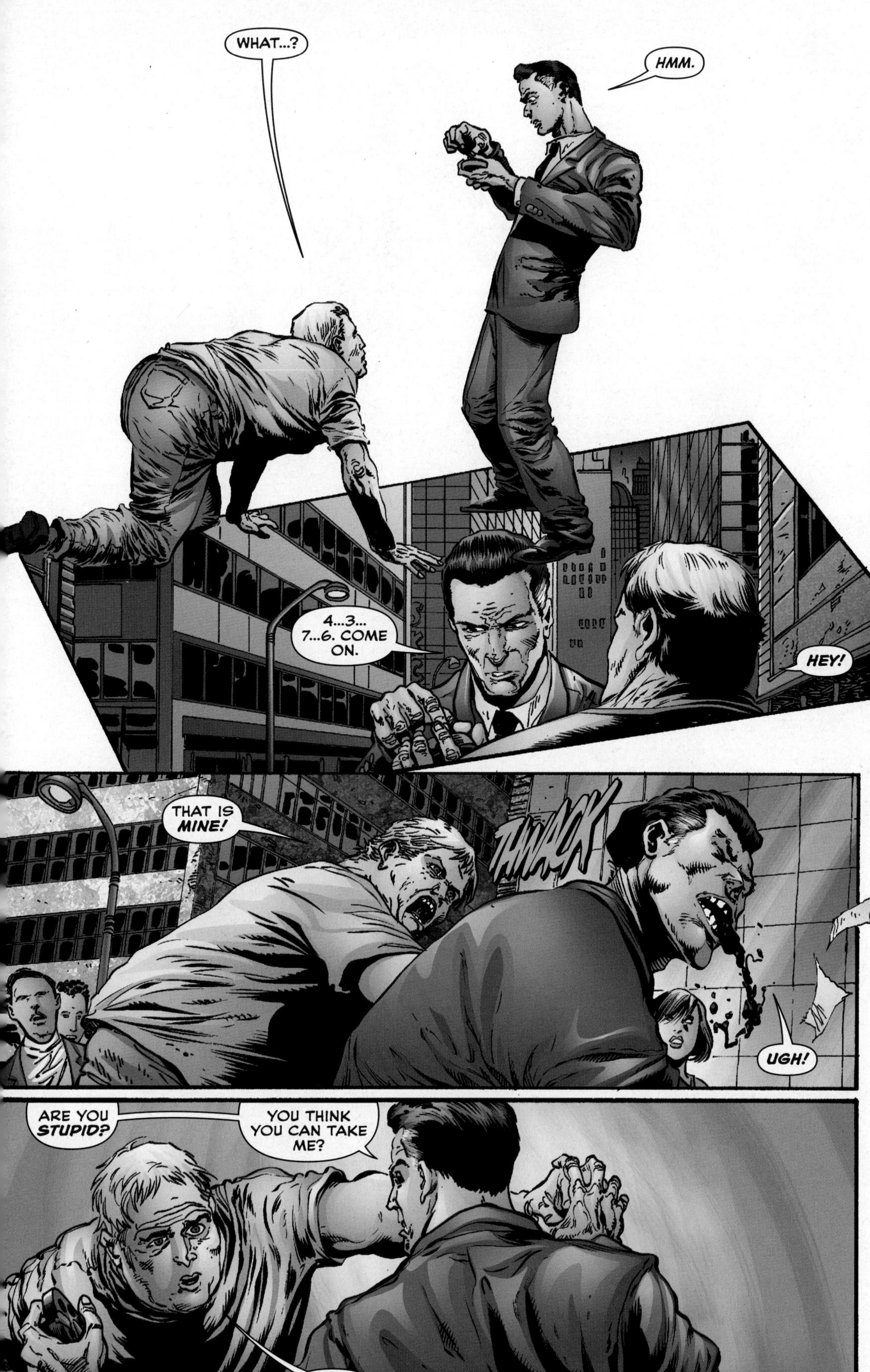
WHAT...?
HMM.
4...3... 7...6. COME ON.
HEY!
THAT IS *MINE!*
THWACK
UGH!
ARE YOU *STUPID?*
YOU THINK YOU CAN TAKE ME?
N-NO!

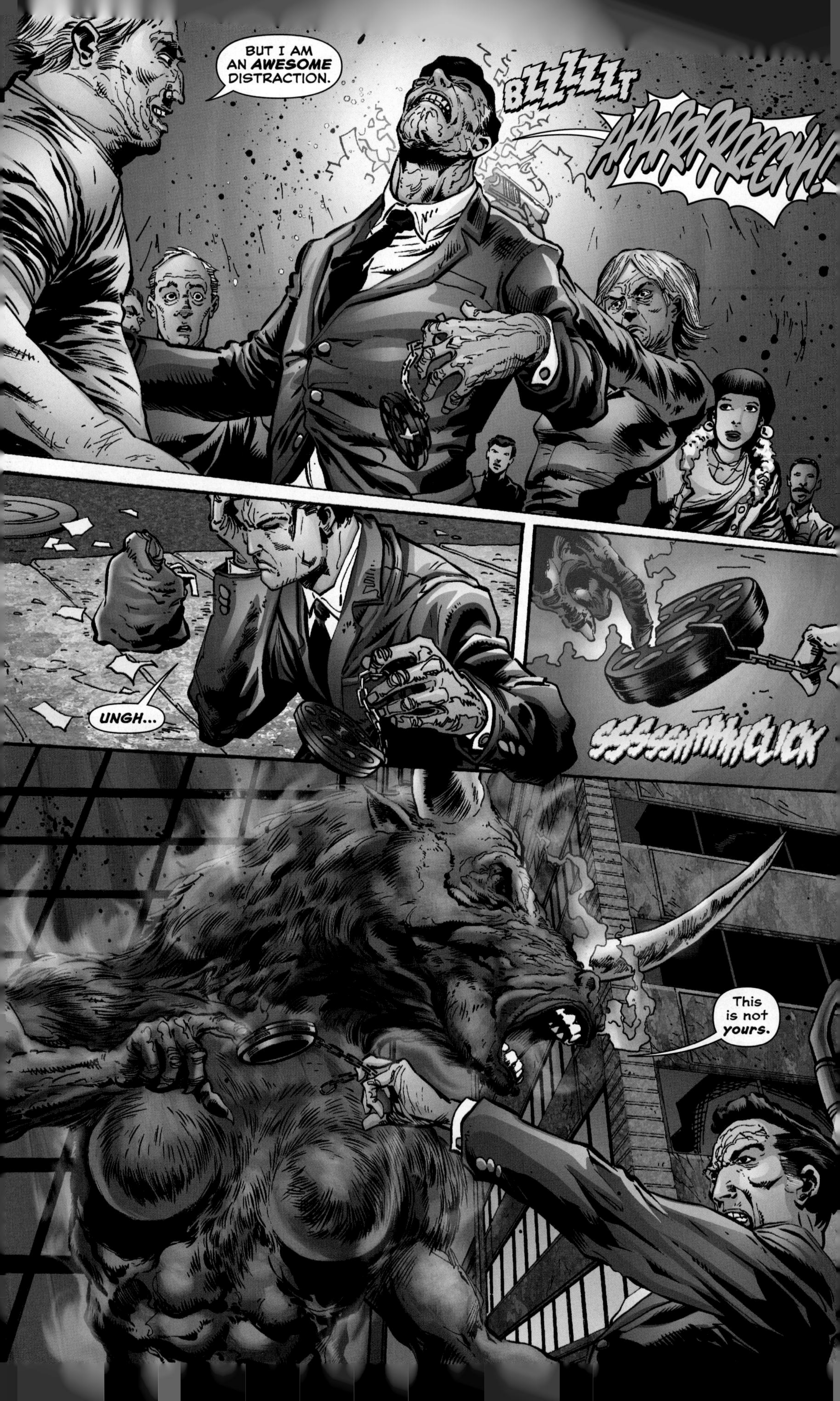

BUT I AM AN AWESOME DISTRACTION.
BZZZZZT
AAARRRRGGHH!
UNGH...
SSSSSHHHHCLICK
This is not yours.

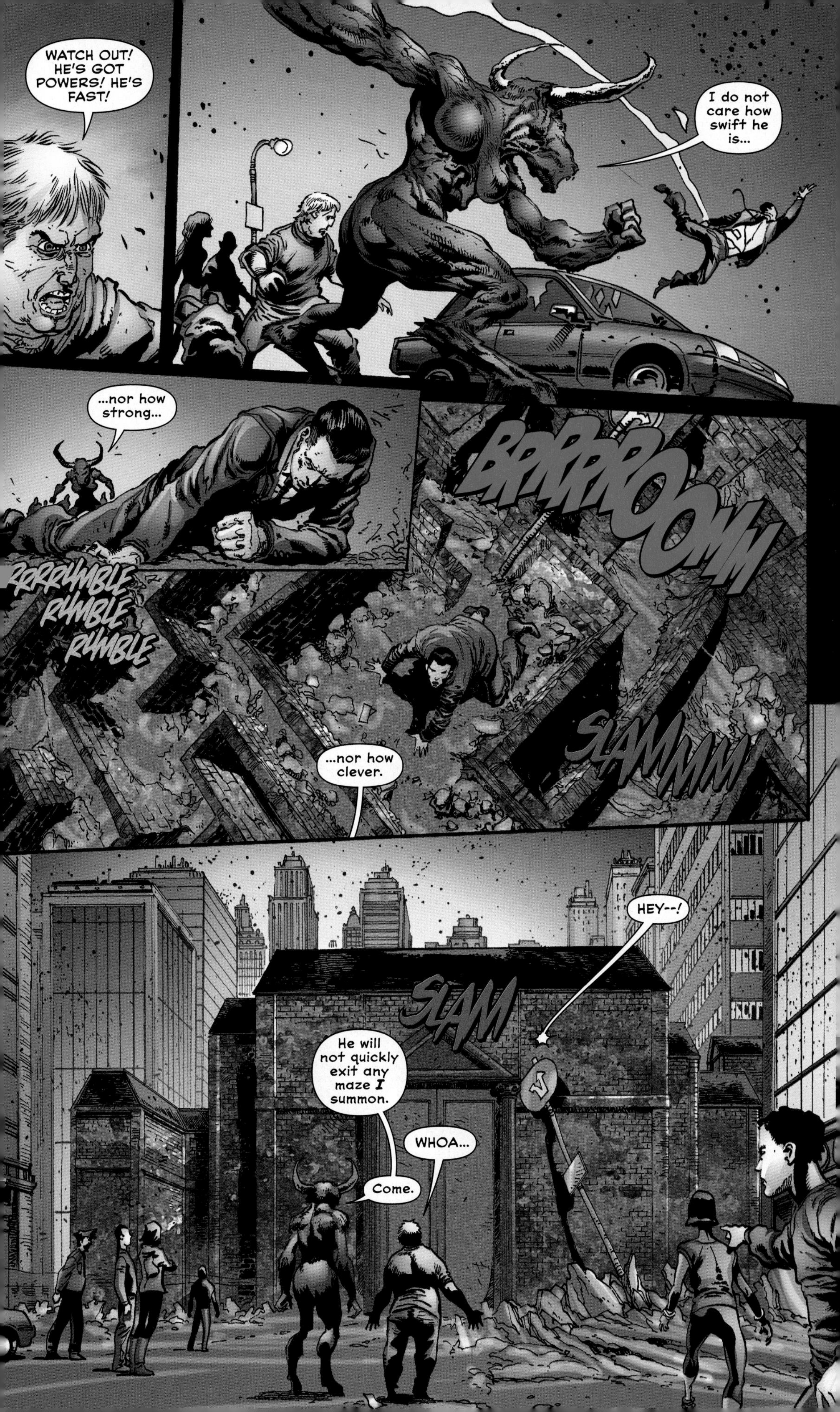
WATCH OUT! HE'S GOT POWERS! HE'S FAST!
I do not care how swift he is...
...nor how strong...
BRRRROOMM
RRRRUMBLE RUMBLE RUMBLE
SLAMMMM
...nor how clever.
HEY--!
SLAM
He will not quickly exit any maze *I* summon.
WHOA...
Come.

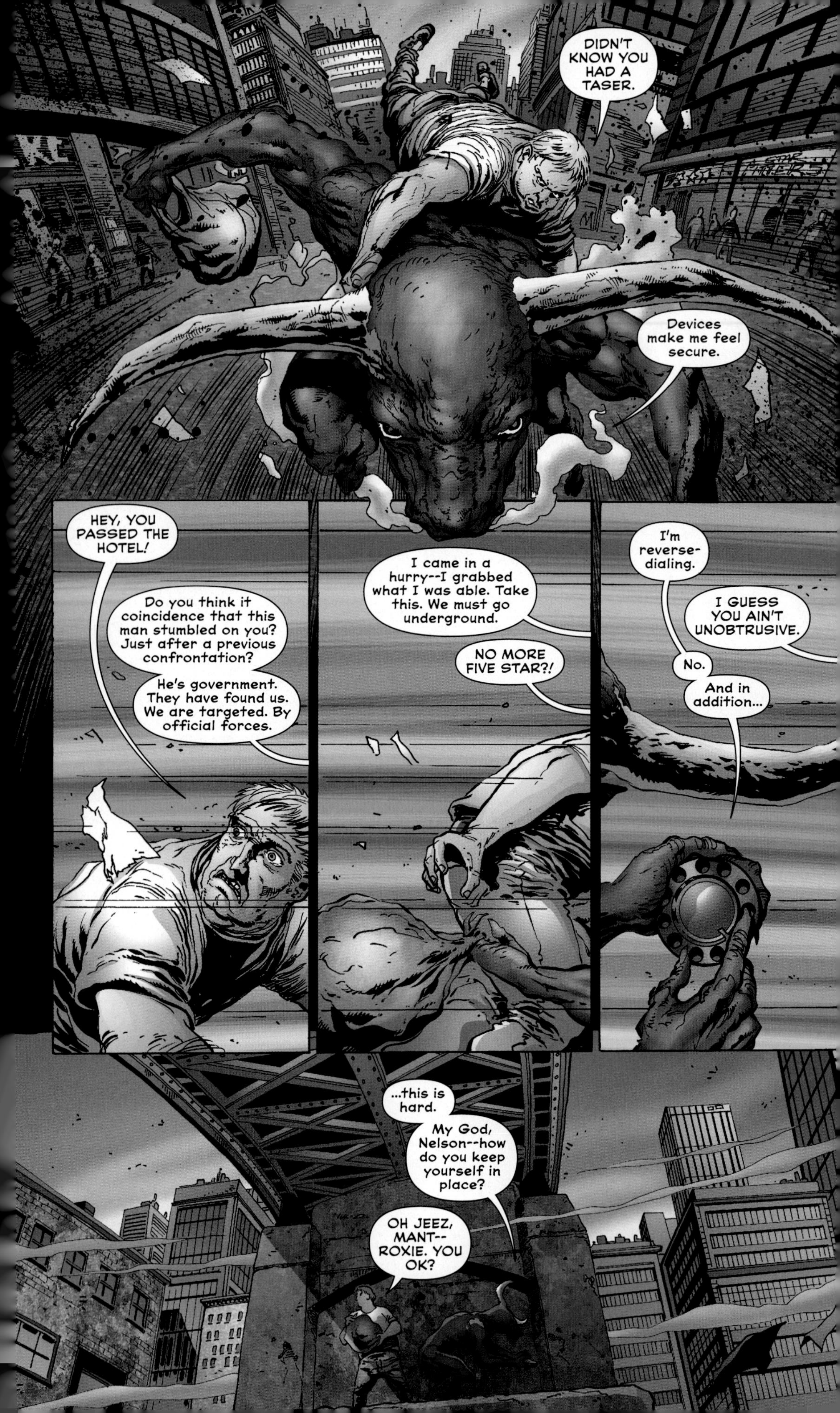
DIDN'T KNOW YOU HAD A TASER.
Devices make me feel secure.
HEY, YOU PASSED THE HOTEL!
Do you think it coincidence that this man stumbled on you? Just after a previous confrontation?
He's government. They have found us. We are targeted. By official forces.
I came in a hurry--I grabbed what I was able. Take this. We must go underground.
NO MORE FIVE STAR?!
I'm reverse-dialing.
I GUESS YOU AIN'T UNOBTRUSIVE.
No.
And in addition...
...this is hard.
My God, Nelson--how do you keep yourself in place?
OH JEEZ, MANT--ROXIE. YOU OK?

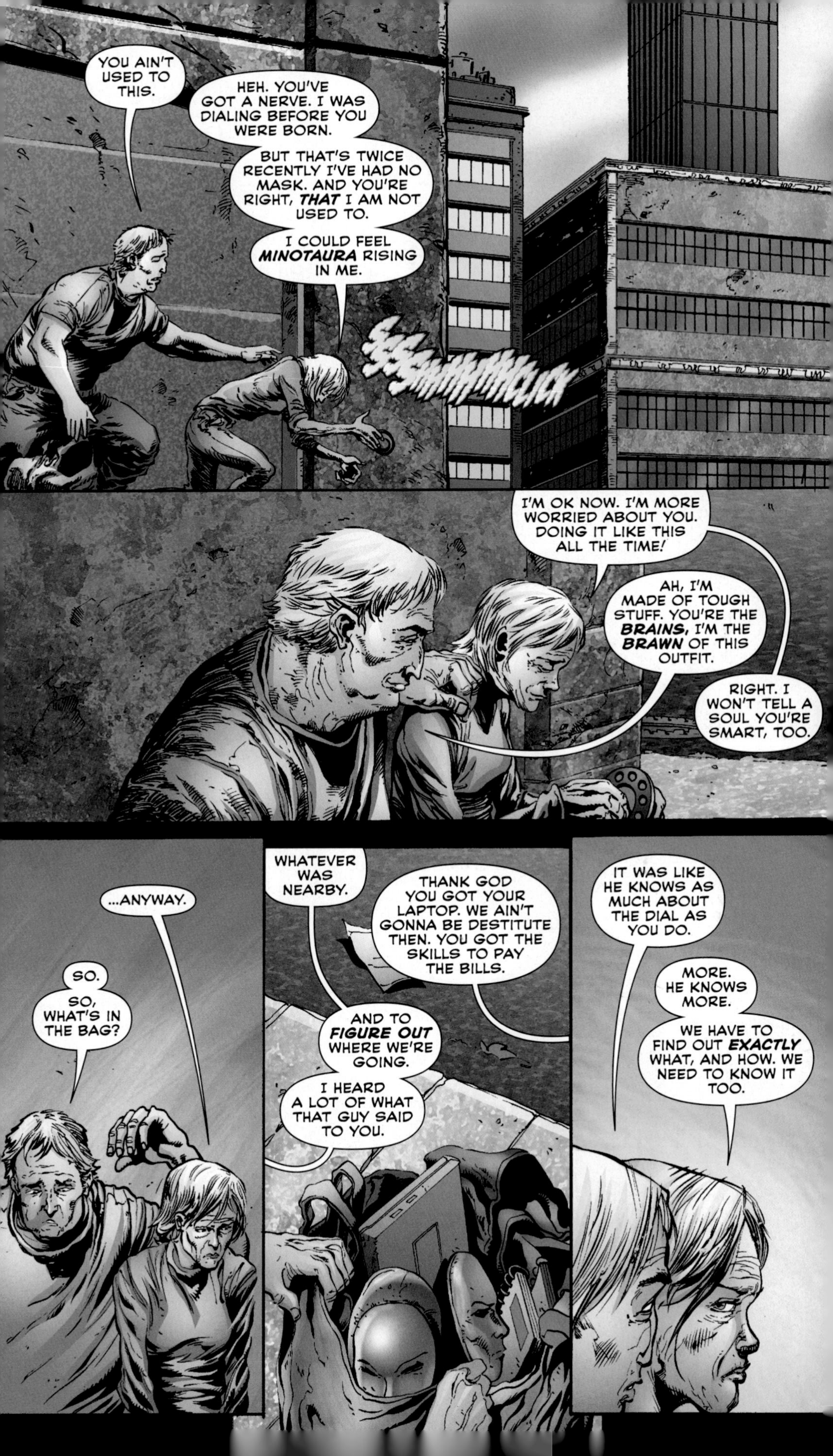
YOU AIN'T USED TO THIS.
HEH. YOU'VE GOT A NERVE. I WAS DIALING BEFORE YOU WERE BORN.
BUT THAT'S TWICE RECENTLY I'VE HAD NO MASK. AND YOU'RE RIGHT, THAT I AM NOT USED TO.
I COULD FEEL MINOTAURA RISING IN ME.
SSSHHHHTTTCLICK
I'M OK NOW. I'M MORE WORRIED ABOUT YOU. DOING IT LIKE THIS ALL THE TIME!
AH, I'M MADE OF TOUGH STUFF. YOU'RE THE BRAINS, I'M THE BRAWN OF THIS OUTFIT.
RIGHT. I WON'T TELL A SOUL YOU'RE SMART, TOO.
...ANYWAY.
SO.
SO, WHAT'S IN THE BAG?
WHATEVER WAS NEARBY.
THANK GOD YOU GOT YOUR LAPTOP. WE AIN'T GONNA BE DESTITUTE THEN. YOU GOT THE SKILLS TO PAY THE BILLS.
AND TO FIGURE OUT WHERE WE'RE GOING.
I HEARD A LOT OF WHAT THAT GUY SAID TO YOU.
IT WAS LIKE HE KNOWS AS MUCH ABOUT THE DIAL AS YOU DO.
MORE. HE KNOWS MORE.
WE HAVE TO FIND OUT EXACTLY WHAT, AND HOW. WE NEED TO KNOW IT TOO.

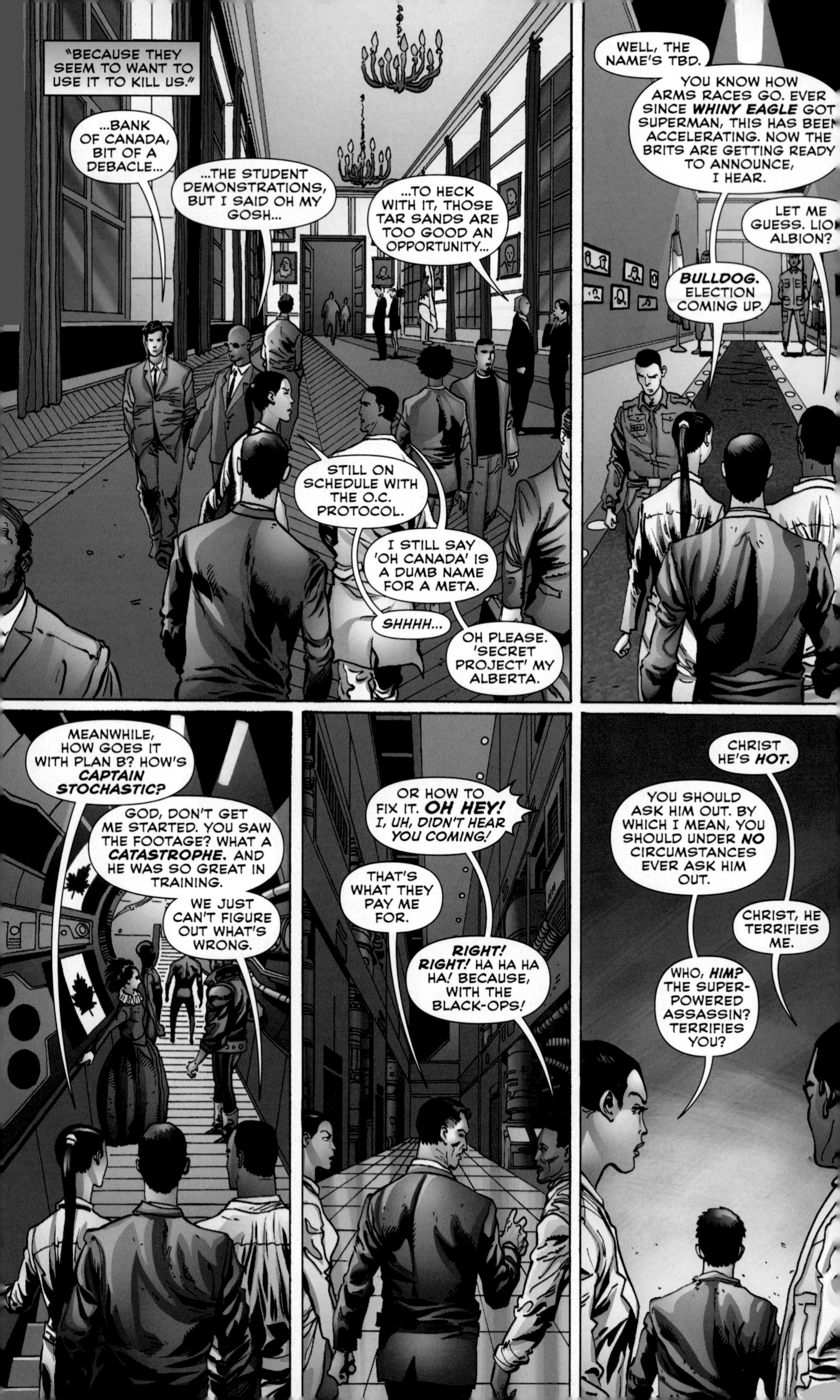

"BECAUSE THEY SEEM TO WANT TO USE IT TO KILL US."
...BANK OF CANADA, BIT OF A DEBACLE...
...THE STUDENT DEMONSTRATIONS, BUT I SAID OH MY GOSH...
...TO HECK WITH IT, THOSE TAR SANDS ARE TOO GOOD AN OPPORTUNITY...
STILL ON SCHEDULE WITH THE O.C. PROTOCOL.
I STILL SAY 'OH CANADA' IS A DUMB NAME FOR A META.
SHHHH...
OH PLEASE. 'SECRET PROJECT' MY ALBERTA.
WELL, THE NAME'S TBD.
YOU KNOW HOW ARMS RACES GO. EVER SINCE WHINY EAGLE GOT SUPERMAN, THIS HAS BEEN ACCELERATING. NOW THE BRITS ARE GETTING READY TO ANNOUNCE, I HEAR.
LET ME GUESS. LIO ALBION?
BULLDOG. ELECTION COMING UP.
MEANWHILE, HOW GOES IT WITH PLAN B? HOW'S CAPTAIN STOCHASTIC?
GOD, DON'T GET ME STARTED. YOU SAW THE FOOTAGE? WHAT A CATASTROPHE. AND HE WAS SO GREAT IN TRAINING.
WE JUST CAN'T FIGURE OUT WHAT'S WRONG.
OR HOW TO FIX IT. OH HEY! I, UH, DIDN'T HEAR YOU COMING!
THAT'S WHAT THEY PAY ME FOR.
RIGHT! RIGHT! HA HA HA HA! BECAUSE, WITH THE BLACK-OPS!
CHRIST HE'S HOT.
YOU SHOULD ASK HIM OUT. BY WHICH I MEAN, YOU SHOULD UNDER NO CIRCUMSTANCES EVER ASK HIM OUT.
CHRIST, HE TERRIFIES ME.
WHO, HIM? THE SUPER-POWERED ASSASSIN? TERRIFIES YOU?

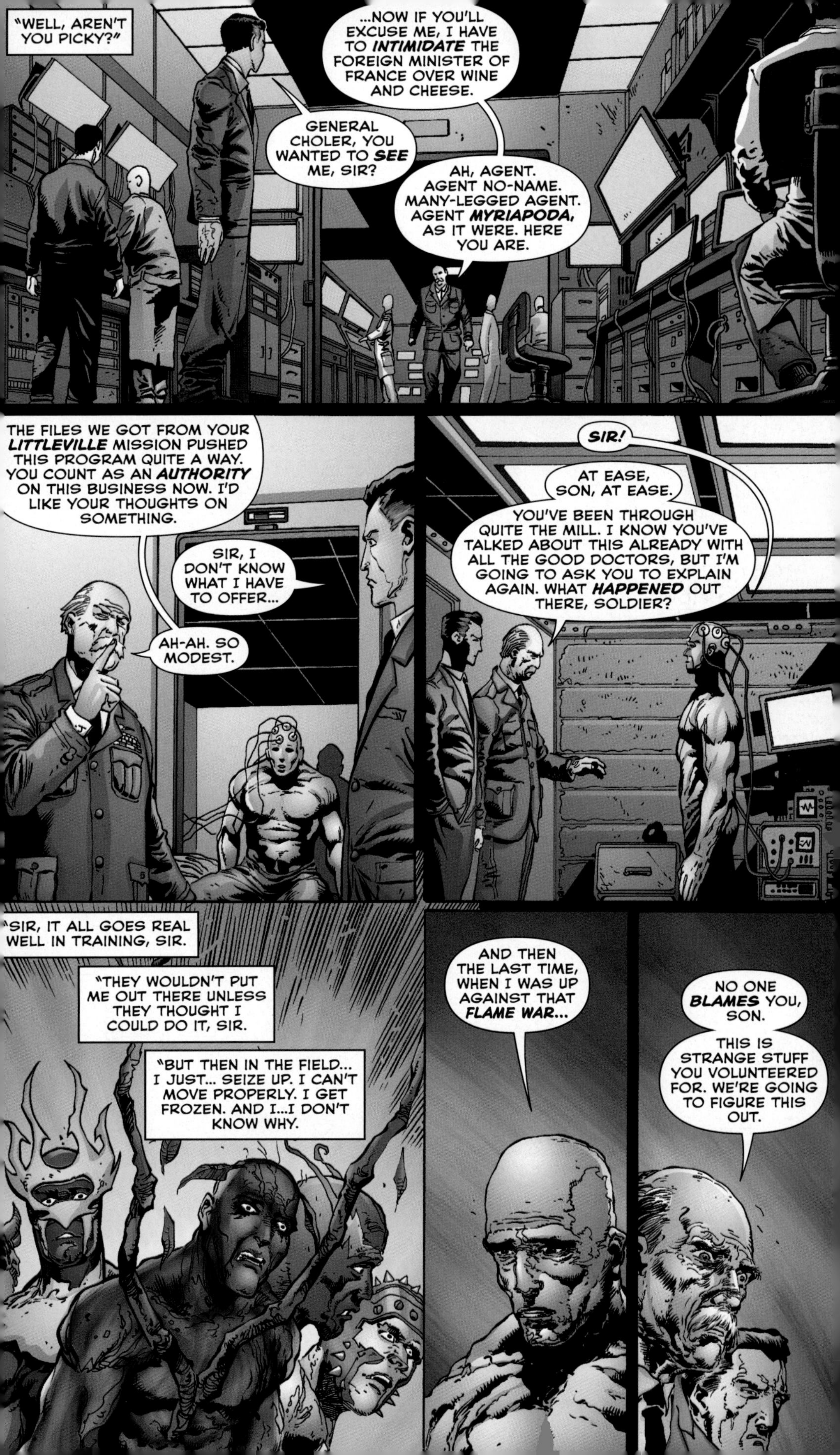
"WELL, AREN'T YOU PICKY?"
...NOW IF YOU'LL EXCUSE ME, I HAVE TO *INTIMIDATE* THE FOREIGN MINISTER OF FRANCE OVER WINE AND CHEESE.
GENERAL CHOLER, YOU WANTED TO *SEE* ME, SIR?
AH, AGENT. AGENT NO-NAME. MANY-LEGGED AGENT. AGENT *MYRIAPODA,* AS IT WERE. HERE YOU ARE.
THE FILES WE GOT FROM YOUR *LITTLEVILLE* MISSION PUSHED THIS PROGRAM QUITE A WAY. YOU COUNT AS AN *AUTHORITY* ON THIS BUSINESS NOW. I'D LIKE YOUR THOUGHTS ON SOMETHING.
SIR, I DON'T KNOW WHAT I HAVE TO OFFER...
AH-AH. SO MODEST.
SIR!
AT EASE, SON, AT EASE.
YOU'VE BEEN THROUGH QUITE THE MILL. I KNOW YOU'VE TALKED ABOUT THIS ALREADY WITH ALL THE GOOD DOCTORS, BUT I'M GOING TO ASK YOU TO EXPLAIN AGAIN. WHAT *HAPPENED* OUT THERE, SOLDIER?
"SIR, IT ALL GOES REAL WELL IN TRAINING, SIR.
"THEY WOULDN'T PUT ME OUT THERE UNLESS THEY THOUGHT I COULD DO IT, SIR.
"BUT THEN IN THE FIELD... I JUST... SEIZE UP. I CAN'T MOVE PROPERLY. I GET FROZEN. AND I...I DON'T KNOW WHY.
AND THEN THE LAST TIME, WHEN I WAS UP AGAINST THAT *FLAME WAR...*
NO ONE *BLAMES* YOU, SON.
THIS IS STRANGE STUFF YOU VOLUNTEERED FOR. WE'RE GOING TO FIGURE THIS OUT.

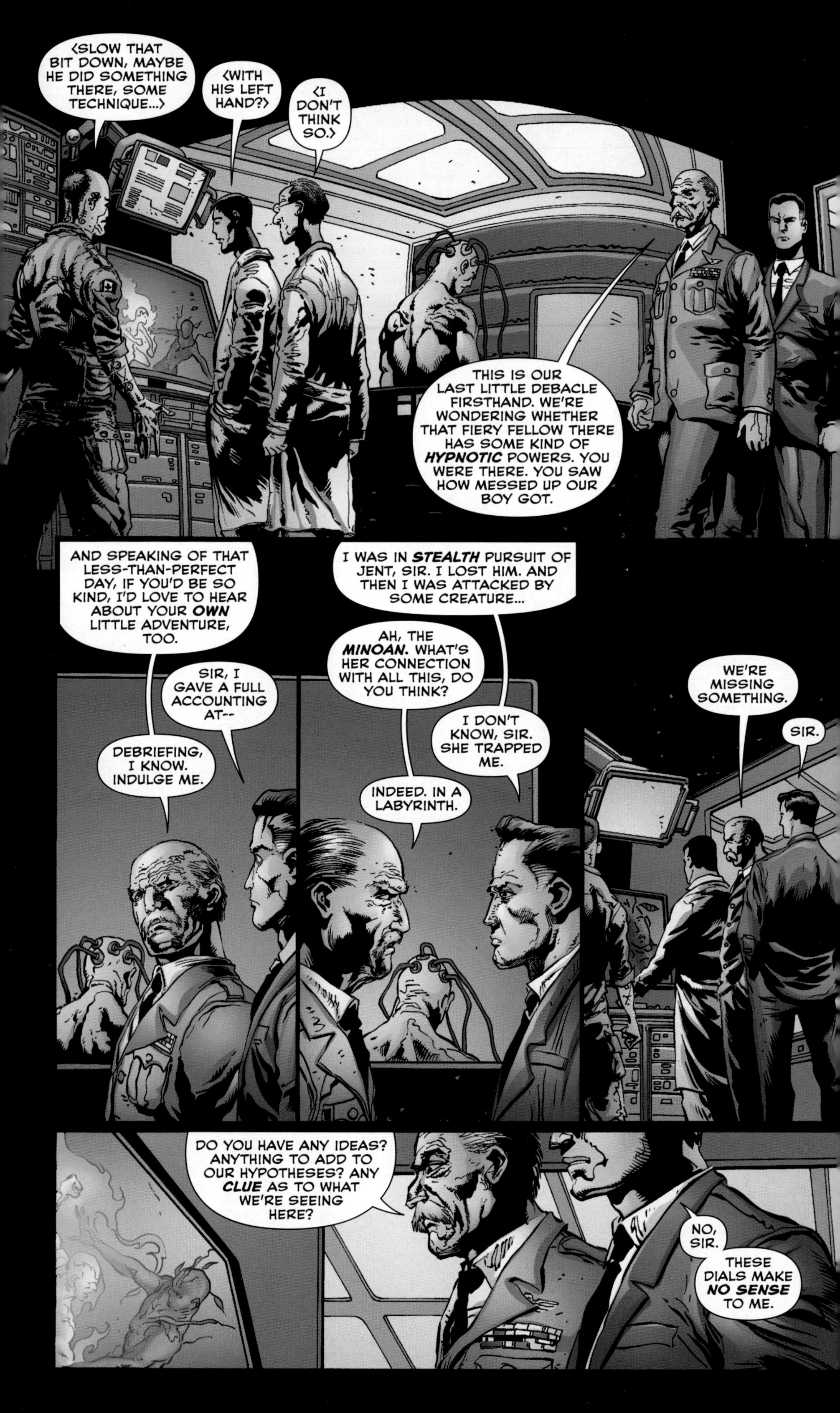
<SLOW THAT BIT DOWN, MAYBE HE DID SOMETHING THERE, SOME TECHNIQUE...>
<WITH HIS LEFT HAND?>
<I DON'T THINK SO.>
THIS IS OUR LAST LITTLE DEBACLE FIRSTHAND. WE'RE WONDERING WHETHER THAT FIERY FELLOW THERE HAS SOME KIND OF ***HYPNOTIC*** POWERS. YOU WERE THERE. YOU SAW HOW MESSED UP OUR BOY GOT.
AND SPEAKING OF THAT LESS-THAN-PERFECT DAY, IF YOU'D BE SO KIND, I'D LOVE TO HEAR ABOUT YOUR ***OWN*** LITTLE ADVENTURE, TOO.
SIR, I GAVE A FULL ACCOUNTING AT--
DEBRIEFING, I KNOW. INDULGE ME.
I WAS IN ***STEALTH*** PURSUIT OF JENT, SIR. I LOST HIM. AND THEN I WAS ATTACKED BY SOME CREATURE...
AH, THE ***MINOAN.*** WHAT'S HER CONNECTION WITH ALL THIS, DO YOU THINK?
I DON'T KNOW, SIR. SHE TRAPPED ME.
INDEED. IN A LABYRINTH.
WE'RE MISSING SOMETHING.
SIR.
DO YOU HAVE ANY IDEAS? ANYTHING TO ADD TO OUR HYPOTHESES? ANY ***CLUE*** AS TO WHAT WE'RE SEEING HERE?
NO, SIR.
THESE DIALS MAKE ***NO SENSE*** TO ME.

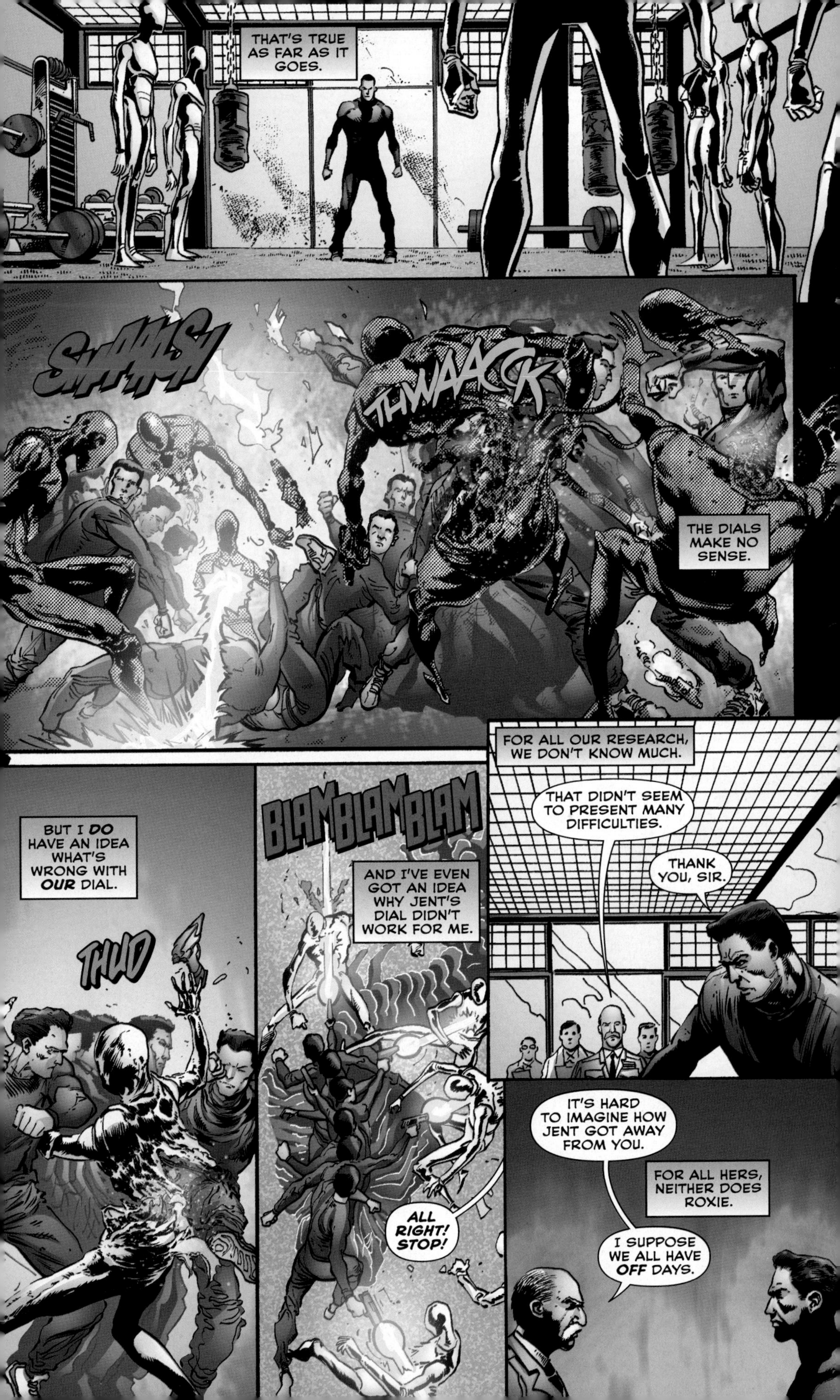
THAT'S TRUE AS FAR AS IT GOES.
SMAASH
THWAACK
THE DIALS MAKE NO SENSE.
FOR ALL OUR RESEARCH, WE DON'T KNOW MUCH.
THAT DIDN'T SEEM TO PRESENT MANY DIFFICULTIES.
THANK YOU, SIR.
BUT I DO HAVE AN IDEA WHAT'S WRONG WITH OUR DIAL.
THUD
BLAM BLAM BLAM
AND I'VE EVEN GOT AN IDEA WHY JENT'S DIAL DIDN'T WORK FOR ME.
ALL RIGHT! STOP!
IT'S HARD TO IMAGINE HOW JENT GOT AWAY FROM YOU.
FOR ALL HERS, NEITHER DOES ROXIE.
I SUPPOSE WE ALL HAVE OFF DAYS.

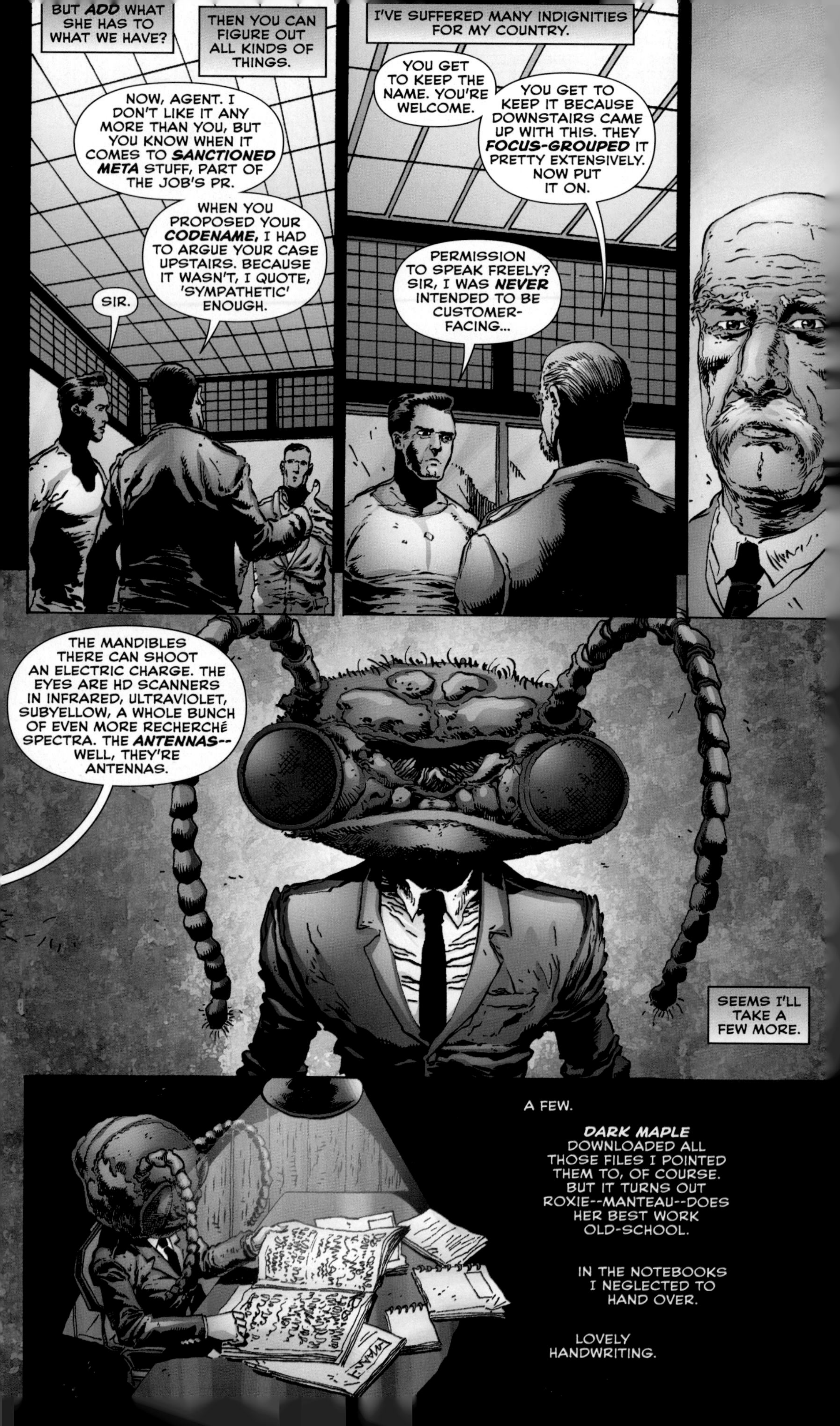
BUT ADD WHAT SHE HAS TO WHAT WE HAVE?
THEN YOU CAN FIGURE OUT ALL KINDS OF THINGS.
NOW, AGENT. I DON'T LIKE IT ANY MORE THAN YOU, BUT YOU KNOW WHEN IT COMES TO SANCTIONED META STUFF, PART OF THE JOB'S PR.
SIR.
WHEN YOU PROPOSED YOUR CODENAME, I HAD TO ARGUE YOUR CASE UPSTAIRS. BECAUSE IT WASN'T, I QUOTE, 'SYMPATHETIC' ENOUGH.
I'VE SUFFERED MANY INDIGNITIES FOR MY COUNTRY.
YOU GET TO KEEP THE NAME. YOU'RE WELCOME.
YOU GET TO KEEP IT BECAUSE DOWNSTAIRS CAME UP WITH THIS. THEY FOCUS-GROUPED IT PRETTY EXTENSIVELY. NOW PUT IT ON.
PERMISSION TO SPEAK FREELY? SIR, I WAS NEVER INTENDED TO BE CUSTOMER-FACING...
THE MANDIBLES THERE CAN SHOOT AN ELECTRIC CHARGE. THE EYES ARE HD SCANNERS IN INFRARED, ULTRAVIOLET, SUBYELLOW, A WHOLE BUNCH OF EVEN MORE RECHERCHÉ SPECTRA. THE ANTENNAS--WELL, THEY'RE ANTENNAS.
SEEMS I'LL TAKE A FEW MORE.
A FEW.
DARK MAPLE DOWNLOADED ALL THOSE FILES I POINTED THEM TO, OF COURSE. BUT IT TURNS OUT ROXIE--MANTEAU--DOES HER BEST WORK OLD-SCHOOL.
IN THE NOTEBOOKS I NEGLECTED TO HAND OVER.
LOVELY HANDWRITING.

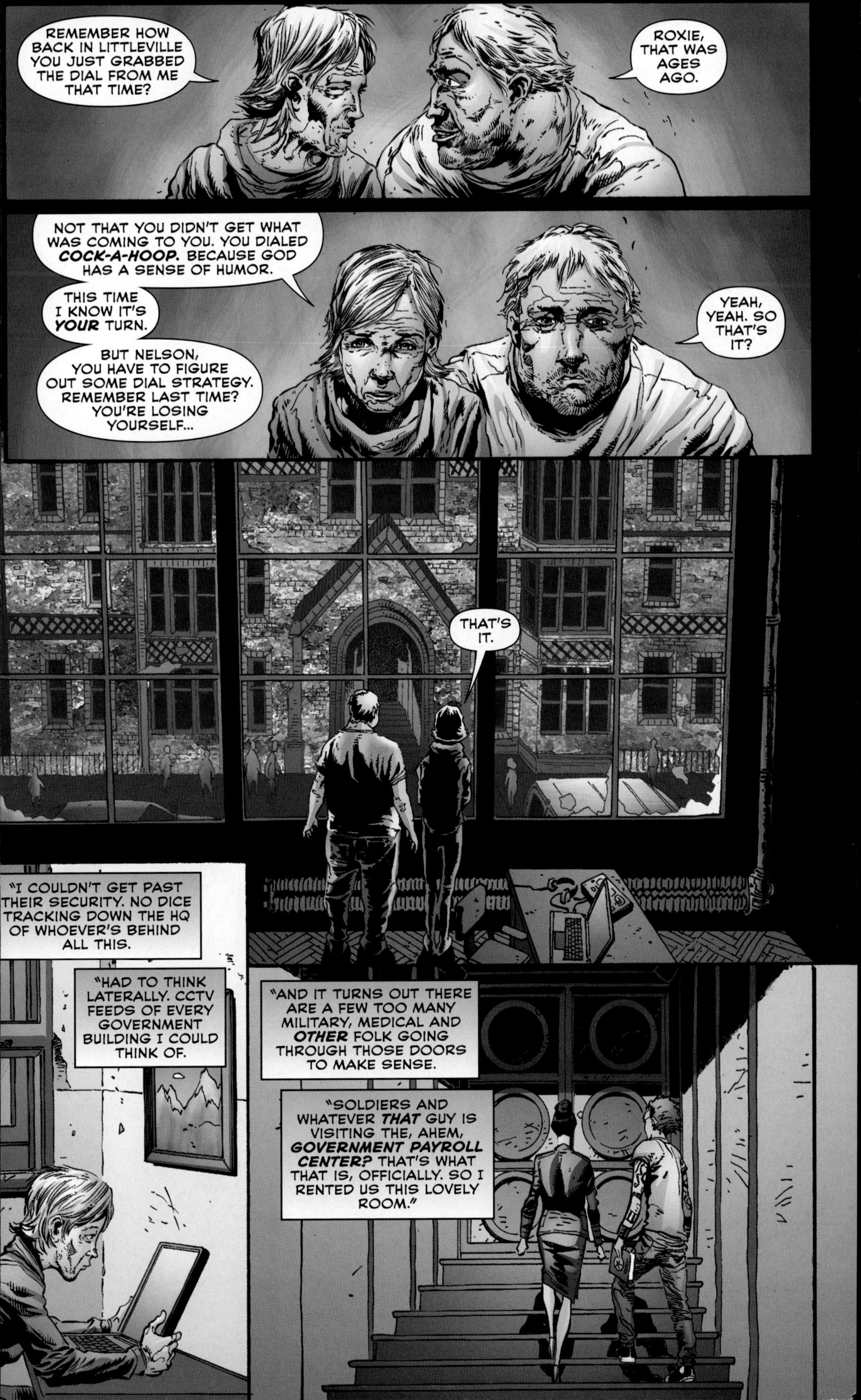
REMEMBER HOW BACK IN LITTLEVILLE YOU JUST GRABBED THE DIAL FROM ME THAT TIME?
ROXIE, THAT WAS AGES AGO.
NOT THAT YOU DIDN'T GET WHAT WAS COMING TO YOU. YOU DIALED COCK-A-HOOP. BECAUSE GOD HAS A SENSE OF HUMOR.
THIS TIME I KNOW IT'S YOUR TURN.
BUT NELSON, YOU HAVE TO FIGURE OUT SOME DIAL STRATEGY. REMEMBER LAST TIME? YOU'RE LOSING YOURSELF...
YEAH, YEAH. SO THAT'S IT?
THAT'S IT.
"I COULDN'T GET PAST THEIR SECURITY. NO DICE TRACKING DOWN THE HQ OF WHOEVER'S BEHIND ALL THIS.
"HAD TO THINK LATERALLY. CCTV FEEDS OF EVERY GOVERNMENT BUILDING I COULD THINK OF.
"AND IT TURNS OUT THERE ARE A FEW TOO MANY MILITARY, MEDICAL AND OTHER FOLK GOING THROUGH THOSE DOORS TO MAKE SENSE.
"SOLDIERS AND WHATEVER THAT GUY IS VISITING THE, AHEM, GOVERNMENT PAYROLL CENTER? THAT'S WHAT THAT IS, OFFICIALLY. SO I RENTED US THIS LOVELY ROOM."

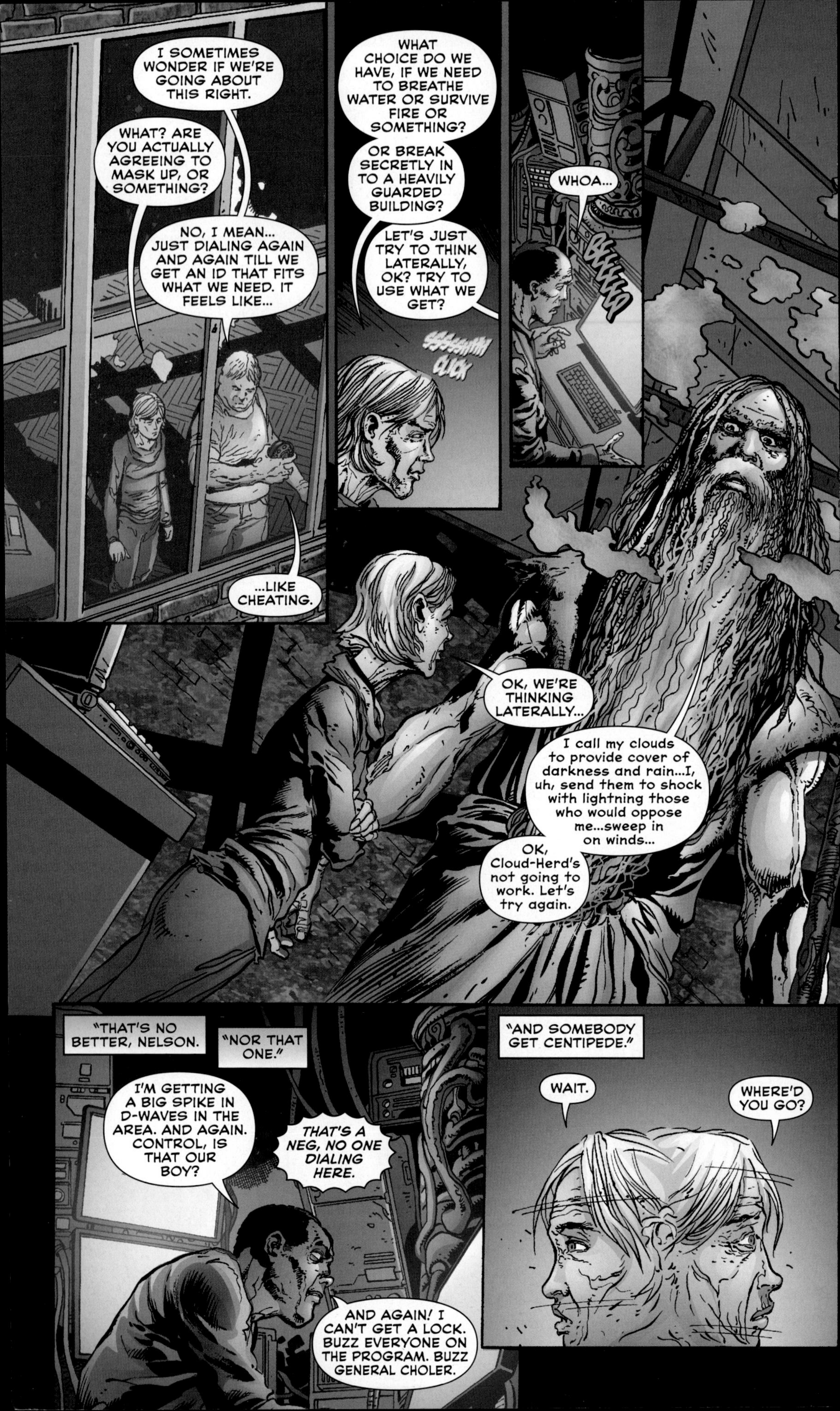

I SOMETIMES WONDER IF WE'RE GOING ABOUT THIS RIGHT.
WHAT? ARE YOU ACTUALLY AGREEING TO MASK UP, OR SOMETHING?
NO, I MEAN... JUST DIALING AGAIN AND AGAIN TILL WE GET AN ID THAT FITS WHAT WE NEED. IT FEELS LIKE...
...LIKE CHEATING.
WHAT CHOICE DO WE HAVE, IF WE NEED TO BREATHE WATER OR SURVIVE FIRE OR SOMETHING?
OR BREAK SECRETLY IN TO A HEAVILY GUARDED BUILDING?
LET'S JUST TRY TO THINK LATERALLY, OK? TRY TO USE WHAT WE GET?
SSSSHHH CLICK
WHOA...
OK, WE'RE THINKING LATERALLY...
I call my clouds to provide cover of darkness and rain...I, uh, send them to shock with lightning those who would oppose me...sweep in on winds...
OK, Cloud-Herd's not going to work. Let's try again.
"THAT'S NO BETTER, NELSON.
"NOR THAT ONE."
I'M GETTING A BIG SPIKE IN D-WAVES IN THE AREA. AND AGAIN. CONTROL, IS THAT OUR BOY?
THAT'S A NEG, NO ONE DIALING HERE.
AND AGAIN! I CAN'T GET A LOCK. BUZZ EVERYONE ON THE PROGRAM. BUZZ GENERAL CHOLER.
"AND SOMEBODY GET CENTIPEDE."
WAIT.
WHERE'D YOU GO?

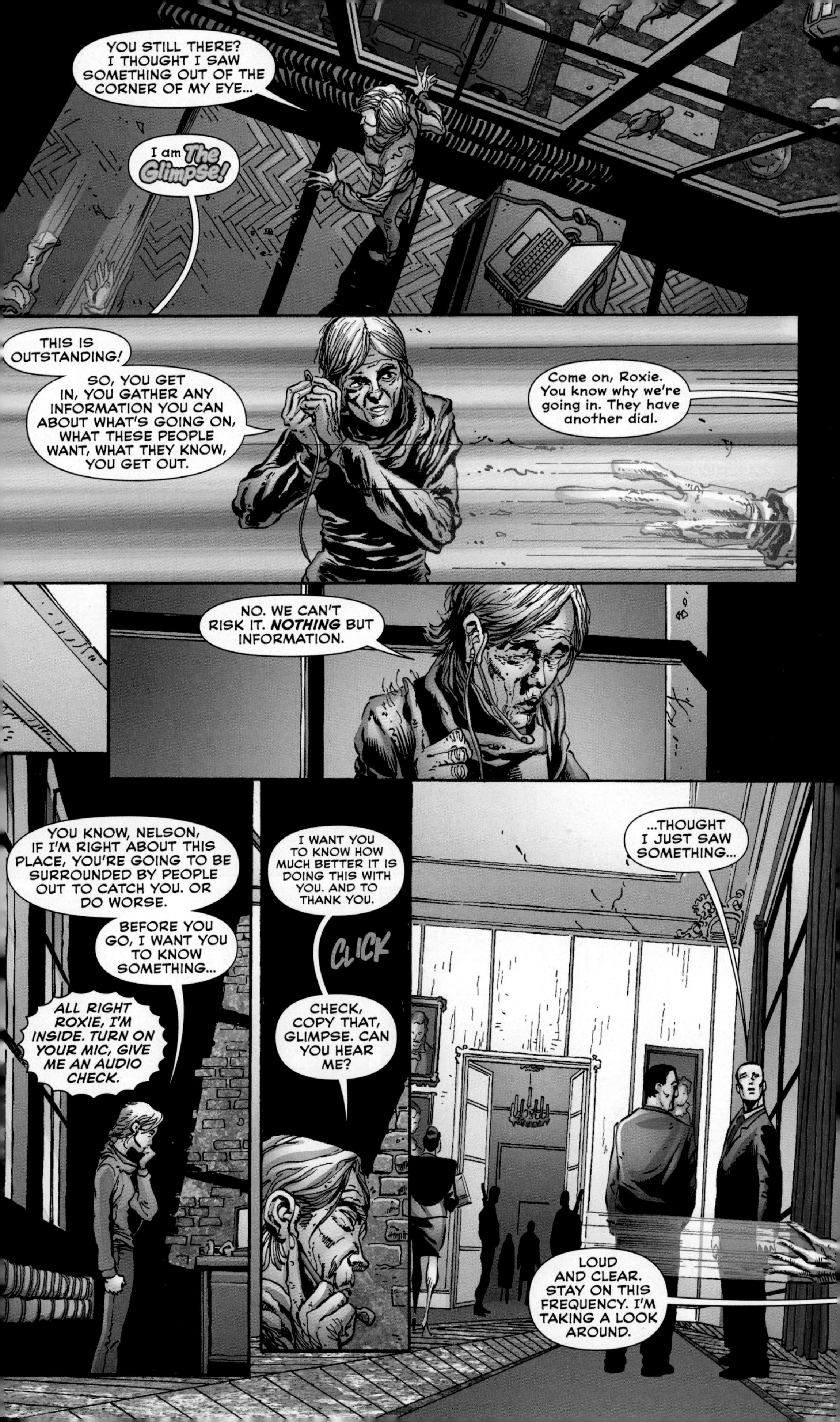

YOU STILL THERE? I THOUGHT I SAW SOMETHING OUT OF THE CORNER OF MY EYE...
I am The Glimpse!
THIS IS OUTSTANDING!
SO, YOU GET IN, YOU GATHER ANY INFORMATION YOU CAN ABOUT WHAT'S GOING ON, WHAT THESE PEOPLE WANT, WHAT THEY KNOW, YOU GET OUT.
Come on, Roxie. You know why we're going in. They have another dial.
NO. WE CAN'T RISK IT. NOTHING BUT INFORMATION.
YOU KNOW, NELSON, IF I'M RIGHT ABOUT THIS PLACE, YOU'RE GOING TO BE SURROUNDED BY PEOPLE OUT TO CATCH YOU. OR DO WORSE.
BEFORE YOU GO, I WANT YOU TO KNOW SOMETHING...
I WANT YOU TO KNOW HOW MUCH BETTER IT IS DOING THIS WITH YOU. AND TO THANK YOU.
CLICK
ALL RIGHT ROXIE, I'M INSIDE. TURN ON YOUR MIC, GIVE ME AN AUDIO CHECK.
CHECK, COPY THAT, GLIMPSE. CAN YOU HEAR ME?
...THOUGHT I JUST SAW SOMETHING...
LOUD AND CLEAR. STAY ON THIS FREQUENCY. I'M TAKING A LOOK AROUND.

HMMM.

THEY'RE TRYING TO KEEP IT CALM, BUT IF YOU KNOW WHERE TO LOOK...

SOMETHING'S GOING ON.

YEAH, OUTSIDE TOO.

BE CAREFUL.

DID YOU SAY SOMETHING?

MAYBE *YOU'RE* WHAT'S GOING ON.

THESE GUYS ARE LIKE A TRAIL OF BREADCRUMBS. I'M FOLLOWING THEM BACK.

BUUUMPP

OH, EXCUSE ME!

I DIDN'T...

...SEE YOU...

...IS SOMEONE THERE?

SHHHHH.

I'M LOSING MY MIND...

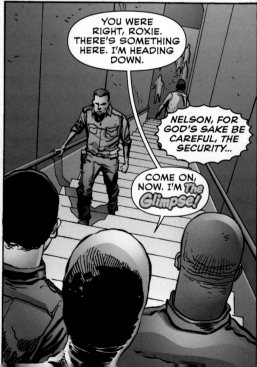

YOU WERE RIGHT, ROXIE. THERE'S SOMETHING HERE. I'M HEADING DOWN.

NELSON, FOR GOD'S SAKE BE CAREFUL, THE SECURITY...

COME ON, NOW. I'M *The Glimpse!*

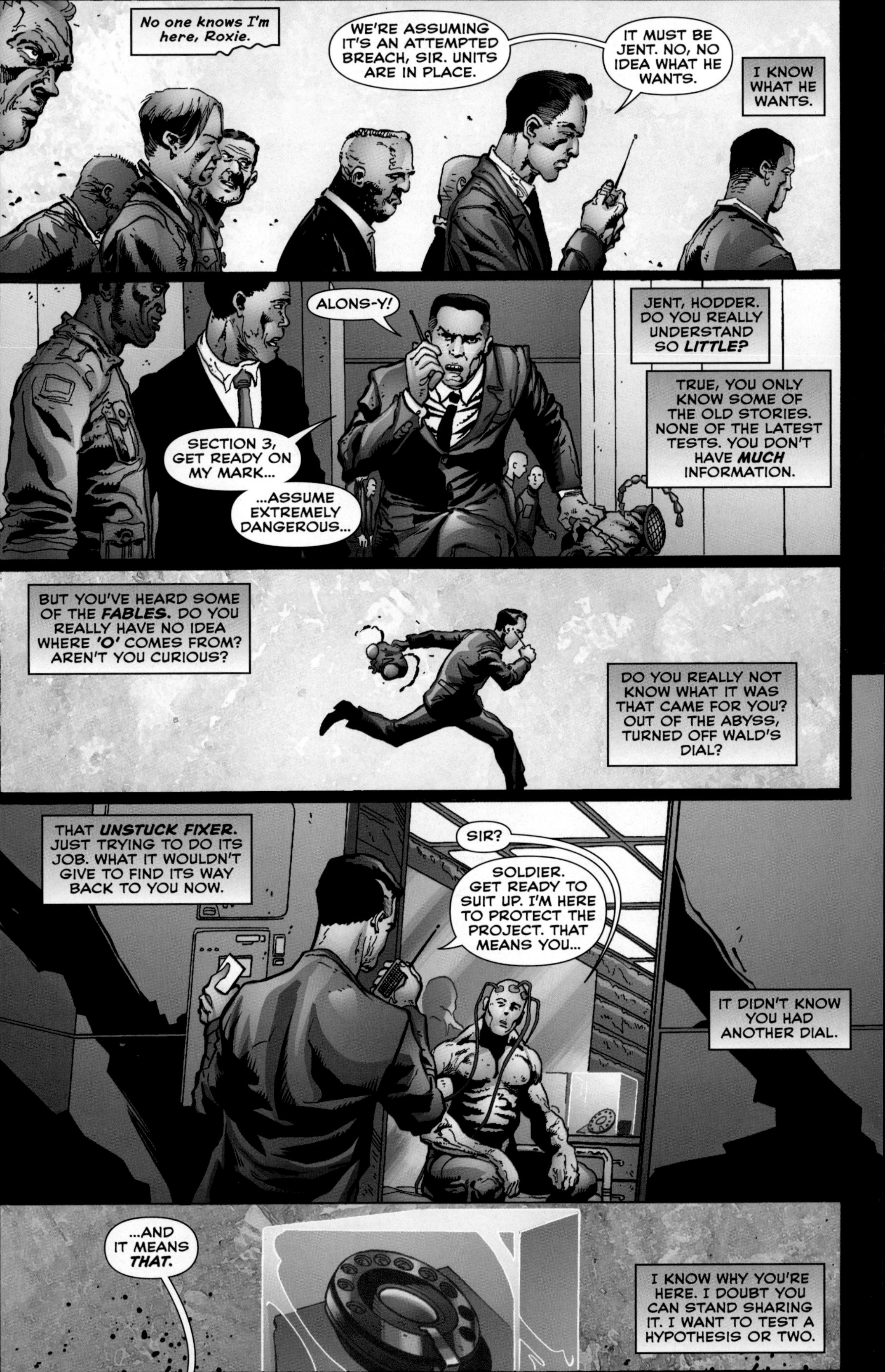
No one knows I'm here, Roxie.
WE'RE ASSUMING IT'S AN ATTEMPTED BREACH, SIR. UNITS ARE IN PLACE.
IT MUST BE JENT. NO, NO IDEA WHAT HE WANTS.
I KNOW WHAT HE WANTS.
ALONS-Y!
JENT, HODDER. DO YOU REALLY UNDERSTAND SO LITTLE?
TRUE, YOU ONLY KNOW SOME OF THE OLD STORIES. NONE OF THE LATEST TESTS. YOU DON'T HAVE MUCH INFORMATION.
SECTION 3, GET READY ON MY MARK...
...ASSUME EXTREMELY DANGEROUS...
BUT YOU'VE HEARD SOME OF THE FABLES. DO YOU REALLY HAVE NO IDEA WHERE 'O' COMES FROM? AREN'T YOU CURIOUS?
DO YOU REALLY NOT KNOW WHAT IT WAS THAT CAME FOR YOU? OUT OF THE ABYSS, TURNED OFF WALD'S DIAL?
THAT UNSTUCK FIXER. JUST TRYING TO DO ITS JOB. WHAT IT WOULDN'T GIVE TO FIND ITS WAY BACK TO YOU NOW.
SIR?
SOLDIER. GET READY TO SUIT UP. I'M HERE TO PROTECT THE PROJECT. THAT MEANS YOU...
IT DIDN'T KNOW YOU HAD ANOTHER DIAL.
...AND IT MEANS THAT.
I KNOW WHY YOU'RE HERE. I DOUBT YOU CAN STAND SHARING IT. I WANT TO TEST A HYPOTHESIS OR TWO.

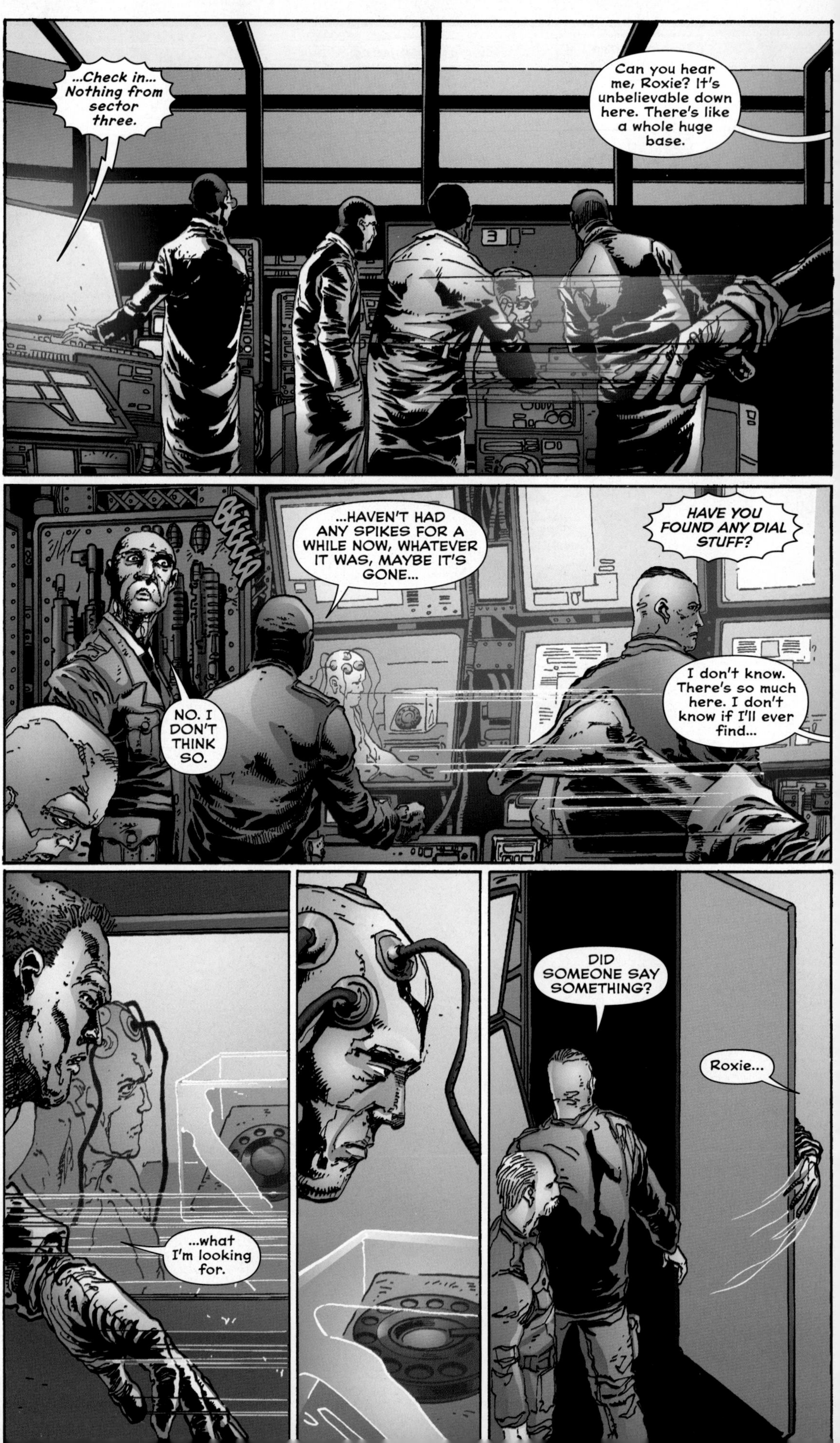
...Check in... Nothing from sector three.
Can you hear me, Roxie? It's unbelievable down here. There's like a whole huge base.
...HAVEN'T HAD ANY SPIKES FOR A WHILE NOW, WHATEVER IT WAS, MAYBE IT'S GONE...
HAVE YOU FOUND ANY DIAL STUFF?
NO. I DON'T THINK SO.
I don't know. There's so much here. I don't know if I'll ever find...
...what I'm looking for.
DID SOMEONE SAY SOMETHING?
Roxie...

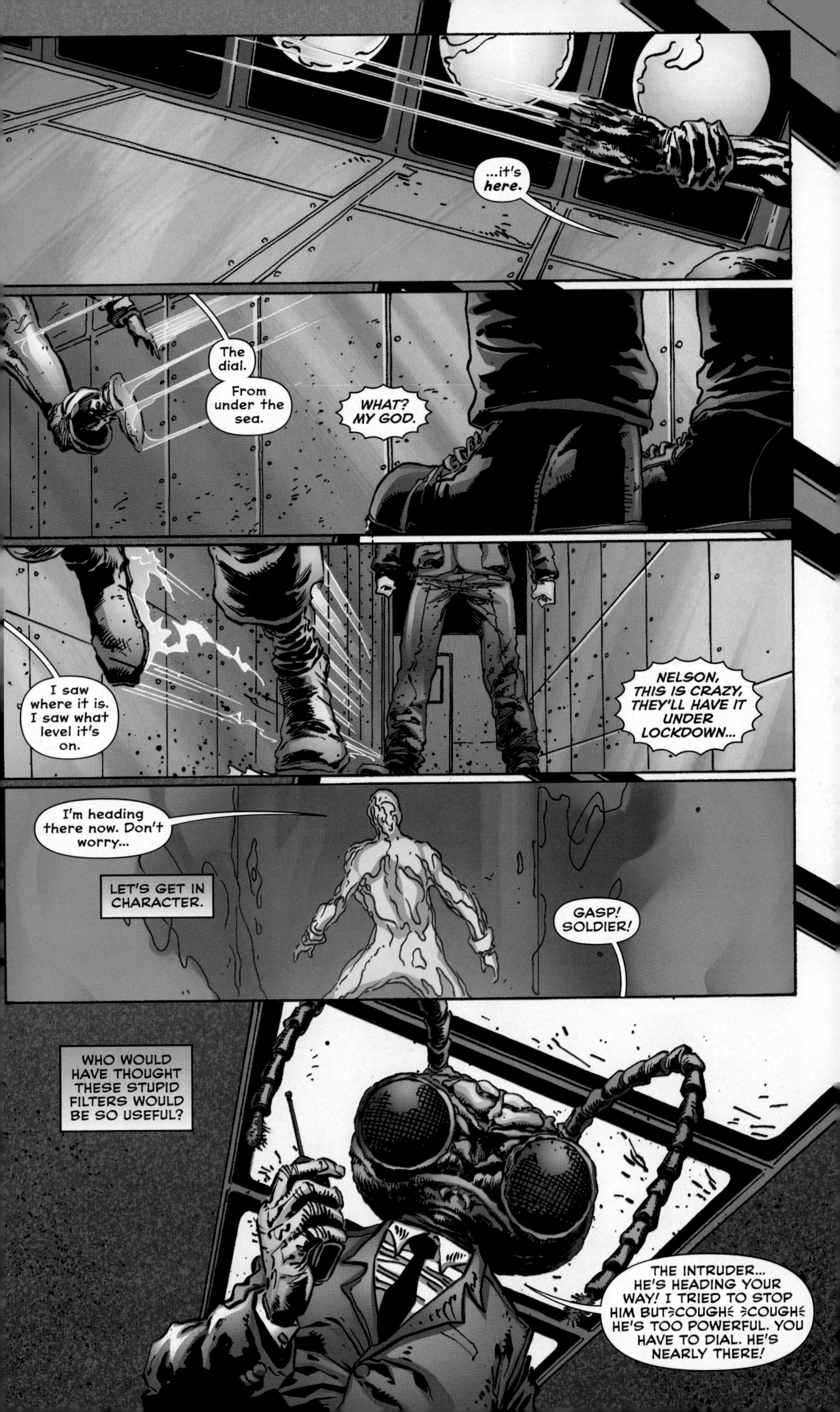

...it's *here.*
The dial.
From under the sea.
WHAT? MY GOD.
I saw where it is. I saw what level it's on.
NELSON, THIS IS CRAZY, THEY'LL HAVE IT UNDER LOCKDOWN...
I'm heading there now. Don't worry...
LET'S GET IN CHARACTER.
GASP! SOLDIER!
WHO WOULD HAVE THOUGHT THESE STUPID FILTERS WOULD BE SO USEFUL?
THE INTRUDER... HE'S HEADING YOUR WAY! I TRIED TO STOP HIM BUT COUGH COUGH HE'S TOO POWERFUL. YOU HAVE TO DIAL. HE'S NEARLY THERE!

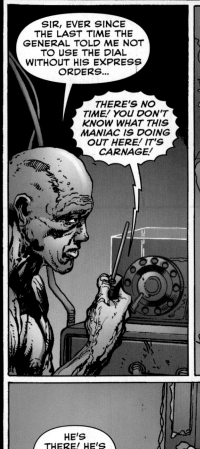

SIR, EVER SINCE THE LAST TIME THE GENERAL TOLD ME NOT TO USE THE DIAL WITHOUT HIS EXPRESS ORDERS...

THERE'S NO TIME! YOU DON'T KNOW WHAT THIS MANIAC IS DOING OUT HERE! IT'S CARNAGE!

I DON'T WANT TO! I FEEL SO *WRONG* WHEN I USE IT, AND MY ORDERS WERE CLEAR....!

OH MY GOD, HE'S COMING! HE'S GOING TO TEAR YOU APART!

HE'S THERE! HE'S OPENING THE DOOR! SAVE YOURSELF!

DIAL!

DIAL!

OH GOD--

SSSHHHHHHHCLICK

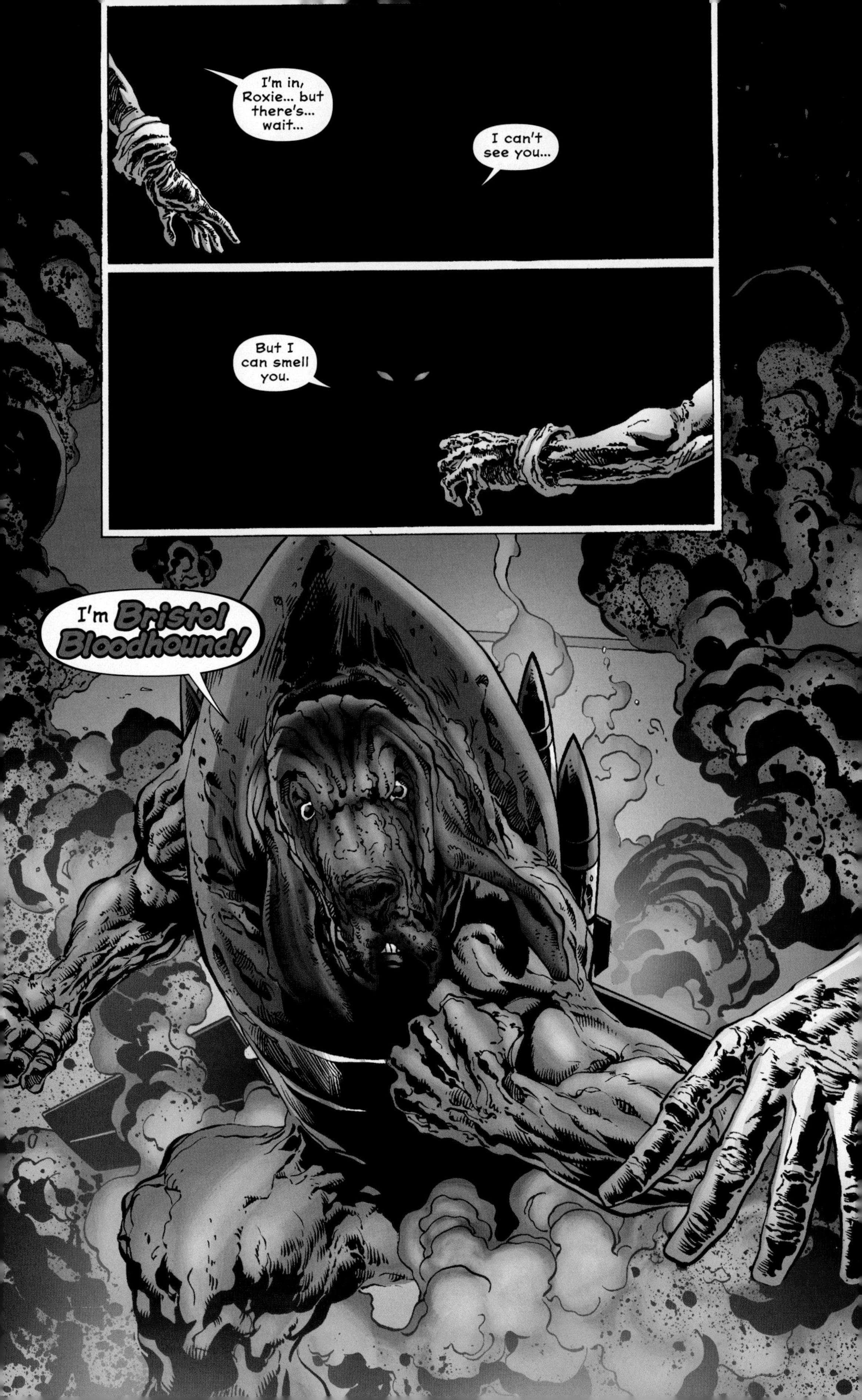
I'm in, Roxie... but there's... wait...
I can't see you...
But I can smell you.
I'm Bristol Bloodhound!

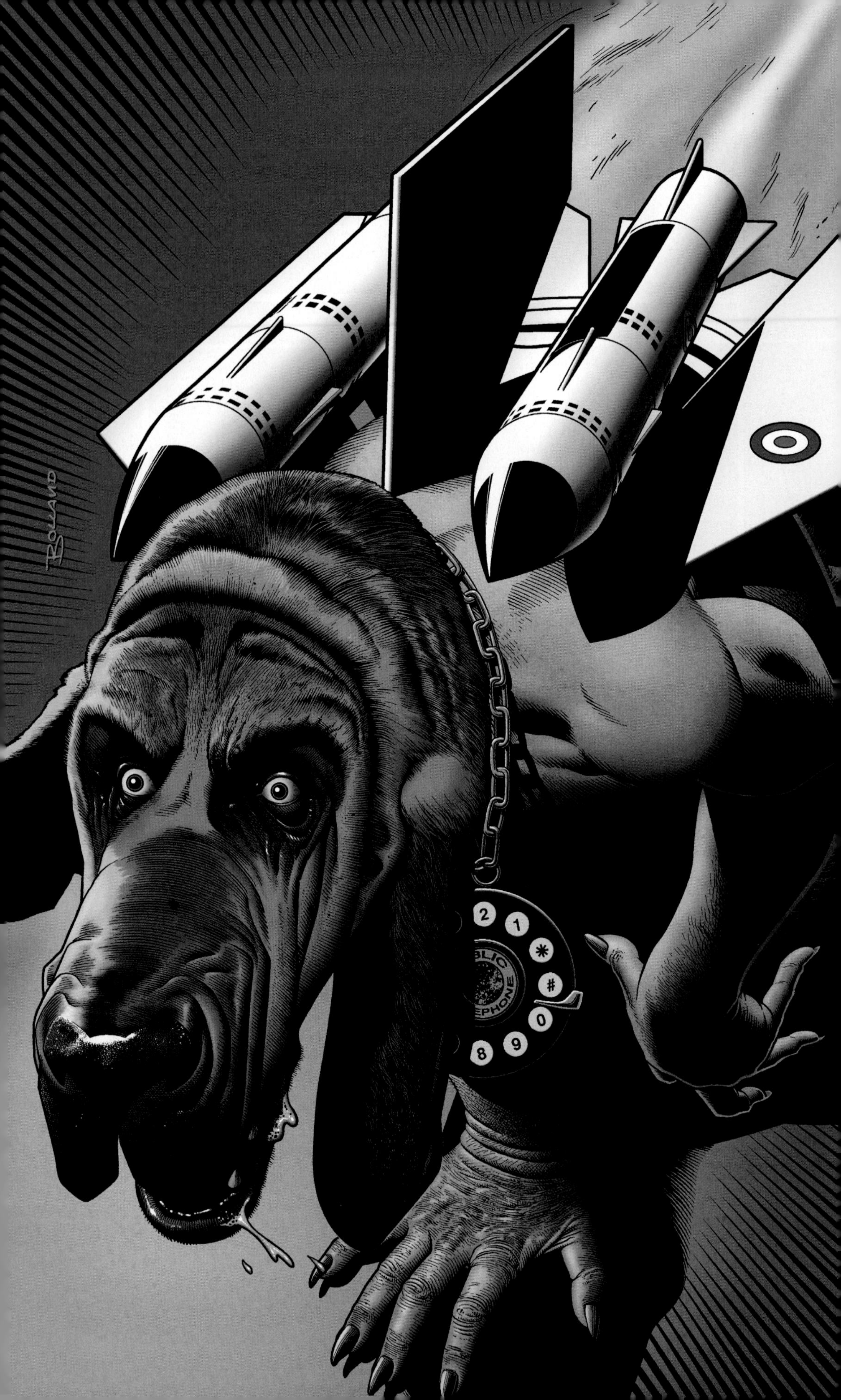
BOLLAND

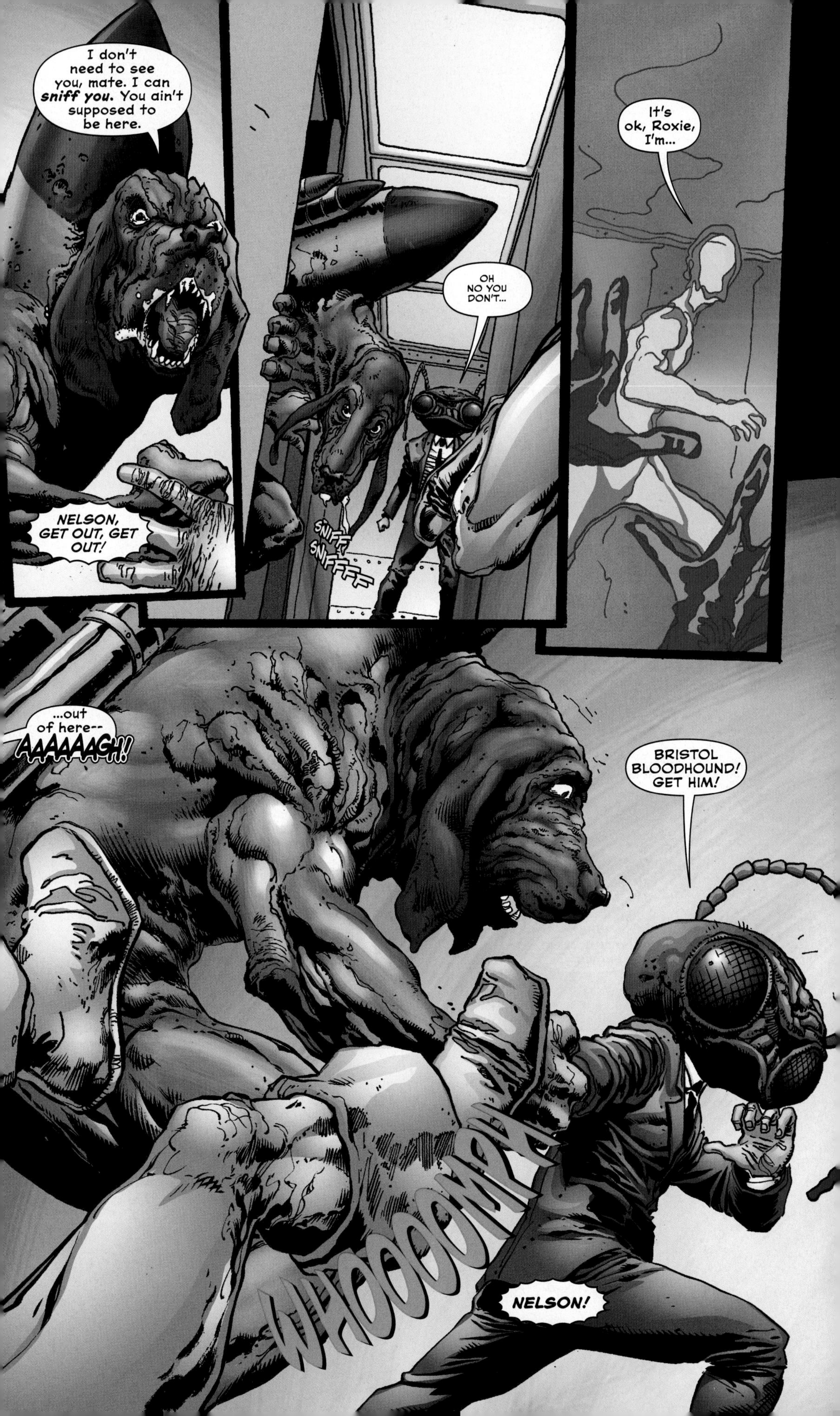
I don't need to see you, mate. I can **sniff you.** You ain't supposed to be here.
NELSON, GET OUT, GET OUT!
SNIFF SNIFF SNIFFFFF
OH NO YOU DON'T...
It's ok, Roxie, I'm...
...out of here-- AAAAAAGH!
BRISTOL BLOODHOUND! GET HIM!
WHOOOOMPH
NELSON!

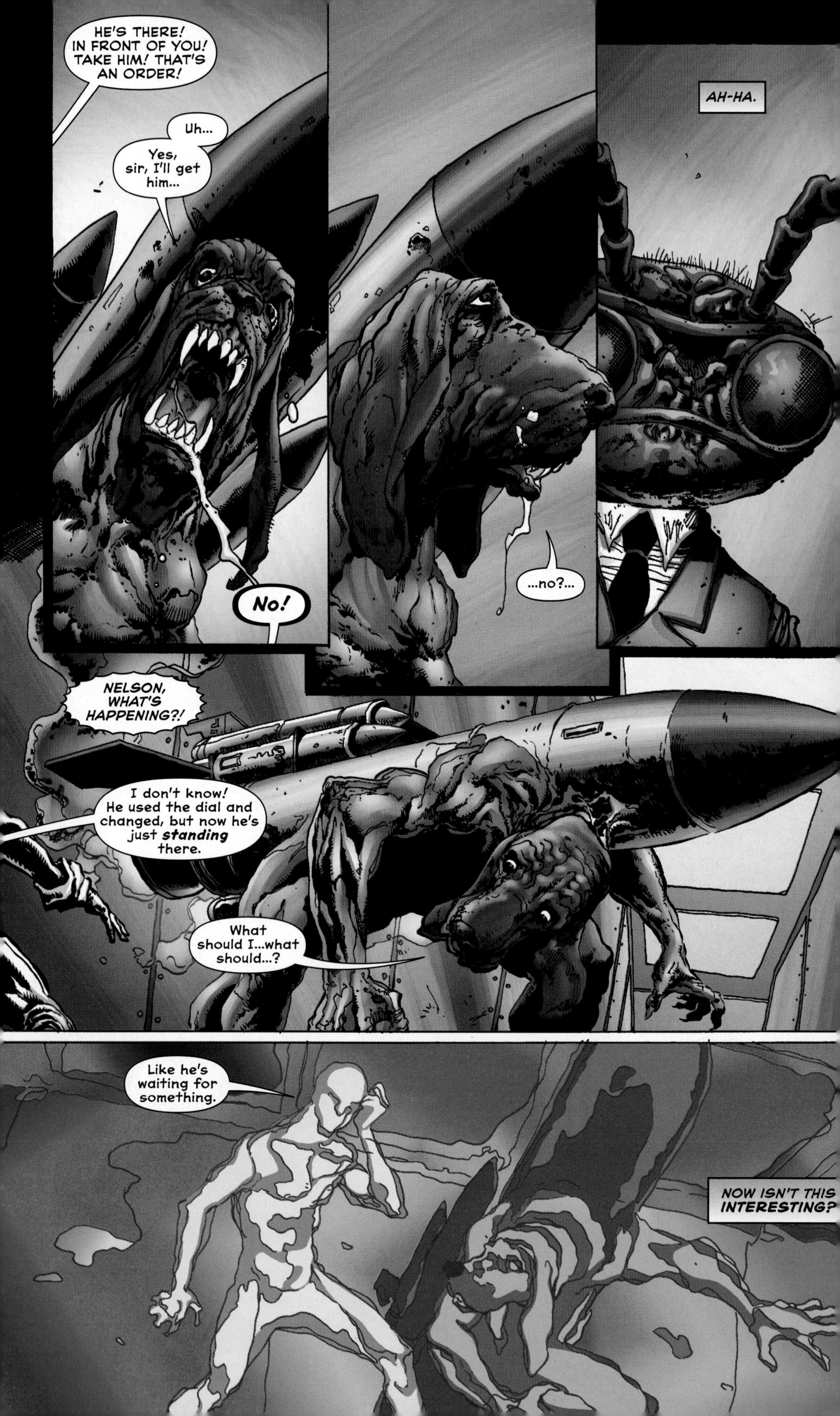
HE'S THERE! IN FRONT OF YOU! TAKE HIM! THAT'S AN ORDER!
Uh...
Yes, sir, I'll get him...
No!
...no?...
AH-HA.
NELSON, WHAT'S HAPPENING?!
I don't know! He used the dial and changed, but now he's just standing there.
What should I...what should...?
Like he's waiting for something.
NOW ISN'T THIS INTERESTING?

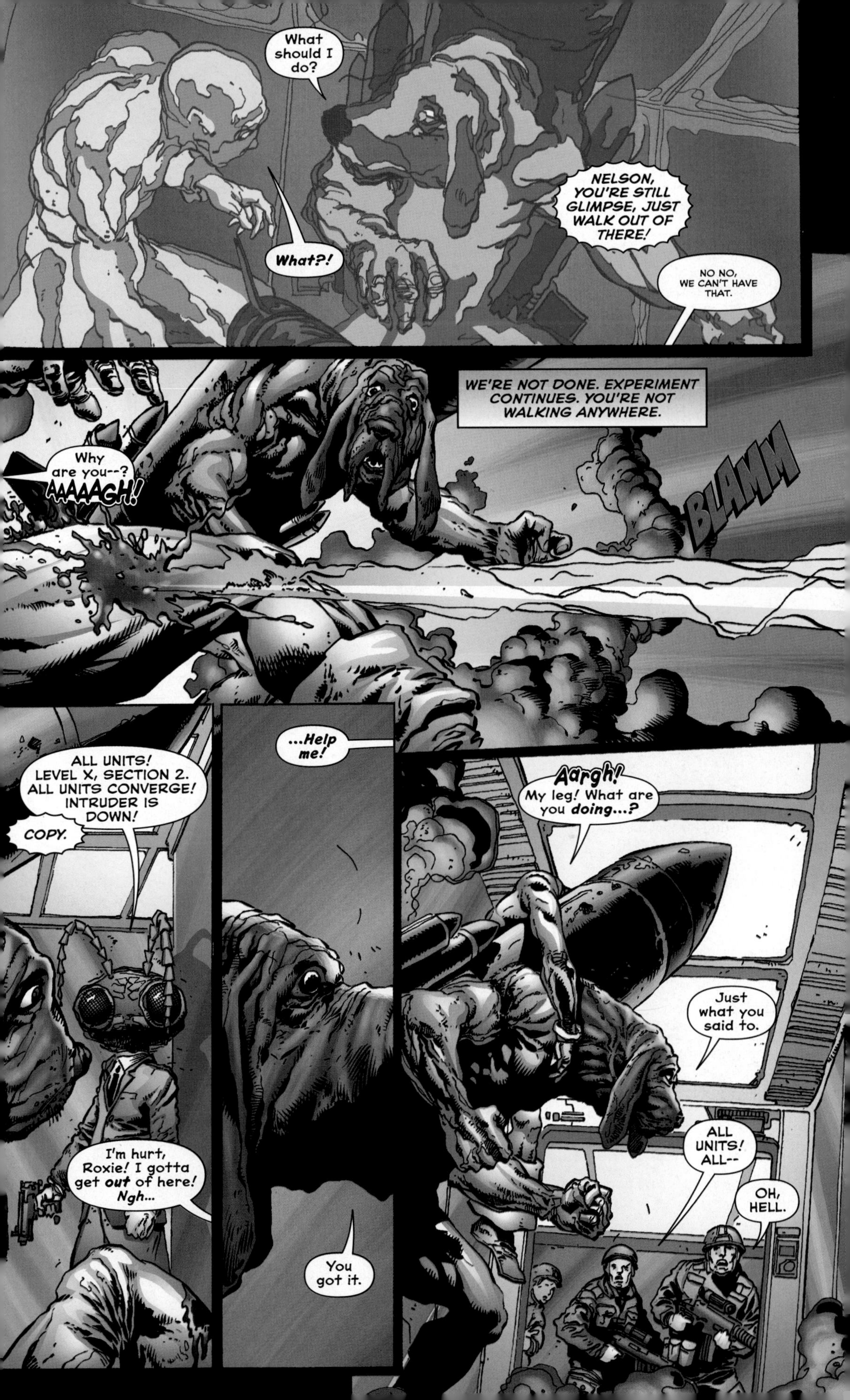

What should I do?
NELSON, YOU'RE STILL GLIMPSE, JUST WALK OUT OF THERE!
What?!
NO NO, WE CAN'T HAVE THAT.
WE'RE NOT DONE. EXPERIMENT CONTINUES. YOU'RE NOT WALKING ANYWHERE.
Why are you--? AAAAAGH!
BLAMM
ALL UNITS! LEVEL X, SECTION 2. ALL UNITS CONVERGE! INTRUDER IS DOWN!
COPY.
...Help me!
Aargh! My leg! What are you doing...?
Just what you said to.
I'm hurt, Roxie! I gotta get out of here! Ngh...
You got it.
ALL UNITS! ALL--
OH, HELL.

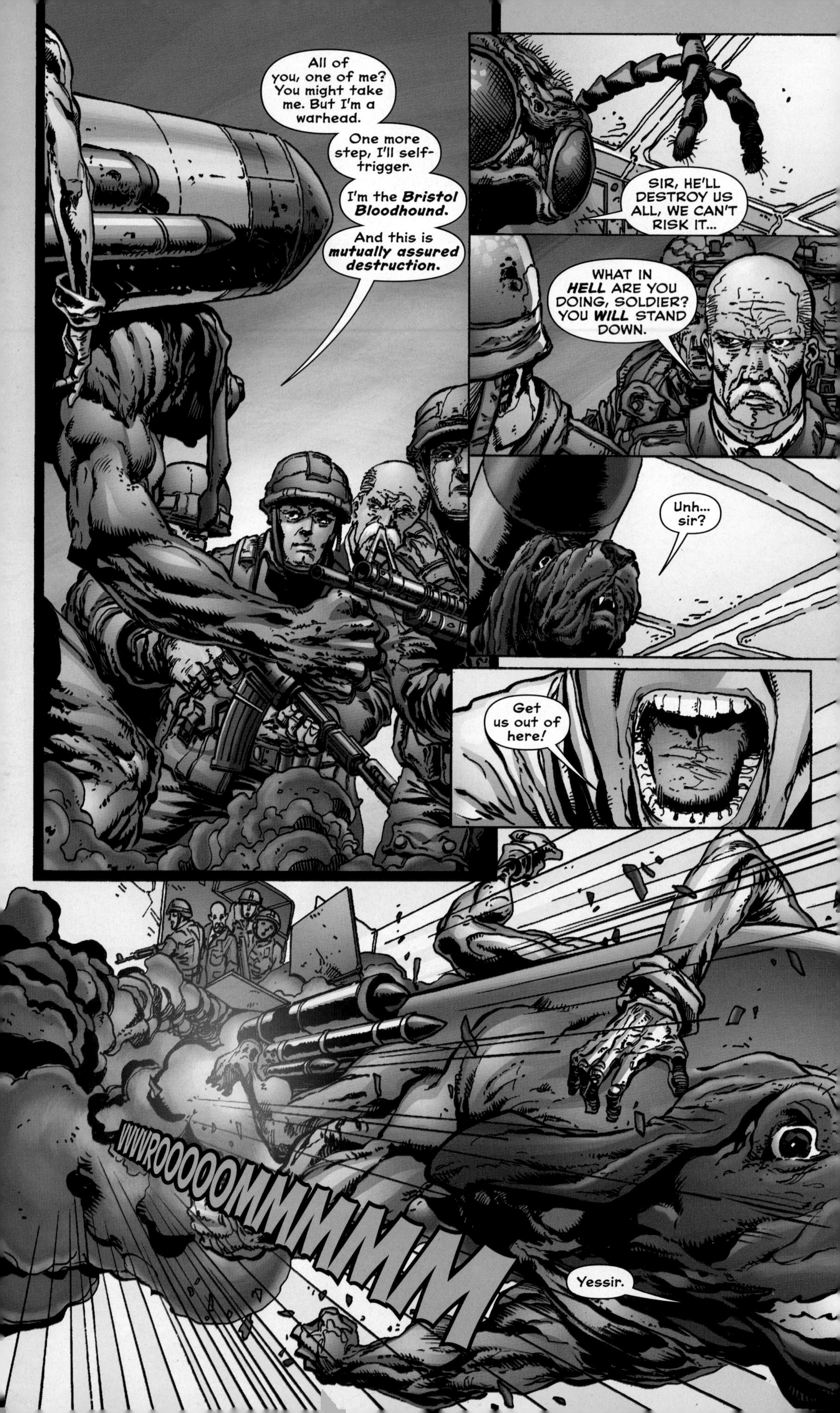
All of you, one of me? You might take me. But I'm a warhead.
One more step, I'll self-trigger.
I'm the *Bristol Bloodhound.*
And this is *mutually assured destruction.*
SIR, HE'LL DESTROY US ALL, WE CAN'T RISK IT...
WHAT IN *HELL* ARE YOU DOING, SOLDIER? YOU *WILL* STAND DOWN.
Unh... sir?
Get us out of here!
VVVVROOOOOOMMMMMMMM
Yessir.

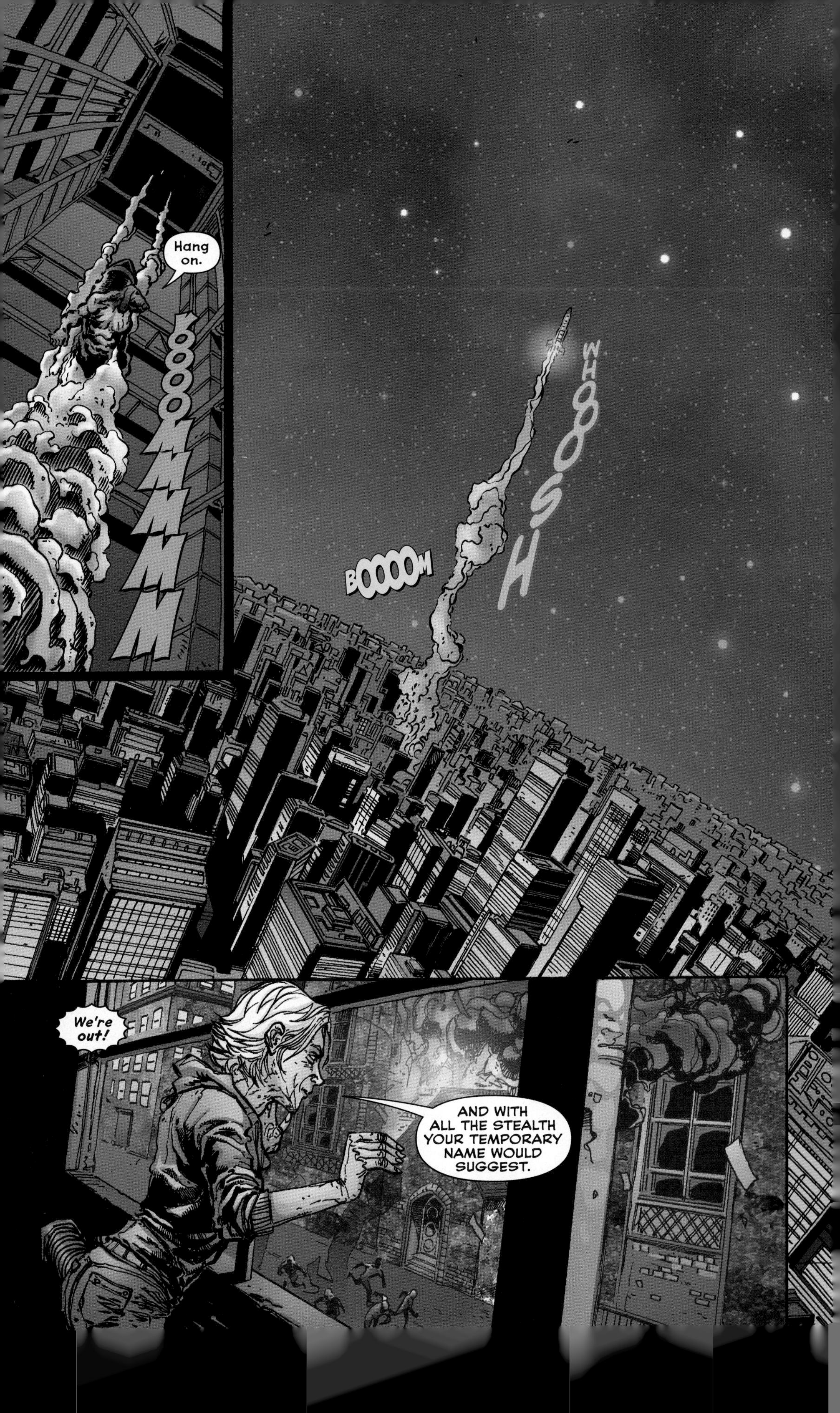

Hang on.
VOOOOMMMMMM
BOOOOM
WHOOOSH
We're out!
AND WITH ALL THE STEALTH YOUR TEMPORARY NAME WOULD SUGGEST.

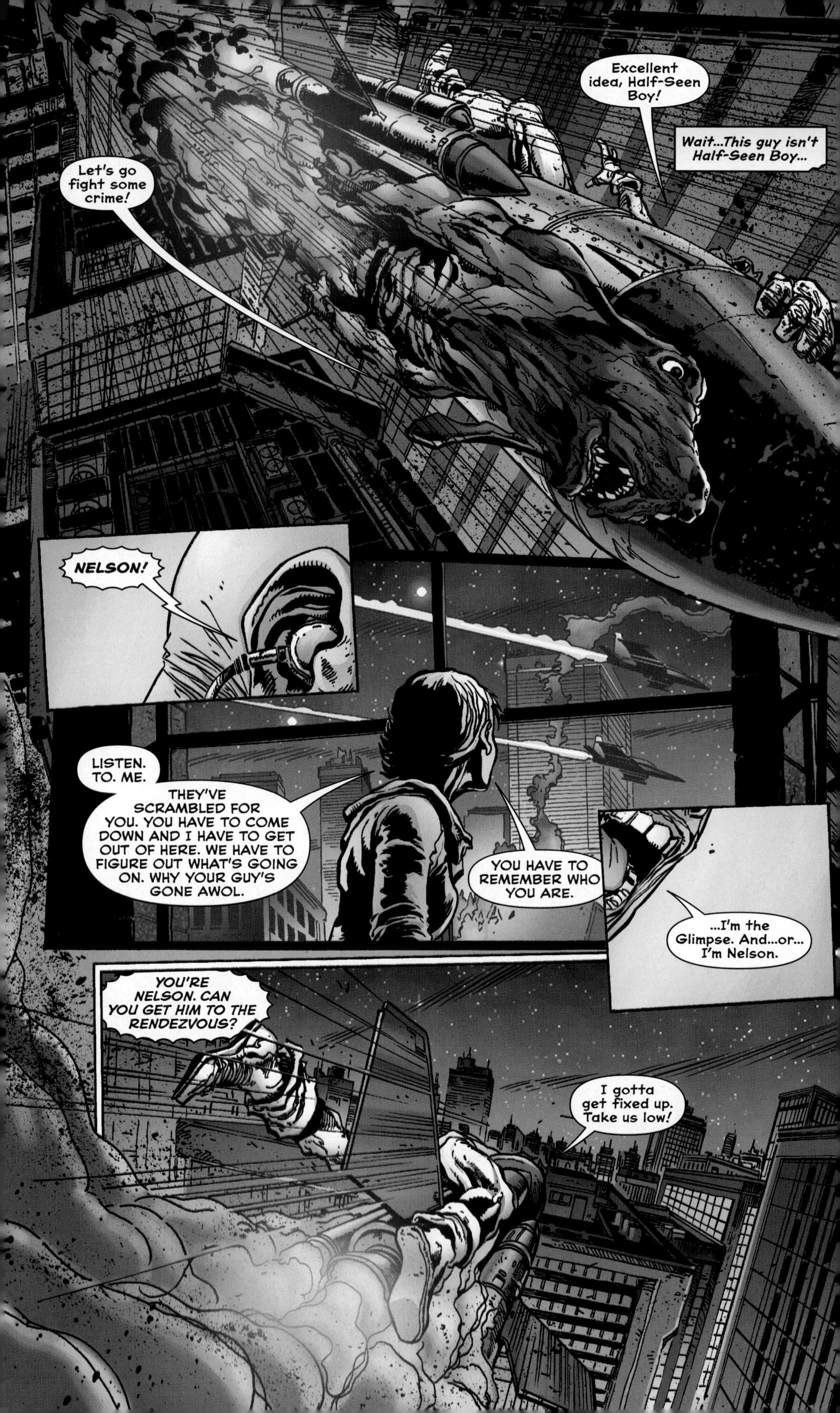
Let's go fight some crime!
Excellent idea, Half-Seen Boy!
Wait...This guy isn't Half-Seen Boy...
NELSON!
LISTEN. TO. ME.
THEY'VE SCRAMBLED FOR YOU. YOU HAVE TO COME DOWN AND I HAVE TO GET OUT OF HERE. WE HAVE TO FIGURE OUT WHAT'S GOING ON. WHY YOUR GUY'S GONE AWOL.
YOU HAVE TO REMEMBER WHO YOU ARE.
...I'm the Glimpse. And...or... I'm Nelson.
YOU'RE NELSON. CAN YOU GET HIM TO THE RENDEZVOUS?
I gotta get fixed up. Take us low!

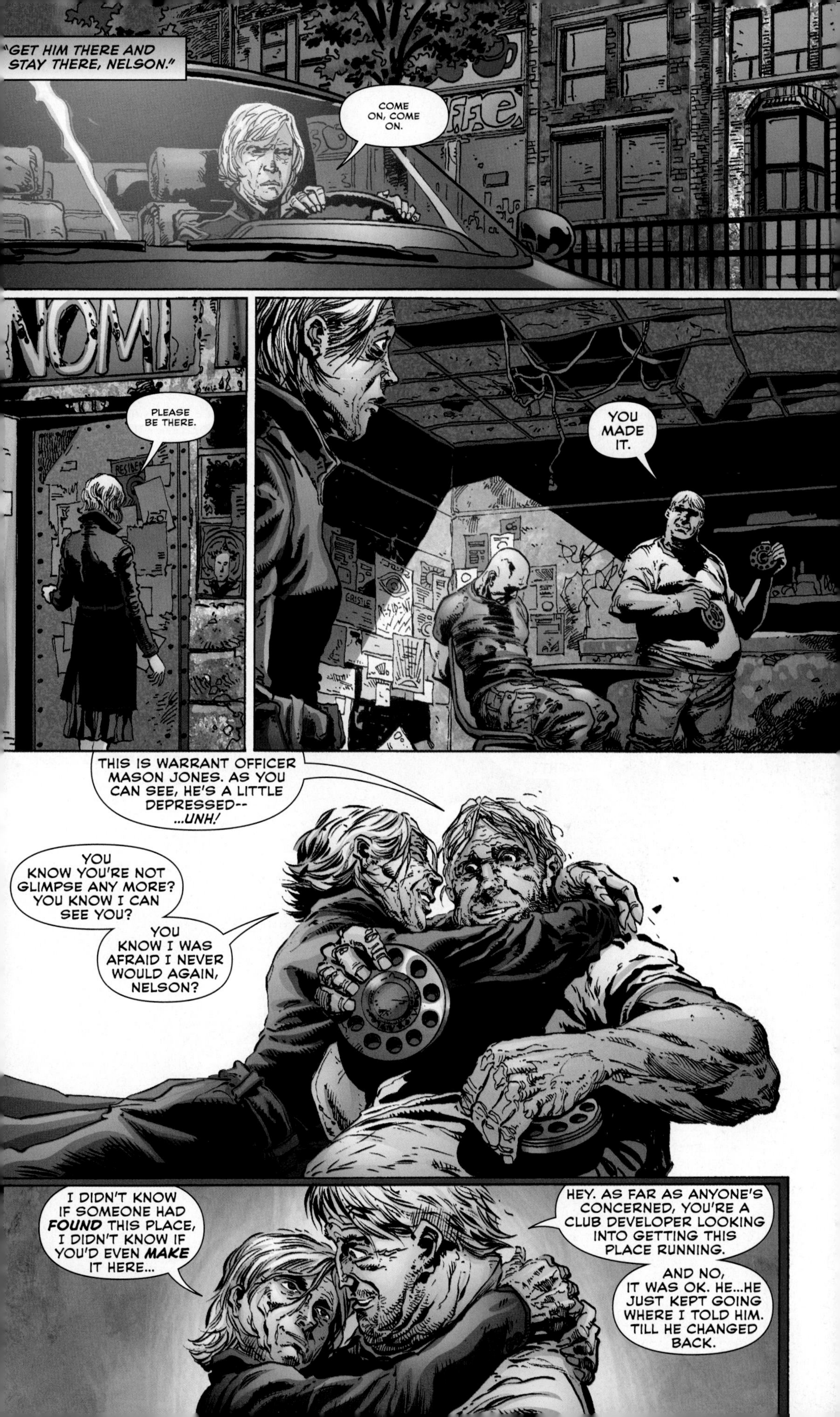
"GET HIM THERE AND STAY THERE, NELSON."
COME ON, COME ON.
PLEASE BE THERE.
YOU MADE IT.
THIS IS WARRANT OFFICER MASON JONES. AS YOU CAN SEE, HE'S A LITTLE DEPRESSED-- ...UNH!
YOU KNOW YOU'RE NOT GLIMPSE ANY MORE? YOU KNOW I CAN SEE YOU?
YOU KNOW I WAS AFRAID I NEVER WOULD AGAIN, NELSON?
I DIDN'T KNOW IF SOMEONE HAD FOUND THIS PLACE, I DIDN'T KNOW IF YOU'D EVEN MAKE IT HERE...
HEY. AS FAR AS ANYONE'S CONCERNED, YOU'RE A CLUB DEVELOPER LOOKING INTO GETTING THIS PLACE RUNNING.
AND NO, IT WAS OK. HE...HE JUST KEPT GOING WHERE I TOLD HIM. TILL HE CHANGED BACK.

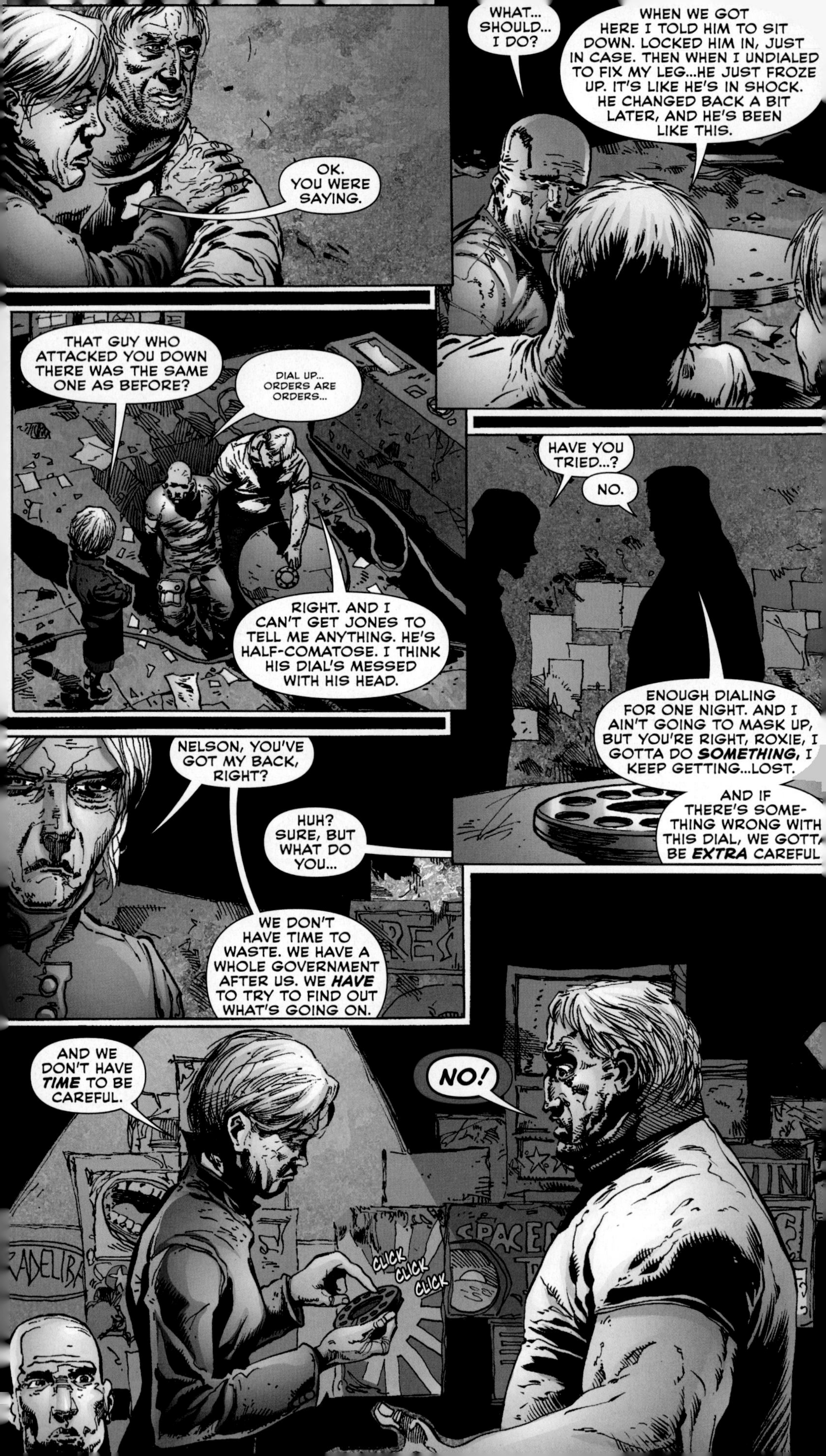
OK. YOU WERE SAYING.
WHAT... SHOULD... I DO?
WHEN WE GOT HERE I TOLD HIM TO SIT DOWN. LOCKED HIM IN, JUST IN CASE. THEN WHEN I UNDIALED TO FIX MY LEG...HE JUST FROZE UP. IT'S LIKE HE'S IN SHOCK. HE CHANGED BACK A BIT LATER, AND HE'S BEEN LIKE THIS.
THAT GUY WHO ATTACKED YOU DOWN THERE WAS THE SAME ONE AS BEFORE?
DIAL UP... ORDERS ARE ORDERS...
RIGHT. AND I CAN'T GET JONES TO TELL ME ANYTHING. HE'S HALF-COMATOSE. I THINK HIS DIAL'S MESSED WITH HIS HEAD.
HAVE YOU TRIED...?
NO.
ENOUGH DIALING FOR ONE NIGHT. AND I AIN'T GOING TO MASK UP, BUT YOU'RE RIGHT, ROXIE, I GOTTA DO *SOMETHING*, I KEEP GETTING...LOST.
AND IF THERE'S SOME-THING WRONG WITH THIS DIAL, WE GOTTA BE *EXTRA* CAREFUL
NELSON, YOU'VE GOT MY BACK, RIGHT?
HUH? SURE, BUT WHAT DO YOU...
WE DON'T HAVE TIME TO WASTE. WE HAVE A WHOLE GOVERNMENT AFTER US. WE *HAVE* TO TRY TO FIND OUT WHAT'S GOING ON.
AND WE DON'T HAVE *TIME* TO BE CAREFUL.
NO!
CLICK CLICK CLICK

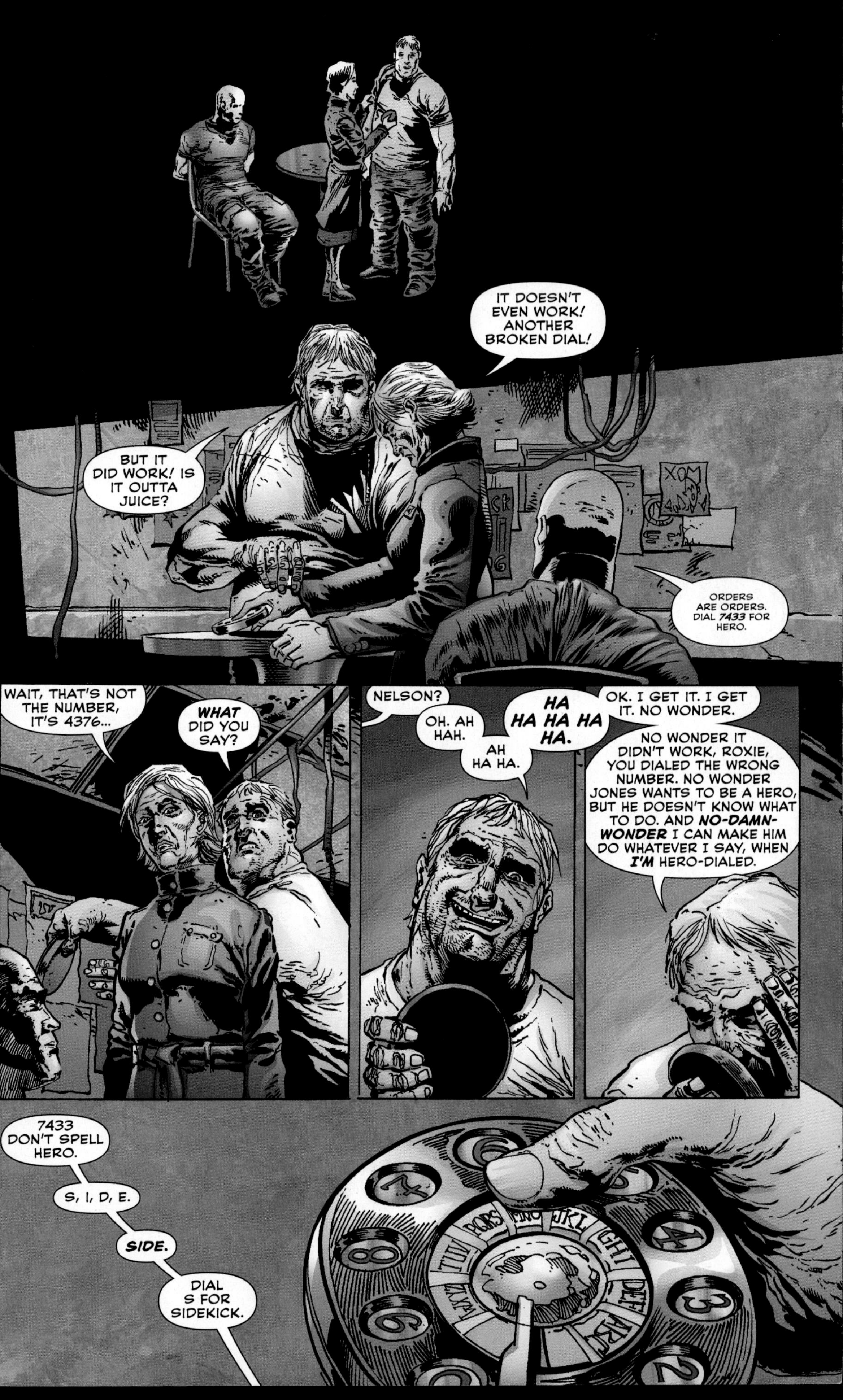
IT DOESN'T EVEN WORK! ANOTHER BROKEN DIAL!
BUT IT DID WORK! IS IT OUTTA JUICE?
ORDERS ARE ORDERS. DIAL 7433 FOR HERO.
WAIT, THAT'S NOT THE NUMBER, IT'S 4376...
WHAT DID YOU SAY?
NELSON?
OH. AH HAH.
AH HA HA.
HA HA HA HA HA.
OK. I GET IT. I GET IT. NO WONDER.
NO WONDER IT DIDN'T WORK, ROXIE, YOU DIALED THE WRONG NUMBER. NO WONDER JONES WANTS TO BE A HERO, BUT HE DOESN'T KNOW WHAT TO DO. AND NO-DAMN-WONDER I CAN MAKE HIM DO WHATEVER I SAY, WHEN I'M HERO-DIALED.
7433 DON'T SPELL HERO.
S, I, D, E.
SIDE.
DIAL S FOR SIDEKICK.

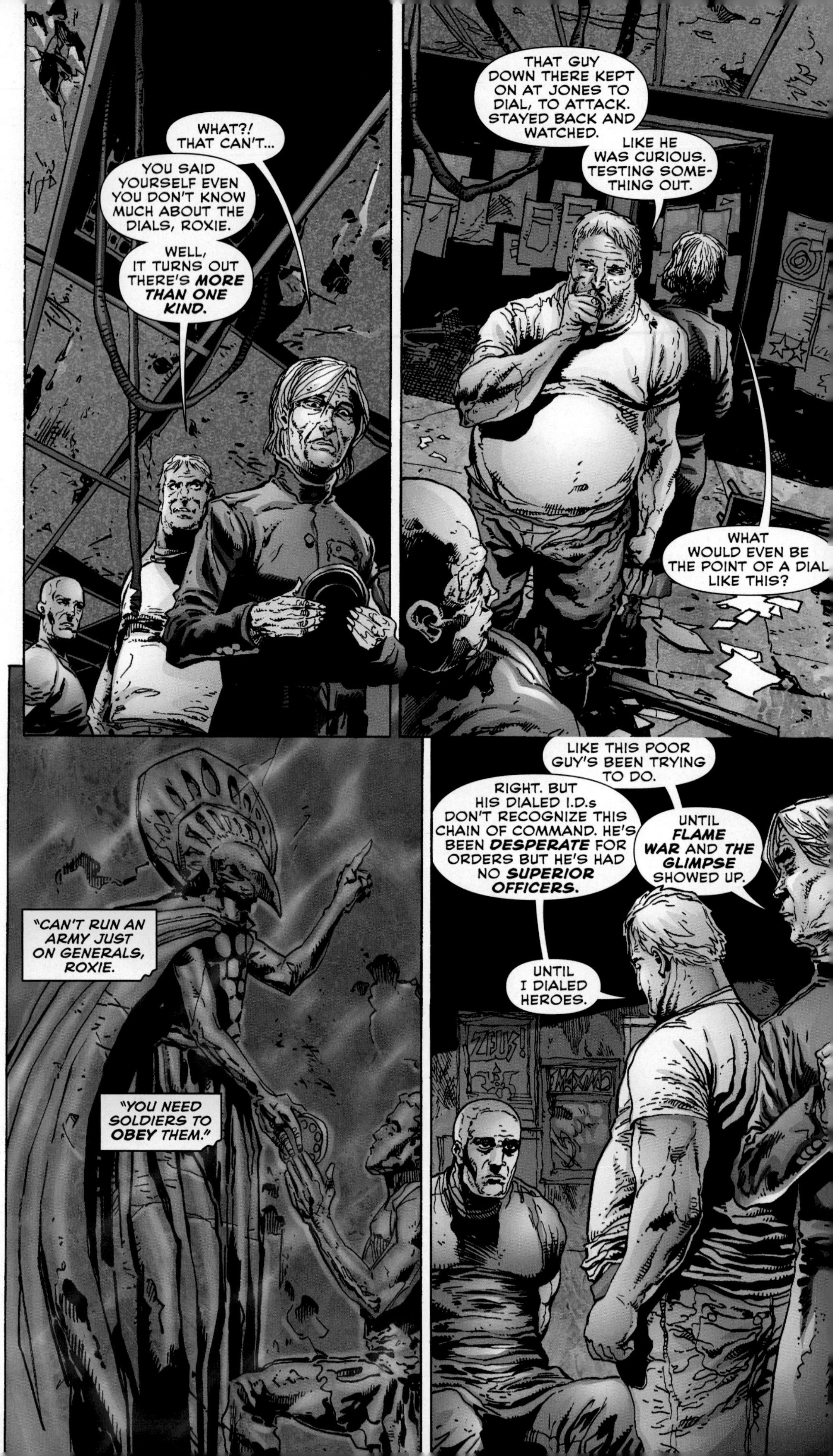
WHAT?! THAT CAN'T...
YOU SAID YOURSELF EVEN YOU DON'T KNOW MUCH ABOUT THE DIALS, ROXIE.
WELL, IT TURNS OUT THERE'S MORE THAN ONE KIND.
THAT GUY DOWN THERE KEPT ON AT JONES TO DIAL, TO ATTACK. STAYED BACK AND WATCHED.
LIKE HE WAS CURIOUS. TESTING SOMETHING OUT.
WHAT WOULD EVEN BE THE POINT OF A DIAL LIKE THIS?
"CAN'T RUN AN ARMY JUST ON GENERALS, ROXIE.
"YOU NEED SOLDIERS TO OBEY THEM."
LIKE THIS POOR GUY'S BEEN TRYING TO DO.
RIGHT. BUT HIS DIALED I.D.s DON'T RECOGNIZE THIS CHAIN OF COMMAND. HE'S BEEN DESPERATE FOR ORDERS BUT HE'S HAD NO SUPERIOR OFFICERS.
UNTIL FLAME WAR AND THE GLIMPSE SHOWED UP.
UNTIL I DIALED HEROES.

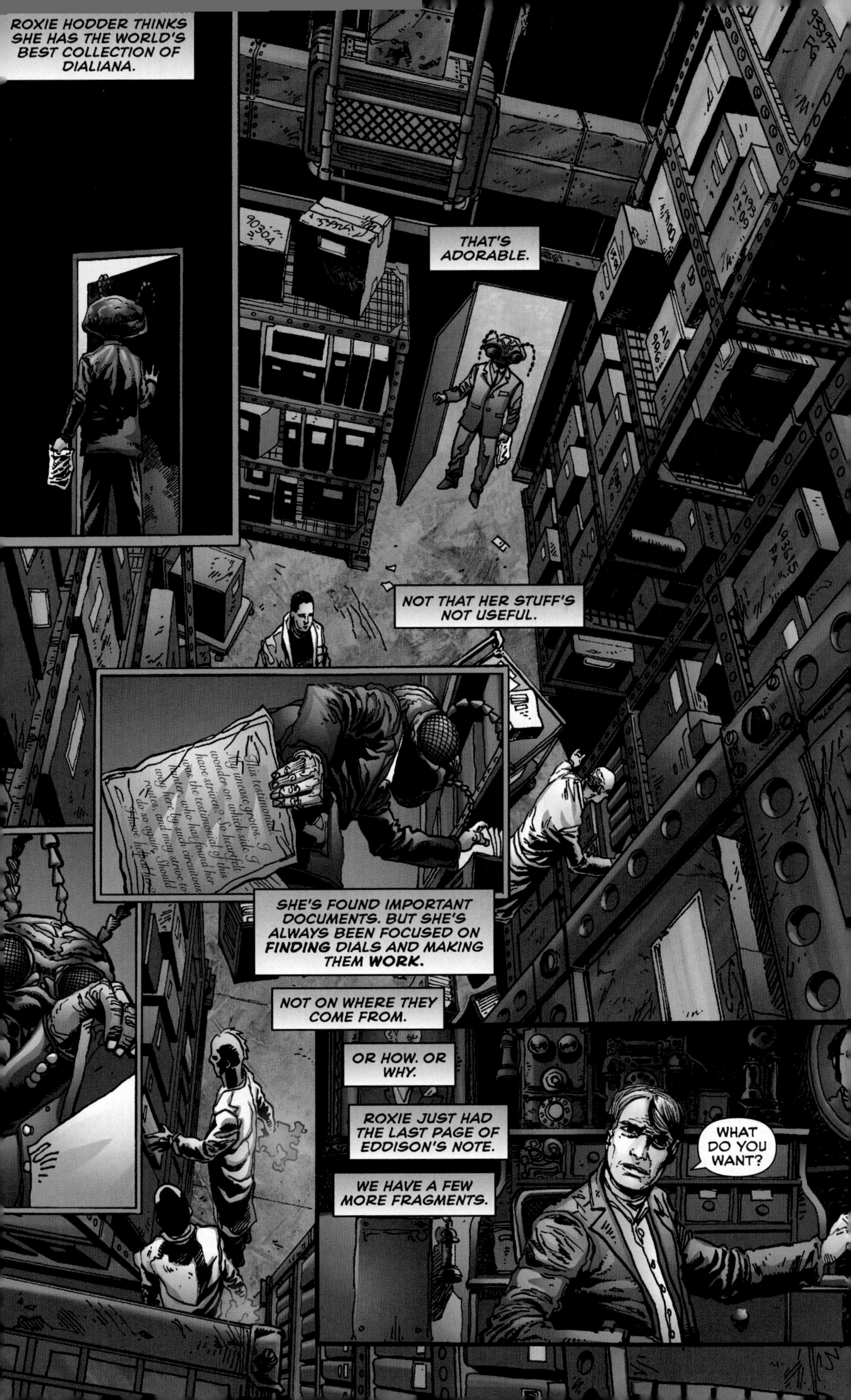
ROXIE HODDER THINKS SHE HAS THE WORLD'S BEST COLLECTION OF DIALIANA.
THAT'S ADORABLE.
NOT THAT HER STUFF'S NOT USEFUL.
SHE'S FOUND IMPORTANT DOCUMENTS. BUT SHE'S ALWAYS BEEN FOCUSED ON FINDING DIALS AND MAKING THEM WORK.
NOT ON WHERE THEY COME FROM.
OR HOW. OR WHY.
ROXIE JUST HAD THE LAST PAGE OF EDDISON'S NOTE.
WE HAVE A FEW MORE FRAGMENTS.
WHAT DO YOU WANT?

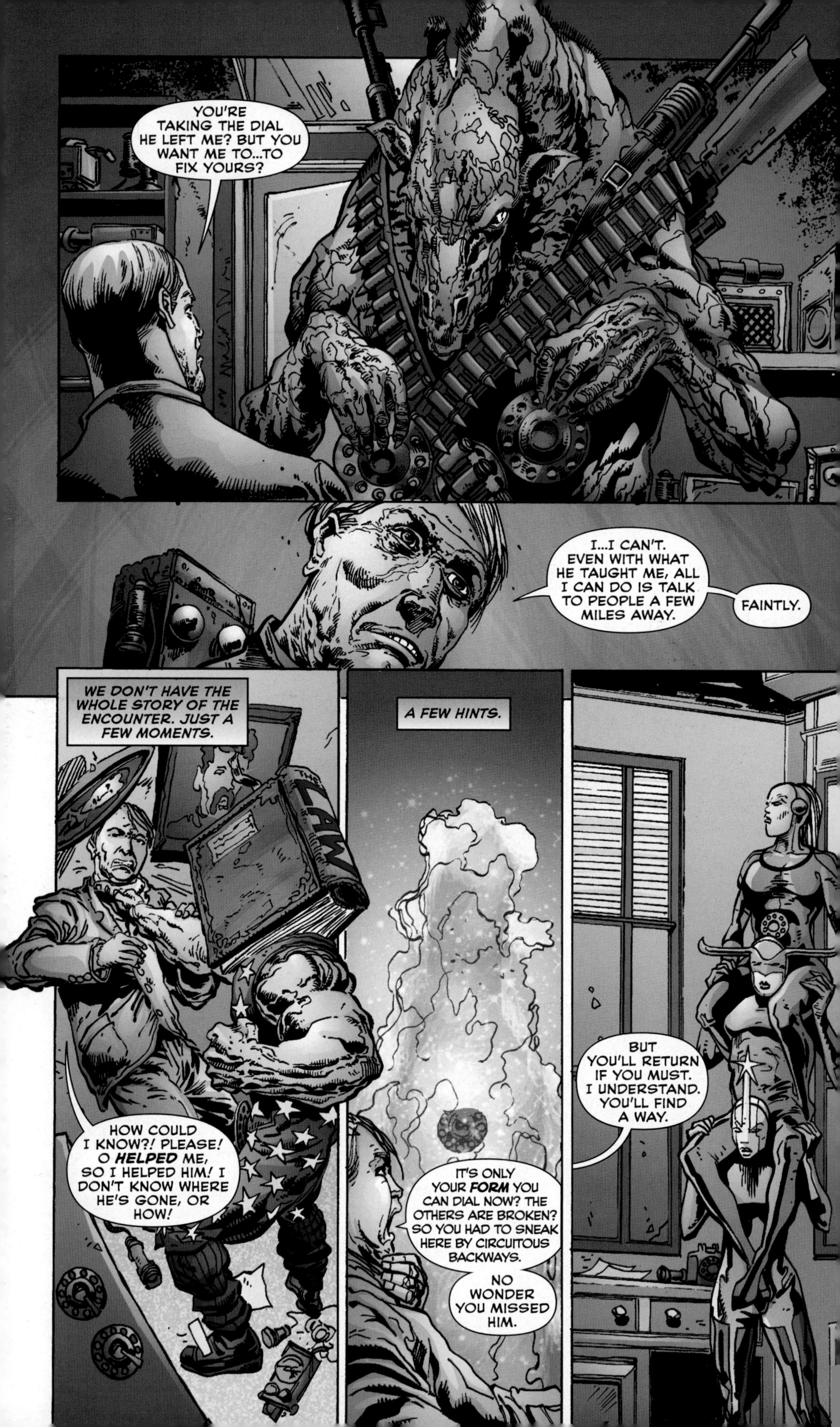
YOU'RE TAKING THE DIAL HE LEFT ME? BUT YOU WANT ME TO...TO FIX YOURS?
I...I CAN'T. EVEN WITH WHAT HE TAUGHT ME, ALL I CAN DO IS TALK TO PEOPLE A FEW MILES AWAY.
FAINTLY.
WE DON'T HAVE THE WHOLE STORY OF THE ENCOUNTER. JUST A FEW MOMENTS.
THE LAW
HOW COULD I KNOW?! PLEASE! O *HELPED* ME, SO I HELPED HIM! I DON'T KNOW WHERE HE'S GONE, OR HOW!
A FEW HINTS.
IT'S ONLY YOUR *FORM* YOU CAN DIAL NOW? THE OTHERS ARE BROKEN? SO YOU HAD TO SNEAK HERE BY CIRCUITOUS BACKWAYS.
NO WONDER YOU MISSED HIM.
BUT YOU'LL RETURN IF YOU MUST. I UNDERSTAND. YOU'LL FIND A WAY.

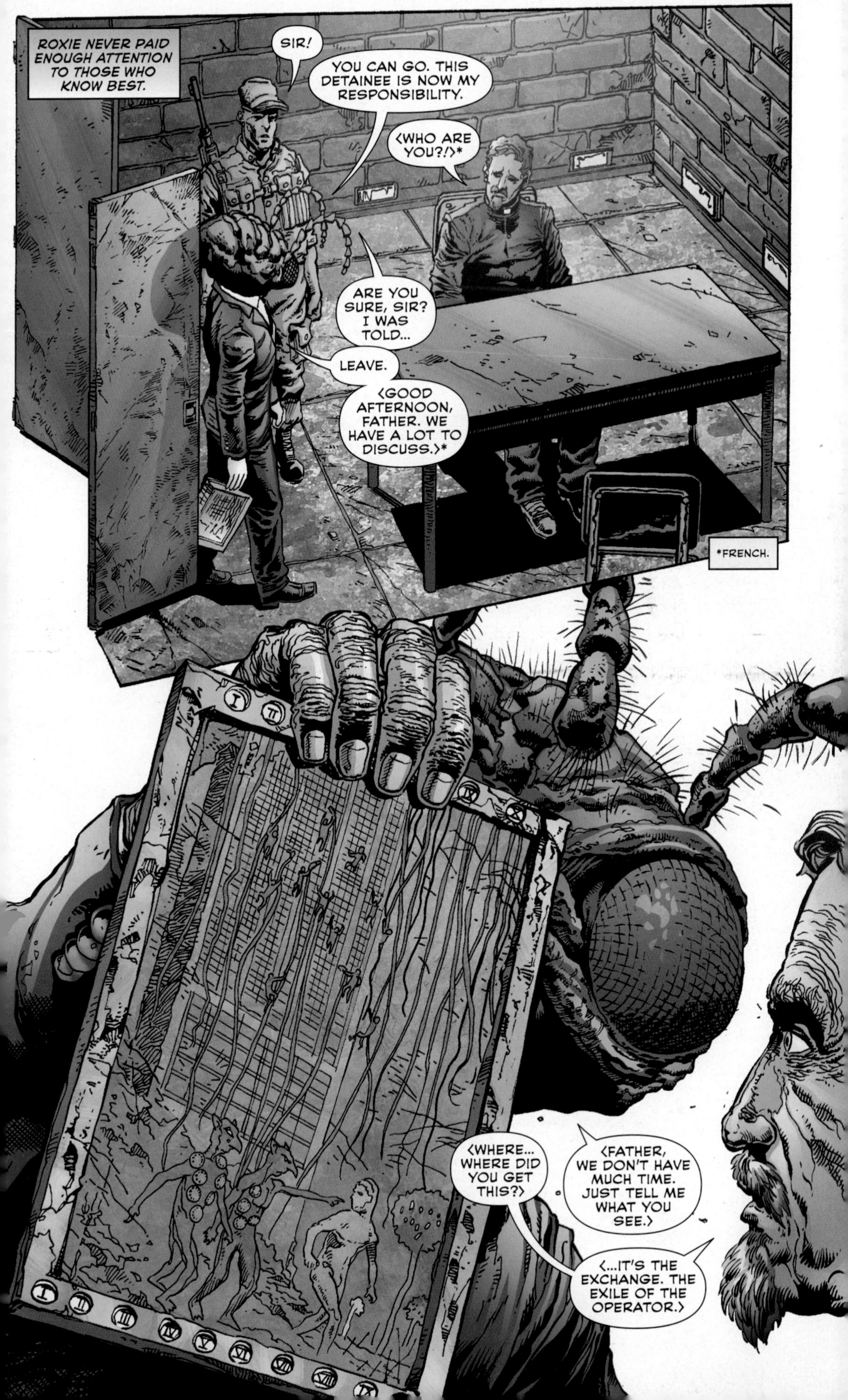
ROXIE NEVER PAID ENOUGH ATTENTION TO THOSE WHO KNOW BEST.
SIR!
YOU CAN GO. THIS DETAINEE IS NOW MY RESPONSIBILITY.
<WHO ARE YOU?!>*
ARE YOU SURE, SIR? I WAS TOLD...
LEAVE.
<GOOD AFTERNOON, FATHER. WE HAVE A LOT TO DISCUSS.>*
*FRENCH.
<FATHER, WE DON'T HAVE MUCH TIME. JUST TELL ME WHAT YOU SEE.>
<WHERE... WHERE DID YOU GET THIS?>
<...IT'S THE EXCHANGE. THE EXILE OF THE OPERATOR.>

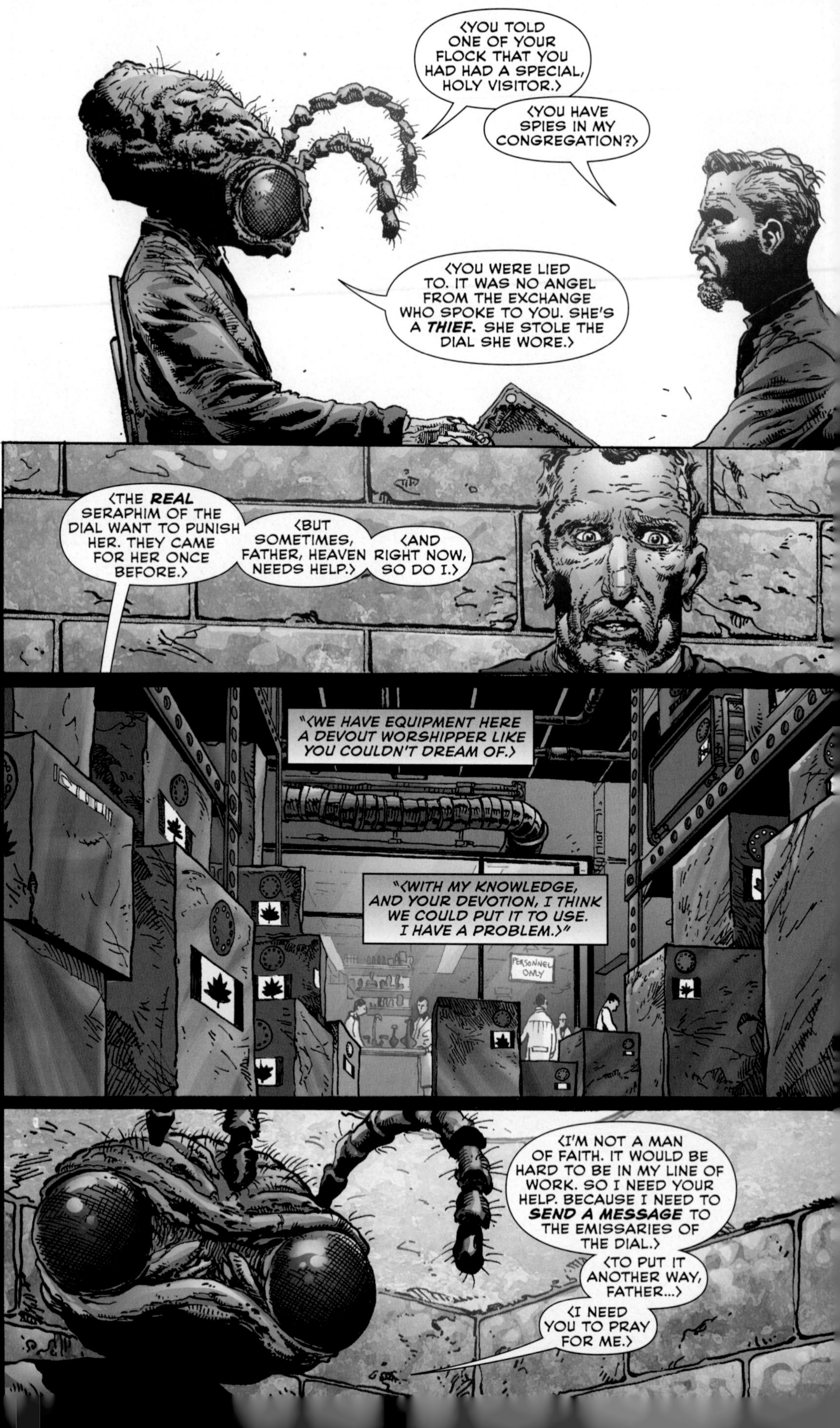

‹YOU TOLD ONE OF YOUR FLOCK THAT YOU HAD HAD A SPECIAL, HOLY VISITOR.›
‹YOU HAVE SPIES IN MY CONGREGATION?›
‹YOU WERE LIED TO. IT WAS NO ANGEL FROM THE EXCHANGE WHO SPOKE TO YOU. SHE'S A *THIEF.* SHE STOLE THE DIAL SHE WORE.›
‹THE *REAL* SERAPHIM OF THE DIAL WANT TO PUNISH HER. THEY CAME FOR HER ONCE BEFORE.›
‹BUT SOMETIMES, FATHER, HEAVEN NEEDS HELP.›
‹AND RIGHT NOW, SO DO I.›
"‹WE HAVE EQUIPMENT HERE A DEVOUT WORSHIPPER LIKE YOU COULDN'T DREAM OF.›
"‹WITH MY KNOWLEDGE, AND YOUR DEVOTION, I THINK WE COULD PUT IT TO USE. I HAVE A PROBLEM.›"
PERSONNEL ONLY
‹I'M NOT A MAN OF FAITH. IT WOULD BE HARD TO BE IN MY LINE OF WORK. SO I NEED YOUR HELP. BECAUSE I NEED TO **SEND A MESSAGE** TO THE EMISSARIES OF THE DIAL.›
‹TO PUT IT ANOTHER WAY, FATHER...›
‹I NEED YOU TO PRAY FOR ME.›

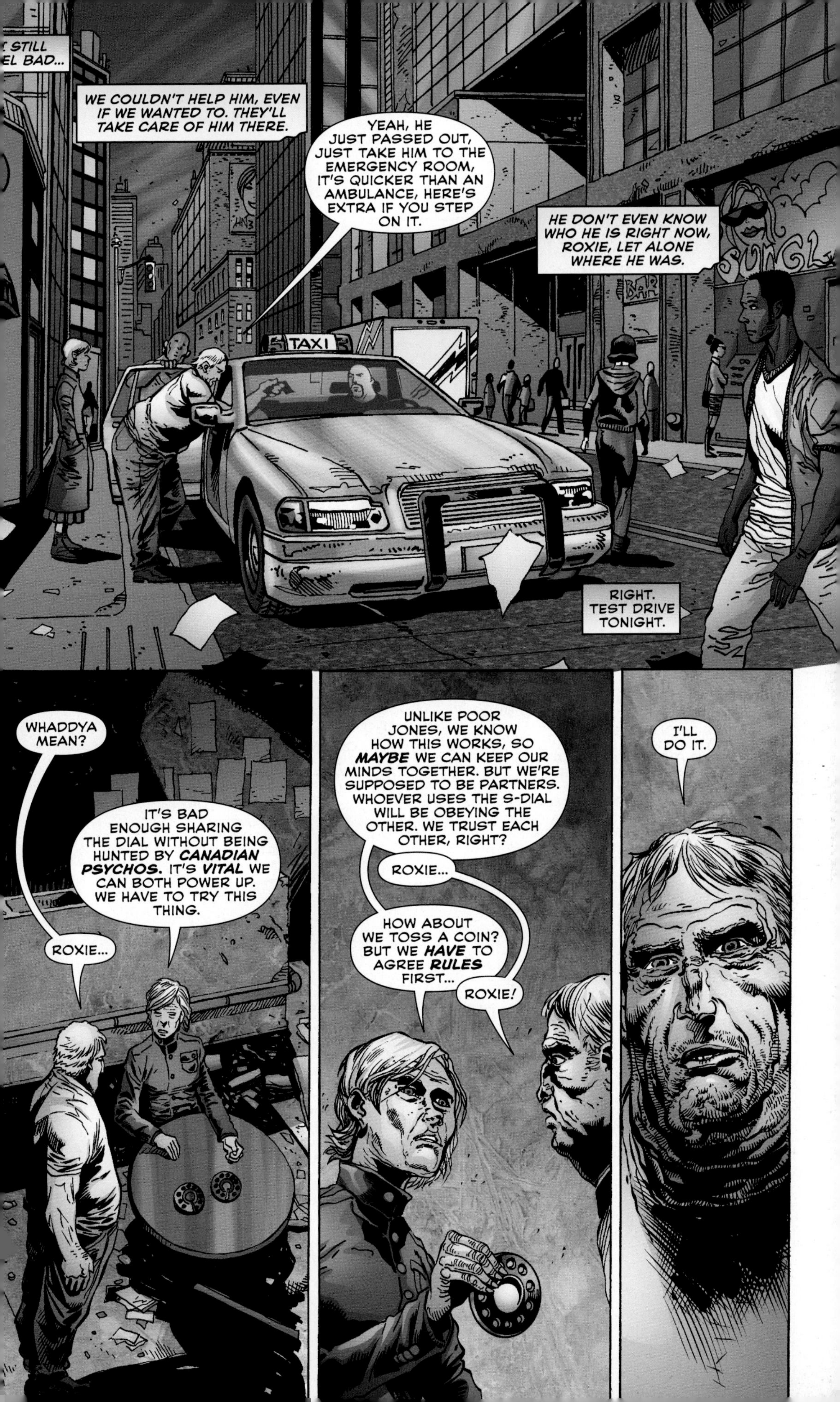

...T STILL ...EL BAD...
WE COULDN'T HELP HIM, EVEN IF WE WANTED TO. THEY'LL TAKE CARE OF HIM THERE.
YEAH, HE JUST PASSED OUT, JUST TAKE HIM TO THE EMERGENCY ROOM, IT'S QUICKER THAN AN AMBULANCE, HERE'S EXTRA IF YOU STEP ON IT.
HE DON'T EVEN KNOW WHO HE IS RIGHT NOW, ROXIE, LET ALONE WHERE HE WAS.
TAXI
RIGHT. TEST DRIVE TONIGHT.
WHADDYA MEAN?
IT'S BAD ENOUGH SHARING THE DIAL WITHOUT BEING HUNTED BY **CANADIAN PSYCHOS.** IT'S **VITAL** WE CAN BOTH POWER UP. WE HAVE TO TRY THIS THING.
ROXIE...
UNLIKE POOR JONES, WE KNOW HOW THIS WORKS, SO **MAYBE** WE CAN KEEP OUR MINDS TOGETHER. BUT WE'RE SUPPOSED TO BE PARTNERS. WHOEVER USES THE S-DIAL WILL BE OBEYING THE OTHER. WE TRUST EACH OTHER, RIGHT?
ROXIE...
HOW ABOUT WE TOSS A COIN? BUT WE **HAVE** TO AGREE **RULES** FIRST...
ROXIE!
I'LL DO IT.

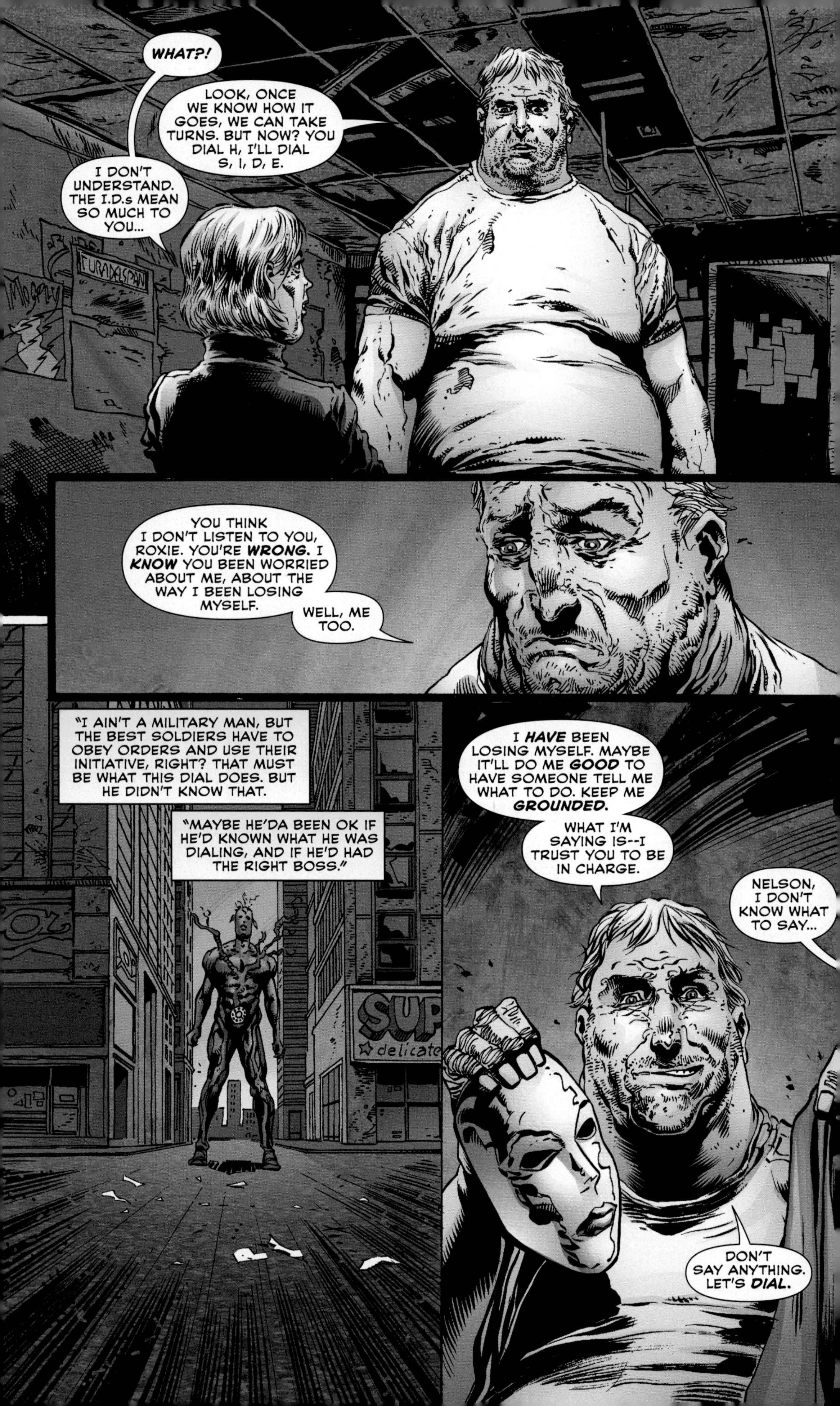

WHAT?!
LOOK, ONCE WE KNOW HOW IT GOES, WE CAN TAKE TURNS. BUT NOW? YOU DIAL H, I'LL DIAL S, I, D, E.
I DON'T UNDERSTAND. THE I.D.s MEAN SO MUCH TO YOU...
YOU THINK I DON'T LISTEN TO YOU, ROXIE. YOU'RE WRONG. I KNOW YOU BEEN WORRIED ABOUT ME, ABOUT THE WAY I BEEN LOSING MYSELF.
WELL, ME TOO.
"I AIN'T A MILITARY MAN, BUT THE BEST SOLDIERS HAVE TO OBEY ORDERS AND USE THEIR INITIATIVE, RIGHT? THAT MUST BE WHAT THIS DIAL DOES. BUT HE DIDN'T KNOW THAT.
"MAYBE HE'DA BEEN OK IF HE'D KNOWN WHAT HE WAS DIALING, AND IF HE'D HAD THE RIGHT BOSS."
SUP
delicate
I HAVE BEEN LOSING MYSELF. MAYBE IT'LL DO ME GOOD TO HAVE SOMEONE TELL ME WHAT TO DO. KEEP ME GROUNDED.
WHAT I'M SAYING IS--I TRUST YOU TO BE IN CHARGE.
NELSON, I DON'T KNOW WHAT TO SAY...
DON'T SAY ANYTHING. LET'S DIAL.

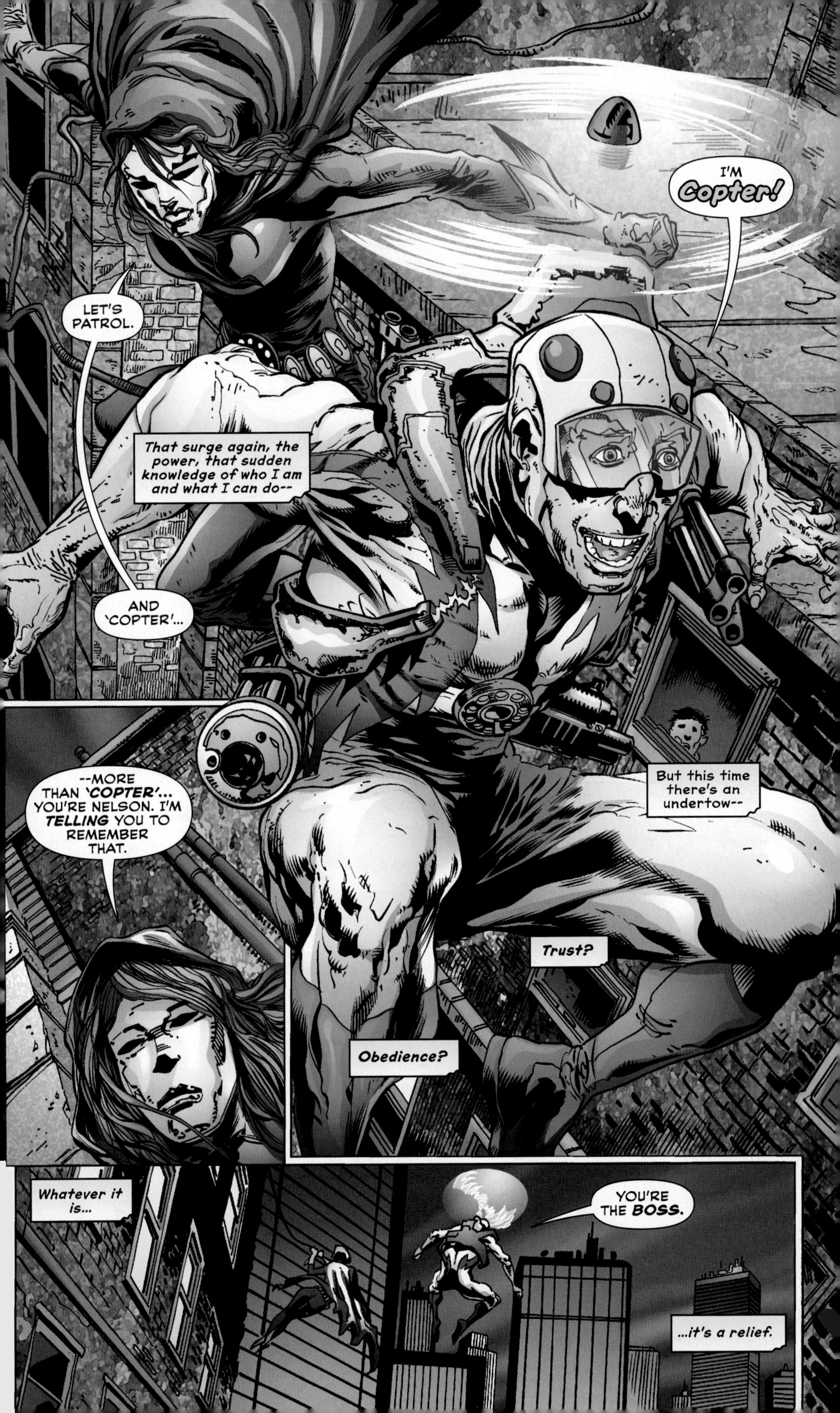
I'M Copter!
LET'S PATROL.
That surge again, the power, that sudden knowledge of who I am and what I can do--
AND 'COPTER'...
--MORE THAN 'COPTER'... YOU'RE NELSON. I'M TELLING YOU TO REMEMBER THAT.
But this time there's an undertow--
Trust?
Obedience?
Whatever it is...
YOU'RE THE BOSS.
...it's a relief.

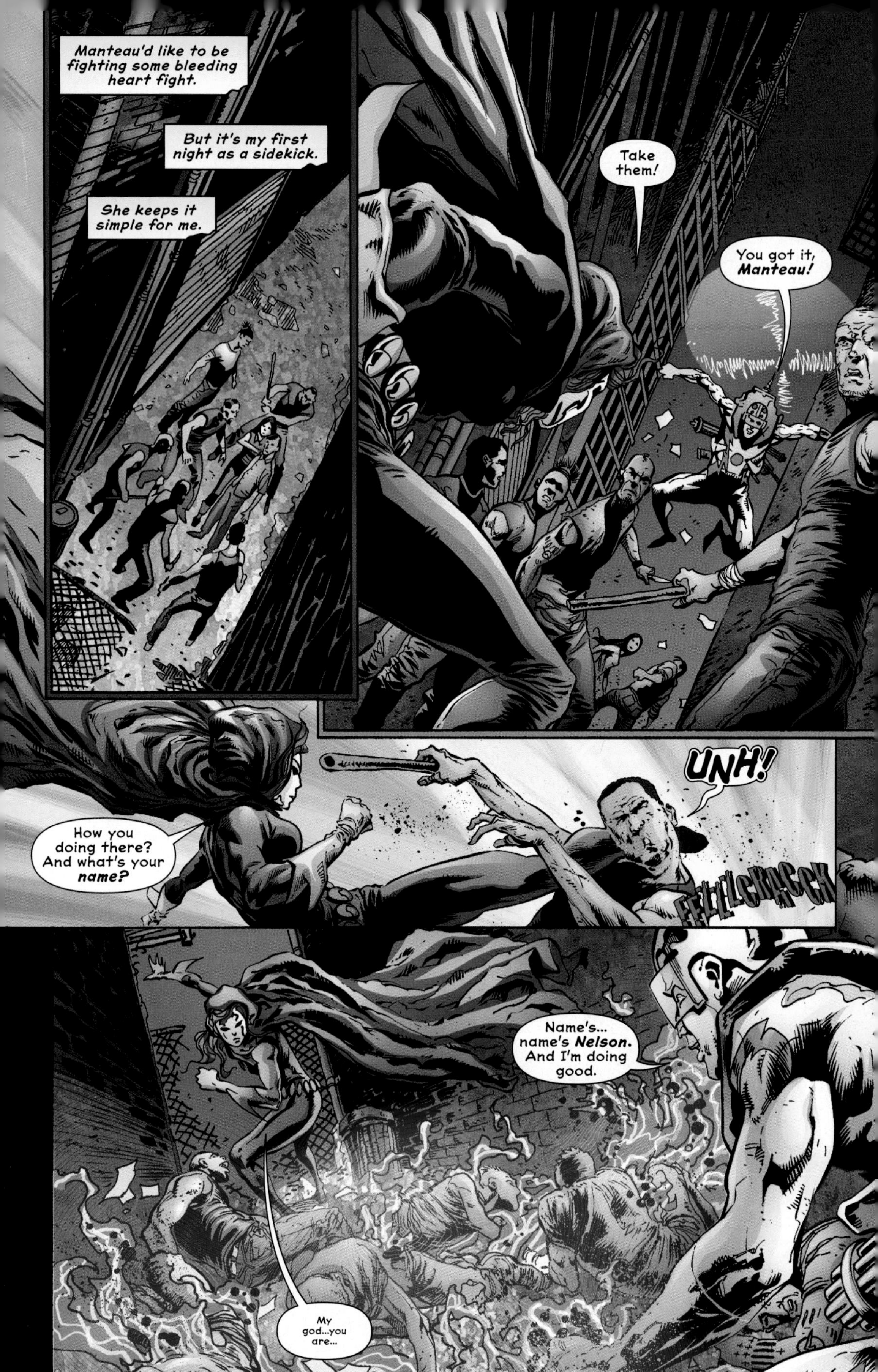

Manteau'd like to be fighting some bleeding heart fight.
But it's my first night as a sidekick.
She keeps it simple for me.
Take them!
You got it, **Manteau!**
How you doing there? And what's your **name?**
UNH!
FFLLLCRACCH
Name's... name's **Nelson.** And I'm doing good.
My god...you are...

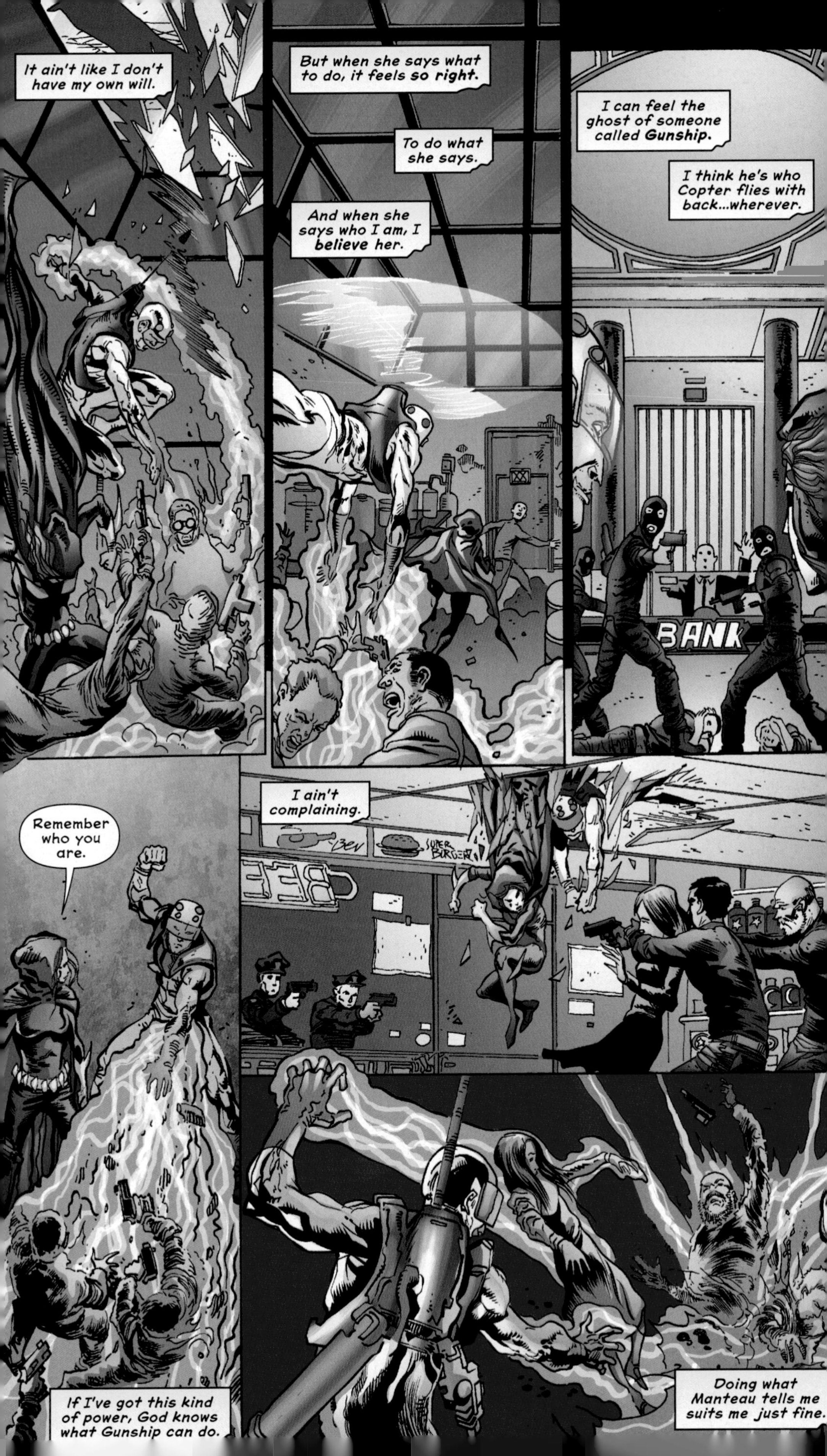
It ain't like I don't have my own will.
But when she says what to do, it feels so right.
To do what she says.
And when she says who I am, I believe her.
I can feel the ghost of someone called Gunship.
I think he's who Copter flies with back...wherever.
BANK
Remember who you are.
If I've got this kind of power, God knows what Gunship can do.
I ain't complaining.
SUPER BURGER
Doing what Manteau tells me suits me just fine.

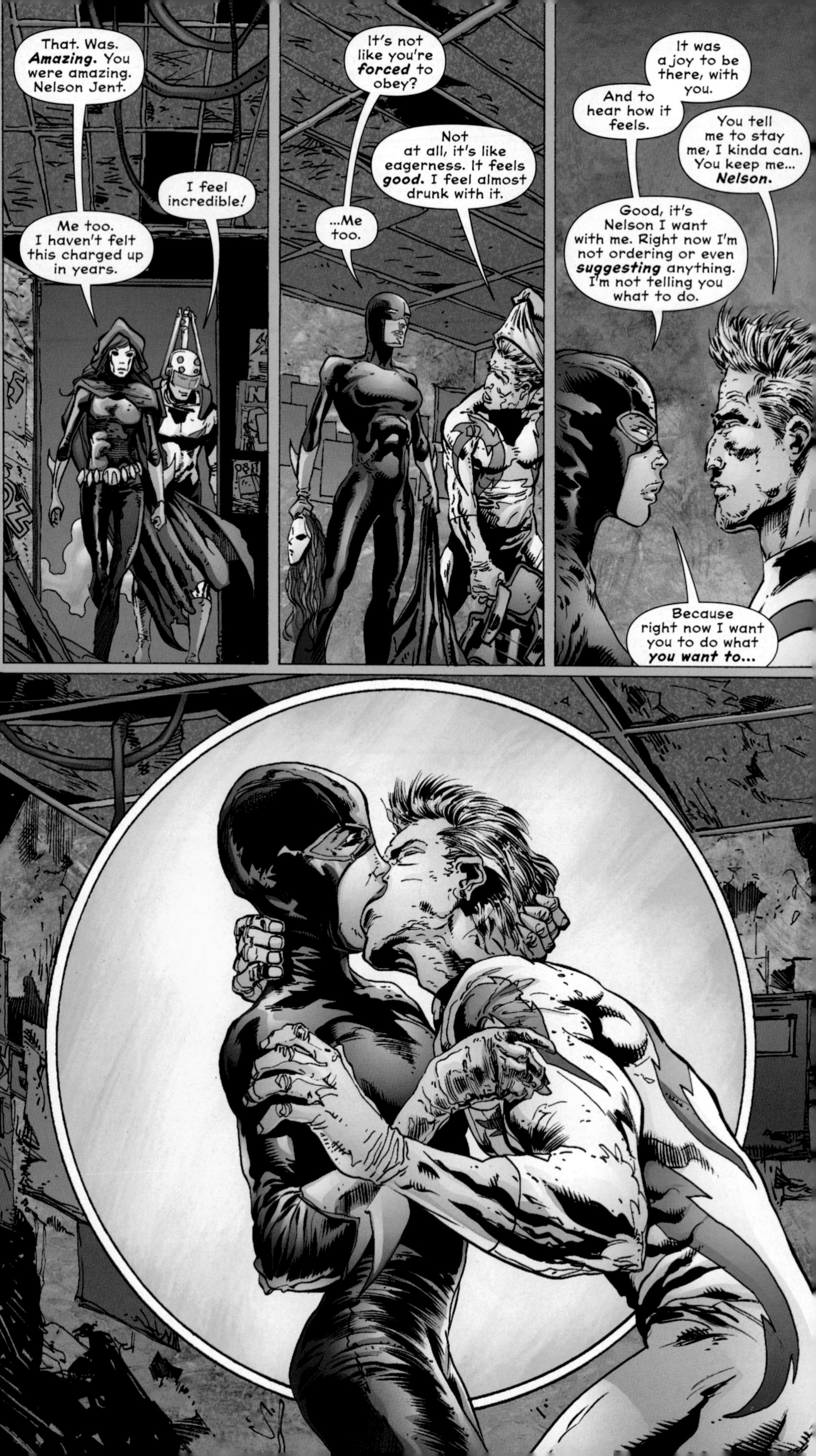
That. Was. ***Amazing.*** You were amazing. Nelson Jent.
Me too. I haven't felt this charged up in years.
I feel incredible!
It's not like you're ***forced*** to obey?
...Me too.
Not at all, it's like eagerness. It feels ***good.*** I feel almost drunk with it.
It was a joy to be there, with you.
And to hear how it feels.
You tell me to stay me, I kinda can. You keep me... ***Nelson.***
Good, it's Nelson I want with me. Right now I'm not ordering or even ***suggesting*** anything. I'm not telling you what to do.
Because right now I want you to do what ***you want to...***

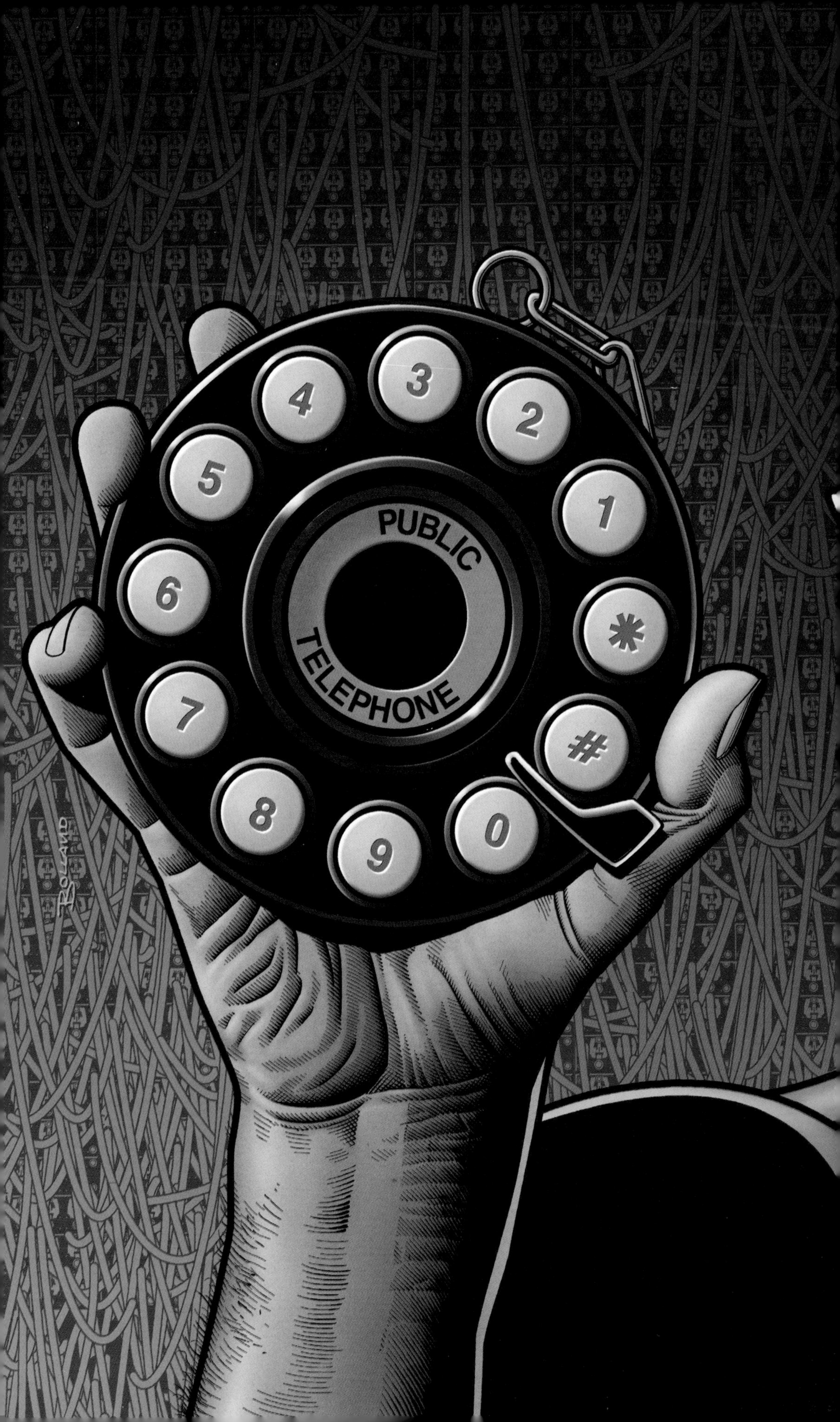

PUBLIC
TELEPHONE
BOLLAND

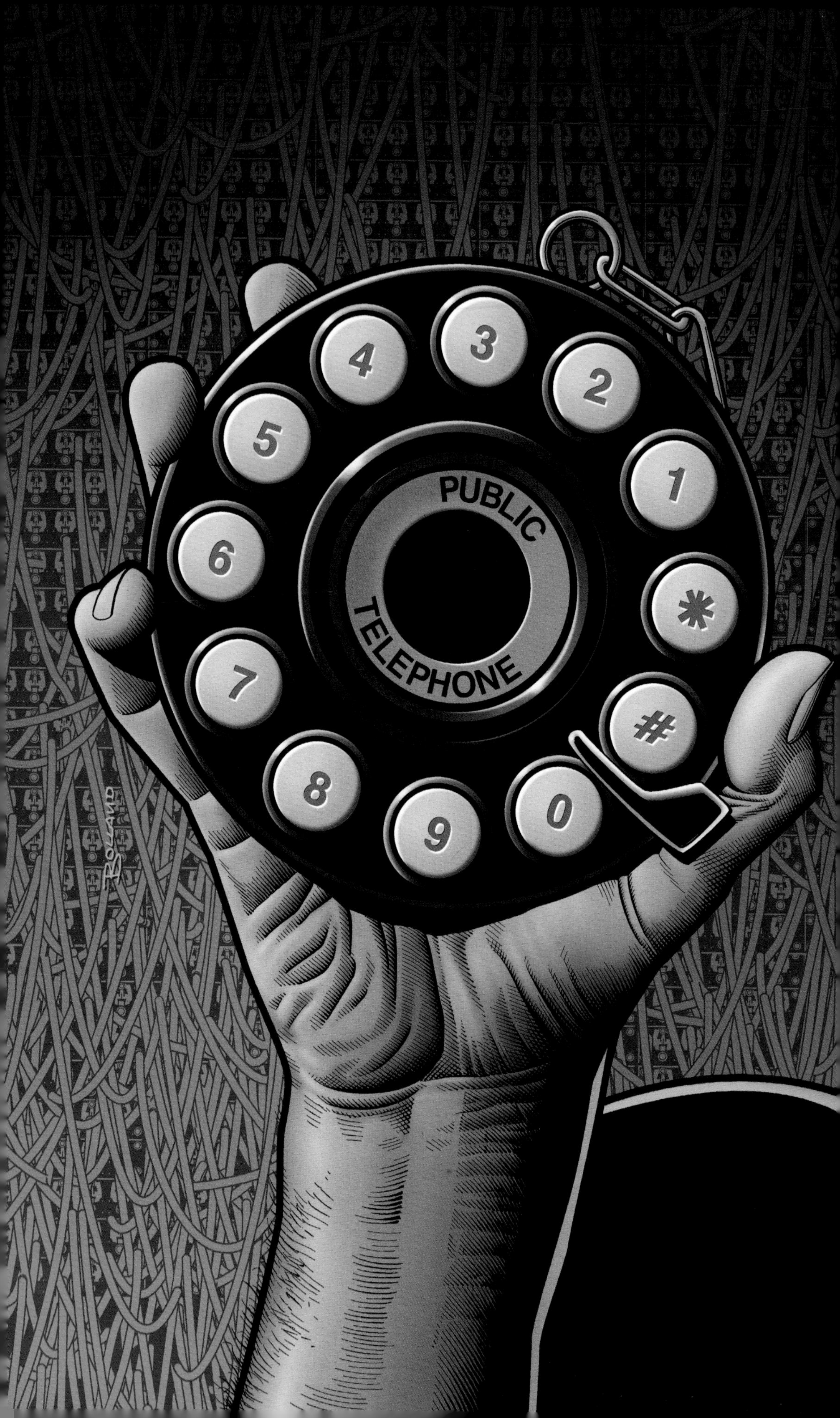
PUBLIC
TELEPHONE
BOLLAND

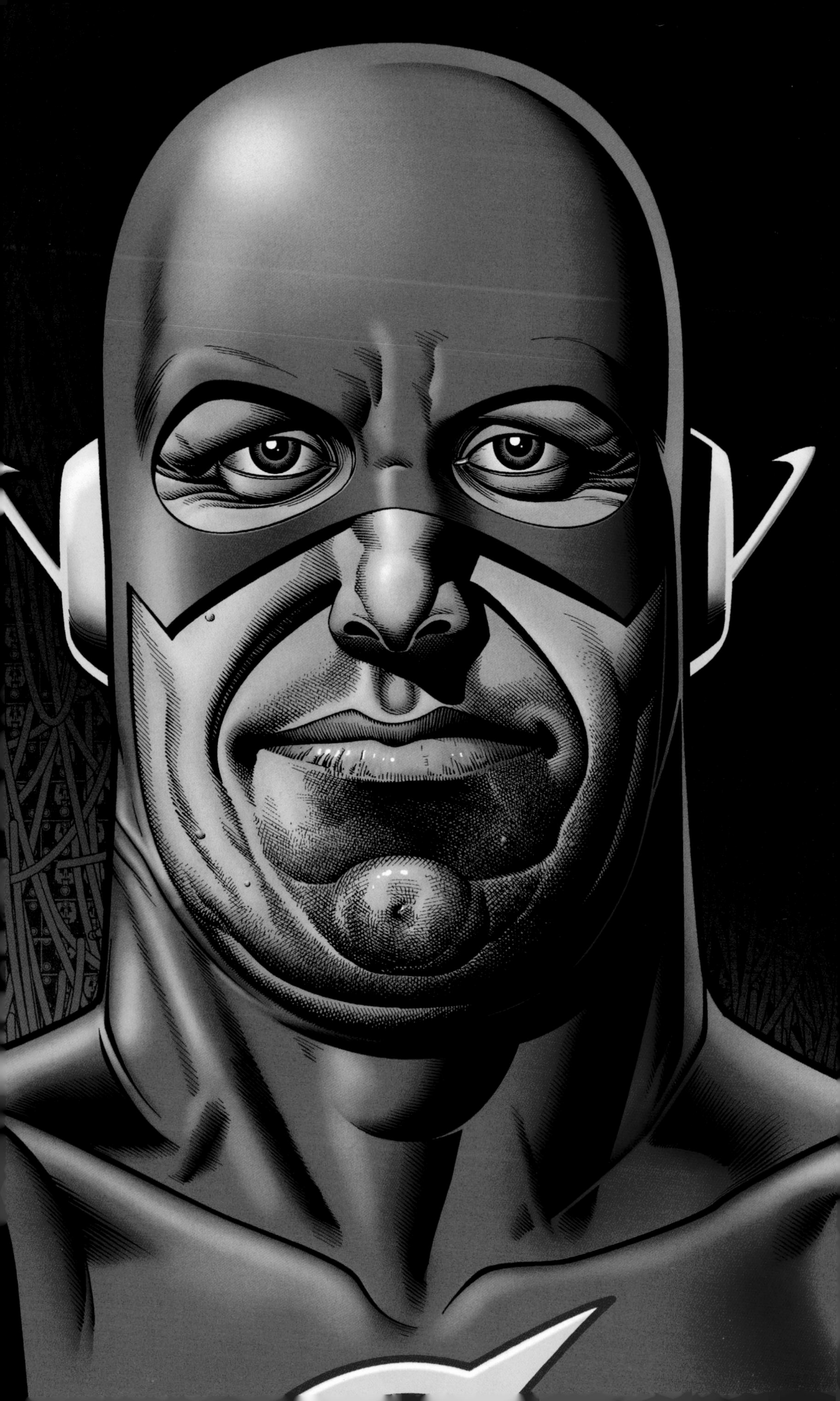

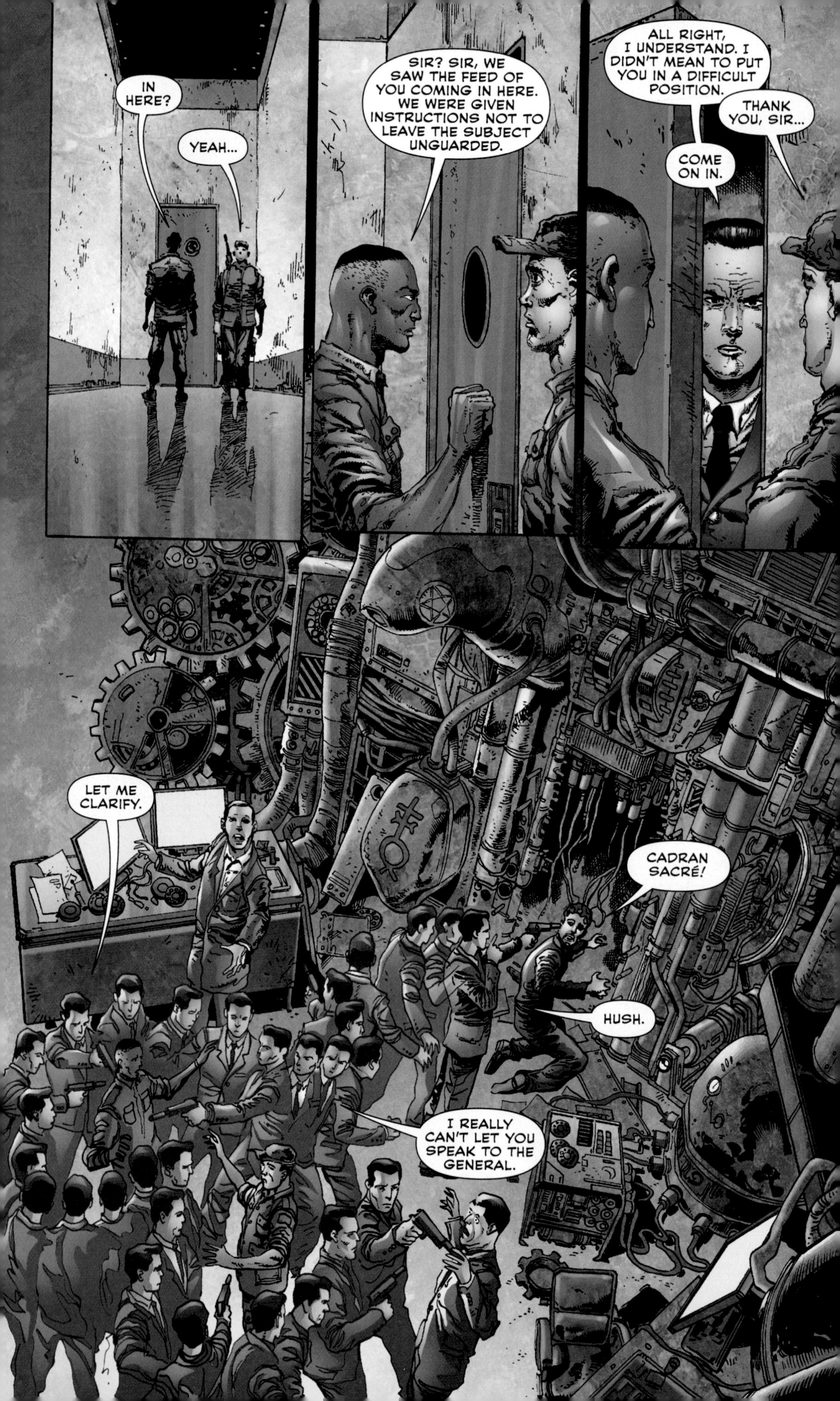

IN HERE?
YEAH...
SIR? SIR, WE SAW THE FEED OF YOU COMING IN HERE. WE WERE GIVEN INSTRUCTIONS NOT TO LEAVE THE SUBJECT UNGUARDED.
ALL RIGHT, I UNDERSTAND. I DIDN'T MEAN TO PUT YOU IN A DIFFICULT POSITION.
THANK YOU, SIR...
COME ON IN.
LET ME CLARIFY.
CADRAN SACRÉ!
HUSH.
I REALLY CAN'T LET YOU SPEAK TO THE GENERAL.

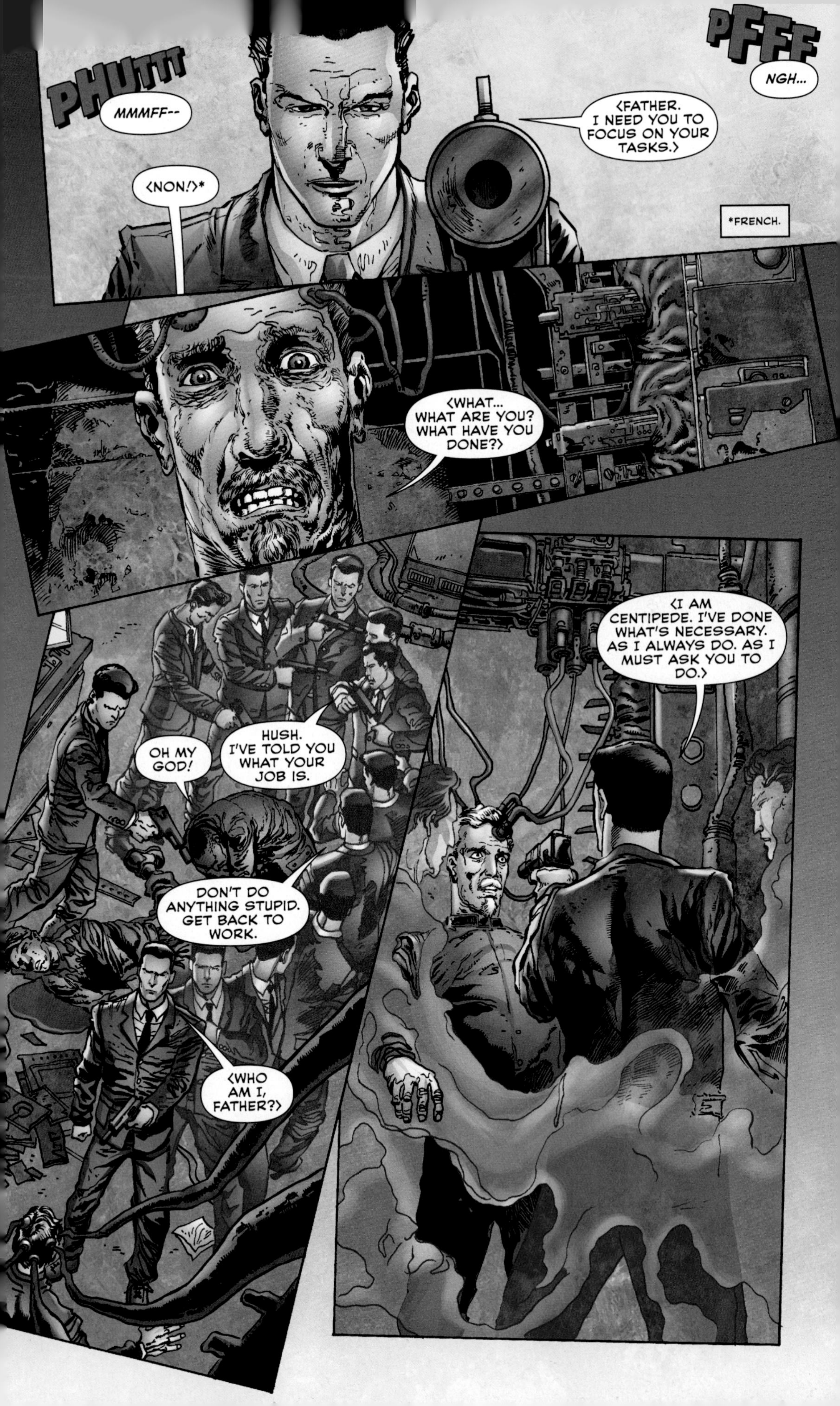
PHUTTT
MMMFF--
<NON!>*
<FATHER. I NEED YOU TO FOCUS ON YOUR TASKS.>
PFFF
NGH...
*FRENCH.
<WHAT... WHAT ARE YOU? WHAT HAVE YOU DONE?>
OH MY GOD!
HUSH. I'VE TOLD YOU WHAT YOUR JOB IS.
DON'T DO ANYTHING STUPID. GET BACK TO WORK.
<WHO AM I, FATHER?>
<I AM CENTIPEDE. I'VE DONE WHAT'S NECESSARY. AS I ALWAYS DO. AS I MUST ASK YOU TO DO.>

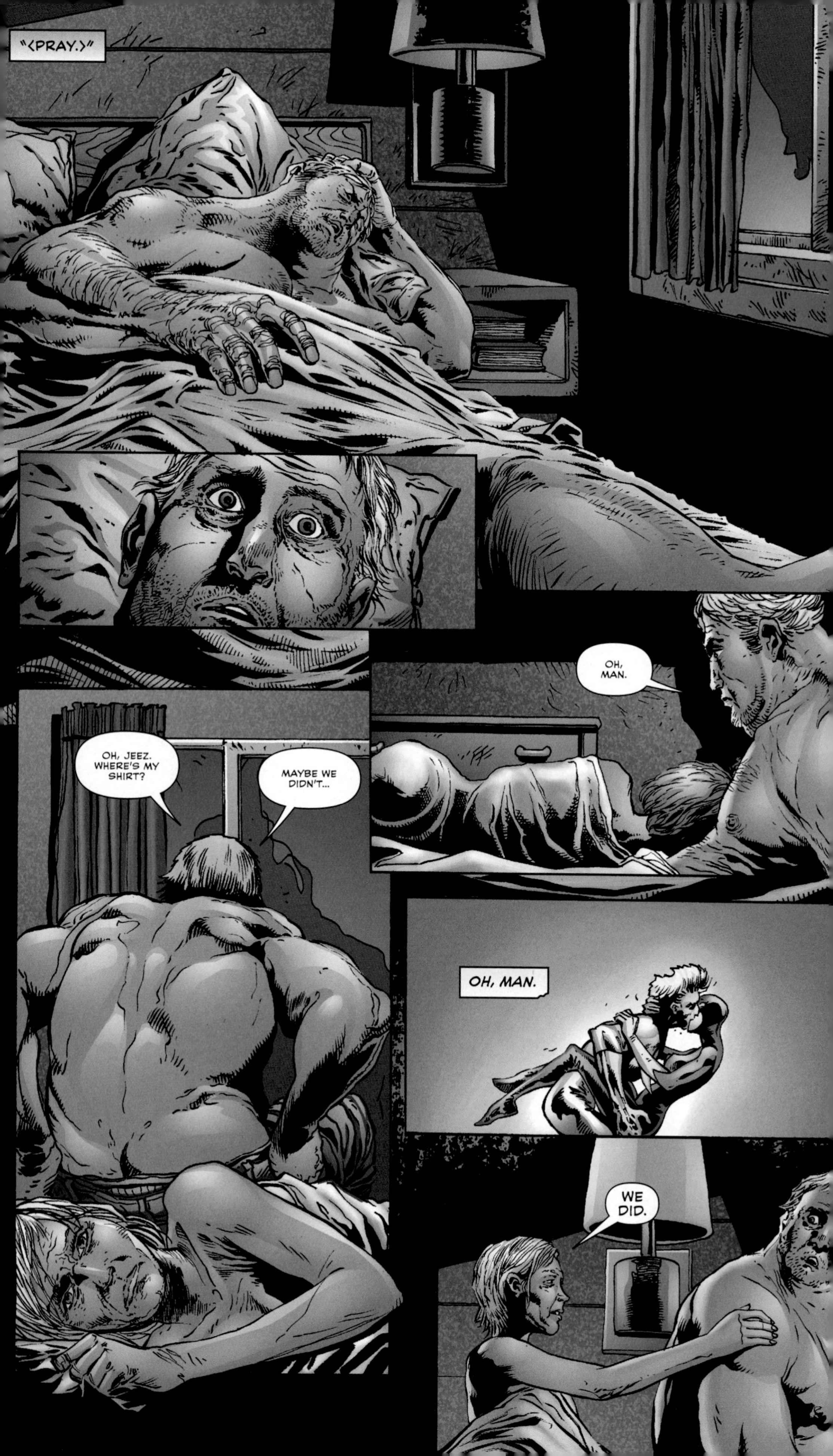
"<PRAY.>"
OH, JEEZ. WHERE'S MY SHIRT?
MAYBE WE DIDN'T...
OH, MAN.
OH, MAN.
WE DID.

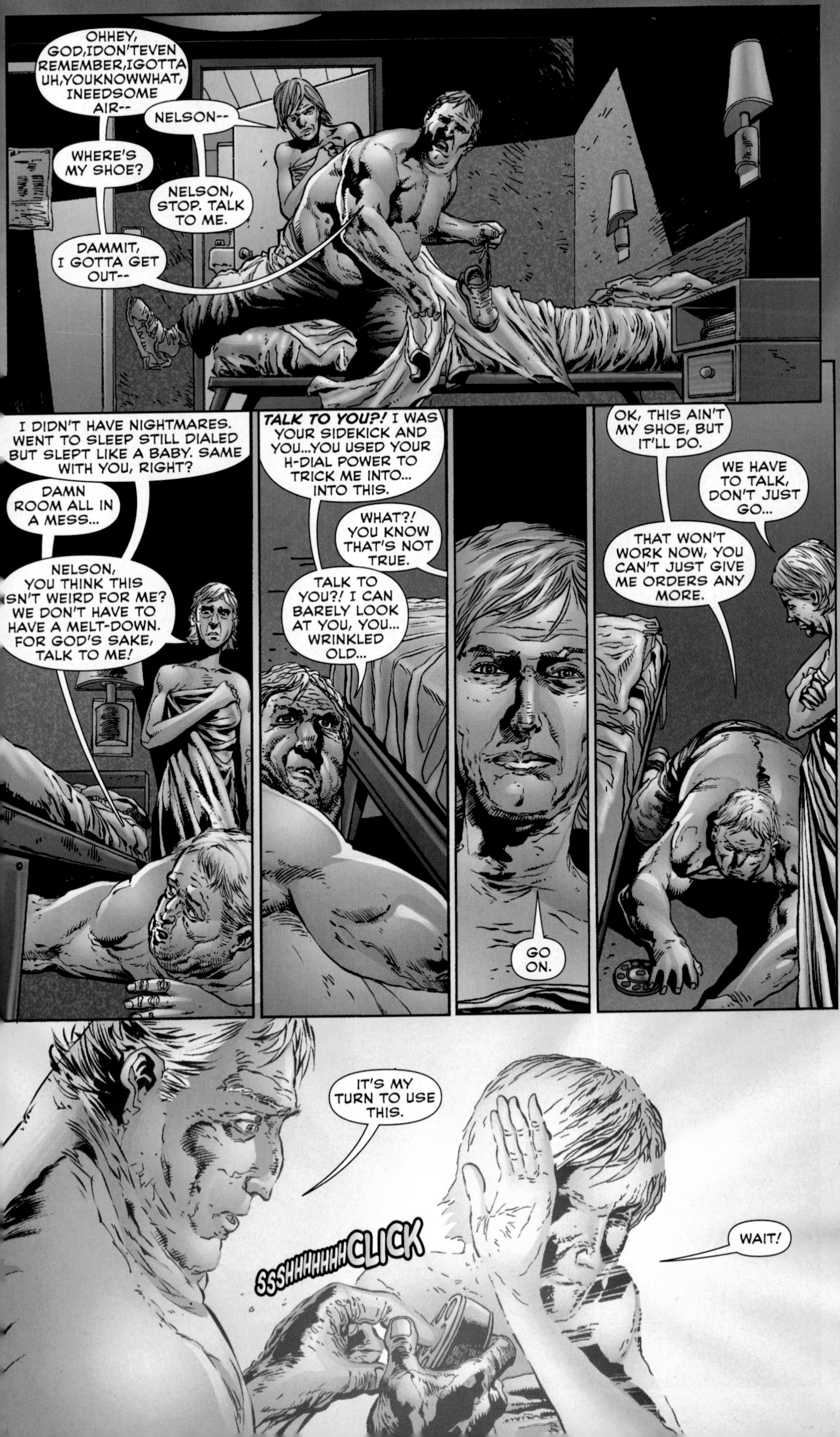
OHHEY, GOD,IDON'TEVEN REMEMBER,IGOTTA UH,YOUKNOWWHAT, INEEDSOME AIR--
NELSON--
WHERE'S MY SHOE?
NELSON, STOP. TALK TO ME.
DAMMIT, I GOTTA GET OUT--
I DIDN'T HAVE NIGHTMARES. WENT TO SLEEP STILL DIALED BUT SLEPT LIKE A BABY. SAME WITH YOU, RIGHT?
DAMN ROOM ALL IN A MESS...
NELSON, YOU THINK THIS ISN'T WEIRD FOR ME? WE DON'T HAVE TO HAVE A MELT-DOWN. FOR GOD'S SAKE, TALK TO ME!
TALK TO YOU?! I WAS YOUR SIDEKICK AND YOU...YOU USED YOUR H-DIAL POWER TO TRICK ME INTO... INTO THIS.
WHAT?! YOU KNOW THAT'S NOT TRUE.
TALK TO YOU?! I CAN BARELY LOOK AT YOU, YOU... WRINKLED OLD...
GO ON.
OK, THIS AIN'T MY SHOE, BUT IT'LL DO.
WE HAVE TO TALK, DON'T JUST GO...
THAT WON'T WORK NOW, YOU CAN'T JUST GIVE ME ORDERS ANY MORE.
IT'S MY TURN TO USE THIS.
SSSHHHHHHHCLICK
WAIT!

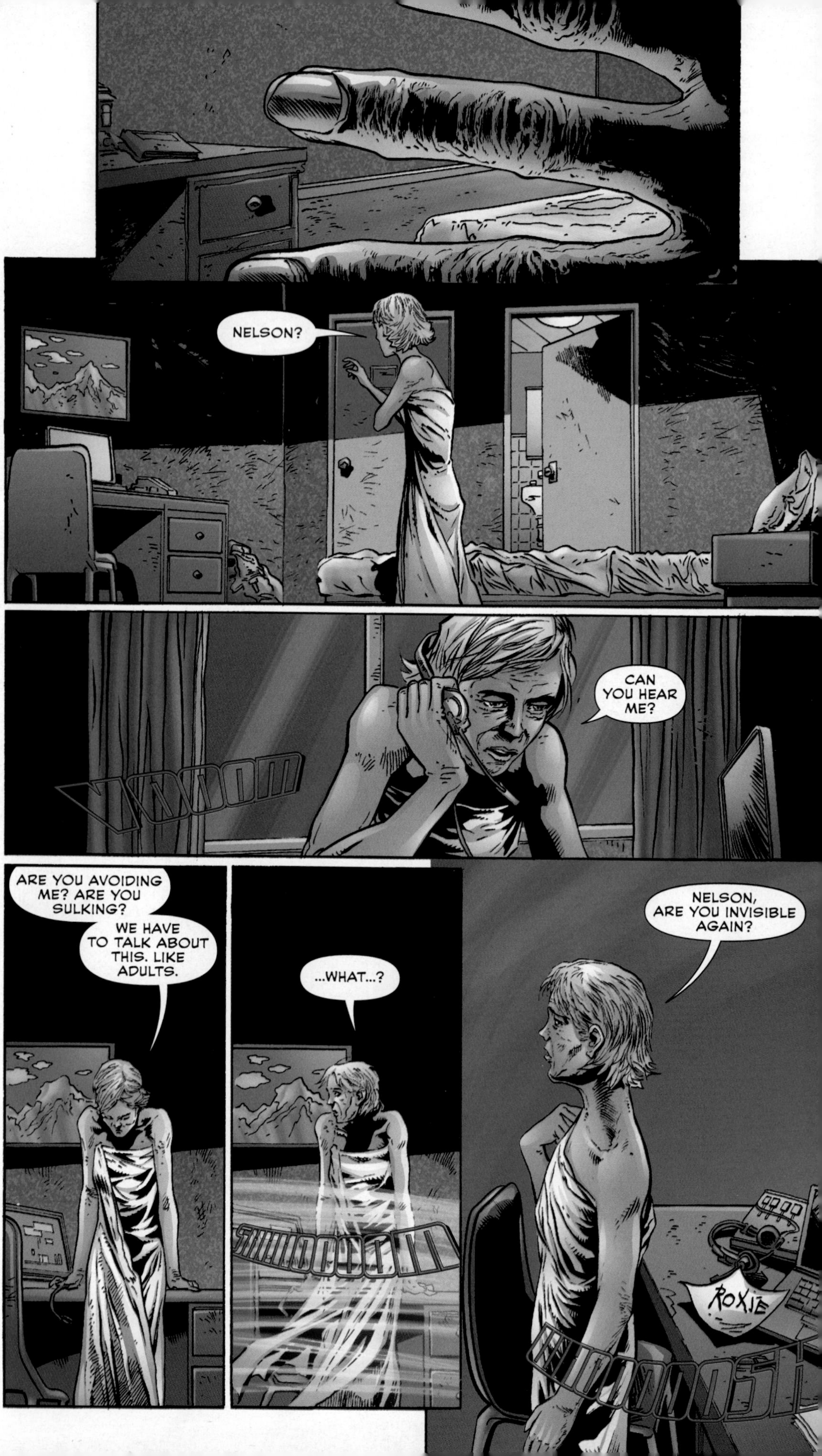
NELSON?
CAN YOU HEAR ME?
VRRROOM
ARE YOU AVOIDING ME? ARE YOU SULKING?
WE HAVE TO TALK ABOUT THIS. LIKE ADULTS.
...WHAT...?
NELSON, ARE YOU INVISIBLE AGAIN?
ROXIE

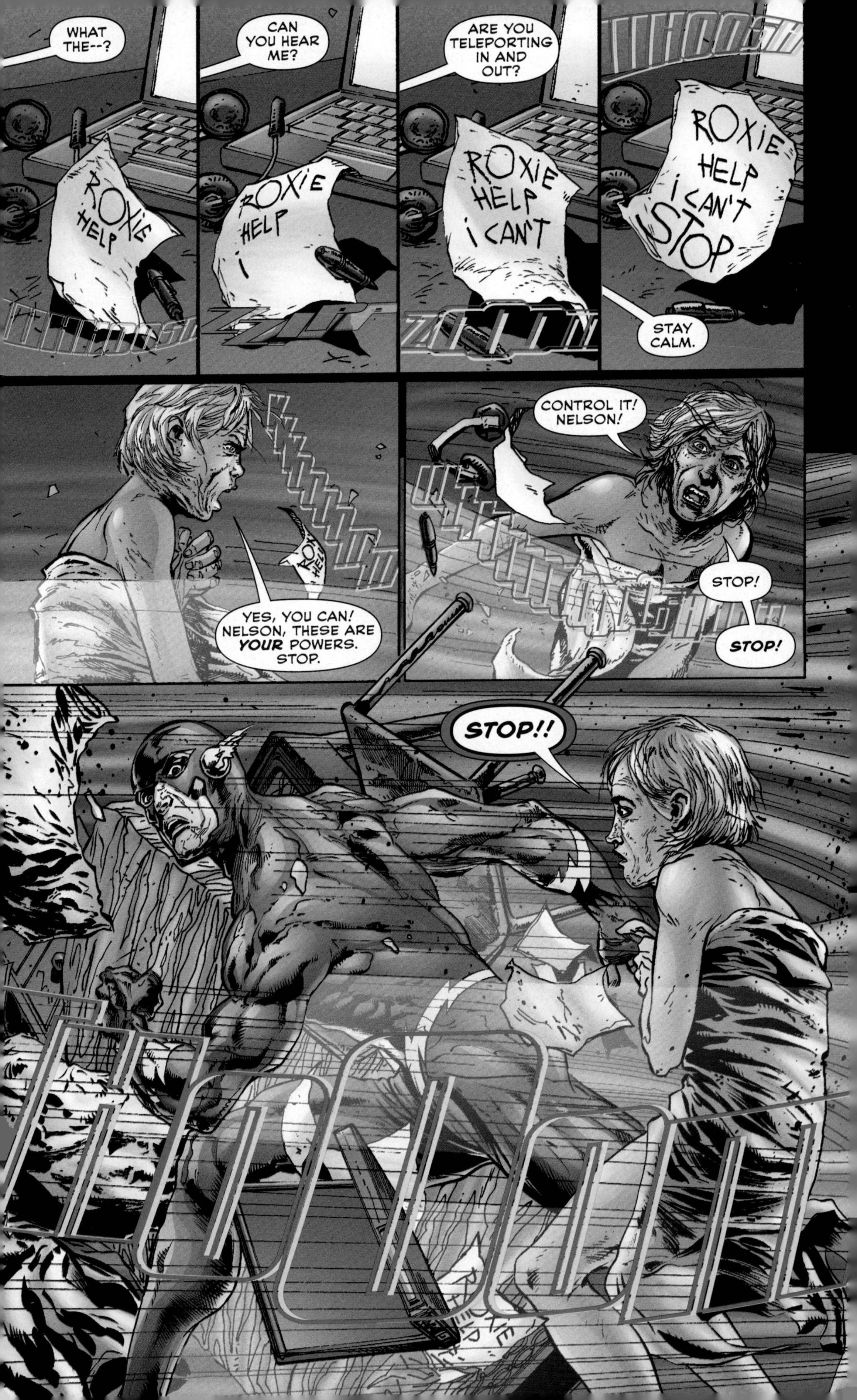
WHAT THE--?
ROXIE HELP
CAN YOU HEAR ME?
ROXIE HELP I
ARE YOU TELEPORTING IN AND OUT?
ROXIE HELP I CAN'T
ROXIE HELP I CAN'T STOP
STAY CALM.
YES, YOU CAN! NELSON, THESE ARE YOUR POWERS. STOP.
CONTROL IT! NELSON!
STOP!
STOP!
STOP!!

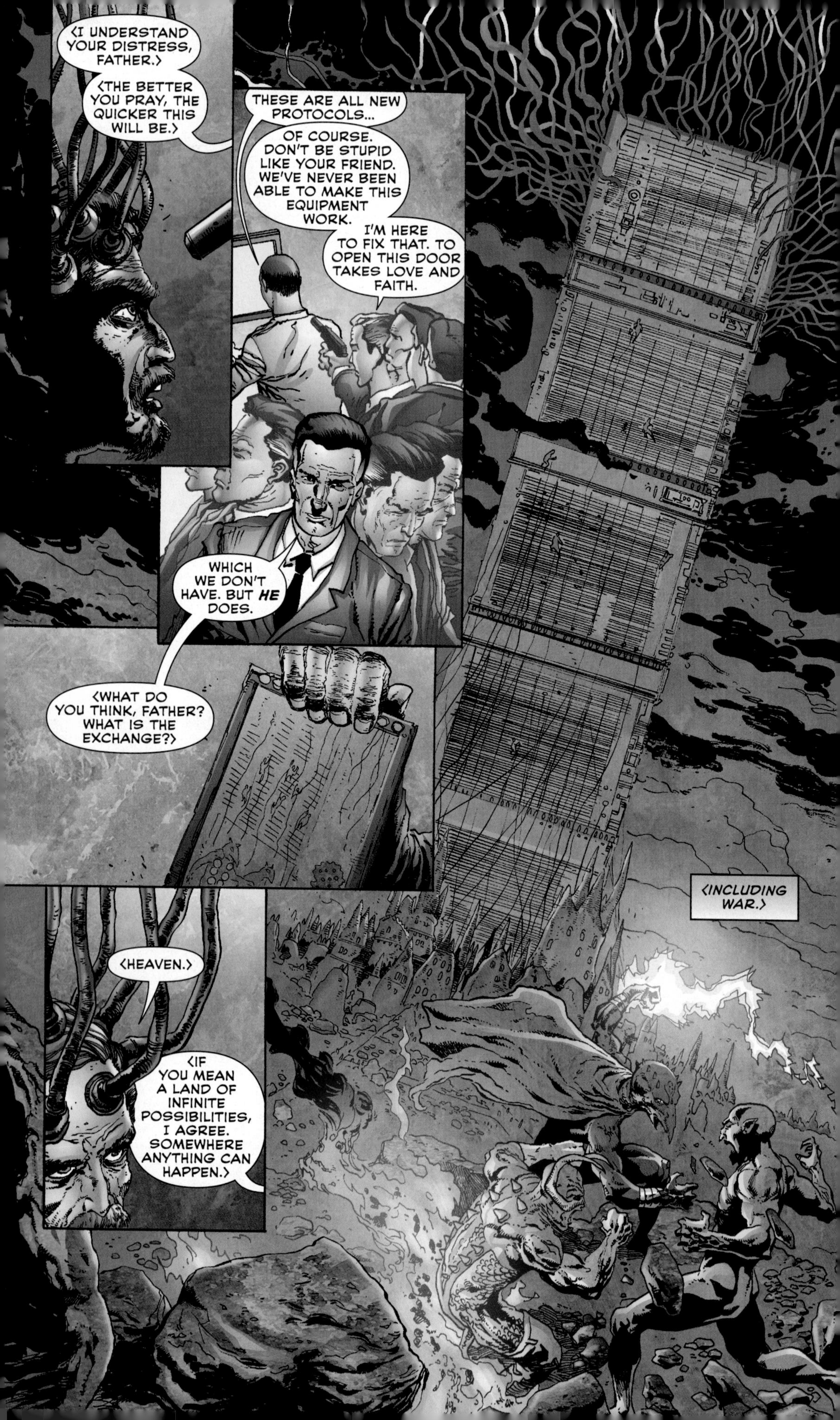
<I UNDERSTAND YOUR DISTRESS, FATHER.>
<THE BETTER YOU PRAY, THE QUICKER THIS WILL BE.>
THESE ARE ALL NEW PROTOCOLS...
OF COURSE. DON'T BE STUPID LIKE YOUR FRIEND. WE'VE NEVER BEEN ABLE TO MAKE THIS EQUIPMENT WORK.
I'M HERE TO FIX THAT. TO OPEN THIS DOOR TAKES LOVE AND FAITH.
WHICH WE DON'T HAVE. BUT *HE* DOES.
<WHAT DO YOU THINK, FATHER? WHAT IS THE EXCHANGE?>
<HEAVEN.>
<IF YOU MEAN A LAND OF INFINITE POSSIBILITIES, I AGREE. SOMEWHERE ANYTHING CAN HAPPEN.>
<INCLUDING WAR.>

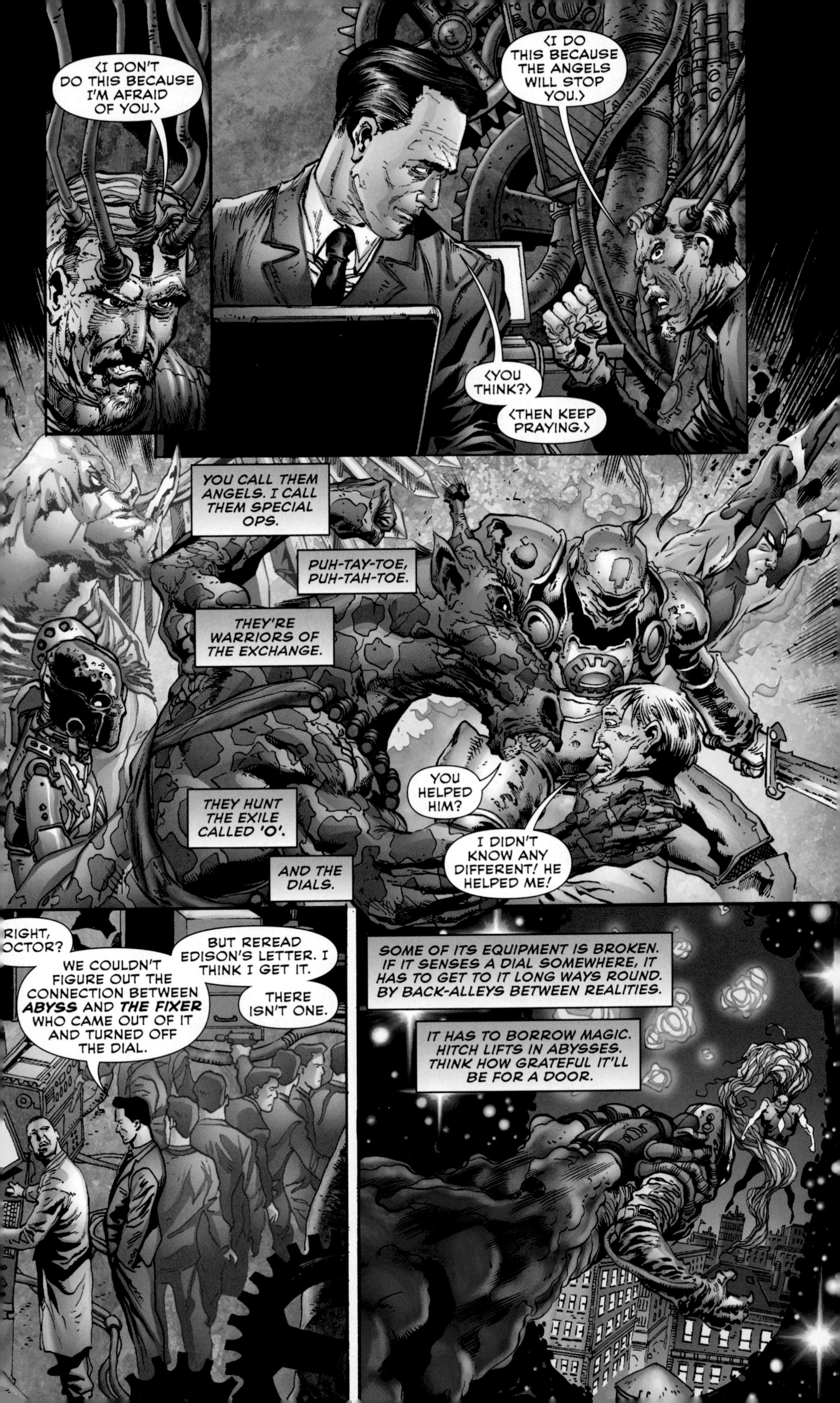

<I DON'T DO THIS BECAUSE I'M AFRAID OF YOU.>
<I DO THIS BECAUSE THE ANGELS WILL STOP YOU.>
<YOU THINK?>
<THEN KEEP PRAYING.>
YOU CALL THEM ANGELS. I CALL THEM SPECIAL OPS.
PUH-TAY-TOE, PUH-TAH-TOE.
THEY'RE WARRIORS OF THE EXCHANGE.
YOU HELPED HIM?
THEY HUNT THE EXILE CALLED 'O'.
I DIDN'T KNOW ANY DIFFERENT! HE HELPED ME!
AND THE DIALS.
RIGHT, OCTOR?
WE COULDN'T FIGURE OUT THE CONNECTION BETWEEN ABYSS AND THE FIXER WHO CAME OUT OF IT AND TURNED OFF THE DIAL.
BUT REREAD EDISON'S LETTER. I THINK I GET IT.
THERE ISN'T ONE.
SOME OF ITS EQUIPMENT IS BROKEN. IF IT SENSES A DIAL SOMEWHERE, IT HAS TO GET TO IT LONG WAYS ROUND. BY BACK-ALLEYS BETWEEN REALITIES.
IT HAS TO BORROW MAGIC. HITCH LIFTS IN ABYSSES. THINK HOW GRATEFUL IT'LL BE FOR A DOOR.

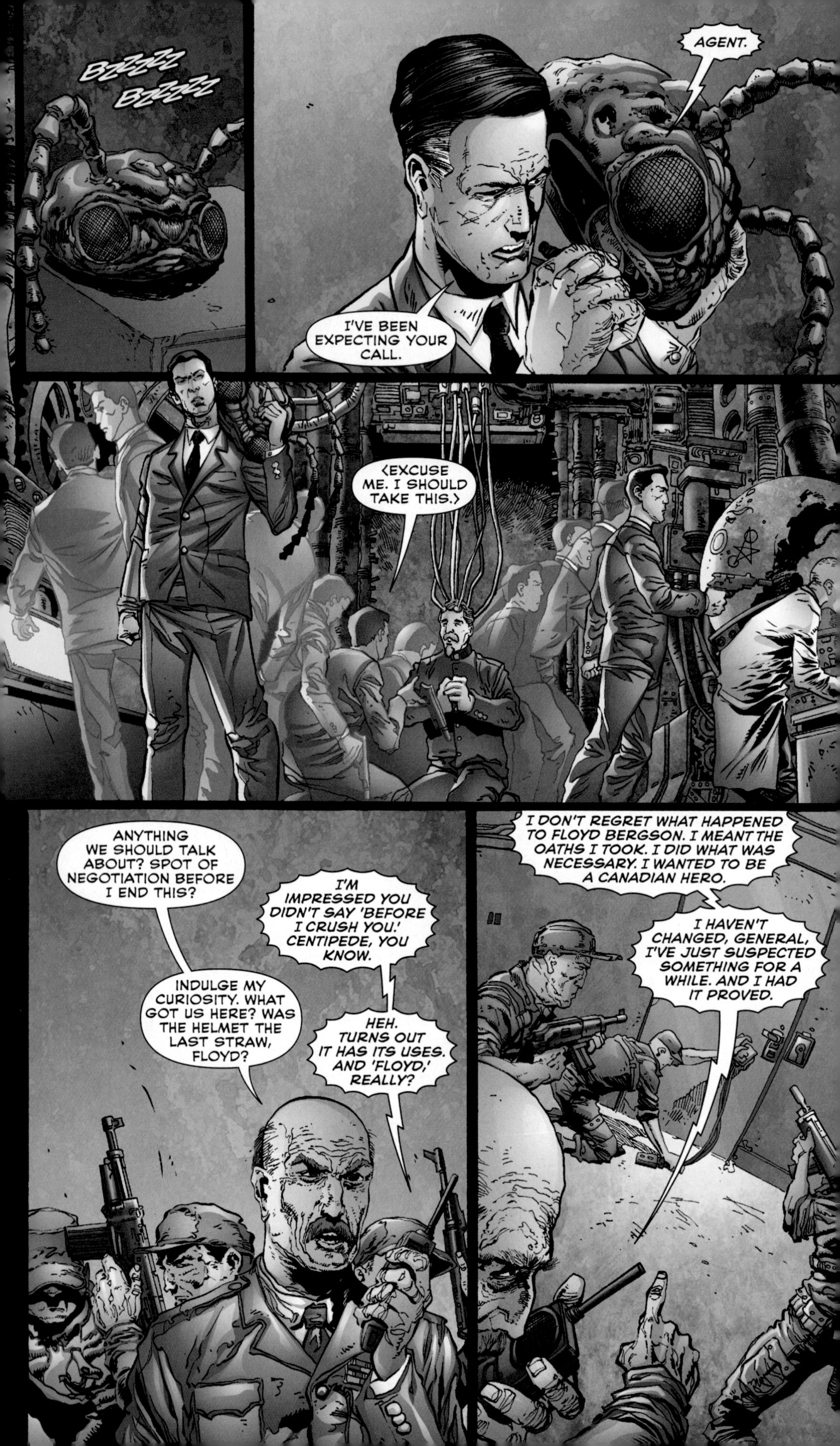
BZZZZ
BZZZZ
AGENT.
I'VE BEEN EXPECTING YOUR CALL.
‹EXCUSE ME. I SHOULD TAKE THIS.›
ANYTHING WE SHOULD TALK ABOUT? SPOT OF NEGOTIATION BEFORE I END THIS?
I'M IMPRESSED YOU DIDN'T SAY 'BEFORE I CRUSH YOU.' CENTIPEDE, YOU KNOW.
INDULGE MY CURIOSITY. WHAT GOT US HERE? WAS THE HELMET THE LAST STRAW, FLOYD?
HEH. TURNS OUT IT HAS ITS USES. AND 'FLOYD,' REALLY?
I DON'T REGRET WHAT HAPPENED TO FLOYD BERGSON. I MEANT THE OATHS I TOOK. I DID WHAT WAS NECESSARY. I WANTED TO BE A CANADIAN HERO.
I HAVEN'T CHANGED, GENERAL, I'VE JUST SUSPECTED SOMETHING FOR A WHILE. AND I HAD IT PROVED.

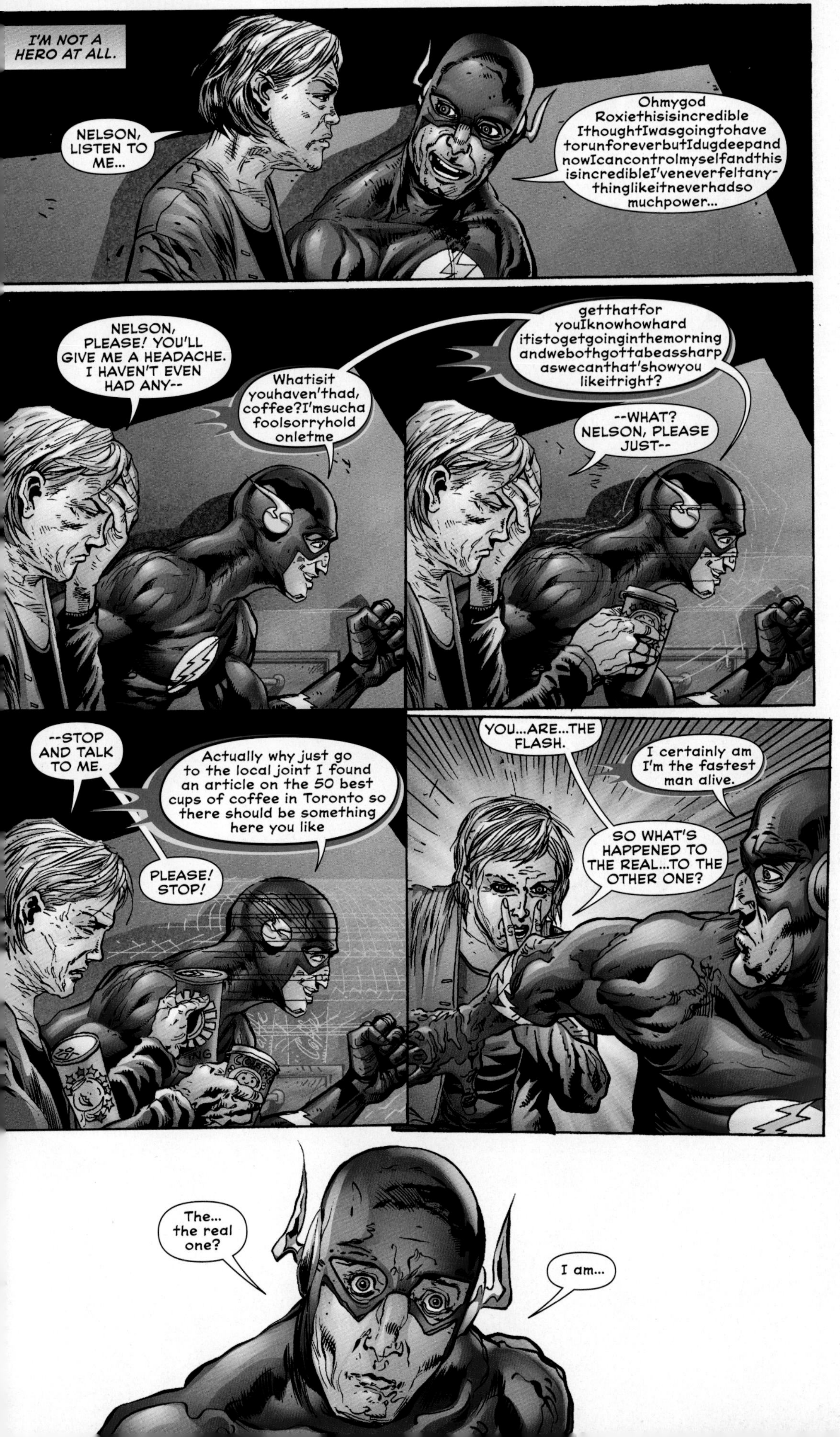
I'M NOT A HERO AT ALL.
NELSON, LISTEN TO ME...
Ohmygod RoxiethisisincredibleIthoughtIwasgoingtohave torunforeverbutIdugdeepand nowIcancontrolmyselfandthis isincredibleI'veneverfeltany-thinglikeitneverhadso muchpower...
NELSON, PLEASE! YOU'LL GIVE ME A HEADACHE. I HAVEN'T EVEN HAD ANY--
Whatisit youhaven'thad, coffee?I'msucha foolsorryhold onletme
getthatfor youIknowhowhard itistogetgoinginthemorning andwebothgottabeassharp aswecanthat'showyou likeitright?
--WHAT? NELSON, PLEASE JUST--
--STOP AND TALK TO ME.
Actually why just go to the local joint I found an article on the 50 best cups of coffee in Toronto so there should be something here you like
PLEASE! STOP!
YOU...ARE...THE FLASH.
I certainly am I'm the fastest man alive.
SO WHAT'S HAPPENED TO THE REAL...TO THE OTHER ONE?
The... the real one?
I am...

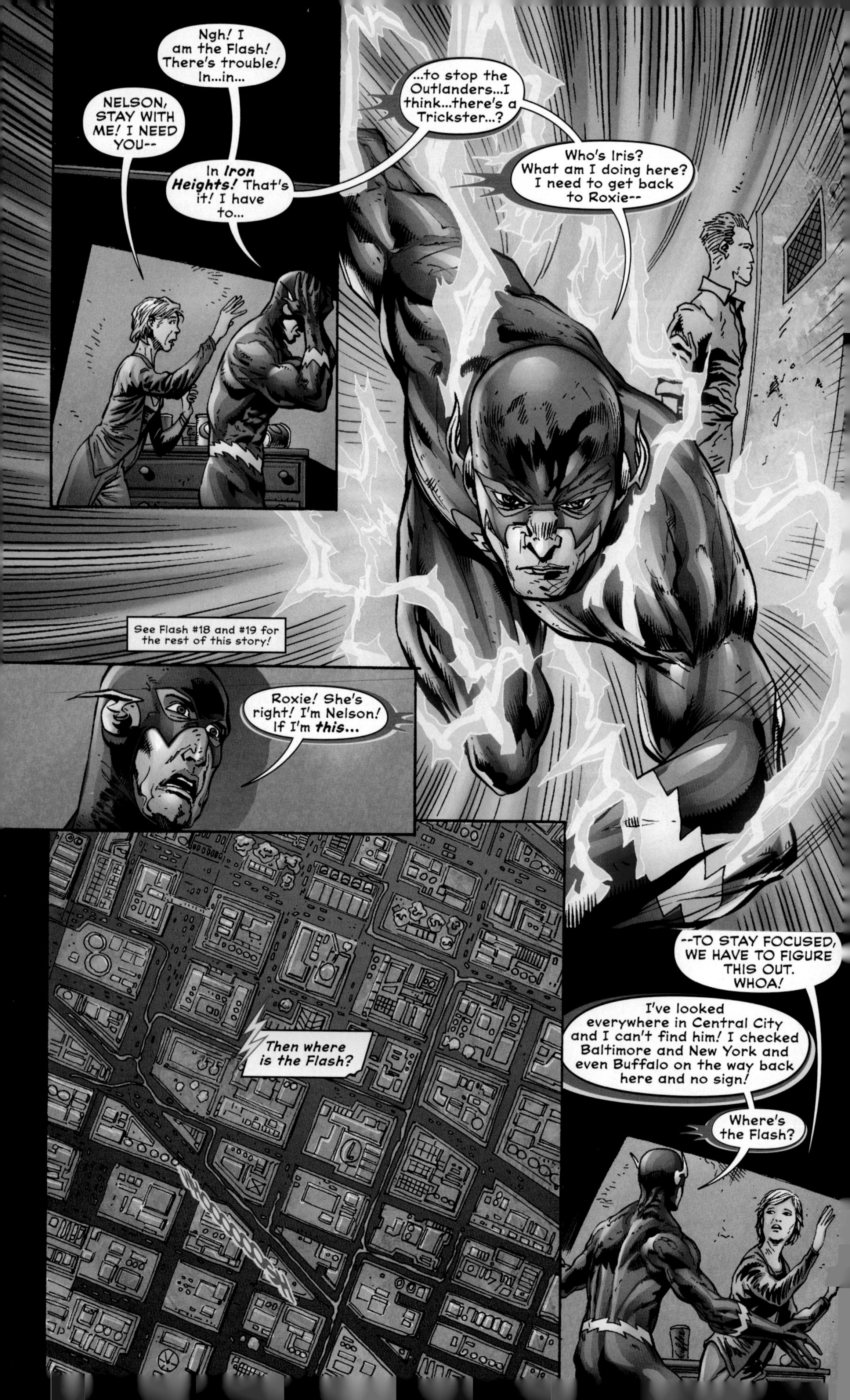
NELSON, STAY WITH ME! I NEED YOU--
Ngh! I am the Flash! There's trouble! In...in...
In **Iron Heights!** That's it! I have to...
...to stop the Outlanders...I think...there's a Trickster...?
Who's Iris? What am I doing here? I need to get back to Roxie--
See Flash #18 and #19 for the rest of this story!
Roxie! She's right! I'm Nelson! If I'm **this...**
Then where is the Flash?
--TO STAY FOCUSED, WE HAVE TO FIGURE THIS OUT. WHOA!
I've looked everywhere in Central City and I can't find him! I checked Baltimore and New York and even Buffalo on the way back here and no sign!
Where's the Flash?

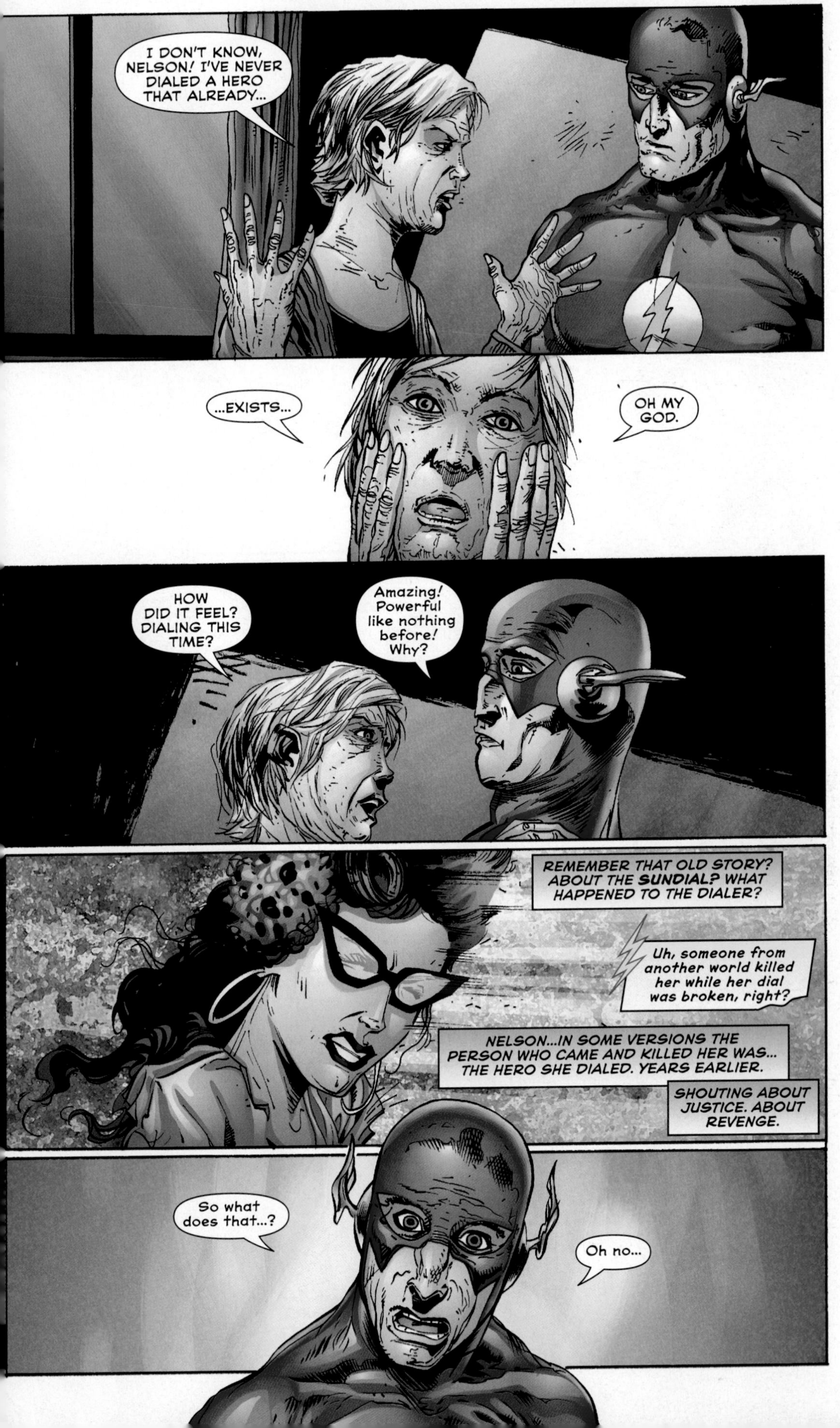
I DON'T KNOW, NELSON! I'VE NEVER DIALED A HERO THAT ALREADY...
...EXISTS...
OH MY GOD.
HOW DID IT FEEL? DIALING THIS TIME?
Amazing! Powerful like nothing before! Why?
REMEMBER THAT OLD STORY? ABOUT THE SUNDIAL? WHAT HAPPENED TO THE DIALER?
Uh, someone from another world killed her while her dial was broken, right?
NELSON...IN SOME VERSIONS THE PERSON WHO CAME AND KILLED HER WAS... THE HERO SHE DIALED. YEARS EARLIER.
SHOUTING ABOUT JUSTICE. ABOUT REVENGE.
So what does that...?
Oh no...

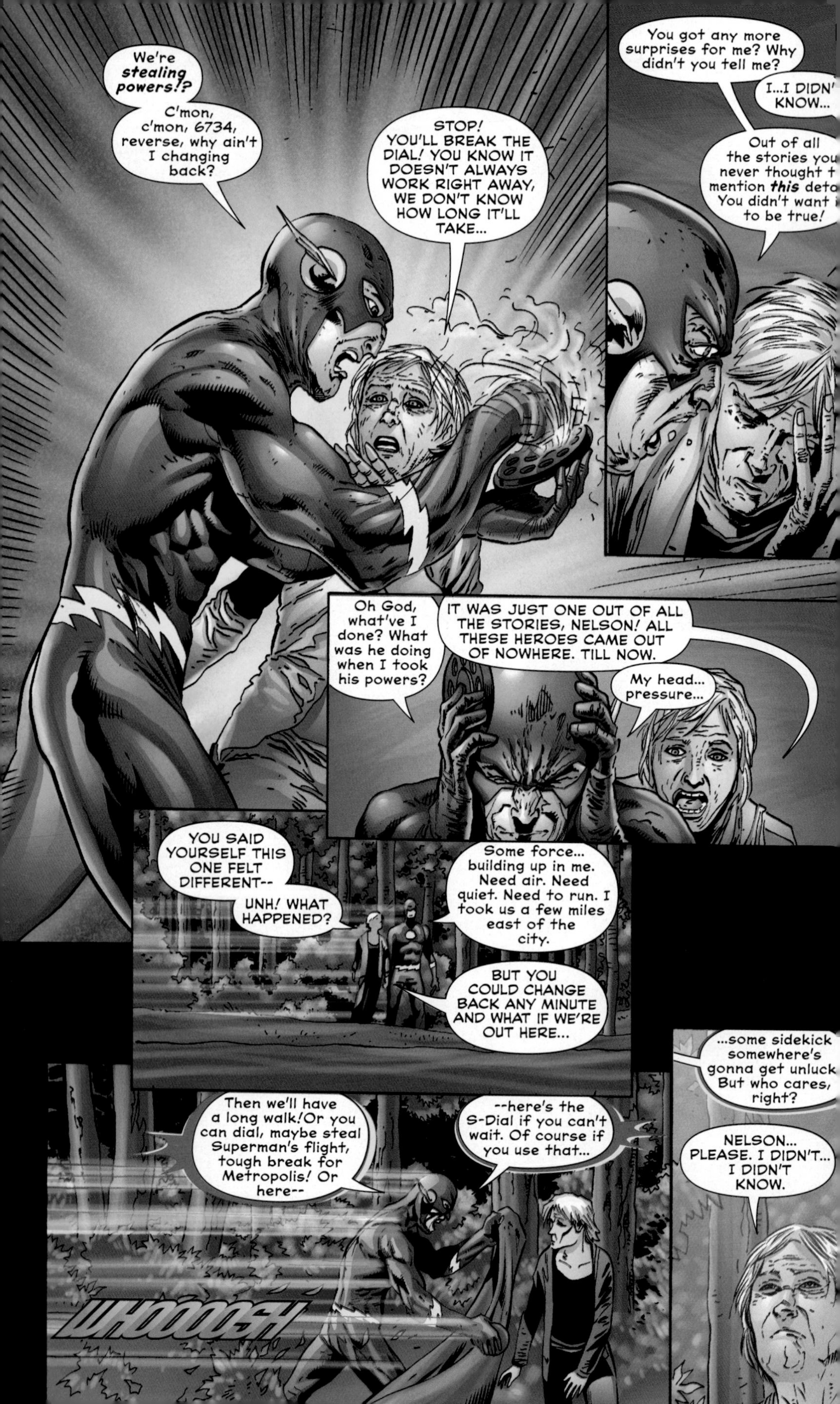
We're *stealing powers!?*
C'mon, c'mon, 6734, reverse, why ain't I changing back?
STOP! YOU'LL BREAK THE DIAL! YOU KNOW IT DOESN'T ALWAYS WORK RIGHT AWAY, WE DON'T KNOW HOW LONG IT'LL TAKE...
You got any more surprises for me? Why didn't you tell me?
I...I DIDN' KNOW...
Out of all the stories you never thought t mention *this* deta You didn't want i to be true!
Oh God, what've I done? What was he doing when I took his powers?
IT WAS JUST ONE OUT OF ALL THE STORIES, NELSON! ALL THESE HEROES CAME OUT OF NOWHERE. TILL NOW.
My head... pressure...
YOU SAID YOURSELF THIS ONE FELT DIFFERENT--
UNH! WHAT HAPPENED?
Some force... building up in me. Need air. Need quiet. Need to run. I took us a few miles east of the city.
BUT YOU COULD CHANGE BACK ANY MINUTE AND WHAT IF WE'RE OUT HERE...
Then we'll have a long walk! Or you can dial, maybe steal Superman's flight, tough break for Metropolis! Or here--
--here's the S-Dial if you can't wait. Of course if you use that...
WHOOOOSH
...some sidekick somewhere's gonna get unluck But who cares, right?
NELSON... PLEASE. I DIDN'T... I DIDN'T KNOW.

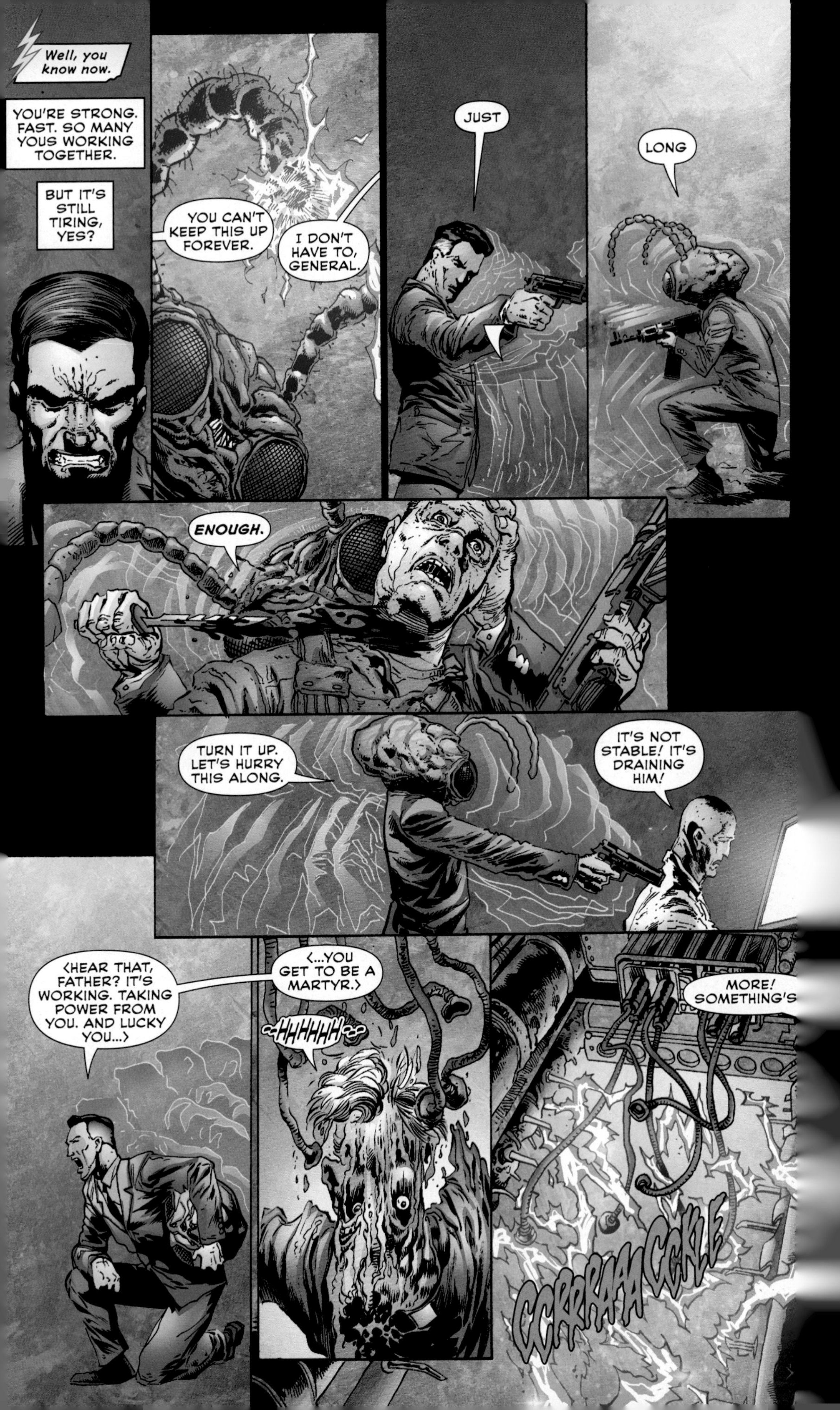

Well, you know now.
YOU'RE STRONG. FAST. SO MANY YOUS WORKING TOGETHER.
BUT IT'S STILL TIRING, YES?
YOU CAN'T KEEP THIS UP FOREVER.
I DON'T HAVE TO, GENERAL.
JUST
LONG
ENOUGH.
TURN IT UP. LET'S HURRY THIS ALONG.
IT'S NOT STABLE! IT'S DRAINING HIM!
<HEAR THAT, FATHER? IT'S WORKING. TAKING POWER FROM YOU. AND LUCKY YOU...>
<...YOU GET TO BE A MARTYR.>
-HHHHHH-
MORE! SOMETHING'S
CCRRRAAACCKLE

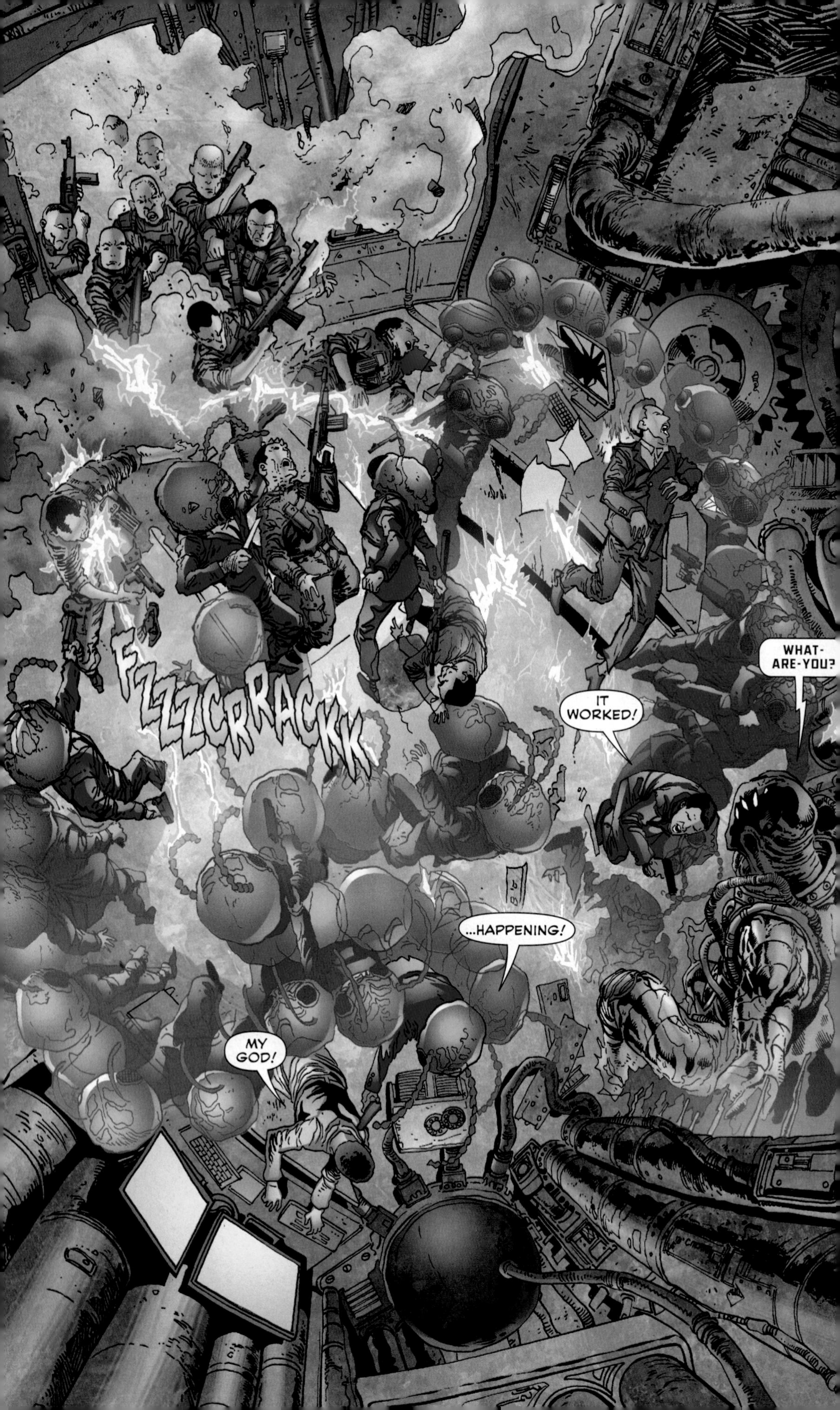
FZZZCRRACKK
WHAT-ARE-YOU?
IT WORKED!
...HAPPENING!
MY GOD!

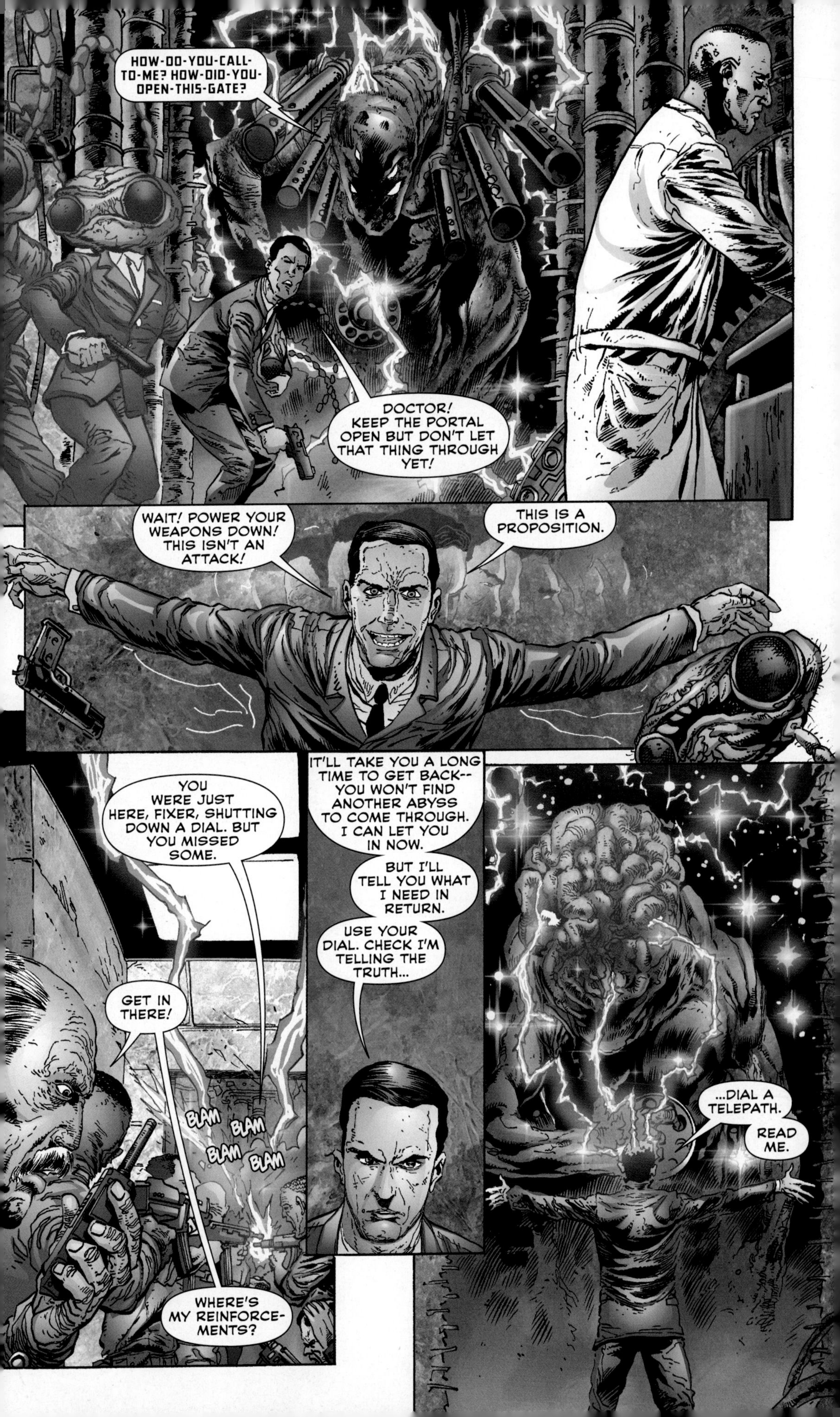
HOW-DO-YOU-CALL-TO-ME? HOW-DID-YOU-OPEN-THIS-GATE?
DOCTOR! KEEP THE PORTAL OPEN BUT DON'T LET THAT THING THROUGH YET!
WAIT! POWER YOUR WEAPONS DOWN! THIS ISN'T AN ATTACK!
THIS IS A PROPOSITION.
YOU WERE JUST HERE, FIXER, SHUTTING DOWN A DIAL. BUT YOU MISSED SOME.
GET IN THERE!
BLAM
BLAM
BLAM
BLAM
WHERE'S MY REINFORCEMENTS?
IT'LL TAKE YOU A LONG TIME TO GET BACK-- YOU WON'T FIND ANOTHER ABYSS TO COME THROUGH. I CAN LET YOU IN NOW.
BUT I'LL TELL YOU WHAT I NEED IN RETURN.
USE YOUR DIAL. CHECK I'M TELLING THE TRUTH...
...DIAL A TELEPATH.
READ ME.

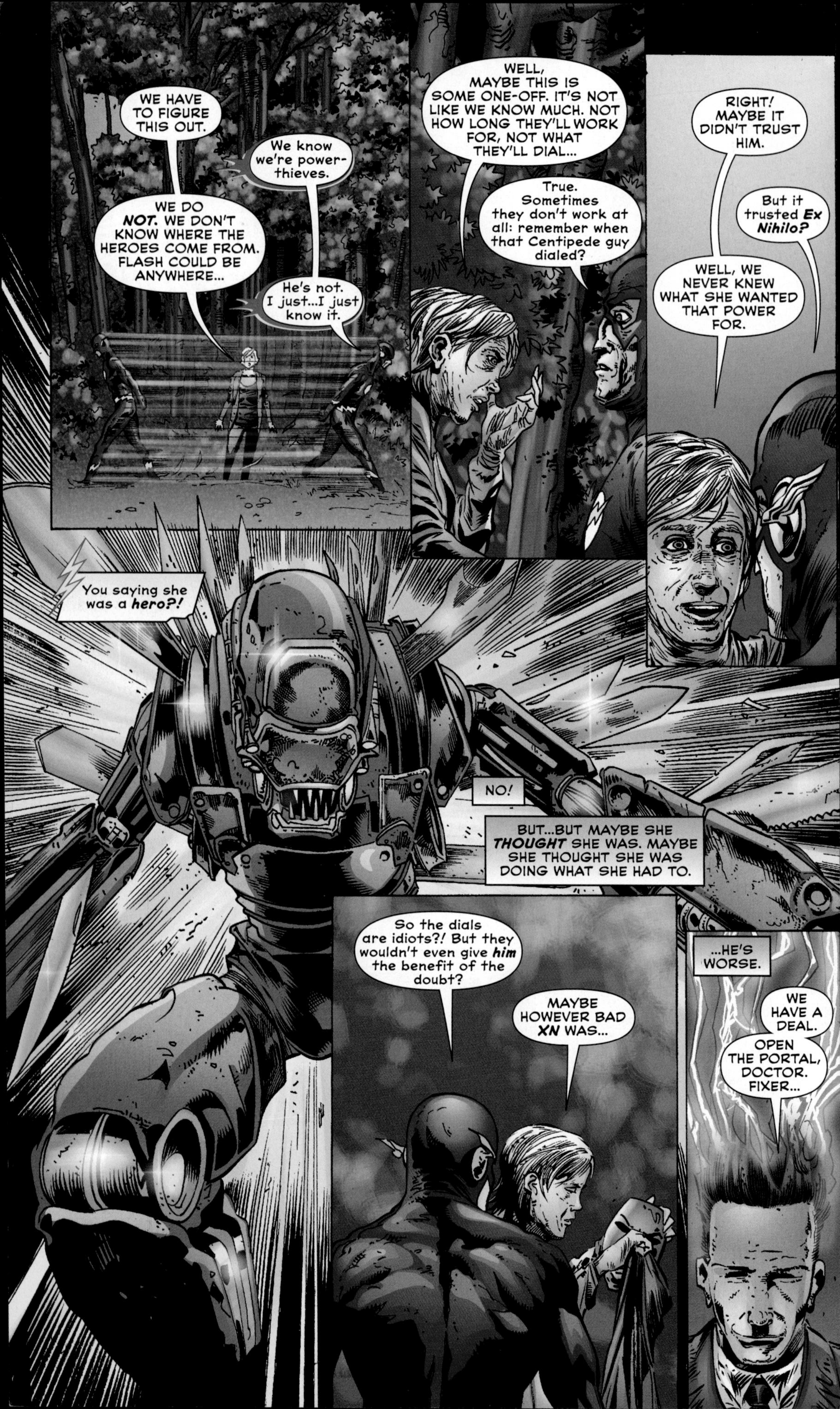
WE HAVE TO FIGURE THIS OUT.
We know we're power-thieves.
WE DO NOT. WE DON'T KNOW WHERE THE HEROES COME FROM. FLASH COULD BE ANYWHERE...
He's not. I just...I just know it.
WELL, MAYBE THIS IS SOME ONE-OFF. IT'S NOT LIKE WE KNOW MUCH. NOT HOW LONG THEY'LL WORK FOR, NOT WHAT THEY'LL DIAL...
True. Sometimes they don't work at all: remember when that Centipede guy dialed?
RIGHT! MAYBE IT DIDN'T TRUST HIM.
But it trusted Ex Nihilo?
WELL, WE NEVER KNEW WHAT SHE WANTED THAT POWER FOR.
You saying she was a hero?!
NO!
BUT...BUT MAYBE SHE THOUGHT SHE WAS. MAYBE SHE THOUGHT SHE WAS DOING WHAT SHE HAD TO.
So the dials are idiots?! But they wouldn't even give him the benefit of the doubt?
MAYBE HOWEVER BAD XN WAS...
...HE'S WORSE.
WE HAVE A DEAL.
OPEN THE PORTAL, DOCTOR. FIXER...

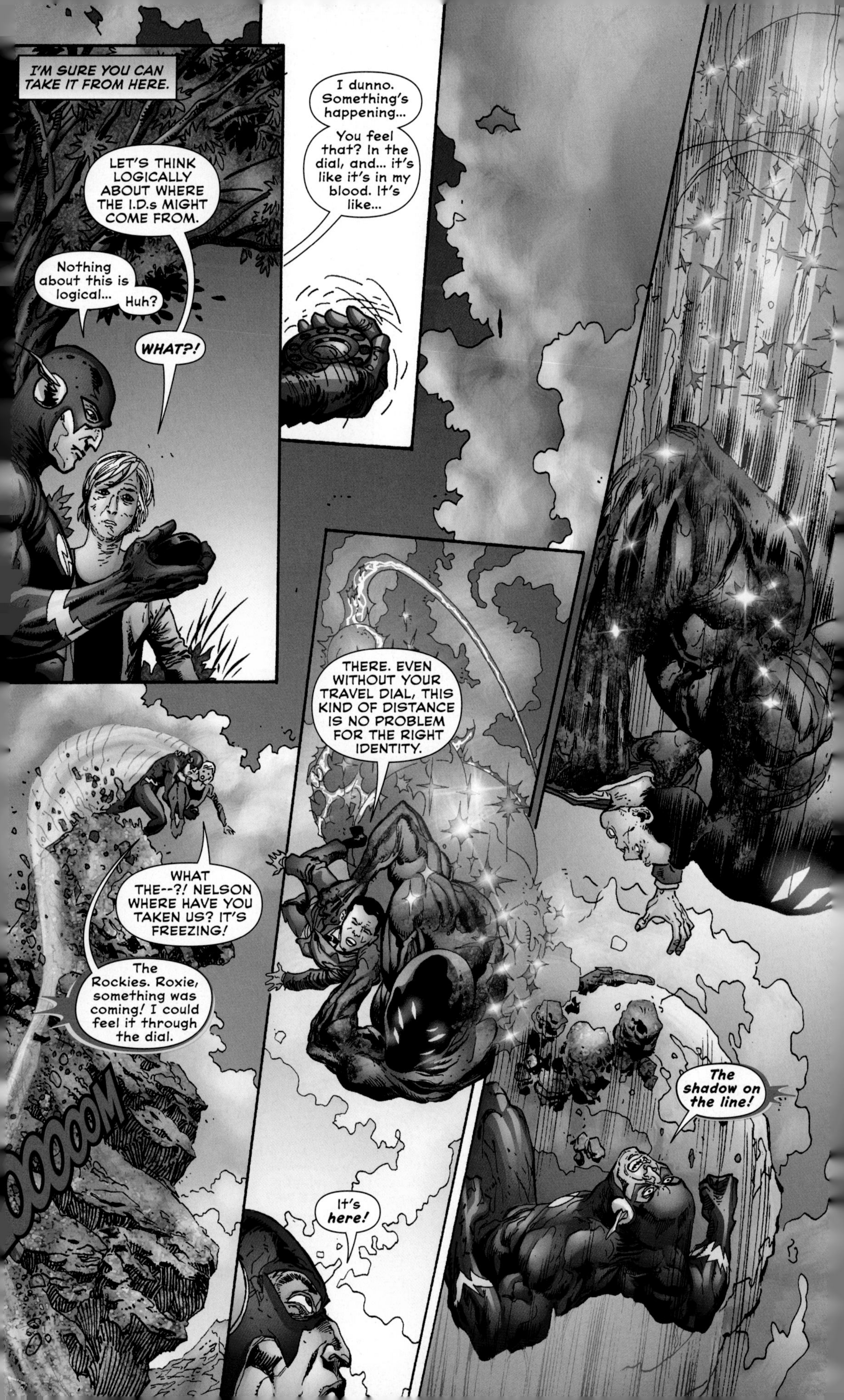
I'M SURE YOU CAN TAKE IT FROM HERE.
LET'S THINK LOGICALLY ABOUT WHERE THE I.D.s MIGHT COME FROM.
Nothing about this is logical...
Huh?
WHAT?!
I dunno. Something's happening...
You feel that? In the dial, and... it's like it's in my blood. It's like...
THERE. EVEN WITHOUT YOUR TRAVEL DIAL, THIS KIND OF DISTANCE IS NO PROBLEM FOR THE RIGHT IDENTITY.
WHAT THE--?! NELSON WHERE HAVE YOU TAKEN US? IT'S FREEZING!
The Rockies. Roxie, something was coming! I could feel it through the dial.
OOOOOM
It's here!
The shadow on the line!

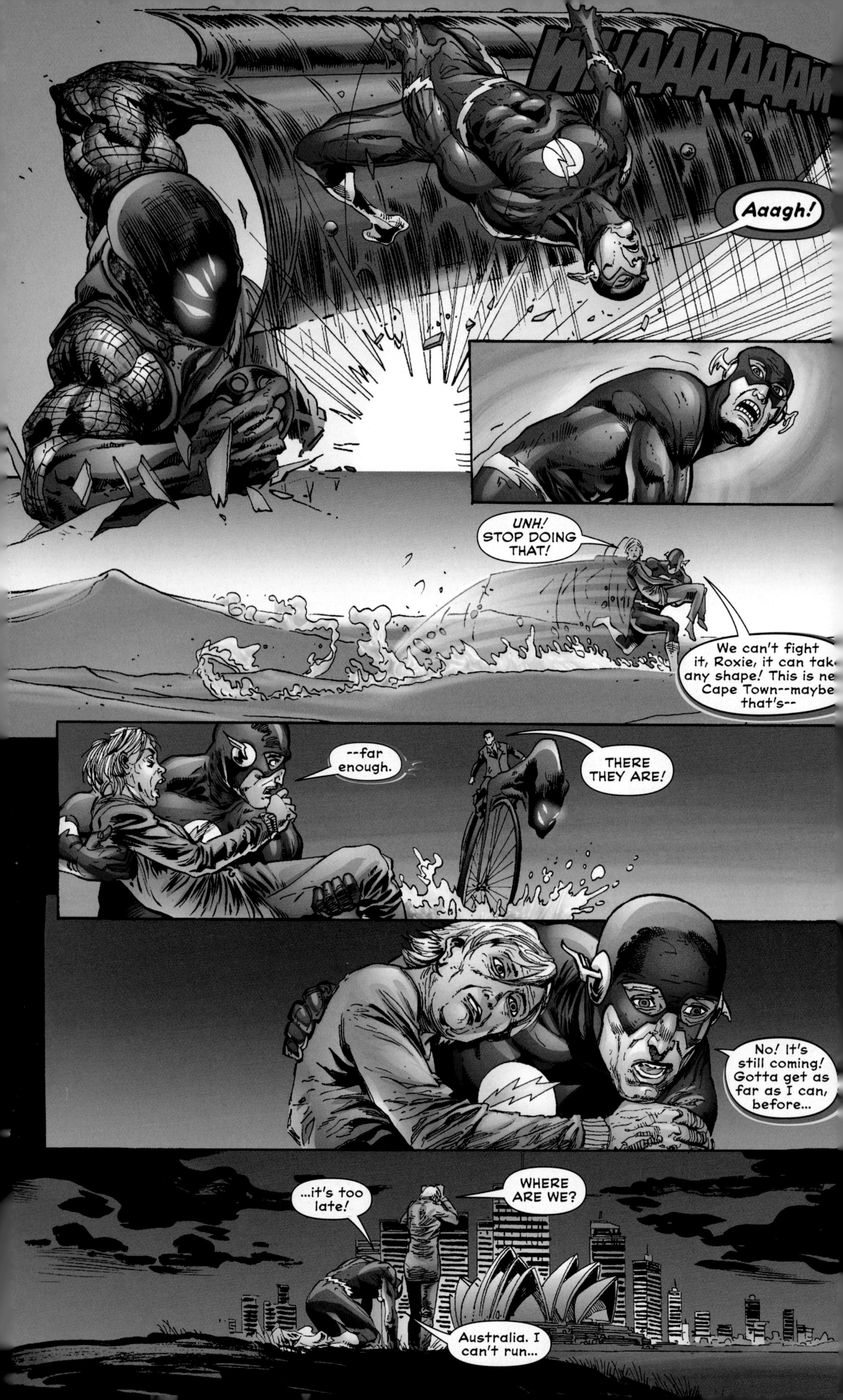
WHAAAAAAM
Aaagh!
UNH! STOP DOING THAT!
We can't fight it, Roxie, it can take any shape! This is ne Cape Town--maybe that's--
--far enough.
THERE THEY ARE!
No! It's still coming! Gotta get as far as I can, before...
...it's too late!
WHERE ARE WE?
Australia. I can't run...

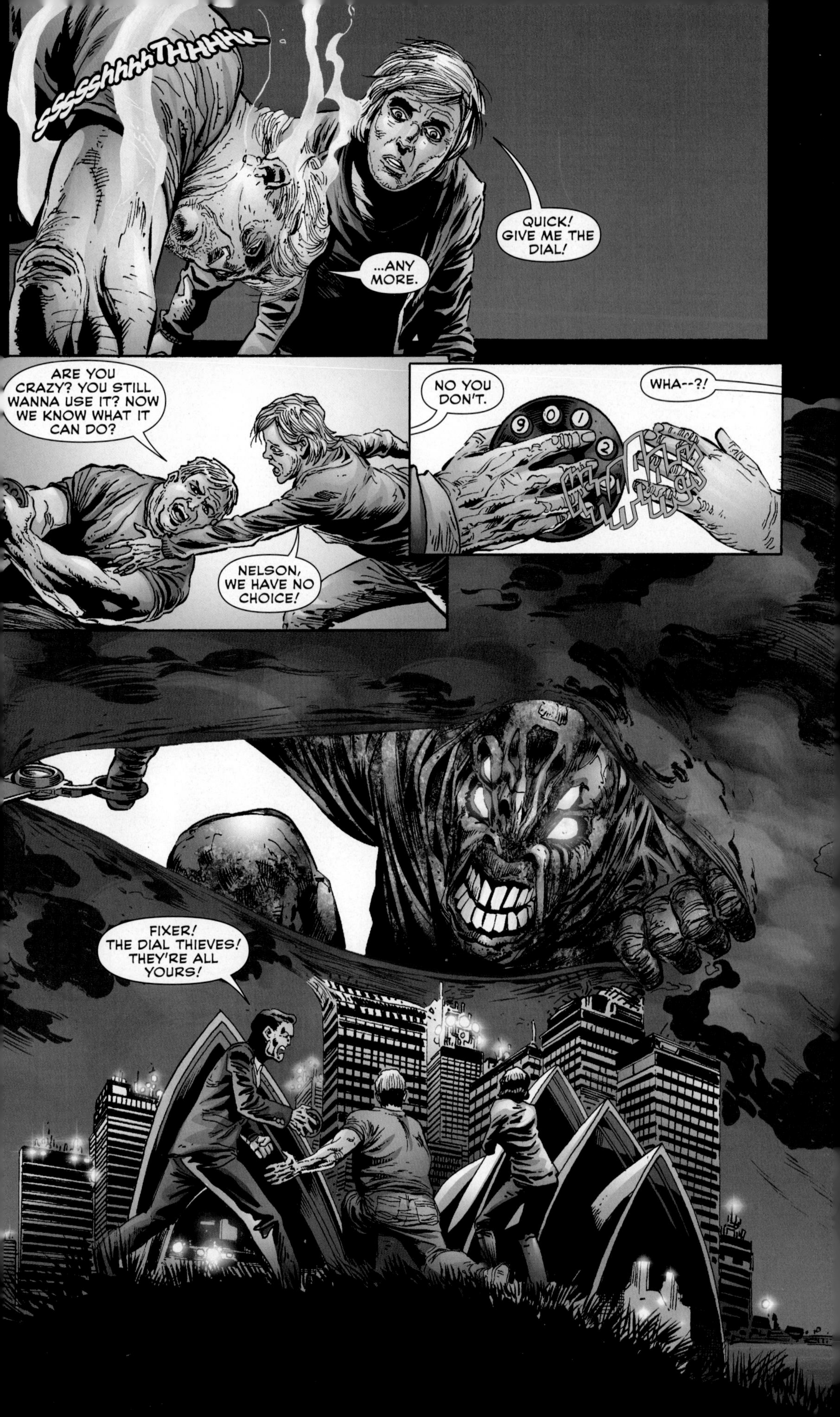
SSSSSHHHHTHHHHK
QUICK! GIVE ME THE DIAL!
...ANY MORE.
ARE YOU CRAZY? YOU STILL WANNA USE IT? NOW WE KNOW WHAT IT CAN DO?
NELSON, WE HAVE NO CHOICE!
NO YOU DON'T.
WHA--?!
FIXER! THE DIAL THIEVES! THEY'RE ALL YOURS!

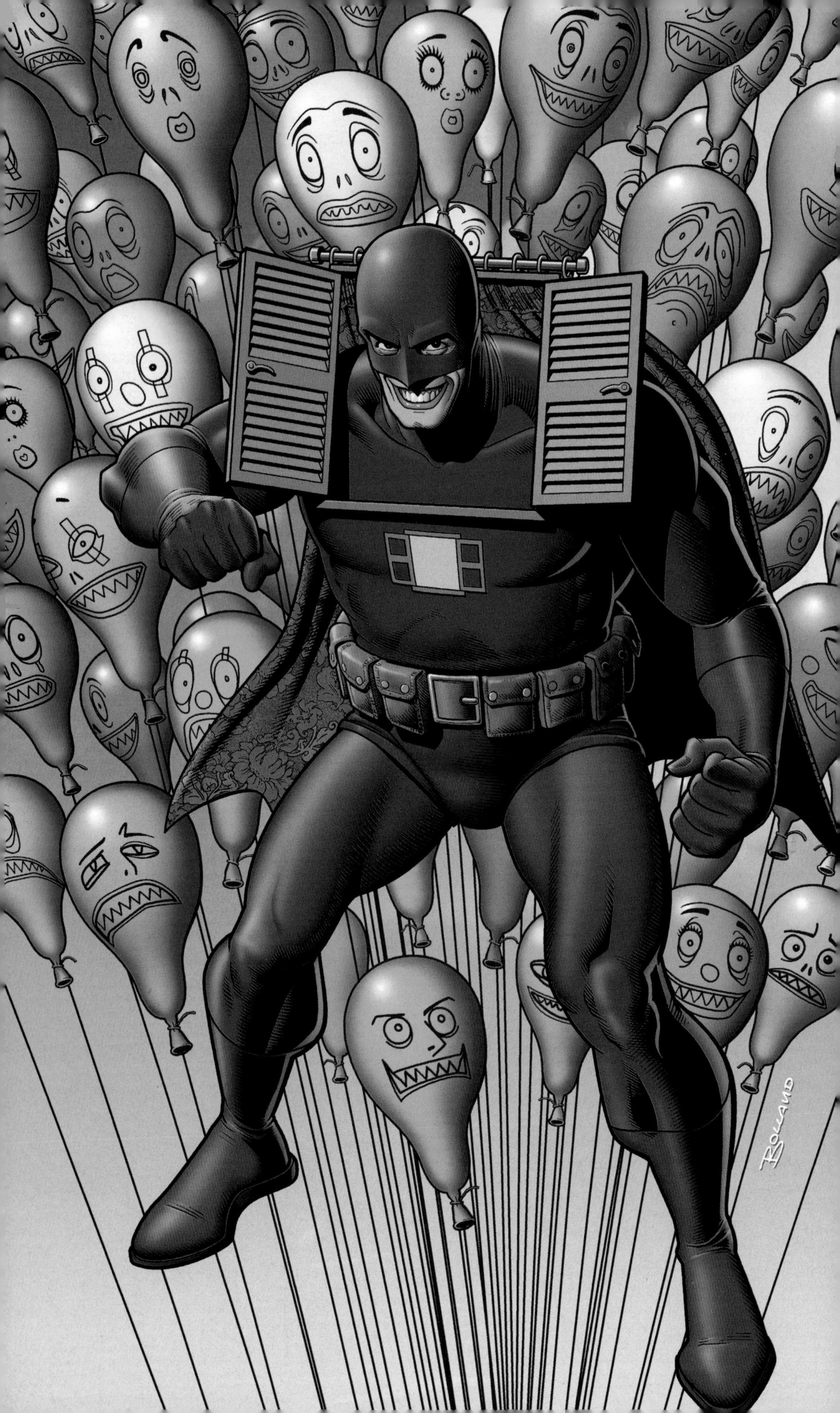
BOLLAND

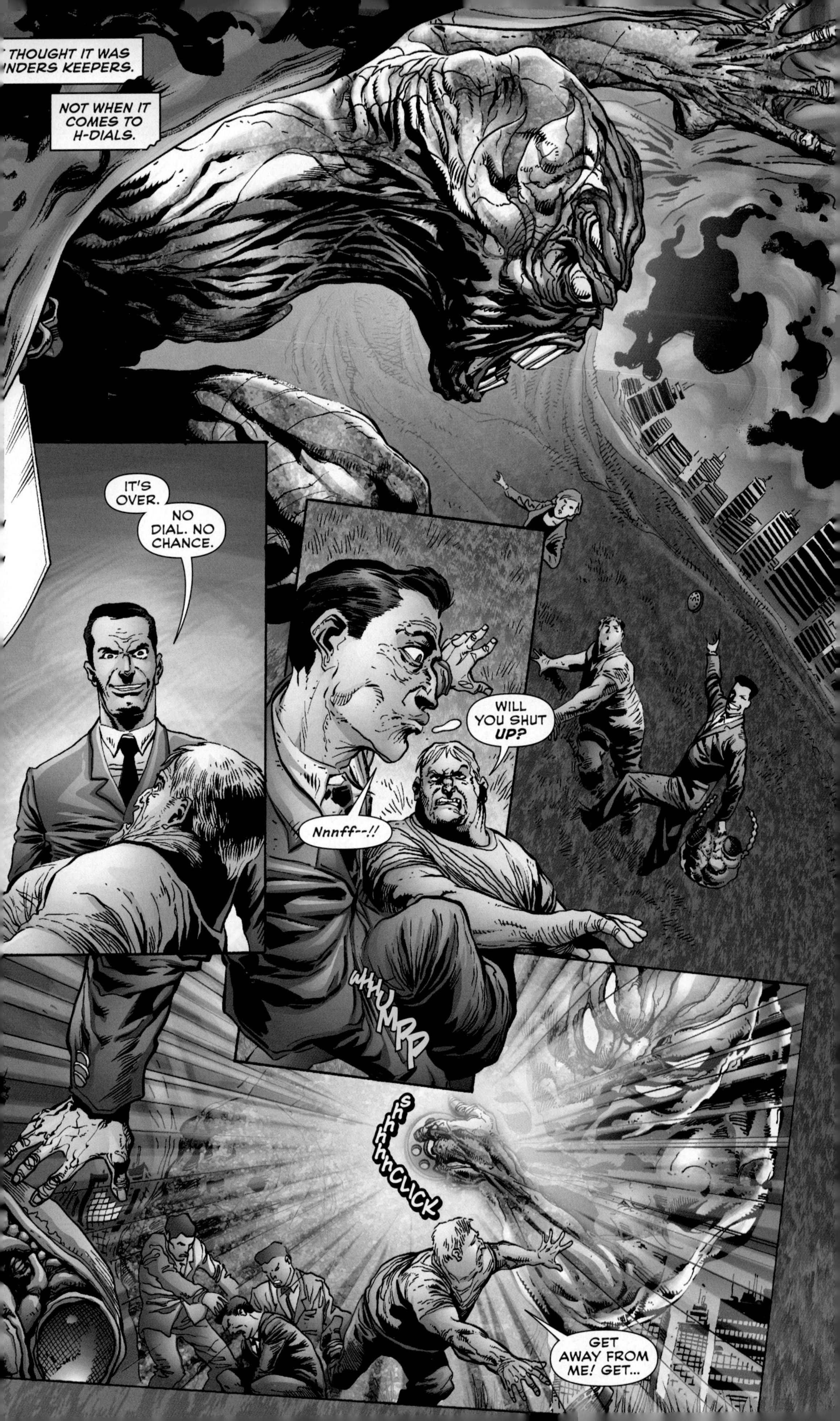
THOUGHT IT WAS
NDERS KEEPERS.
NOT WHEN IT COMES TO H-DIALS.
IT'S OVER.
NO DIAL. NO CHANCE.
WILL YOU SHUT UP?
Nnnff--!!
WHHUMPP
SHHHRRCLICK
GET AWAY FROM ME! GET...

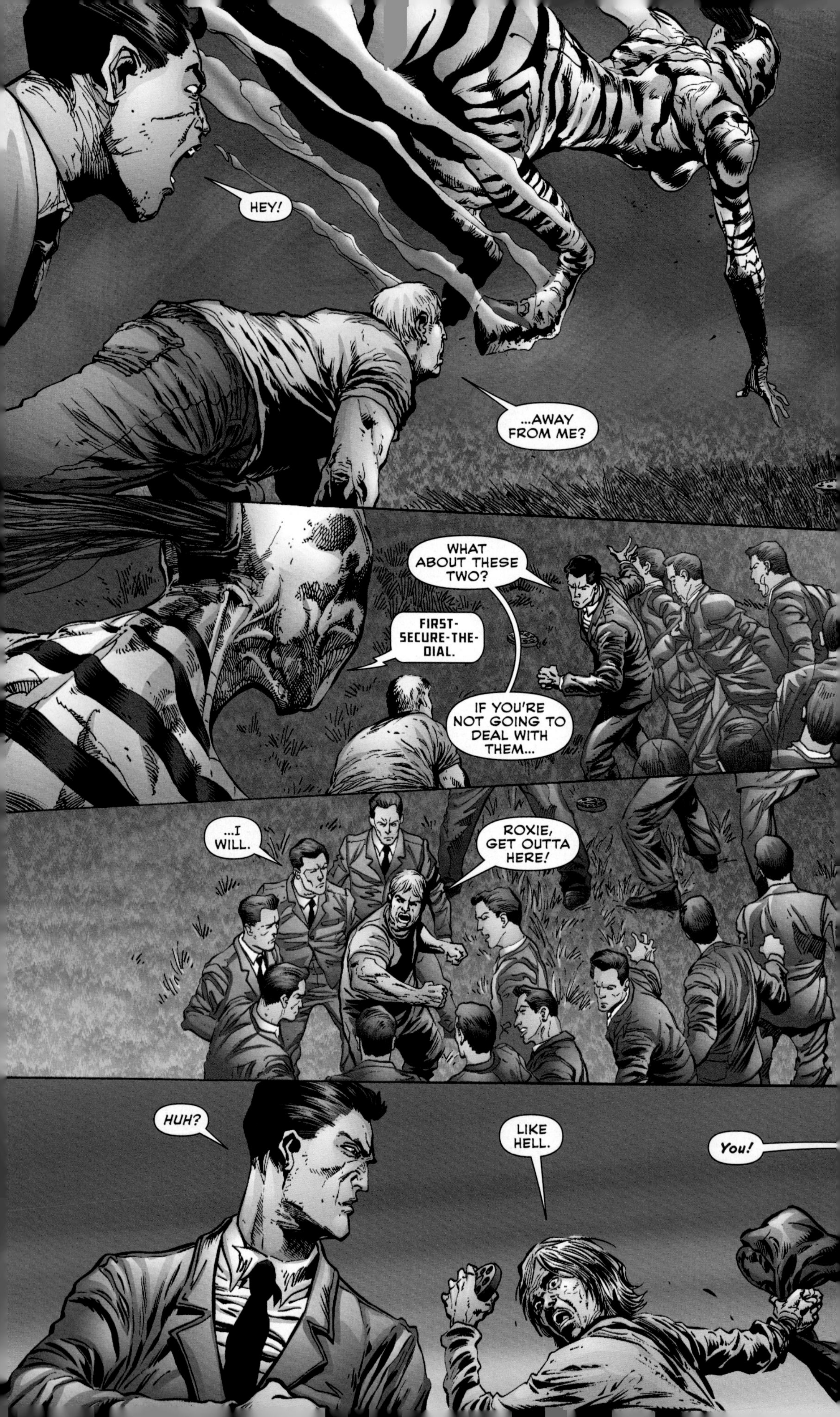
HEY!
...AWAY FROM ME?
WHAT ABOUT THESE TWO?
FIRST-SECURE-THE-DIAL.
IF YOU'RE NOT GOING TO DEAL WITH THEM...
...I WILL.
ROXIE, GET OUTTA HERE!
HUH?
LIKE HELL.
You!

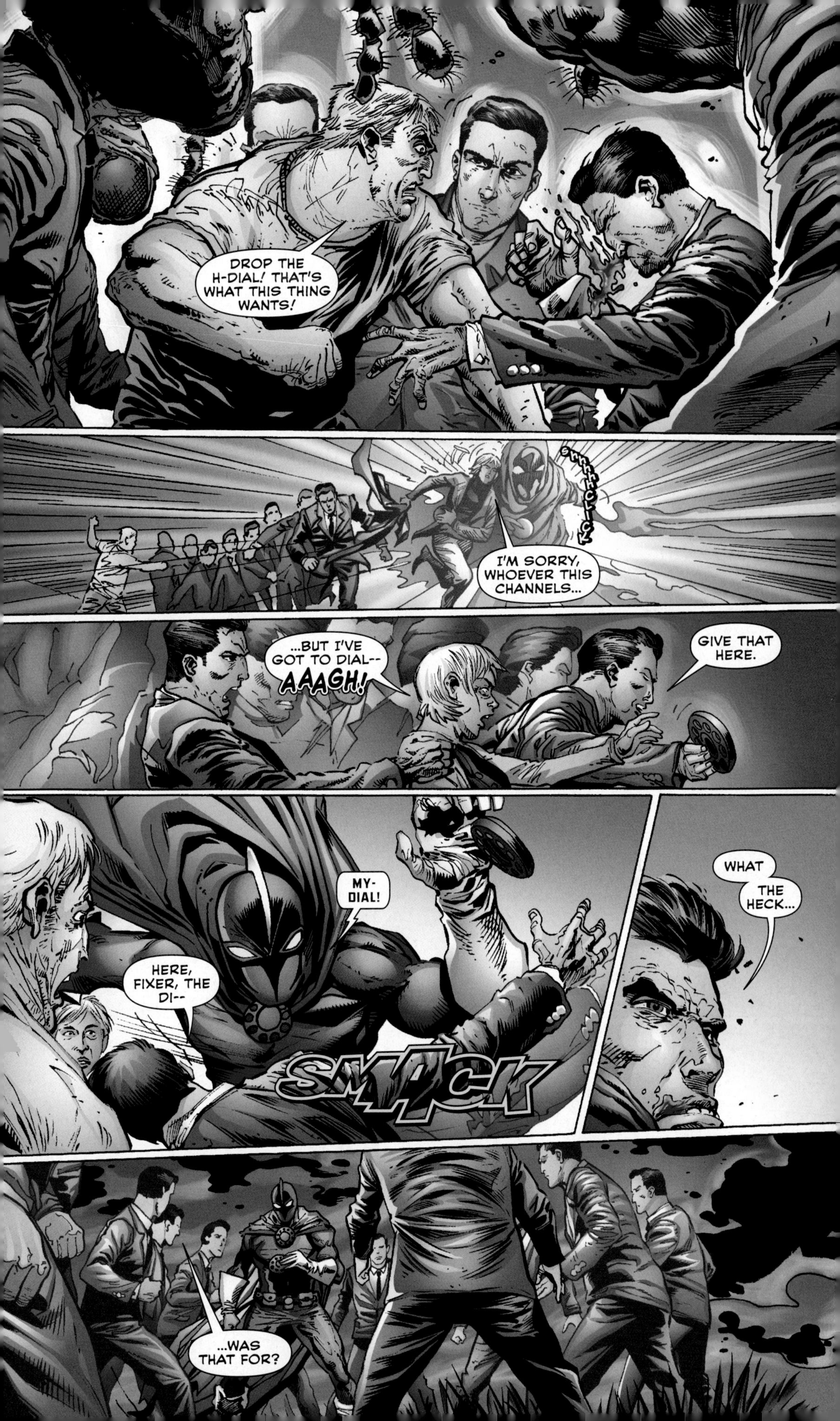
DROP THE H-DIAL! THAT'S WHAT THIS THING WANTS!
I'M SORRY, WHOEVER THIS CHANNELS...
...BUT I'VE GOT TO DIAL-- AAAGH!
GIVE THAT HERE.
MY-DIAL!
HERE, FIXER, THE DI--
SMACK
WHAT THE HECK...
...WAS THAT FOR?

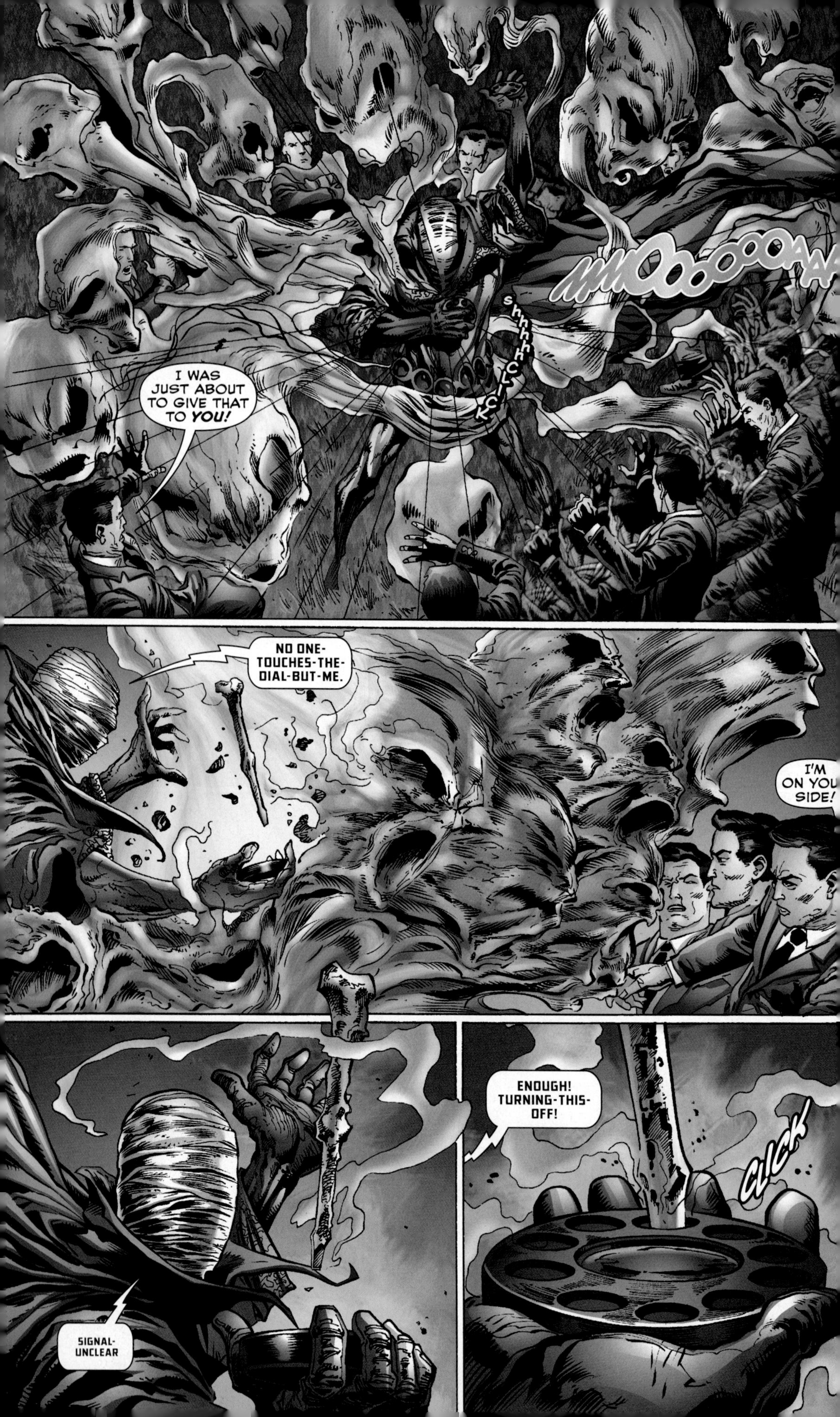

AWOOOOOOOAAA
ShhhhCLICK
I WAS JUST ABOUT TO GIVE THAT TO YOU!
NO ONE-TOUCHES-THE-DIAL-BUT-ME.
I'M ON YOU SIDE!
SIGNAL-UNCLEAR
ENOUGH! TURNING-THIS-OFF!
CLICK

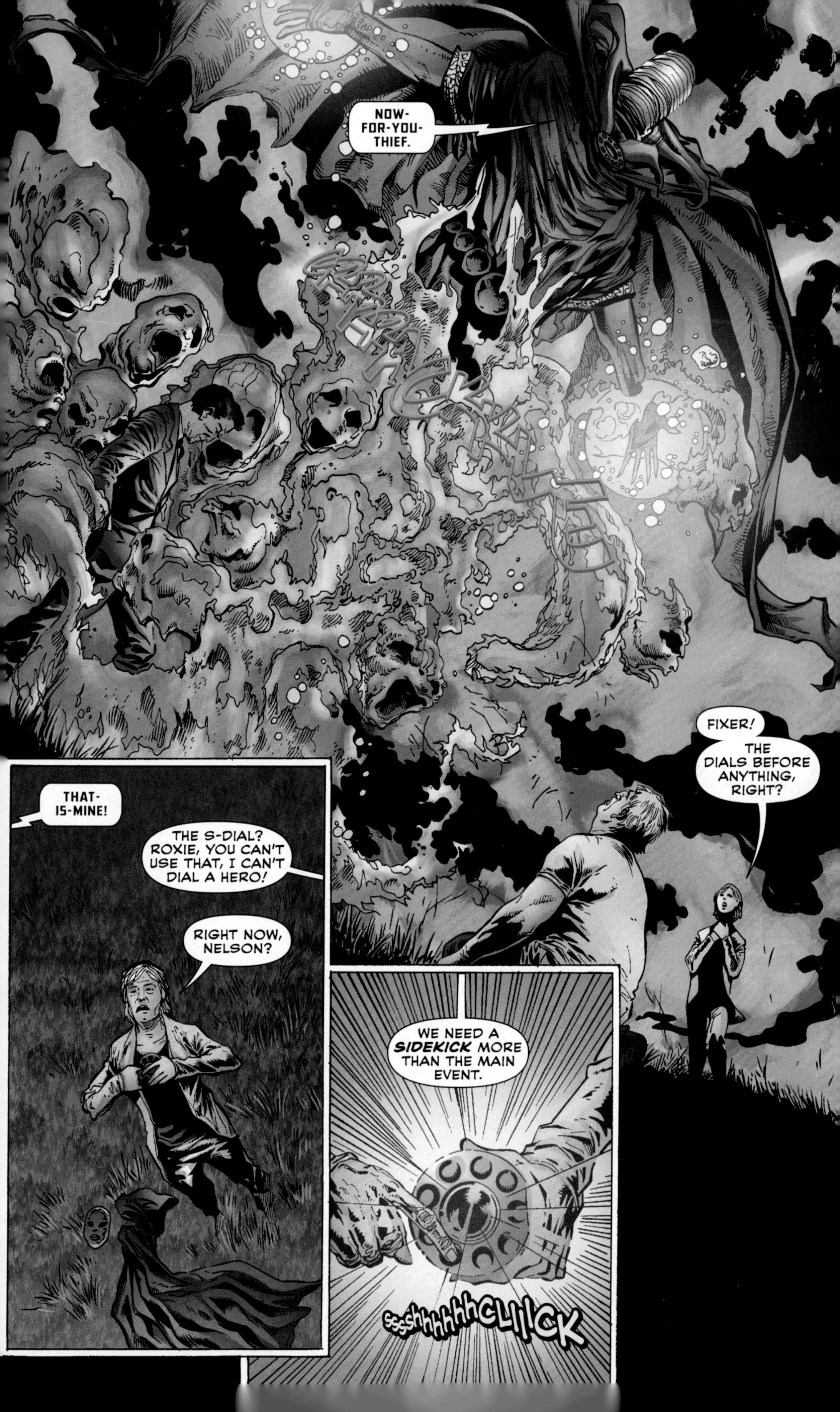
NOW-FOR-YOU-THIEF.
FIXER!
THE DIALS BEFORE ANYTHING, RIGHT?
THAT-IS-MINE!
THE S-DIAL? ROXIE, YOU CAN'T USE THAT, I CAN'T DIAL A HERO!
RIGHT NOW, NELSON?
WE NEED A *SIDEKICK* MORE THAN THE MAIN EVENT.
ssshhhhhCLIIICK

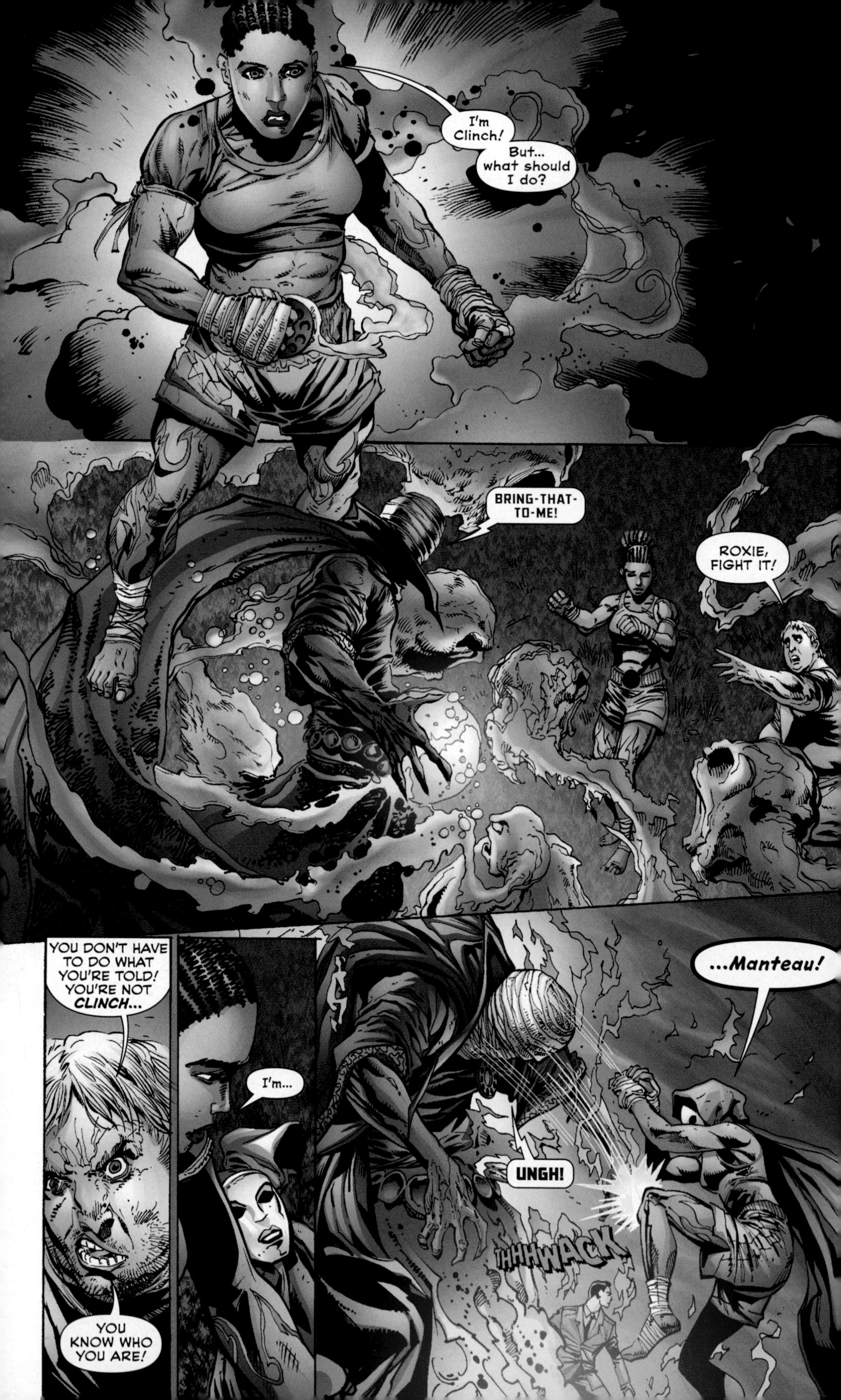
I'm Clinch!
But... what should I do?
BRING-THAT-TO-ME!
ROXIE, FIGHT IT!
YOU DON'T HAVE TO DO WHAT YOU'RE TOLD! YOU'RE NOT *CLINCH*...
YOU KNOW WHO YOU ARE!
I'm...
...*Manteau!*
UNGH!
THHHWACK

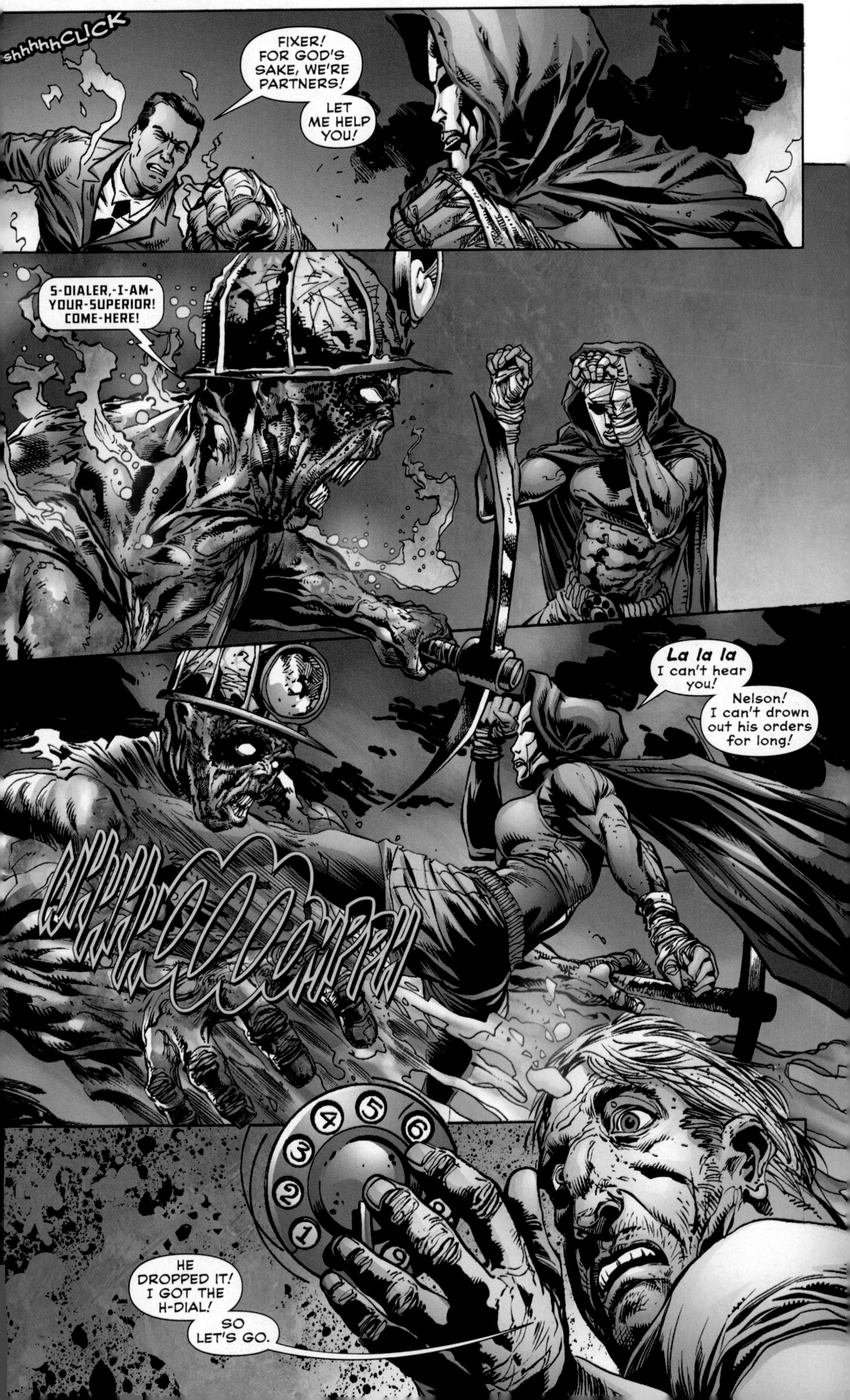

shhhhhCLICK
FIXER! FOR GOD'S SAKE, WE'RE PARTNERS!
LET ME HELP YOU!
S-DIALER,-I-AM-YOUR-SUPERIOR! COME-HERE!
La la la I can't hear you!
Nelson! I can't drown out his orders for long!
HE DROPPED IT! I GOT THE H-DIAL!
SO LET'S GO.

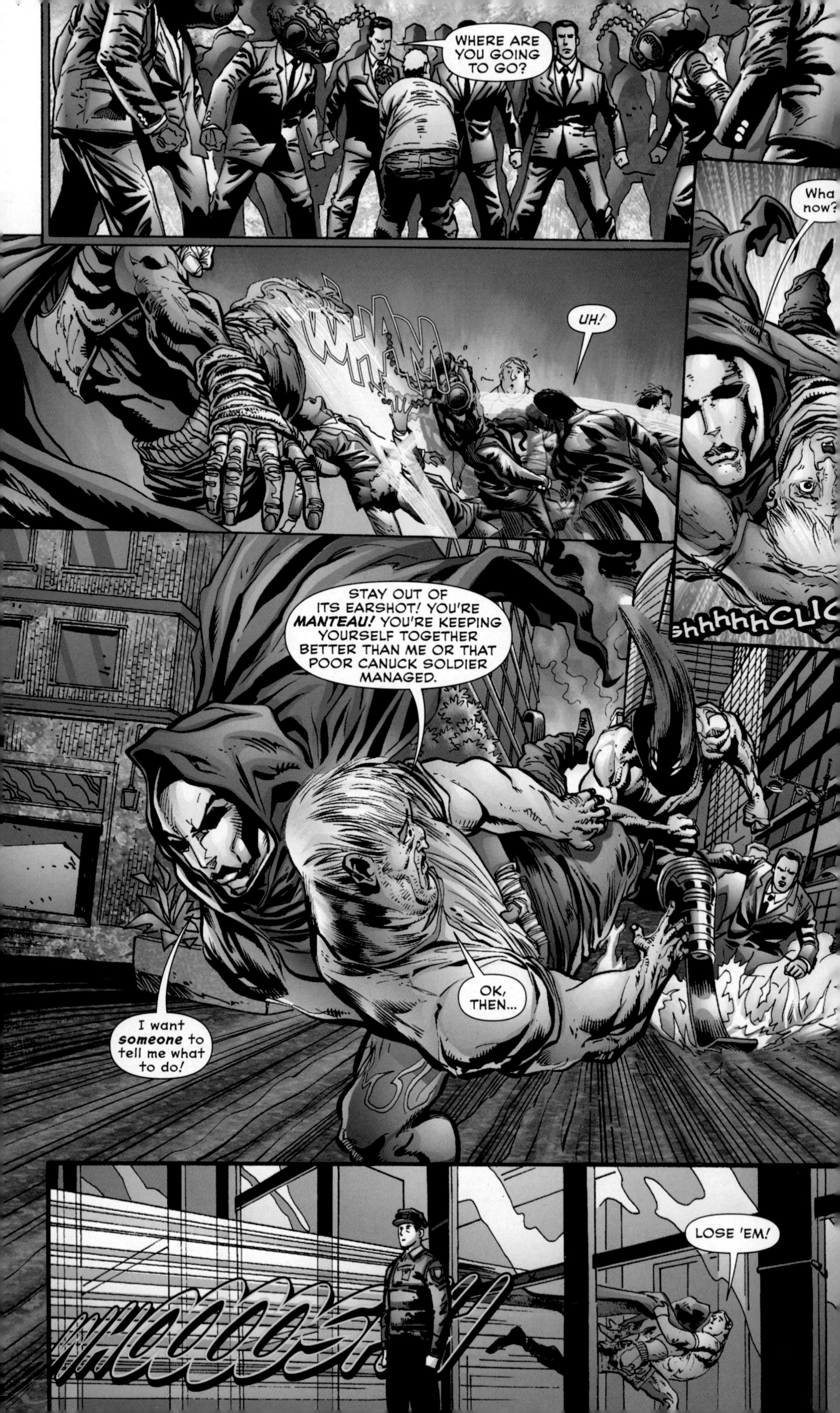
WHERE ARE YOU GOING TO GO?
Wha now?
WHAM
UH!
shhhhhCLIC
STAY OUT OF ITS EARSHOT! YOU'RE MANTEAU! YOU'RE KEEPING YOURSELF TOGETHER BETTER THAN ME OR THAT POOR CANUCK SOLDIER MANAGED.
I want someone to tell me what to do!
OK, THEN...
LOSE 'EM!

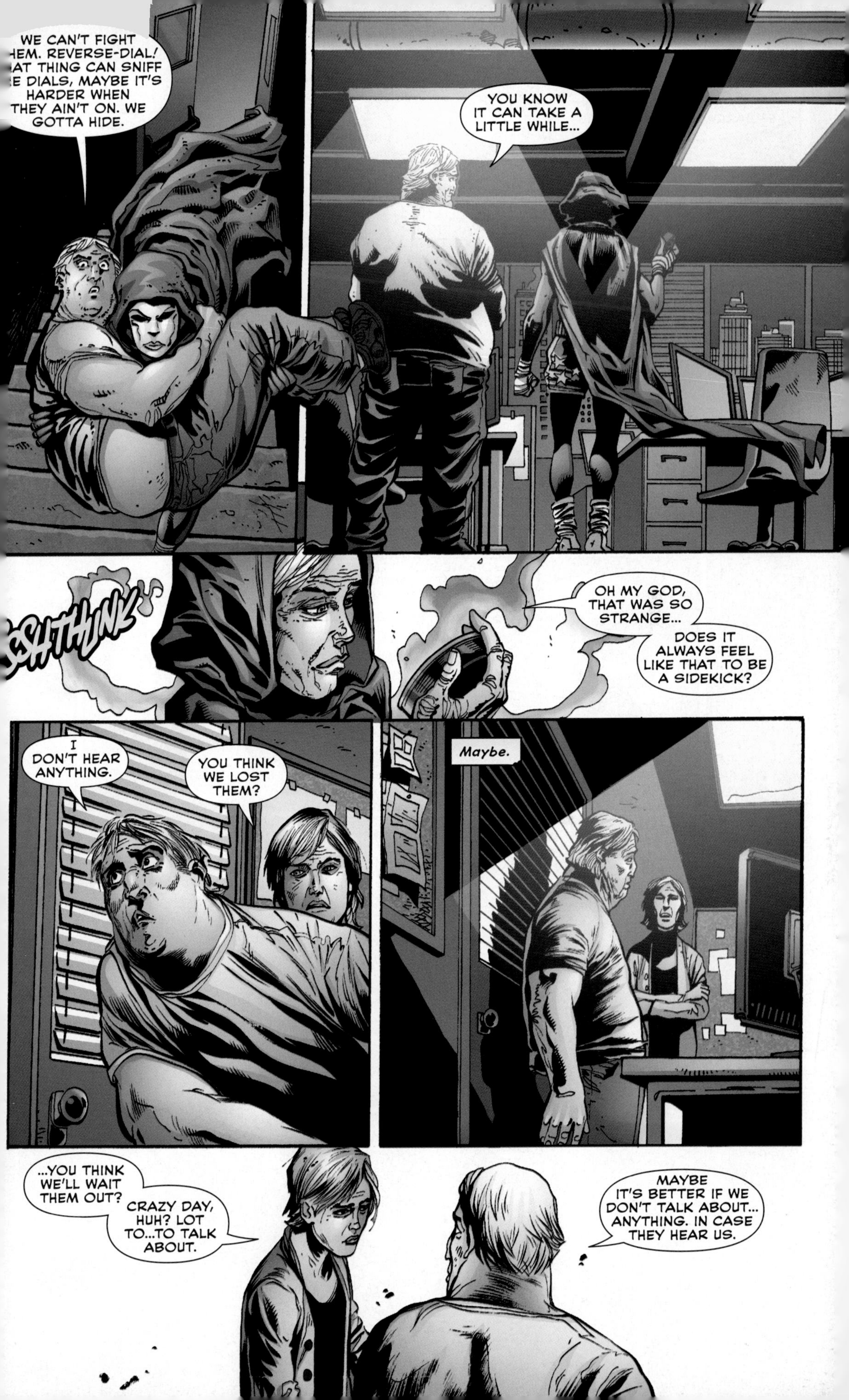

WE CAN'T FIGHT
HEM. REVERSE-DIAL!
AT THING CAN SNIFF
E DIALS, MAYBE IT'S
HARDER WHEN
THEY AIN'T ON. WE
GOTTA HIDE.
YOU KNOW IT CAN TAKE A LITTLE WHILE...
SHTHUNK
OH MY GOD, THAT WAS SO STRANGE...
DOES IT ALWAYS FEEL LIKE THAT TO BE A SIDEKICK?
I DON'T HEAR ANYTHING.
YOU THINK WE LOST THEM?
Maybe.
...YOU THINK WE'LL WAIT THEM OUT?
CRAZY DAY, HUH? LOT TO...TO TALK ABOUT.
MAYBE IT'S BETTER IF WE DON'T TALK ABOUT... ANYTHING. IN CASE THEY HEAR US.

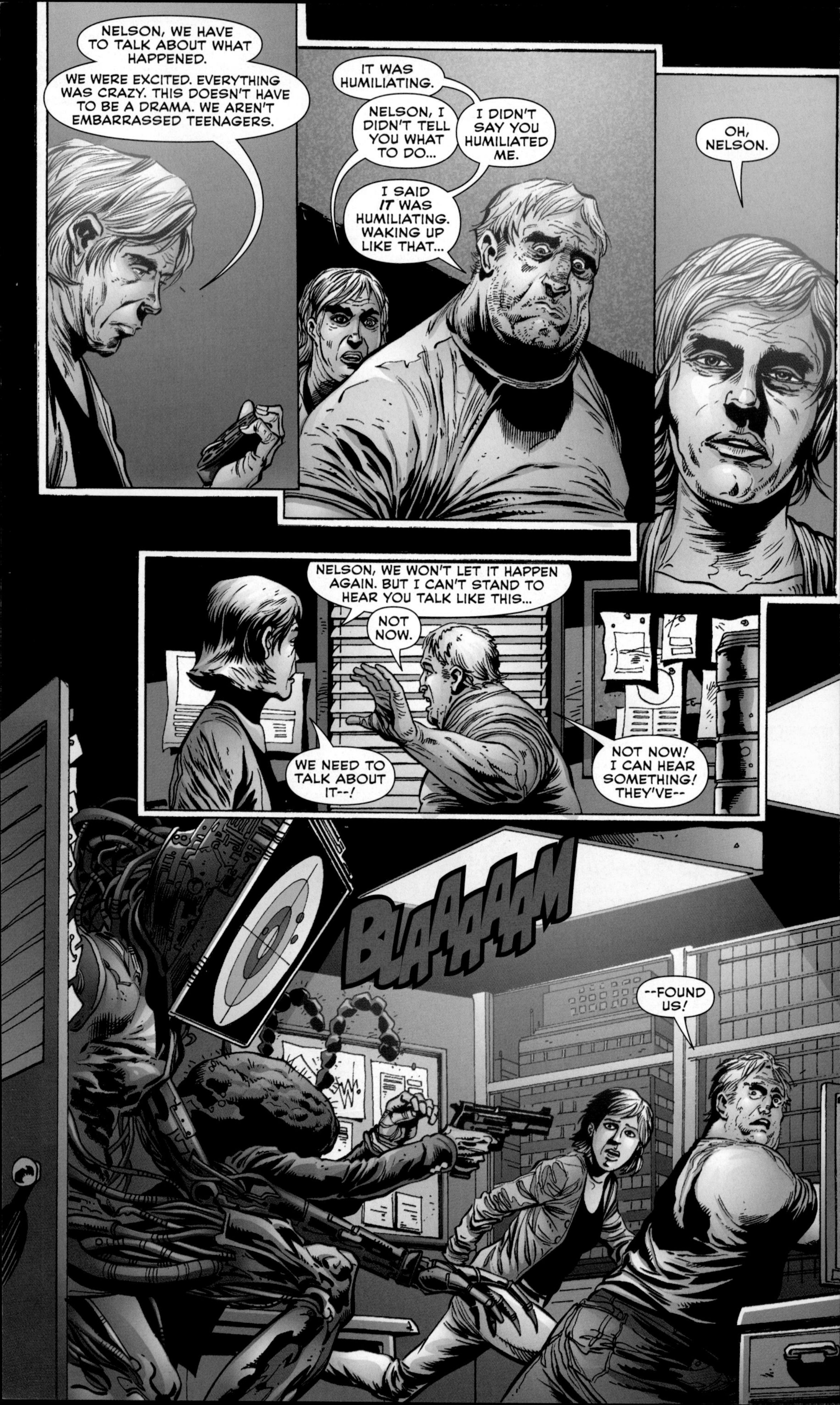
NELSON, WE HAVE TO TALK ABOUT WHAT HAPPENED.
WE WERE EXCITED. EVERYTHING WAS CRAZY. THIS DOESN'T HAVE TO BE A DRAMA. WE AREN'T EMBARRASSED TEENAGERS.
IT WAS HUMILIATING.
NELSON, I DIDN'T TELL YOU WHAT TO DO...
I DIDN'T SAY YOU HUMILIATED ME.
I SAID *IT* WAS HUMILIATING. WAKING UP LIKE THAT...
OH, NELSON.
NELSON, WE WON'T LET IT HAPPEN AGAIN. BUT I CAN'T STAND TO HEAR YOU TALK LIKE THIS...
NOT NOW.
WE NEED TO TALK ABOUT IT--!
NOT NOW! I CAN HEAR SOMETHING! THEY'VE--
BLAAAAAM
--FOUND US!

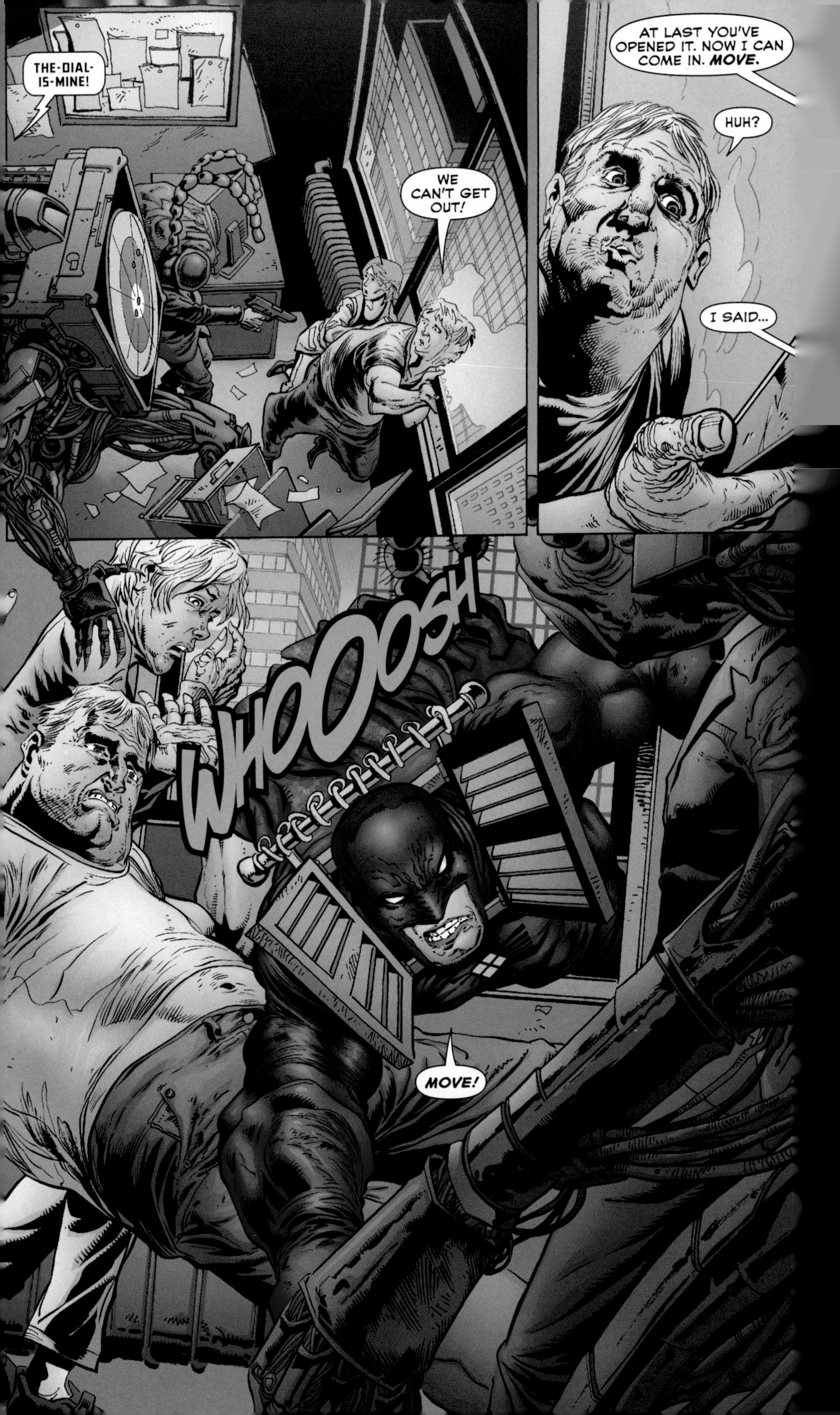
THE-DIAL-IS-MINE!
WE CAN'T GET OUT!
AT LAST YOU'VE OPENED IT. NOW I CAN COME IN. MOVE.
HUH?
I SAID...
WHOOOOSH
MOVE!

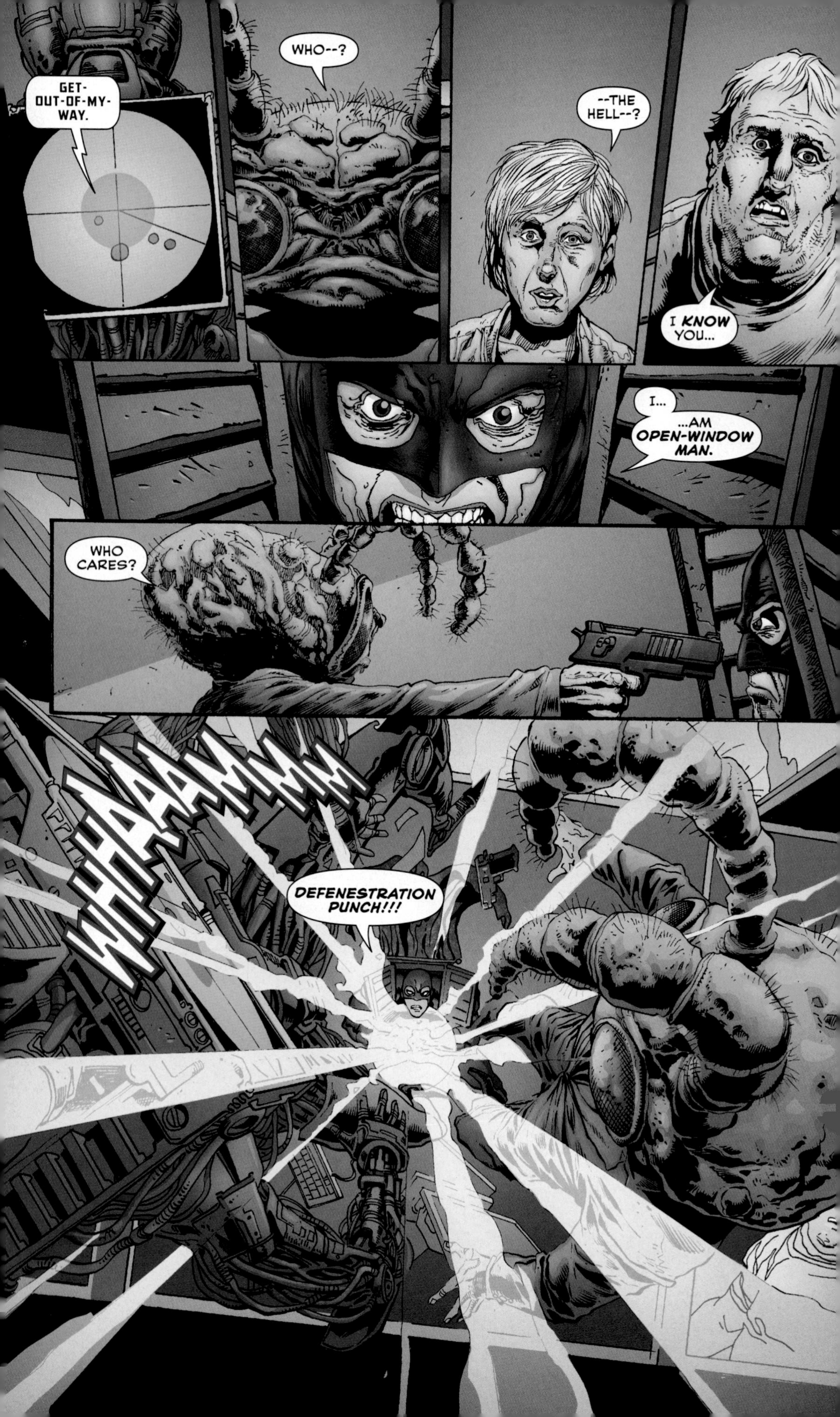
GET-
OUT-OF-MY-
WAY.
WHO--?
--THE
HELL--?
I KNOW
YOU...
I...
...AM
OPEN-WINDOW
MAN.
WHO
CARES?
WHHAAMMM
DEFENESTRATION
PUNCH!!!

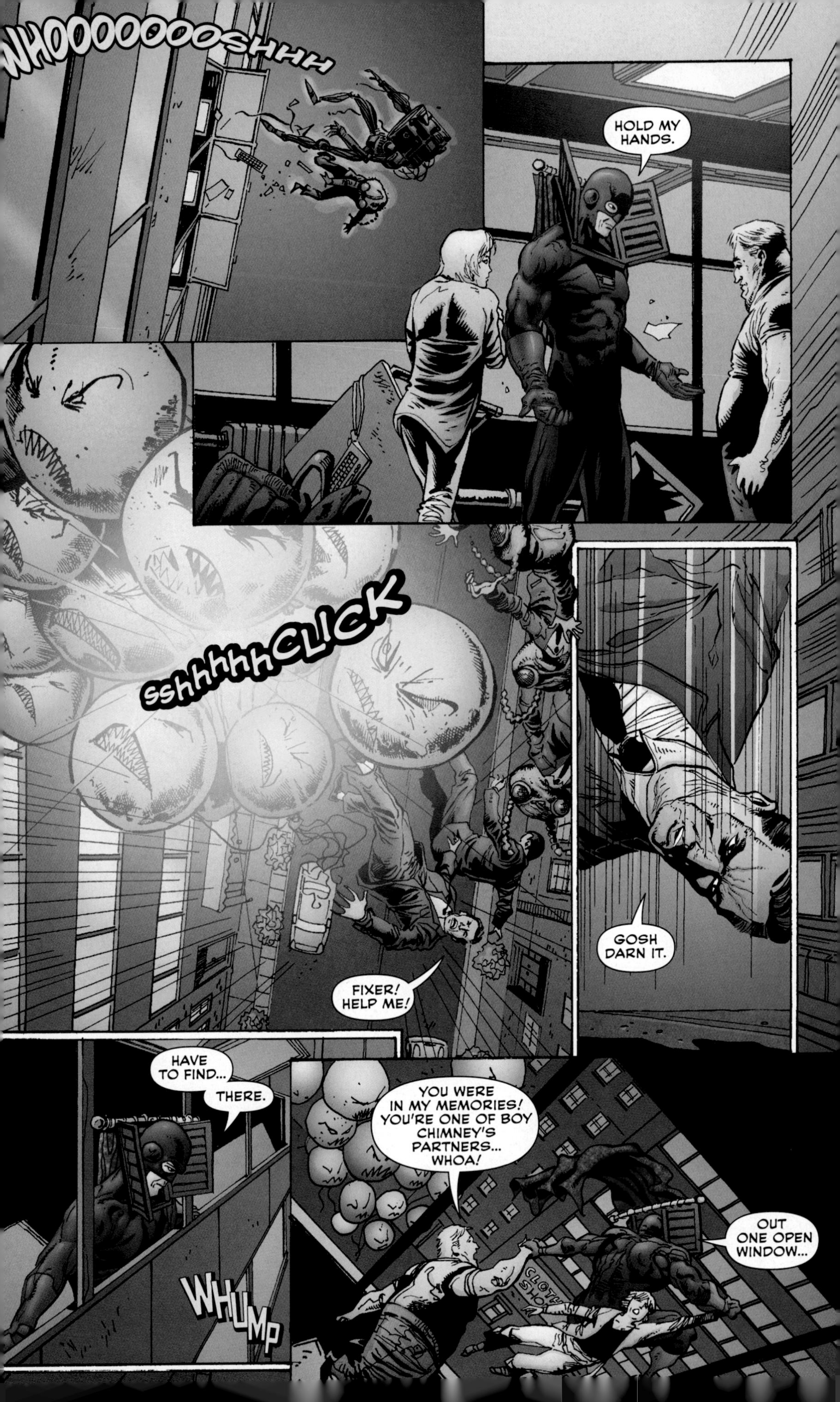
WHOOOOOOOOSHHH
HOLD MY HANDS.
sshhhhhCLICK
FIXER! HELP ME!
GOSH DARN IT.
HAVE TO FIND...
THERE.
WHUMP
YOU WERE IN MY MEMORIES! YOU'RE ONE OF BOY CHIMNEY'S PARTNERS... WHOA!
OUT ONE OPEN WINDOW...

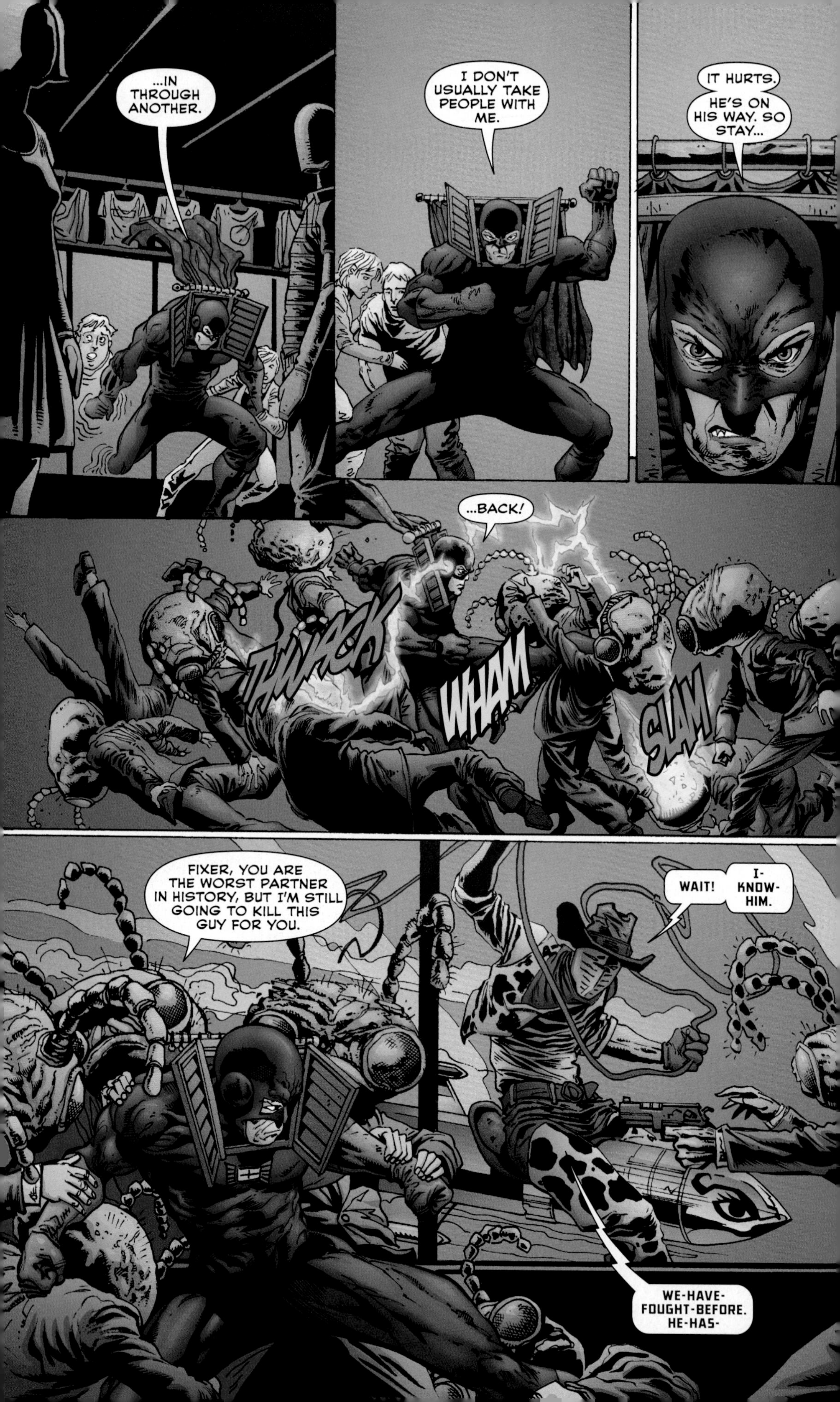
...IN THROUGH ANOTHER.
I DON'T USUALLY TAKE PEOPLE WITH ME.
IT HURTS.
HE'S ON HIS WAY. SO STAY...
...BACK!
THWACK
WHAM
SLAM
FIXER, YOU ARE THE WORST PARTNER IN HISTORY, BUT I'M STILL GOING TO KILL THIS GUY FOR YOU.
WAIT!
I-KNOW-HIM.
WE-HAVE-FOUGHT-BEFORE. HE-HAS-

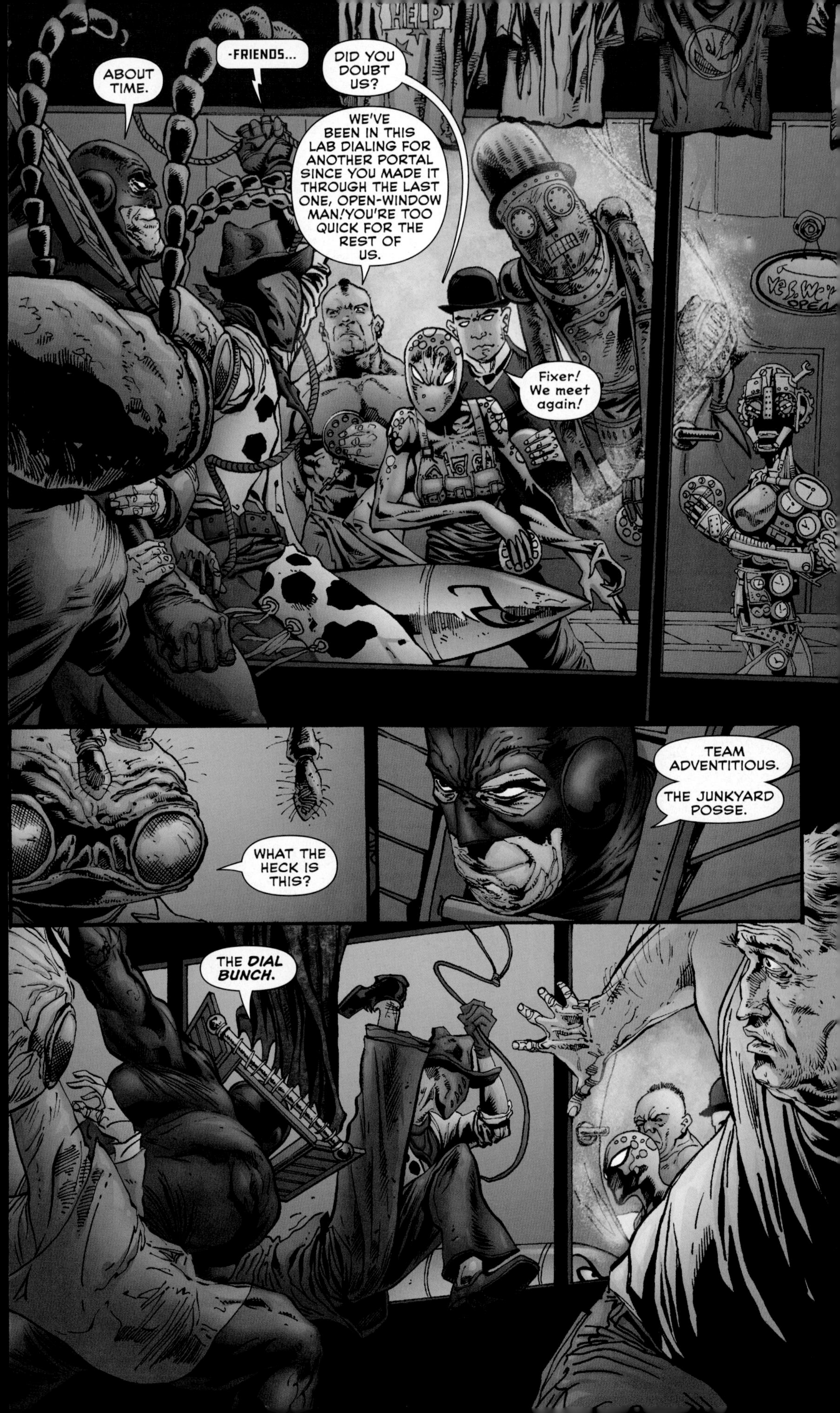

ABOUT TIME.
-FRIENDS...
DID YOU DOUBT US?
WE'VE BEEN IN THIS LAB DIALING FOR ANOTHER PORTAL SINCE YOU MADE IT THROUGH THE LAST ONE, OPEN-WINDOW MAN! YOU'RE TOO QUICK FOR THE REST OF US.
HELP
Fixer! We meet again!
WHAT THE HECK IS THIS?
TEAM ADVENTITIOUS.
THE JUNKYARD POSSE.
THE *DIAL BUNCH*.

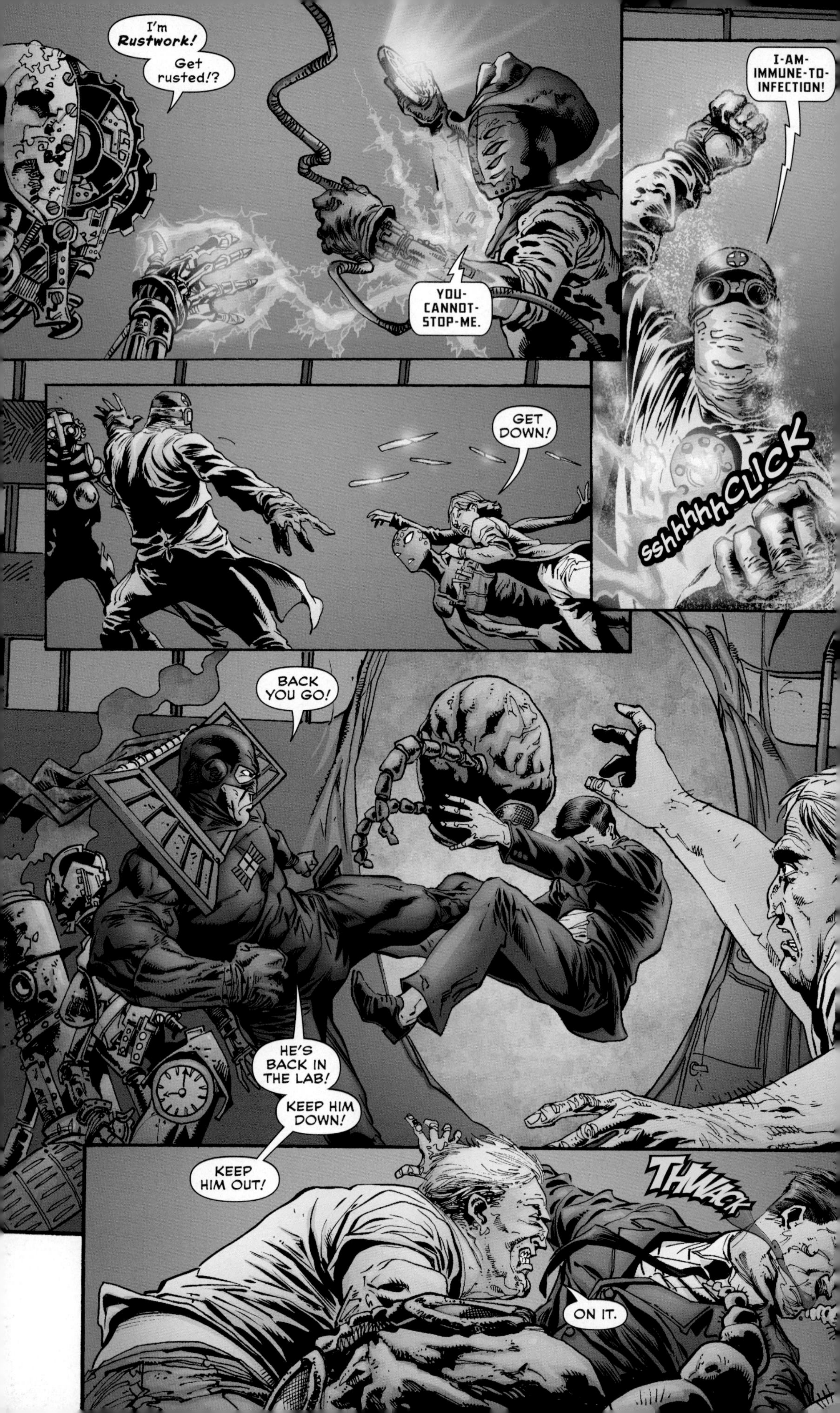
I'm *Rustwork!* Get rusted!?
YOU-CANNOT-STOP-ME.
I-AM-IMMUNE-TO-INFECTION!
sshhhhhCLICK
GET DOWN!
BACK YOU GO!
HE'S BACK IN THE LAB!
KEEP HIM DOWN!
KEEP HIM OUT!
THWACK
ON IT.

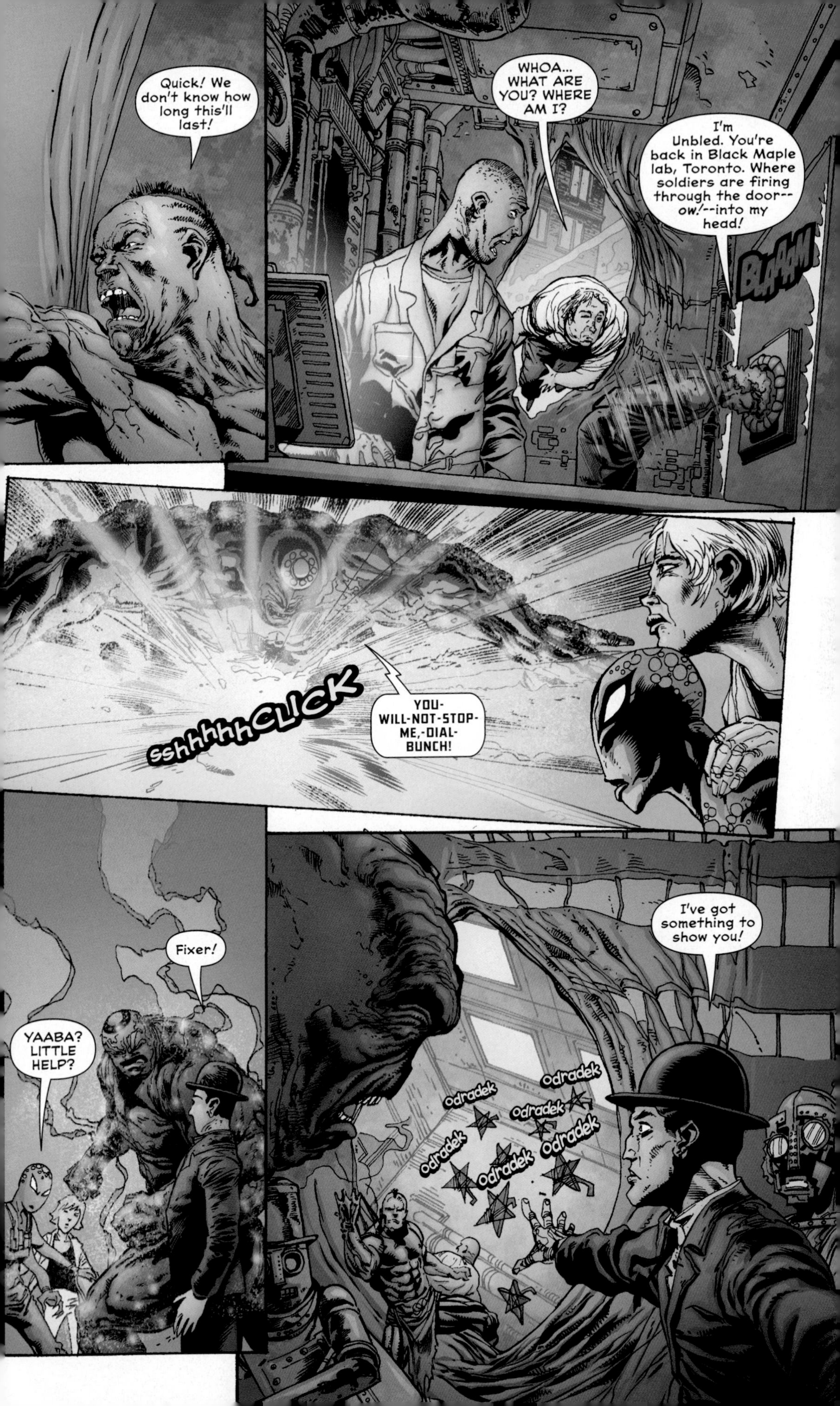

Quick! We don't know how long this'll last!
WHOA... WHAT ARE YOU? WHERE AM I?
I'm Unbled. You're back in Black Maple lab, Toronto. Where soldiers are firing through the door--ow!--into my head!
BLAAAM
SSHHHHCLICK
YOU-WILL-NOT-STOP-ME,-DIAL-BUNCH!
Fixer!
YAABA? LITTLE HELP?
I've got something to show you!
odradek
odradek
odradek
odradek
odradek
odradek

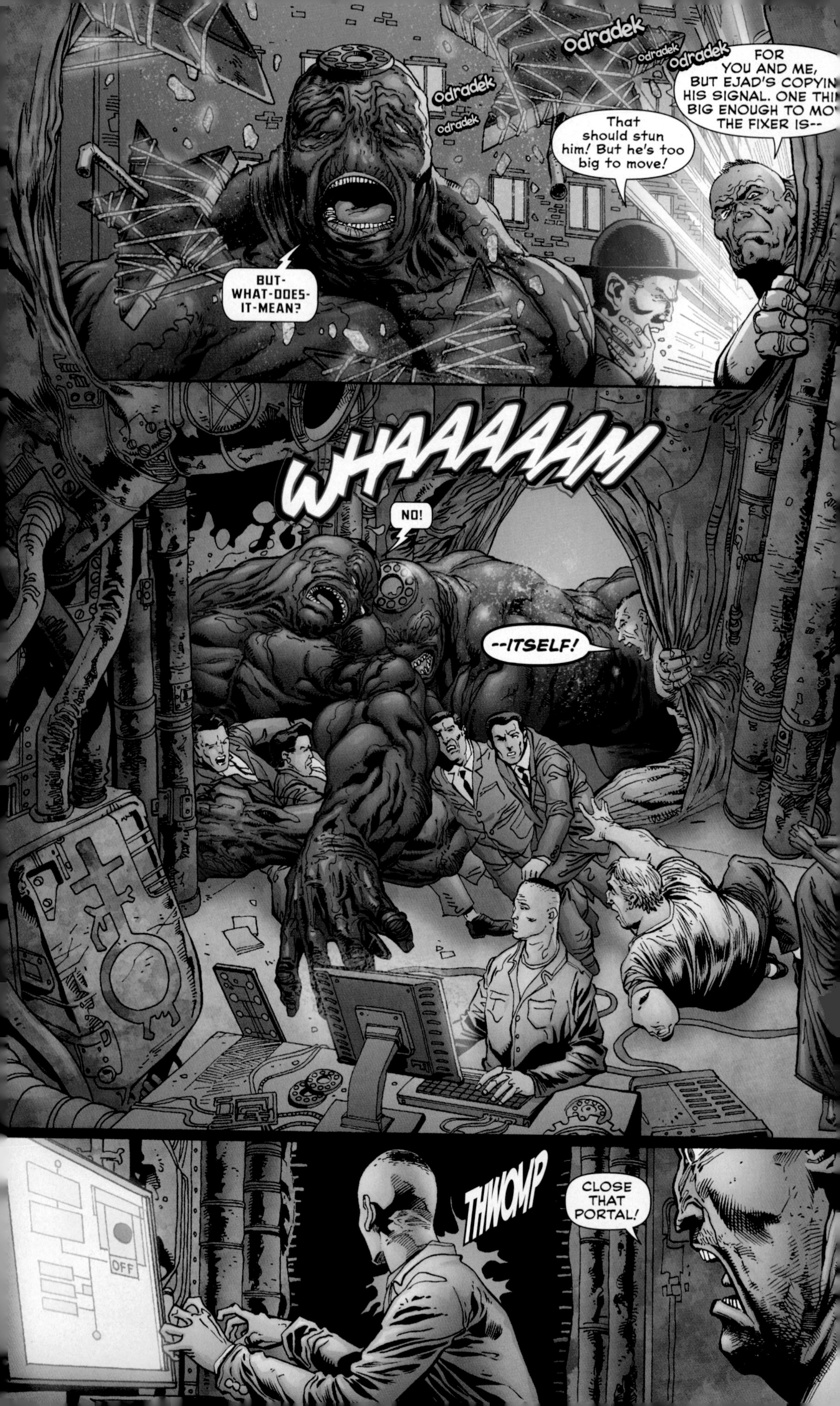
odradek
odradek
odradek
odradek
odradek
BUT-WHAT-DOES-IT-MEAN?
That should stun him! But he's too big to move!
FOR YOU AND ME, BUT EJAD'S COPYIN HIS SIGNAL. ONE THI BIG ENOUGH TO MO THE FIXER IS--
WHAAAAAM
NO!
--ITSELF!
OFF
THWOMP
CLOSE THAT PORTAL!

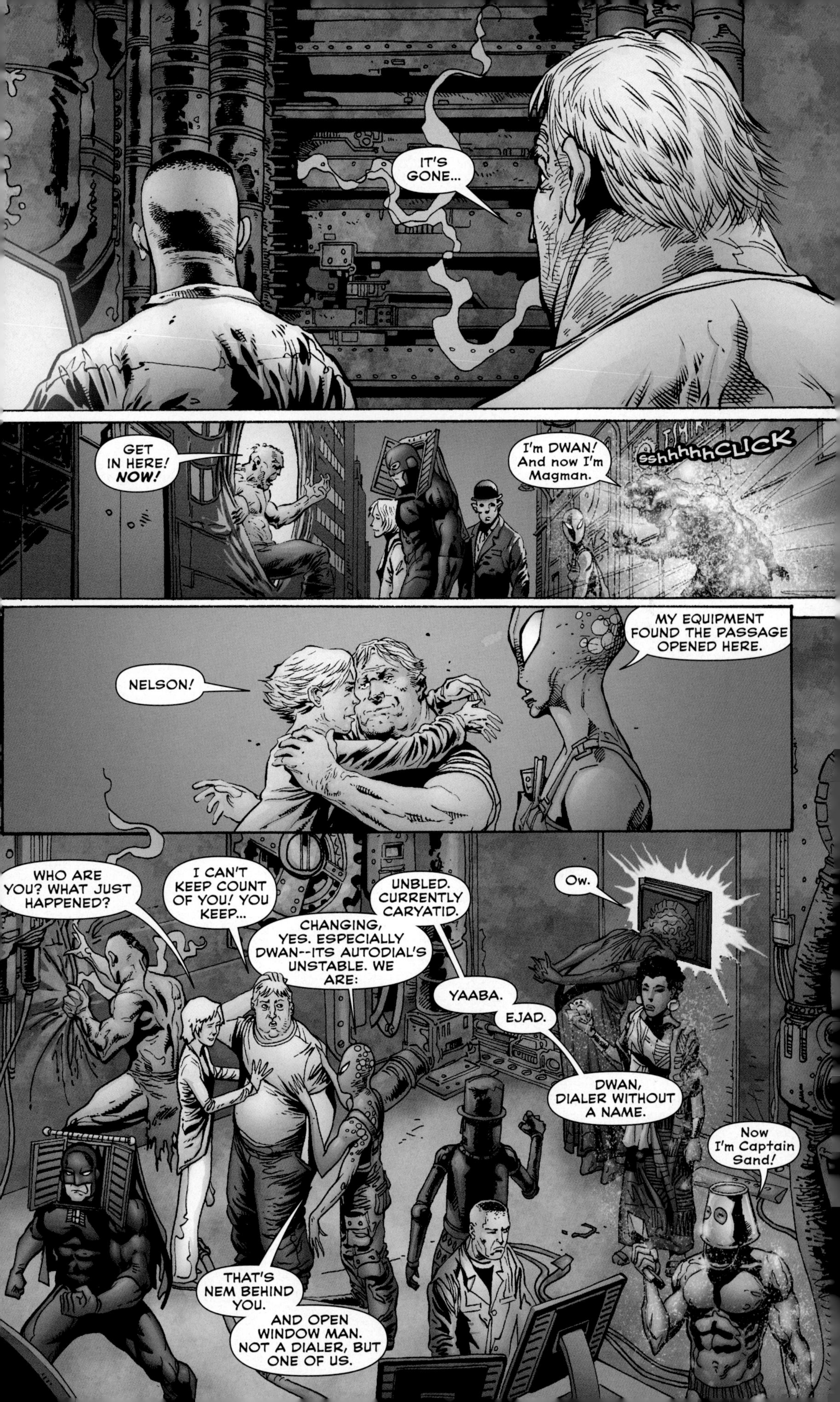
IT'S GONE...
GET IN HERE! *NOW!*
I'm DWAN! And now I'm Magman.
sshhhhhCLICK
NELSON!
MY EQUIPMENT FOUND THE PASSAGE OPENED HERE.
WHO ARE YOU? WHAT JUST HAPPENED?
I CAN'T KEEP COUNT OF YOU! YOU KEEP...
CHANGING, YES. ESPECIALLY DWAN--ITS AUTODIAL'S UNSTABLE. WE ARE:
UNBLED. CURRENTLY CARYATID.
YAABA.
EJAD.
DWAN, DIALER WITHOUT A NAME.
THAT'S NEM BEHIND YOU.
AND OPEN WINDOW MAN. NOT A DIALER, BUT ONE OF US.
Ow.
Now I'm Captain Sand!

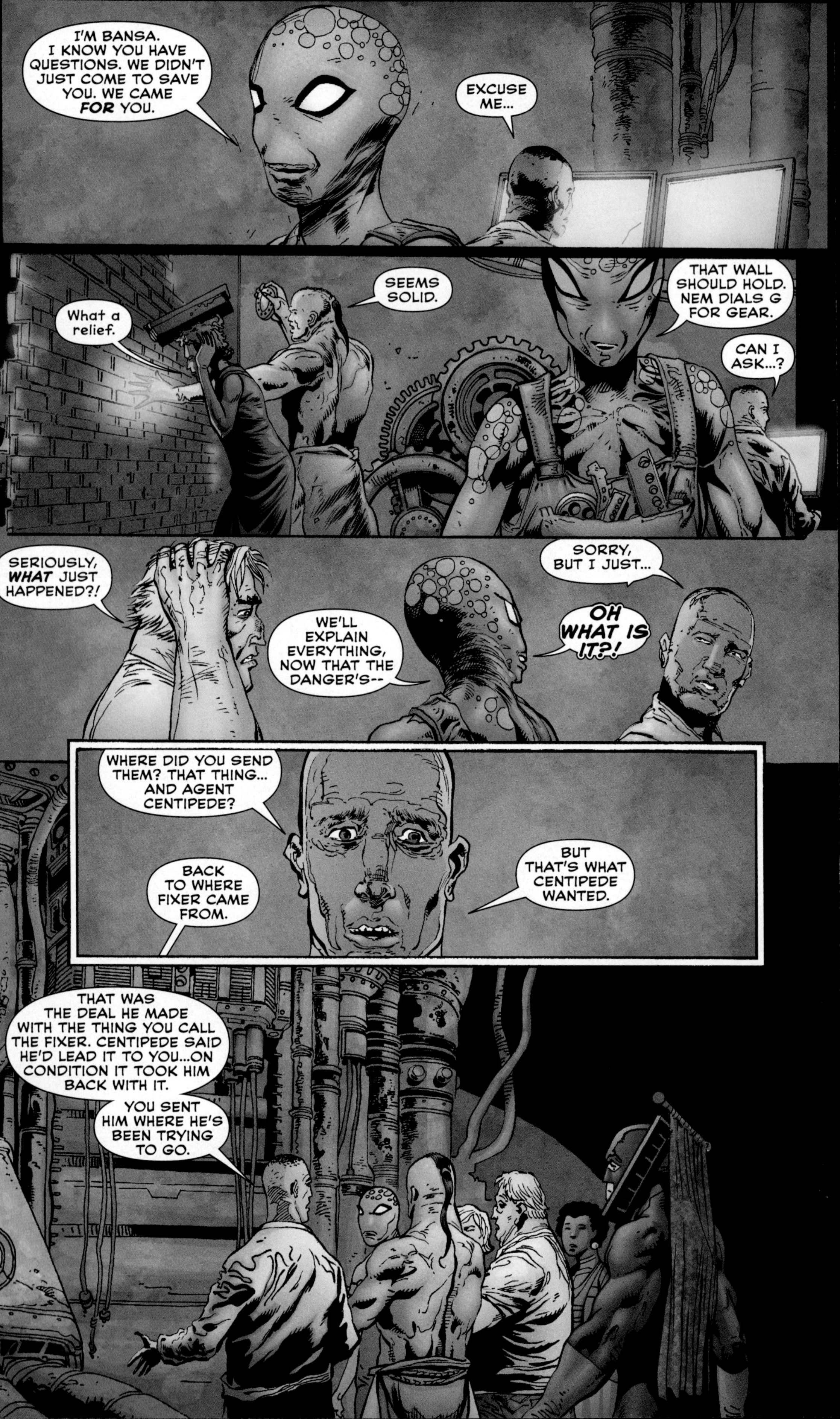
I'M BANSA. I KNOW YOU HAVE QUESTIONS. WE DIDN'T JUST COME TO SAVE YOU. WE CAME FOR YOU.
EXCUSE ME...
What a relief.
SEEMS SOLID.
THAT WALL SHOULD HOLD. NEM DIALS G FOR GEAR.
CAN I ASK...?
SERIOUSLY, WHAT JUST HAPPENED?!
WE'LL EXPLAIN EVERYTHING, NOW THAT THE DANGER'S--
SORRY, BUT I JUST...
OH WHAT IS IT?!
WHERE DID YOU SEND THEM? THAT THING... AND AGENT CENTIPEDE?
BACK TO WHERE FIXER CAME FROM.
BUT THAT'S WHAT CENTIPEDE WANTED.
THAT WAS THE DEAL HE MADE WITH THE THING YOU CALL THE FIXER. CENTIPEDE SAID HE'D LEAD IT TO YOU...ON CONDITION IT TOOK HIM BACK WITH IT.
YOU SENT HIM WHERE HE'S BEEN TRYING TO GO.

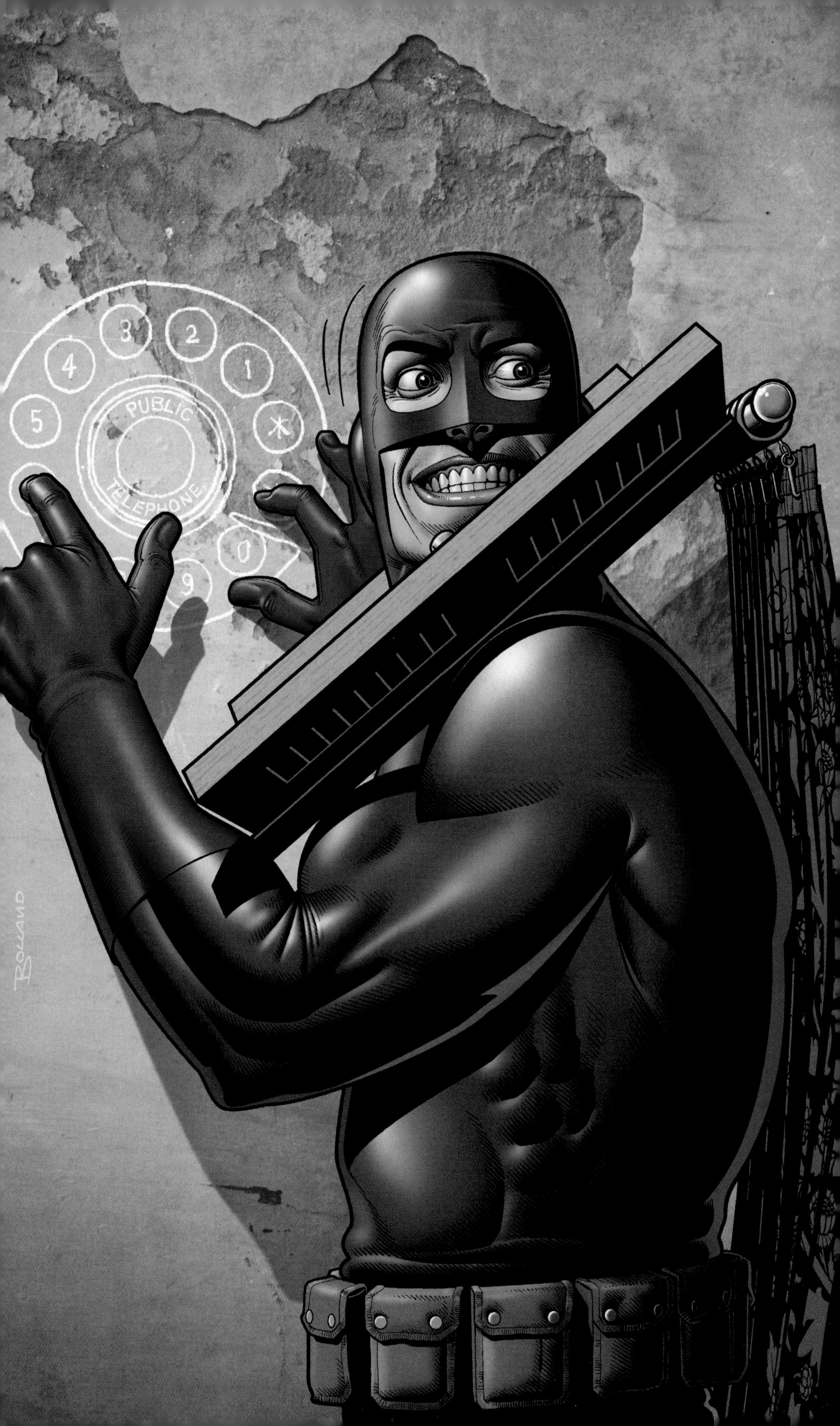
PUBLIC
TELEPHONE.
BOLLAND

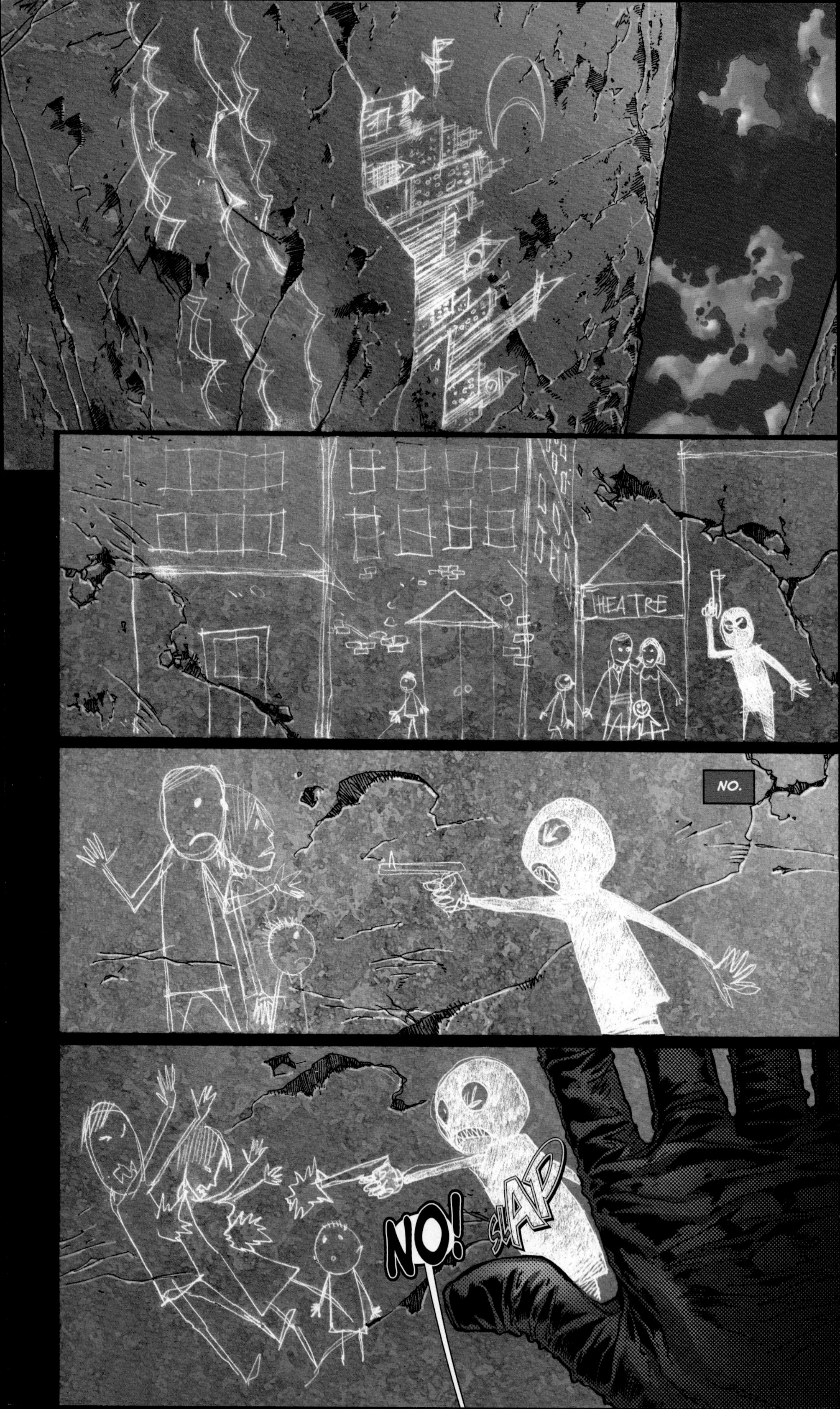

THEATRE
NO.
NO!
SLAP

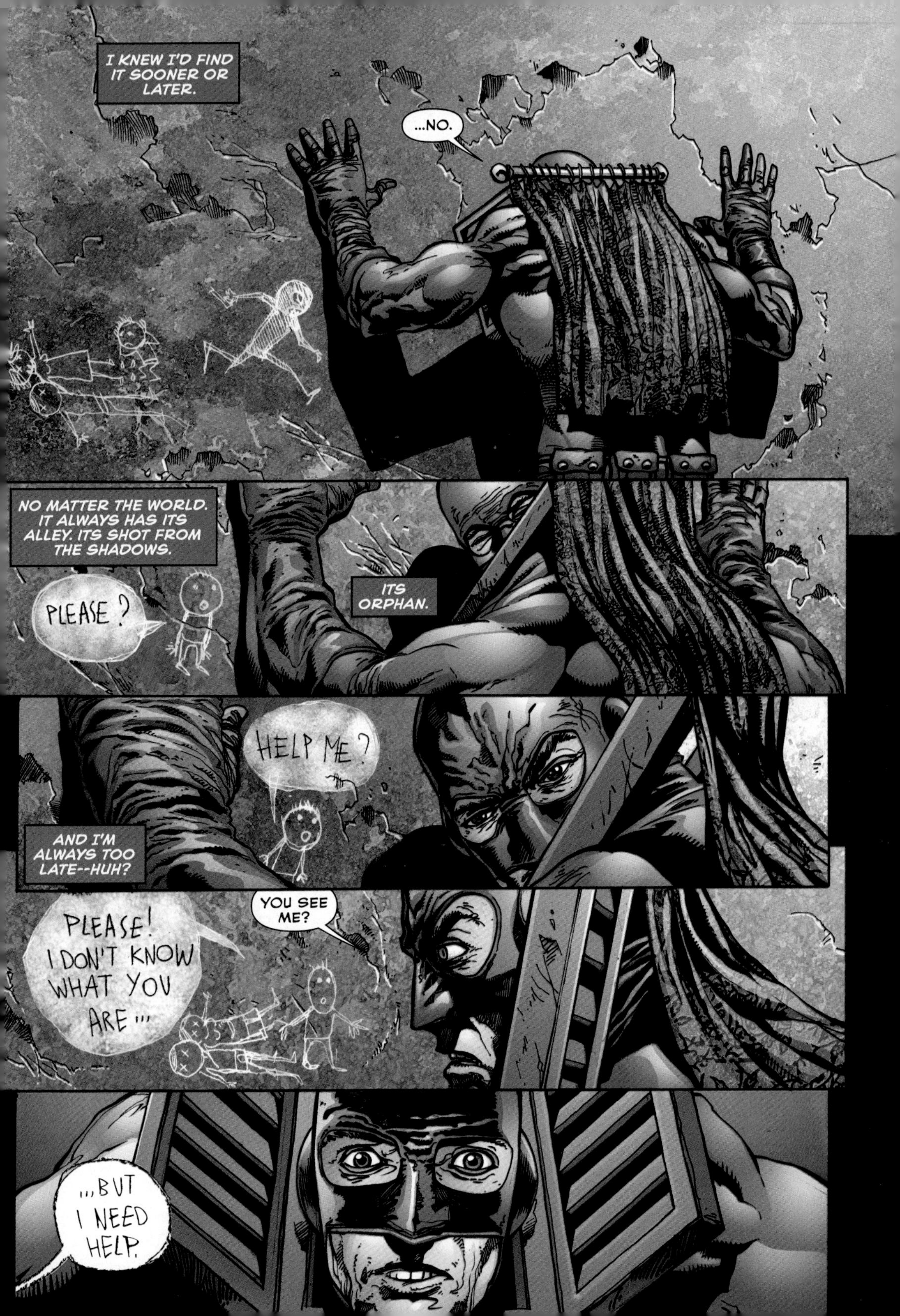

I KNEW I'D FIND IT SOONER OR LATER.
...NO.
NO MATTER THE WORLD. IT ALWAYS HAS ITS ALLEY. ITS SHOT FROM THE SHADOWS.
PLEASE?
ITS ORPHAN.
HELP ME?
AND I'M ALWAYS TOO LATE--HUH?
PLEASE! I DON'T KNOW WHAT YOU ARE...
YOU SEE ME?
...BUT I NEED HELP.

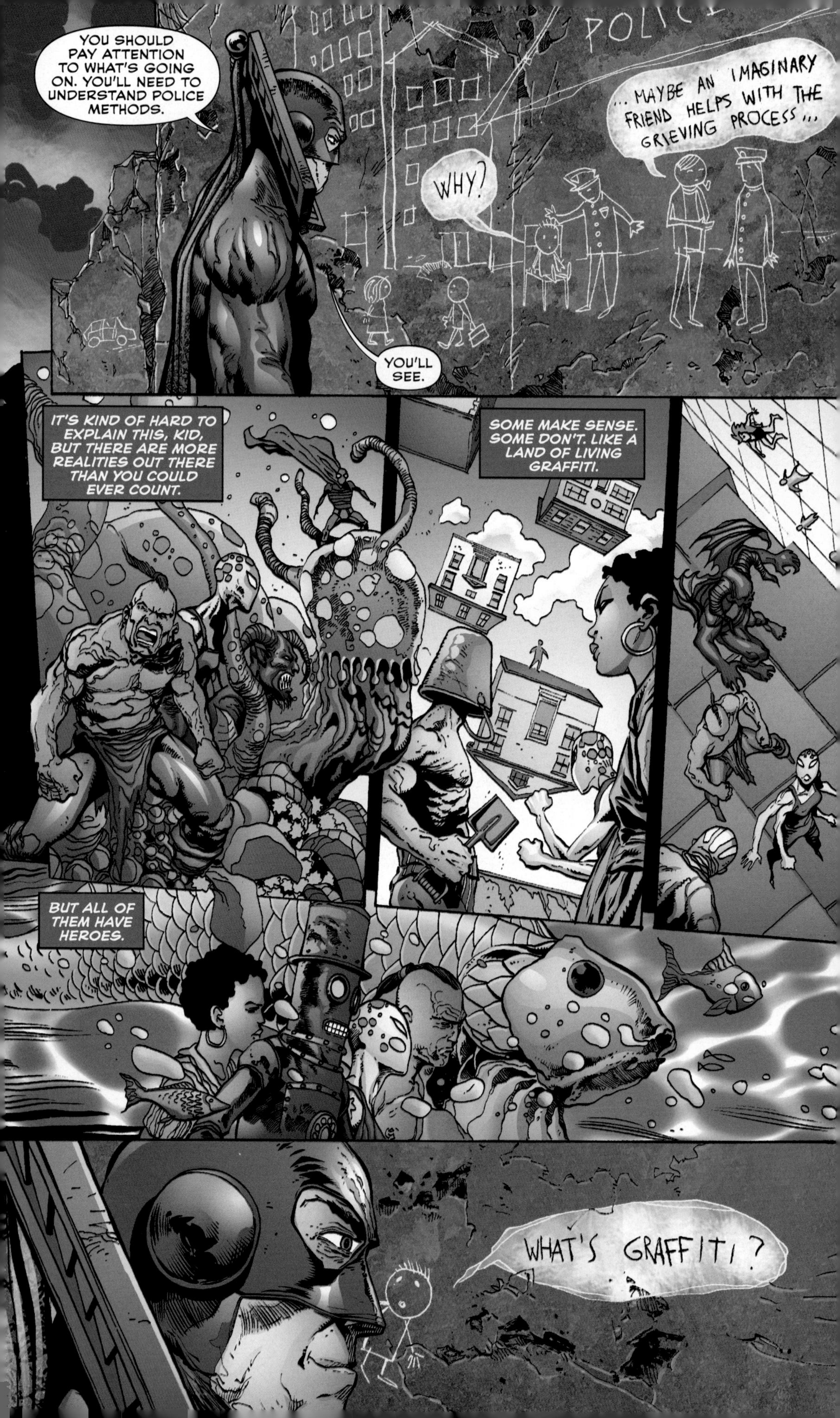
YOU SHOULD PAY ATTENTION TO WHAT'S GOING ON. YOU'LL NEED TO UNDERSTAND POLICE METHODS.
POLIC
WHY?
...MAYBE AN IMAGINARY FRIEND HELPS WITH THE GRIEVING PROCESS...
YOU'LL SEE.
IT'S KIND OF HARD TO EXPLAIN THIS, KID, BUT THERE ARE MORE REALITIES OUT THERE THAN YOU COULD EVER COUNT.
SOME MAKE SENSE. SOME DON'T. LIKE A LAND OF LIVING GRAFFITI.
BUT ALL OF THEM HAVE HEROES.
WHAT'S GRAFFITI?

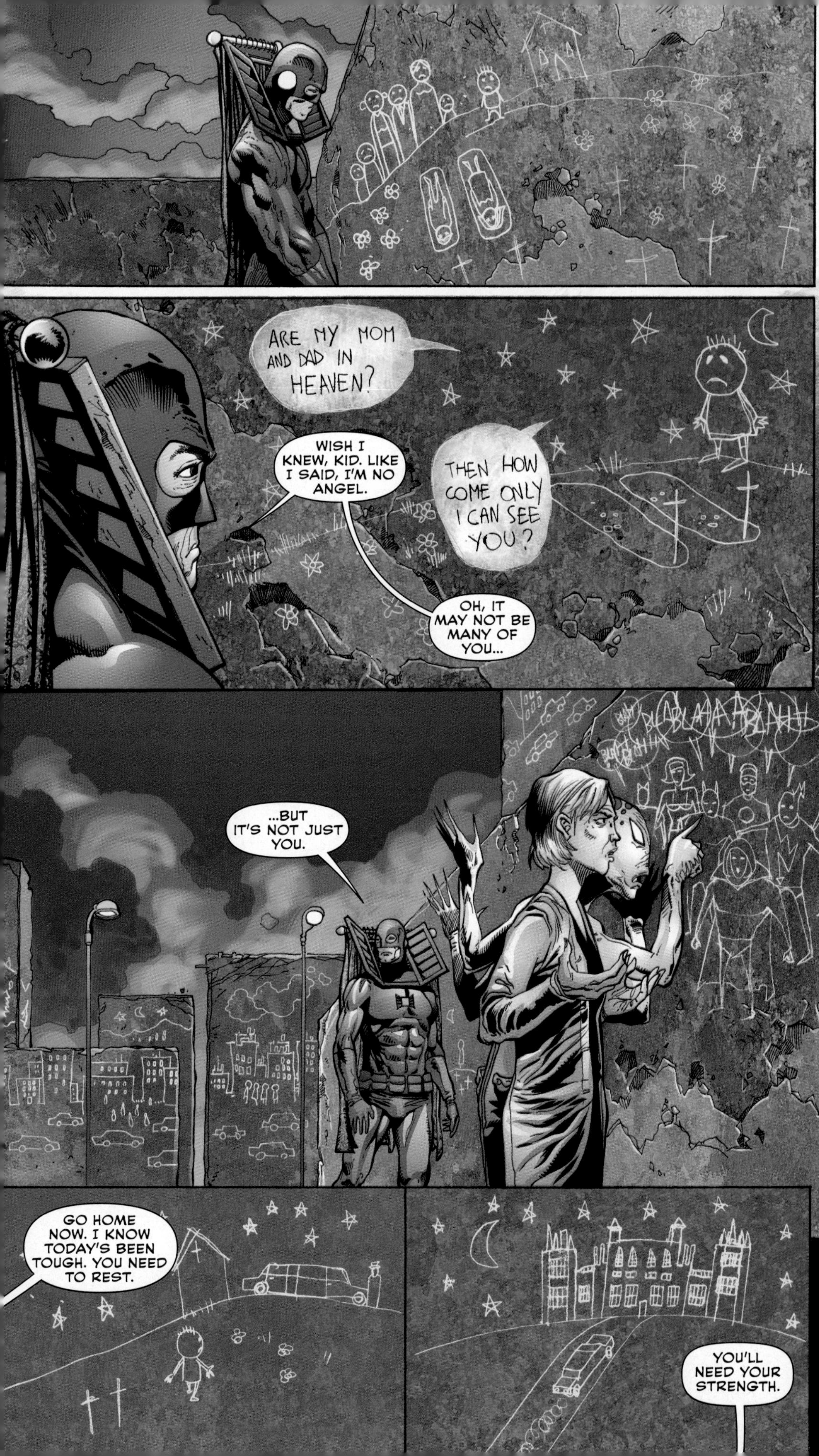
ARE MY MOM AND DAD IN HEAVEN?
WISH I KNEW, KID. LIKE I SAID, I'M NO ANGEL.
THEN HOW COME ONLY I CAN SEE YOU?
OH, IT MAY NOT BE MANY OF YOU...
...BUT IT'S NOT JUST YOU.
GO HOME NOW. I KNOW TODAY'S BEEN TOUGH. YOU NEED TO REST.
YOU'LL NEED YOUR STRENGTH.

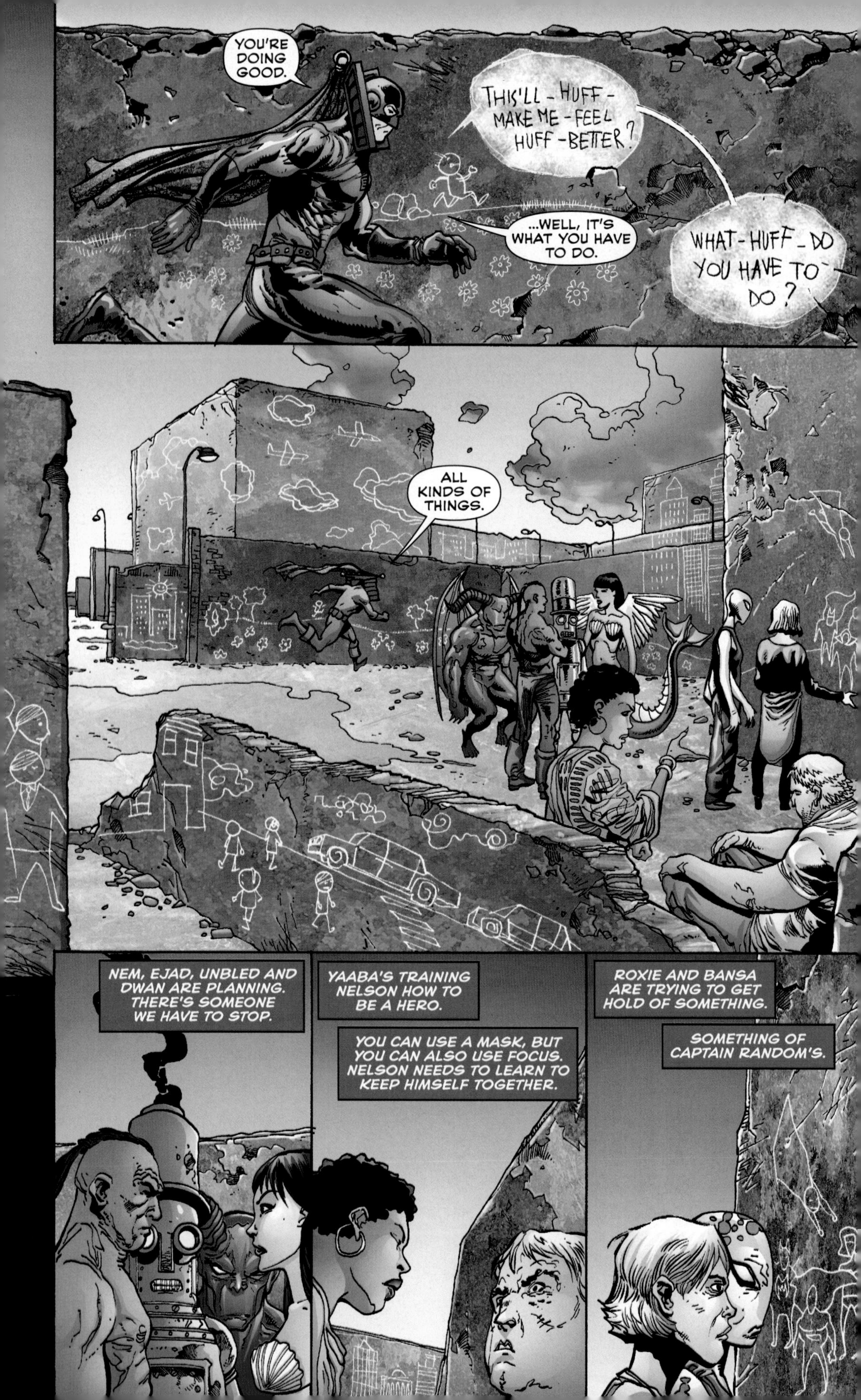
YOU'RE DOING GOOD.
THIS'LL - HUFF - MAKE ME - FEEL HUFF - BETTER?
...WELL, IT'S WHAT YOU HAVE TO DO.
WHAT - HUFF - DO YOU HAVE TO DO?
ALL KINDS OF THINGS.
NEM, EJAD, UNBLED AND DWAN ARE PLANNING. THERE'S SOMEONE WE HAVE TO STOP.
YAABA'S TRAINING NELSON HOW TO BE A HERO.
YOU CAN USE A MASK, BUT YOU CAN ALSO USE FOCUS. NELSON NEEDS TO LEARN TO KEEP HIMSELF TOGETHER.
ROXIE AND BANSA ARE TRYING TO GET HOLD OF SOMETHING.
SOMETHING OF CAPTAIN RANDOM'S.

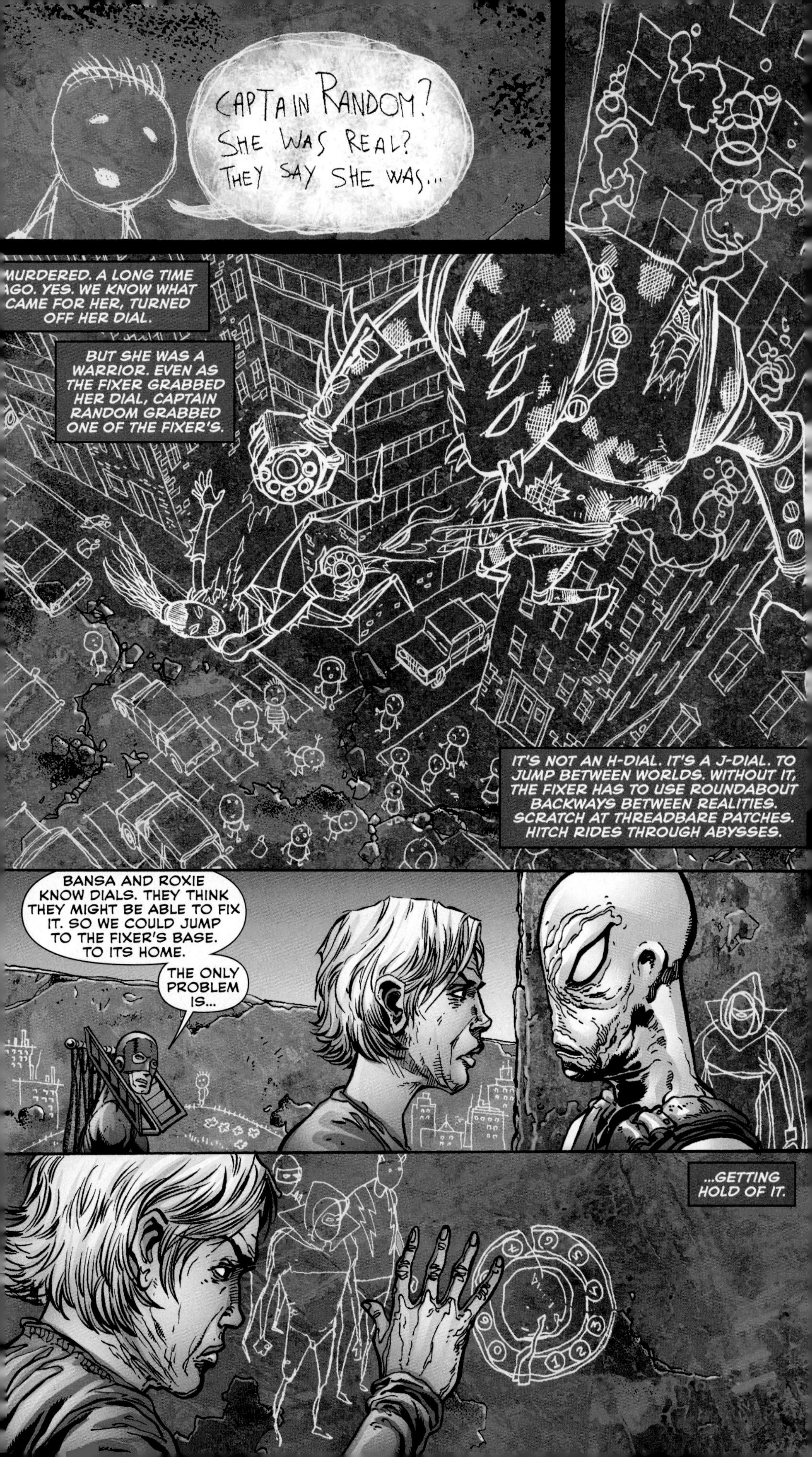
CAPTAIN RANDOM? SHE WAS REAL? THEY SAY SHE WAS...
MURDERED. A LONG TIME AGO. YES. WE KNOW WHAT CAME FOR HER, TURNED OFF HER DIAL.
BUT SHE WAS A WARRIOR. EVEN AS THE FIXER GRABBED HER DIAL, CAPTAIN RANDOM GRABBED ONE OF THE FIXER'S.
IT'S NOT AN H-DIAL. IT'S A J-DIAL. TO JUMP BETWEEN WORLDS. WITHOUT IT, THE FIXER HAS TO USE ROUNDABOUT BACKWAYS BETWEEN REALITIES. SCRATCH AT THREADBARE PATCHES. HITCH RIDES THROUGH ABYSSES.
BANSA AND ROXIE KNOW DIALS. THEY THINK THEY MIGHT BE ABLE TO FIX IT. SO WE COULD JUMP TO THE FIXER'S BASE. TO ITS HOME.
THE ONLY PROBLEM IS...
...GETTING HOLD OF IT.

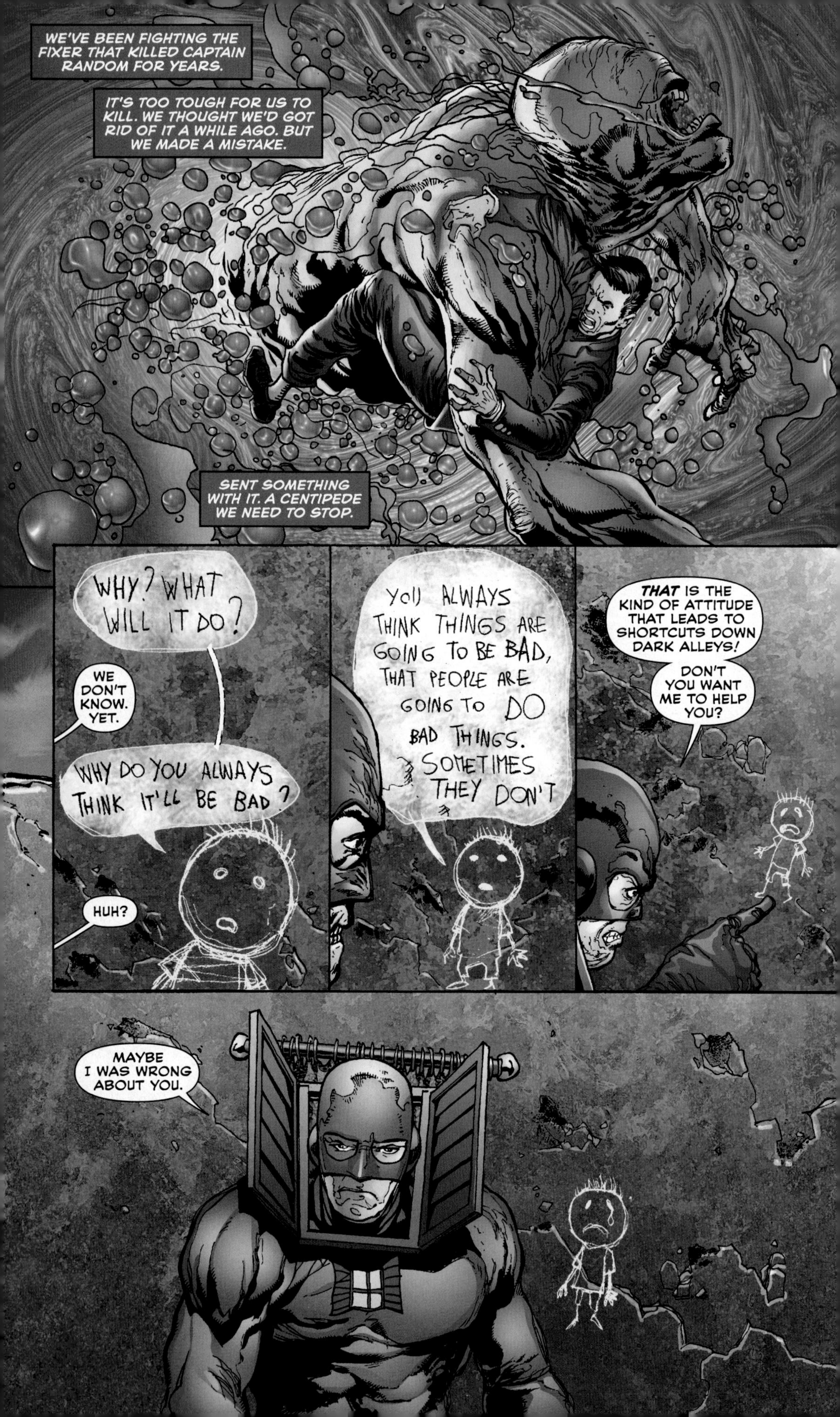
WE'VE BEEN FIGHTING THE FIXER THAT KILLED CAPTAIN RANDOM FOR YEARS.
IT'S TOO TOUGH FOR US TO KILL. WE THOUGHT WE'D GOT RID OF IT A WHILE AGO. BUT WE MADE A MISTAKE.
SENT SOMETHING WITH IT. A CENTIPEDE WE NEED TO STOP.
WHY? WHAT WILL IT DO?
WE DON'T KNOW. YET.
WHY DO YOU ALWAYS THINK IT'LL BE BAD?
HUH?
YOU ALWAYS THINK THINGS ARE GOING TO BE BAD, THAT PEOPLE ARE GOING TO DO BAD THINGS. SOMETIMES THEY DON'T
THAT IS THE KIND OF ATTITUDE THAT LEADS TO SHORTCUTS DOWN DARK ALLEYS!
DON'T YOU WANT ME TO HELP YOU?
MAYBE I WAS WRONG ABOUT YOU.

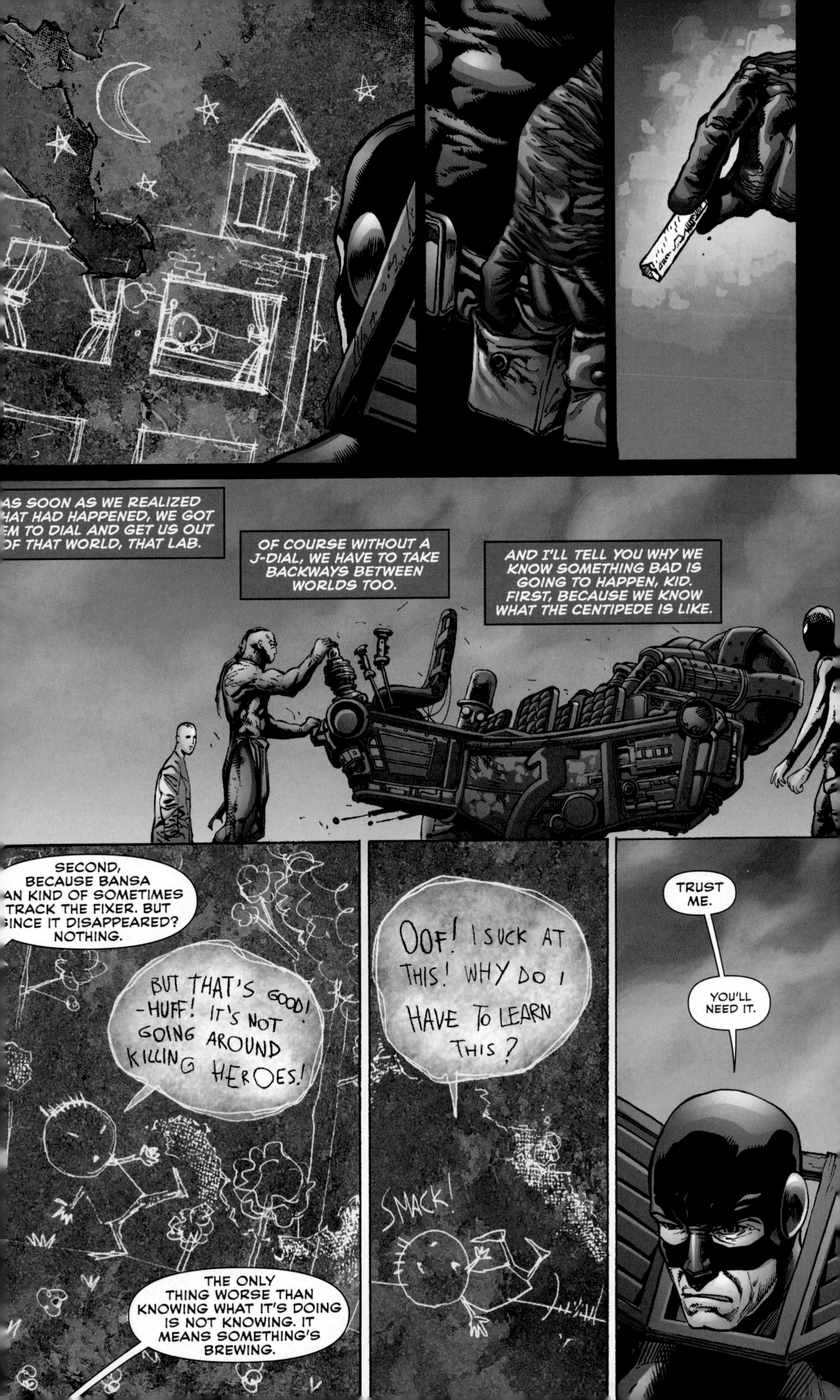
AS SOON AS WE REALIZED HAT HAD HAPPENED, WE GOT EM TO DIAL AND GET US OUT OF THAT WORLD, THAT LAB.
OF COURSE WITHOUT A J-DIAL, WE HAVE TO TAKE BACKWAYS BETWEEN WORLDS TOO.
AND I'LL TELL YOU WHY WE KNOW SOMETHING BAD IS GOING TO HAPPEN, KID. FIRST, BECAUSE WE KNOW WHAT THE CENTIPEDE IS LIKE.
SECOND, BECAUSE BANSA AN KIND OF SOMETIMES TRACK THE FIXER. BUT INCE IT DISAPPEARED? NOTHING.
BUT THAT'S GOOD! -HUFF! IT'S NOT GOING AROUND KILLING HEROES!
THE ONLY THING WORSE THAN KNOWING WHAT IT'S DOING IS NOT KNOWING. IT MEANS SOMETHING'S BREWING.
OOF! I SUCK AT THIS! WHY DO I HAVE TO LEARN THIS?
SMACK!
TRUST ME.
YOU'LL NEED IT.

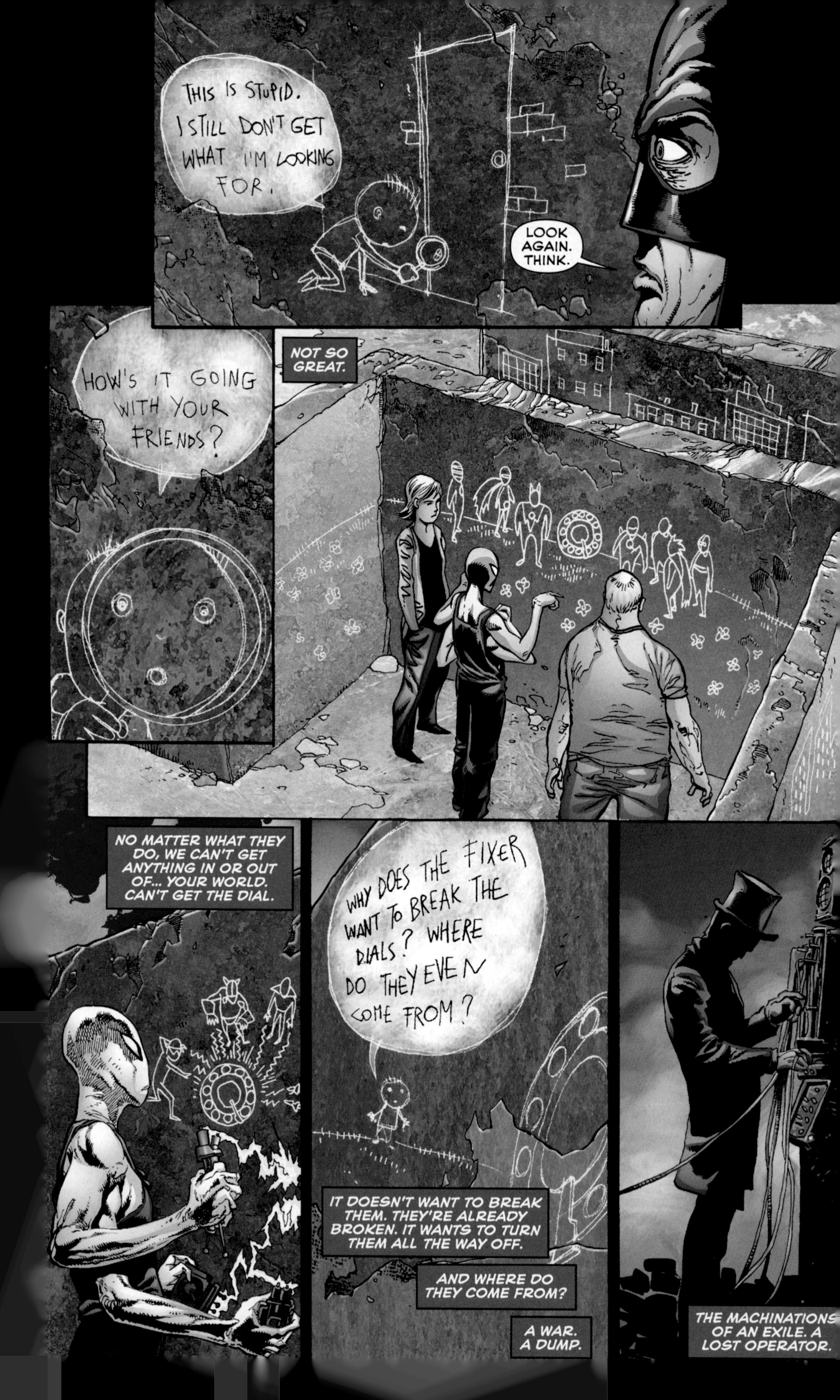

THIS IS STUPID. I STILL DON'T GET WHAT I'M LOOKING FOR.
LOOK AGAIN. THINK.
HOW'S IT GOING WITH YOUR FRIENDS?
NOT SO GREAT.
NO MATTER WHAT THEY DO, WE CAN'T GET ANYTHING IN OR OUT OF... YOUR WORLD. CAN'T GET THE DIAL.
WHY DOES THE FIXER WANT TO BREAK THE DIALS? WHERE DO THEY EVEN COME FROM?
IT DOESN'T WANT TO BREAK THEM. THEY'RE ALREADY BROKEN. IT WANTS TO TURN THEM ALL THE WAY OFF.
AND WHERE DO THEY COME FROM?
A WAR. A DUMP.
THE MACHINATIONS OF AN EXILE. A LOST OPERATOR.

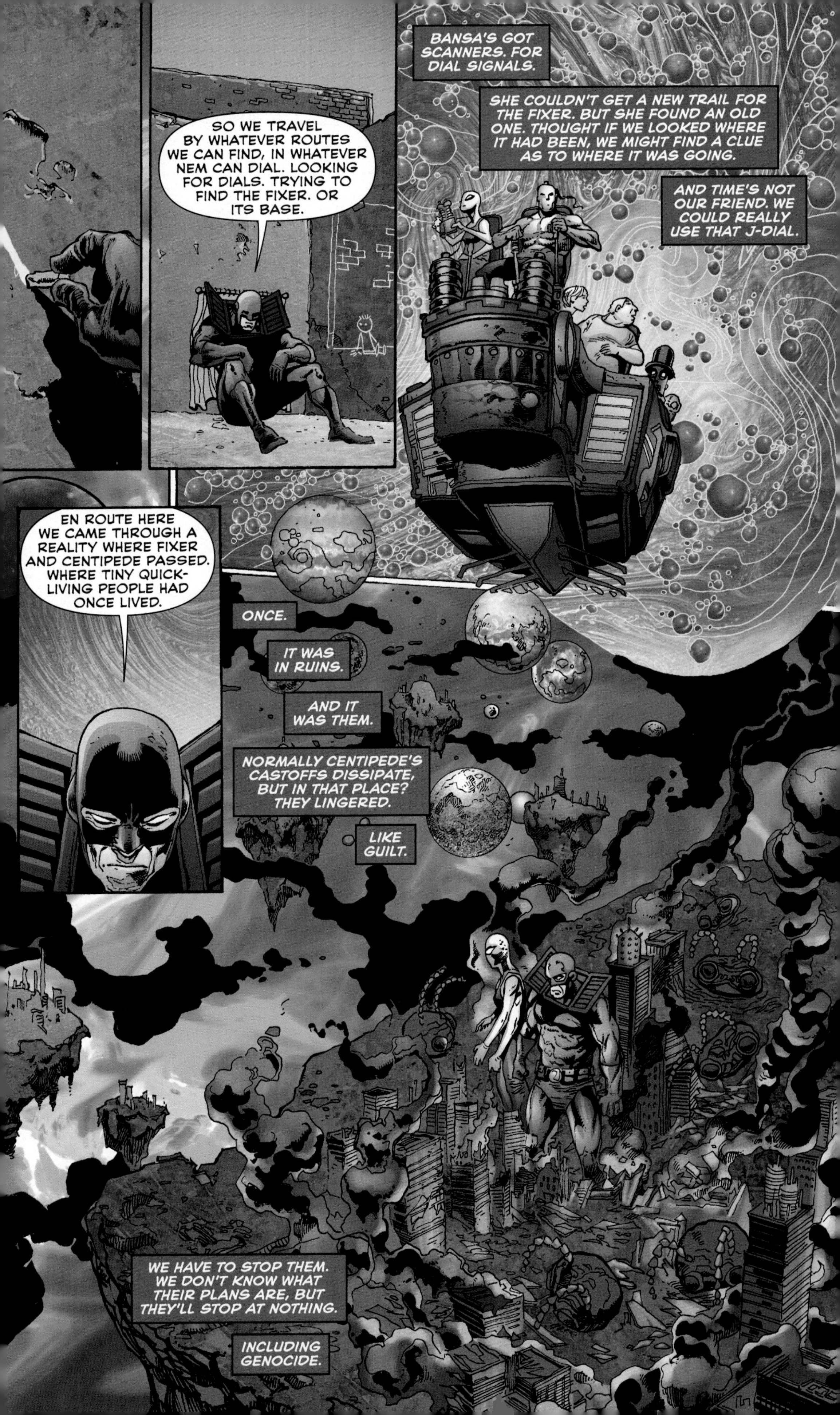
SO WE TRAVEL BY WHATEVER ROUTES WE CAN FIND, IN WHATEVER NEM CAN DIAL. LOOKING FOR DIALS. TRYING TO FIND THE FIXER. OR ITS BASE.
BANSA'S GOT SCANNERS. FOR DIAL SIGNALS.
SHE COULDN'T GET A NEW TRAIL FOR THE FIXER. BUT SHE FOUND AN OLD ONE. THOUGHT IF WE LOOKED WHERE IT HAD BEEN, WE MIGHT FIND A CLUE AS TO WHERE IT WAS GOING.
AND TIME'S NOT OUR FRIEND. WE COULD REALLY USE THAT J-DIAL.
EN ROUTE HERE WE CAME THROUGH A REALITY WHERE FIXER AND CENTIPEDE PASSED. WHERE TINY QUICK-LIVING PEOPLE HAD ONCE LIVED.
ONCE.
IT WAS IN RUINS.
AND IT WAS THEM.
NORMALLY CENTIPEDE'S CASTOFFS DISSIPATE, BUT IN THAT PLACE? THEY LINGERED.
LIKE GUILT.
WE HAVE TO STOP THEM. WE DON'T KNOW WHAT THEIR PLANS ARE, BUT THEY'LL STOP AT NOTHING.
INCLUDING GENOCIDE.

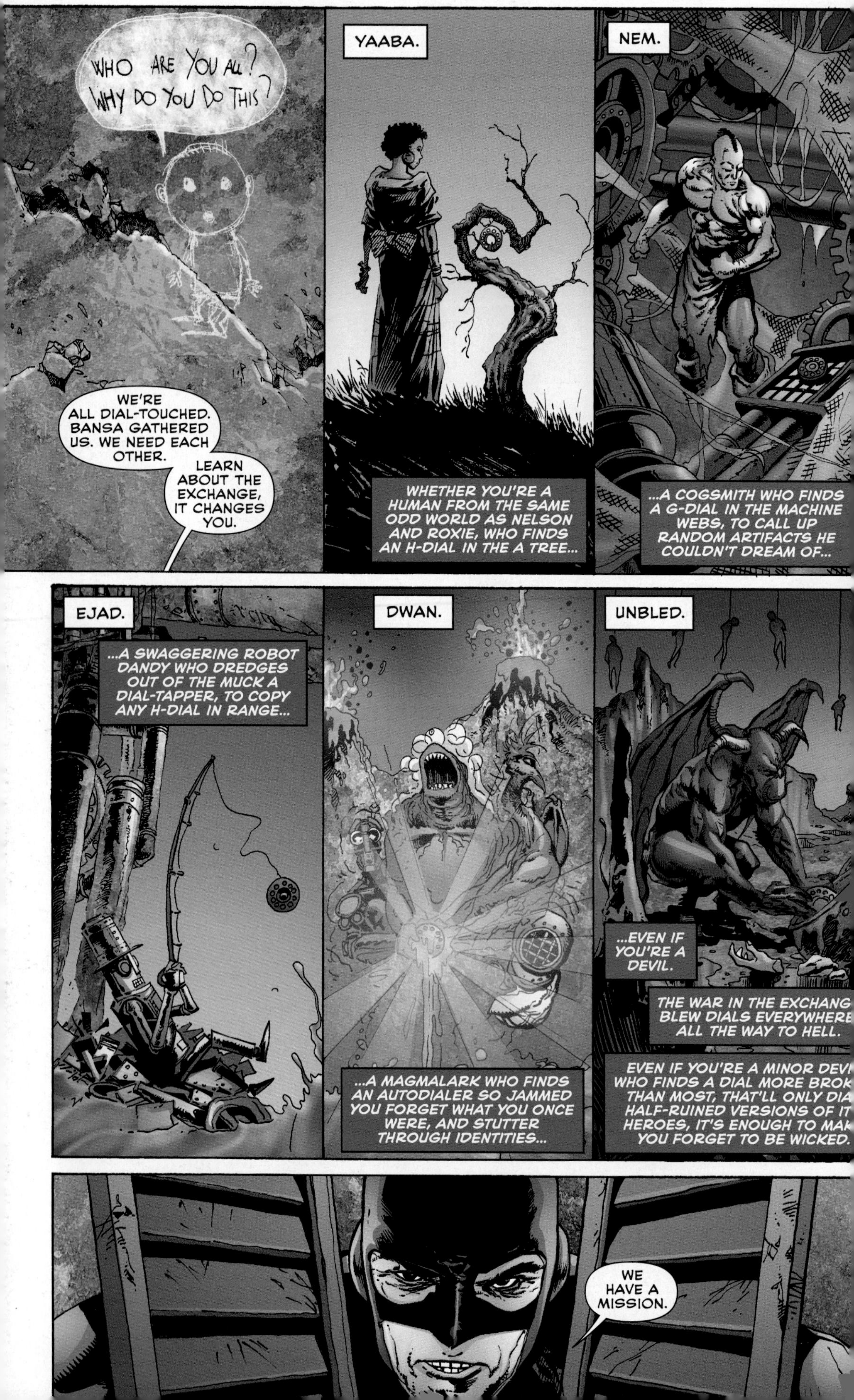
WHO ARE YOU ALL? WHY DO YOU DO THIS?
WE'RE ALL DIAL-TOUCHED. BANSA GATHERED US. WE NEED EACH OTHER.
LEARN ABOUT THE EXCHANGE, IT CHANGES YOU.
YAABA.
WHETHER YOU'RE A HUMAN FROM THE SAME ODD WORLD AS NELSON AND ROXIE, WHO FINDS AN H-DIAL IN THE A TREE...
NEM.
...A COGSMITH WHO FINDS A G-DIAL IN THE MACHINE WEBS, TO CALL UP RANDOM ARTIFACTS HE COULDN'T DREAM OF...
EJAD.
...A SWAGGERING ROBOT DANDY WHO DREDGES OUT OF THE MUCK A DIAL-TAPPER, TO COPY ANY H-DIAL IN RANGE...
DWAN.
...A MAGMALARK WHO FINDS AN AUTODIALER SO JAMMED YOU FORGET WHAT YOU ONCE WERE, AND STUTTER THROUGH IDENTITIES...
UNBLED.
...EVEN IF YOU'RE A DEVIL.
THE WAR IN THE EXCHANG BLEW DIALS EVERYWHERE ALL THE WAY TO HELL.
EVEN IF YOU'RE A MINOR DEVI WHO FINDS A DIAL MORE BROK THAN MOST, THAT'LL ONLY DIA HALF-RUINED VERSIONS OF IT HEROES, IT'S ENOUGH TO MAK YOU FORGET TO BE WICKED.
WE HAVE A MISSION.

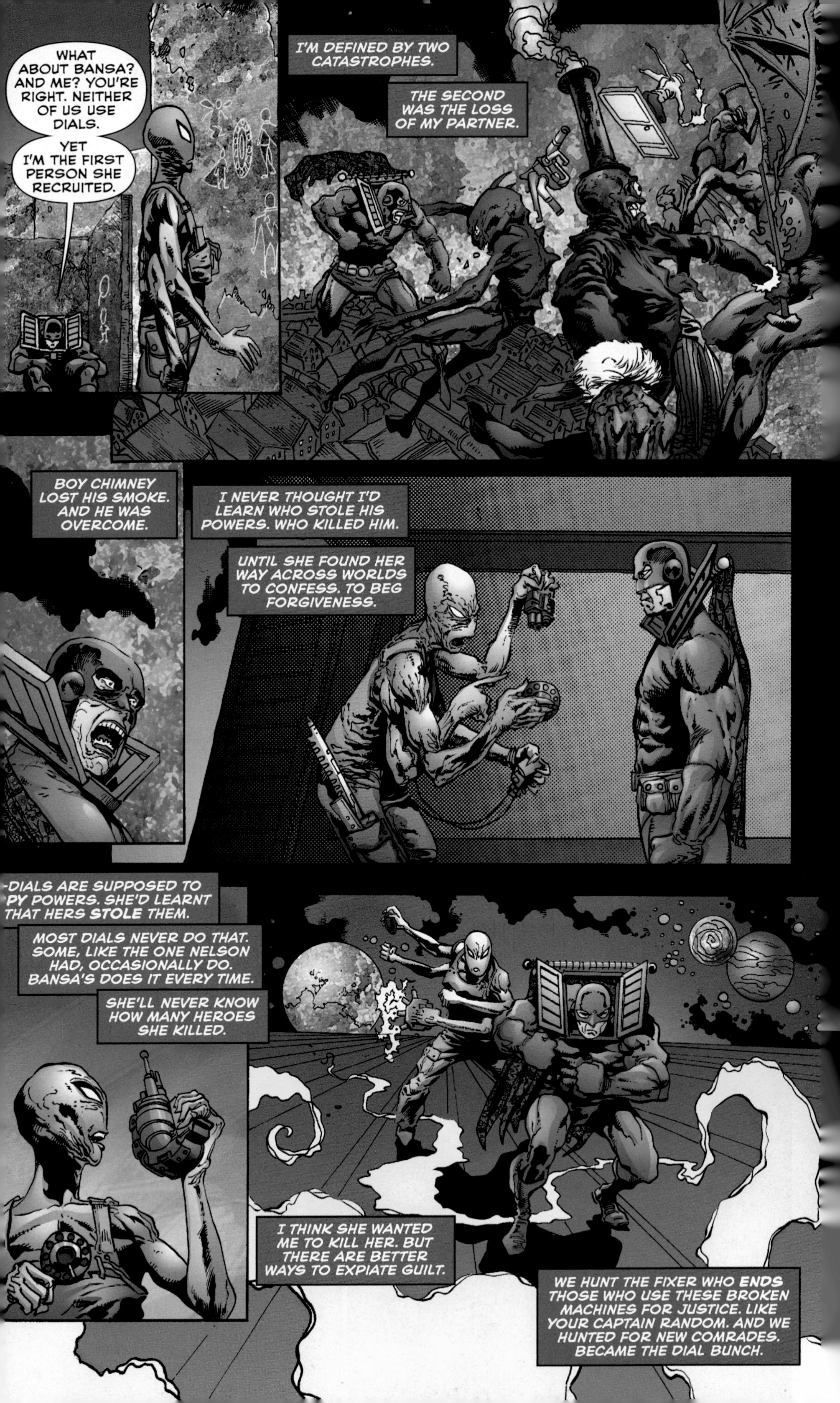

WHAT ABOUT BANSA? AND ME? YOU'RE RIGHT. NEITHER OF US USE DIALS.
YET I'M THE FIRST PERSON SHE RECRUITED.
I'M DEFINED BY TWO CATASTROPHES.
THE SECOND WAS THE LOSS OF MY PARTNER.
BOY CHIMNEY LOST HIS SMOKE. AND HE WAS OVERCOME.
I NEVER THOUGHT I'D LEARN WHO STOLE HIS POWERS. WHO KILLED HIM.
UNTIL SHE FOUND HER WAY ACROSS WORLDS TO CONFESS. TO BEG FORGIVENESS.
-DIALS ARE SUPPOSED TO PY POWERS. SHE'D LEARNT THAT HERS STOLE THEM.
MOST DIALS NEVER DO THAT. SOME, LIKE THE ONE NELSON HAD, OCCASIONALLY DO. BANSA'S DOES IT EVERY TIME.
SHE'LL NEVER KNOW HOW MANY HEROES SHE KILLED.
I THINK SHE WANTED ME TO KILL HER. BUT THERE ARE BETTER WAYS TO EXPIATE GUILT.
WE HUNT THE FIXER WHO ENDS THOSE WHO USE THESE BROKEN MACHINES FOR JUSTICE. LIKE YOUR CAPTAIN RANDOM. AND WE HUNTED FOR NEW COMRADES. BECAME THE DIAL BUNCH.

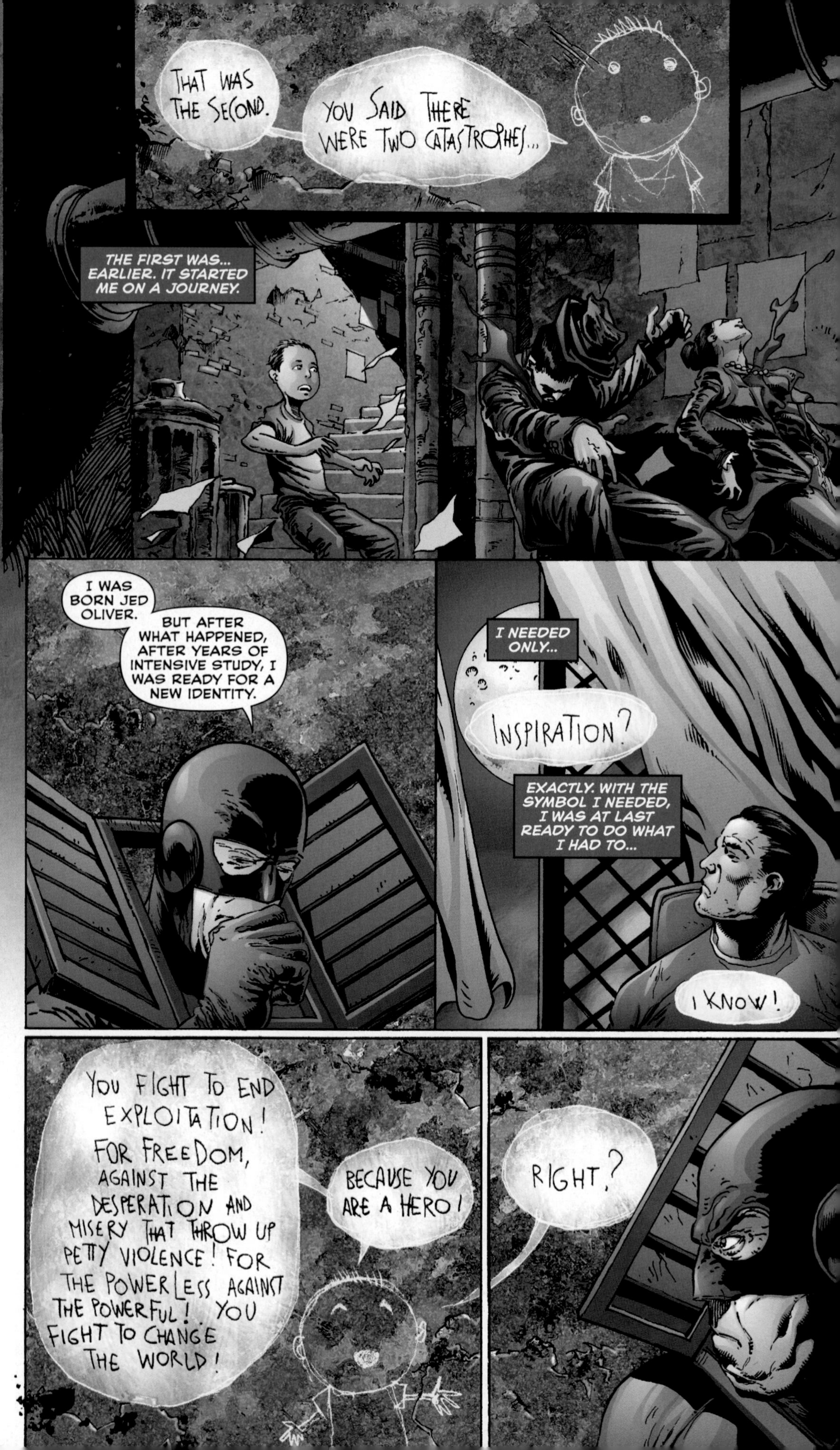
THAT WAS THE SECOND.
YOU SAID THERE WERE TWO CATASTROPHES...
THE FIRST WAS... EARLIER. IT STARTED ME ON A JOURNEY.
I WAS BORN JED OLIVER.
BUT AFTER WHAT HAPPENED, AFTER YEARS OF INTENSIVE STUDY, I WAS READY FOR A NEW IDENTITY.
I NEEDED ONLY...
INSPIRATION?
EXACTLY. WITH THE SYMBOL I NEEDED, I WAS AT LAST READY TO DO WHAT I HAD TO...
I KNOW!
YOU FIGHT TO END EXPLOITATION! FOR FREEDOM, AGAINST THE DESPERATION AND MISERY THAT THROW UP PETTY VIOLENCE! FOR THE POWERLESS AGAINST THE POWERFUL! YOU FIGHT TO CHANGE THE WORLD!
BECAUSE YOU ARE A HERO!
RIGHT?

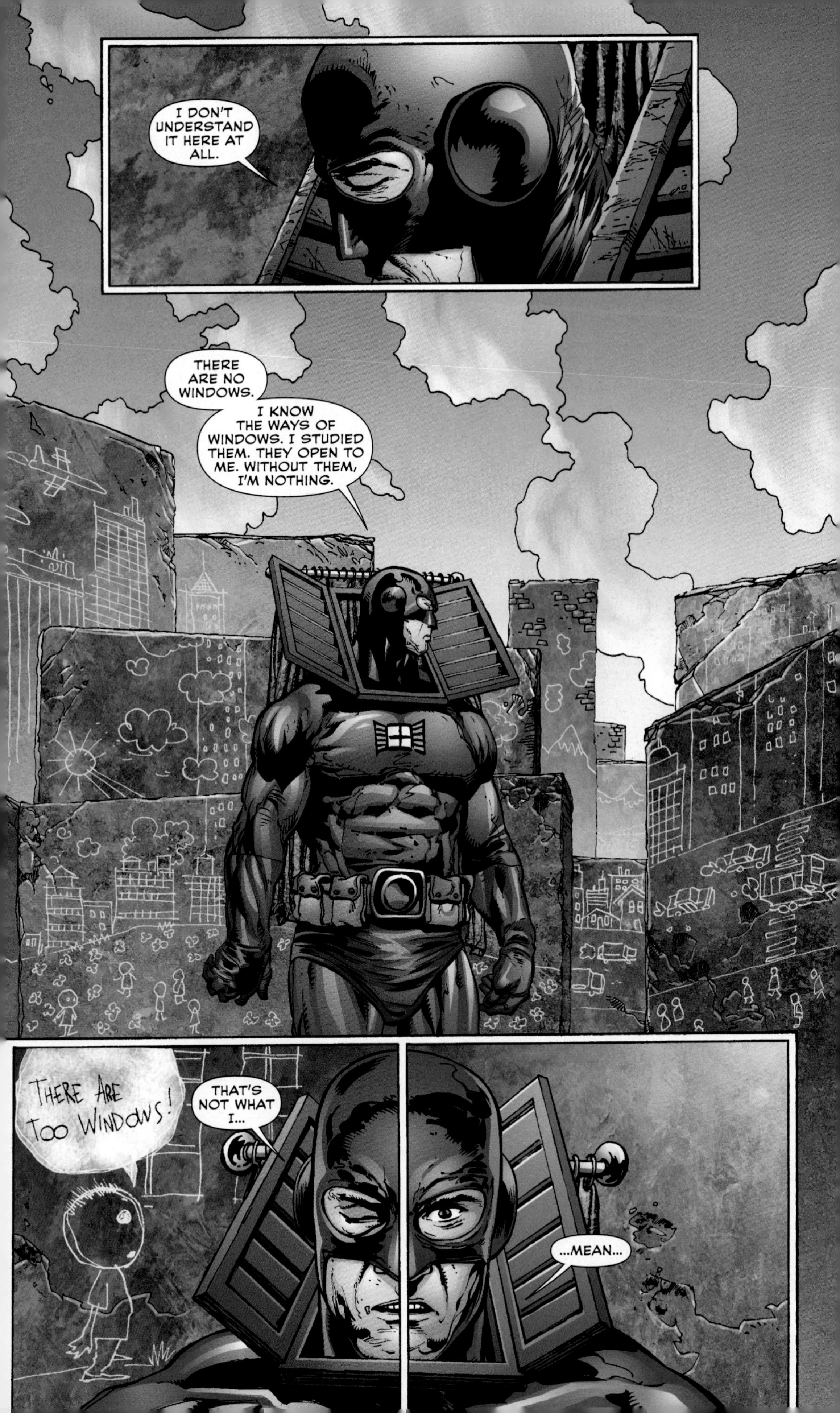
I DON'T UNDERSTAND IT HERE AT ALL.
THERE ARE NO WINDOWS.
I KNOW THE WAYS OF WINDOWS. I STUDIED THEM. THEY OPEN TO ME. WITHOUT THEM, I'M NOTHING.
THERE ARE TOO WINDOWS!
THAT'S NOT WHAT I...
...MEAN...

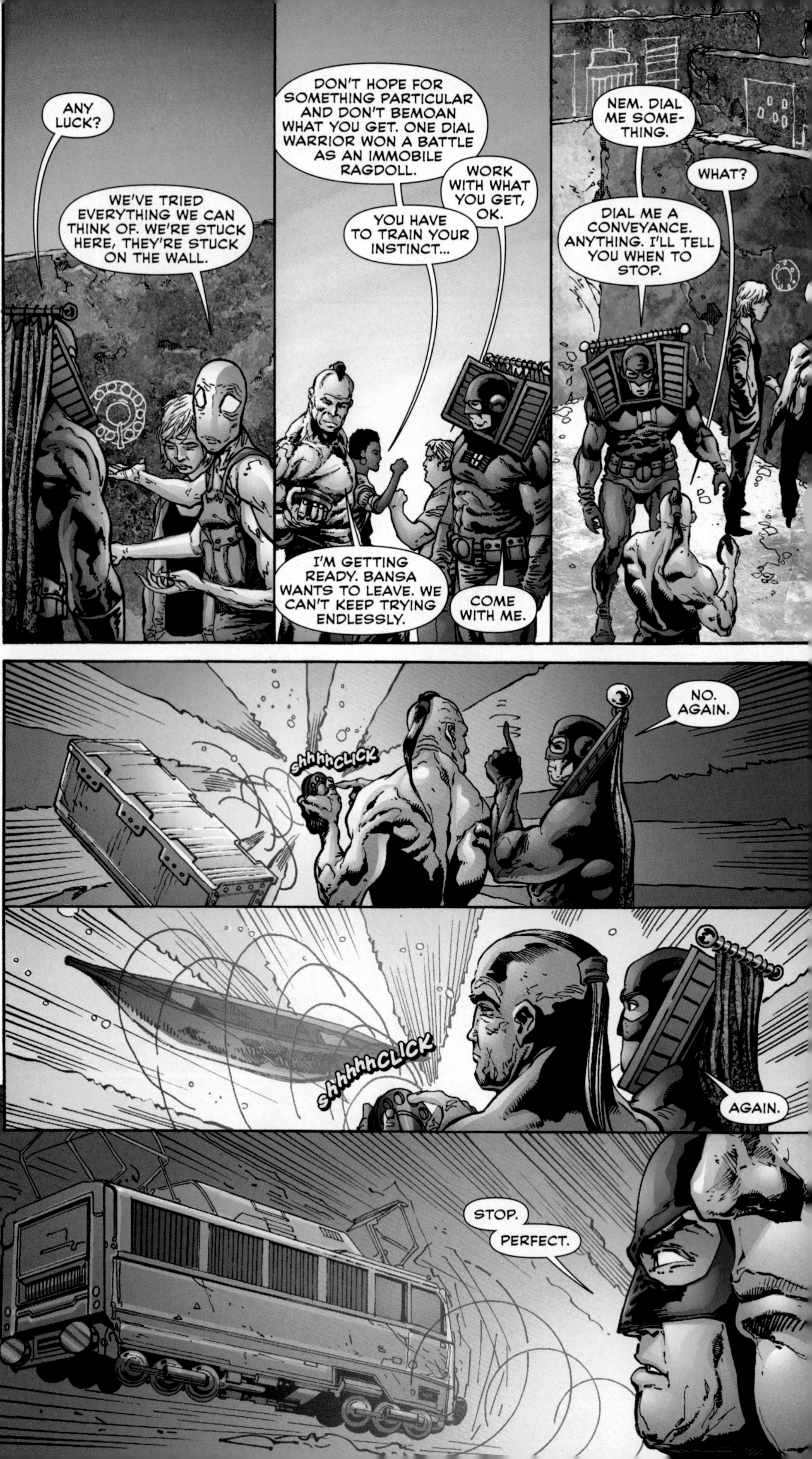
ANY LUCK?
WE'VE TRIED EVERYTHING WE CAN THINK OF. WE'RE STUCK HERE, THEY'RE STUCK ON THE WALL.
DON'T HOPE FOR SOMETHING PARTICULAR AND DON'T BEMOAN WHAT YOU GET. ONE DIAL WARRIOR WON A BATTLE AS AN IMMOBILE RAGDOLL.
YOU HAVE TO TRAIN YOUR INSTINCT...
WORK WITH WHAT YOU GET, OK.
I'M GETTING READY. BANSA WANTS TO LEAVE. WE CAN'T KEEP TRYING ENDLESSLY.
COME WITH ME.
NEM. DIAL ME SOMETHING.
WHAT?
DIAL ME A CONVEYANCE. ANYTHING. I'LL TELL YOU WHEN TO STOP.
shhhhCLICK
NO. AGAIN.
shhhhhCLICK
AGAIN.
STOP.
PERFECT.

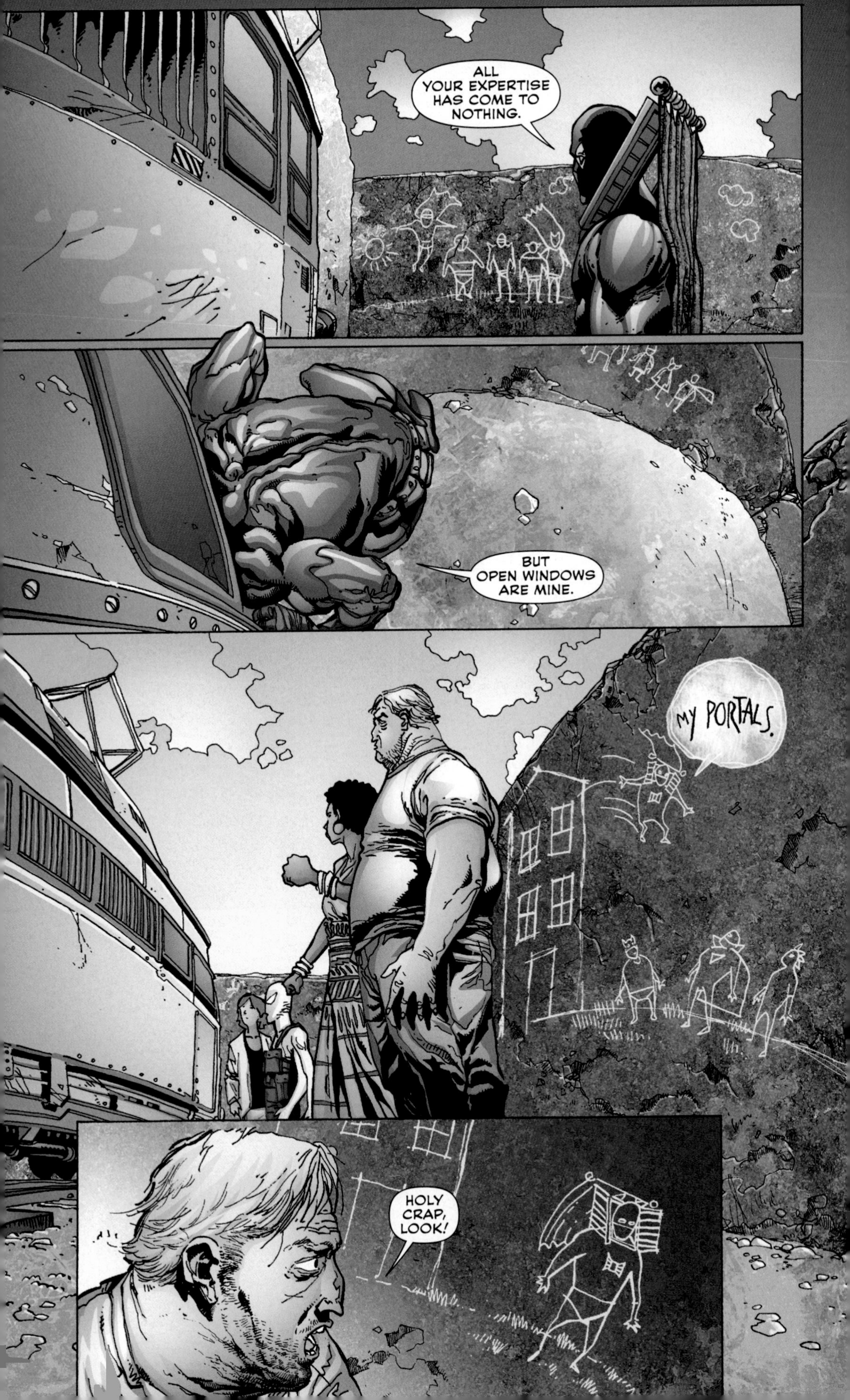
ALL YOUR EXPERTISE HAS COME TO NOTHING.
BUT OPEN WINDOWS ARE MINE.
MY PORTALS.
HOLY CRAP, LOOK!

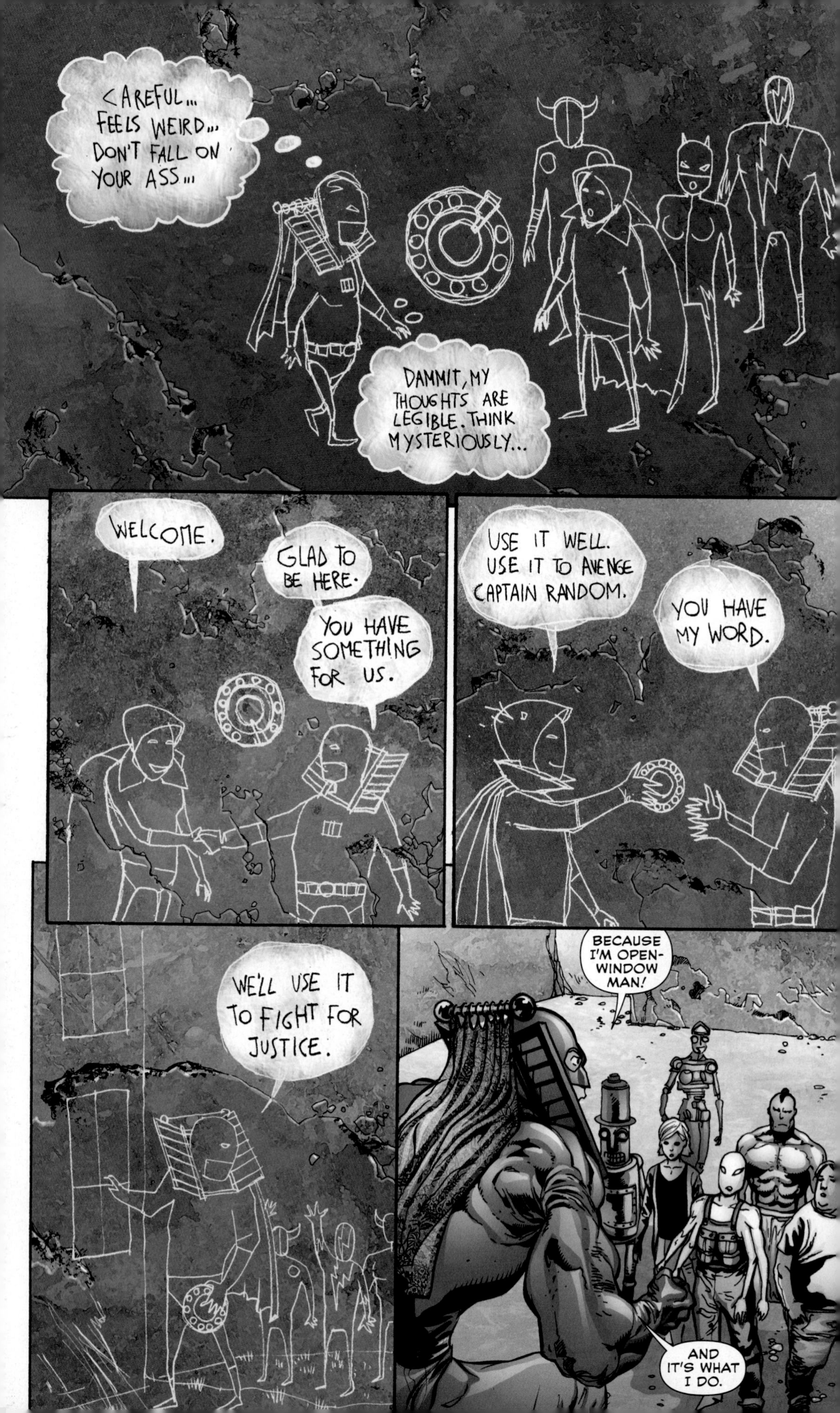
CAREFUL... FEELS WEIRD... DON'T FALL ON YOUR ASS...
DAMMIT, MY THOUGHTS ARE LEGIBLE. THINK MYSTERIOUSLY...
WELCOME.
GLAD TO BE HERE.
YOU HAVE SOMETHING FOR US.
USE IT WELL. USE IT TO AVENGE CAPTAIN RANDOM.
YOU HAVE MY WORD.
WE'LL USE IT TO FIGHT FOR JUSTICE.
BECAUSE I'M OPEN-WINDOW MAN!
AND IT'S WHAT I DO.

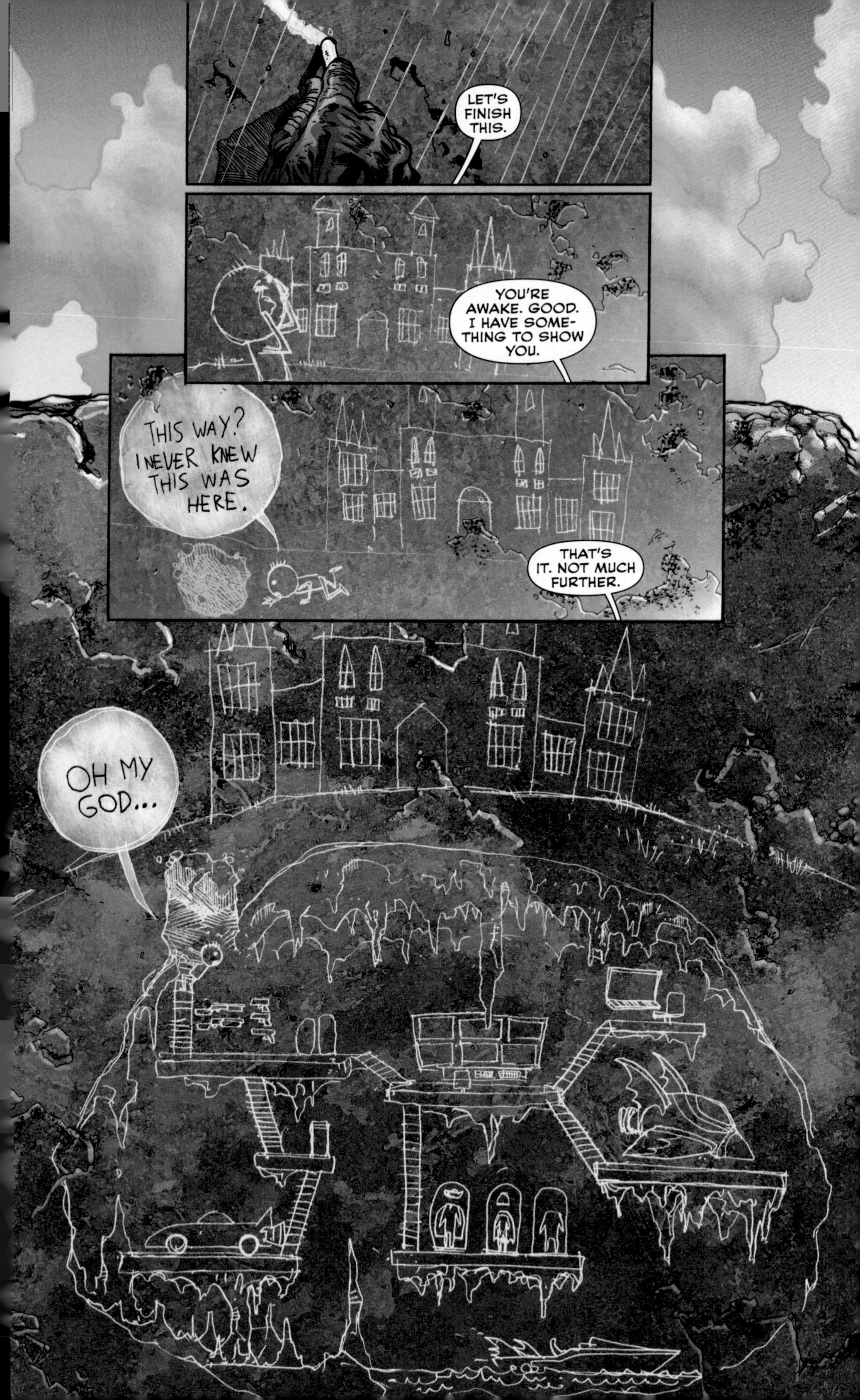
LET'S FINISH THIS.
YOU'RE AWAKE. GOOD. I HAVE SOME-THING TO SHOW YOU.
THIS WAY? I NEVER KNEW THIS WAS HERE.
THAT'S IT. NOT MUCH FURTHER.
OH MY GOD...

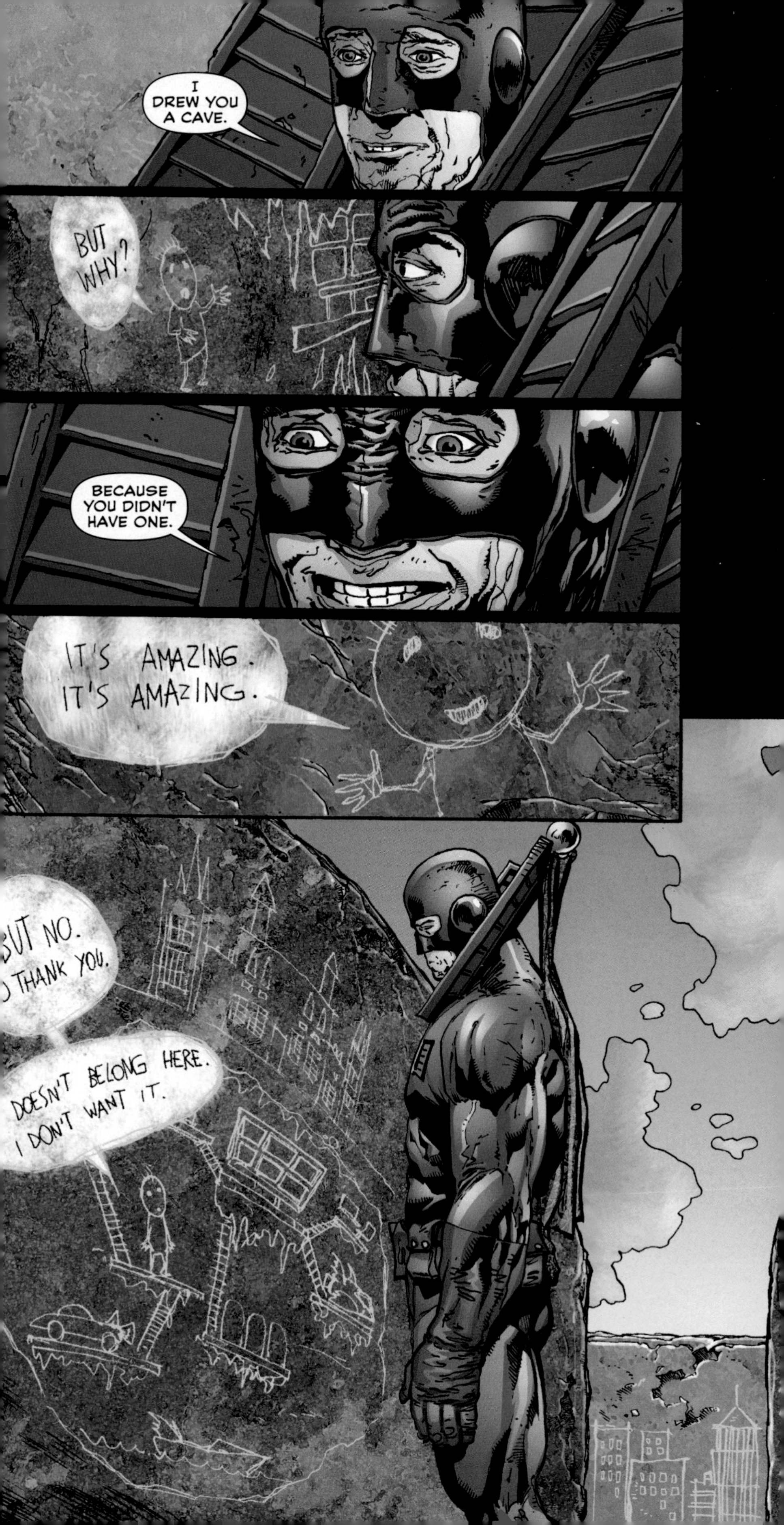
I DREW YOU A CAVE.
BUT WHY?
BECAUSE YOU DIDN'T HAVE ONE.
IT'S AMAZING. IT'S AMAZING.
UT NO. THANK YOU.
DOESN'T BELONG HERE. I DON'T WANT IT.

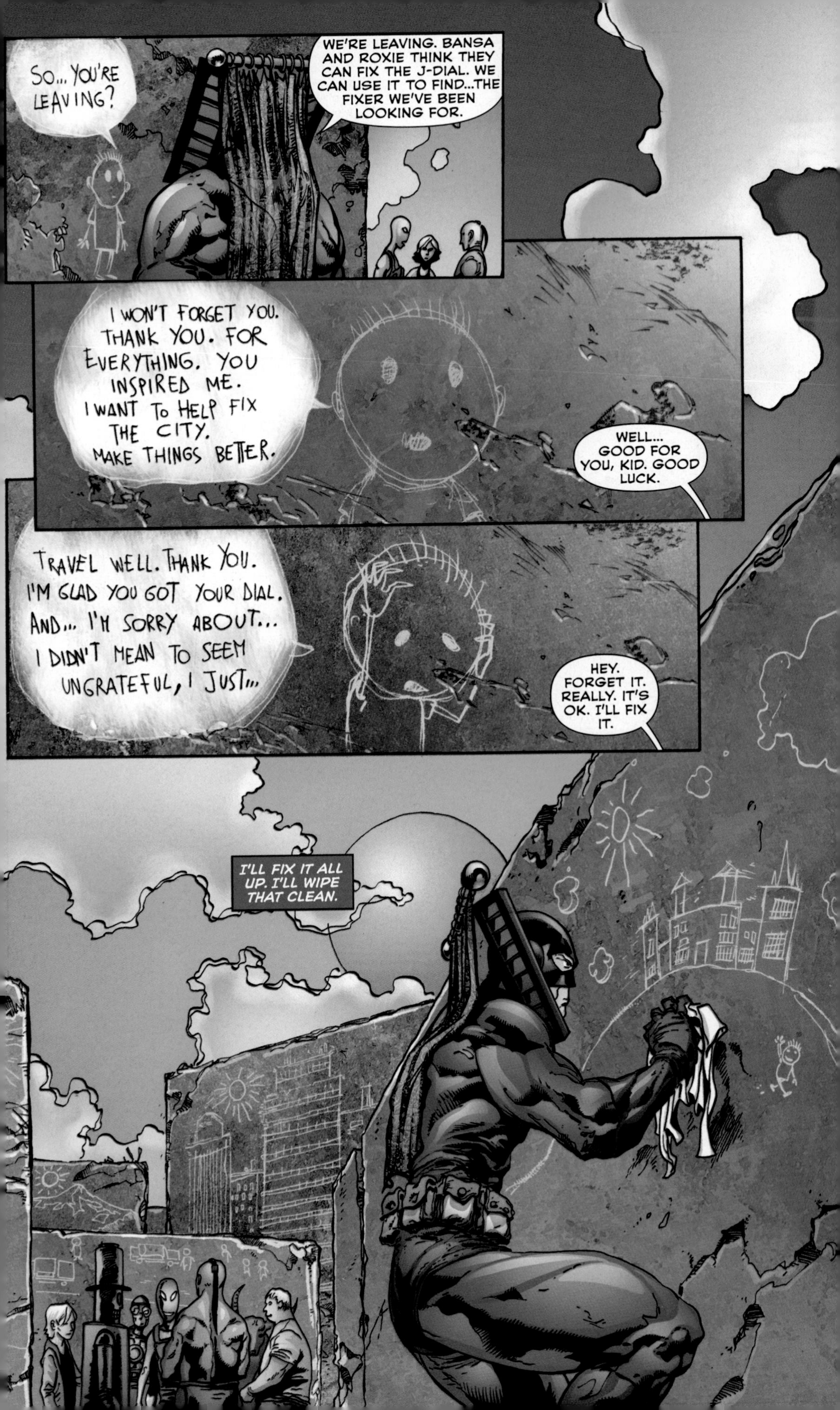
So... you're leaving?
We're leaving. Bansa and Roxie think they can fix the J-Dial. We can use it to find...the Fixer we've been looking for.
I won't forget you. Thank you. For everything. You inspired me. I want to help fix the city. Make things better.
Well... good for you, kid. Good luck.
Travel well. Thank you. I'm glad you got your dial. And... I'm sorry about... I didn't mean to seem ungrateful, I just...
Hey. Forget it. Really. It's OK. I'll fix it.
I'll fix it all up. I'll wipe that clean.

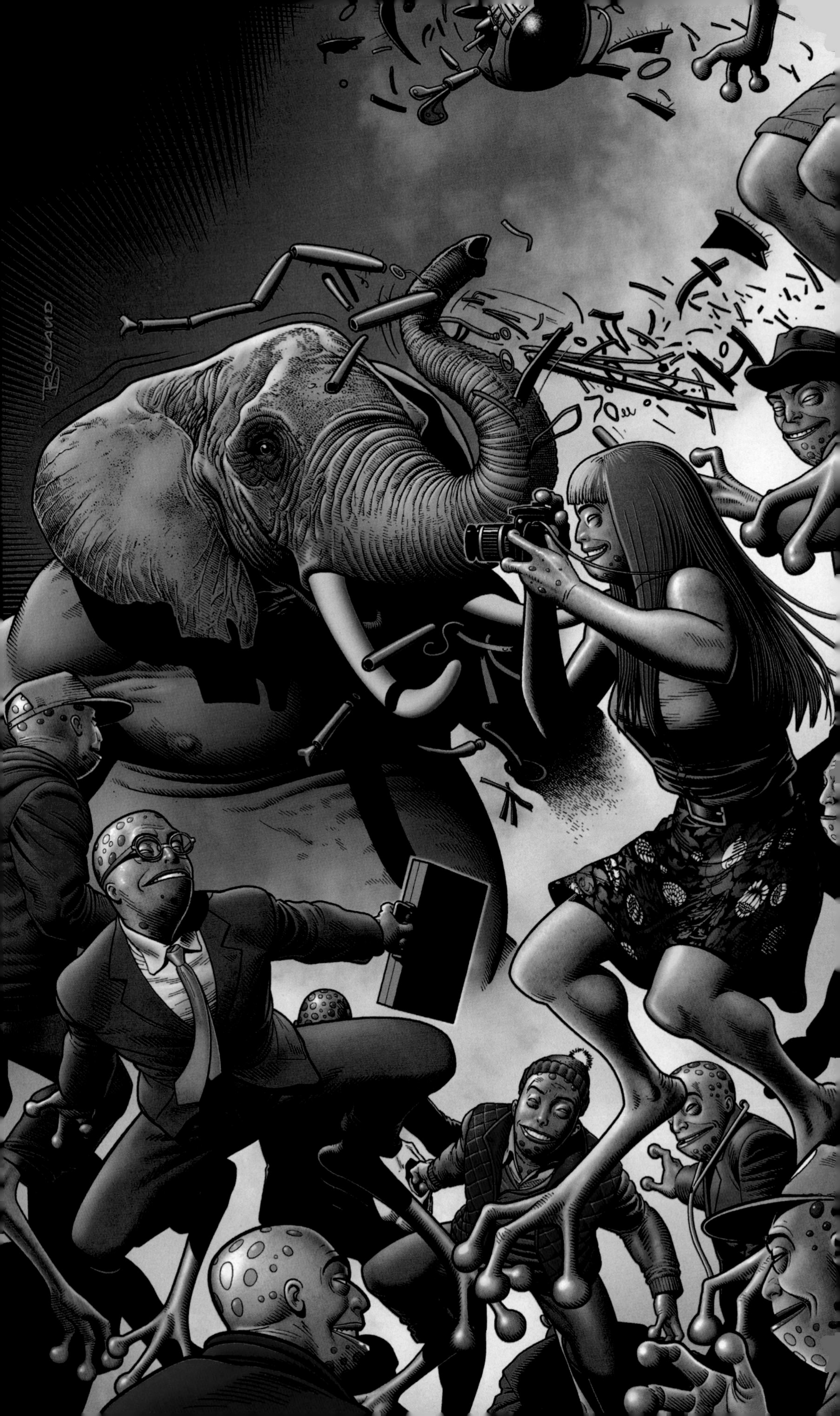
BOLLAND

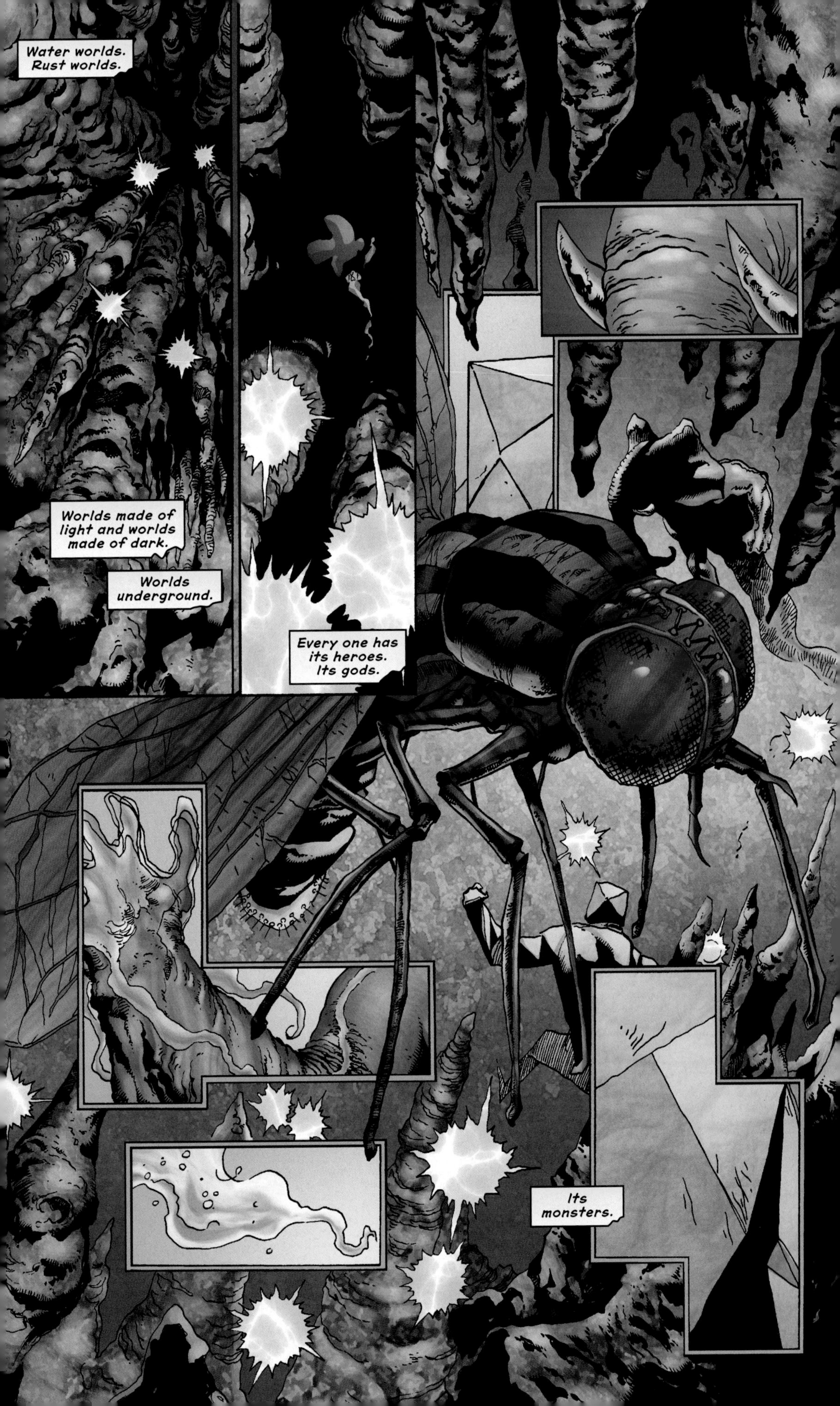
Water worlds. Rust worlds.
Worlds made of light and worlds made of dark.
Worlds underground.
Every one has its heroes. Its gods.
Its monsters.

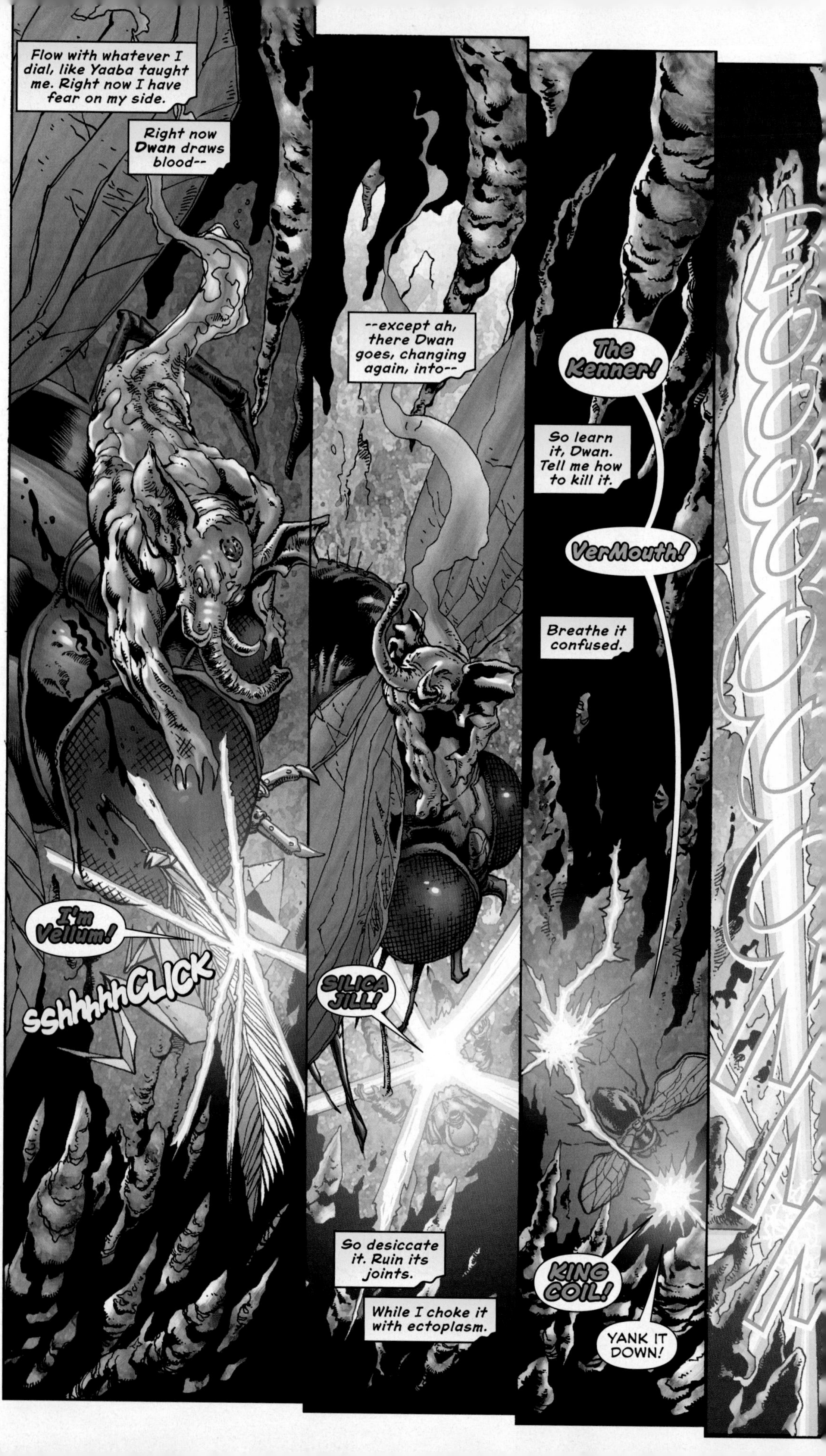
Flow with whatever I dial, like Yaaba taught me. Right now I have fear on my side.
Right now Dwan draws blood--
I'm Vellum!
SSHHHHHCLICK
--except ah, there Dwan goes, changing again, into--
SILICA JILL!
So desiccate it. Ruin its joints.
While I choke it with ectoplasm.
The Kenner!
So learn it, Dwan. Tell me how to kill it.
VerMouth!
Breathe it confused.
KING COIL!
YANK IT DOWN!

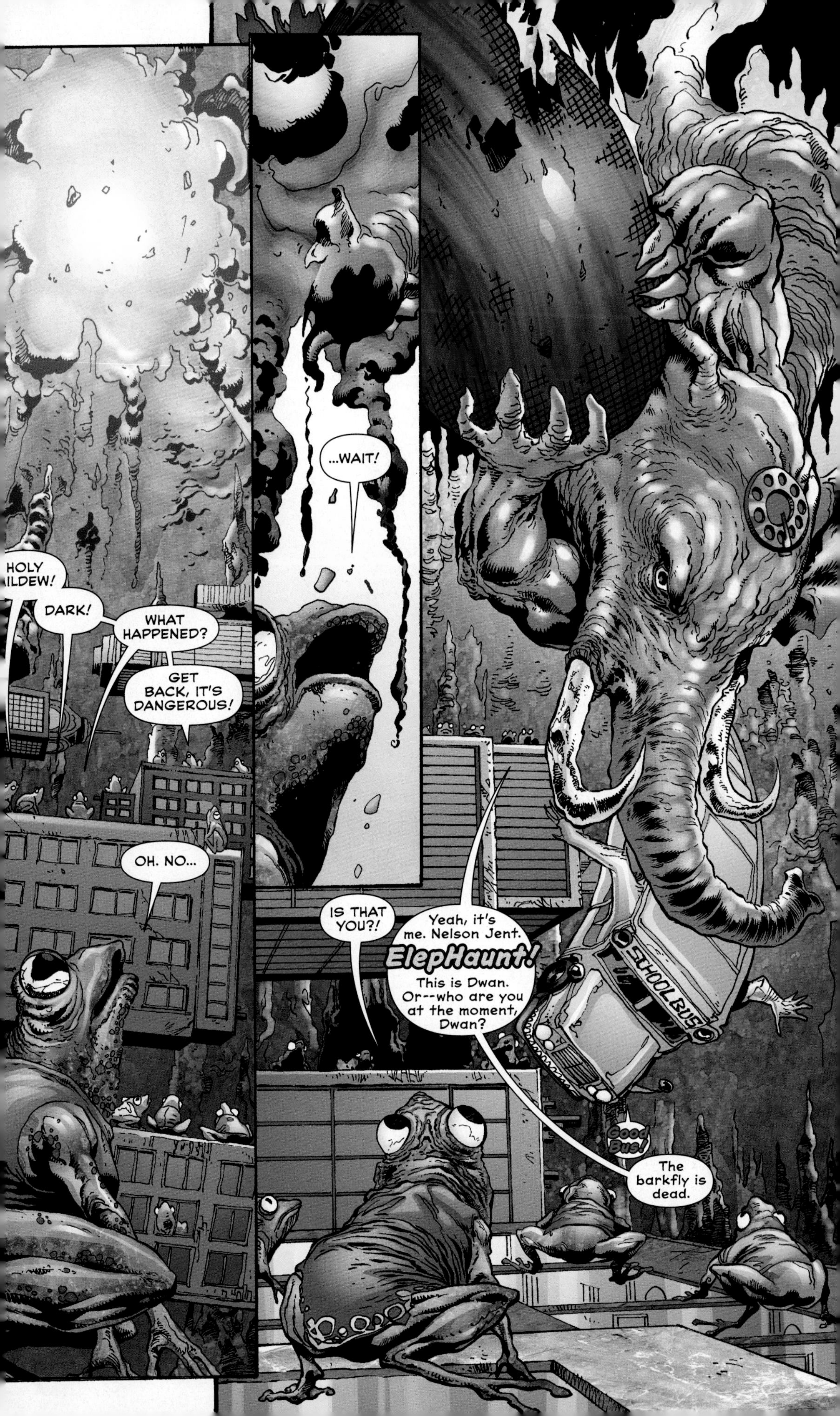
HOLY
ILDEW!
DARK!
WHAT HAPPENED?
GET BACK, IT'S DANGEROUS!
OH. NO...
...WAIT!
IS THAT YOU?!
Yeah, it's me. Nelson Jent.
ElepHaunt!
This is Dwan. Or--who are you at the moment, Dwan?
SCHOOLBUS
Good Bus!
The barkfly is dead.

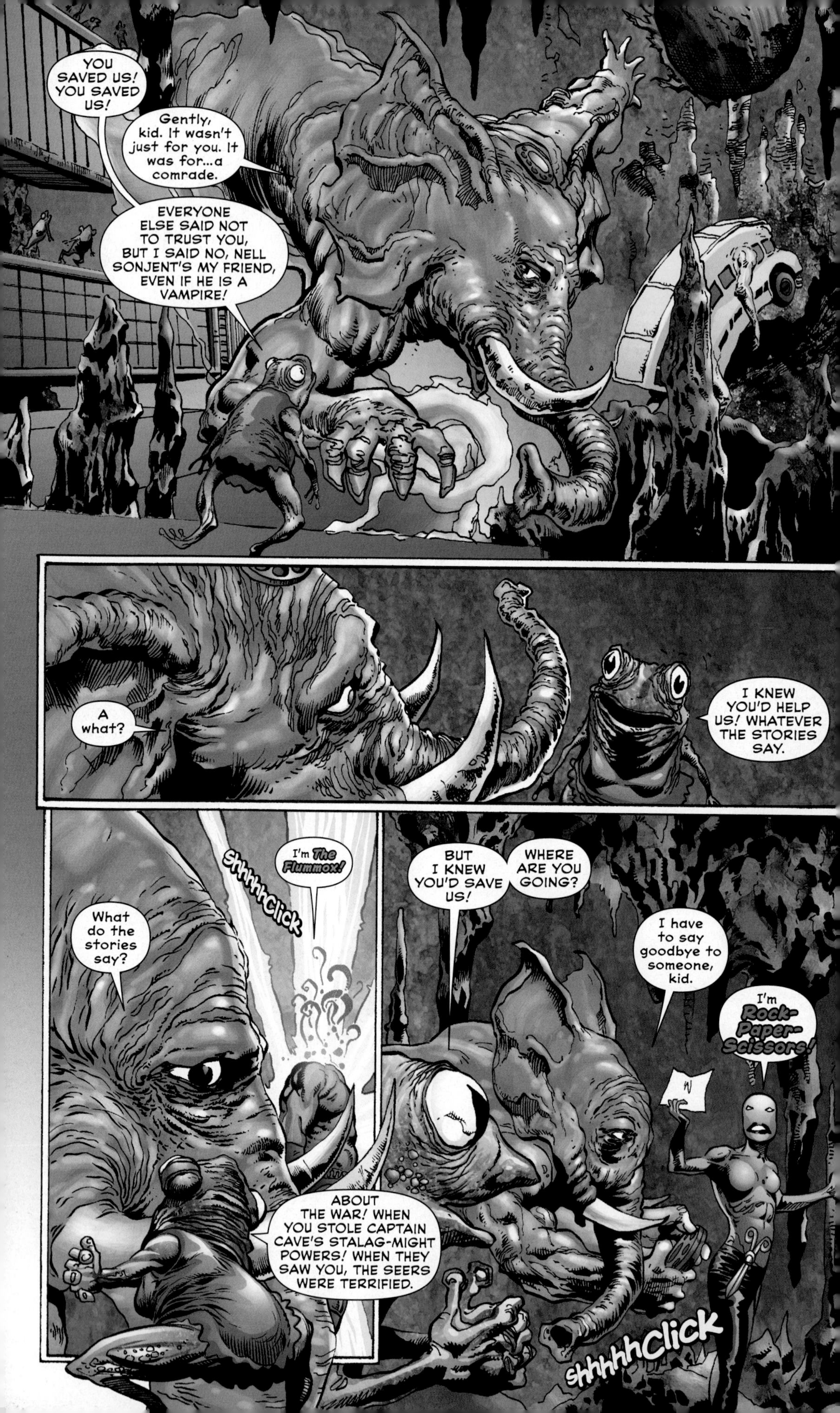
YOU SAVED US! YOU SAVED US!
Gently, kid. It wasn't just for you. It was for...a comrade.
EVERYONE ELSE SAID NOT TO TRUST YOU, BUT I SAID NO, NELL SONJENT'S MY FRIEND, EVEN IF HE IS A VAMPIRE!
A what?
I KNEW YOU'D HELP US! WHATEVER THE STORIES SAY.
What do the stories say?
shhhhhClick
I'm The Flummox!
ABOUT THE WAR! WHEN YOU STOLE CAPTAIN CAVE'S STALAG-MIGHT POWERS! WHEN THEY SAW YOU, THE SEERS WERE TERRIFIED.
BUT I KNEW YOU'D SAVE US!
WHERE ARE YOU GOING?
I have to say goodbye to someone, kid.
I'm Rock-Paper-Scissors!
shhhhhClick

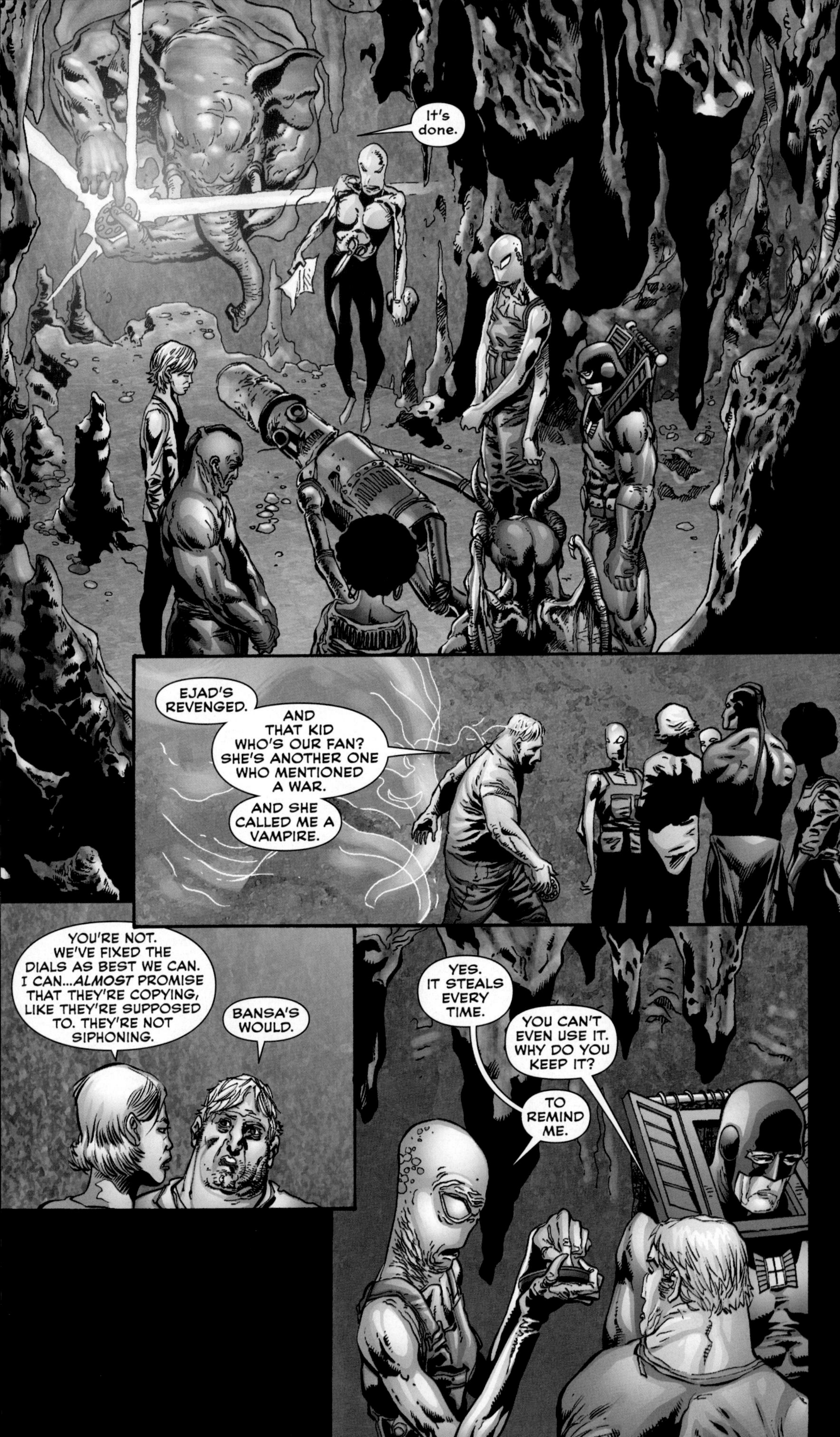
It's done.
EJAD'S REVENGED.
AND THAT KID WHO'S OUR FAN? SHE'S ANOTHER ONE WHO MENTIONED A WAR.
AND SHE CALLED ME A VAMPIRE.
YOU'RE NOT. WE'VE FIXED THE DIALS AS BEST WE CAN. I CAN...*ALMOST* PROMISE THAT THEY'RE COPYING, LIKE THEY'RE SUPPOSED TO. THEY'RE NOT SIPHONING.
BANSA'S WOULD.
YES. IT STEALS EVERY TIME.
YOU CAN'T EVEN USE IT. WHY DO YOU KEEP IT?
TO REMIND ME.

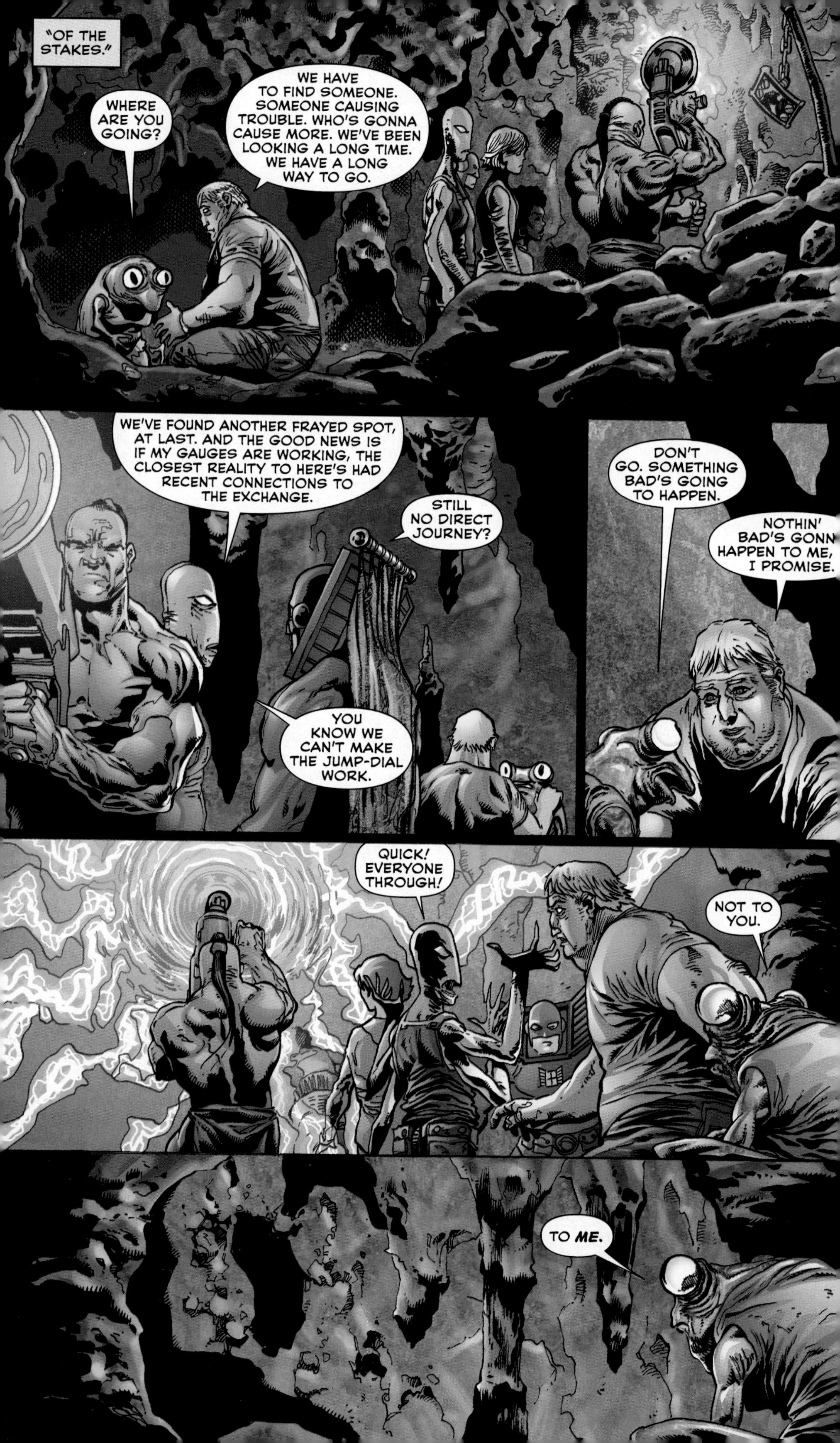
"OF THE STAKES."
WHERE ARE YOU GOING?
WE HAVE TO FIND SOMEONE. SOMEONE CAUSING TROUBLE. WHO'S GONNA CAUSE MORE. WE'VE BEEN LOOKING A LONG TIME. WE HAVE A LONG WAY TO GO.
WE'VE FOUND ANOTHER FRAYED SPOT, AT LAST. AND THE GOOD NEWS IS IF MY GAUGES ARE WORKING, THE CLOSEST REALITY TO HERE'S HAD RECENT CONNECTIONS TO THE EXCHANGE.
STILL NO DIRECT JOURNEY?
YOU KNOW WE CAN'T MAKE THE JUMP-DIAL WORK.
DON'T GO. SOMETHING BAD'S GOING TO HAPPEN.
NOTHIN' BAD'S GONN HAPPEN TO ME, I PROMISE.
QUICK! EVERYONE THROUGH!
NOT TO YOU.
TO *ME*.

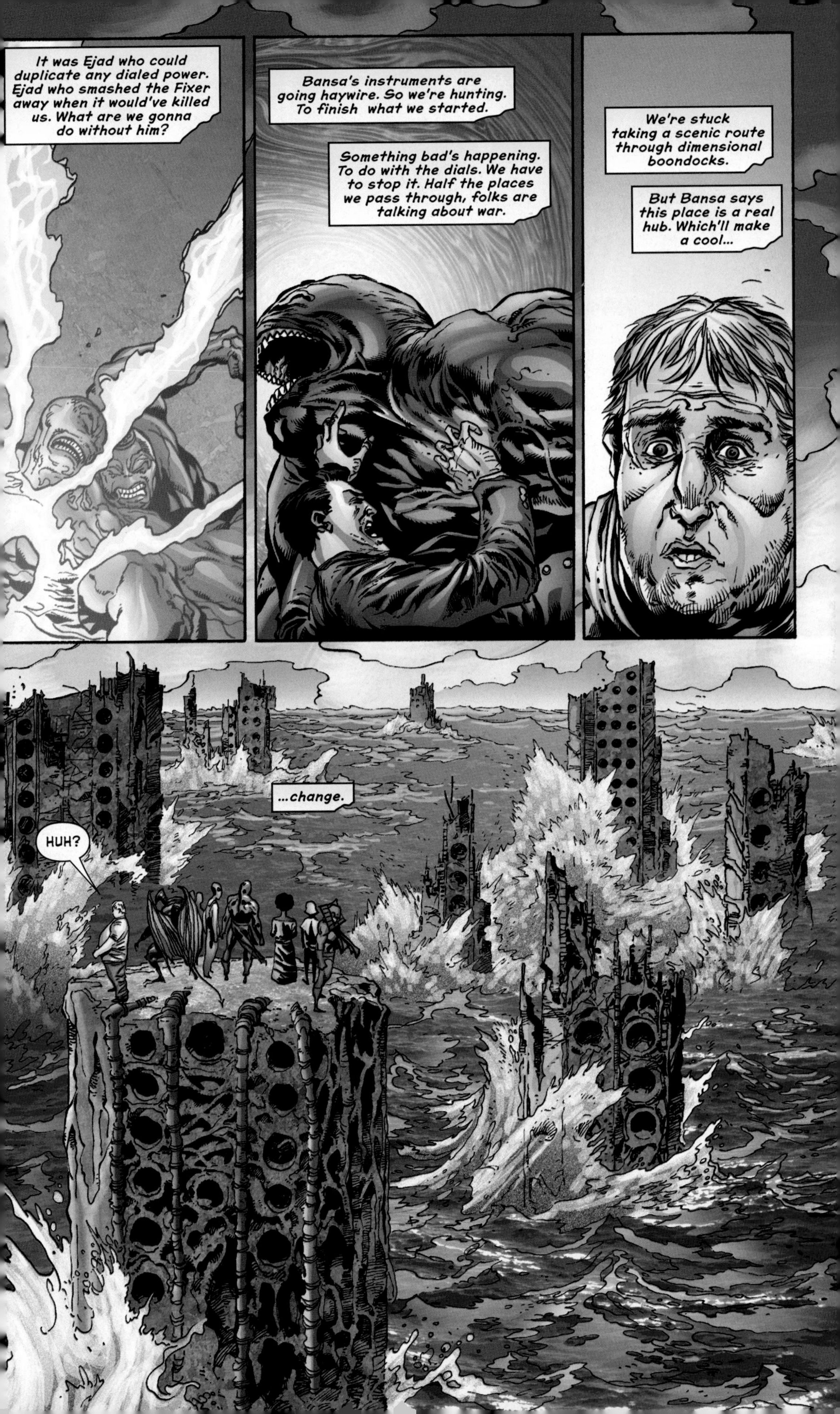
It was Ejad who could duplicate any dialed power. Ejad who smashed the Fixer away when it would've killed us. What are we gonna do without him?
Bansa's instruments are going haywire. So we're hunting. To finish what we started.
Something bad's happening. To do with the dials. We have to stop it. Half the places we pass through, folks are talking about war.
We're stuck taking a scenic route through dimensional boondocks.
But Bansa says this place is a real hub. Which'll make a cool...
...change.
HUH?

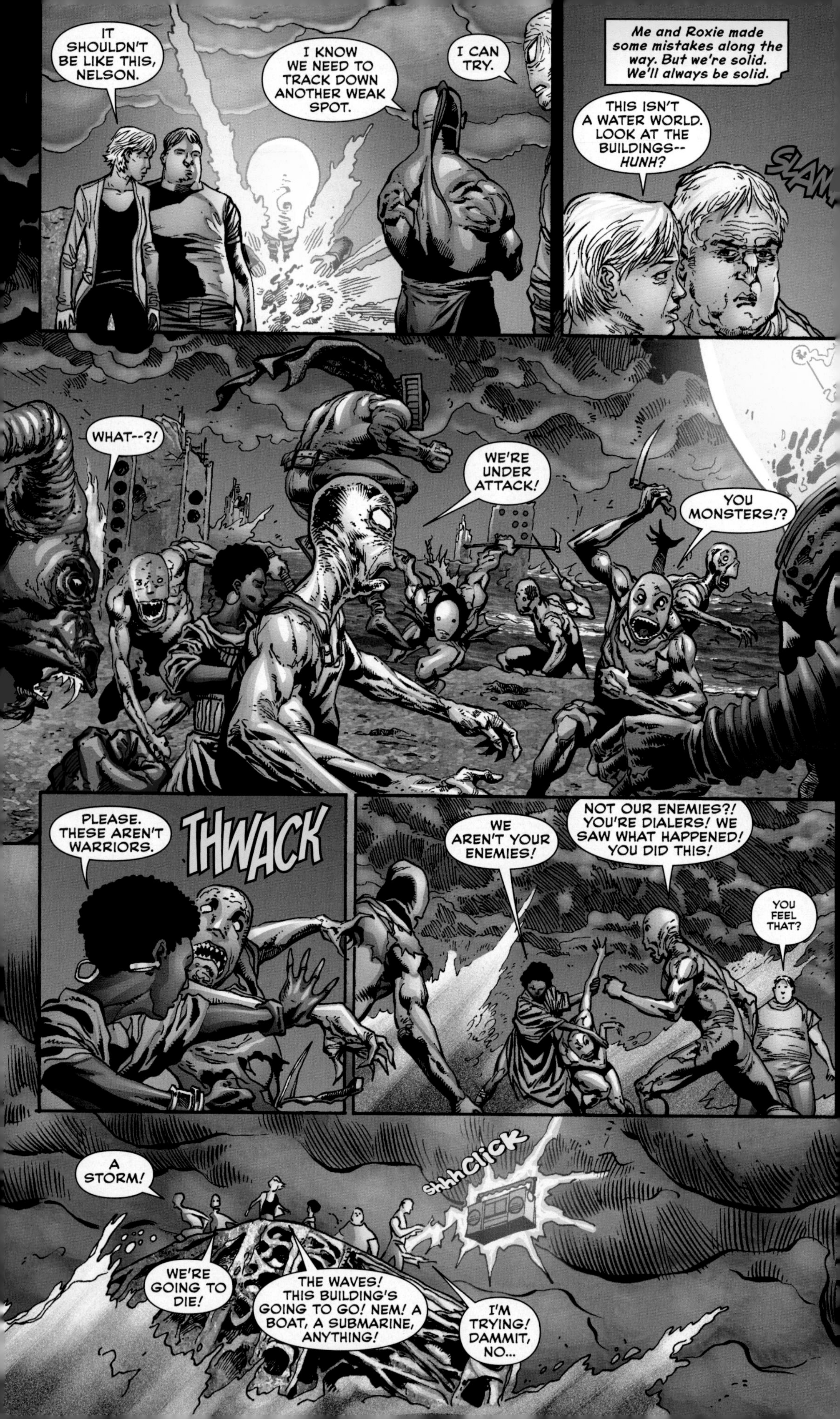
IT SHOULDN'T BE LIKE THIS, NELSON.
I KNOW WE NEED TO TRACK DOWN ANOTHER WEAK SPOT.
I CAN TRY.
Me and Roxie made some mistakes along the way. But we're solid. We'll always be solid.
THIS ISN'T A WATER WORLD. LOOK AT THE BUILDINGS-- *HUNH?*
SLAM
WHAT--?!
WE'RE UNDER ATTACK!
YOU MONSTERS!?
PLEASE. THESE AREN'T WARRIORS.
THWACK
WE AREN'T YOUR ENEMIES!
NOT OUR ENEMIES?! YOU'RE DIALERS! WE SAW WHAT HAPPENED! YOU DID THIS!
YOU FEEL THAT?
A STORM!
ShhhClick
WE'RE GOING TO DIE!
THE WAVES! THIS BUILDING'S GOING TO GO! NEM! A BOAT, A SUBMARINE, ANYTHING!
I'M TRYING! DAMMIT, NO...

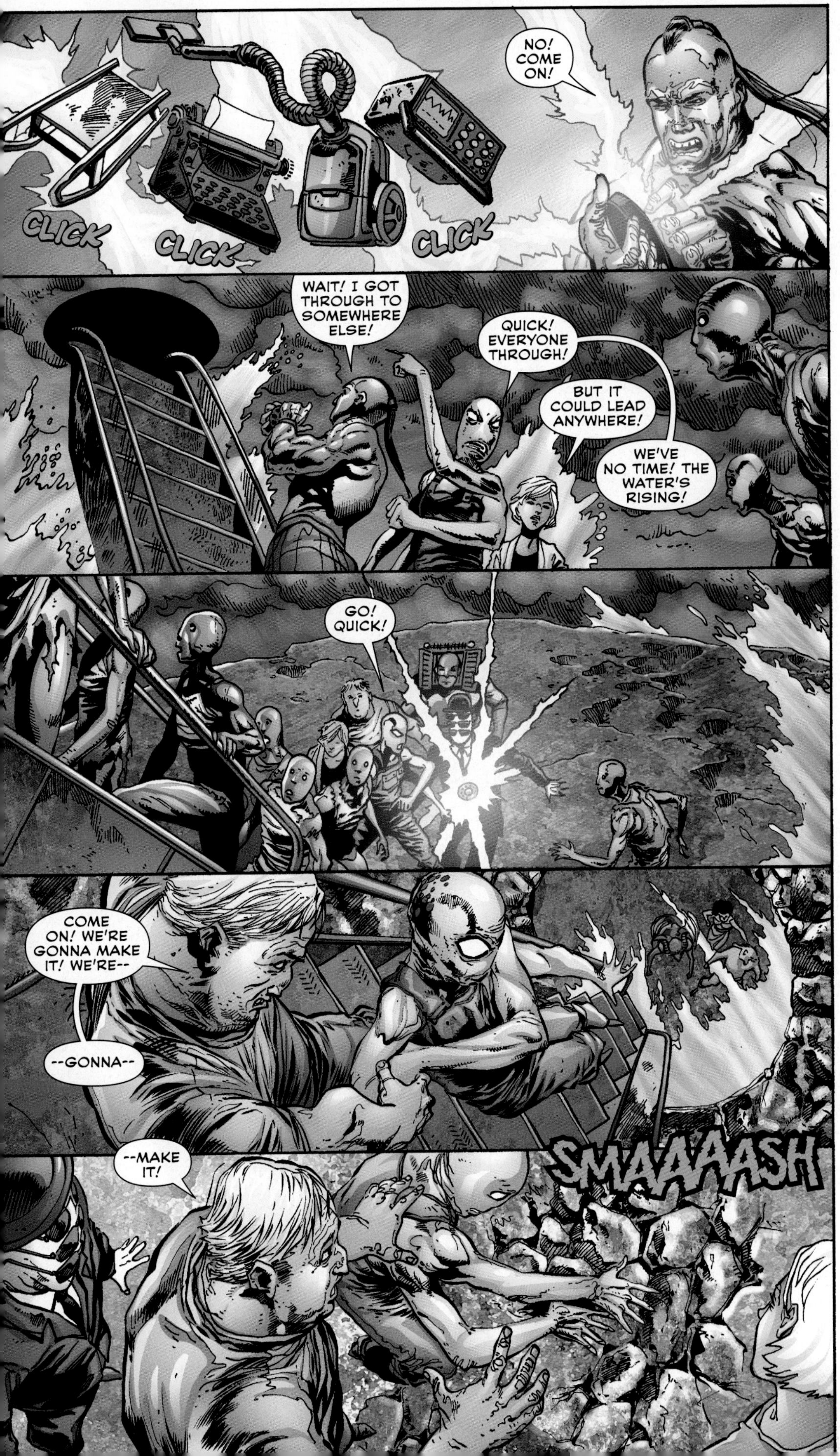

CLICK
CLICK
CLICK
NO! COME ON!
WAIT! I GOT THROUGH TO SOMEWHERE ELSE!
QUICK! EVERYONE THROUGH!
BUT IT COULD LEAD ANYWHERE!
WE'VE NO TIME! THE WATER'S RISING!
GO! QUICK!
COME ON! WE'RE GONNA MAKE IT! WE'RE--
--GONNA--
SMAAAAASH
--MAKE IT!

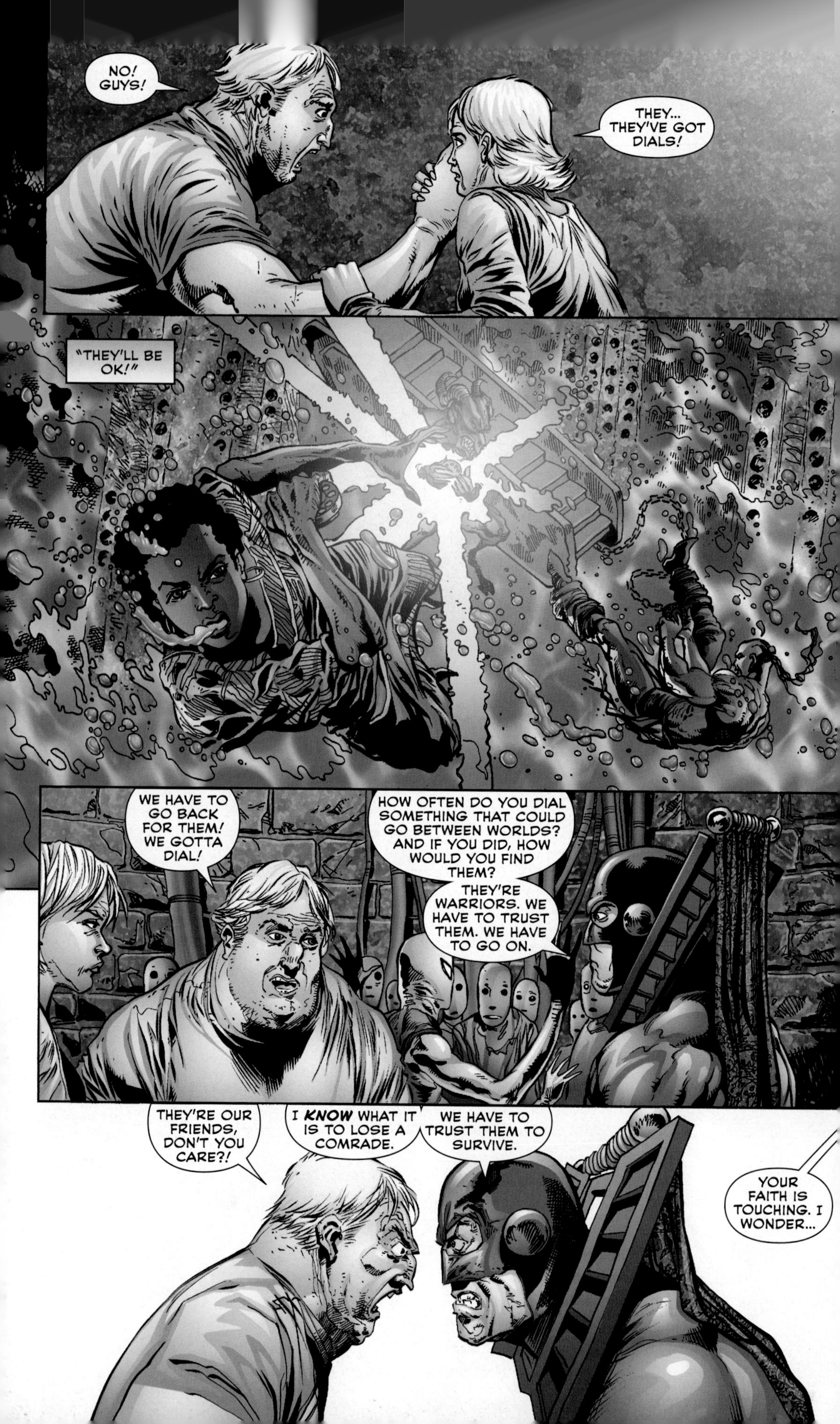
NO! GUYS!
THEY... THEY'VE GOT DIALS!
"THEY'LL BE OK!"
WE HAVE TO GO BACK FOR THEM! WE GOTTA DIAL!
HOW OFTEN DO YOU DIAL SOMETHING THAT COULD GO BETWEEN WORLDS? AND IF YOU DID, HOW WOULD YOU FIND THEM?
THEY'RE WARRIORS. WE HAVE TO TRUST THEM. WE HAVE TO GO ON.
THEY'RE OUR FRIENDS, DON'T YOU CARE?!
I *KNOW* WHAT IT IS TO LOSE A COMRADE.
WE HAVE TO TRUST THEM TO SURVIVE.
YOUR FAITH IS TOUCHING. I WONDER...

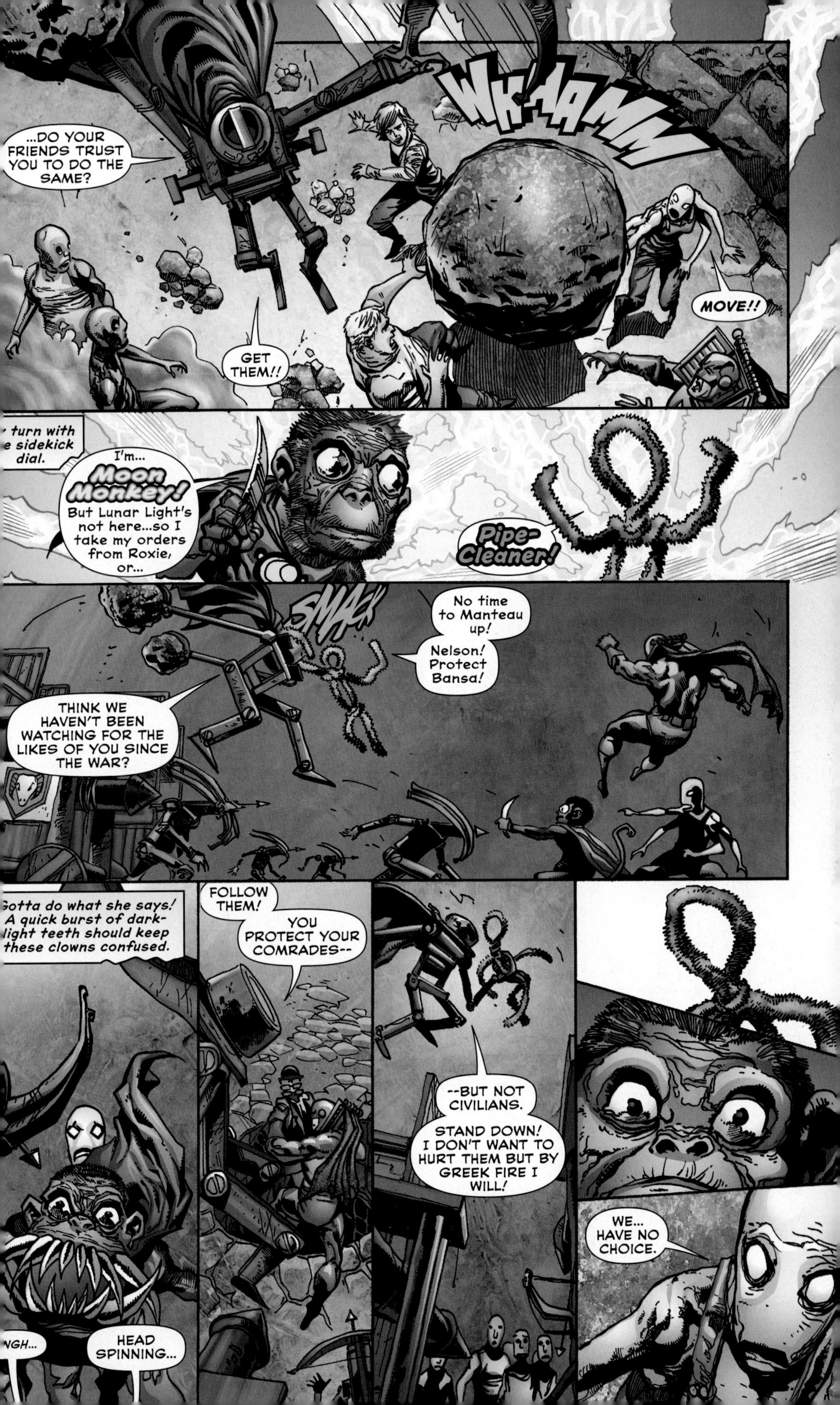
WK-RAMM
...DO YOUR FRIENDS TRUST YOU TO DO THE SAME?
GET THEM!!
MOVE!!
turn with e sidekick dial.
I'm... Moon Monkey! But Lunar Light's not here...so I take my orders from Roxie, or...
Pipe-Cleaner!
SMACK
No time to Manteau up!
Nelson! Protect Bansa!
THINK WE HAVEN'T BEEN WATCHING FOR THE LIKES OF YOU SINCE THE WAR?
Gotta do what she says! A quick burst of dark-light teeth should keep these clowns confused.
NGH...
HEAD SPINNING...
FOLLOW THEM!
YOU PROTECT YOUR COMRADES--
--BUT NOT CIVILIANS.
STAND DOWN! I DON'T WANT TO HURT THEM BUT BY GREEK FIRE I WILL!
WE... HAVE NO CHOICE.

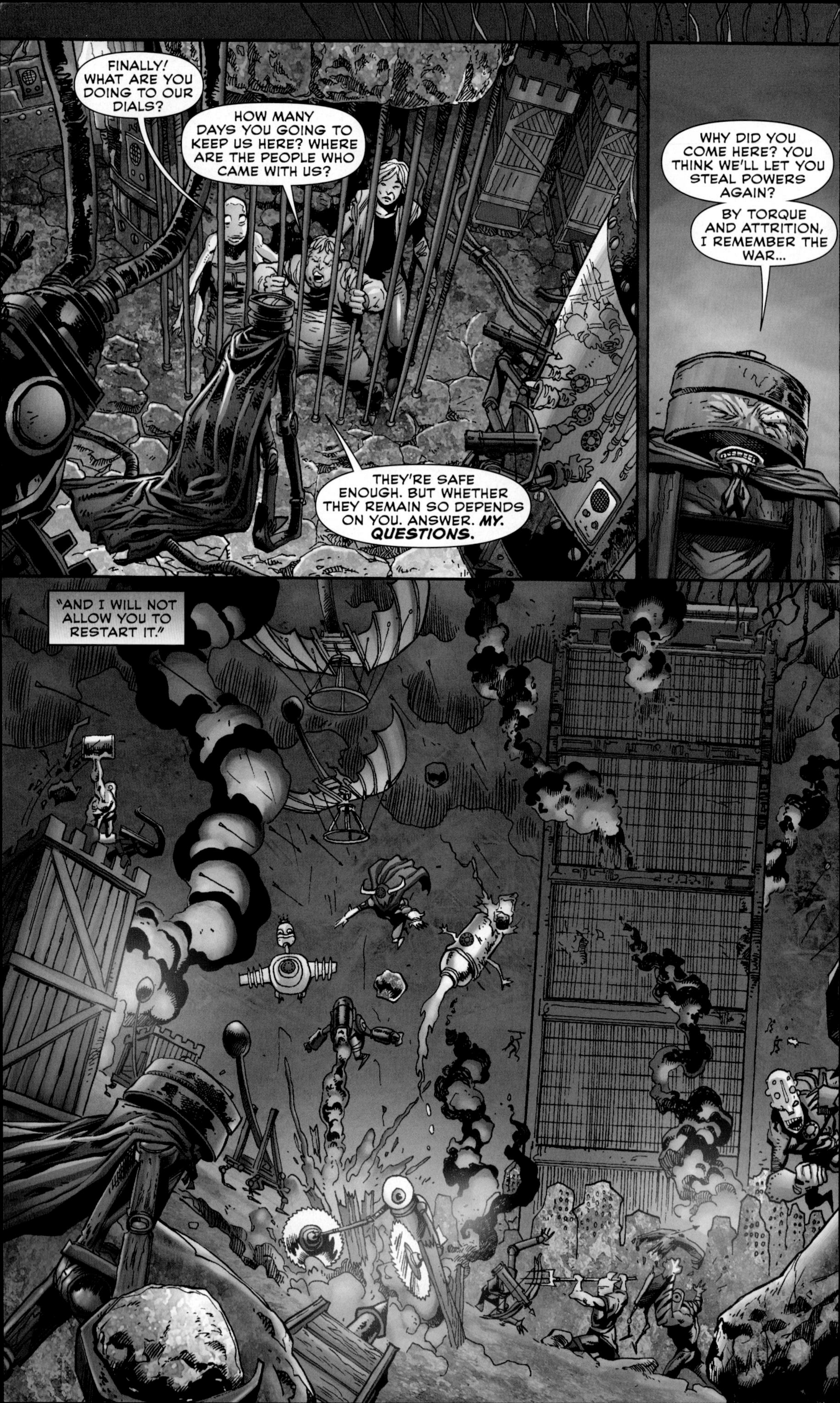
FINALLY! WHAT ARE YOU DOING TO OUR DIALS?
HOW MANY DAYS YOU GOING TO KEEP US HERE? WHERE ARE THE PEOPLE WHO CAME WITH US?
THEY'RE SAFE ENOUGH. BUT WHETHER THEY REMAIN SO DEPENDS ON YOU. ANSWER. **MY. QUESTIONS.**
WHY DID YOU COME HERE? YOU THINK WE'LL LET YOU STEAL POWERS AGAIN?
BY TORQUE AND ATTRITION, I REMEMBER THE WAR...
"AND I WILL NOT ALLOW YOU TO RESTART IT."

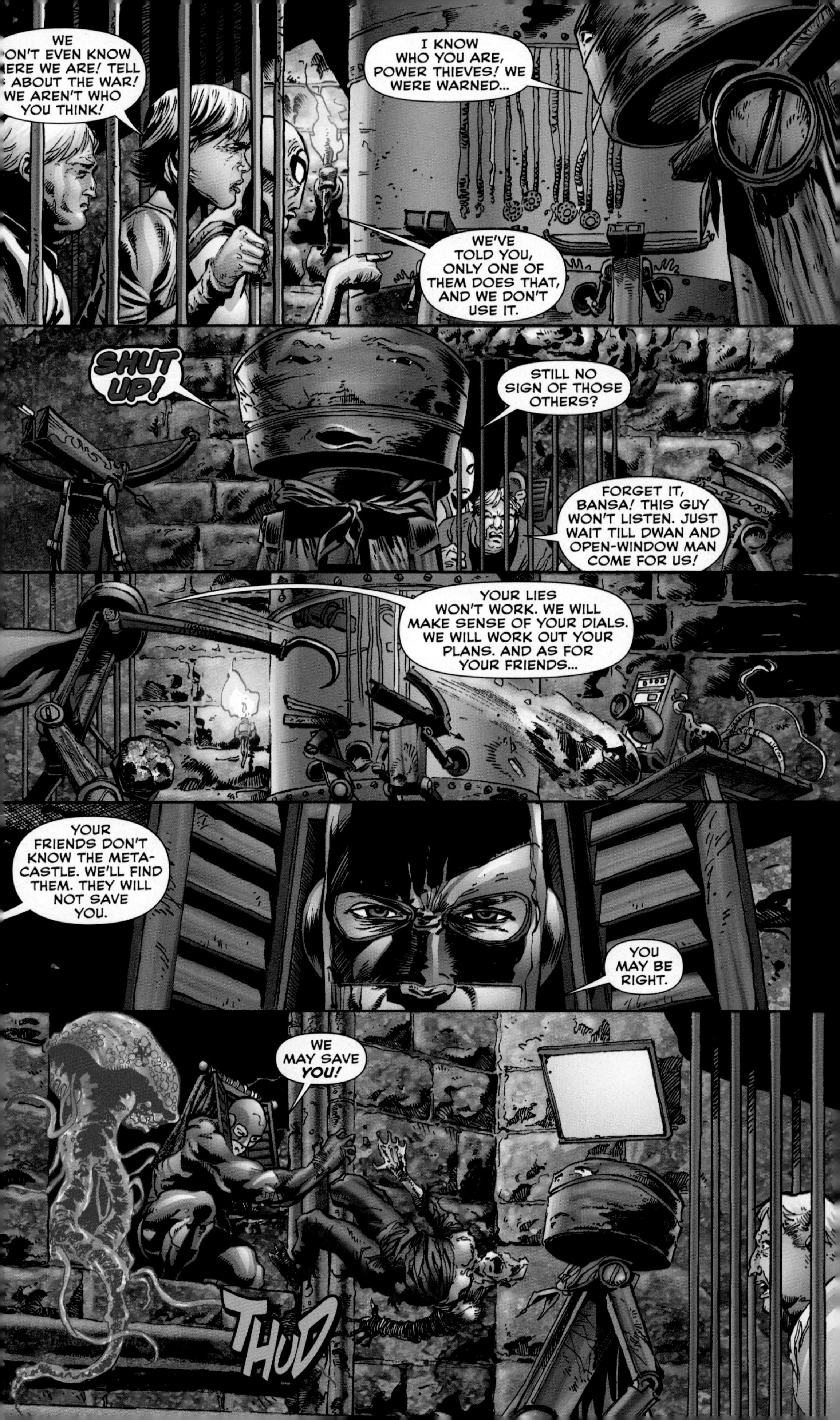
WE ON'T EVEN KNOW ERE WE ARE! TELL ABOUT THE WAR! WE AREN'T WHO YOU THINK!
I KNOW WHO YOU ARE, POWER THIEVES! WE WERE WARNED...
WE'VE TOLD YOU, ONLY ONE OF THEM DOES THAT, AND WE DON'T USE IT.
SHUT UP!
STILL NO SIGN OF THOSE OTHERS?
FORGET IT, BANSA! THIS GUY WON'T LISTEN. JUST WAIT TILL DWAN AND OPEN-WINDOW MAN COME FOR US!
YOUR LIES WON'T WORK. WE WILL MAKE SENSE OF YOUR DIALS. WE WILL WORK OUT YOUR PLANS. AND AS FOR YOUR FRIENDS...
YOUR FRIENDS DON'T KNOW THE META-CASTLE. WE'LL FIND THEM. THEY WILL NOT SAVE YOU.
YOU MAY BE RIGHT.
WE MAY SAVE YOU!
THUD

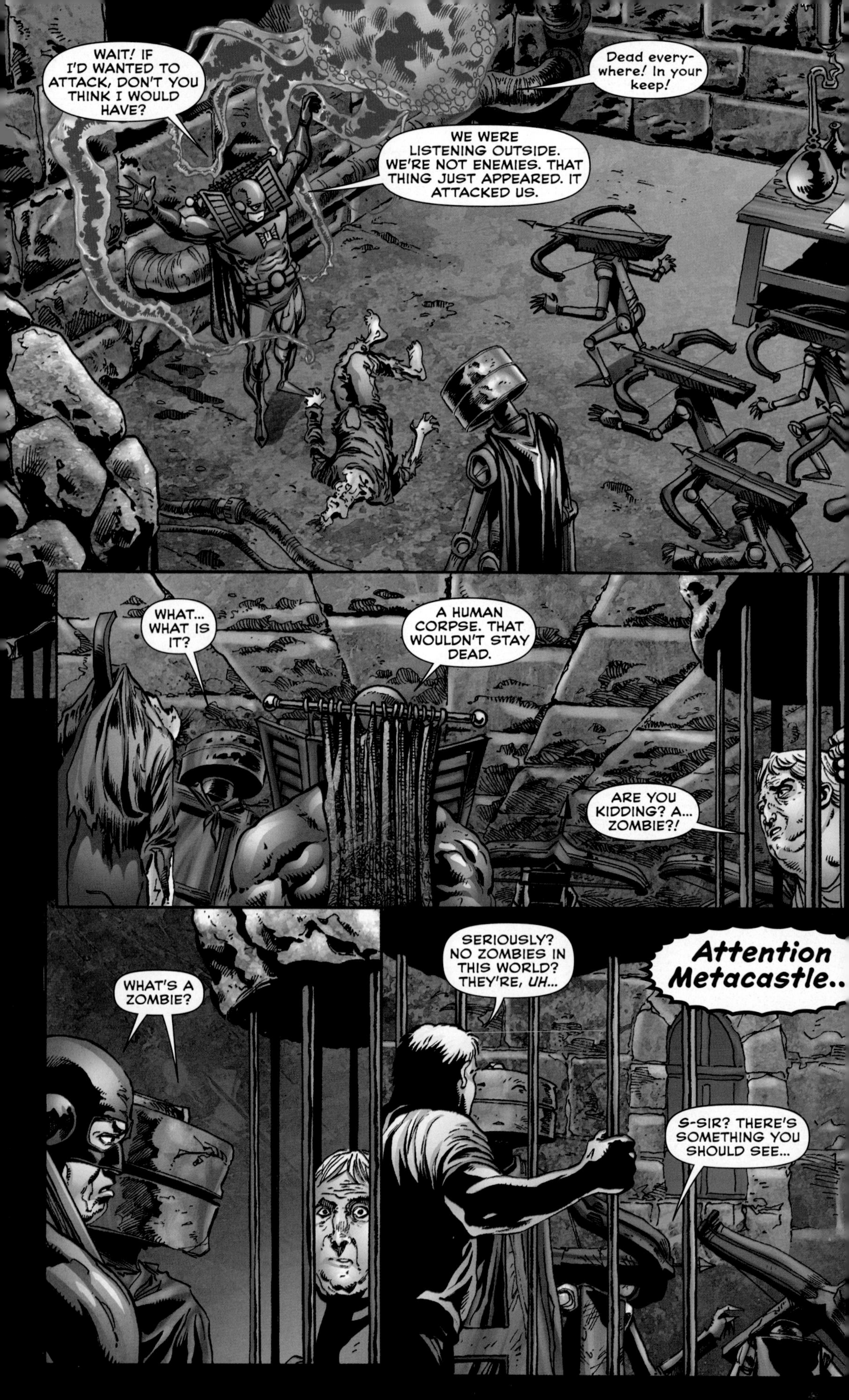
WAIT! IF I'D WANTED TO ATTACK, DON'T YOU THINK I WOULD HAVE?
Dead every-where! In your keep!
WE WERE LISTENING OUTSIDE. WE'RE NOT ENEMIES. THAT THING JUST APPEARED. IT ATTACKED US.
WHAT... WHAT IS IT?
A HUMAN CORPSE. THAT WOULDN'T STAY DEAD.
ARE YOU KIDDING? A... ZOMBIE?!
WHAT'S A ZOMBIE?
SERIOUSLY? NO ZOMBIES IN THIS WORLD? THEY'RE, UH...
Attention Metacastle..
S-SIR? THERE'S SOMETHING YOU SHOULD SEE...

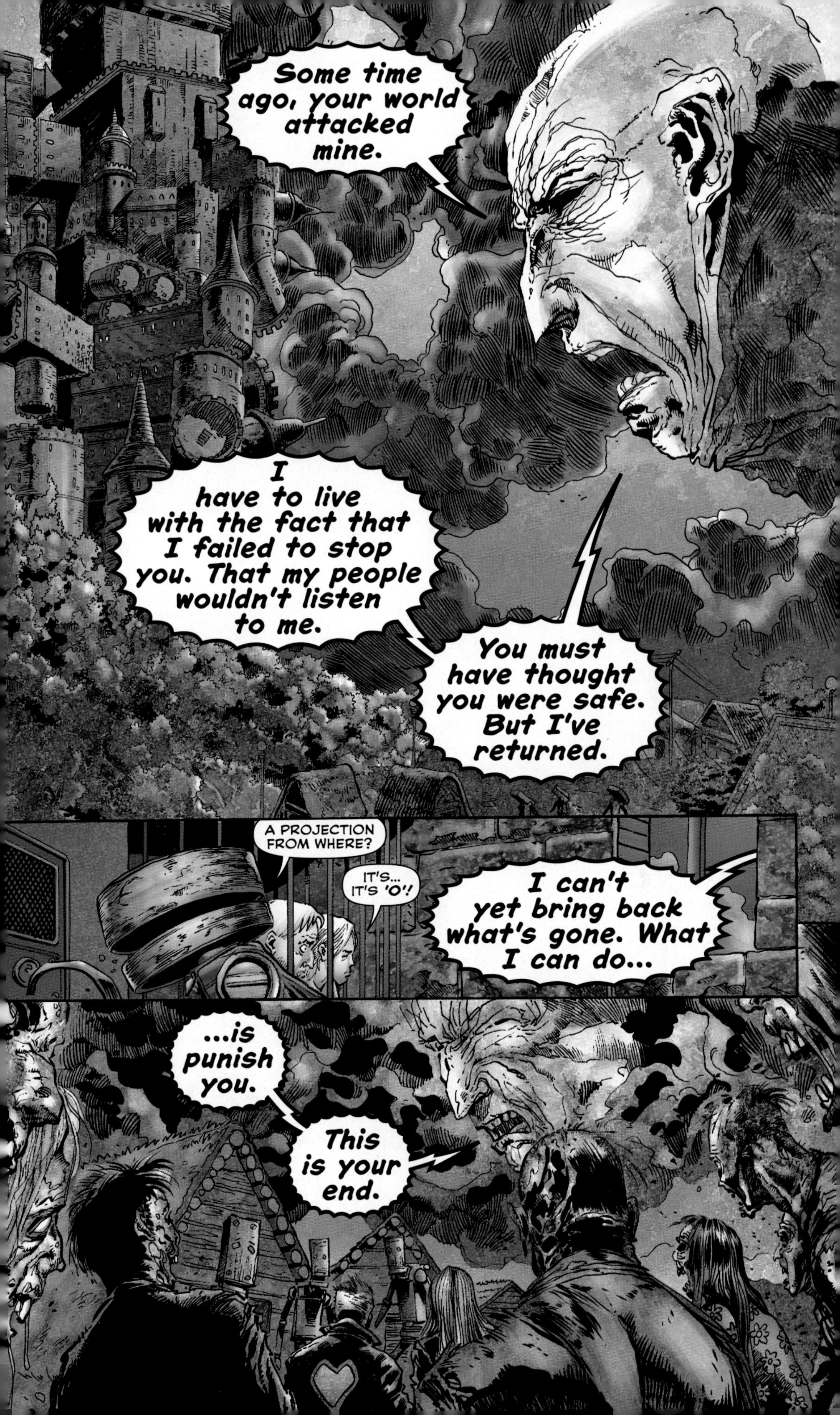
Some time ago, your world attacked mine.
I have to live with the fact that I failed to stop you. That my people wouldn't listen to me.
You must have thought you were safe. But I've returned.
A PROJECTION FROM WHERE?
IT'S... IT'S 'O'!
I can't yet bring back what's gone. What I can do...
...is punish you.
This is your end.

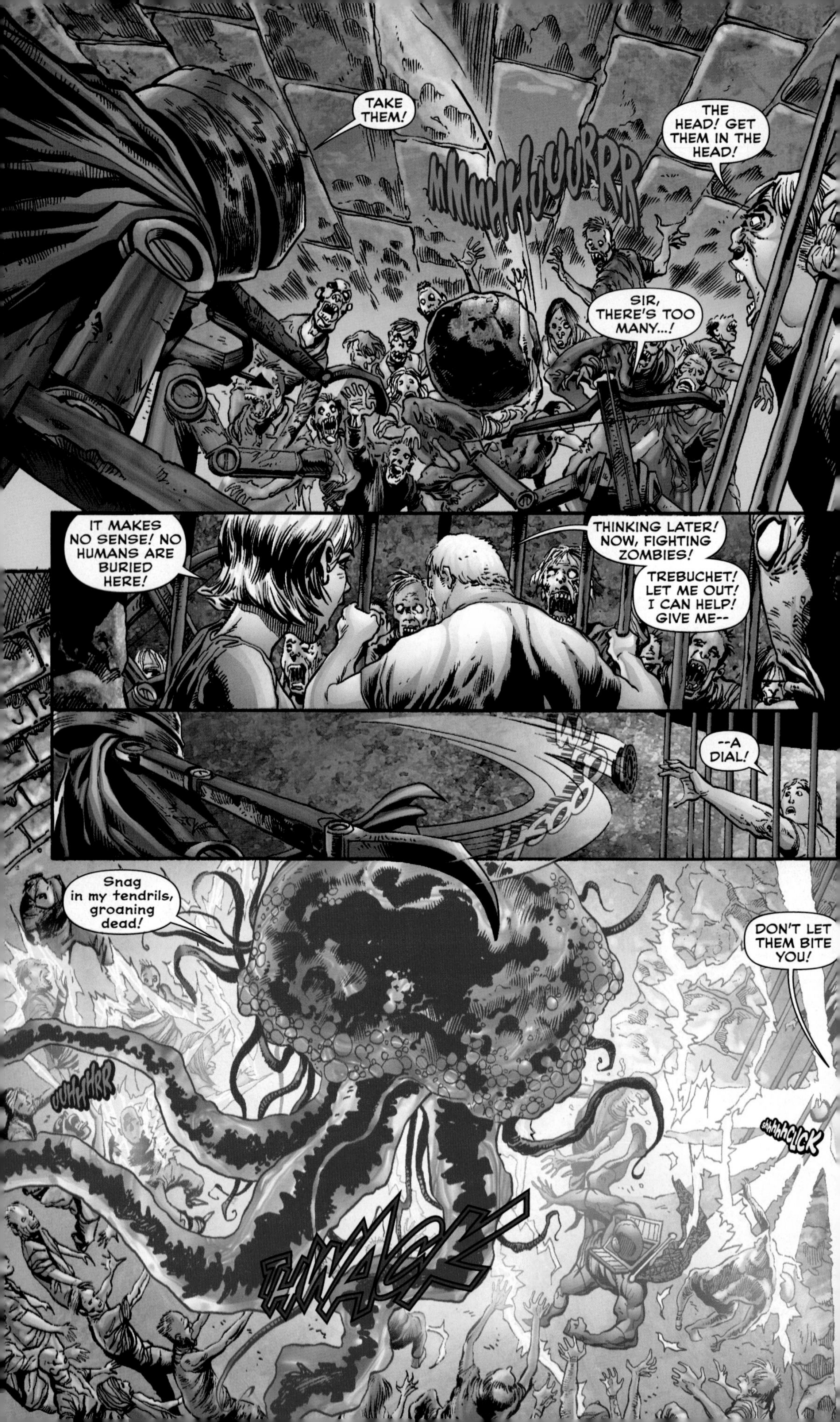
TAKE THEM!
MMMMHHUURRR
THE HEAD! GET THEM IN THE HEAD!
SIR, THERE'S TOO MANY...!
IT MAKES NO SENSE! NO HUMANS ARE BURIED HERE!
THINKING LATER! NOW, FIGHTING ZOMBIES!
TREBUCHET! LET ME OUT! I CAN HELP! GIVE ME--
--A DIAL!
Snag in my tendrils, groaning dead!
DON'T LET THEM BITE YOU!
UUHHHRR
SHHHHCLICK
THWACK

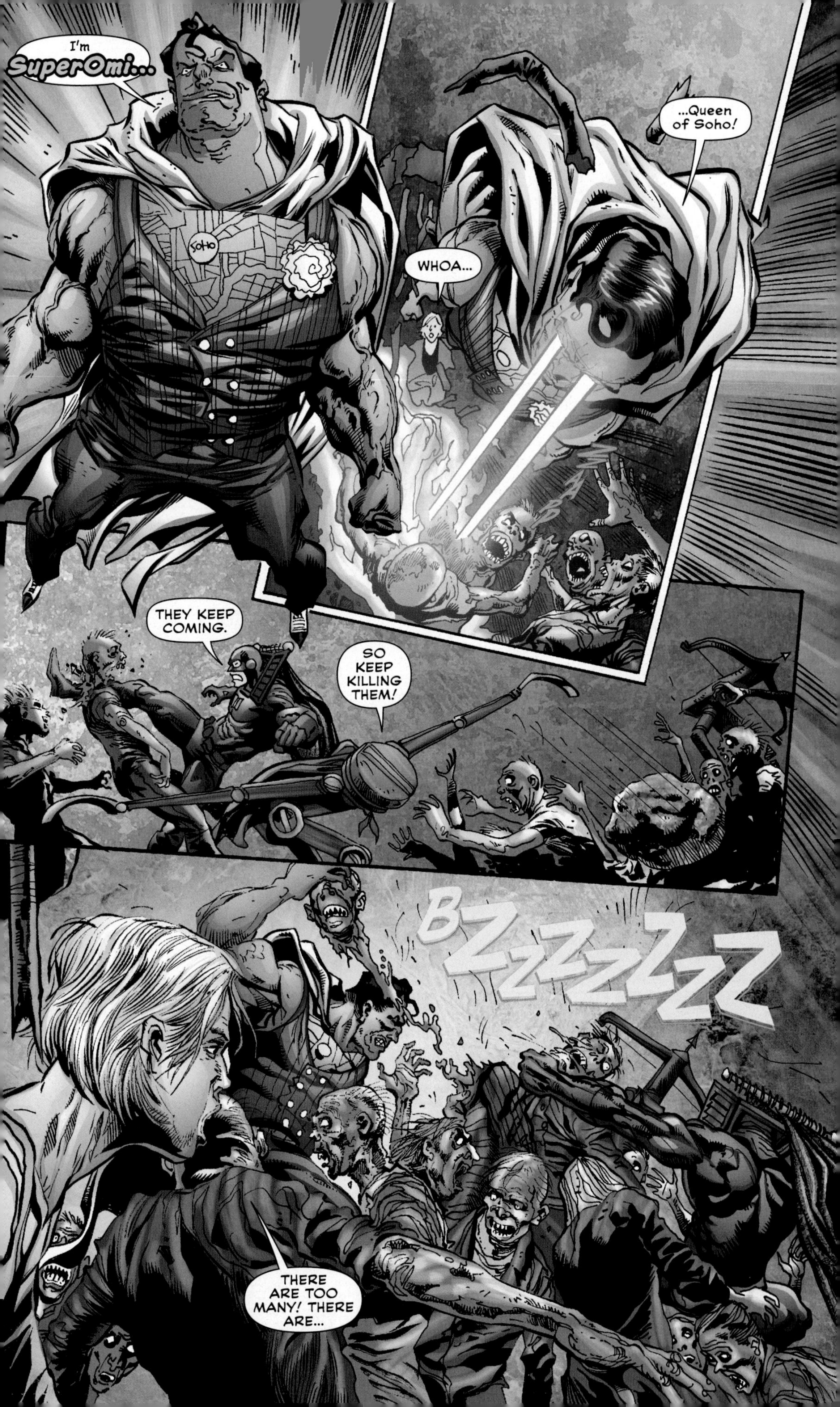
I'm
SuperOmi...
...Queen of Soho!
SOHO
WHOA...
THEY KEEP COMING.
SO KEEP KILLING THEM!
BZZZZZZZ
THERE ARE TOO MANY! THERE ARE...

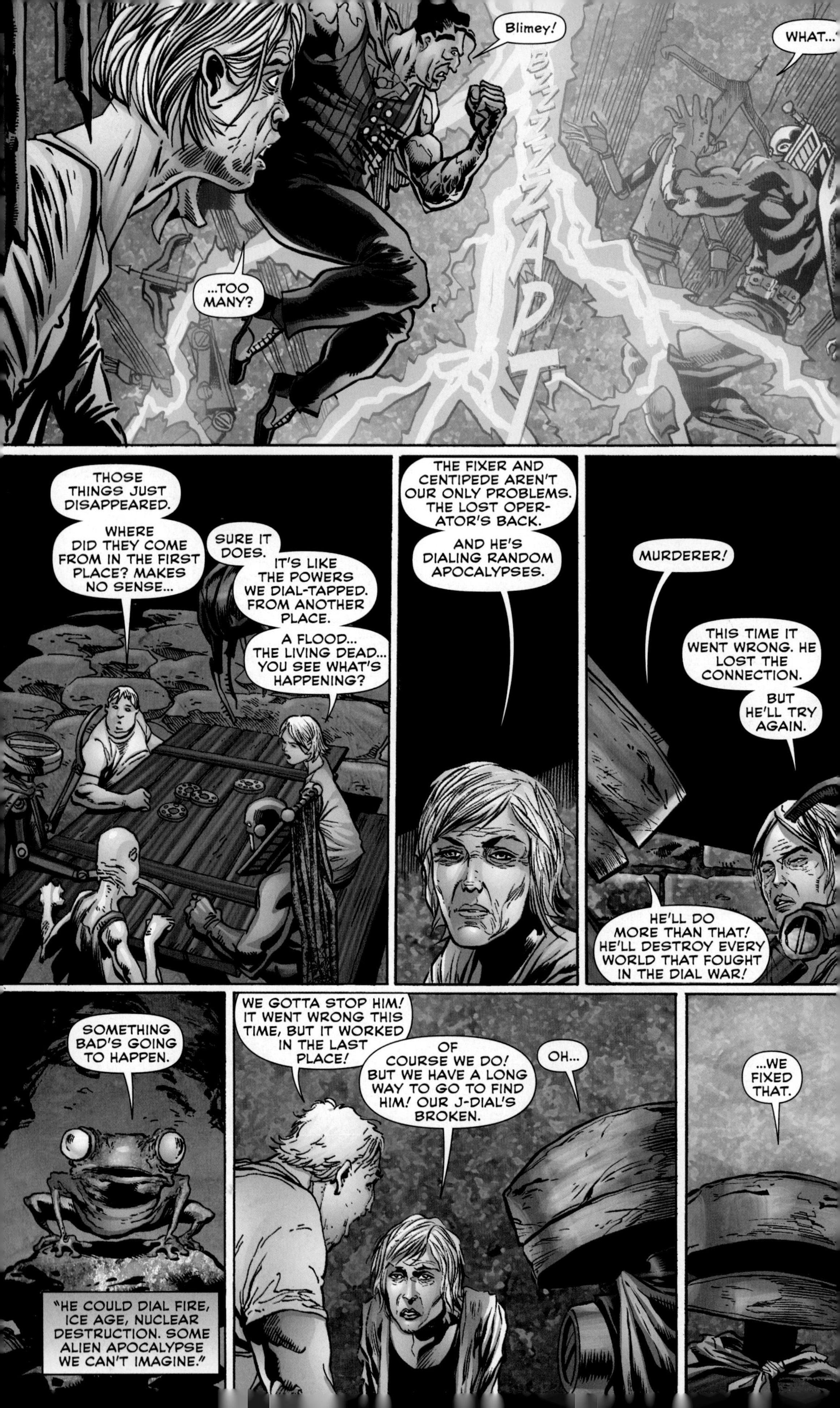
Blimey!
WHAT...
BZZZZZZAPT
...TOO MANY?
THOSE THINGS JUST DISAPPEARED.
WHERE DID THEY COME FROM IN THE FIRST PLACE? MAKES NO SENSE...
SURE IT DOES.
IT'S LIKE THE POWERS WE DIAL-TAPPED. FROM ANOTHER PLACE.
A FLOOD... THE LIVING DEAD... YOU SEE WHAT'S HAPPENING?
THE FIXER AND CENTIPEDE AREN'T OUR ONLY PROBLEMS. THE LOST OPERATOR'S BACK.
AND HE'S DIALING RANDOM APOCALYPSES.
MURDERER!
THIS TIME IT WENT WRONG. HE LOST THE CONNECTION.
BUT HE'LL TRY AGAIN.
HE'LL DO MORE THAN THAT! HE'LL DESTROY EVERY WORLD THAT FOUGHT IN THE DIAL WAR!
SOMETHING BAD'S GOING TO HAPPEN.
"HE COULD DIAL FIRE, ICE AGE, NUCLEAR DESTRUCTION. SOME ALIEN APOCALYPSE WE CAN'T IMAGINE."
WE GOTTA STOP HIM! IT WENT WRONG THIS TIME, BUT IT WORKED IN THE LAST PLACE!
OF COURSE WE DO! BUT WE HAVE A LONG WAY TO GO TO FIND HIM! OUR J-DIAL'S BROKEN.
OH...
...WE FIXED THAT.

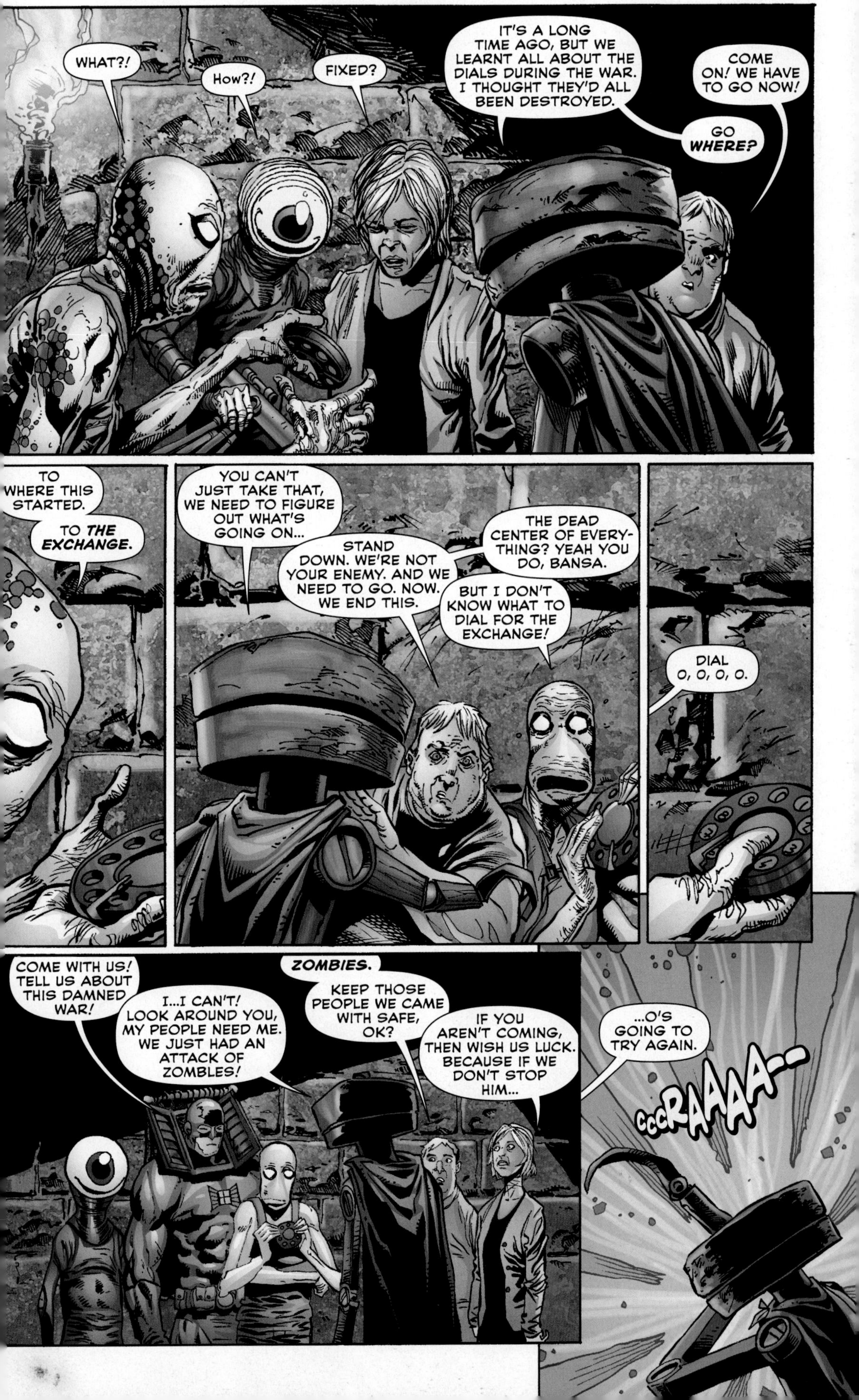
WHAT?!
How?!
FIXED?
IT'S A LONG TIME AGO, BUT WE LEARNT ALL ABOUT THE DIALS DURING THE WAR. I THOUGHT THEY'D ALL BEEN DESTROYED.
GO WHERE?
COME ON! WE HAVE TO GO NOW!
TO WHERE THIS STARTED.
TO THE EXCHANGE.
YOU CAN'T JUST TAKE THAT, WE NEED TO FIGURE OUT WHAT'S GOING ON...
STAND DOWN. WE'RE NOT YOUR ENEMY. AND WE NEED TO GO. NOW. WE END THIS.
THE DEAD CENTER OF EVERY-THING? YEAH YOU DO, BANSA.
BUT I DON'T KNOW WHAT TO DIAL FOR THE EXCHANGE!
DIAL 0, 0, 0, 0.
COME WITH US! TELL US ABOUT THIS DAMNED WAR!
I...I CAN'T! LOOK AROUND YOU, MY PEOPLE NEED ME. WE JUST HAD AN ATTACK OF ZOMBIES!
ZOMBIES.
KEEP THOSE PEOPLE WE CAME WITH SAFE, OK?
IF YOU AREN'T COMING, THEN WISH US LUCK. BECAUSE IF WE DON'T STOP HIM...
...0'S GOING TO TRY AGAIN.
CCCRAAAA--

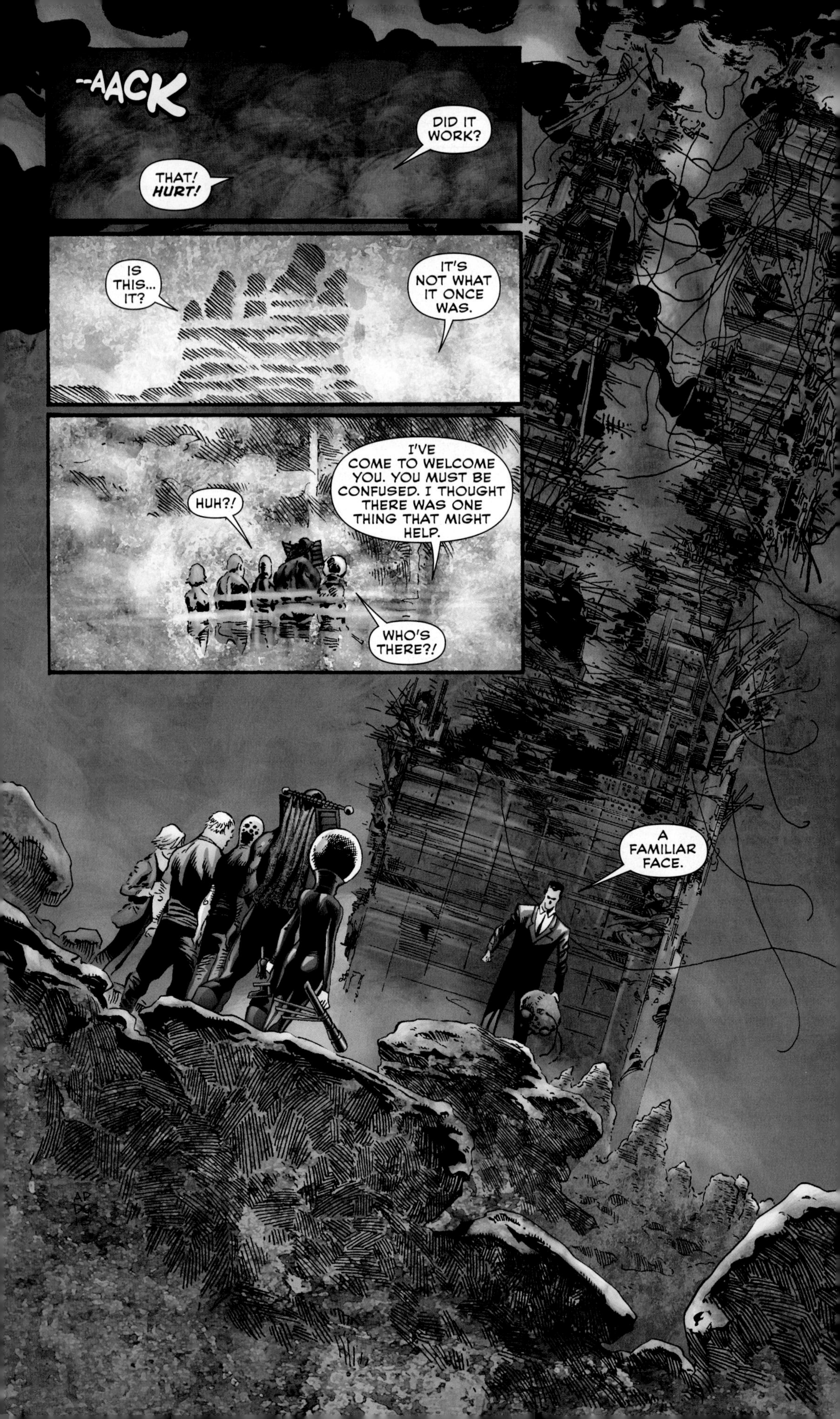
--AACK
DID IT WORK?
THAT! HURT!
IS THIS... IT?
IT'S NOT WHAT IT ONCE WAS.
I'VE COME TO WELCOME YOU. YOU MUST BE CONFUSED. I THOUGHT THERE WAS ONE THING THAT MIGHT HELP.
HUH?!
WHO'S THERE?!
A FAMILIAR FACE.

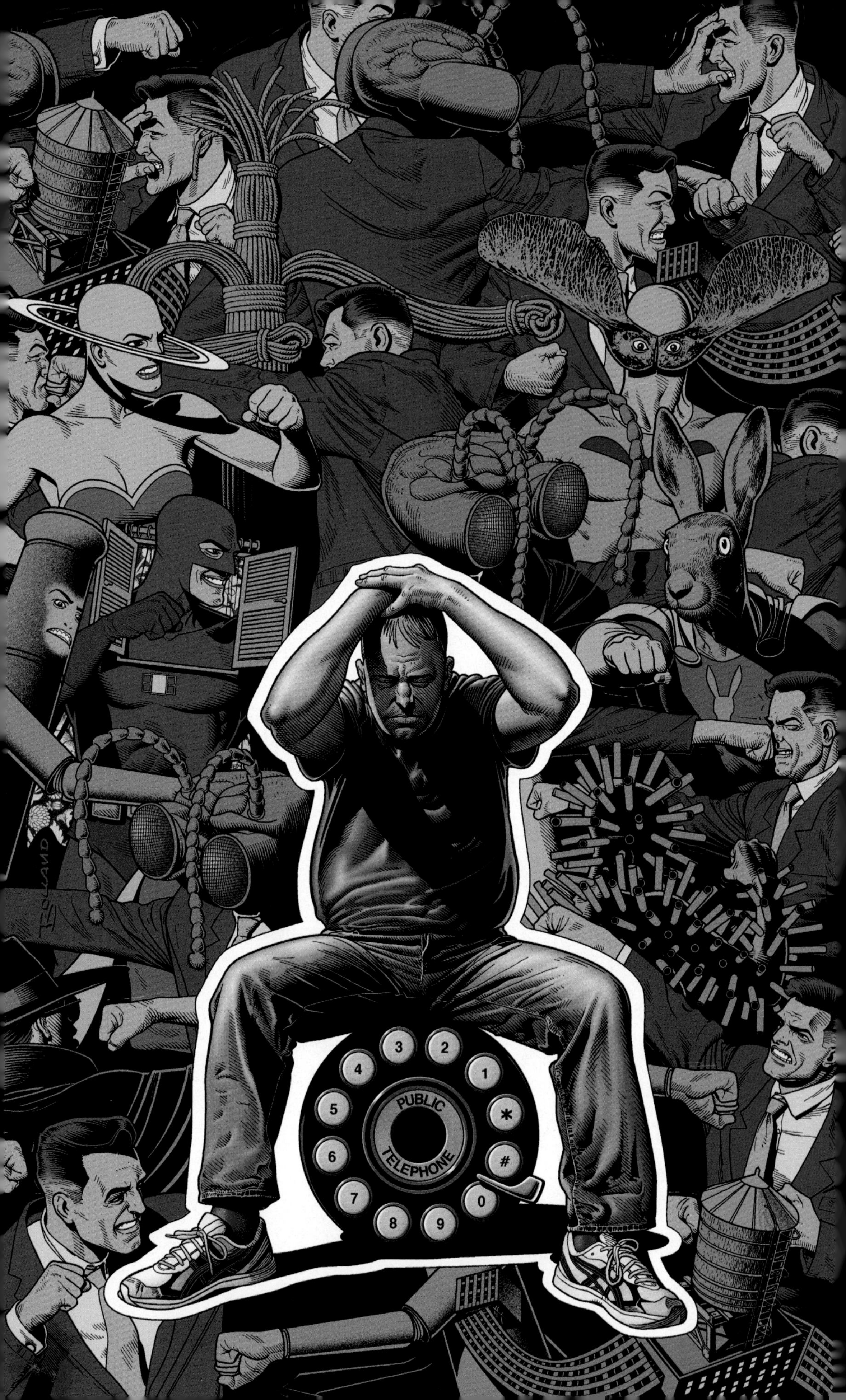
PUBLIC
TELEPHONE
3
2
4
1
5
*
6
#
7
0
8
9
BOLLAND

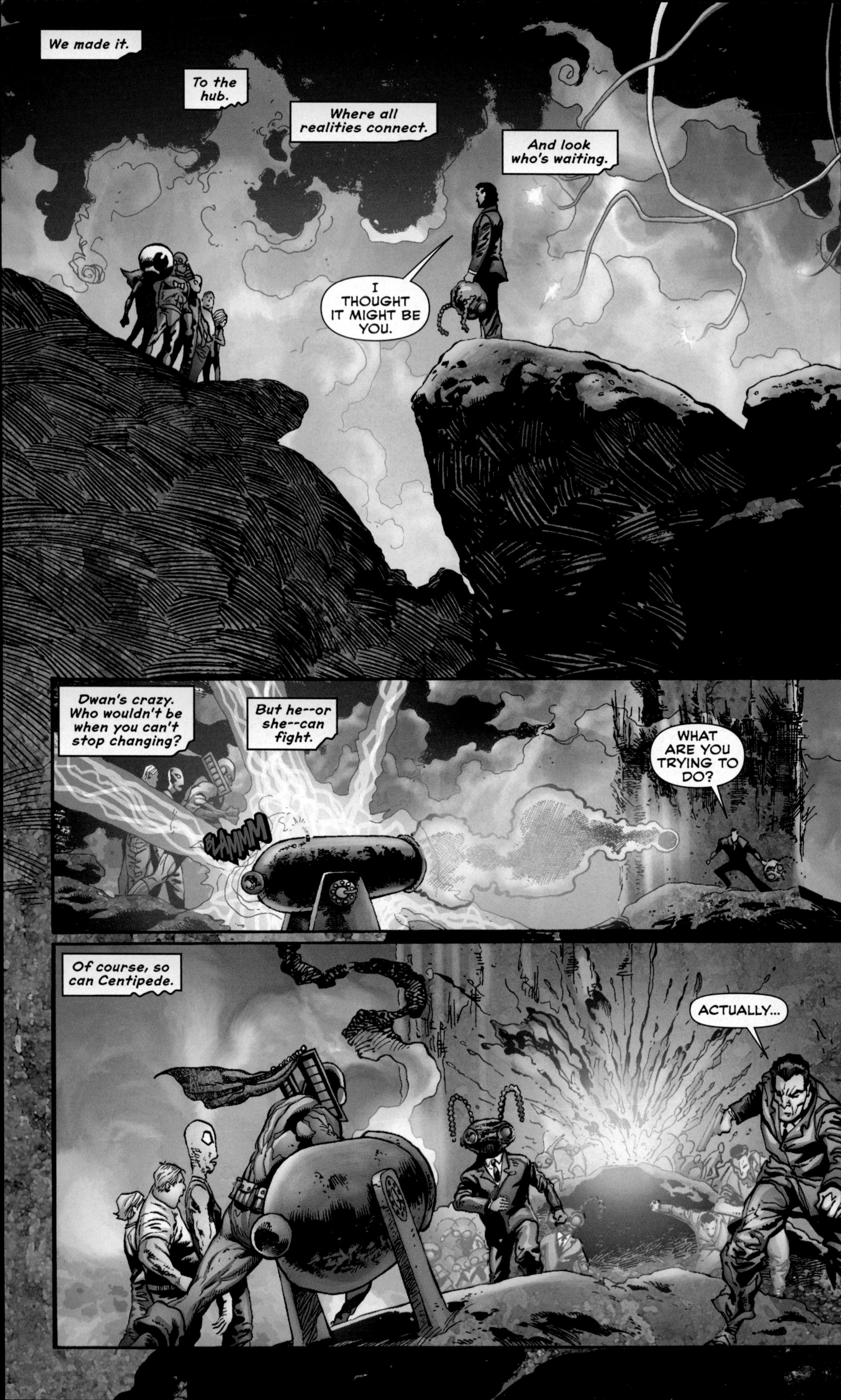
We made it.
To the hub.
Where all realities connect.
And look who's waiting.
I THOUGHT IT MIGHT BE YOU.
Dwan's crazy. Who wouldn't be when you can't stop changing?
But he--or she--can fight.
BLAMMM
WHAT ARE YOU TRYING TO DO?
Of course, so can Centipede.
ACTUALLY...

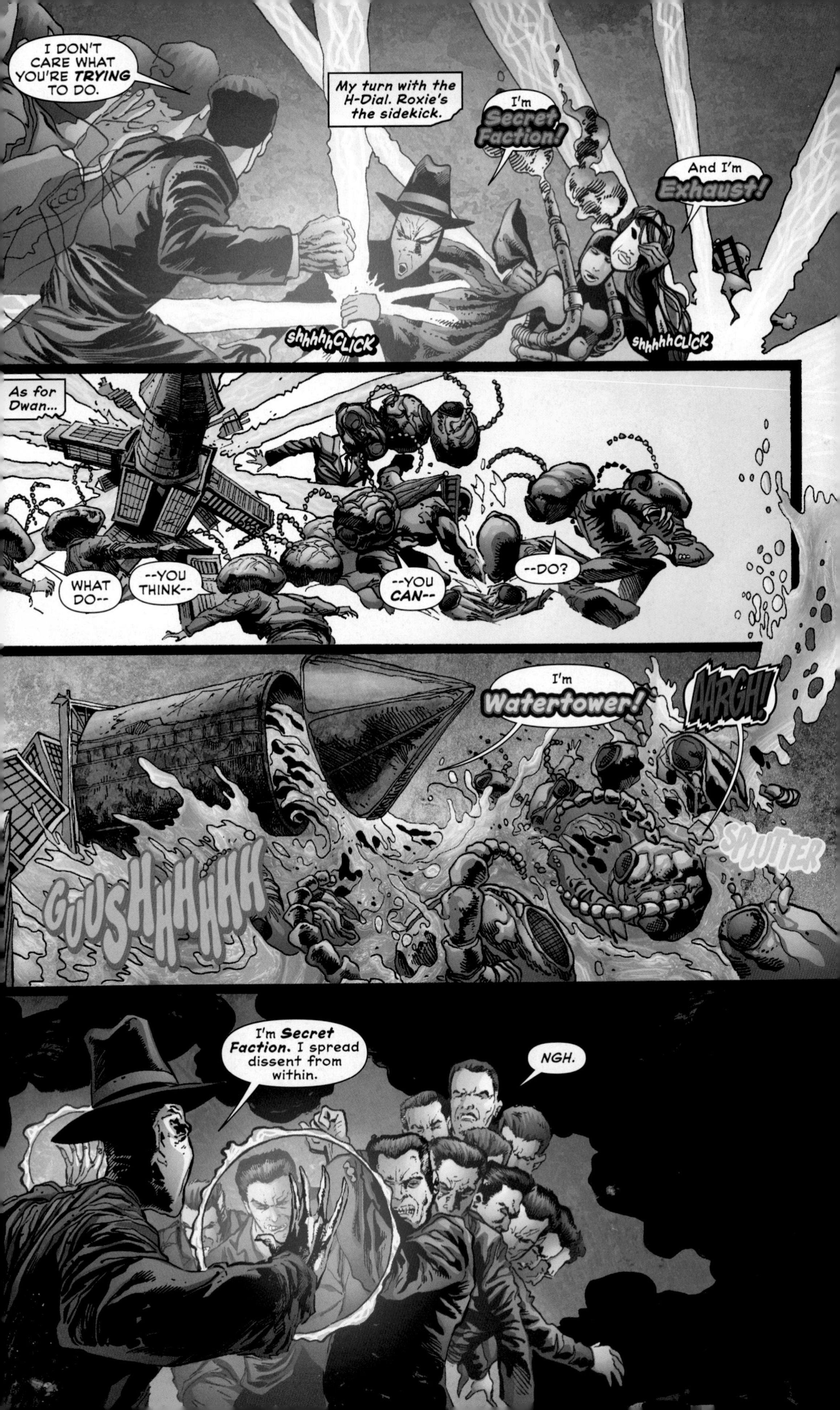
I DON'T CARE WHAT YOU'RE TRYING TO DO.
My turn with the H-Dial. Roxie's the sidekick.
I'm Secret Faction!
And I'm Exhaust!
shhhhhCLICK
shhhhhCLICK
As for Dwan...
WHAT DO--
--YOU THINK--
--YOU CAN--
--DO?
I'm Watertower!
AARGH!
SPLUTTER
GUUSHHHHHH
I'm Secret Faction. I spread dissent from within.
NGH.

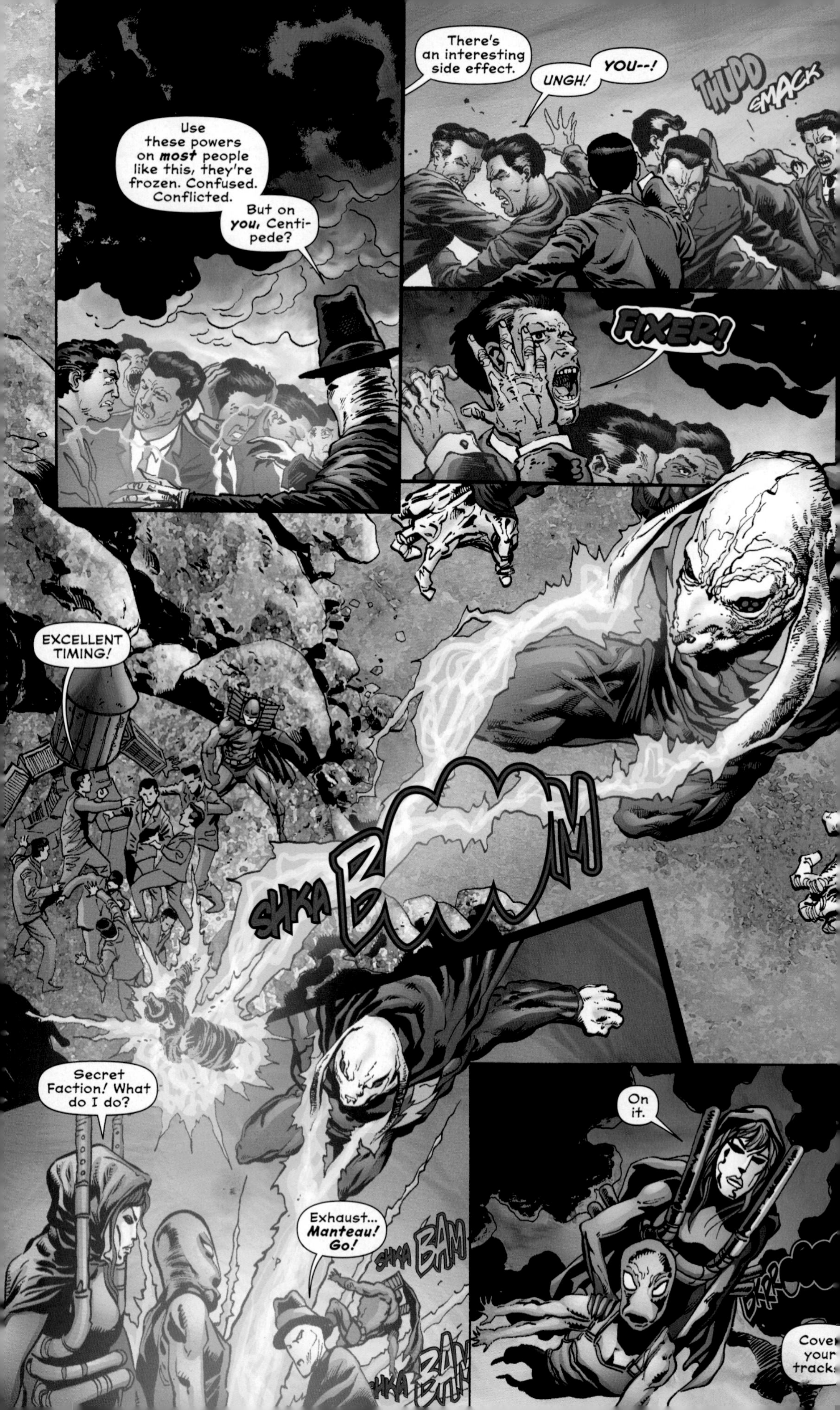
Use these powers on *most* people like this, they're frozen. Confused. Conflicted.
But on *you,* Centipede?
There's an interesting side effect.
UNGH!
YOU--!
THUDD
SMACK
FIXER!
EXCELLENT TIMING!
SHKA BOOM
Secret Faction! What do I do?
Exhaust... *Manteau! Go!*
SHKA BAM
SHKA BAM
On it.
Cover your tracks

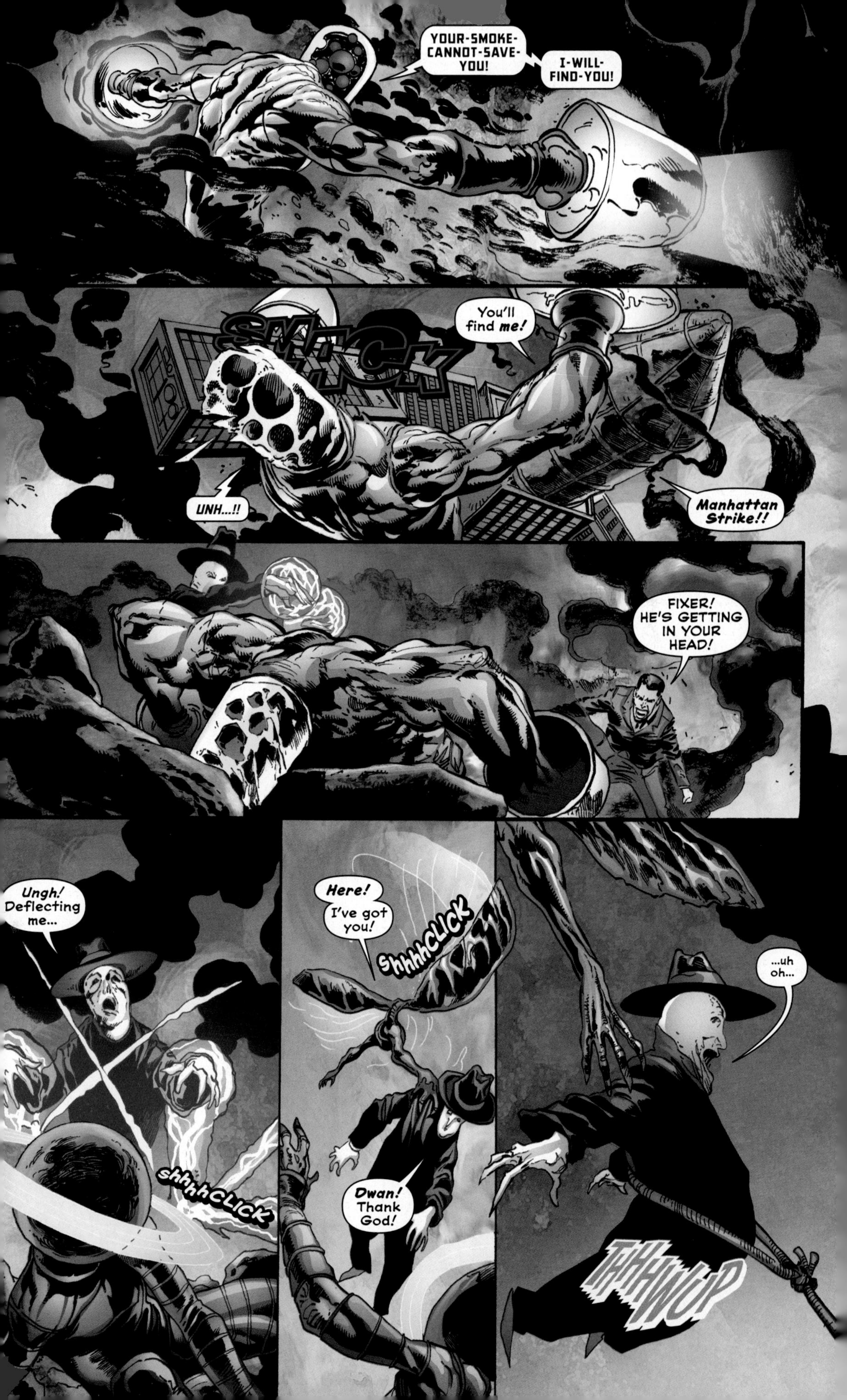

YOUR-SMOKE-CANNOT-SAVE-YOU!
I-WILL-FIND-YOU!
You'll find *me*!
SMACK
UNH...!!
Manhattan Strike!!
FIXER! HE'S GETTING IN YOUR HEAD!
Ungh! Deflecting me...
shhhhCLICK
Here!
I've got you!
ShhhhCLICK
Dwan! Thank God!
...uh oh...
THHWUP

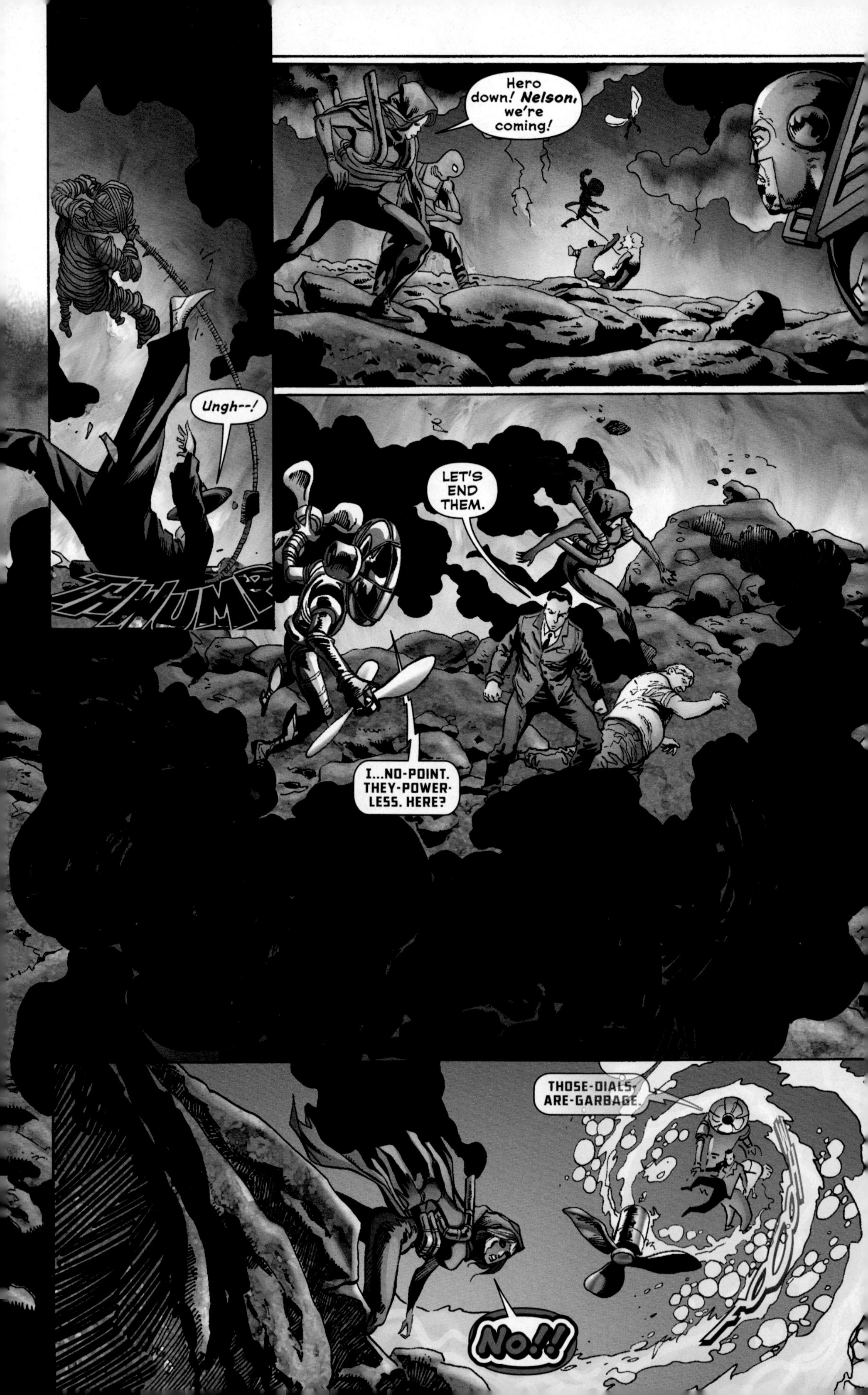
Ungh--!
THWUMP
Hero down! Nelson, we're coming!
LET'S END THEM.
I...NO-POINT. THEY-POWERLESS. HERE?
THOSE-DIALS-ARE-GARBAGE.
No!!

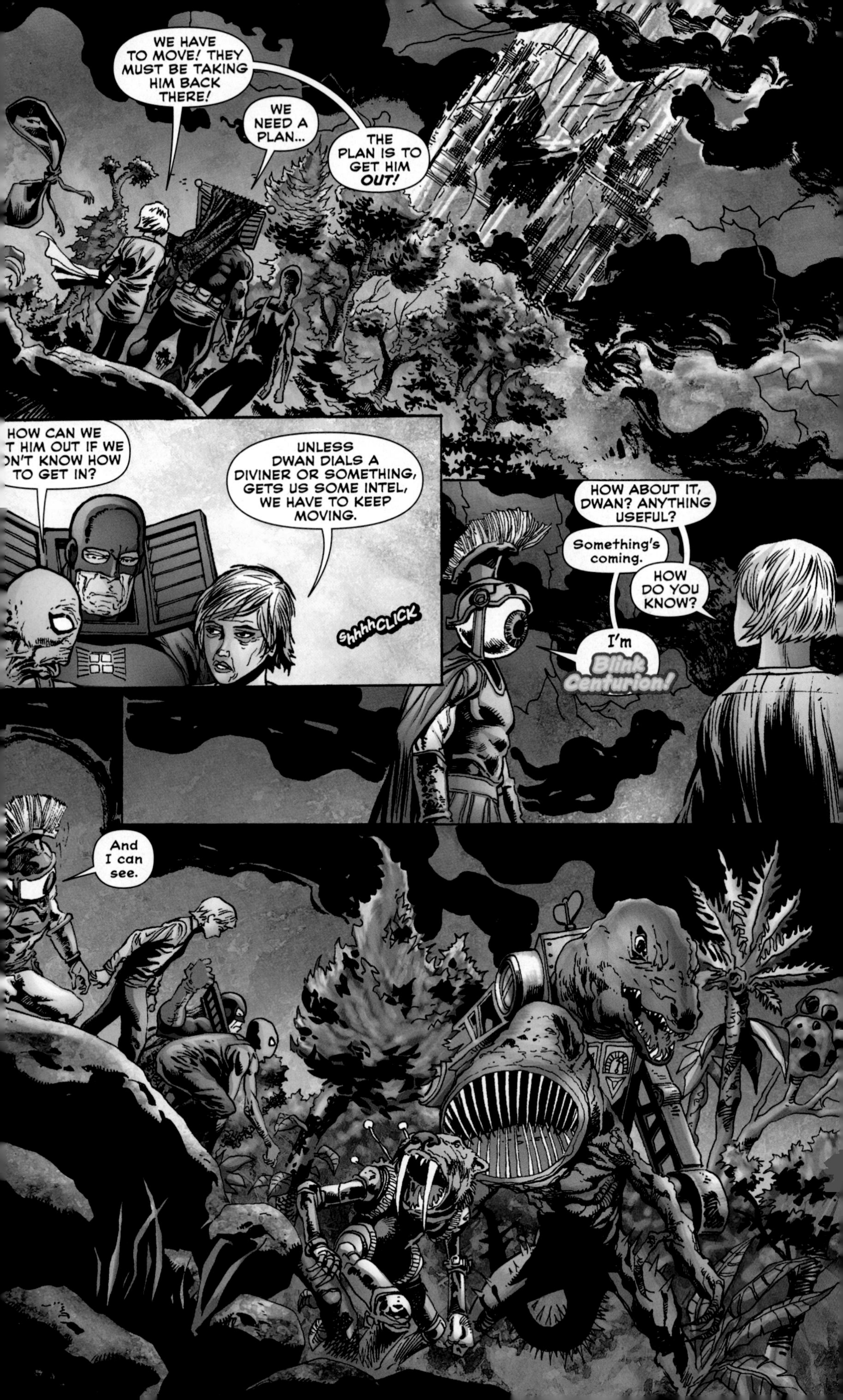

WE HAVE TO MOVE! THEY MUST BE TAKING HIM BACK THERE!
WE NEED A PLAN...
THE PLAN IS TO GET HIM OUT!
HOW CAN WE T HIM OUT IF WE N'T KNOW HOW TO GET IN?
UNLESS DWAN DIALS A DIVINER OR SOMETHING, GETS US SOME INTEL, WE HAVE TO KEEP MOVING.
ShhhhCLICK
HOW ABOUT IT, DWAN? ANYTHING USEFUL?
Something's coming.
HOW DO YOU KNOW?
I'm Blink Centurion!
And I can see.

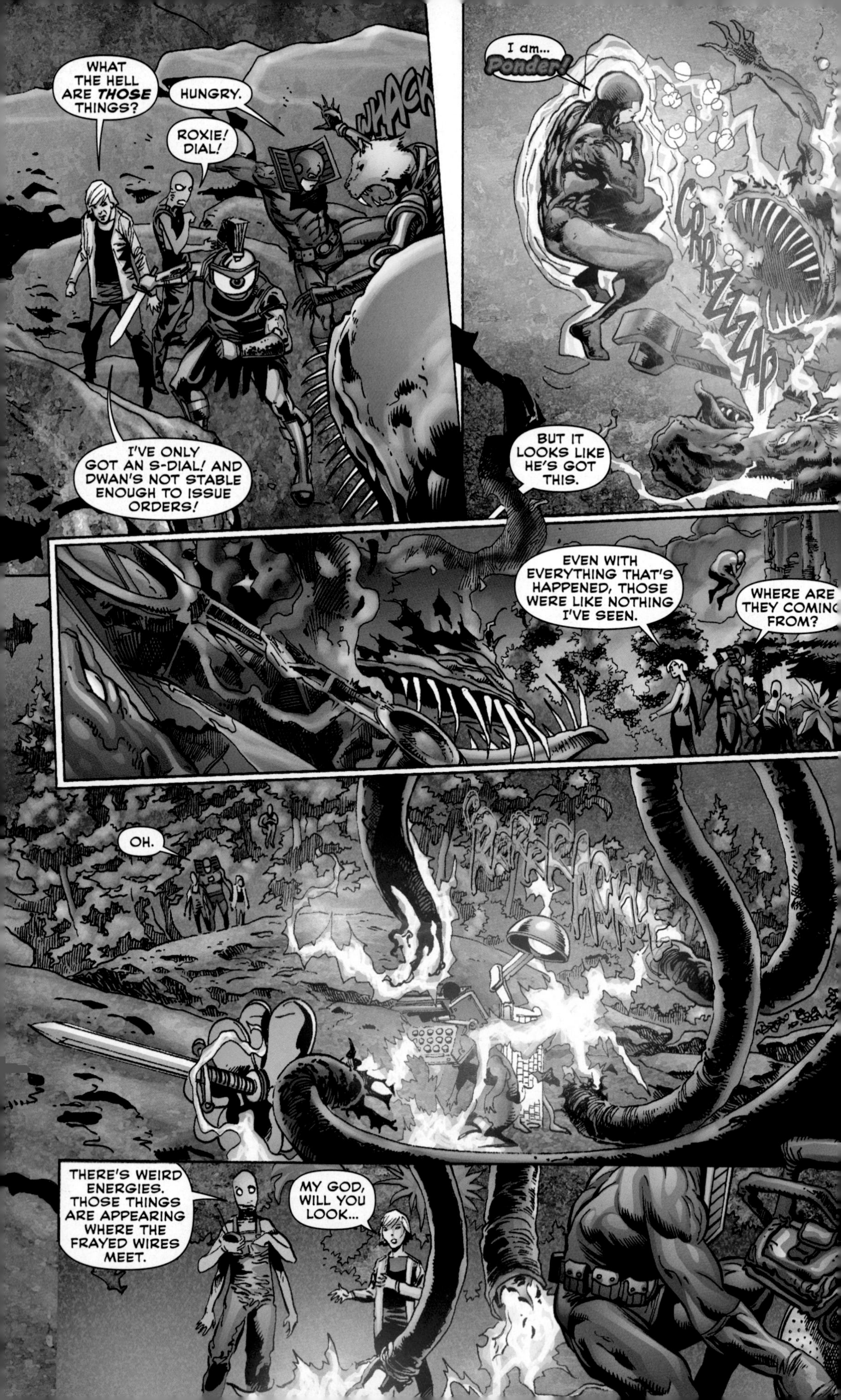
WHAT THE HELL ARE *THOSE* THINGS?
HUNGRY.
ROXIE! DIAL!
WHACK
I'VE ONLY GOT AN S-DIAL! AND DWAN'S NOT STABLE ENOUGH TO ISSUE ORDERS!
I am... Ponder!
CRRZZZZAP
BUT IT LOOKS LIKE HE'S GOT THIS.
EVEN WITH EVERYTHING THAT'S HAPPENED, THOSE WERE LIKE NOTHING I'VE SEEN.
WHERE ARE THEY COMING FROM?
OH.
THERE'S WEIRD ENERGIES. THOSE THINGS ARE APPEARING WHERE THE FRAYED WIRES MEET.
MY GOD, WILL YOU LOOK...

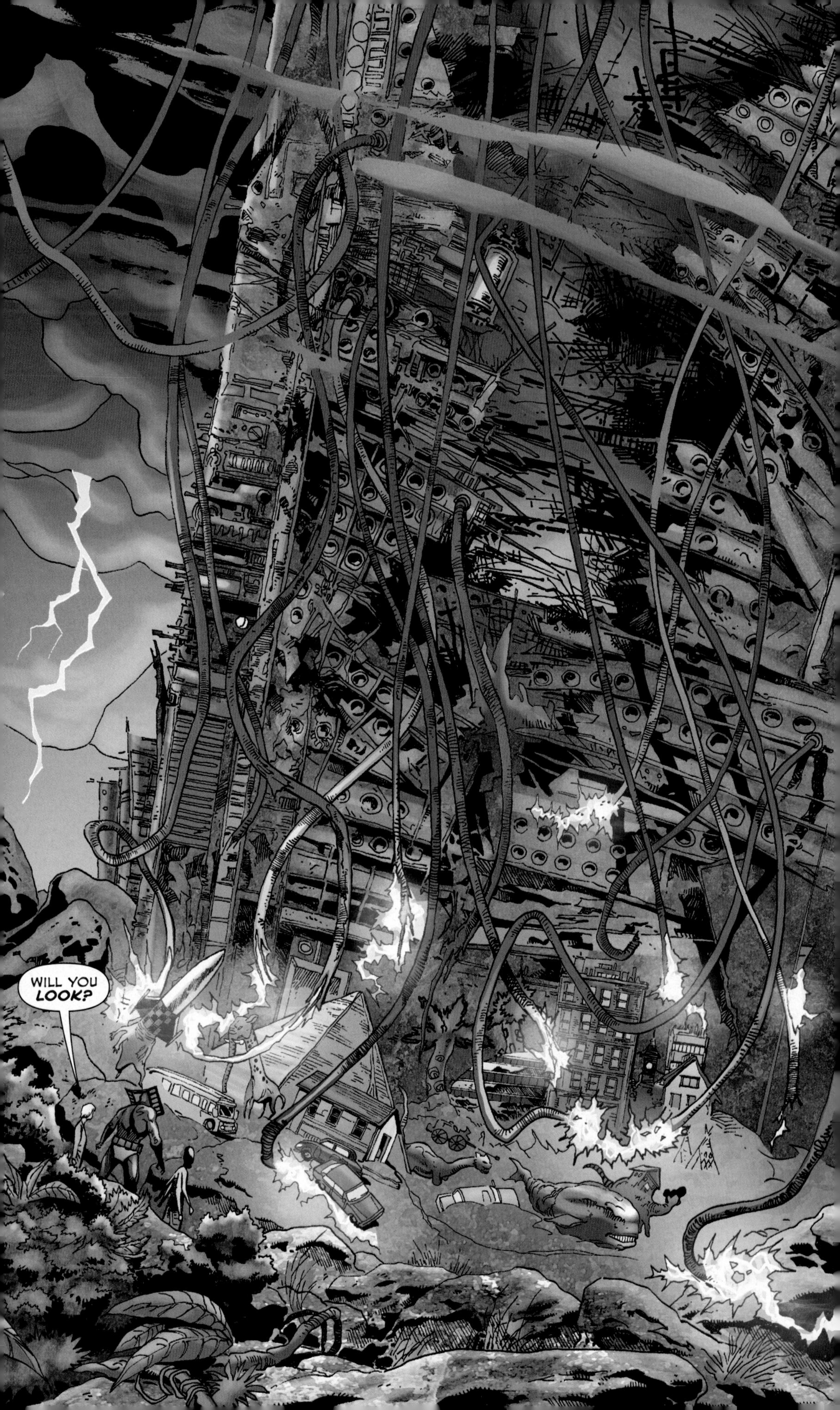
WILL YOU LOOK?

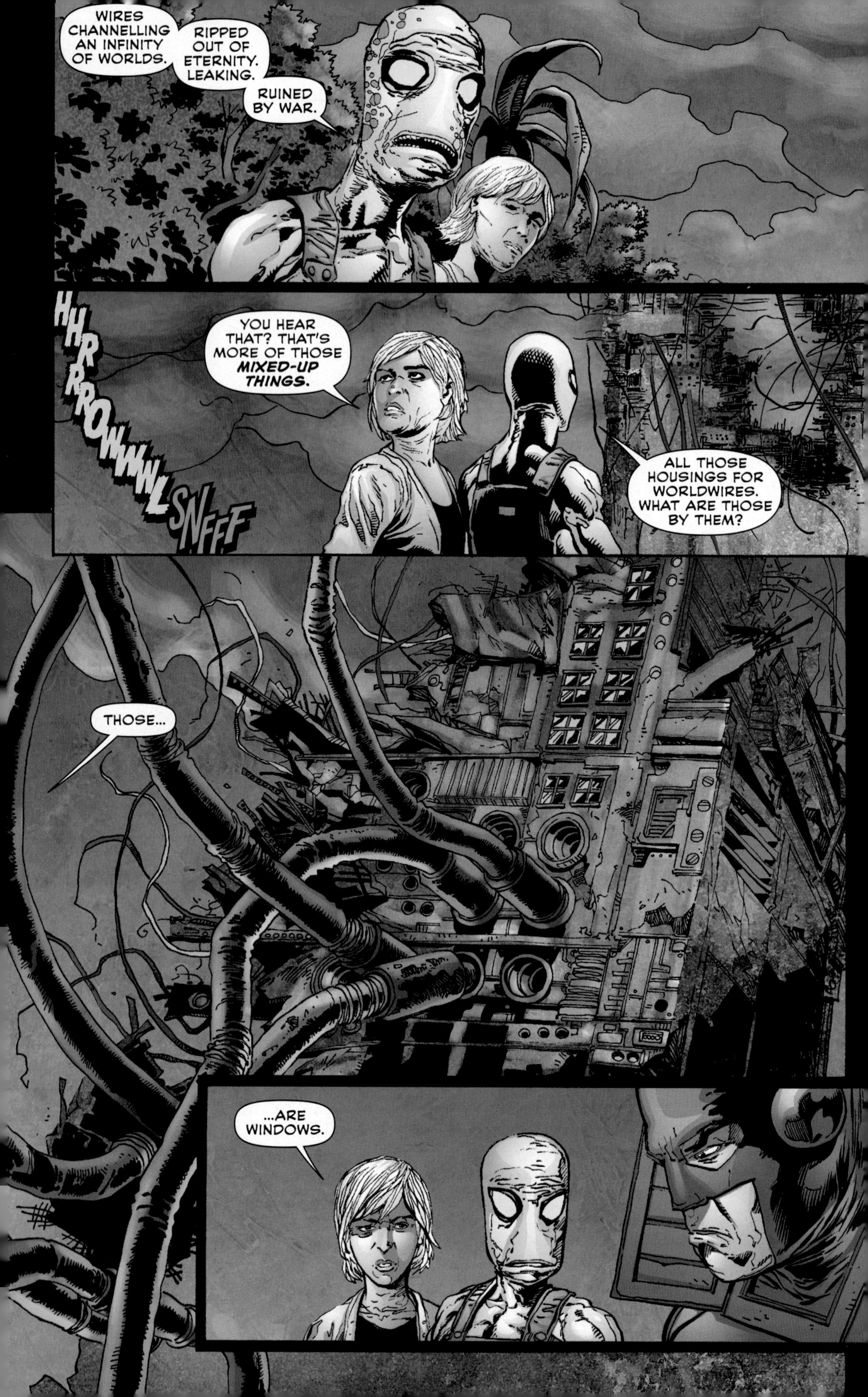
WIRES CHANNELLING AN INFINITY OF WORLDS.
RIPPED OUT OF ETERNITY. LEAKING.
RUINED BY WAR.
HHRRROWWWL SNFFF
YOU HEAR THAT? THAT'S MORE OF THOSE ***MIXED-UP THINGS.***
ALL THOSE HOUSINGS FOR WORLDWIRES. WHAT ARE THOSE BY THEM?
THOSE...
...ARE WINDOWS.

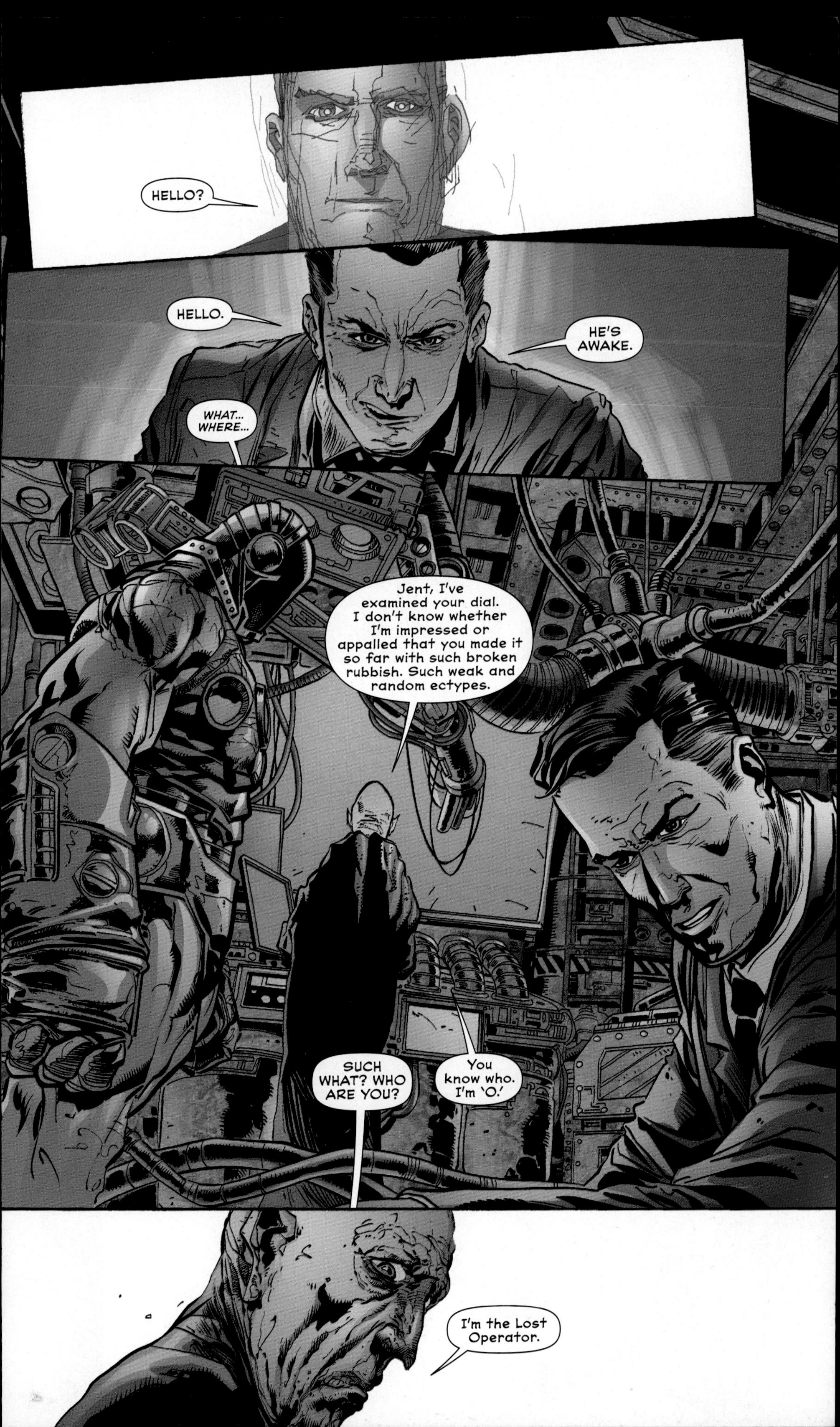
HELLO?
HELLO.
HE'S AWAKE.
WHAT... WHERE...
Jent, I've examined your dial. I don't know whether I'm impressed or appalled that you made it so far with such broken rubbish. Such weak and random ectypes.
SUCH WHAT? WHO ARE YOU?
You know who. I'm 'O.'
I'm the Lost Operator.

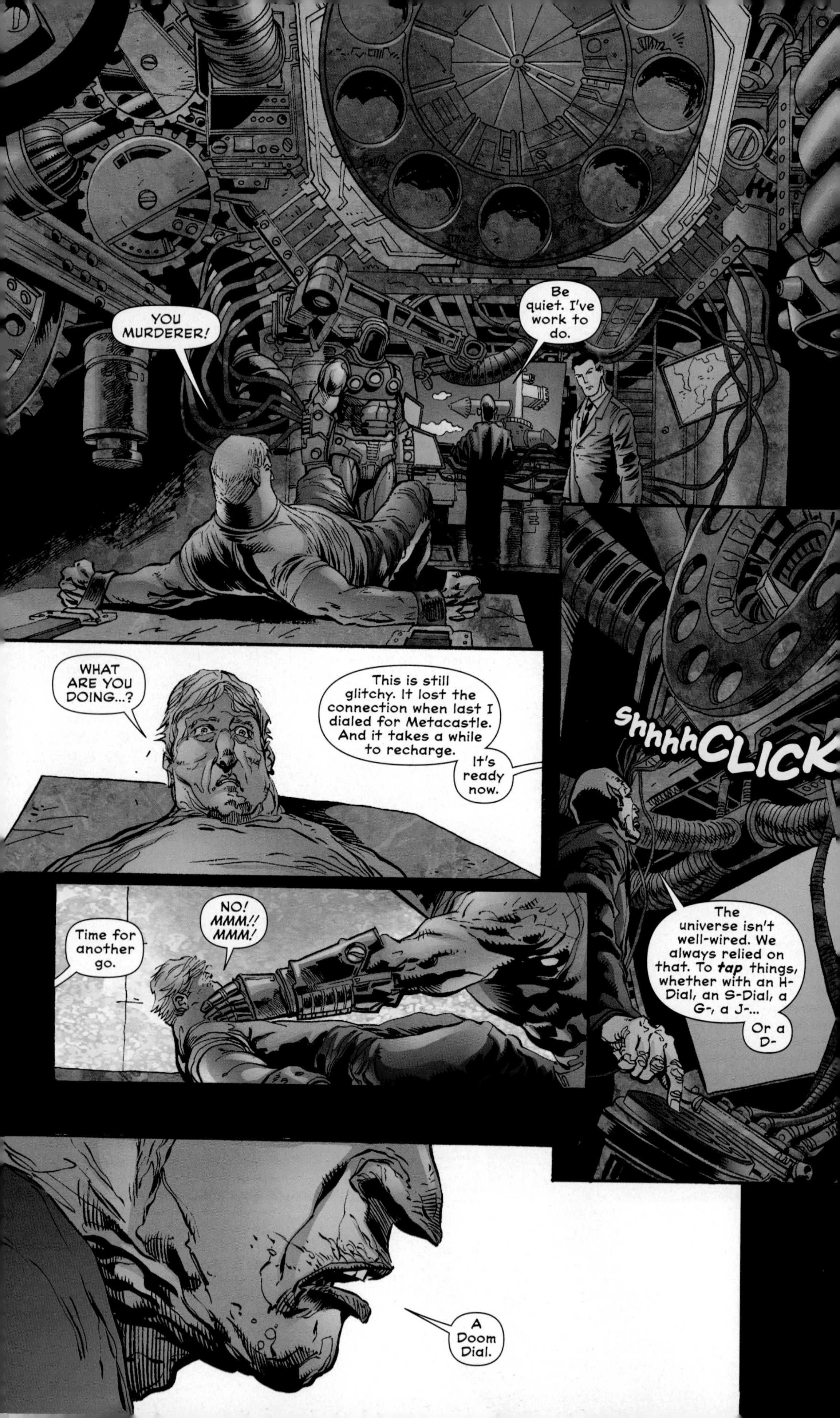
YOU MURDERER!
Be quiet. I've work to do.
WHAT ARE YOU DOING...?
This is still glitchy. It lost the connection when last I dialed for Metacastle. And it takes a while to recharge.
It's ready now.
Time for another go.
NO! MMM!! MMM!
shhhhCLICK
The universe isn't well-wired. We always relied on that. To *tap* things, whether with an H-Dial, an S-Dial, a G-, a J-...
Or a D-
A Doom Dial.

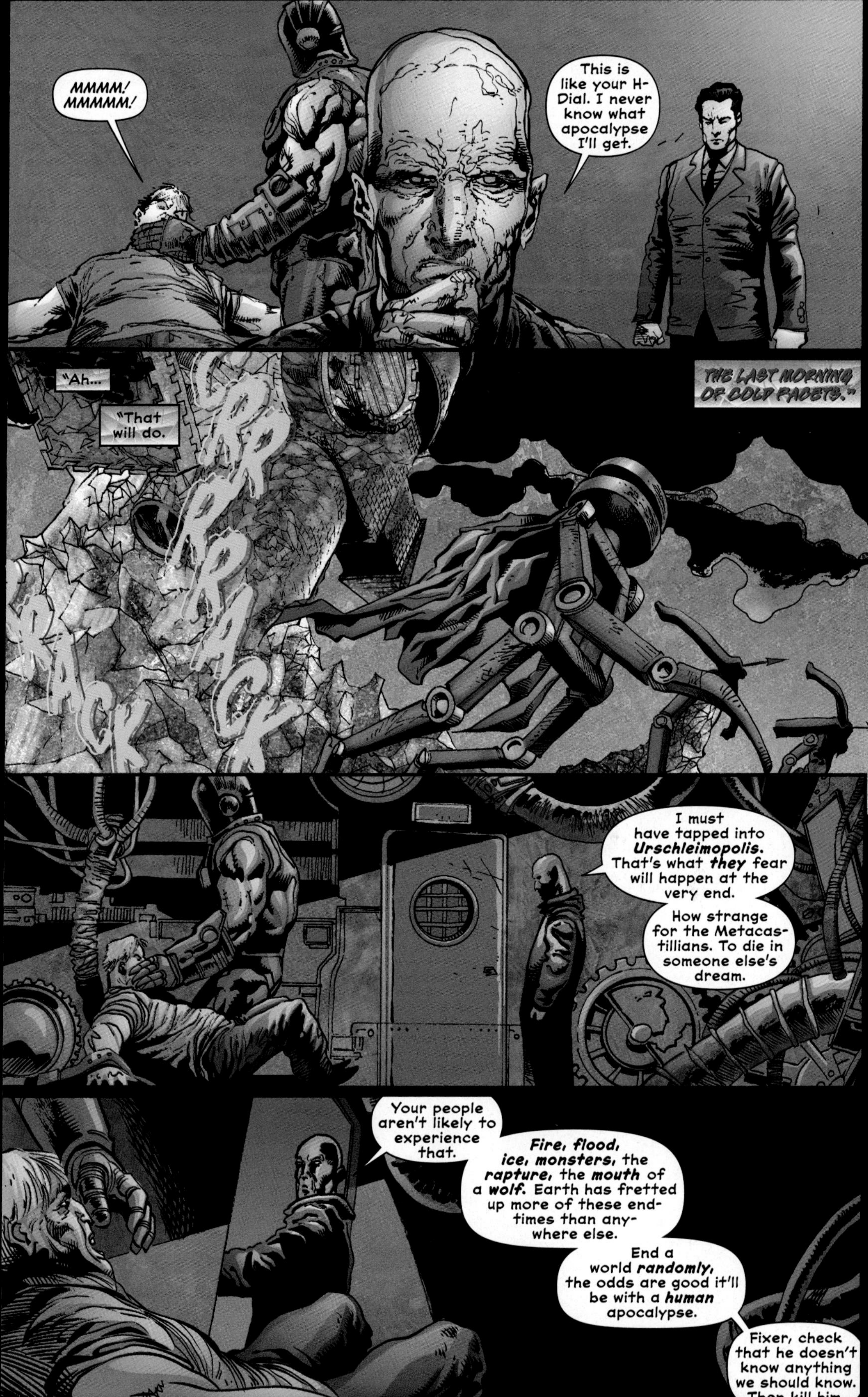
MMMM! MMMMM!
This is like your H-Dial. I never know what apocalypse I'll get.
"Ah...
"That will do.
CRRRACK
CRRACK
RRACK
THE LAST MORNING OF COLD FACETS."
I must have tapped into *Urschleimopolis*. That's what *they* fear will happen at the very end.
How strange for the Metacastillians. To die in someone else's dream.
Your people aren't likely to experience that.
Fire, flood, ice, monsters, the *rapture,* the *mouth* of a *wolf.* Earth has fretted up more of these end-times than anywhere else.
End a world *randomly,* the odds are good it'll be with a *human* apocalypse.
Fixer, check that he doesn't know anything we should know.

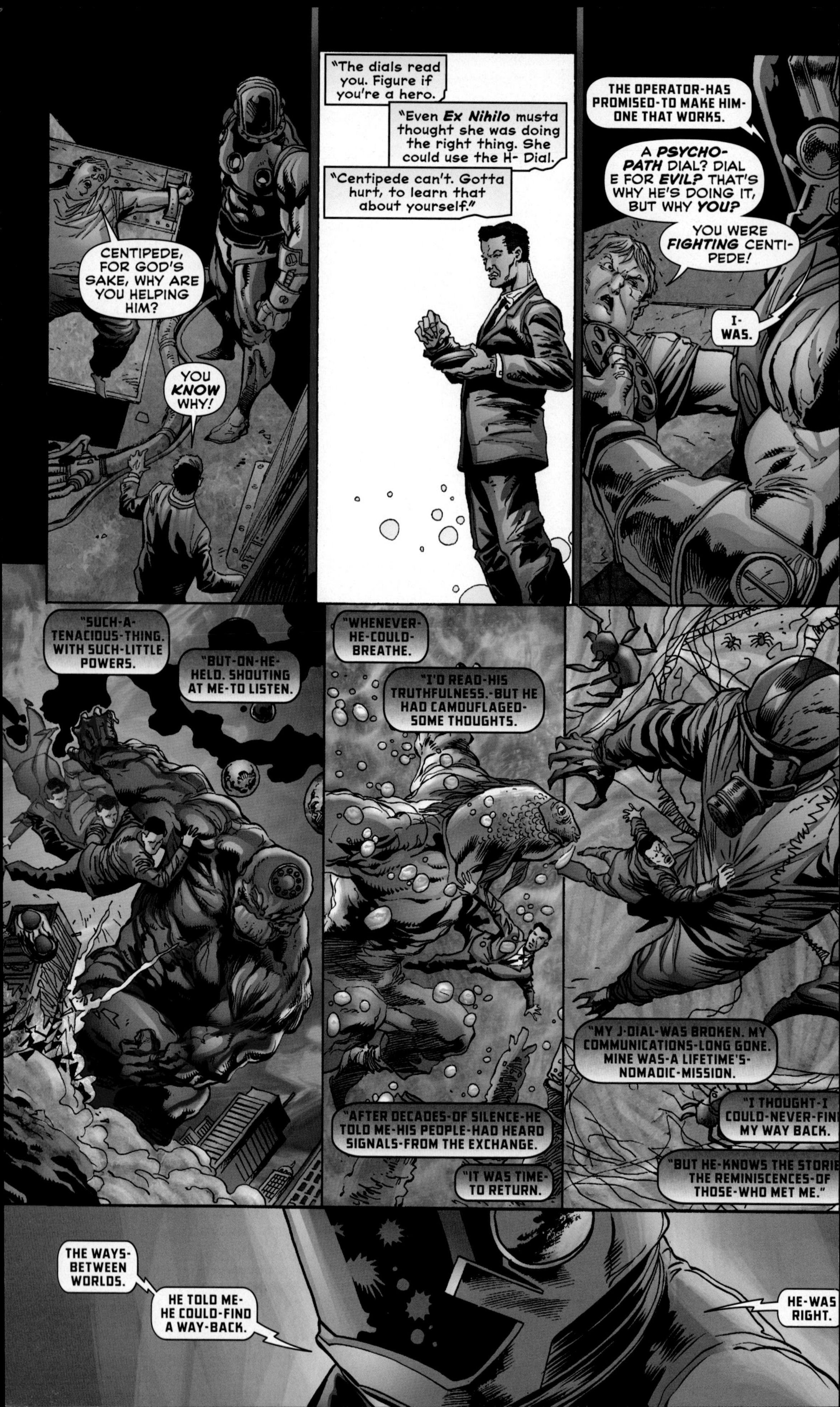

CENTIPEDE, FOR GOD'S SAKE, WHY ARE YOU HELPING HIM?
YOU KNOW WHY!
"The dials read you. Figure if you're a hero.
"Even Ex Nihilo musta thought she was doing the right thing. She could use the H- Dial.
"Centipede can't. Gotta hurt, to learn that about yourself."
THE OPERATOR-HAS PROMISED-TO MAKE HIM-ONE THAT WORKS.
A PSYCHO-PATH DIAL? DIAL E FOR EVIL? THAT'S WHY HE'S DOING IT, BUT WHY YOU?
YOU WERE FIGHTING CENTI-PEDE!
I-WAS.
"SUCH-A-TENACIOUS-THING. WITH SUCH-LITTLE POWERS.
"BUT-ON-HE-HELD. SHOUTING AT ME-TO LISTEN.
"WHENEVER-HE-COULD-BREATHE.
"I'D READ-HIS TRUTHFULNESS.-BUT HE HAD CAMOUFLAGED-SOME THOUGHTS.
"AFTER DECADES-OF SILENCE-HE TOLD ME-HIS PEOPLE-HAD HEARD SIGNALS-FROM THE EXCHANGE.
"IT WAS TIME-TO RETURN.
"MY J-DIAL-WAS BROKEN. MY COMMUNICATIONS-LONG GONE. MINE WAS-A LIFETIME'S-NOMADIC-MISSION.
"I THOUGHT-I COULD-NEVER-FIN MY WAY BACK.
"BUT HE-KNOWS THE STORIE THE REMINISCENCES-OF THOSE-WHO MET ME."
THE WAYS-BETWEEN WORLDS.
HE TOLD ME-HE COULD-FIND A WAY-BACK.
HE-WAS RIGHT.

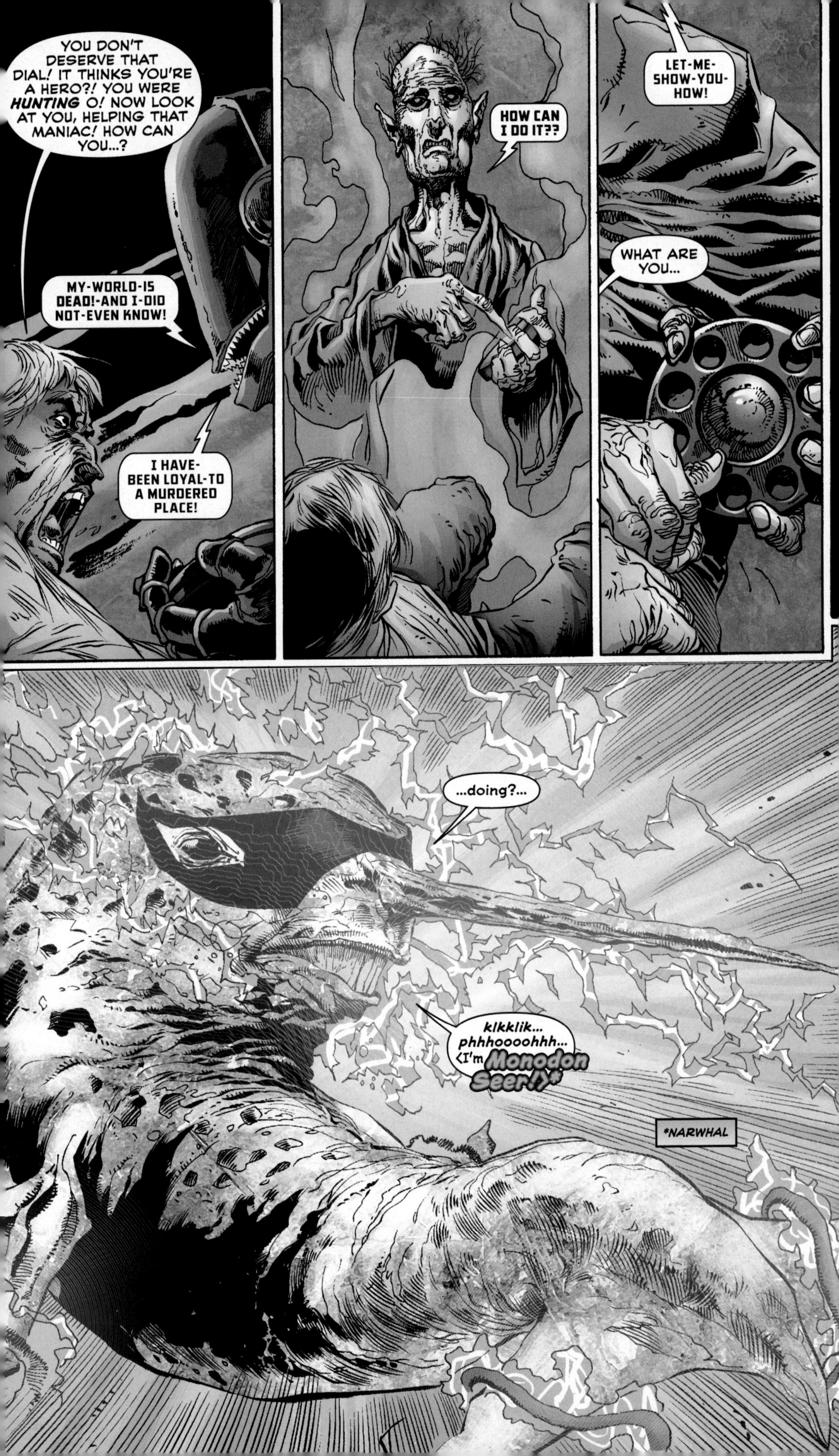
YOU DON'T DESERVE THAT DIAL! IT THINKS YOU'RE A HERO?! YOU WERE HUNTING O! NOW LOOK AT YOU, HELPING THAT MANIAC! HOW CAN YOU...?
MY-WORLD-IS DEAD!-AND I-DID NOT-EVEN KNOW!
I HAVE-BEEN LOYAL-TO A MURDERED PLACE!
HOW CAN I DO IT??
LET-ME-SHOW-YOU-HOW!
WHAT ARE YOU...
...doing?...
klkklik... phhhoooohhh... <I'm Monodon Seer!>*
*NARWHAL

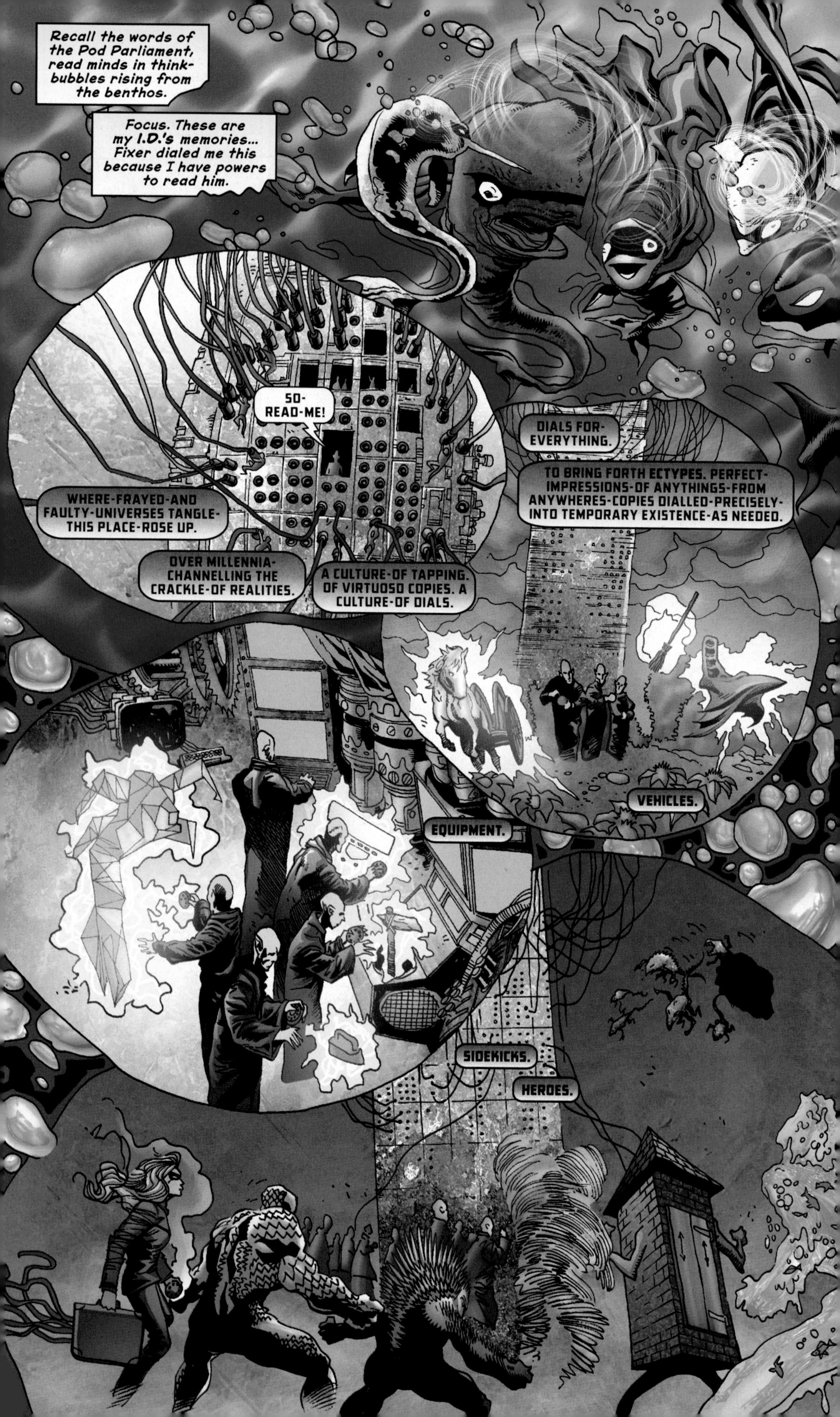
Recall the words of the Pod Parliament, read minds in think-bubbles rising from the benthos.
Focus. These are my I.D.'s memories... Fixer dialed me this because I have powers to read him.
SO-READ-ME!
WHERE-FRAYED-AND FAULTY-UNIVERSES TANGLE-THIS PLACE-ROSE UP.
OVER MILLENNIA-CHANNELLING THE CRACKLE-OF REALITIES.
A CULTURE-OF TAPPING. OF VIRTUOSO COPIES. A CULTURE-OF DIALS.
DIALS FOR-EVERYTHING.
TO BRING FORTH ECTYPES. PERFECT-IMPRESSIONS-OF ANYTHINGS-FROM ANYWHERES-COPIES DIALLED-PRECISELY-INTO TEMPORARY EXISTENCE-AS NEEDED.
VEHICLES.
EQUIPMENT.
SIDEKICKS.
HEROES.

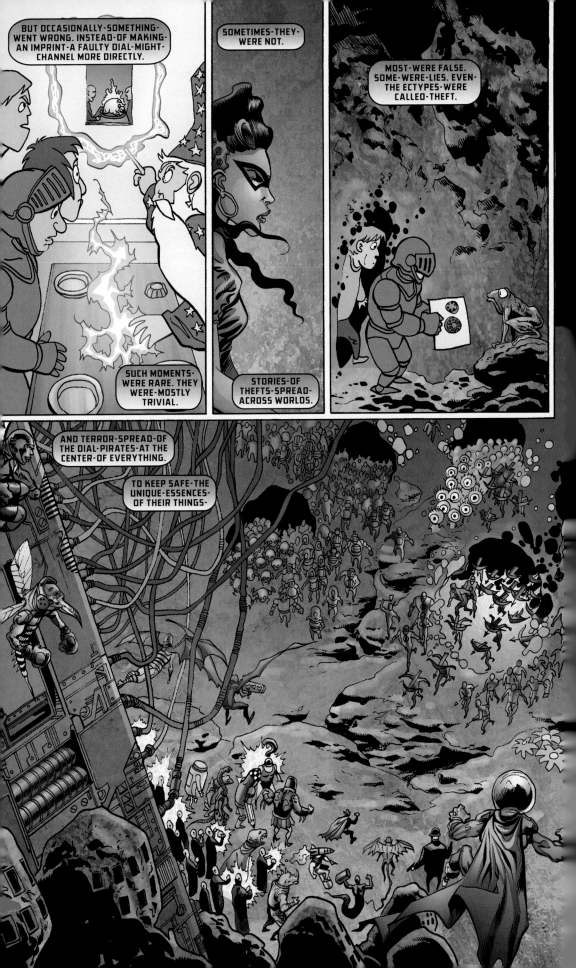

BUT·OCCASIONALLY·SOMETHING· WENT·WRONG.·INSTEAD·OF·MAKING· AN·IMPRINT·A·FAULTY·DIAL·MIGHT· CHANNEL·MORE·DIRECTLY.

SUCH·MOMENTS· WERE·RARE.·THEY· WERE·MOSTLY· TRIVIAL.

SOMETIMES·THEY· WERE·NOT.

STORIES·OF· THEFTS·SPREAD· ACROSS·WORLDS.

MOST·WERE·FALSE. SOME·WERE·LIES.·EVEN· THE·ECTYPES·WERE· CALLED·THEFT.

AND·TERROR·SPREAD·OF· THE·DIAL·PIRATES·AT·THE· CENTER·OF·EVERYTHING.

TO·KEEP·SAFE·THE· UNIQUE·ESSENCES· OF·THEIR·THINGS·

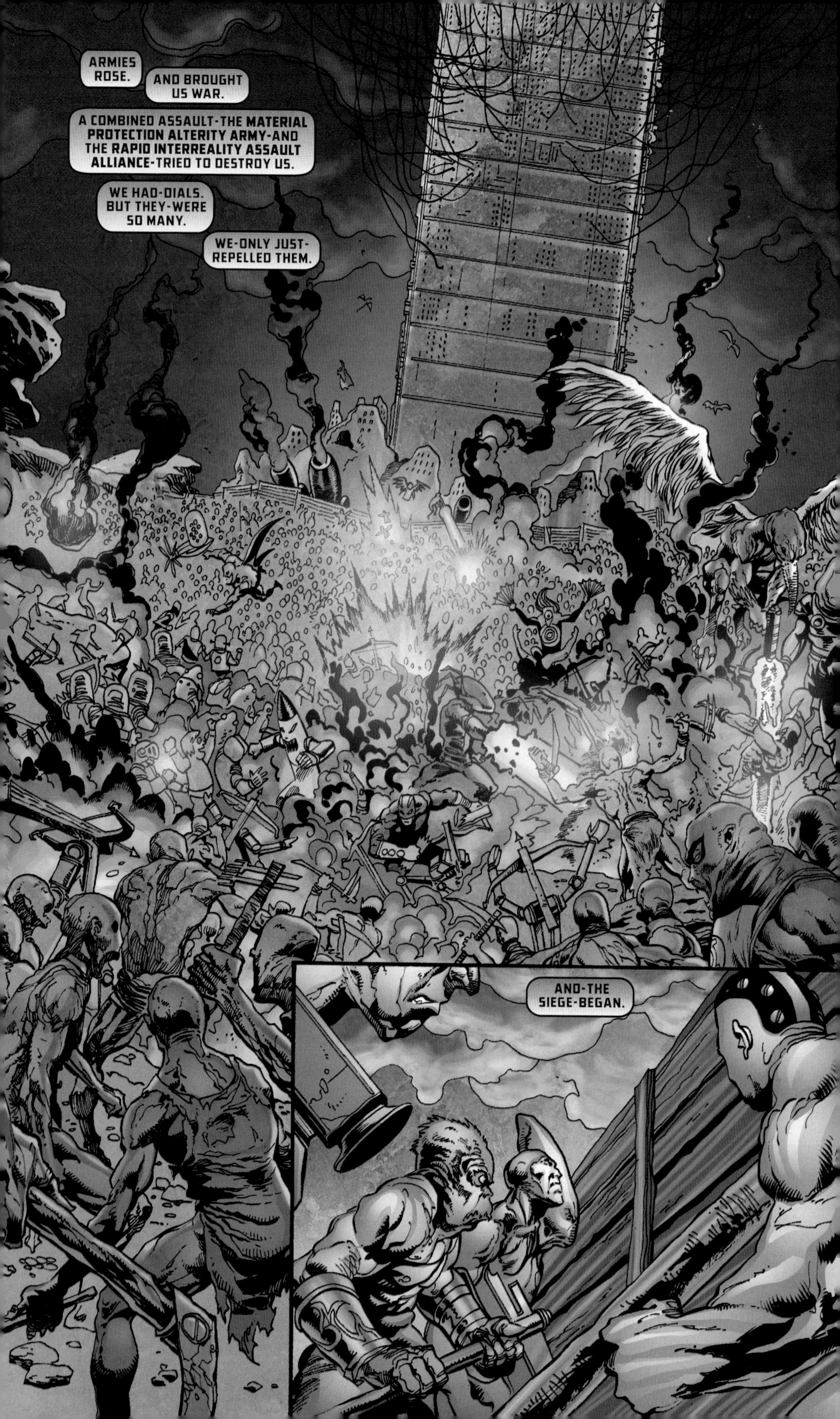
ARMIES ROSE.
AND BROUGHT US WAR.
A COMBINED ASSAULT-THE MATERIAL PROTECTION ALTERITY ARMY-AND THE RAPID INTERREALITY ASSAULT ALLIANCE-TRIED TO DESTROY US.
WE HAD-DIALS. BUT THEY-WERE SO MANY.
WE-ONLY JUST-REPELLED THEM.
AND-THE SIEGE-BEGAN.

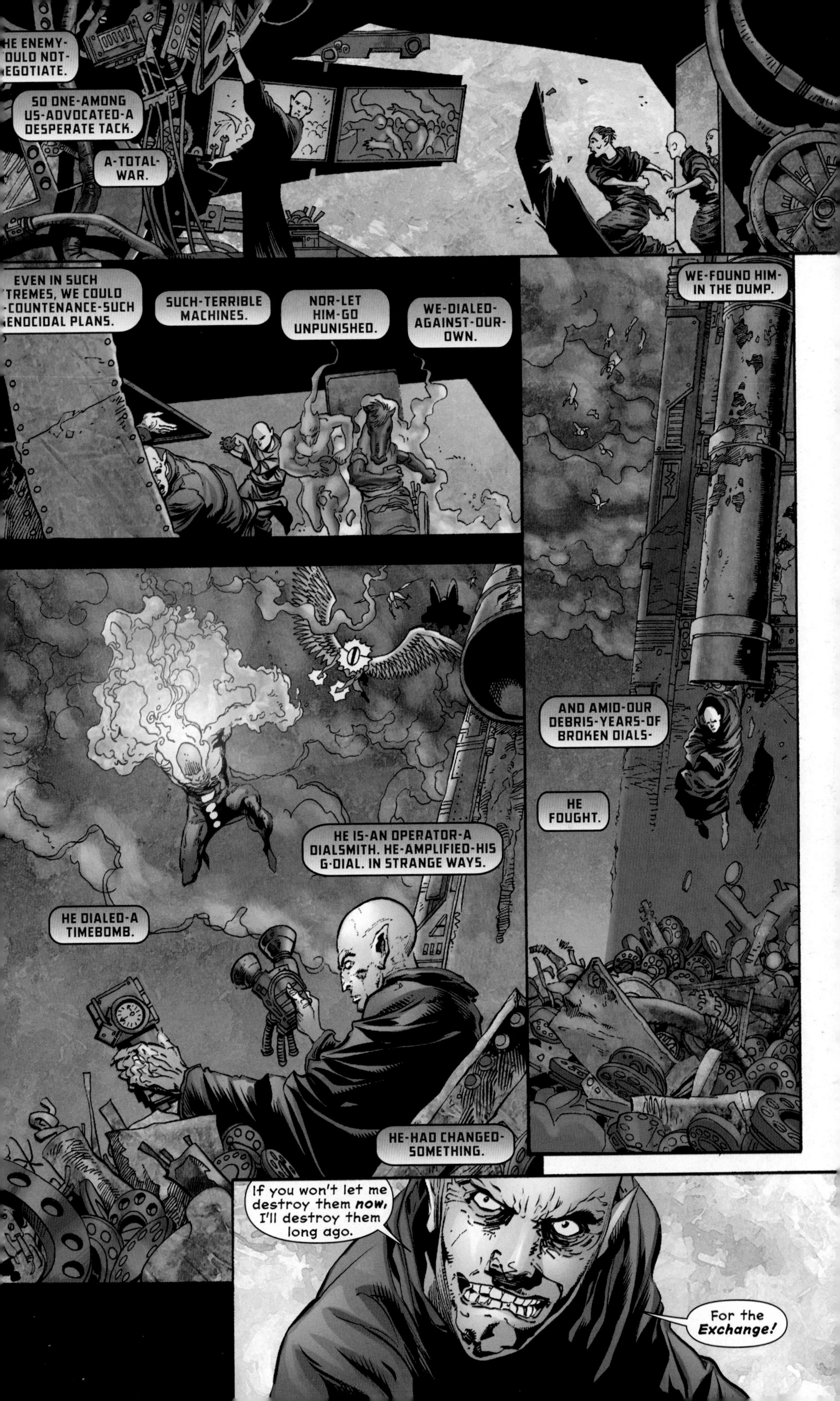

HE ENEMY-
OULD NOT-
EGOTIATE.
SO ONE-AMONG US-ADVOCATED-A DESPERATE TACK.
A-TOTAL-WAR.
EVEN IN SUCH
TREMES, WE COULD
-COUNTENANCE-SUCH
ENOCIDAL PLANS.
SUCH-TERRIBLE MACHINES.
NOR-LET HIM-GO UNPUNISHED.
WE-DIALED-AGAINST-OUR-OWN.
WE-FOUND HIM-IN THE DUMP.
AND AMID-OUR DEBRIS-YEARS-OF BROKEN DIALS-
HE FOUGHT.
HE IS-AN OPERATOR-A DIALSMITH. HE-AMPLIFIED-HIS G-DIAL. IN STRANGE WAYS.
HE DIALED-A TIMEBOMB.
HE-HAD CHANGED-SOMETHING.
If you won't let me destroy them *now,* I'll destroy them long ago.
For the *Exchange!*

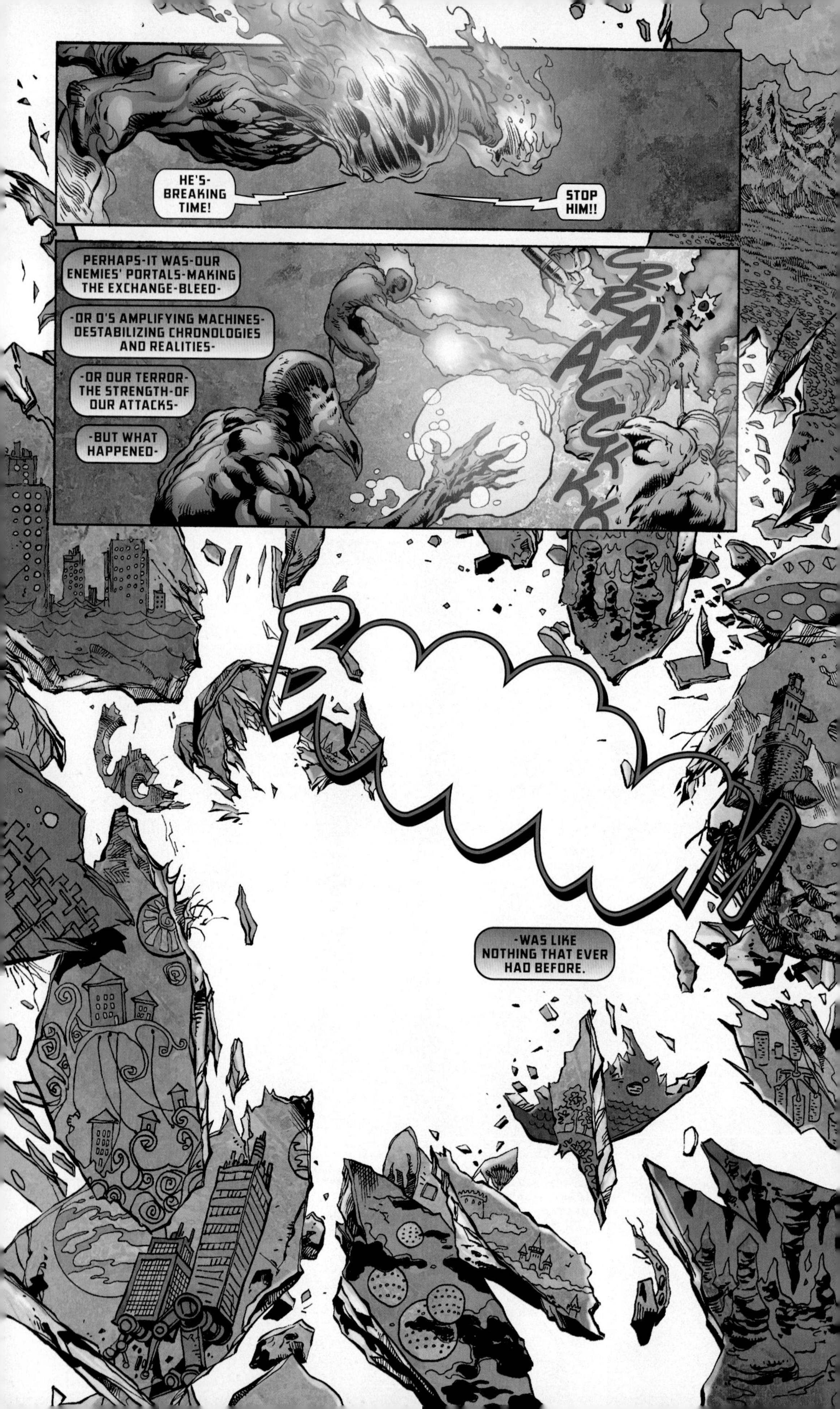
HE'S-
BREAKING
TIME!
STOP
HIM!!
PERHAPS-IT WAS-OUR ENEMIES' PORTALS-MAKING THE EXCHANGE-BLEED-
-OR O'S AMPLIFYING MACHINES-DESTABILIZING CHRONOLOGIES AND REALITIES-
-OR OUR TERROR-THE STRENGTH-OF OUR ATTACKS-
-BUT WHAT HAPPENED-
KRRAAACKKK
BOOOM
-WAS LIKE NOTHING THAT EVER HAD BEFORE.

O WAS GONE.

WITH THE BROKEN RUBBISH OF THE DUMP BLOWN ACROSS HISTORY AND REALITIES.

FOR YOU TO FIND.

THE DIALS HAVE VEIL TECH AND MORE THEY TWISTED YOUR HISTORY.

IT STRETCHED TO ACCOMMODATE THEM. THEY WERE HIDDEN IN SIGHT THEY SHED INFLUENCE.

TELEPHONE

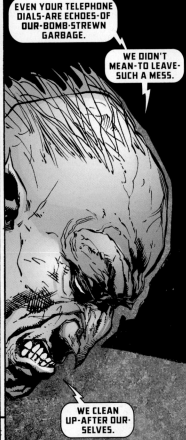

EVEN YOUR TELEPHONE DIALS ARE ECHOES OF OUR BOMB STREWN GARBAGE.

WE DIDN'T MEAN TO LEAVE SUCH A MESS.

WE CLEAN UP AFTER OUR SELVES.

'GO' THEY TOLD US. 'WHEN WE WIN WE WILL SING YOUR NAMES.'

IT WAS A LIFETIME'S MISSION. TO TRACK DOWN THE BROKEN DIALS.

AND BRING TO JUSTICE THE LOST OPERATOR.

SO WHY IN HELL YOU WITH HIM NOW!?

BECAUSE I JUST RETURNED! AND THIS IS WHAT I FOUND!

BECAUSE HE WAS RIGHT!

BECAUSE DAYS AFTER I LEFT—

—THE EXCHANGE FELL.

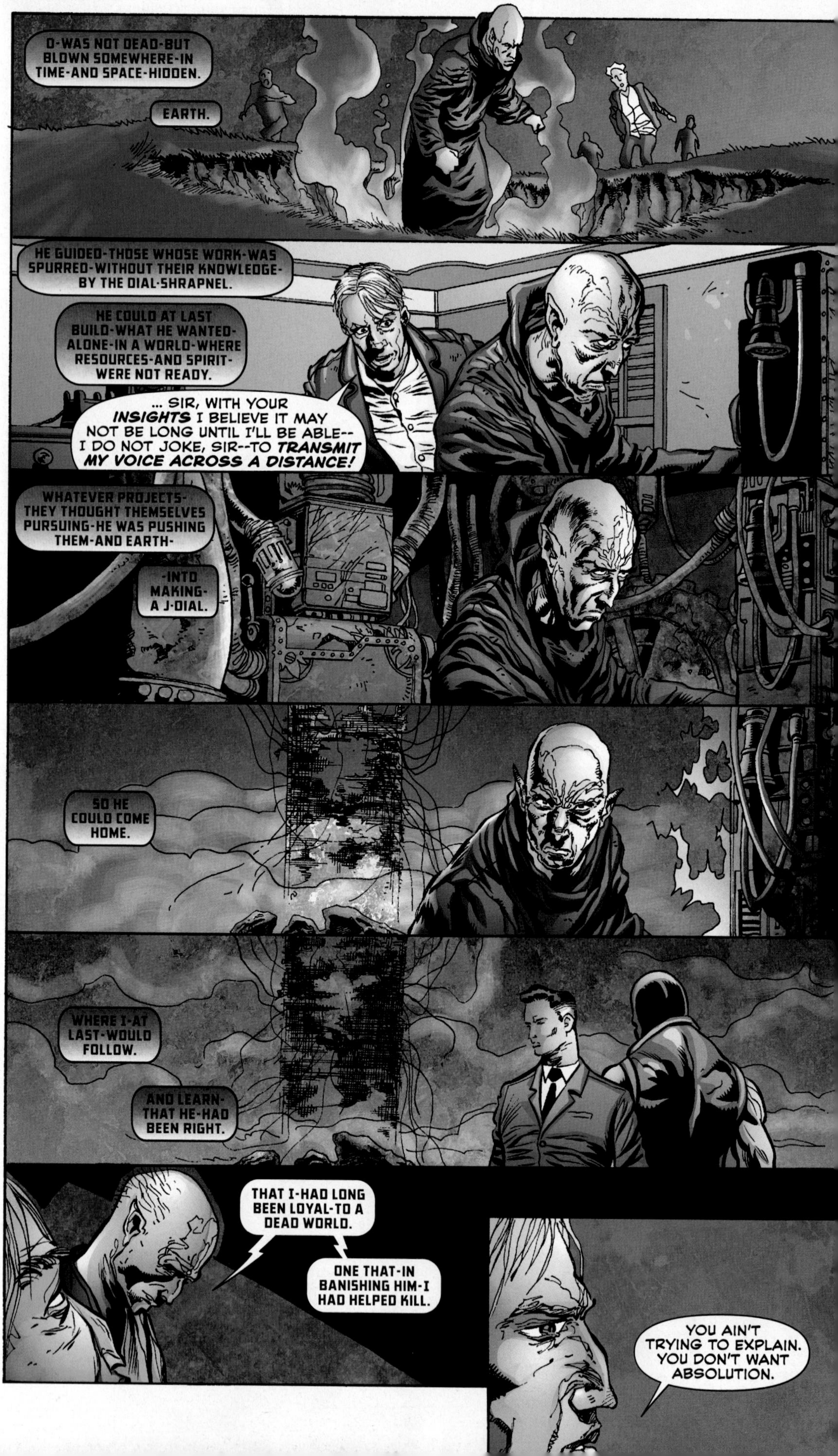
O-WAS NOT DEAD-BUT BLOWN SOMEWHERE-IN TIME-AND SPACE-HIDDEN.
EARTH.
HE GUIDED-THOSE WHOSE WORK-WAS SPURRED-WITHOUT THEIR KNOWLEDGE-BY THE DIAL-SHRAPNEL.
HE COULD AT LAST BUILD-WHAT HE WANTED-ALONE-IN A WORLD-WHERE RESOURCES-AND SPIRIT-WERE NOT READY.
... SIR, WITH YOUR INSIGHTS I BELIEVE IT MAY NOT BE LONG UNTIL I'LL BE ABLE-- I DO NOT JOKE, SIR--TO TRANSMIT MY VOICE ACROSS A DISTANCE!
WHATEVER PROJECTS-THEY THOUGHT THEMSELVES PURSUING-HE WAS PUSHING THEM-AND EARTH-
-INTO MAKING-A J-DIAL.
SO HE COULD COME HOME.
WHERE I-AT LAST-WOULD FOLLOW.
AND LEARN-THAT HE-HAD BEEN RIGHT.
THAT I-HAD LONG BEEN LOYAL-TO A DEAD WORLD.
ONE THAT-IN BANISHING HIM-I HAD HELPED KILL.
YOU AIN'T TRYING TO EXPLAIN. YOU DON'T WANT ABSOLUTION.

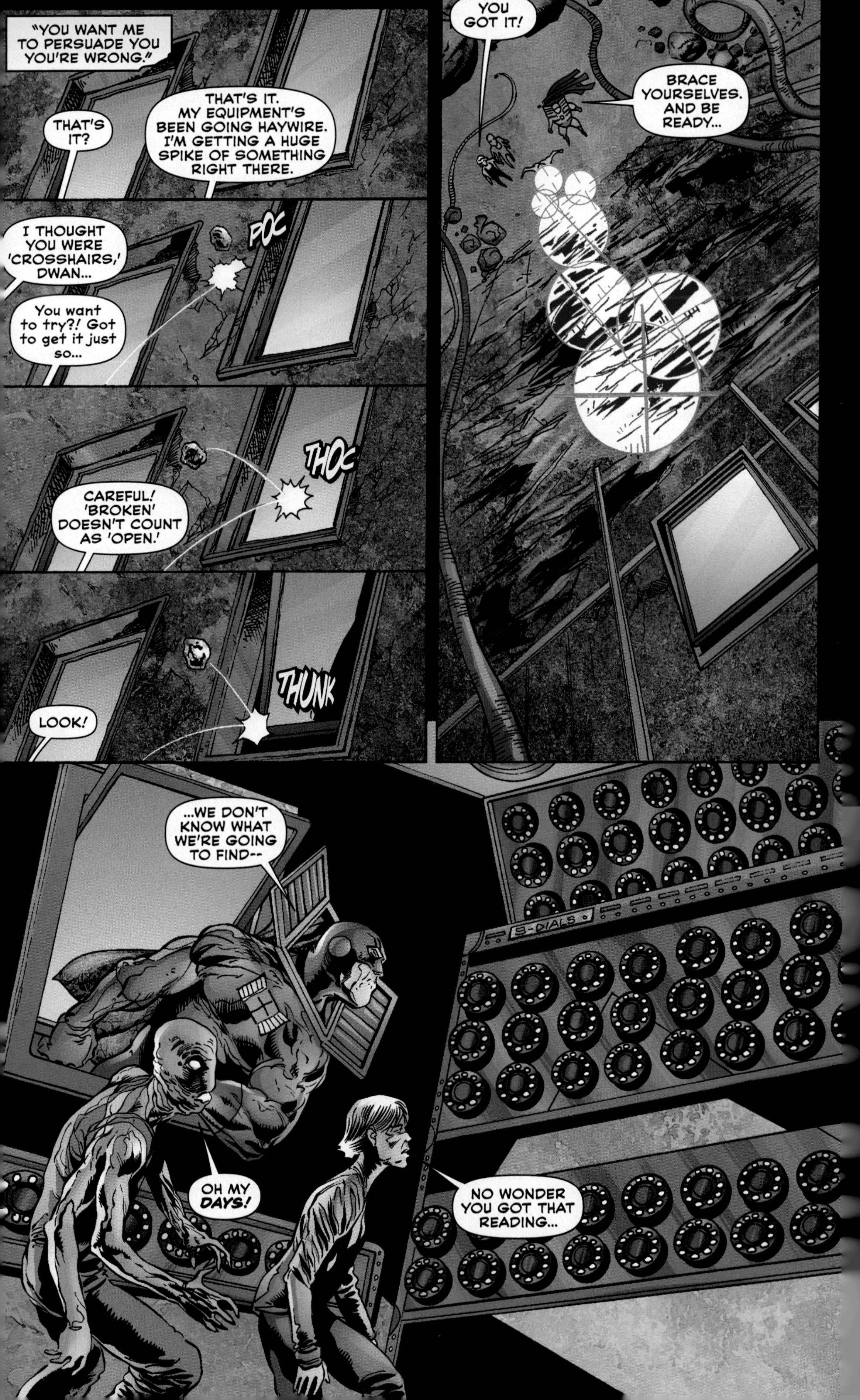
"YOU WANT ME TO PERSUADE YOU YOU'RE WRONG."
THAT'S IT?
THAT'S IT. MY EQUIPMENT'S BEEN GOING HAYWIRE. I'M GETTING A HUGE SPIKE OF SOMETHING RIGHT THERE.
I THOUGHT YOU WERE 'CROSSHAIRS,' DWAN...
POC
You want to try?! Got to get it just so...
THOC
CAREFUL! 'BROKEN' DOESN'T COUNT AS 'OPEN.'
THUNK
LOOK!
YOU GOT IT!
BRACE YOURSELVES. AND BE READY...
...WE DON'T KNOW WHAT WE'RE GOING TO FIND--
S-DIALS
OH MY DAYS!
NO WONDER YOU GOT THAT READING...

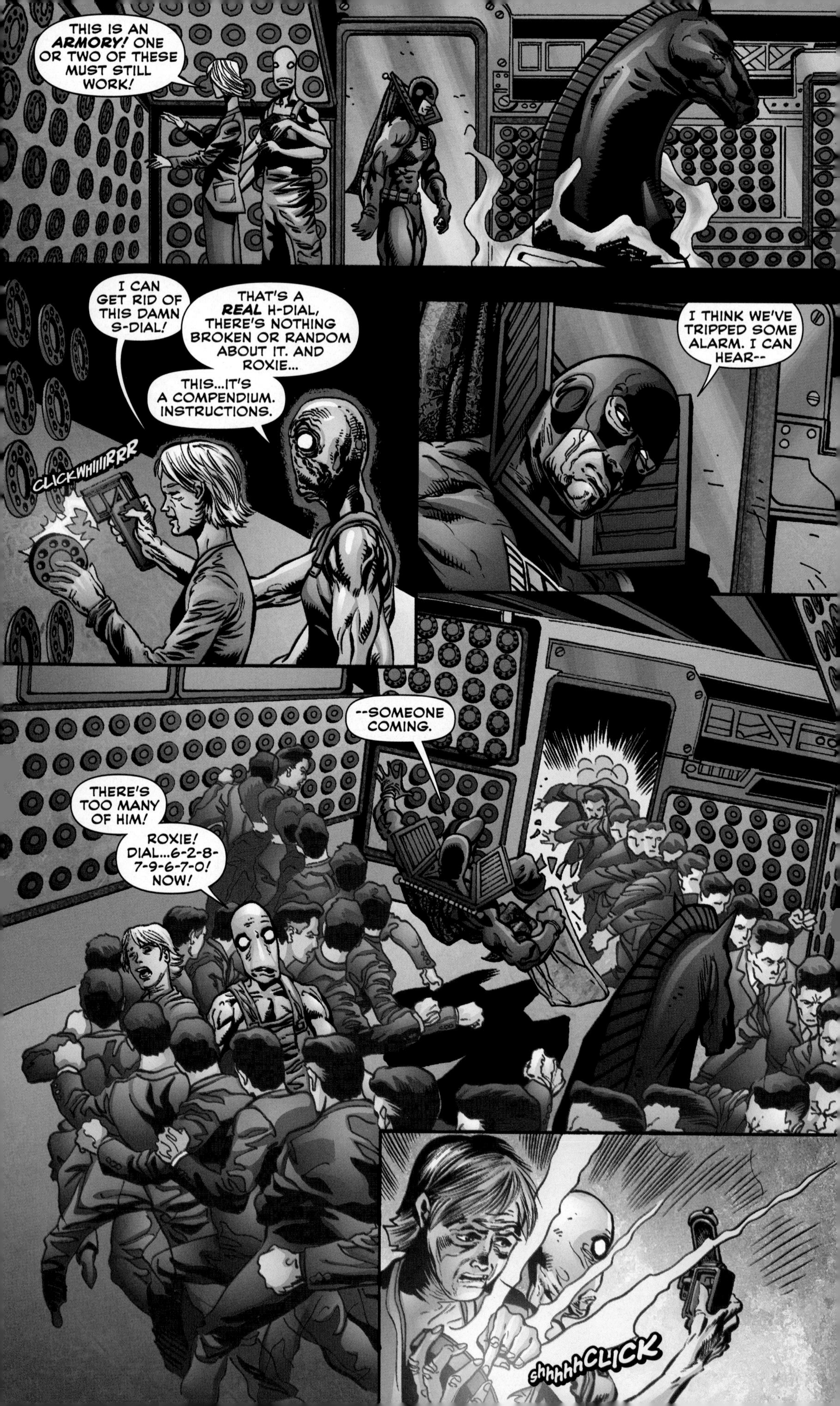
THIS IS AN ARMORY! ONE OR TWO OF THESE MUST STILL WORK!
I CAN GET RID OF THIS DAMN S-DIAL!
THAT'S A REAL H-DIAL, THERE'S NOTHING BROKEN OR RANDOM ABOUT IT. AND ROXIE...
THIS...IT'S A COMPENDIUM. INSTRUCTIONS.
CLICKWHIIIIRRR
I THINK WE'VE TRIPPED SOME ALARM. I CAN HEAR--
--SOMEONE COMING.
THERE'S TOO MANY OF HIM!
ROXIE! DIAL...6-2-8-7-9-6-7-0! NOW!
shhhhhCLICK

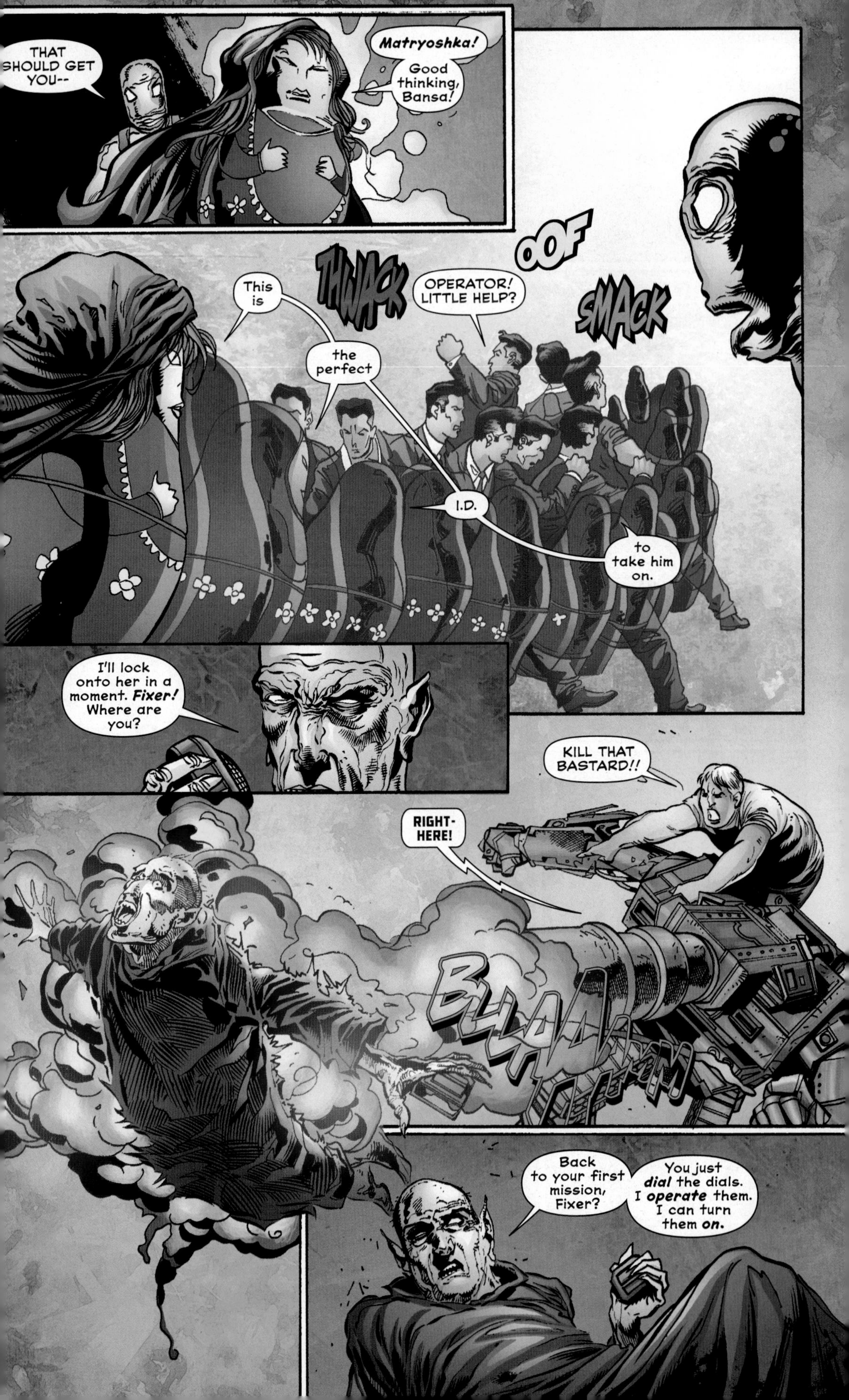
THAT SHOULD GET YOU--
Matryoshka!
Good thinking, Bansa!
THWACK
OOF
This is
the perfect
I.D.
to take him on.
OPERATOR! LITTLE HELP?
SMACK
I'll lock onto her in a moment. Fixer! Where are you?
KILL THAT BASTARD!!
RIGHT-HERE!
BLAAAMM
Back to your first mission, Fixer?
You just dial the dials. I operate them. I can turn them on.

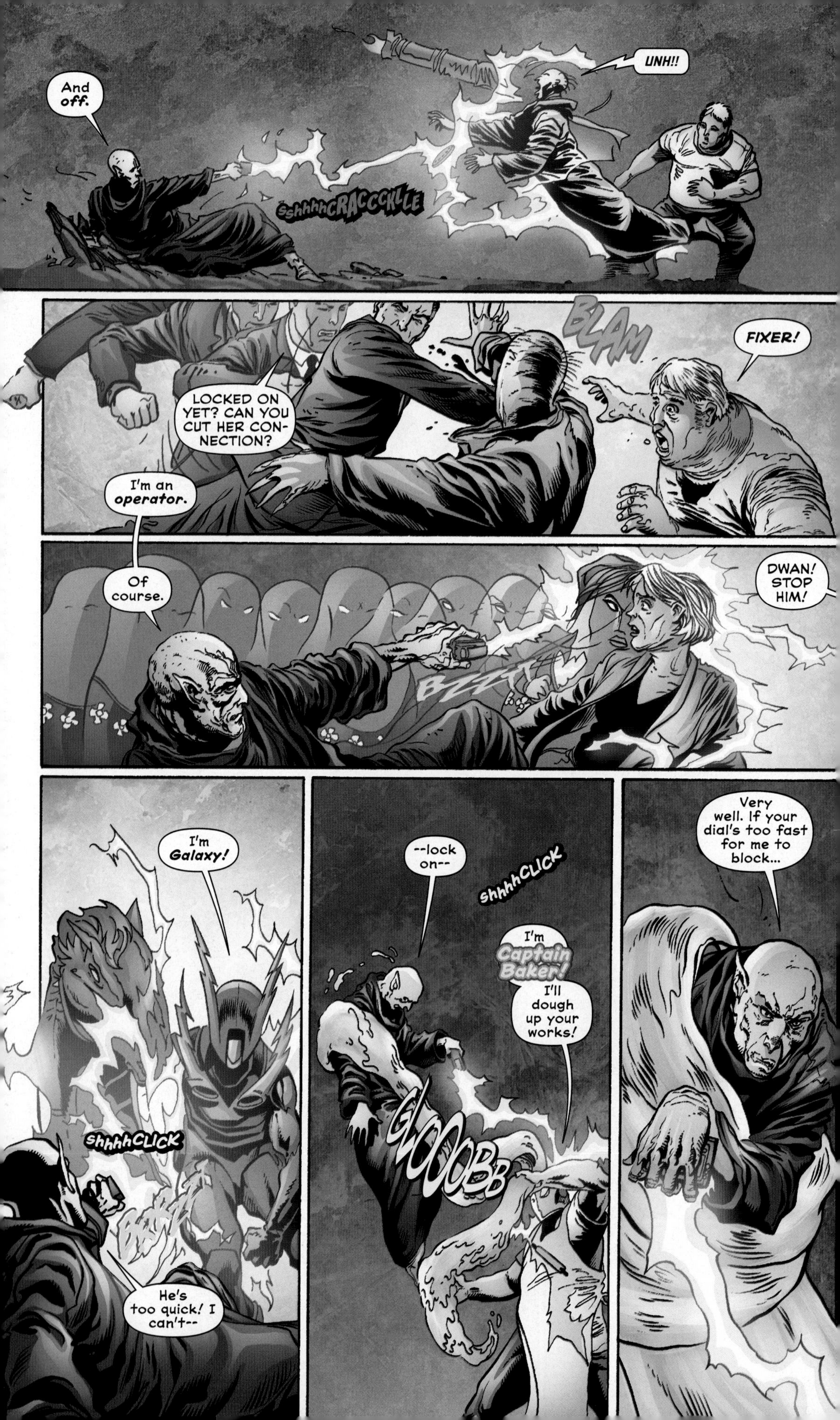
And off.
SHHHHCRACCCKLLE
UNH!!
LOCKED ON YET? CAN YOU CUT HER CONNECTION?
I'm an operator.
BLAM
FIXER!
Of course.
BZZT
DWAN! STOP HIM!
I'm Galaxy!
SHHHHCLICK
He's too quick! I can't--
--lock on--
SHHHHCLICK
I'm Captain Baker! I'll dough up your works!
GLOOOBB
Very well. If your dial's too fast for me to block...

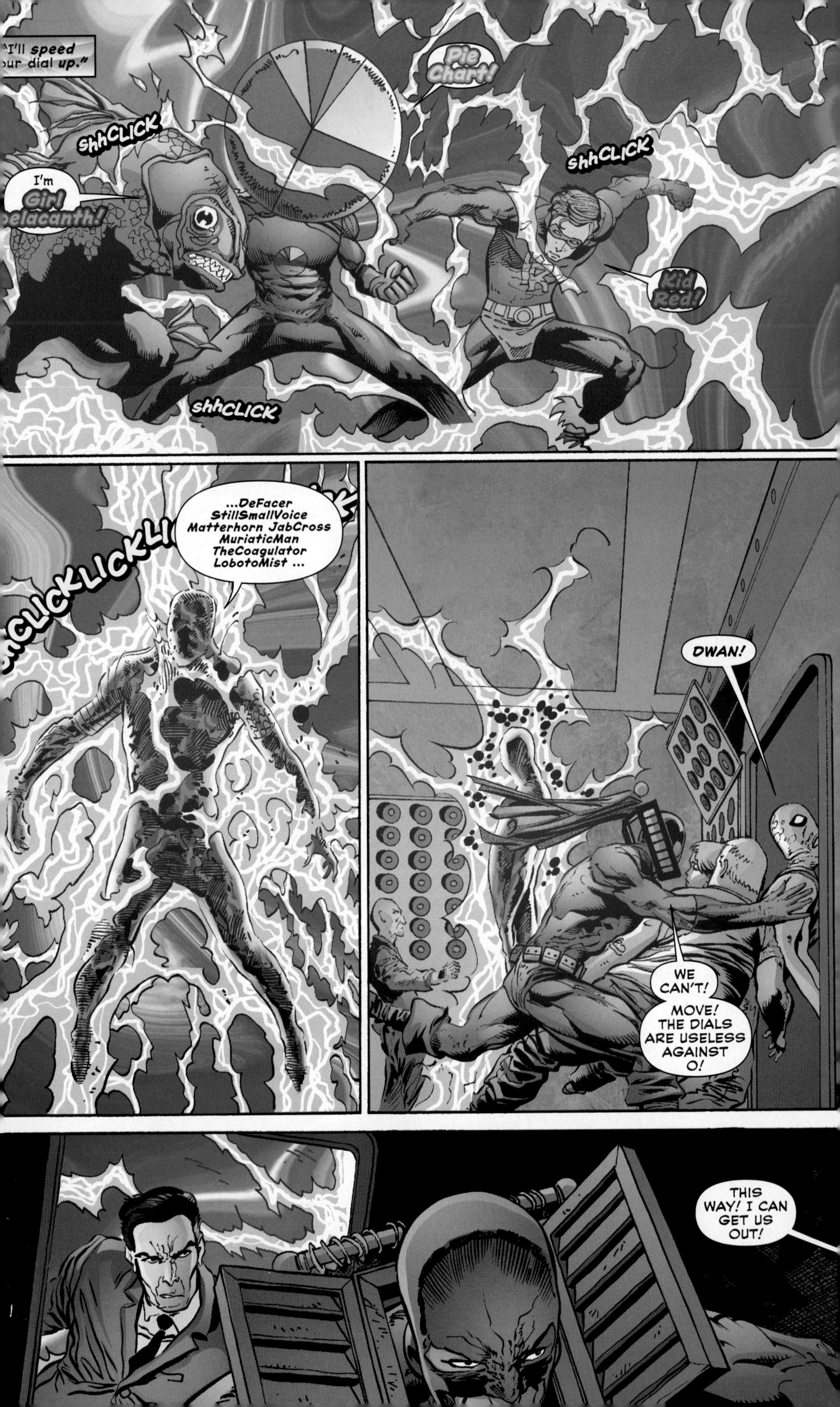
"I'll speed
our dial up."
Pie
Chart!
shhCLICK
I'm
Girl
Coelacanth!
shhCLICK
Kid
Red!
shhCLICK
CLICKLICKLI
...DeFacer
StillSmallVoice
Matterhorn JabCross
MuriaticMan
TheCoagulator
LobotoMist ...
DWAN!
WE
CAN'T!
MOVE!
THE DIALS
ARE USELESS
AGAINST
O!
THIS
WAY! I CAN
GET US
OUT!

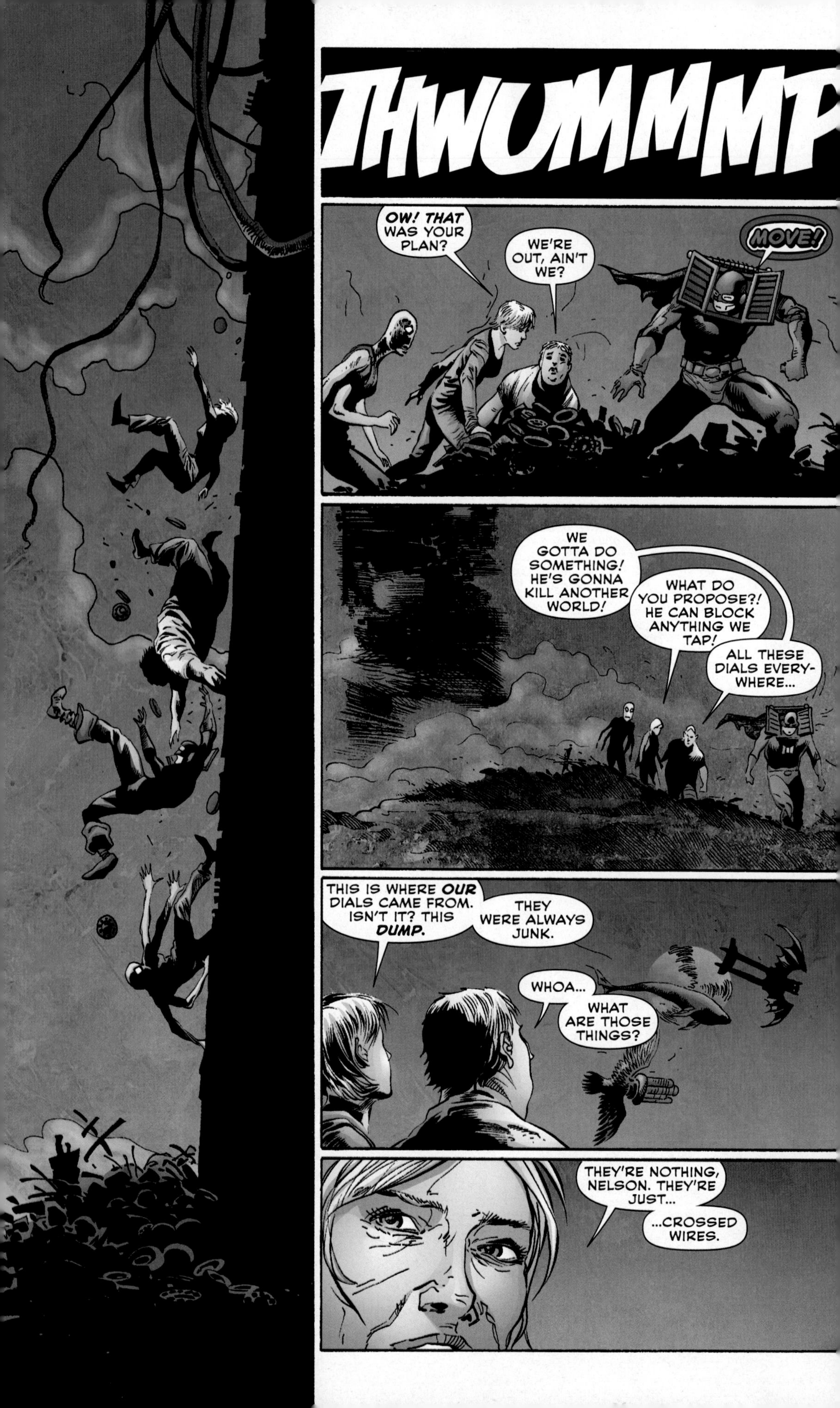
THWUMMMP
OW! THAT WAS YOUR PLAN?
WE'RE OUT, AIN'T WE?
MOVE!
WE GOTTA DO SOMETHING! HE'S GONNA KILL ANOTHER WORLD!
WHAT DO YOU PROPOSE?! HE CAN BLOCK ANYTHING WE TAP!
ALL THESE DIALS EVERY-WHERE...
THIS IS WHERE OUR DIALS CAME FROM. ISN'T IT? THIS DUMP.
THEY WERE ALWAYS JUNK.
WHOA...
WHAT ARE THOSE THINGS?
THEY'RE NOTHING, NELSON. THEY'RE JUST...
...CROSSED WIRES.

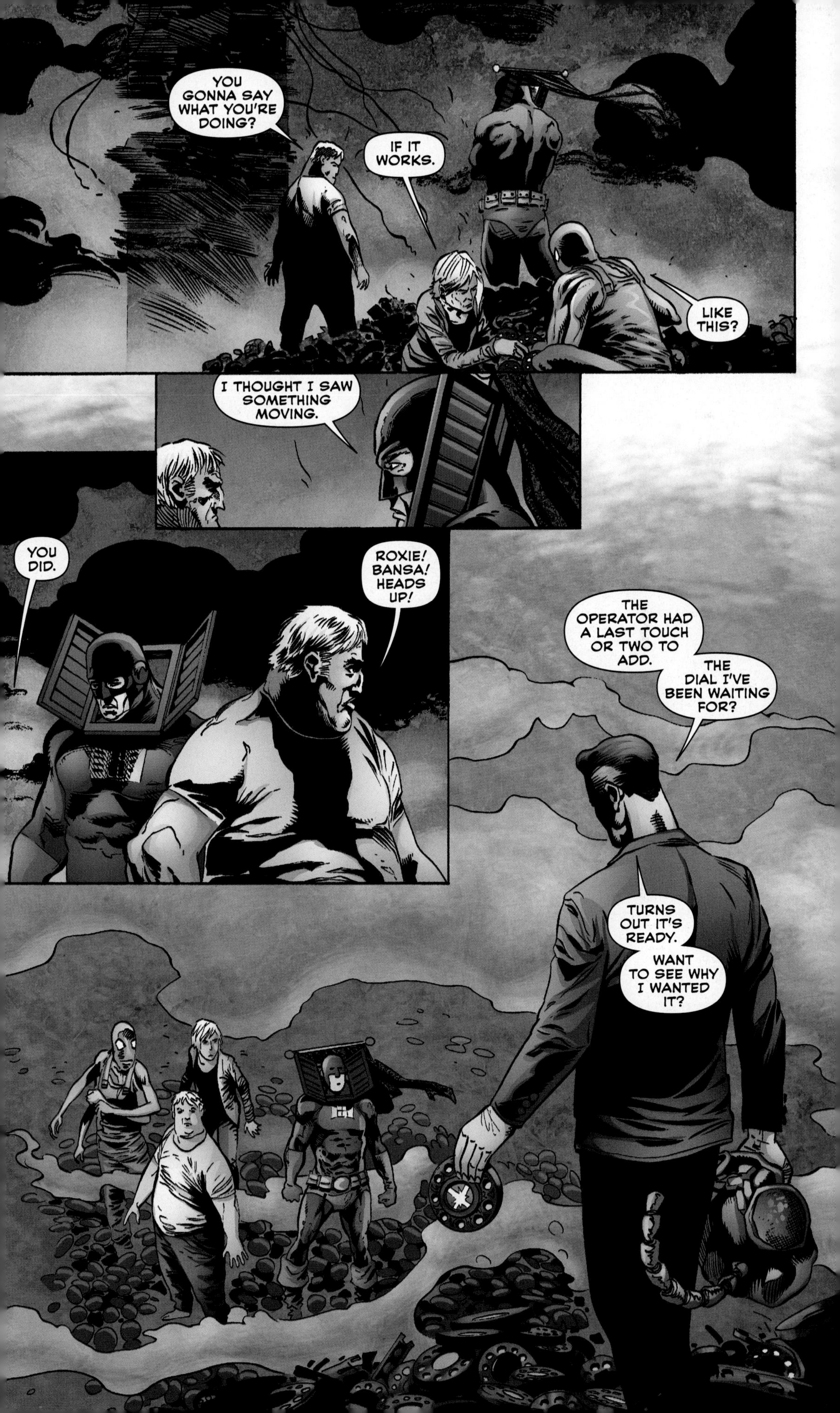
YOU GONNA SAY WHAT YOU'RE DOING?
IF IT WORKS.
LIKE THIS?
I THOUGHT I SAW SOMETHING MOVING.
YOU DID.
ROXIE! BANSA! HEADS UP!
THE OPERATOR HAD A LAST TOUCH OR TWO TO ADD.
THE DIAL I'VE BEEN WAITING FOR?
TURNS OUT IT'S READY.
WANT TO SEE WHY I WANTED IT?

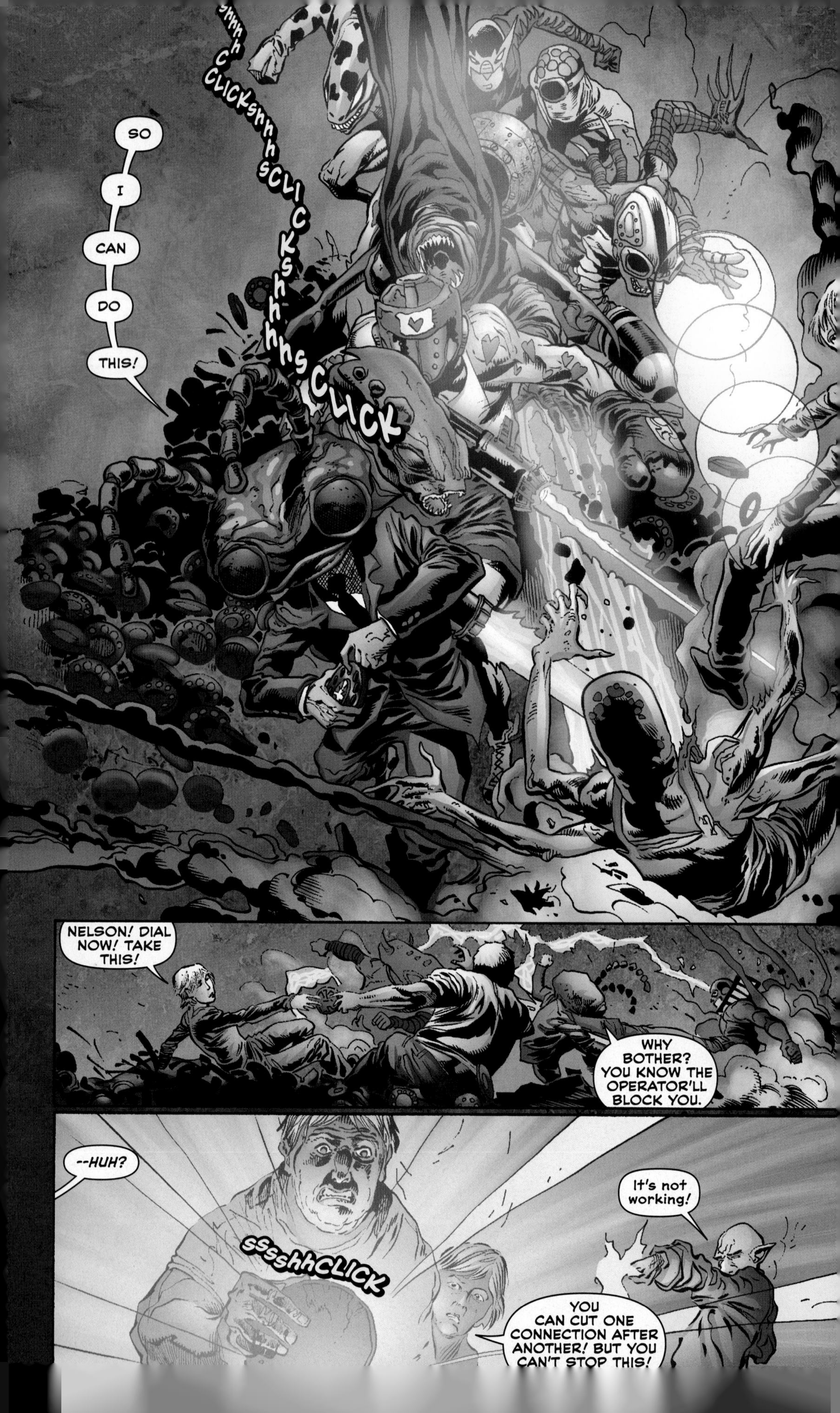
SO I CAN DO THIS!
shhh CLICKshhhh sCLICKshhhhhsCLICK
NELSON! DIAL NOW! TAKE THIS!
WHY BOTHER? YOU KNOW THE OPERATOR'LL BLOCK YOU.
--HUH?
SSSShhCLICK
It's not working!
YOU CAN CUT ONE CONNECTION AFTER ANOTHER! BUT YOU CAN'T STOP THIS!

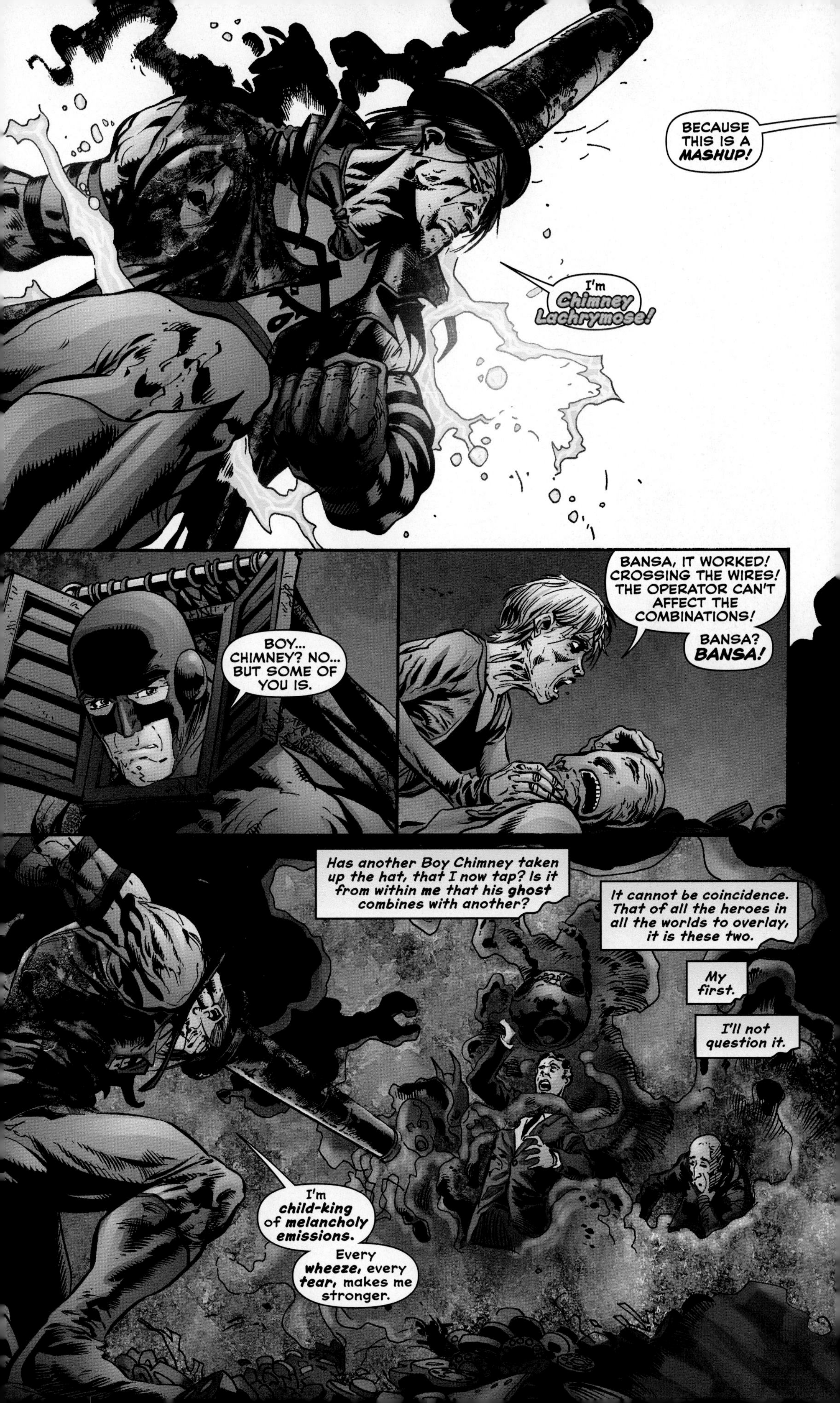
BECAUSE THIS IS A MASHUP!
I'm Chimney Lachrymose!
BOY... CHIMNEY? NO... BUT SOME OF YOU IS.
BANSA, IT WORKED! CROSSING THE WIRES! THE OPERATOR CAN'T AFFECT THE COMBINATIONS!
BANSA? BANSA!
Has another Boy Chimney taken up the hat, that I now tap? Is it from within me that his ghost combines with another?
It cannot be coincidence. That of all the heroes in all the worlds to overlay, it is these two.
My first.
I'll not question it.
I'm child-king of melancholy emissions.
Every wheeze, every tear, makes me stronger.

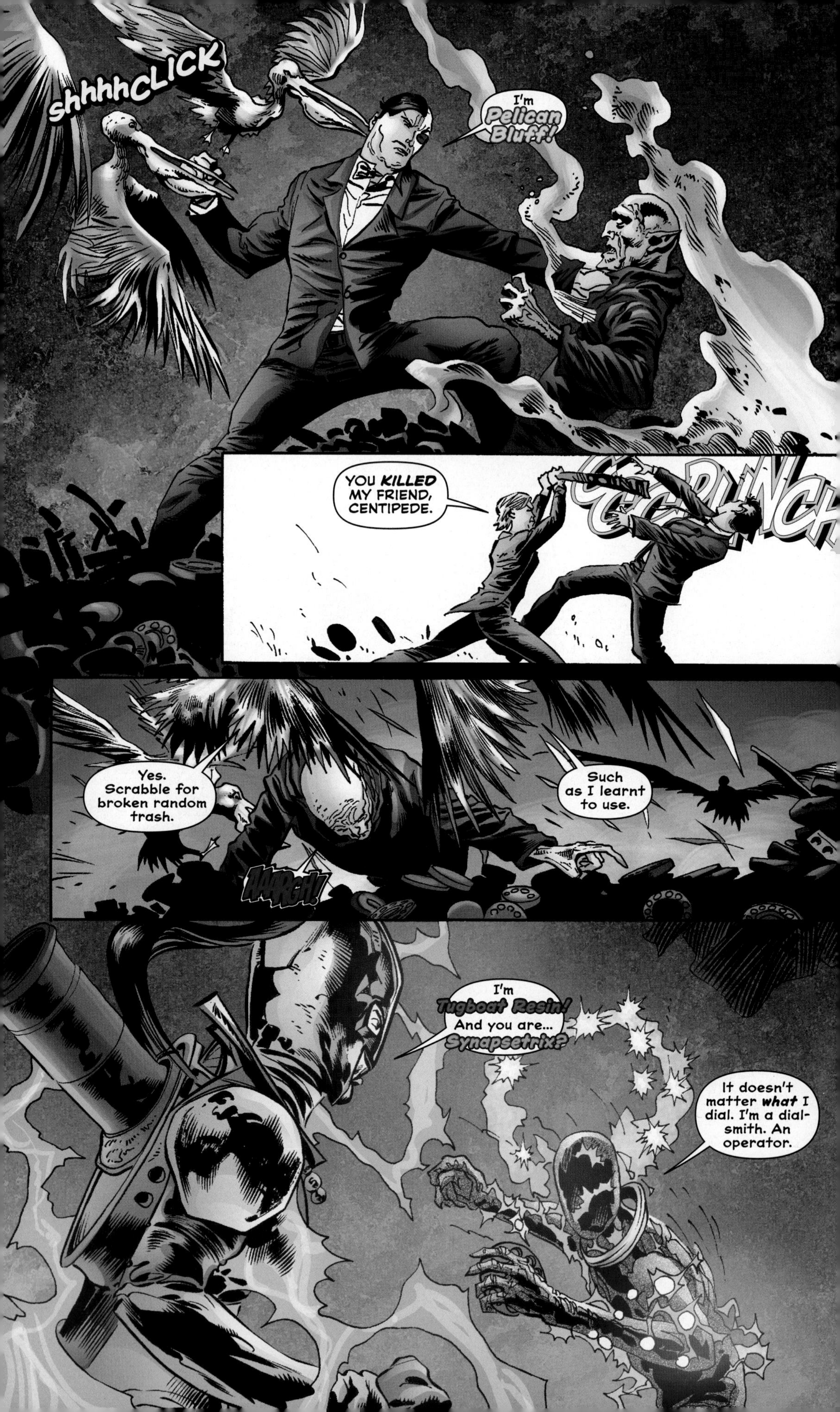
shhhhCLICK
I'm Pelican Bluff!
YOU KILLED MY FRIEND, CENTIPEDE.
Yes. Scrabble for broken random trash.
Such as I learnt to use.
AAARGH!
I'm Tugboat Resin! And you are... Synapsetrix?
It doesn't matter what I dial. I'm a dial-smith. An operator.

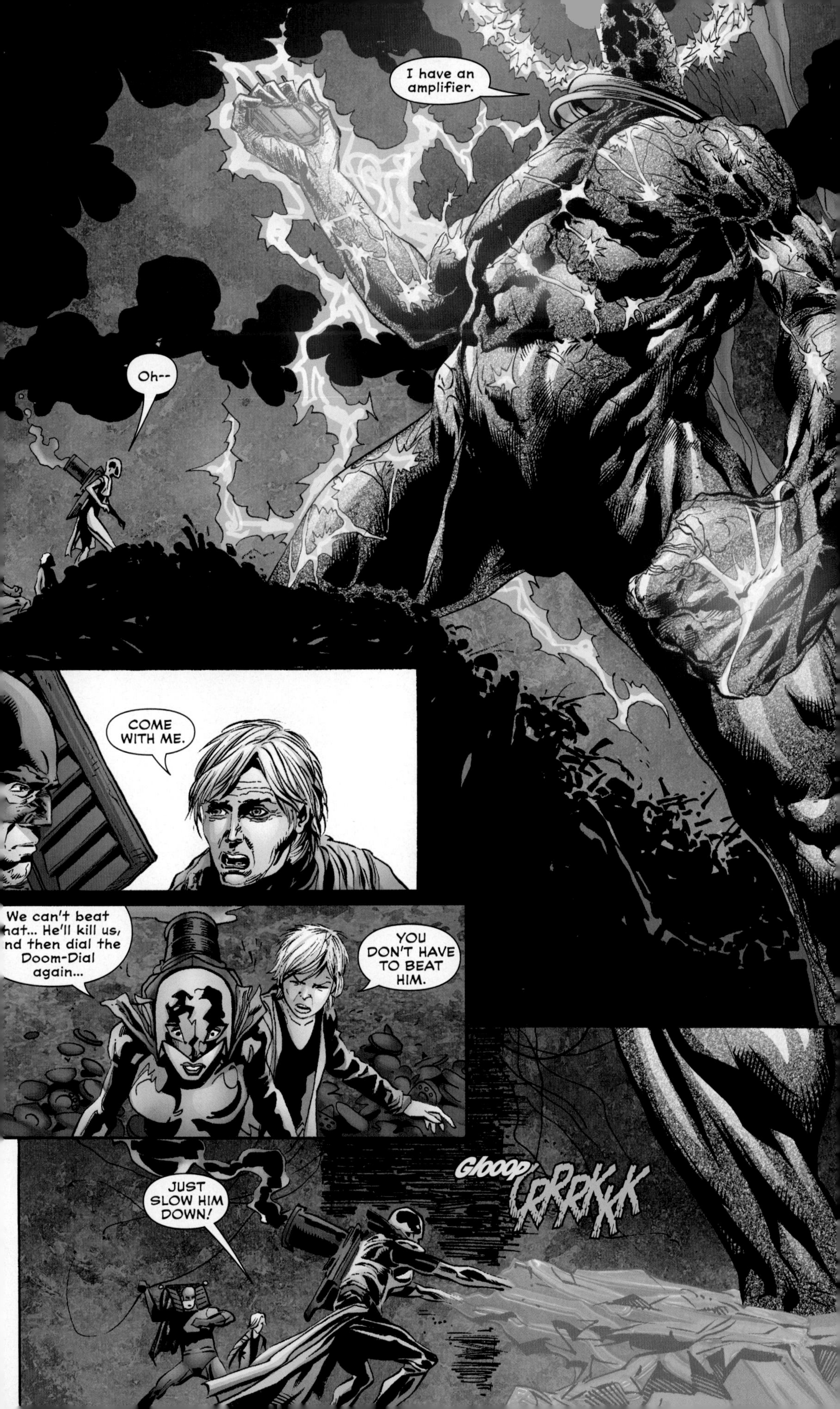
I have an amplifier.
Oh--
COME WITH ME.
We can't beat hat... He'll kill us, nd then dial the Doom-Dial again...
YOU DON'T HAVE TO BEAT HIM.
JUST SLOW HIM DOWN!
GLOOP!
CRRKKK

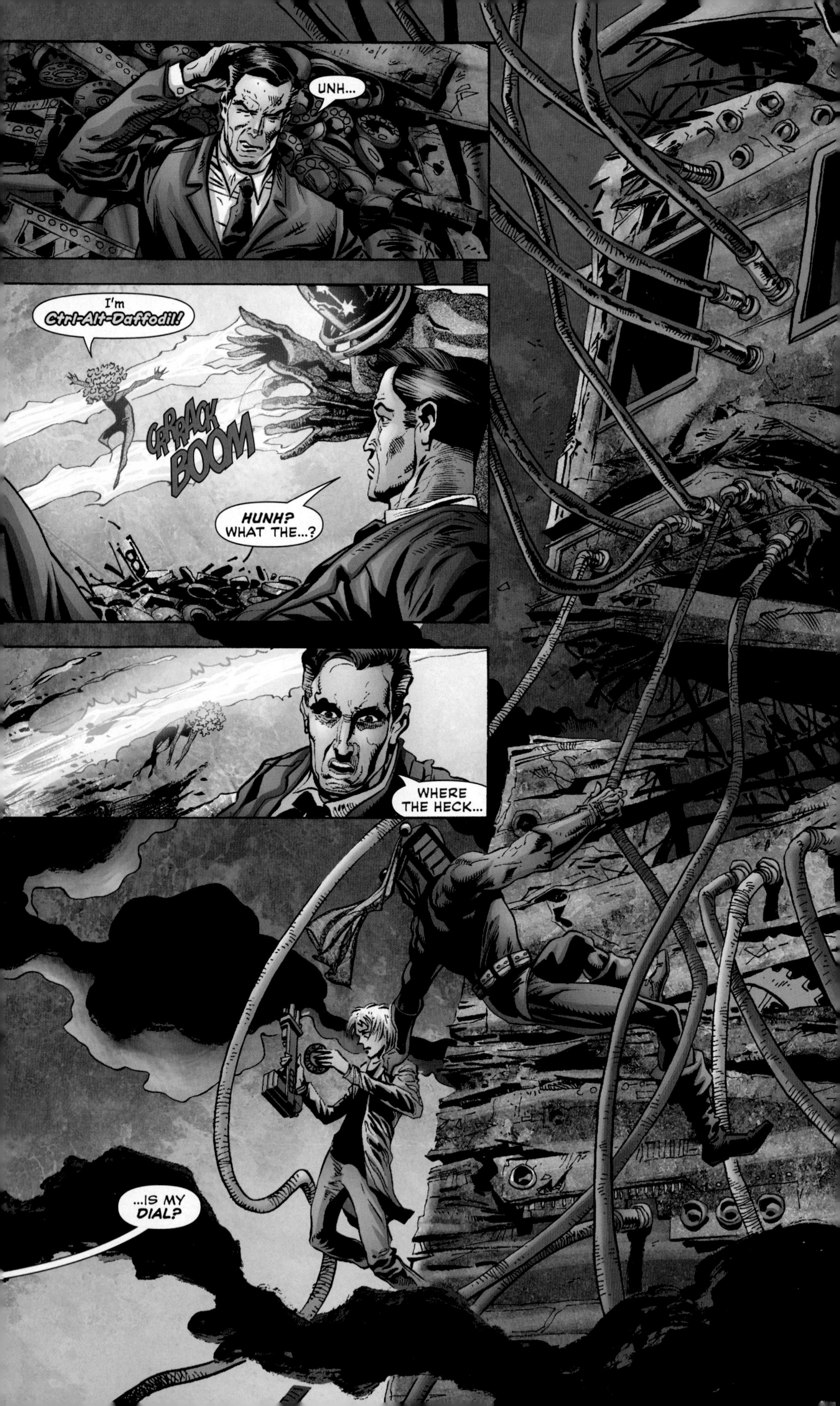
UNH...
I'm Ctrl-Alt-Daffodil!
CRRRACK BOOM
HUNH? WHAT THE...?
WHERE THE HECK...
...IS MY DIAL?

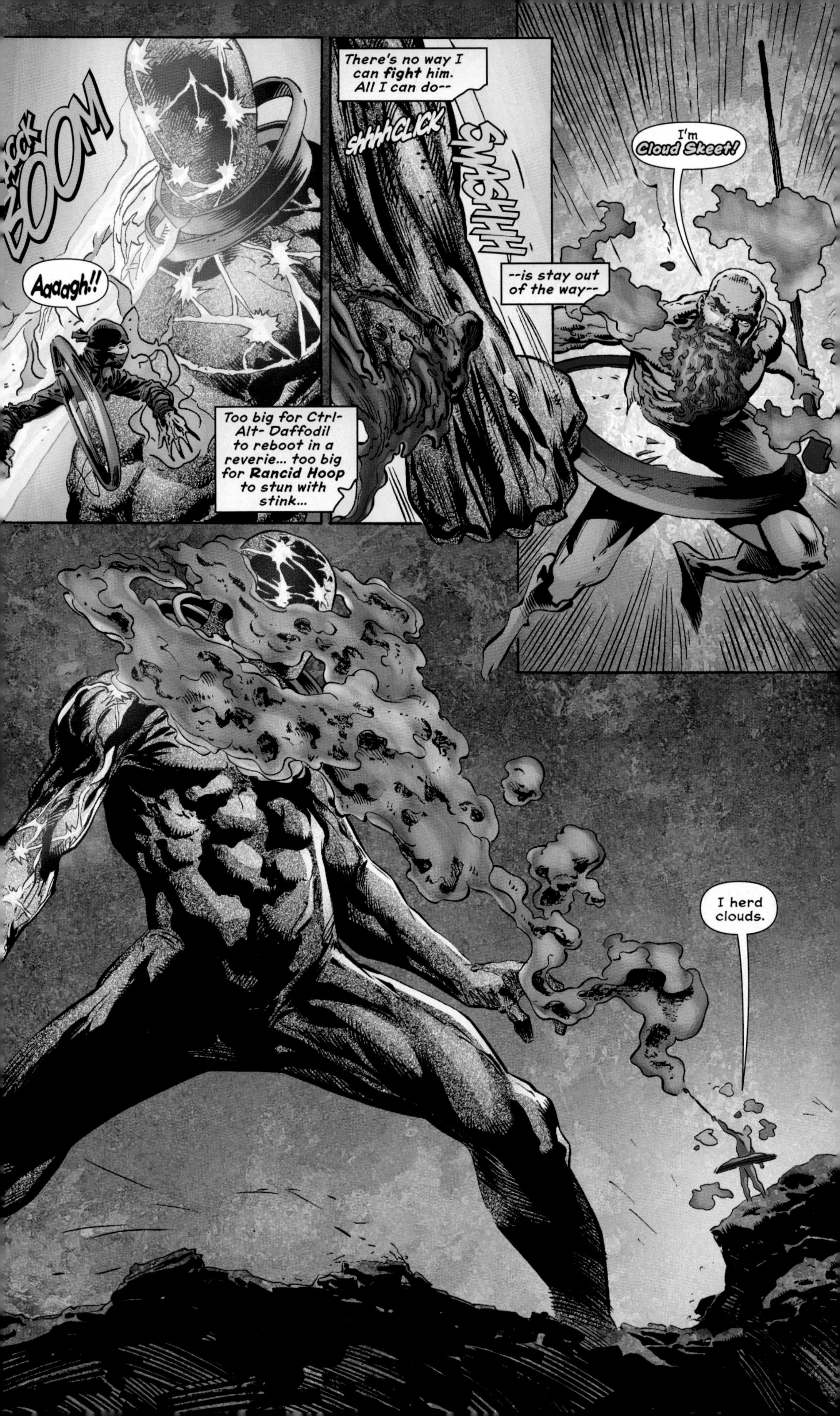
KRAKK
BOOM
Aaaagh!!
Too big for Ctrl-Alt-Daffodil to reboot in a reverie... too big for Rancid Hoop to stun with stink...
There's no way I can fight him. All I can do--
shhhhCLICK
SMASHHH
--is stay out of the way--
I'm Cloud Skeet!
I herd clouds.

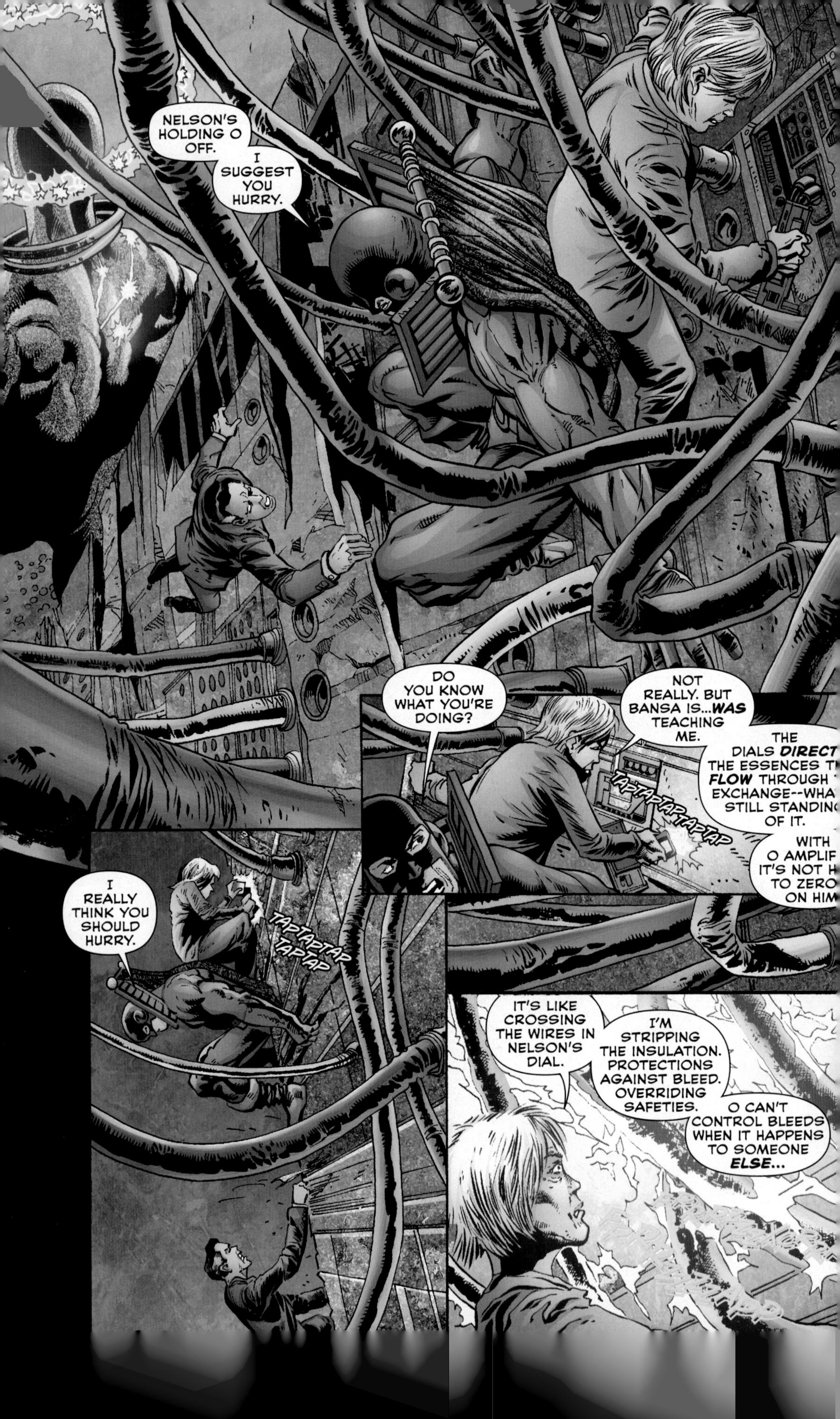

NELSON'S HOLDING O OFF.
I SUGGEST YOU HURRY.
DO YOU KNOW WHAT YOU'RE DOING?
NOT REALLY. BUT BANSA IS...WAS TEACHING ME.
TAPTAPTAPTAPTAPTAP
I REALLY THINK YOU SHOULD HURRY.
TAPTAPTAP TAPTAP
IT'S LIKE CROSSING THE WIRES IN NELSON'S DIAL.
I'M STRIPPING THE INSULATION. PROTECTIONS AGAINST BLEED. OVERRIDING SAFETIES.
O CAN'T CONTROL BLEEDS WHEN IT HAPPENS TO SOMEONE ELSE...

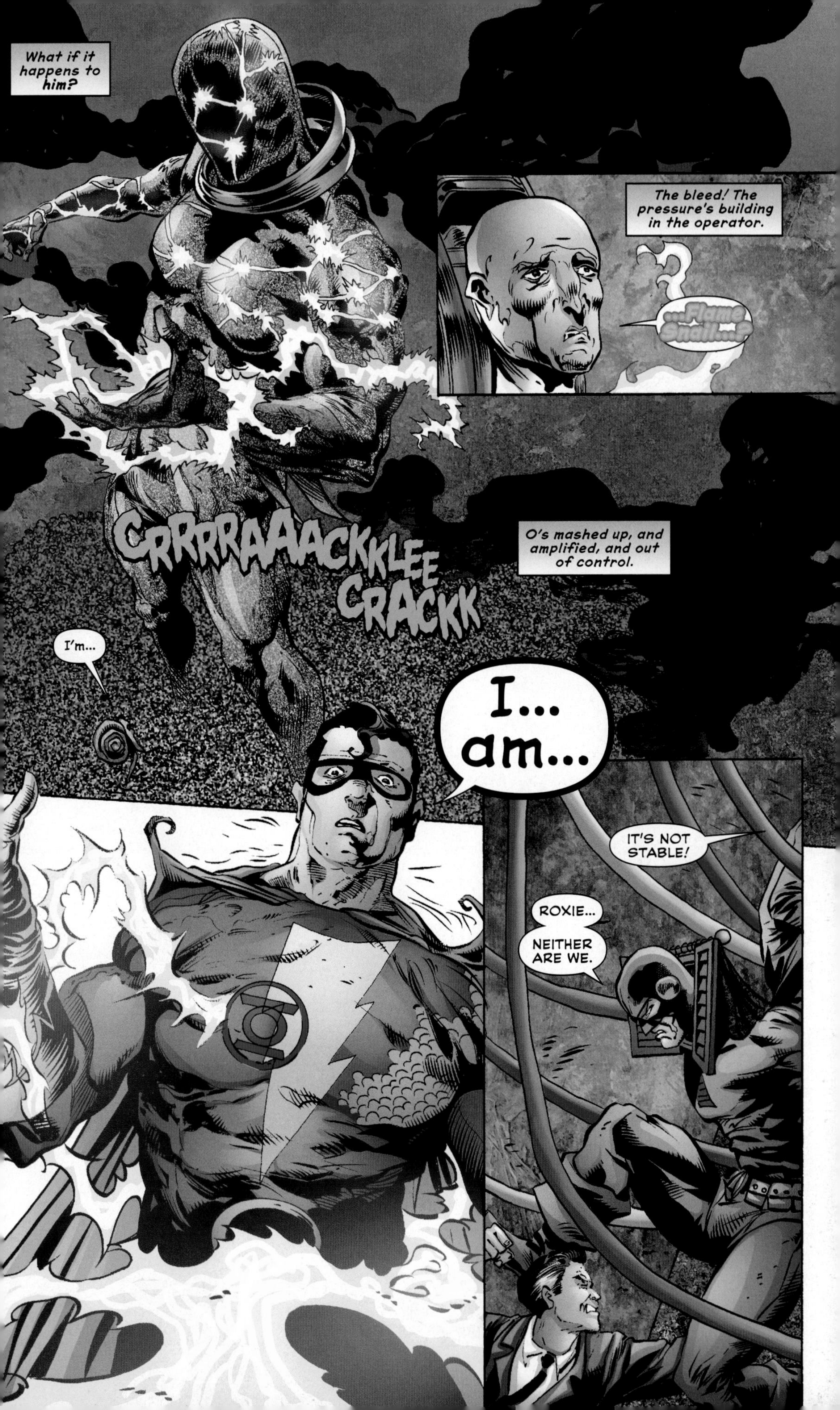
What if it happens to him?
The bleed! The pressure's building in the operator.
...Flame Snail...?
CRRRRAAACKKLEE CRACKK
O's mashed up, and amplified, and out of control.
I'm...
I... am...
IT'S NOT STABLE!
ROXIE...
NEITHER ARE WE.

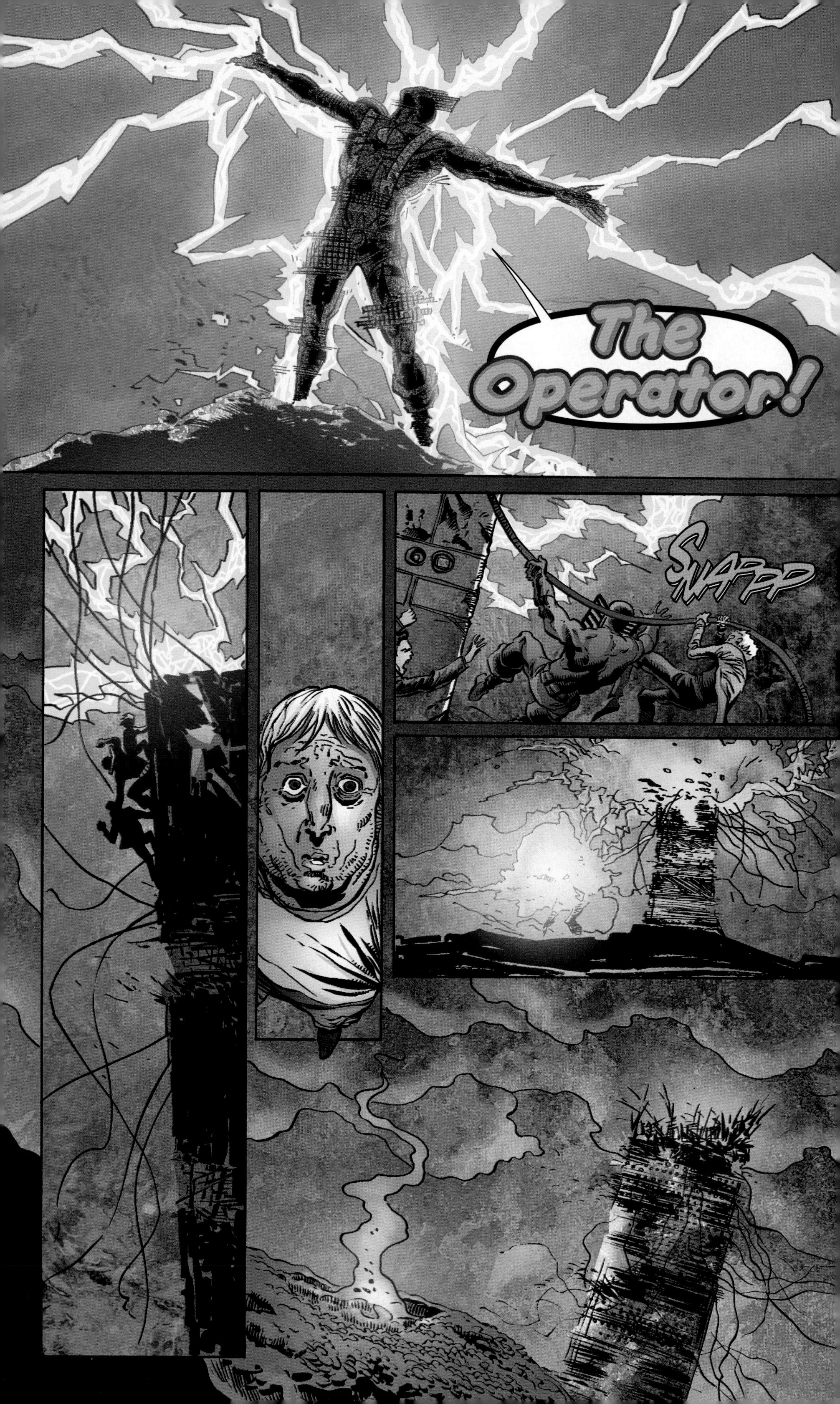
The Operator!
SNAPPP

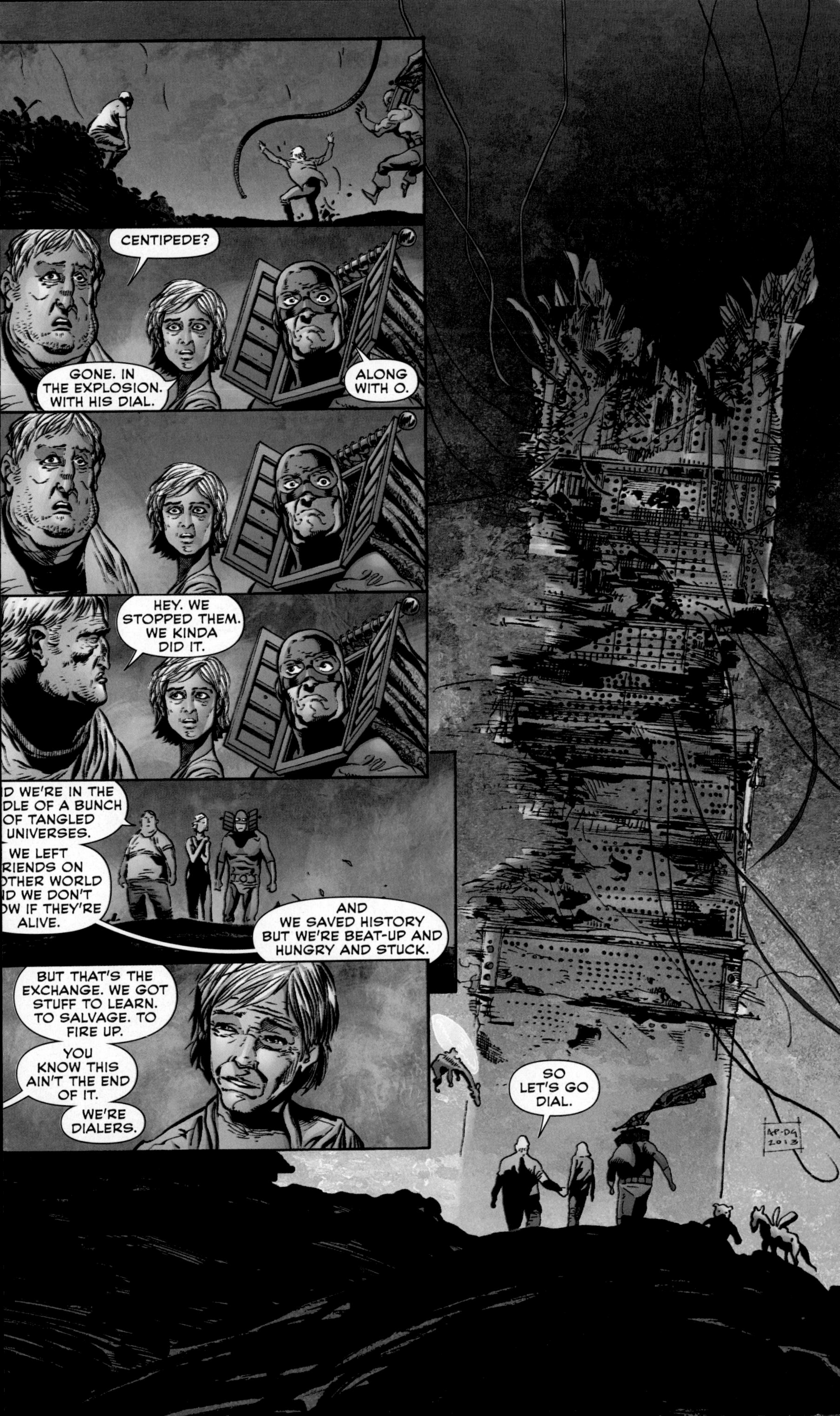
CENTIPEDE?
GONE. IN THE EXPLOSION. WITH HIS DIAL.
ALONG WITH O.
HEY. WE STOPPED THEM. WE KINDA DID IT.
D WE'RE IN THE DLE OF A BUNCH OF TANGLED UNIVERSES.
WE LEFT RIENDS ON OTHER WORLD D WE DON'T OW IF THEY'RE ALIVE.
AND WE SAVED HISTORY BUT WE'RE BEAT-UP AND HUNGRY AND STUCK.
BUT THAT'S THE EXCHANGE. WE GOT STUFF TO LEARN. TO SALVAGE. TO FIRE UP.
YOU KNOW THIS AIN'T THE END OF IT.
WE'RE DIALERS.
SO LET'S GO DIAL.
AP-DG 2013

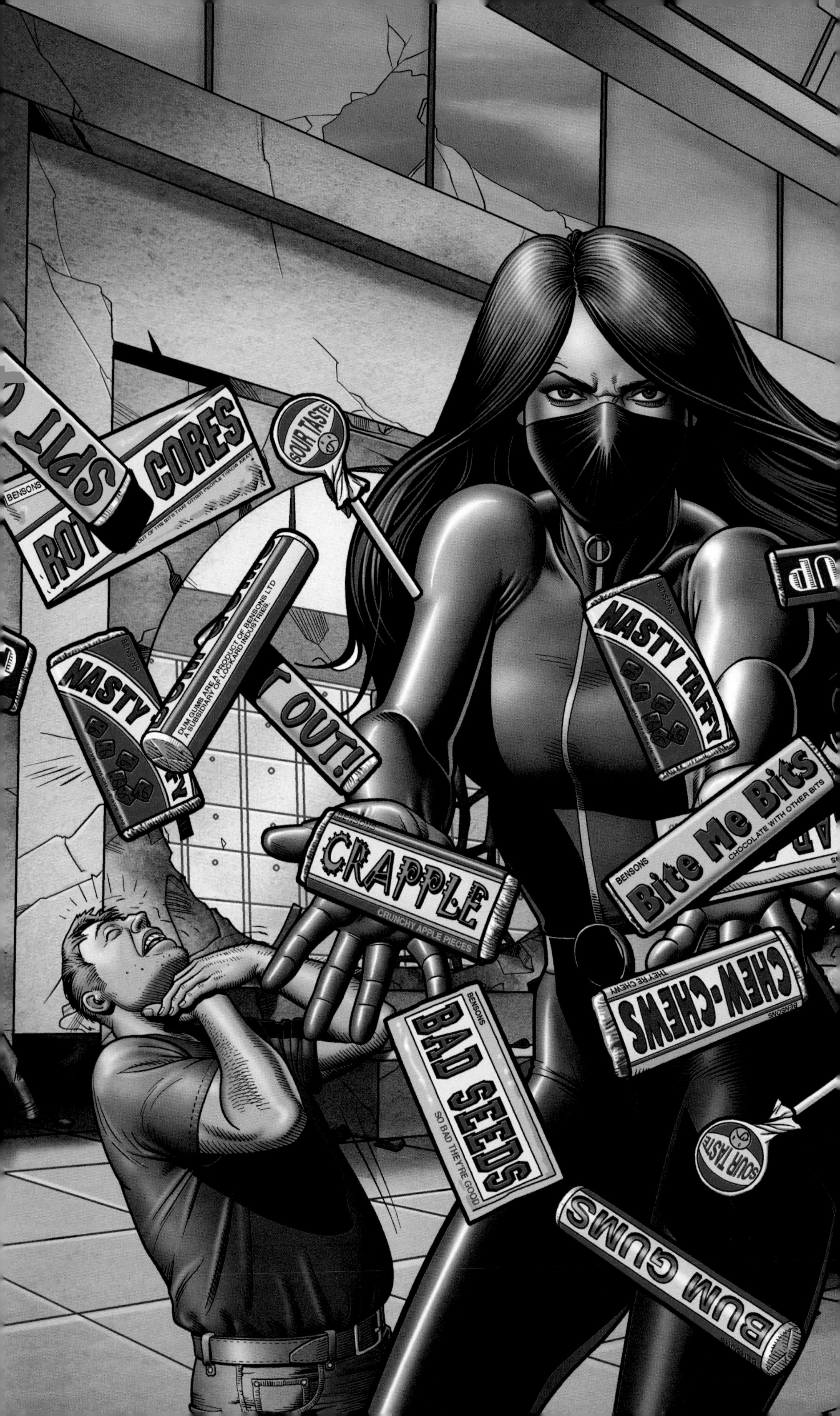
CORES
BENSONS
SOUR TASTE
DUM GUMS ARE A PRODUCT OF BENSONS LTD
A SUBSIDIARY OF LOCKARD INDUSTRIES.
BENSONS
NASTY TAFFY
BENSONS
CRAPPLE
CRUNCHY APPLE PIECES
BENSONS
Bite Me Bits
CHOCOLATE WITH OTHER BITS
CHEW-CHEWS
THEY'RE CHEWY
BENSONS
BENSONS
BAD SEEDS
SO BAD THEY'RE GOOD
SOUR TASTE
BUM GUMS

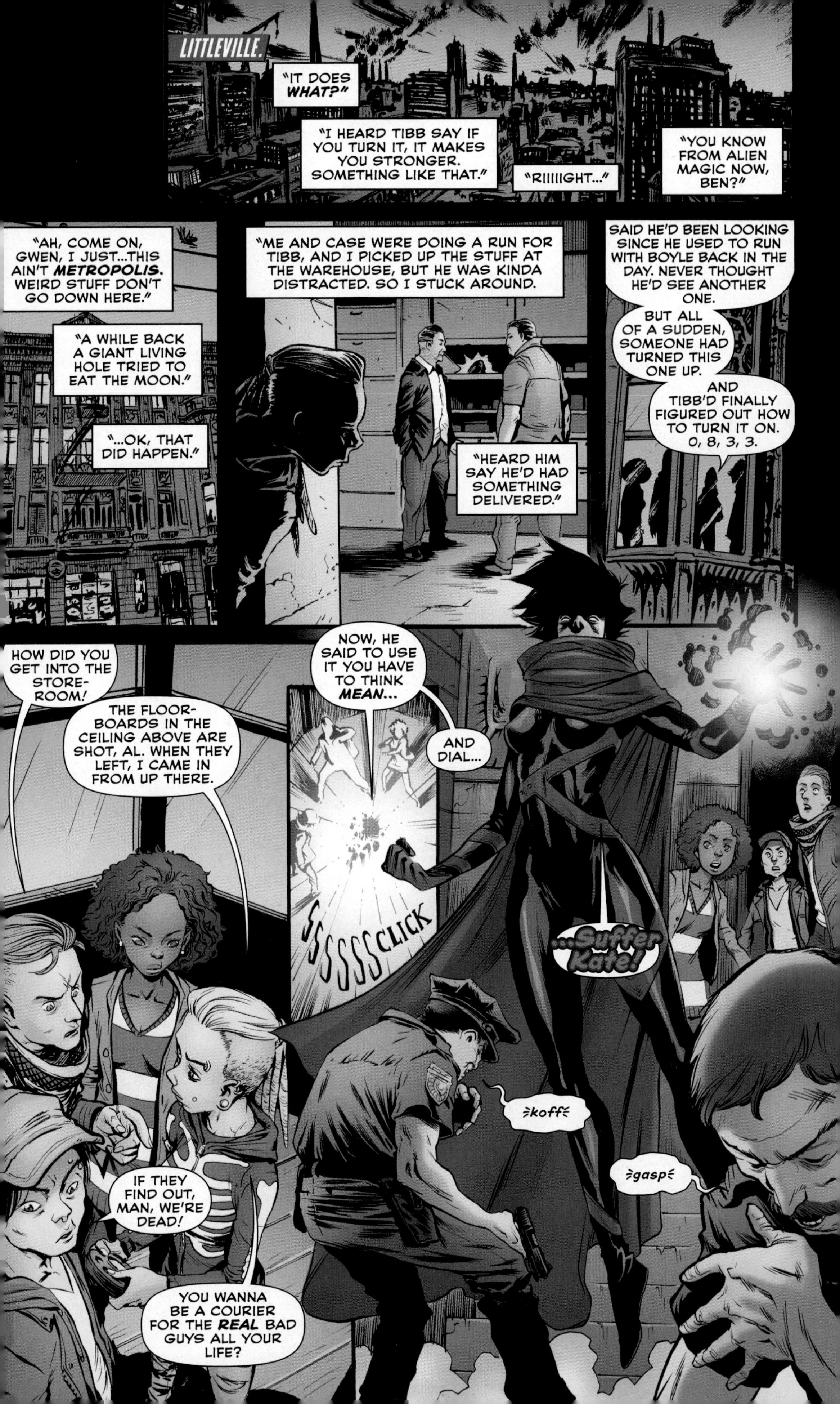

LITTLEVILLE.
"IT DOES WHAT?"
"I HEARD TIBB SAY IF YOU TURN IT, IT MAKES YOU STRONGER. SOMETHING LIKE THAT."
"RIIIIGHT..."
"YOU KNOW FROM ALIEN MAGIC NOW, BEN?"
"AH, COME ON, GWEN, I JUST...THIS AIN'T METROPOLIS. WEIRD STUFF DON'T GO DOWN HERE."
"A WHILE BACK A GIANT LIVING HOLE TRIED TO EAT THE MOON."
"...OK, THAT DID HAPPEN."
"ME AND CASE WERE DOING A RUN FOR TIBB, AND I PICKED UP THE STUFF AT THE WAREHOUSE, BUT HE WAS KINDA DISTRACTED. SO I STUCK AROUND.
"HEARD HIM SAY HE'D HAD SOMETHING DELIVERED."
SAID HE'D BEEN LOOKING SINCE HE USED TO RUN WITH BOYLE BACK IN THE DAY. NEVER THOUGHT HE'D SEE ANOTHER ONE.
BUT ALL OF A SUDDEN, SOMEONE HAD TURNED THIS ONE UP.
AND TIBB'D FINALLY FIGURED OUT HOW TO TURN IT ON. 0, 8, 3, 3.
HOW DID YOU GET INTO THE STORE-ROOM!
THE FLOOR-BOARDS IN THE CEILING ABOVE ARE SHOT, AL. WHEN THEY LEFT, I CAME IN FROM UP THERE.
NOW, HE SAID TO USE IT YOU HAVE TO THINK MEAN...
AND DIAL...
SSSSSCLICK
...Suffer Kate!
koff
gasp
IF THEY FIND OUT, MAN, WE'RE DEAD!
YOU WANNA BE A COURIER FOR THE REAL BAD GUYS ALL YOUR LIFE?

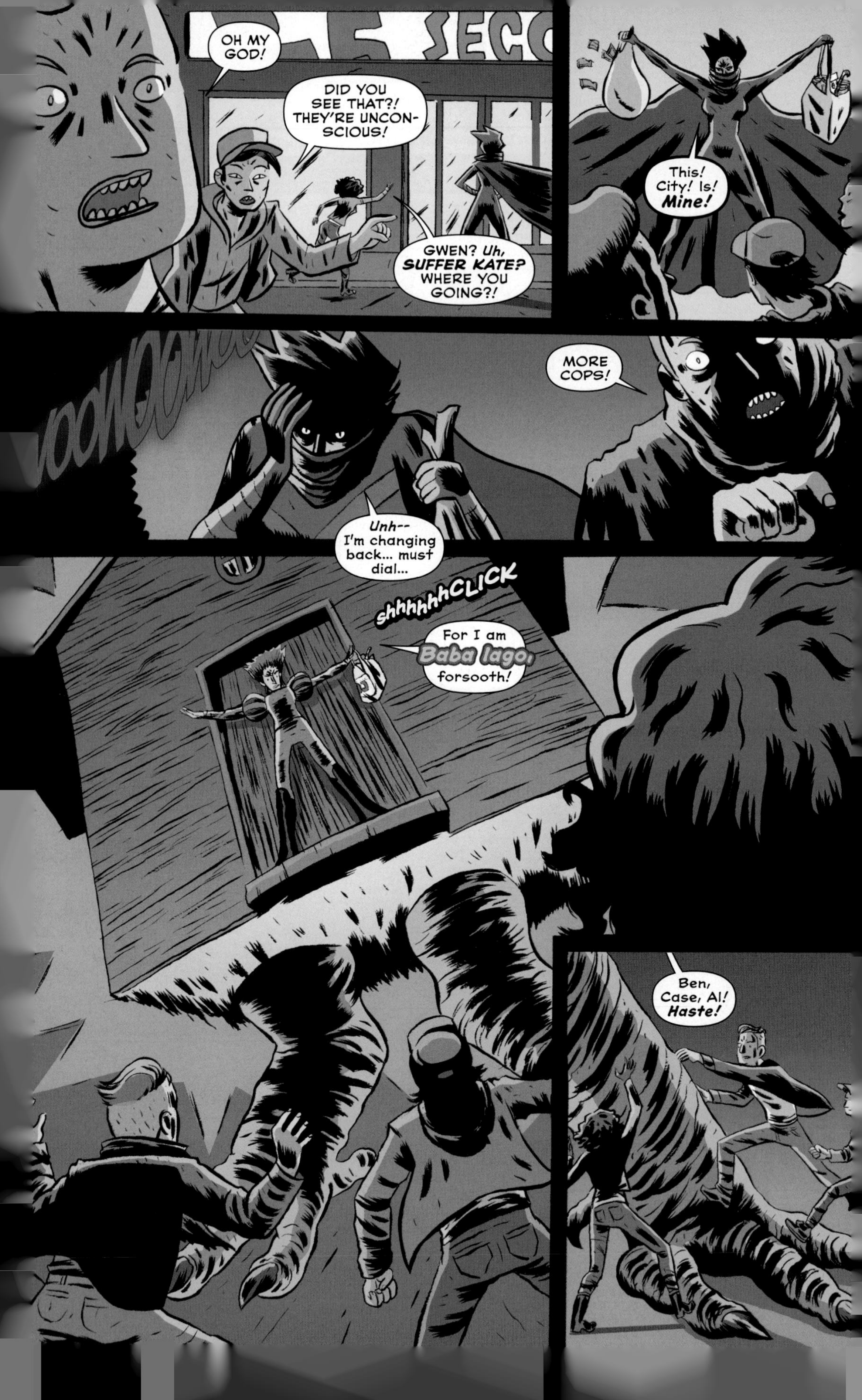
SECO
OH MY GOD!
DID YOU SEE THAT?! THEY'RE UNCON-SCIOUS!
GWEN? *Uh,* **SUFFER KATE?** WHERE YOU GOING?!
This! City! Is! ***Mine!***
MORE COPS!
Unh-- I'm changing back... must dial...
shhhhhhCLICK
For I am *Baba Iago,* forsooth!
Ben, Case, Al! ***Haste!***

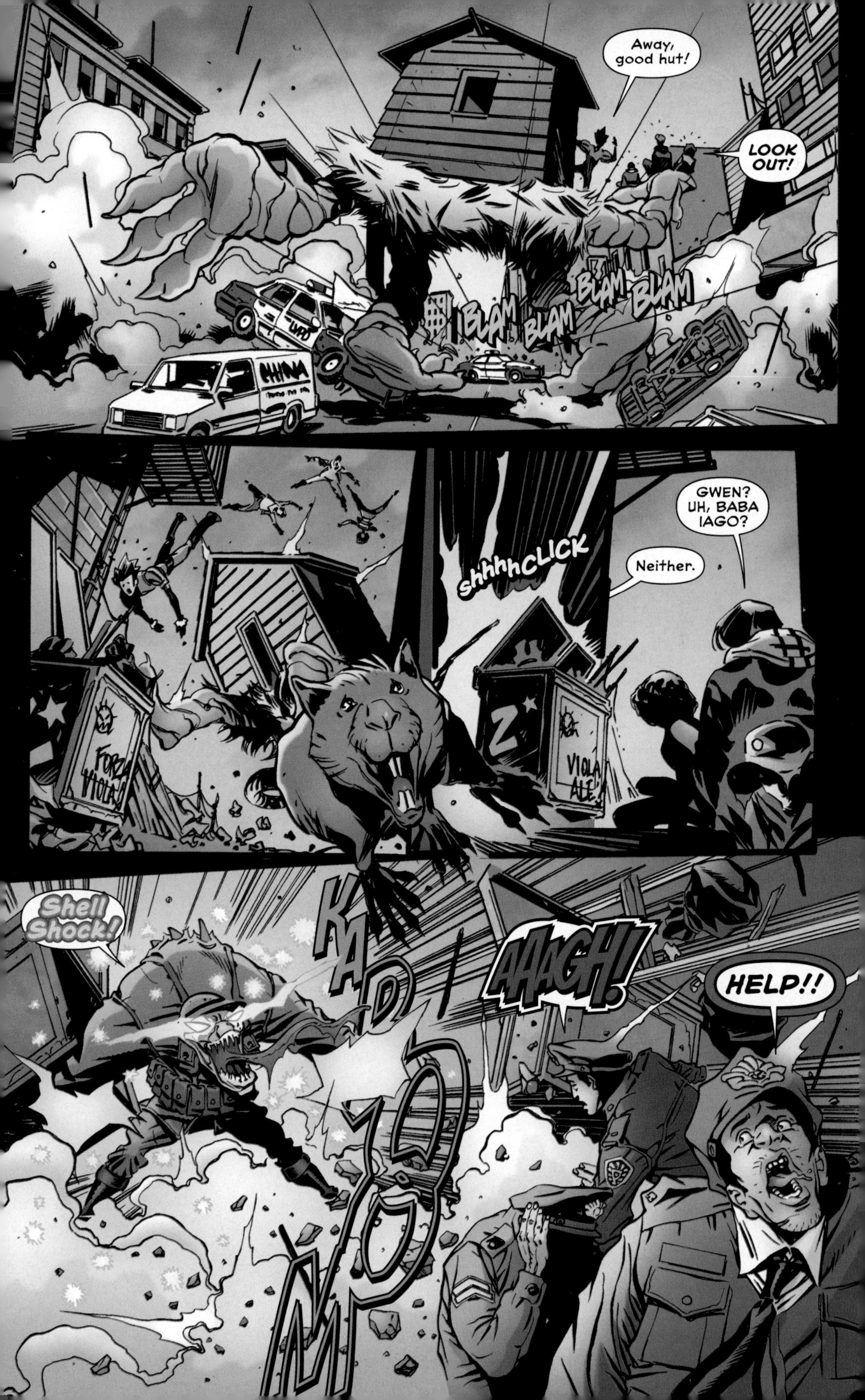
Away, good hut!
LOOK OUT!
BLAM BLAM BLAM BLAM
GWEN? UH, BABA IAGO?
shhhhCLICK
Neither.
FORZA VIOLA
VIOLA ALE
Shell Shock!
KA-DOOOM
AAAGH!
HELP!!

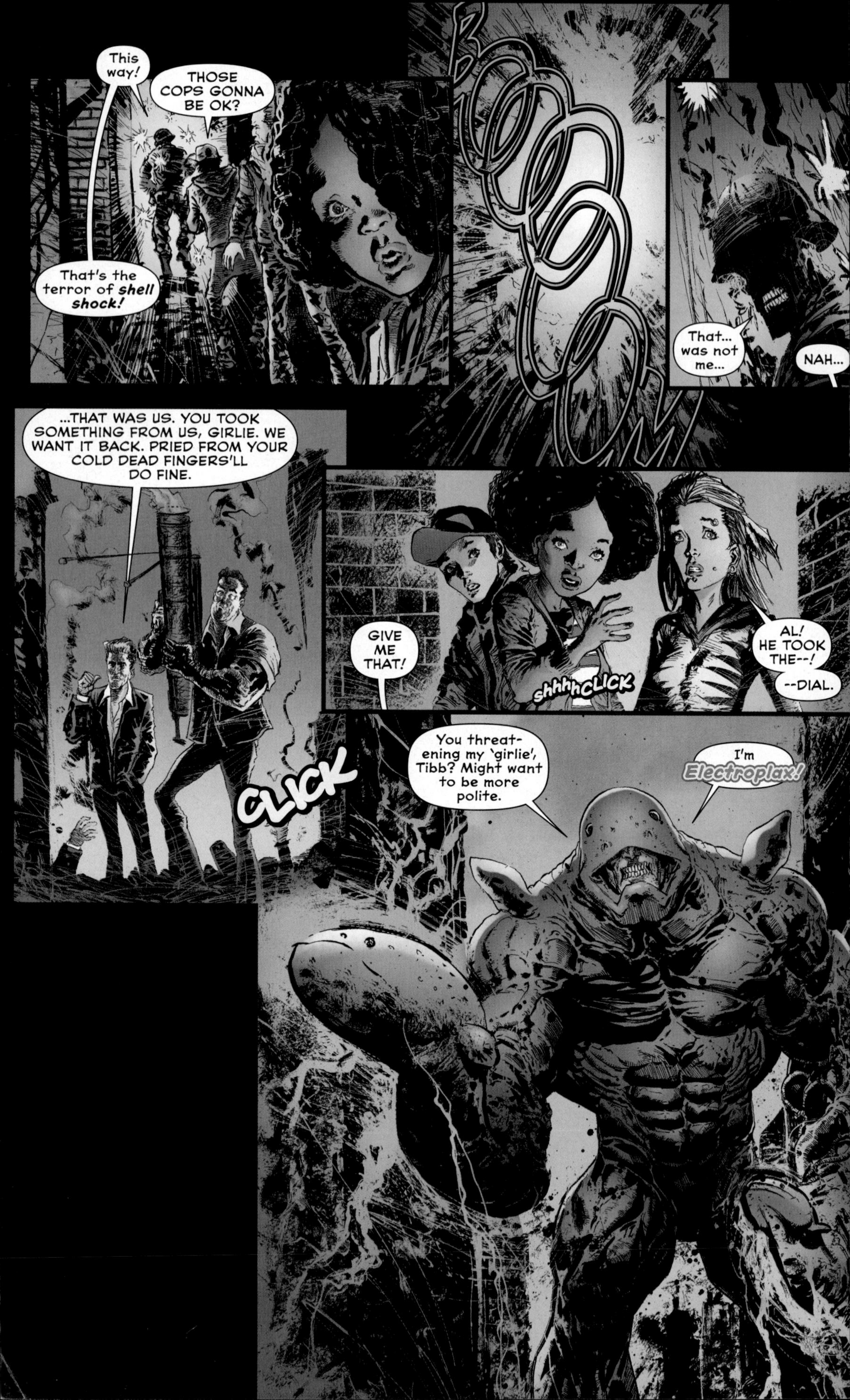
This way!
THOSE COPS GONNA BE OK?
That's the terror of ***shell shock!***
BOOOOOOM
That... was not me...
NAH...
...THAT WAS US. YOU TOOK SOMETHING FROM US, GIRLIE. WE WANT IT BACK. PRIED FROM YOUR COLD DEAD FINGERS'LL DO FINE.
GIVE ME THAT!
shhhhCLICK
AL! HE TOOK THE--!
--DIAL.
CLICK
You threat-ening my 'girlie', Tibb? Might want to be more polite.
I'm Electroplax!

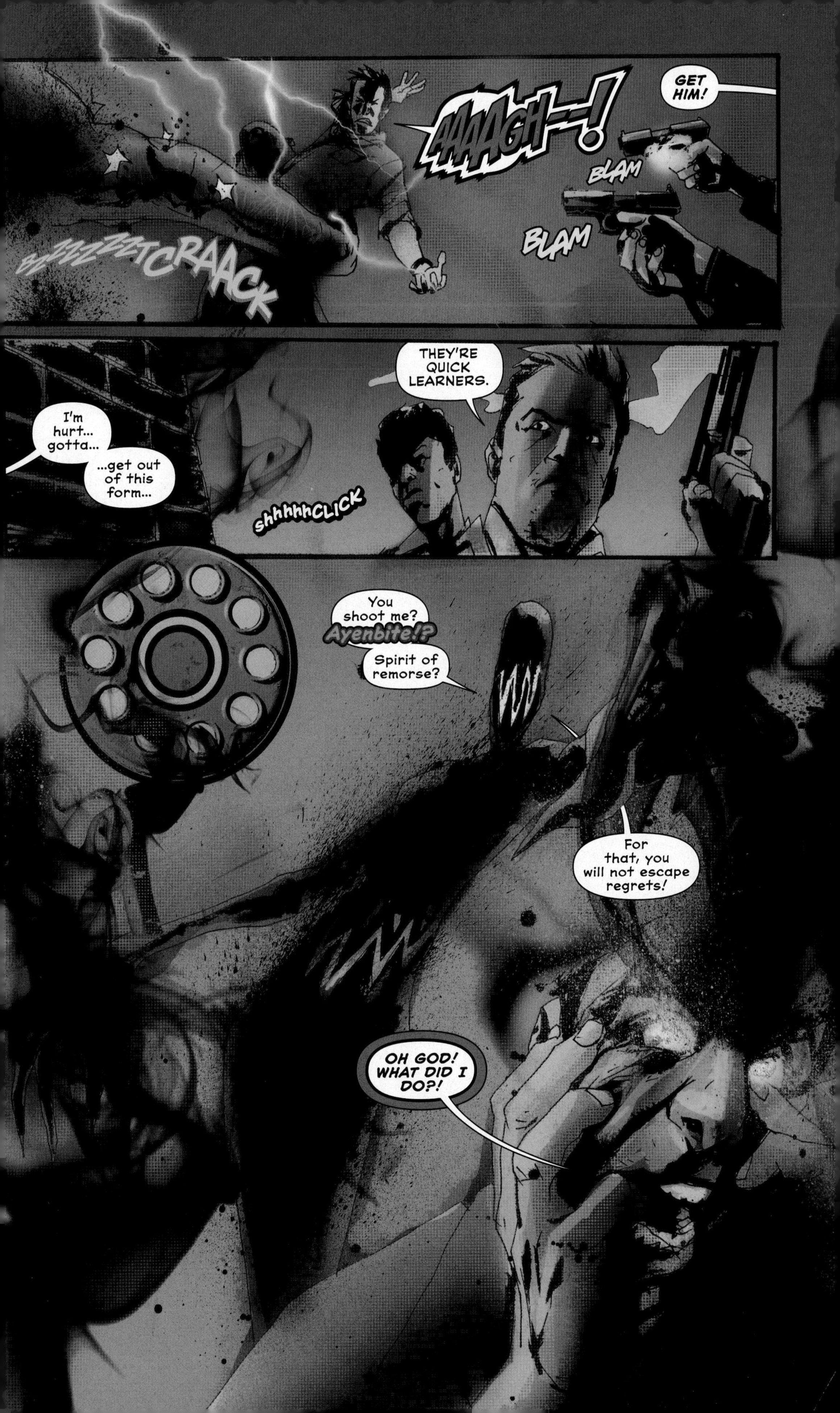
BZZZZZZZZTCRAAACK
AAAAGH--!
GET HIM!
BLAM
BLAM
I'm hurt... gotta...
...get out of this form...
THEY'RE QUICK LEARNERS.
shhhhhCLICK
You shoot me? Ayenbite!?
Spirit of remorse?
For that, you will not escape regrets!
OH GOD! WHAT DID I DO?!

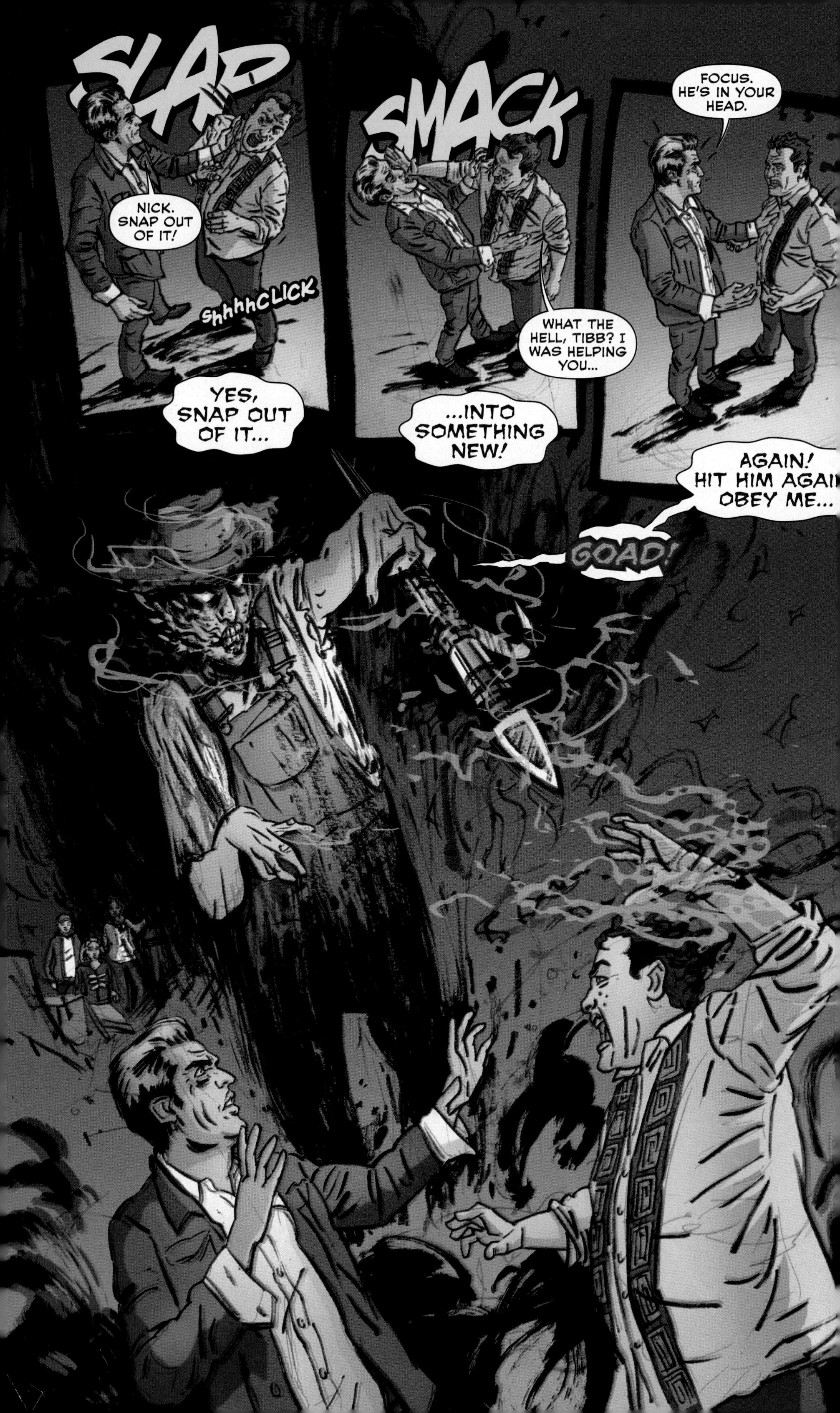
SLAP
NICK. SNAP OUT OF IT!
ShhhhCLICK
YES, SNAP OUT OF IT...
SMACK
WHAT THE HELL, TIBB? I WAS HELPING YOU...
...INTO SOMETHING NEW!
FOCUS. HE'S IN YOUR HEAD.
AGAIN! HIT HIM AGAI OBEY ME...
GOAD!

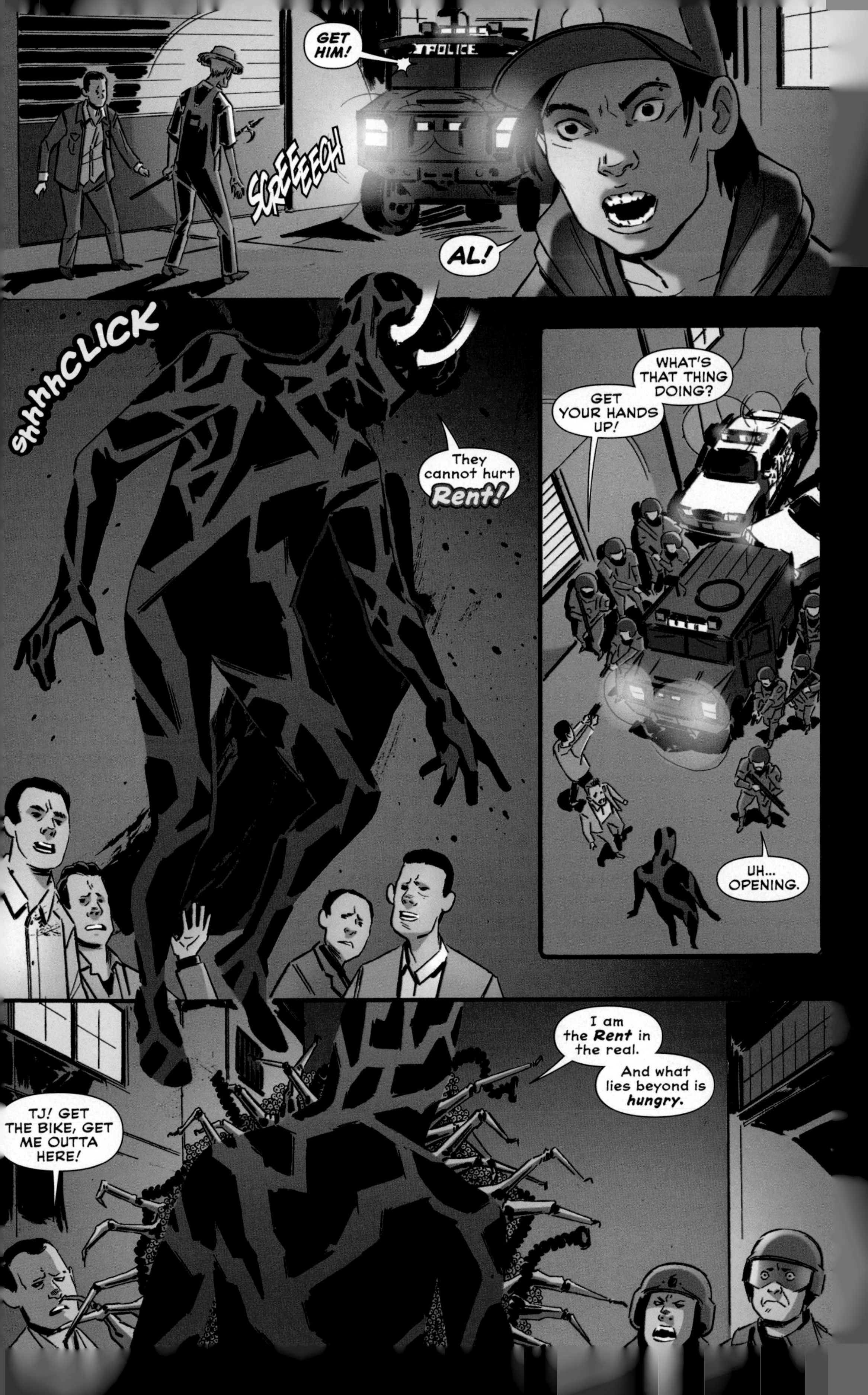
GET HIM!
SCREEEEECH
AL!
shhhhCLICK
They cannot hurt Rent!
GET YOUR HANDS UP!
WHAT'S THAT THING DOING?
UH... OPENING.
TJ! GET THE BIKE, GET ME OUTTA HERE!
I am the Rent in the real.
And what lies beyond is hungry.

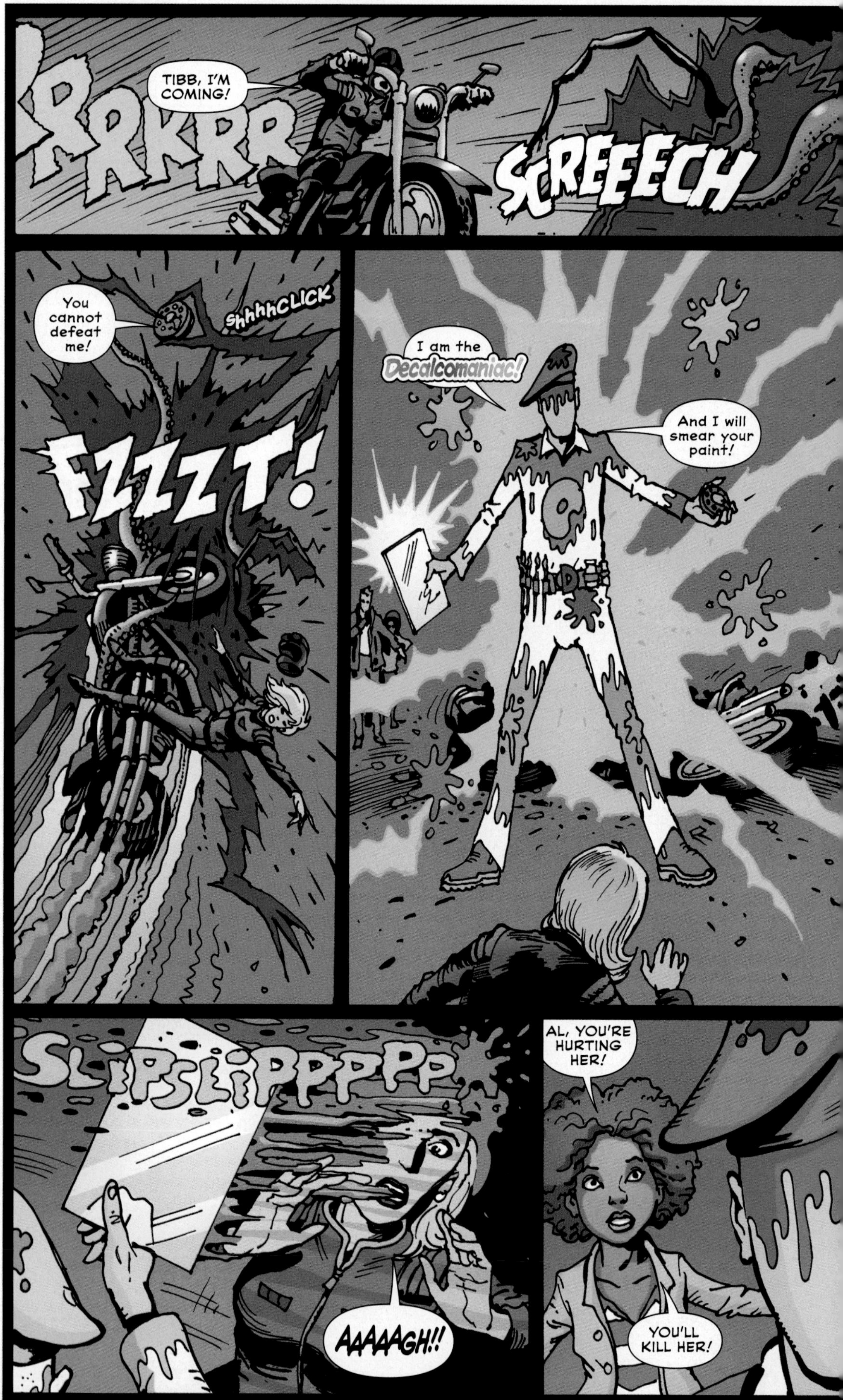

RRKRR
TIBB, I'M COMING!
SCREEECH
You cannot defeat me!
ShhhhCLICK
FZZZT!
I am the Decalcomaniac!
And I will smear your paint!
SLIPSLIPPPPP
AAAAAGH!!
AL, YOU'RE HURTING HER!
YOU'LL KILL HER!

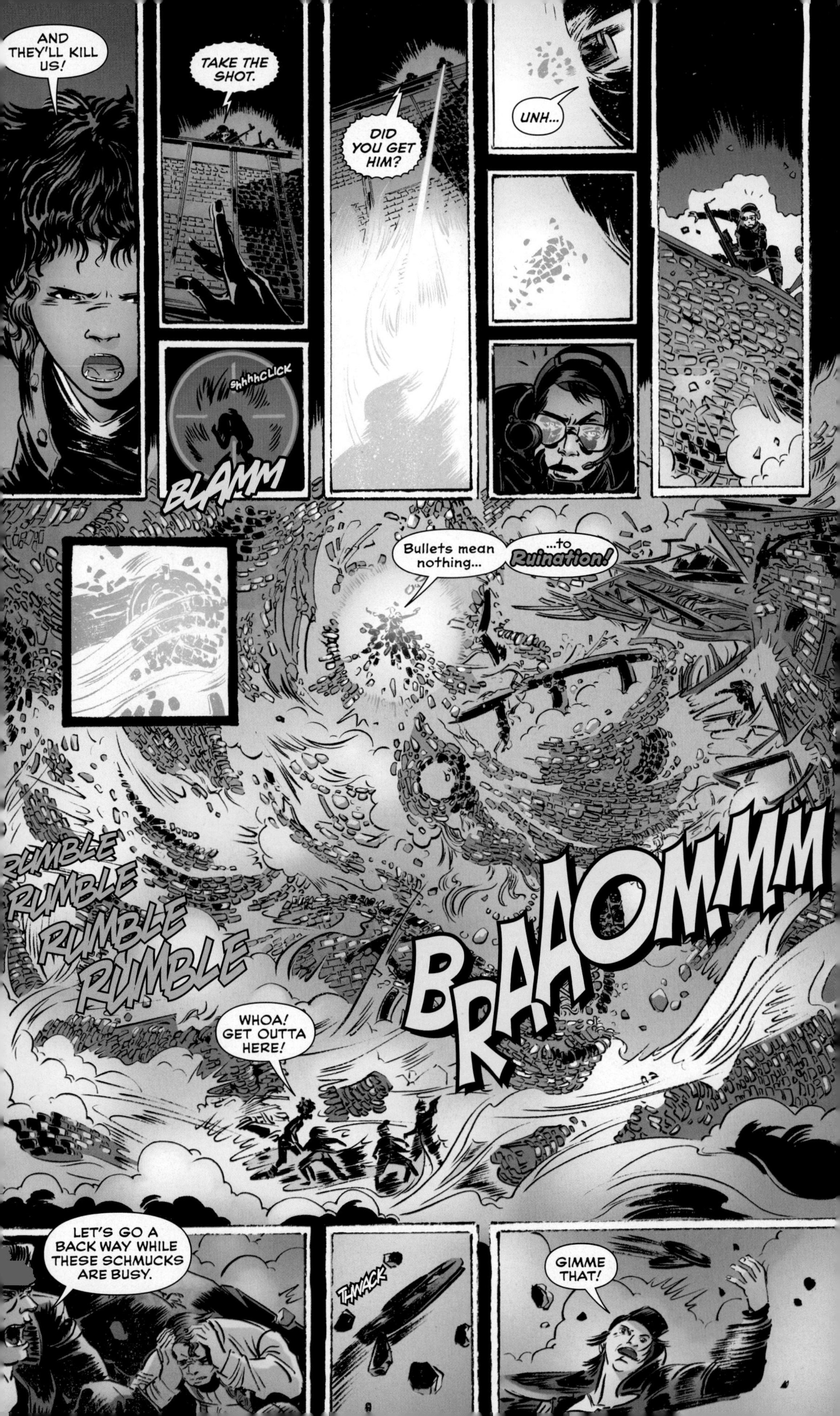
AND THEY'LL KILL US!
TAKE THE SHOT.
SHHHHCLICK
BLAMM
DID YOU GET HIM?
UNH...
Bullets mean nothing...
...to Ruination!
RUMBLE
RUMBLE
RUMBLE
RUMBLE
BRAAOMMM
WHOA! GET OUTTA HERE!
LET'S GO A BACK WAY WHILE THESE SCHMUCKS ARE BUSY.
THWACK
GIMME THAT!

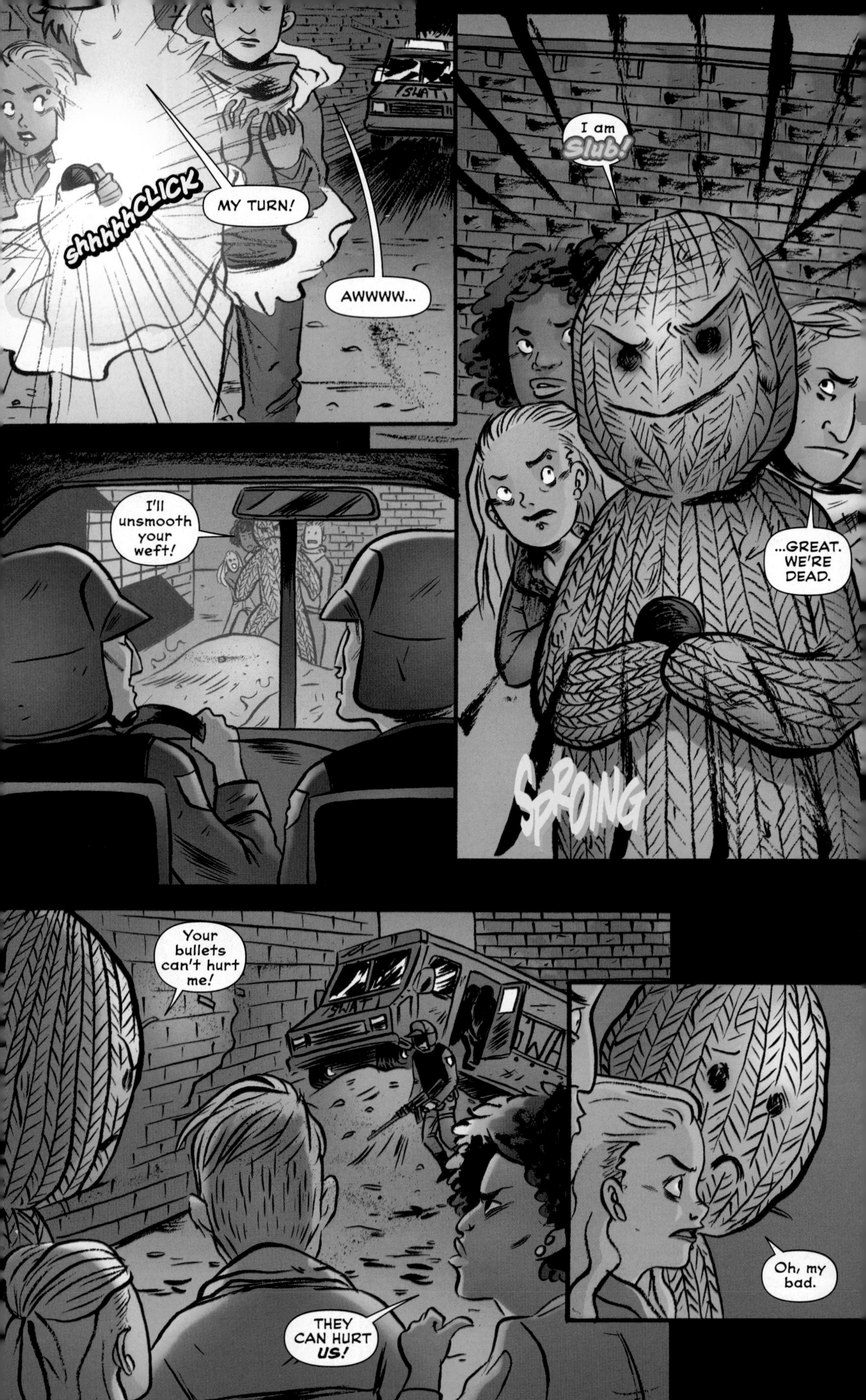

shhhhCLICK
MY TURN!
AWWWW...
I am Slub!
...GREAT. WE'RE DEAD.
SPROING
I'll unsmooth your weft!
Your bullets can't hurt me!
THEY CAN HURT US!
Oh, my bad.

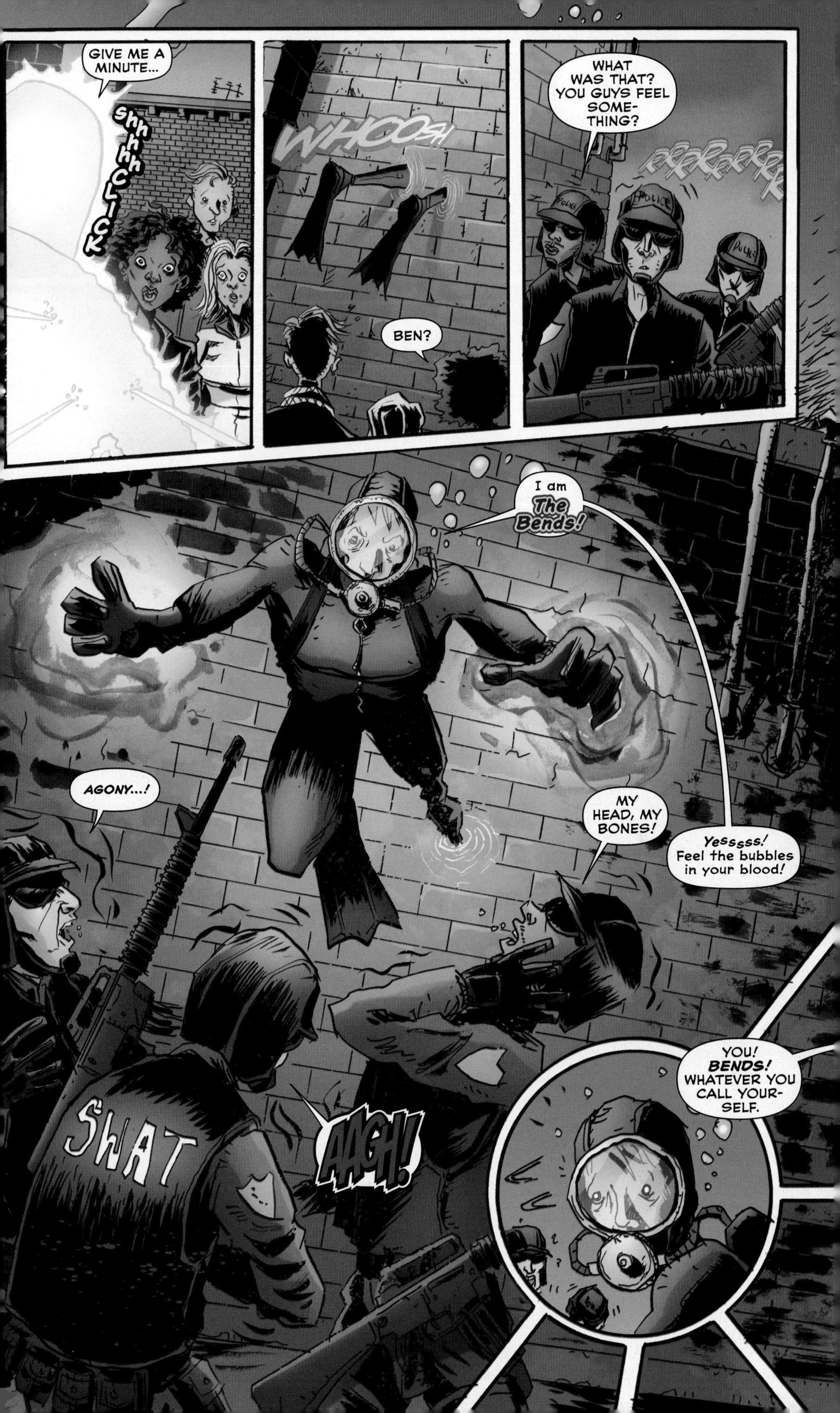

GIVE ME A MINUTE...
ShhhhCLICK
WHOOSH
BEN?
WHAT WAS THAT? YOU GUYS FEEL SOME-THING?
RRRRRRRRR
I am The Bends!
AGONY...!
MY HEAD, MY BONES!
Yessssss! Feel the bubbles in your blood!
SWAT
AAGH!
YOU! BENDS! WHATEVER YOU CALL YOUR-SELF.

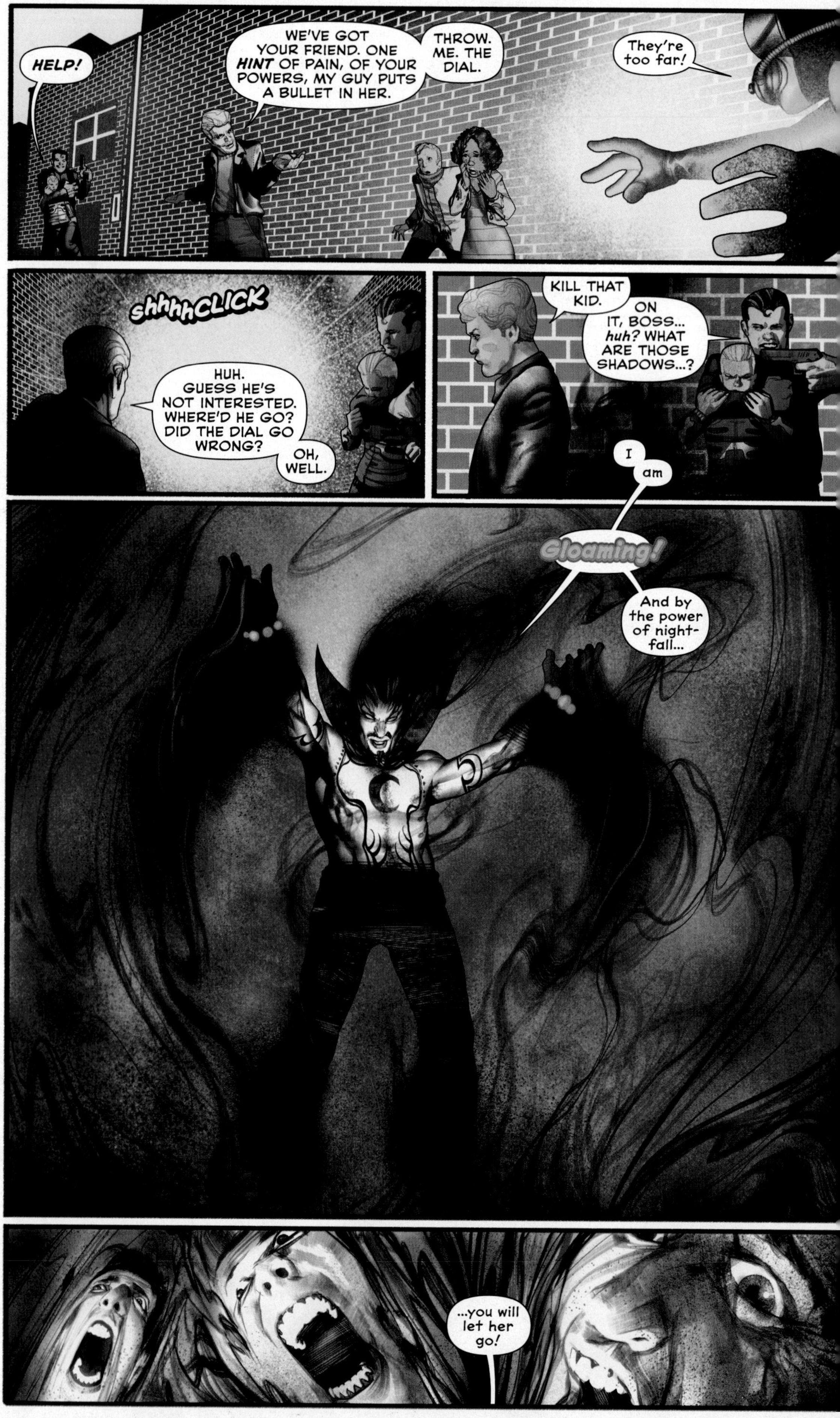
HELP!
WE'VE GOT YOUR FRIEND. ONE HINT OF PAIN, OF YOUR POWERS, MY GUY PUTS A BULLET IN HER.
THROW. ME. THE DIAL.
They're too far!
shhhhCLICK
HUH. GUESS HE'S NOT INTERESTED. WHERE'D HE GO? DID THE DIAL GO WRONG?
OH, WELL.
KILL THAT KID.
ON IT, BOSS... huh? WHAT ARE THOSE SHADOWS...?
I am
Gloaming!
And by the power of night-fall...
...you will let her go!

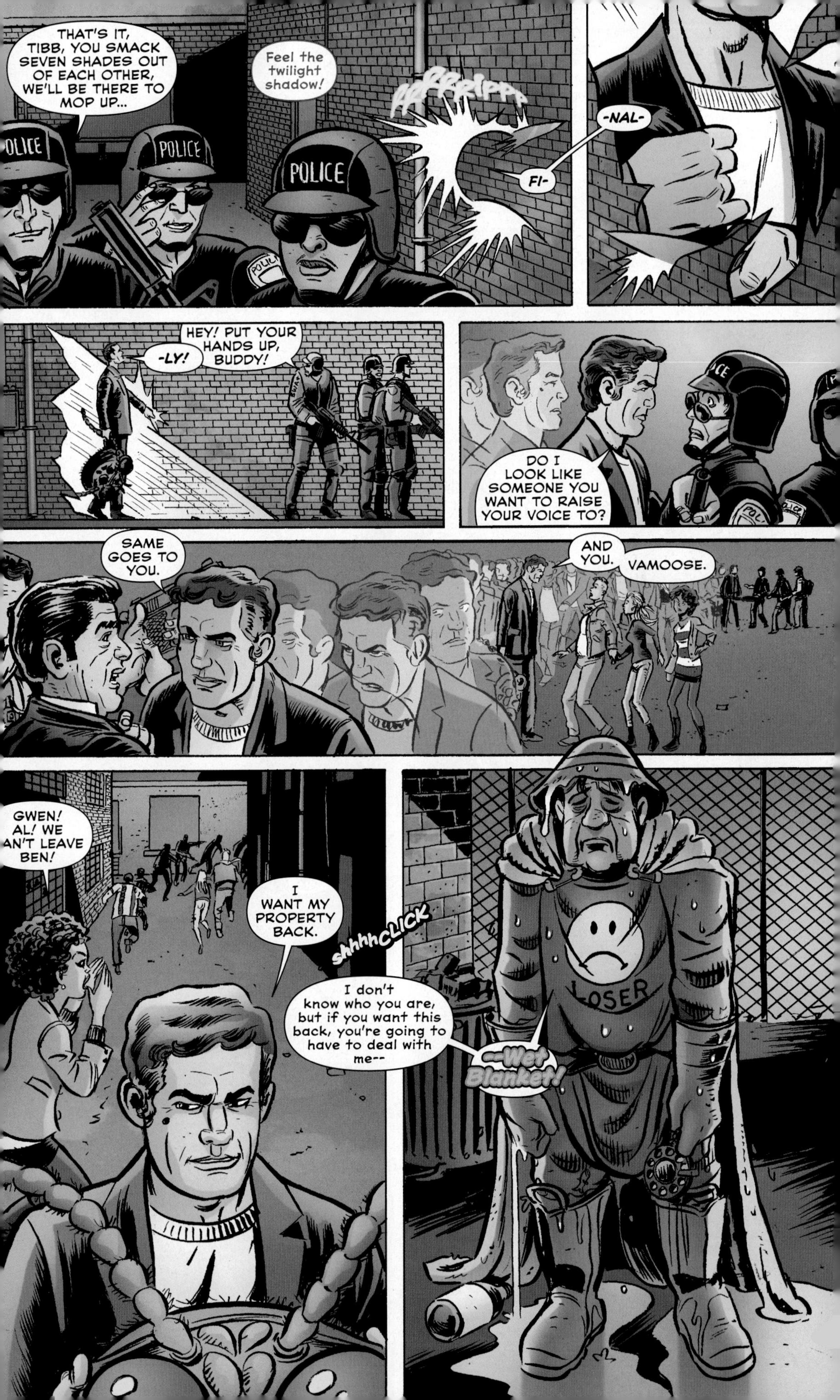
THAT'S IT, TIBB, YOU SMACK SEVEN SHADES OUT OF EACH OTHER, WE'LL BE THERE TO MOP UP...
POLICE
POLICE
POLICE
Feel the twilight shadow!
RRRRRIPPP
-NAL-
FI-
-LY!
HEY! PUT YOUR HANDS UP, BUDDY!
DO I LOOK LIKE SOMEONE YOU WANT TO RAISE YOUR VOICE TO?
SAME GOES TO YOU.
AND YOU.
VAMOOSE.
GWEN! AL! WE AN'T LEAVE BEN!
I WANT MY PROPERTY BACK.
shhhhCLICK
I don't know who you are, but if you want this back, you're going to have to deal with me--
--Wet Blanket!
LOSER

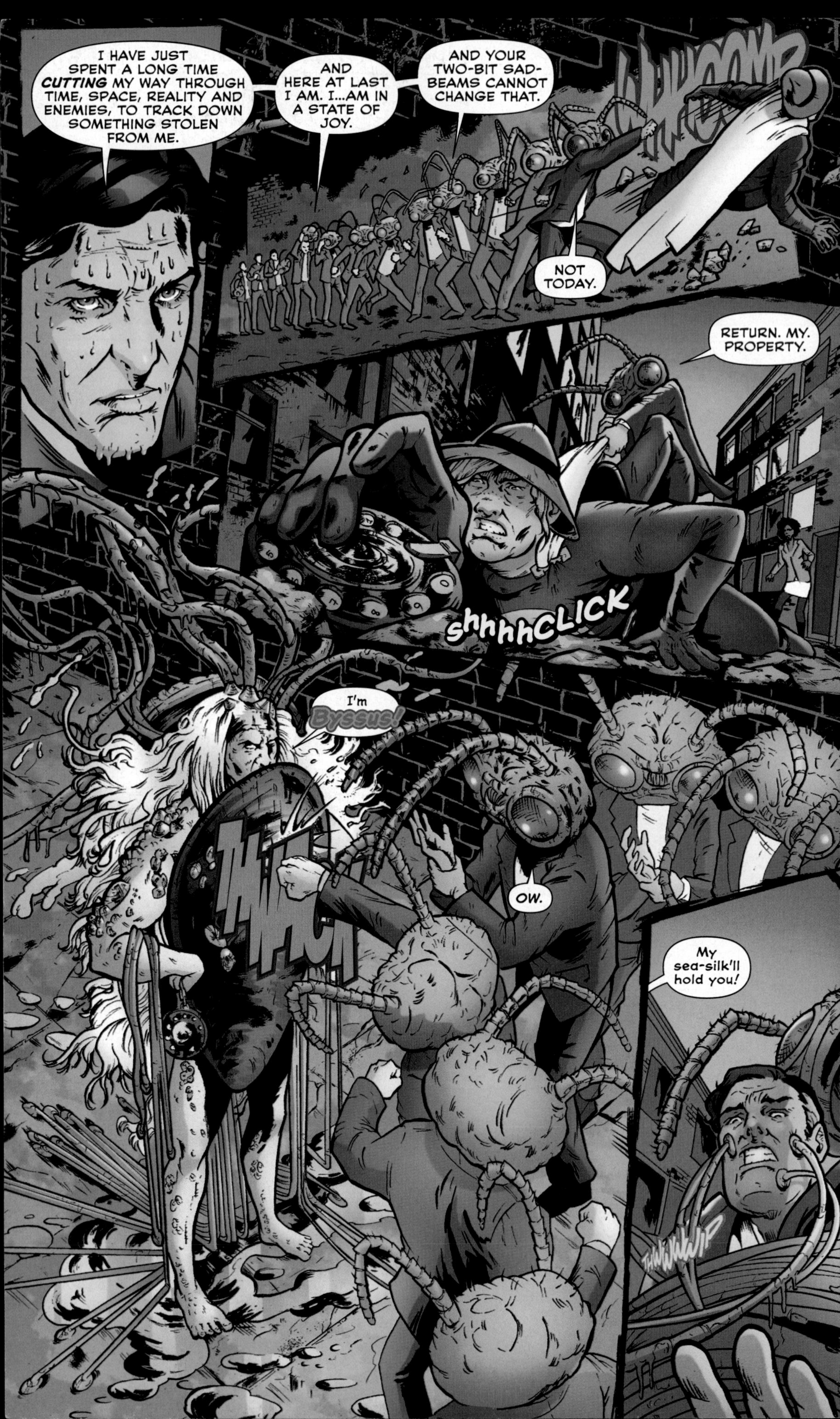
WHUMP
I HAVE JUST SPENT A LONG TIME CUTTING MY WAY THROUGH TIME, SPACE, REALITY AND ENEMIES, TO TRACK DOWN SOMETHING STOLEN FROM ME.
AND HERE AT LAST I AM. I...AM IN A STATE OF JOY.
AND YOUR TWO-BIT SAD-BEAMS CANNOT CHANGE THAT.
NOT TODAY.
RETURN. MY. PROPERTY.
shhhhCLICK
I'm Byssus!
THWACK
OW.
My sea-silk'll hold you!
THWWWWIP

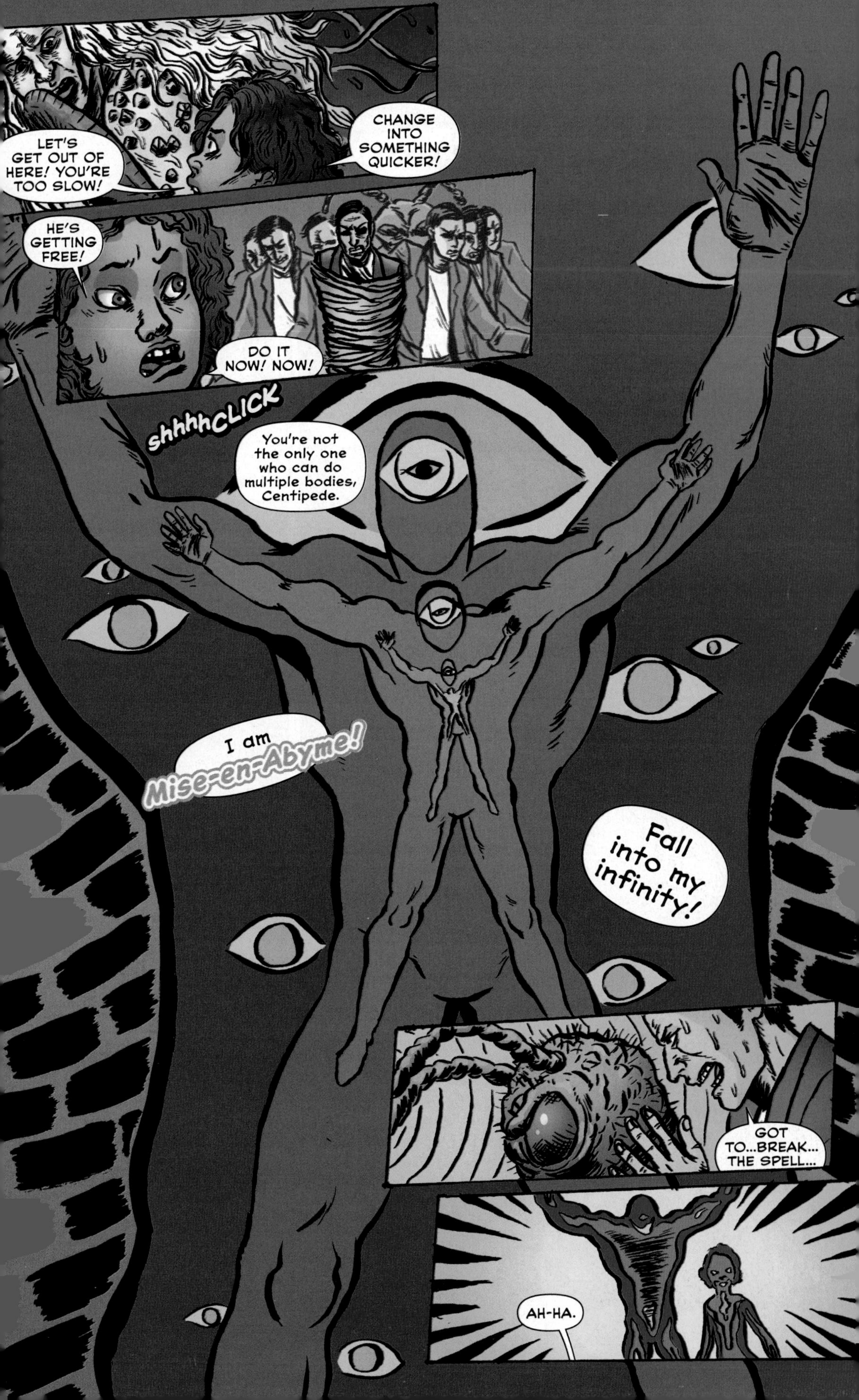

CHANGE INTO SOMETHING QUICKER!
LET'S GET OUT OF HERE! YOU'RE TOO SLOW!
HE'S GETTING FREE!
DO IT NOW! NOW!
shhhhCLICK
You're not the only one who can do multiple bodies, Centipede.
I am Mise-en-Abyme!
Fall into my infinity!
GOT TO...BREAK... THE SPELL...
AH-HA.

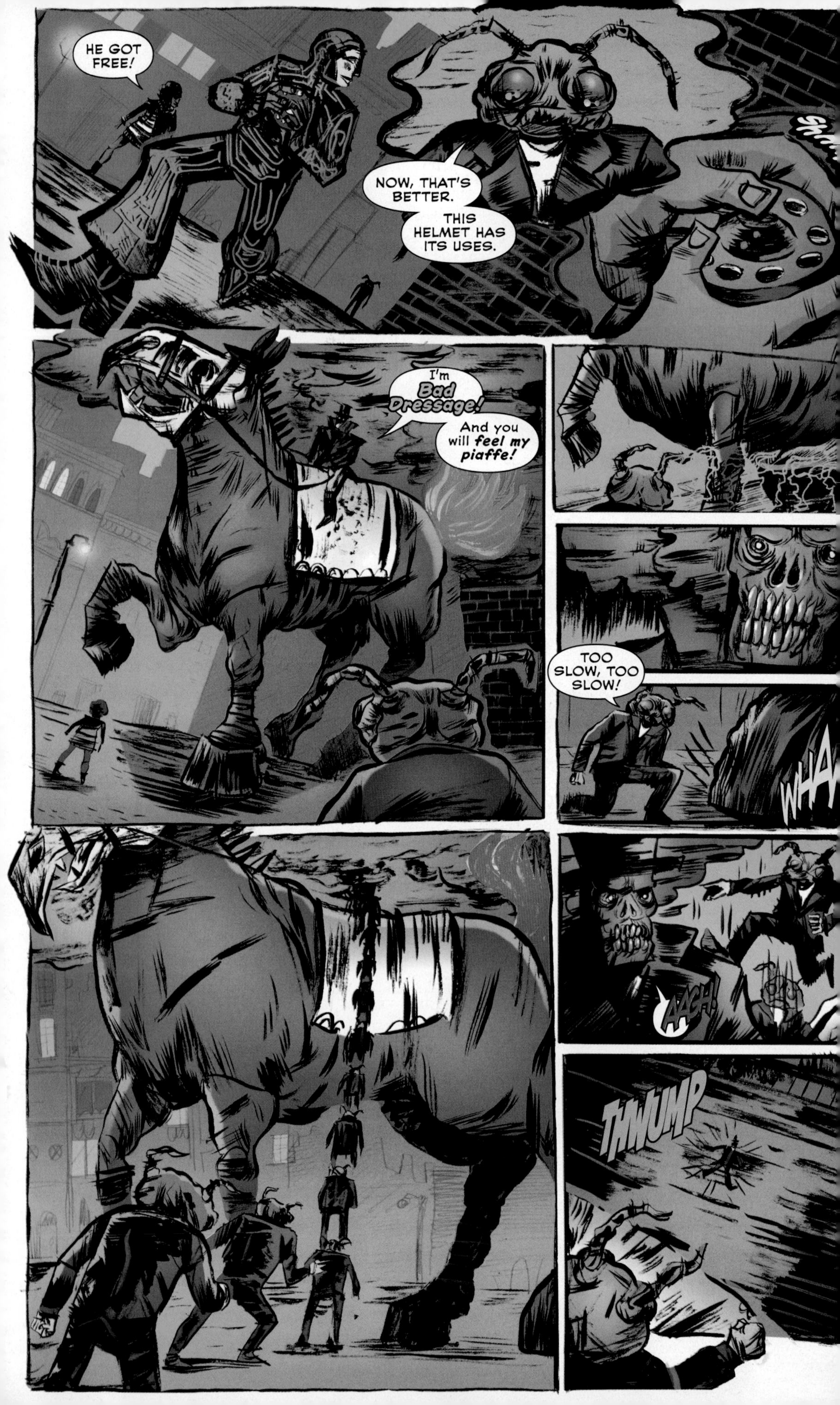

HE GOT FREE!
NOW, THAT'S BETTER.
THIS HELMET HAS ITS USES.
I'm Bad Dressage!
And you will feel my piaffe!
TOO SLOW, TOO SLOW!
AACH!
THWUMP

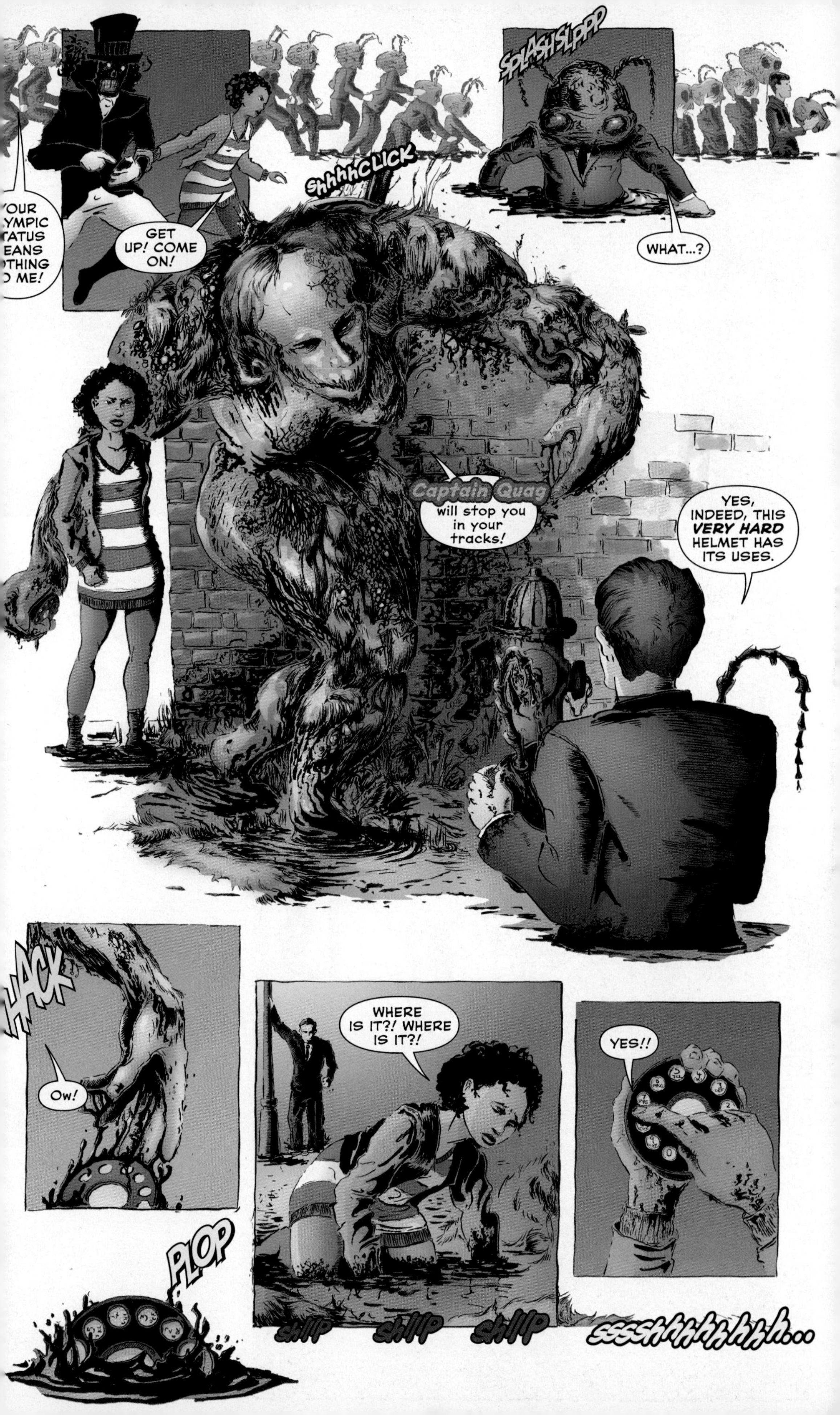

YOUR
YMPIC
TATUS
EANS
OTHING
O ME!
GET UP! COME ON!
ShhhhCLICK
SPLASHSLPPP
WHAT...?
Captain Quag will stop you in your tracks!
YES, INDEED, THIS VERY HARD HELMET HAS ITS USES.
HACK
Ow!
PLOP
WHERE IS IT?! WHERE IS IT?!
YES!!
shllp
shllp
shllp
ssssshhhhhhh...

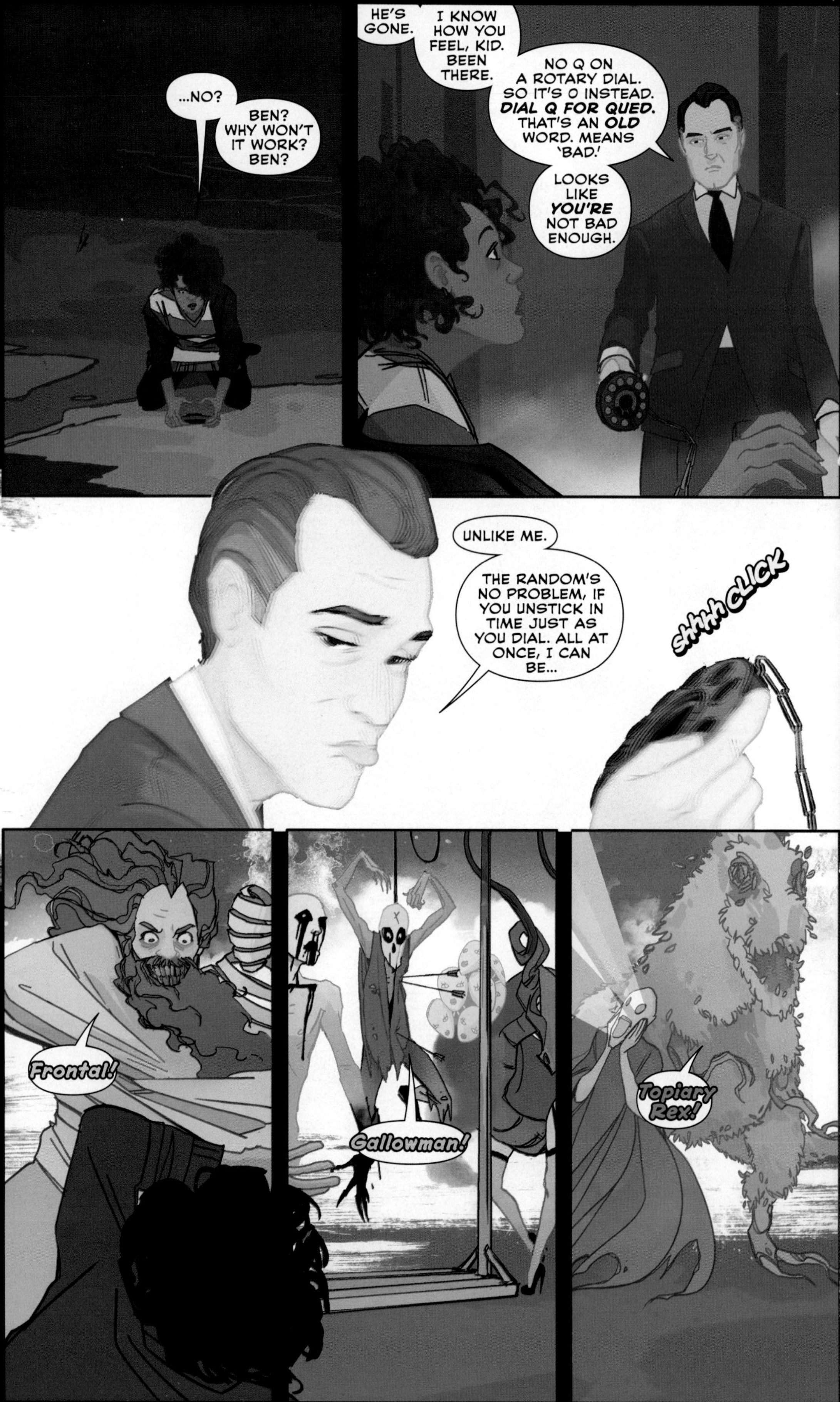
...NO?
BEN? WHY WON'T IT WORK? BEN?
HE'S GONE.
I KNOW HOW YOU FEEL, KID. BEEN THERE.
NO Q ON A ROTARY DIAL. SO IT'S 0 INSTEAD. DIAL Q FOR QUED. THAT'S AN OLD WORD. MEANS 'BAD.'
LOOKS LIKE YOU'RE NOT BAD ENOUGH.
UNLIKE ME.
THE RANDOM'S NO PROBLEM, IF YOU UNSTICK IN TIME JUST AS YOU DIAL. ALL AT ONCE, I CAN BE...
shhhh CLICK
Frontal!
Gallowman!
Topiary Rex!

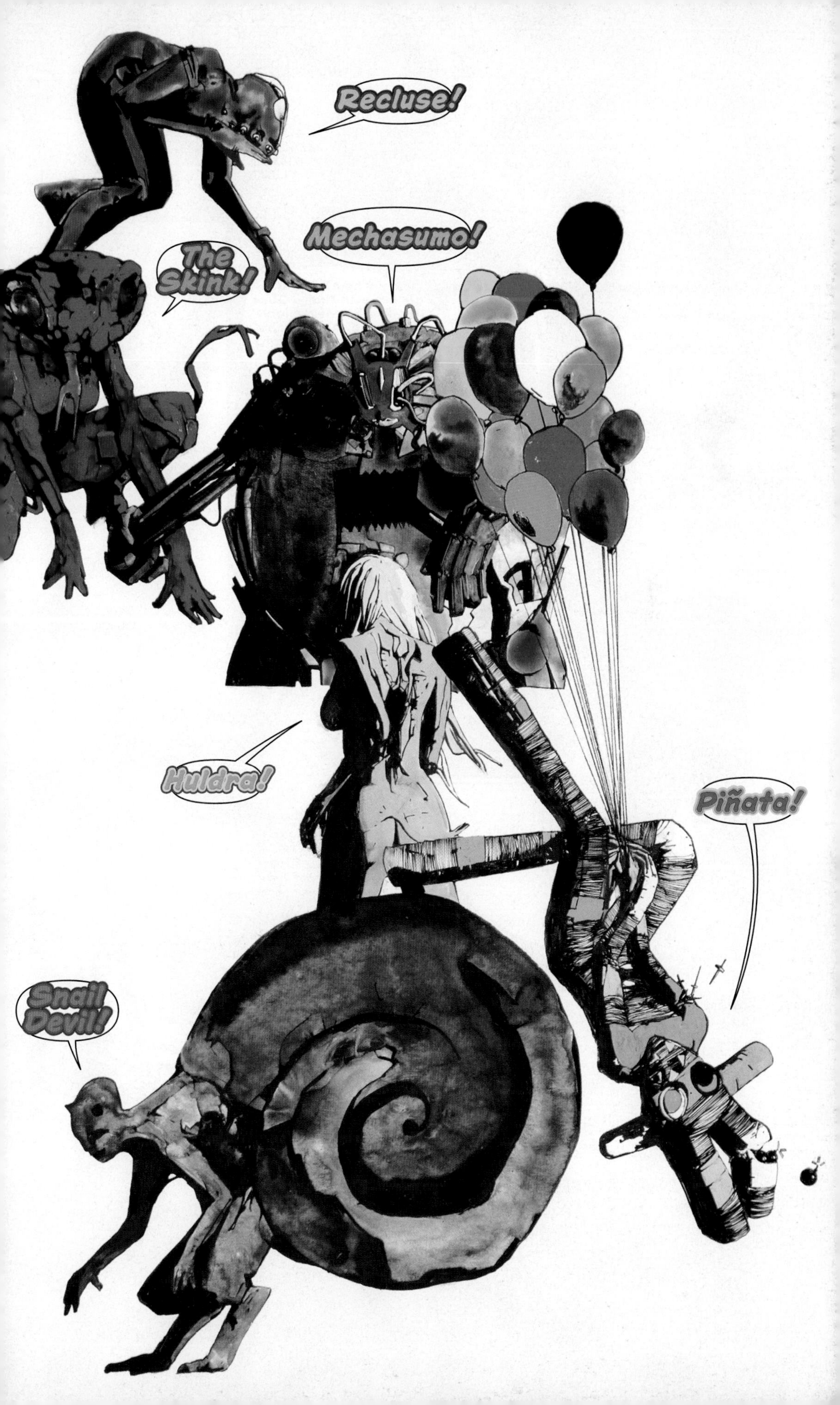
Recluse!
Mechasumo!
The Skink!
Huldra!
Piñata!
Snail Devil!

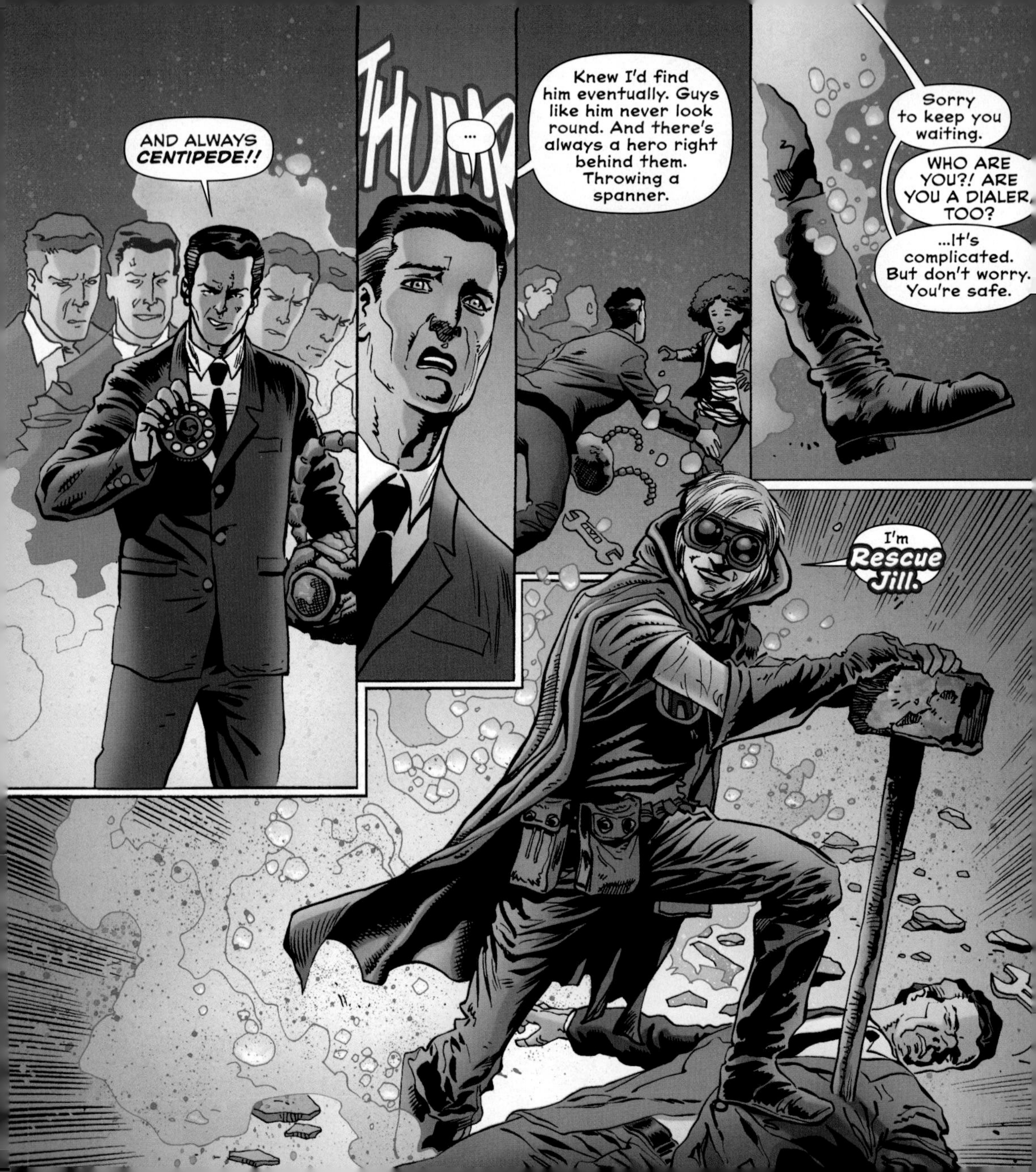
AND ALWAYS CENTIPEDE!!
THUMP
...
Knew I'd find him eventually. Guys like him never look round. And there's always a hero right behind them. Throwing a spanner.
Sorry to keep you waiting.
WHO ARE YOU?! ARE YOU A DIALER, TOO?
...It's complicated. But don't worry. You're safe.
I'm Rescue Jill.

Issue #11

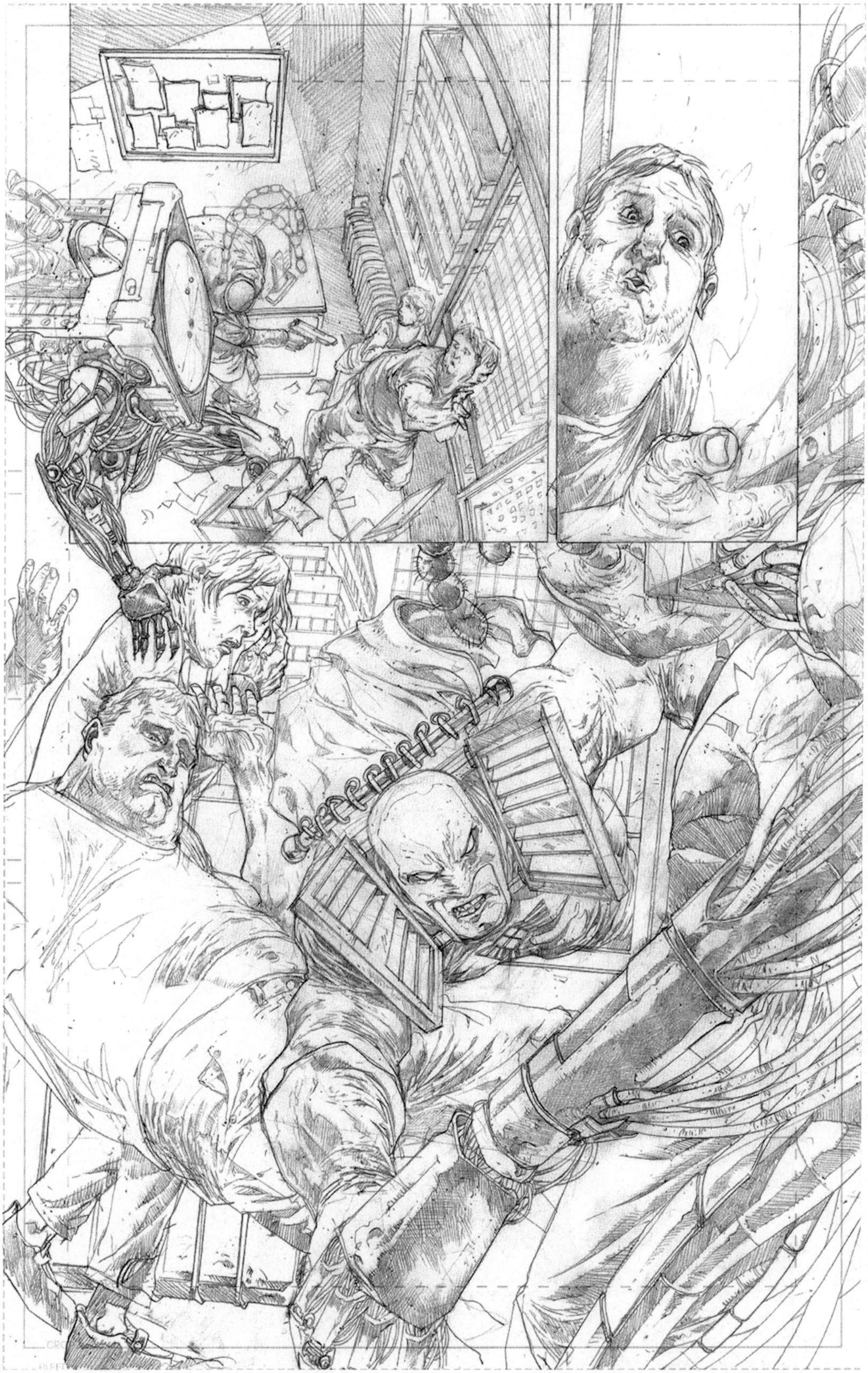

Issue #13

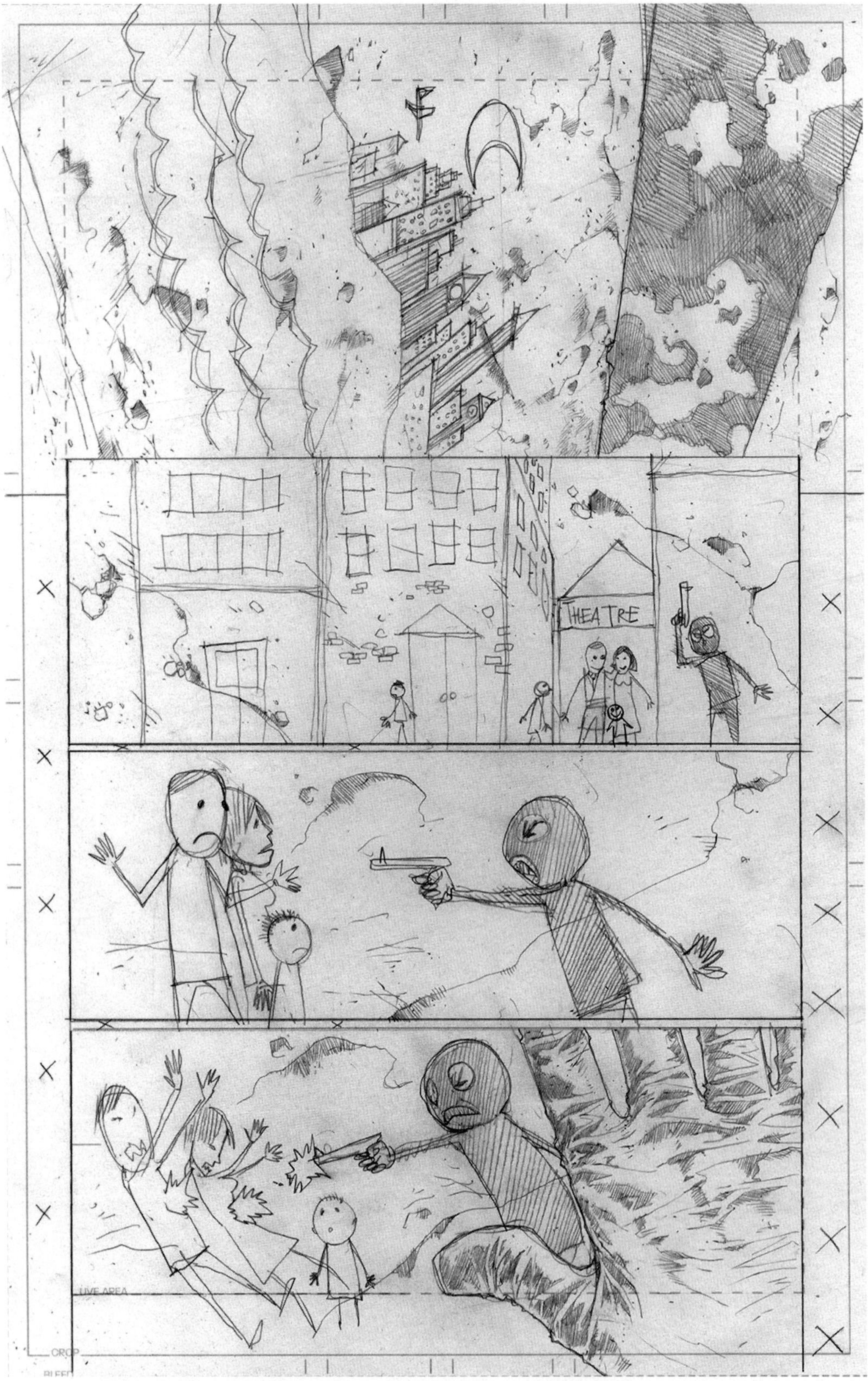

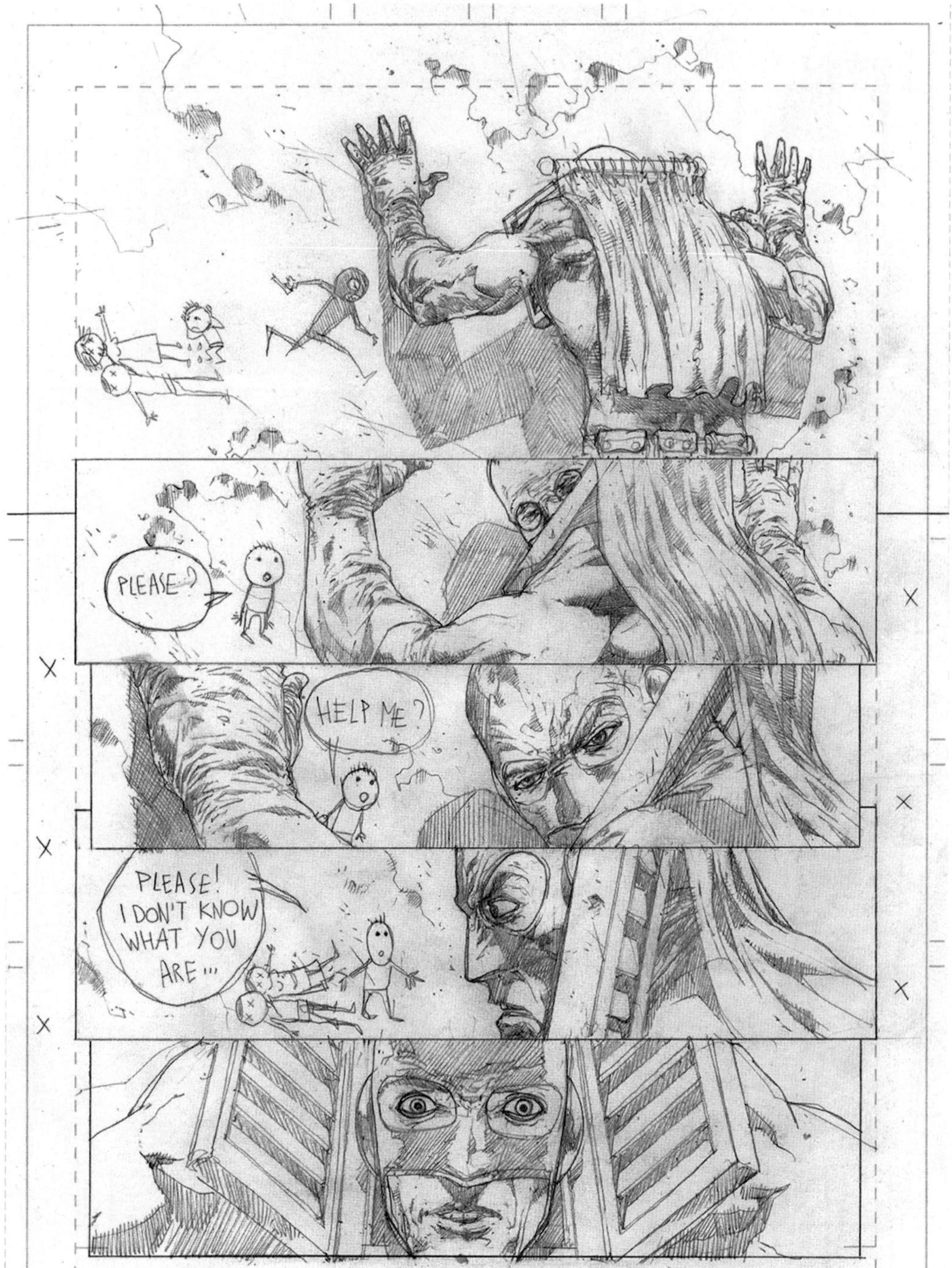
PLEASE?
HELP ME?
PLEASE! I DON'T KNOW WHAT YOU ARE...
LIVE AREA
CROP
BLEED

JUSTICE LEAGUE #23.3
PENCILS BY MARLEY ZARCONE

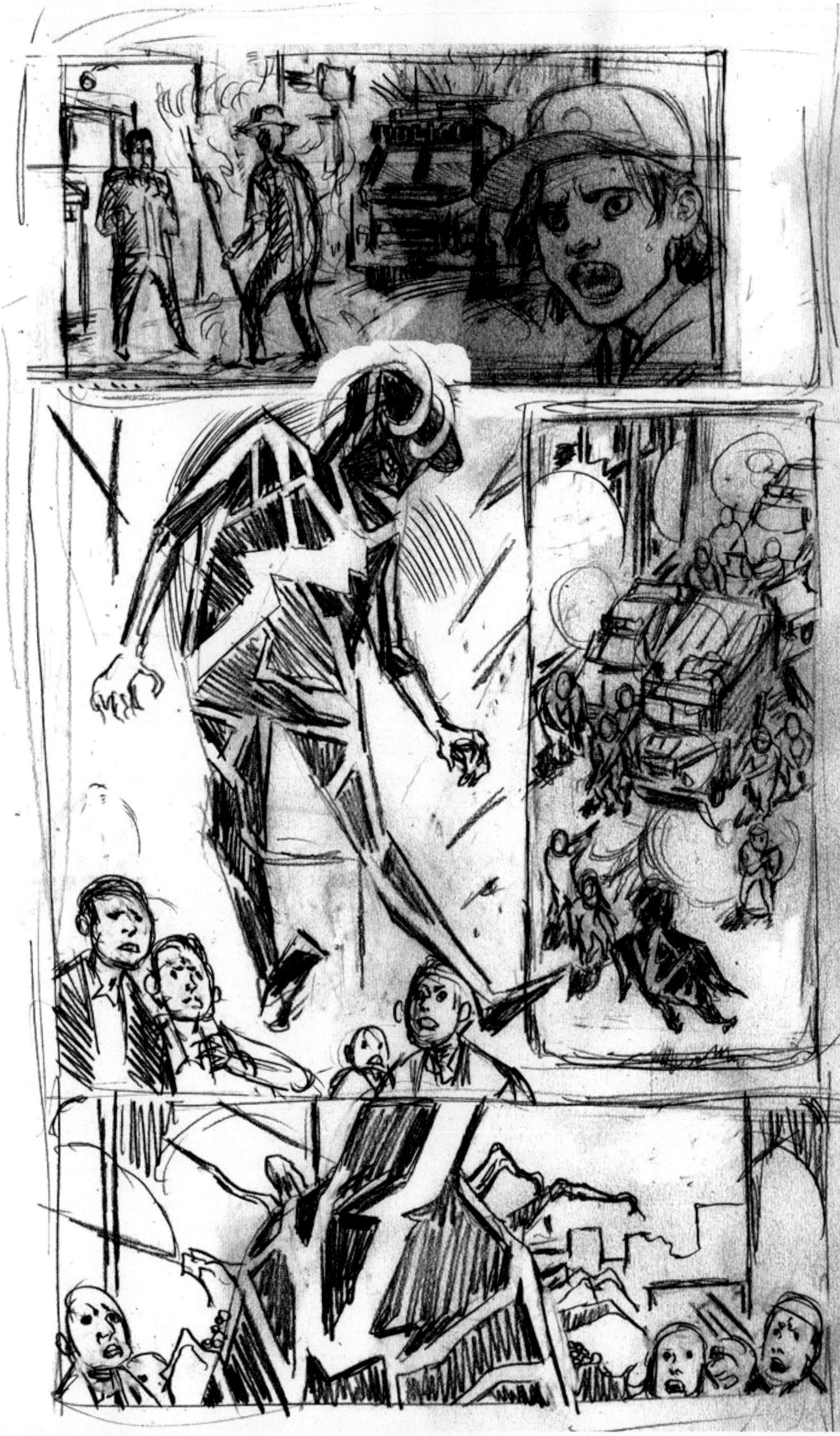

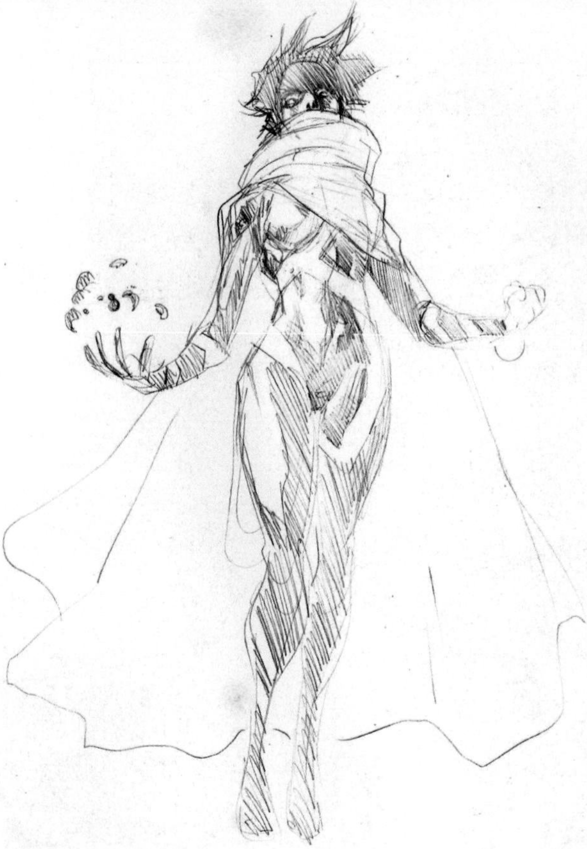

Suffer Kate and The Kids
by Mateus Santoloucco

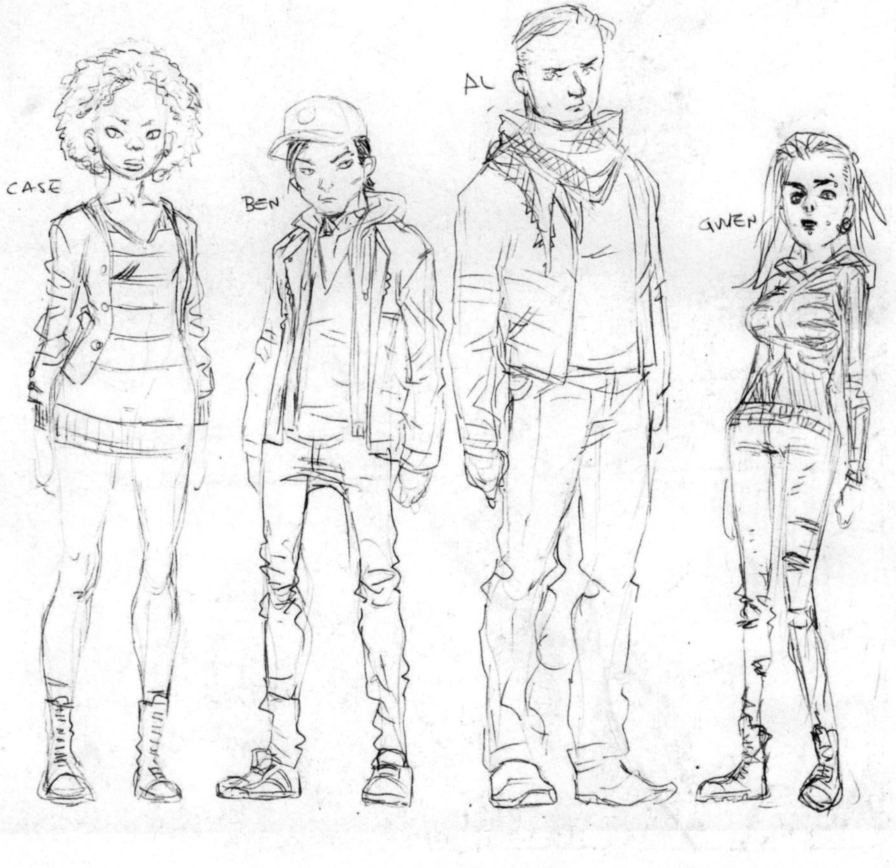

CASE
BEN
AL
GWEN

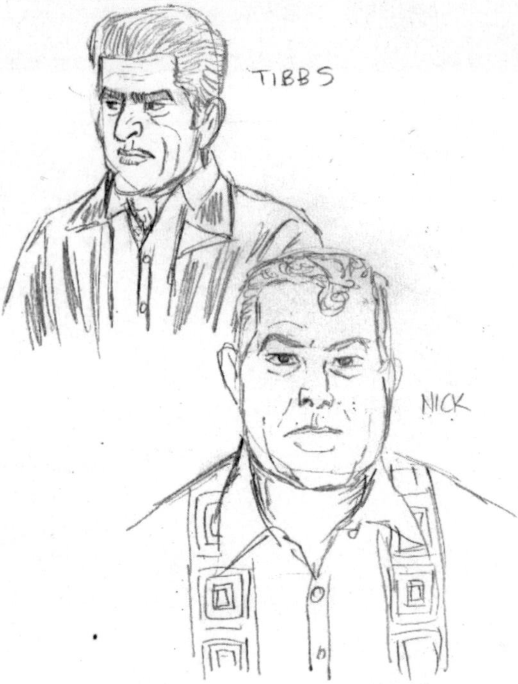
TIBBS
NICK

Tibbs and Nick by David Lapham

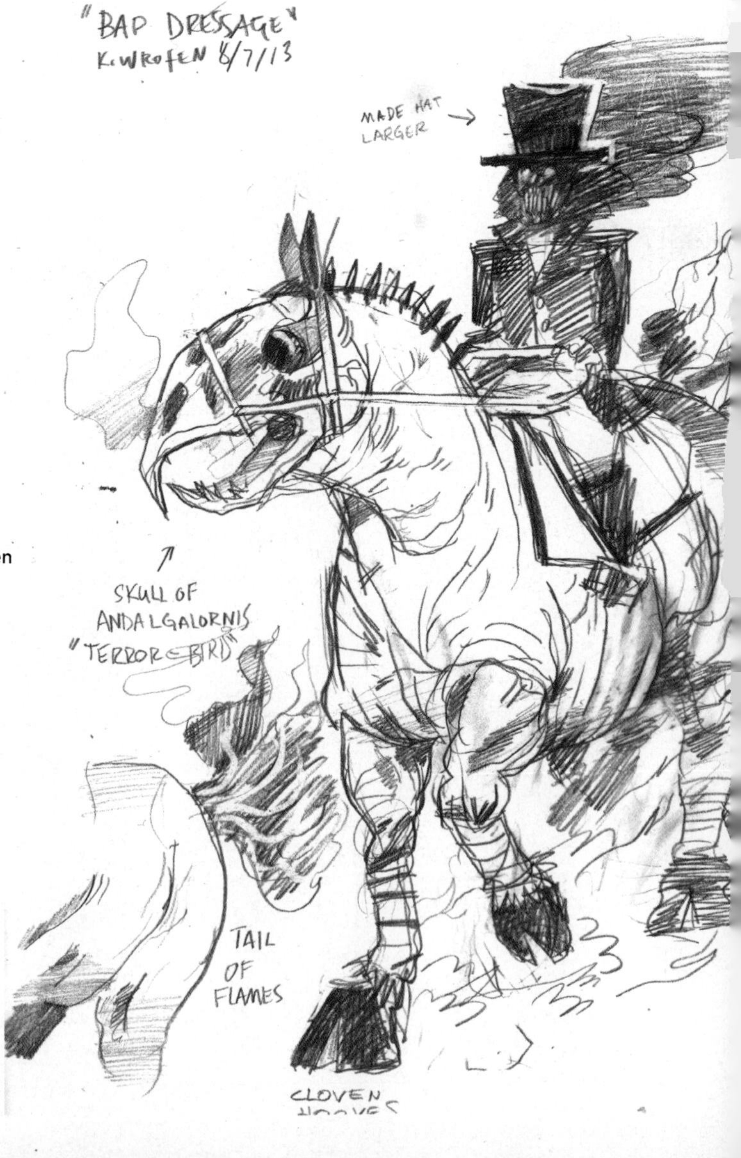
"BAD DRESSAGE"
K. WROTEN 8/7/13
MADE HAT LARGER
SKULL OF
ANDALGALORNIS
"TERROR BIRD"
TAIL
OF
FLAMES
CLOVEN

Bad Dressage by Kelsey Wroten